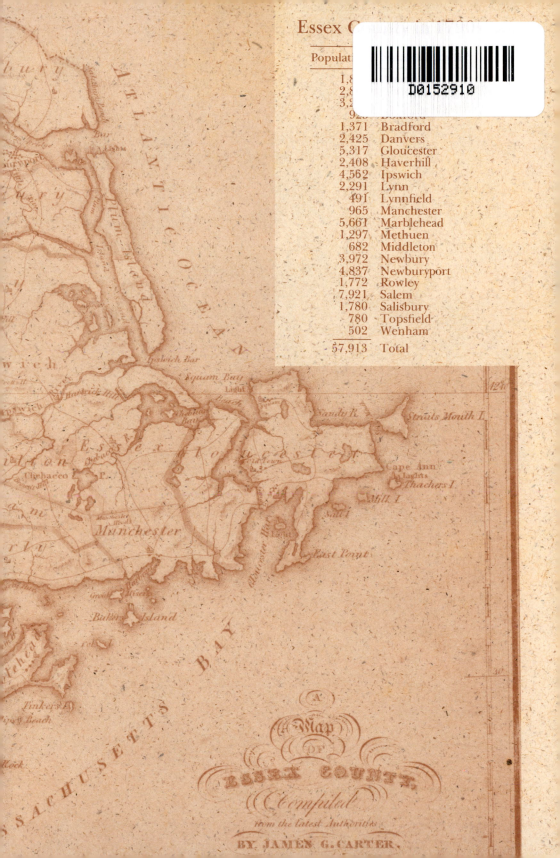

Essex C...... 179.

Populat...	
1,8..	
2,8..	
3,9..	
920	Boxford
1,371	Bradford
2,425	Danvers
5,317	Gloucester
2,408	Haverhill
4,562	Ipswich
2,291	Lynn
491	Lynnfield
965	Manchester
5,661	Marblehead
1,297	Methuen
682	Middleton
3,972	Newbury
4,837	Newburyport
1,772	Rowley
7,921	Salem
1,780	Salisbury
780	Topsfield
502	Wenham
57,913	Total

A Map OF ESSEX COUNTY, Compiled from the latest Authorities BY JAMES G. CARTER.

THE WORLD
TURNED
UPSIDE DOWN

THE WORLD
TURNED
UPSIDE DOWN

Essex County During America's
Turbulent Years, 1763–1790

By

RONALD N. TAGNEY

ESSEX COUNTY HISTORY
1989

Essex County History
P.O. Box 418
West Newbury, MA 01985

Developmental Editor: Louise M. Sullivan
Production Coordinator: Anne M. Imhoff
Cover Designer: David Ford
Interior Designer: Dorothy A. Lovering
Photo Researcher: Ann Knight
Map Illustrator: David A. Marshall
Indexer: Janice Matula
Endpapers: Courtesy, Essex Institute, Salem, Mass.

Type set in Baskerville by DEKR Corporation;
printing and binding by Hamilton Printing Co.

Printed in the United States of America
ISBN 0-9623792-0-4
Library of Congress No. 89-085400

PREFACE

The World Turned Upside Down, Essex County During America's Turbulent Years, 1763–1790 focuses on the rich heritage of Essex County, Massachusetts, and traces the American experience from the first stirrings of revolution, through the War of Independence, to the shaping of the Federal period. This book, which has been three years in the making, commemorates Essex County's and this country's bicentennial under our Republic.

In this chronicle of the most stormy period in American history, I have attempted to portray, in the microcosm of Essex County, a clear picture of this nation's birth. I also hope to offer the reader a new perspective through an understanding of the regional events, forces, and personalities that helped shape United States Revolutionary history. Indeed, Essex County's endowment to this period is momentous; possibly, unequaled.

In the works cited in each chapter, the first reference contains full bibliographical details. A shorter form—omitting publisher, place, and date of printing—is used for serial collections of documentary materials, namely: *Massachusetts Soldiers and Sailors of the Revolutionary War*, published by the Commonwealth of Massachusetts in seventeen volumes (1896–1908); Peter Force, ed., *American Archives* manuscript history, nine volumes, 1839–1853; William Bell Clark, ed., *Naval Documents of the American Revolution*, in nine volumes, Department of the Navy, Washington, D.C., 1964–1986; *The Writings of George Washington*, from original manuscript sources, John C. Fitzpatrick, ed., thirty-nine volumes, published in Washington, D.C., Government Printing Office, 1931–1944; Massachusetts' acts and resolves printed for the commonwealth between 1888 and 1918.

Acknowledgment

This book was made possible by the assistance, guidance, and support of many people, including friends, local historians, city and town clerks, volunteers and staffs of archival centers, historical societies, and libraries. I give special acknowledgment to the American

Antiquarian Society, the Beverly Historical Society, the Boston Athenaeum, the Massachusetts Historical Society, the Massachusetts State Archives, the Newburyport Public Library, the Peabody Museum of Salem, and to my daughter, Lisa Tagney, for her research assistance. Additionally, I am grateful to Nancy G. Lewis for proofreading the original manuscript. I am especially indebted to Richard Fyffe, Librarian/Curator of Books and Printed Materials and to the talented staff and volunteers of the Essex Institute of Salem—a veritable treasure-trove for a researcher. Also, for the good humor, sound judgment, and valuable developmental assistance of Louise M. Sullivan. Most of all, and once again, I thank my wife, Brooke, and my family for their patience and understanding while I have been sequestered preparing this book.

Ronald N. Tagney
West Newbury, Massachusetts
May 1989

CONTENTS

Profile medallion of George Washington, carved by Samuel McIntire after drawings he made during the President's visit to Salem on October 29, 1789. Placed on the west gate of Salem Common, c. 1805–1806. Courtesy, Essex Institute, Salem, Mass.

CHAPTER ONE

WASHINGTON'S HISTORIC TOUR

On October 15, 1789, President George Washington, then fifty-seven years and in office just six months, left the temporary capital on Manhattan Island to tour New England. The first Congress was in recess. Slowly recovering from a protracted illness, the chief executive needed a sojourn to restore his health. More to the purpose, he wanted to familiarize himself with "the face of the Country, the growth and agriculture thereof—and the temper and disposition of the inhabitants towards the new government."[1] In this, Washington's first visit to the northeast since the siege of Boston in 1775–76, he would spend several memorable days in Essex County.

To Essex County

Washington left Boston on Thursday, October 29 for Cambridge, where President Joseph Willard of Harvard College, the former pastor of Beverly's First Parish, received him. Then Washington resumed his tour, traveling out of North Cambridge, through Mystic (now Medford) and Malden to Saugus Parish in Lynn, the Essex County line.

Here Revolutionary soldier Major General Jonathan Titcomb of Newburyport, leader of the Essex brigade, greeted President Washington. Titcomb had ordered that America's commander in chief be afforded "every military honor." Capt. Peter Osgood's Andover horse troop, decked in new crimson uniforms and caps furnished by Samuel Phillips, Jr., proudly stepped out to escort the President, who was seated in state in a carriage drawn by four horses and accompanied by Major William Jackson, his private secretary. Another close aide, Col. Tobias Lear, had traveled to Boston with the President, but had gone on alone to his native Portsmouth. Behind the carriage were six Negro attendants in a baggage wagon, followed by Washington's great white charger, ridden by a young black man.[2]

The cavalcade drove down the old Boston road, through Lynn village, past about one hundred modest clapboard homes and clusters of well wishers. The President noted in his diary that four hundred Lynn workmen made about 175,000 pairs of mostly women's shoes, annually. Beside many houses were ten- to fourteen-foot-square shoe shops, where resident cordwainers turned their craft.[3]

To Marblehead and Salem

Marblehead was four miles off Washington's direct route, but he had been invited and "wanted to see it." During the war, its brave amphibious regiment had served him well. He took the Essex Street route, through Swampscott and past present Vinnin Square. At the town line, a large reception committee greeted him, including the eight selectmen. One was Washington's old friend Gen. John Glover. Amid wild, joyous demonstrations, he was ushered through Marblehead to Mrs. Jeremiah Lee's elegant Georgian home on present Washington Street. The President enjoyed a "cold collation" with the committee, clergy, and other distinguished townspeople; then he strolled along the narrow, curving streets toward the harbor and observed a fish yard lined with cod-curing flakes. He noted the fisheries engage "about 110 vessels and 800 men and boys."[4]

Since the war, Marblehead had not risen above water; in fact, during the last two years conditions had worsened. This was painfully apparent when Washington noted "the appearance of antiquity; the Houses are old; the streets are dirty; and the common people not very clean." Selectmen explained apologetically: "The too visible decay and poverty of this town must be their excuse" for not having "a reception more answerable to his dignity, and more expressive of their own veneration." They predicted that the establishment "of a secure and efficient" federal government would result in "gradual revival of our Fishery and Commerce."[5]

The President left Marblehead for Salem. At the town line by the Forest River bridge, he was received by Salem's arrangements committee—Jacob Ashton, John Fish, Nathan Goodale, Benjamin Goodhue, and John Treadwell—and escorted to town.

His approach was flag-telegraphed to old Fort Pickering on Winter Island, at the harbor entrance, where a second flag was hoisted. With this cue, three 12-pounders at Fort Lee on Salem Neck facing toward

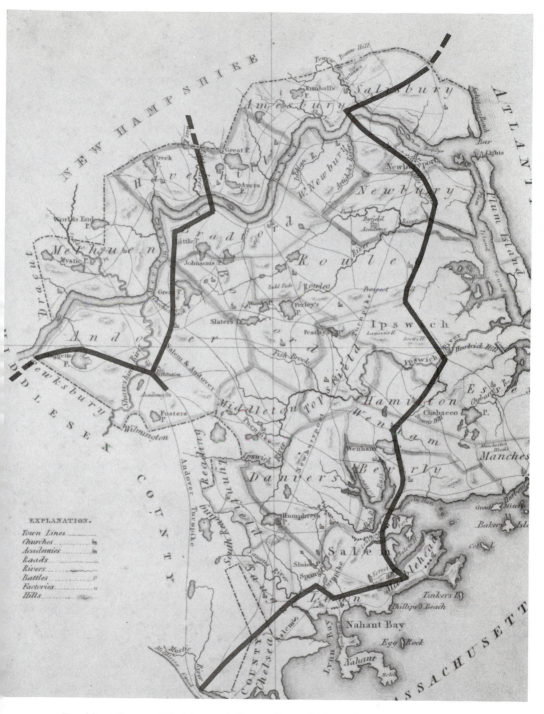

President George Washington's Route through Essex County.

town roared thirteen blasts—a federal discharge—announcing the historic arrival, which was followed by booms from the artillery on Back Street.

By one o'clock, townspeople had assembled in narrow Court (now Washington) Street and formed a procession. With a band leading, they paraded—first, town officials; followed by clergy, merchants, shipmasters, mechanics, seamen, and schoolmasters with children— to west Main (now Essex) Street at Buffum's Corner, where they opened ranks on opposite sides of the streets.

Within sight, on Back Street (since 1792 called Federal), under Brig. General John Fisk, the colorfully outfitted militia prepared for review: the Salem 1st Regiment in rifle frocks, under Col. Stephen Abbott; the 5th Regiment of Lynn commanded by Colonel Breed; Ipswich's horse troop dressed in blue with hats; Salem's scarlet-and-white uniformed Independent Cadets led by Major John Saunders; the artillery of Salem, under Capt. Zadock Buffington, in scarlet and black.

Washington rode down a narrow lane, now Lafayette Street, over New Mills bridge to High Street and Summer, across Main, and past the North Meetinghouse to Back Street. About two o'clock, church bells started signaling the honored guest's approach. The Salem welcoming committee conducted Washington to the line of troops, who saluted as he passed. Escorted by the Andover troops, Bailey Bartlett, Essex County sheriff, and Jonathan Jackson, recently named U. S. marshal of Massachusetts, Washington proceeded toward Buffum's Corner. As the escort came to open order, the President cantered on his white charger toward the procession.

With Salem's Independent Corps of Cadets in front, the selectmen greeted him, and Chairman William Northey, a Quaker, with head covered, spoke: *"Friend Washington, we are glad to see thee, and in behalf of the inhabitants bid thee a hearty welcome to Salem!"* As the President passed through, lines formed and moved toward the recently completed Court House on Court Street, which had been designed by the renowned Salem architect Samuel McIntire. The President was conducted to its balcony, in full view of the crowd. From a specially built gallery, elegantly covered with Persian carpets and hung with damask curtains, a choir sang an ode composed in his honor. Cong. Benjamin Goodhue conveyed the town's welcome. The President responded warmly, expressing high aspirations for Salem: "May your navigation and commerce flourish—your industry, in all its applications, be rewarded—your happiness, here, be as perfect as belongs to the lot of humanity—and your eternal felicity be complete!"[6] The ecstatic crowd wildly cheered and shouted.

The Salem Cadets escorted Washington to his lodging, the Joshua

Ward house at the south end of Court Street, where he had requested to stay. Erected in the 1780s, the large brick mansion was a fine Salem home. Ward, a prominent merchant, presumably was chairman of the arrangements committee. Washington held a reception, noting afterward: "Rec'd the Compliments of many differ't. classes of People."[7]

That evening, the Court House was lighted resplendently, as a joyous Salem was celebrating. The highlight was the Concert Hall ball. As Washington left the Ward house, thirteen glaring rockets streamed into the sky. First, the President visited the home of Major John Saunders, commander of the Cadets, and took tea, thanking the well-known attorney for his escort. (The private company, composed of older men, had been formed in 1786 prior to Shays's Rebellion.) As Washington stepped down from his carriage to enter, a second volley of thirteen rockets "appeared at once in the air." Upon retiring, about nine o'clock, he was treated to a repeat salvo.

The Concert Hall or Assembly House, located on present Federal Street, originally was built in 1769 as a clubhouse for many distinguished and wealthy local residents. It featured a grand hall that measured forty by thirty feet and two "handsome" adjoining drawing rooms. In the brightly illuminated main room, strikingly decorated with leaves and flowers, many Salem gentlemen and about one hundred fashionably dressed women wearing black velvet "Washington Sashes" eagerly awaited their honored guest.

About seven o'clock, attired in black velvet, with his hair powdered, and accompanied by his attendants, Washington made his entrance. The company moved to the sides, bowing and curtsying. With his accustomed dignity and grace, the President bowed and took the seat of honor—a special armchair lent for the occasion by Elias Hasket Derby, Salem's leading merchant. It was the most memorable social event in Salem's history.[8]

To Beverly and Ipswich

On Friday morning, October 30, at about nine o'clock, Washington left town on horseback, strutting down Essex Street "escorted by Capt. Osgood's and Capt. Brown's Horse [from Ipswich], and accompanied by many respectable gentlemen." In his diary, Washington pictured Salem a "neat Town," which "exports chiefly Fish, Lumber, and Provisions. They have in the East India Trade at this time 13 Sail of Vessels." The commander in chief passed down Ives Lane to Capt. Francis Boardman's newly constructed mansion, situated northeasterly of the Common, where Boardman had offered him lodging. In response, the President rode past and saluted Boardman at

Woodcut of the new Essex Bridge with Fish Flake Hill shown in background.

his doorstep. Washington traveled along Winter Street turning onto Ferry lane, which led to the magnificent, year-old Essex Bridge. As he dismounted to observe the draw, crowds of bystanders cheered. The President noted its "handsome appearance," colorfully decked out with flags borrowed from ships moored in the harbor.[9]

He breakfasted with George Cabot, Beverly's most prosperous merchant, whose mansion stood a short distance up present Cabot Street. Afterwards, they traveled to the "Cotton Manufactory" in North Beverly, owned by Cabot and other local investors. A fascinated Washington wrote: "In short the whole seemed perfect, and the cotton stuffs w'ch they [machines] turn out, excellent of their kind."[10]

Washington then boarded his carriage and rode toward Ipswich village, about ten miles away, escorted by General Titcomb and the two horse troops. At the Wenham-Hamlet line, they were met by the selectmen, who led the procession down the Boston road into town. Col. Nathaniel Wade's regiment paraded under arms. Wade and Colonel Heard, both local war heros, stood beside the President as he was welcomed. Town officials, clergy, school masters, businessmen, and many others received greetings from the legendary Washington. In three hours, after "a cold collation" at Mrs. Homan's tavern, on Poplar Street near the south village green, he left for Newburyport, accompanied by Senator Tristram Dalton and other prominent Newburyport-area people. Lines of cheering onlookers bid him farewell.[11]

To Newburyport

To prepare for Washington's visit, voters of the northern trading town of Newburyport had met on October 21. It was decided that the eminent attorney, Theophilus Parsons, would write a welcoming address (which, in fact, was actually authored in part by his student, John Quincy Adams). Five famed Newburyporters were to present it: Judge Benjamin Greenleaf, Marshal Jonathan Jackson, State Senator Jonathan Greenleaf, Dr. Micajah Sawyer, and Col. Edward Wigglesworth. Artillery and militia were to be allocated adequate powder to assure a fitting salute.[12]

With his entourage and escort, Washington traveled through Rowley, passing tidal salt marshes and cultivated fields, and over the Parker River bridge to Old Town, Newbury. At the upper green, for a grand-style entrance, he mounted his white steed. With his dignified bearing and exceptional six-foot-two-inch frame, the famed soldier always presented an impressive profile. On horseback, Washington was even more inspiring. At about three o'clock, he reached the Newburyport town line (the present Bromfield and High streets), where an eager crowd of spectators awaited. Years later, a woman bystander recalled: "He rode through the crowd so majestic in his appearance, and, in his manner, so humble, that all were deeply impressed. What was very striking, amid all the crowd there was not the least noise."[13]

Alice Tucker of Newbury's First Parish, pastor John Tucker's thirty-eight-year-old maiden daughter, was not as star-struck. She noted in her diary: "The great Man the Monarch of the Earth, has just pass'd along escorted by his own Train and one or two Troop of Horse, his arrival is proclaimed by the ringing of Bells, and the firing of Cannon. But I drop my Pen for I have nothing more to say for this is not the Seat of action," she wrote, "and I have not curiosity enough to carry me to Town to be an observer of the transactions there."[14]

The Newburyport artillery company fired a federal salute, and a chorus of young men sang an ode, which began:

> *He comes, He comes! the HERO comes!*
> *Sound, Sound your Trumpets, beat, beat your Drums:*
> *From Port, to Port, let Cannons roar,*
> *He's welcome to New-England's shore!*

As the lyrics were sung, drums beat and cannon fired. The stirring tribute is said to have moved Washington to tears.[15]

In a procession similar to those in Salem and—earlier—in Boston, Washington rode past townspeople lined in order: militia, musicians,

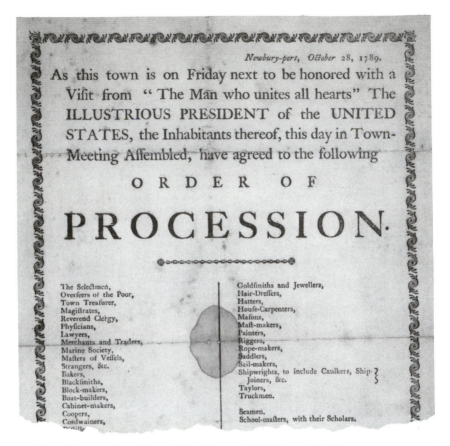

Newbury-port, October 28, 1789.

As this town is on Friday next to be honored with a Visit from " The Man who unites all hearts" The ILLUSTRIOUS PRESIDENT of the UNITED STATES, the Inhabitants thereof, this day in Town-Meeting Assembled, have agreed to the following

ORDER OF

PROCESSION.

The Selectmen,	Goldsmiths and Jewellers,
Overseers of the Poor,	Hair-Dressers,
Town Treasurer,	Hatters,
Magistrates,	House-Carpenters,
Reverend Clergy,	Masons,
Physicians,	Mast-makers,
Lawyers,	Painters,
Merchants and Traders,	Riggers,
Marine Society,	Rope-makers,
Masters of Vessels,	Saddlers,
Strangers, &c.	Sail-makers,
Bakers,	Shipwrights, to include Caulkers, Ship-Joiners, &c.
Blacksmiths,	Taylors,
Block-makers,	Truckmen.
Boat-builders,	
Cabinet-makers,	
Coopers,	Seamen.
Cordwainers,	School-masters, with their Scholars.

Order of procession planned for George Washington's visit to Newburyport. Courtesy, Essex Institute, Salem, Mass.

town officials, ministers, physicians . . . and, lastly, four hundred and twenty students, led by their preceptors, quills grasped in their hands. Once Washington had passed, they closed ranks and joined in the procession honoring "the man who united all hearts." The President was escorted to the Tracy house, an imposing brick mansion on Fish (now State) Street, presently the Newburyport Public Library. Washington slept the night here, after an evening reception at Marshal Jonathan Jackson's exquisite High Street residence.

The delegation read Parsons's welcome, which began: "Sir, When by the unanimous suffrages of your countrymen, you were called to preside over their public councils, the citizens of the Town of Newburyport participated in the general joy, that arose from anticipating an administration, conducted by the man, to whose wisdom and valor they owed their liberties." Washington graciously replied: "In visiting the Town of Newburyport, I have obeyed a favorite inclination, and I am much gratified by the indulgence—In expressing a sincere wish for its prosperity, and the happiness of its inhabitants, I do Justice to my own sentiments and their merit."[16]

Militia companies pridefully fired a feu-de-joie. In the evening, reveling townspeople and visitors celebrated as fireworks burst and rockets soared skyward. All "man and beast" arriving in town to help commemorate the historic occasion were "provided for gratis."[17] The November 4 *Essex Journal* praised the public "for their orderly behaviour through day and evening."

On Saturday morning, Washington and invited guests, including Rev. John Tucker and young Quincy Adams, breakfasted at Senator Dalton's State Street home. Afterwards, as the President rode along High Street toward Amesbury ferry, he bid farewell to Newburyport, which he described as "pleasantly situated on the Merrimack River." Two miles above, the Newburyport Marine Society awaited in a barge, splendidly canopied with rugs and draped with curtains. With the celebrated merchant William Coombs as cockswain, eight senior shipmasters dressed in white rowed Washington to the opposite shore. During the river crossing, Capt. Joseph A. deMurrietta of Tenerife, Canary Islands, fired a twenty-one gun salute from his "elegantly dressed" vessel moored in the harbor.[18]

Washington disembarked at Amesbury landing, near Ebenezer Pearson's tavern, and crossed to the north side of Merrimac Street. There, in an open field, stood militia, children clothed in white, and townspeople, waiting to see the President. It was a brief but memorable meeting. Over the Powow River, along Salisbury Point, birthplace of many Revolutionary War vessels including the frigate *Alliance*, Washington and company turned up Rocky Hill Road to the training field in West Salisbury. Here the Amesbury militia, with Jonathan Morrill, captain, and the Salisbury militia, captained by Isaac Merrill, were on dress parade. A veteran, that day, recalled that Washington "passed through the soldiers filed on either side, with his hat in his hand, a tall noble looking man." He took the Portsmouth road; Gen. John Sullivan, chief executive of New Hampshire, waited at the New Hampshire line with four light horse companies. Washington bid adieu to Senator Dalton, General Titcomb, his troop escort, and the many other military and distinguished Newburyport personages.[19]

To Haverhill and Andover

After three days of extensive sight-seeing, which included a boat ride and festive dinners and receptions, on Wednesday morning, November 4, Washington and party left Portsmouth and turned south toward the state's "second town," Exeter. They reached their destination by ten o'clock. Six miles further, in Kingston hamlet, lived Dr. Josiah Bartlett, the Amesbury-born physician, who, in 1790, would become president of New Hampshire. Washington stopped briefly to see his old patriot friend, a signer of the Declaration of Independence and delegate to the Continental Congress, and then resumed his southerly course.

A trumpet blast pierced through Haverhill village as Timothy Osgood galloped his frothing horse down the hill shouting, between shrill notes, "Washington is coming!" Originally, townspeople had expected the President, then they heard his plans had changed. As the parish bell dispelled the rumor, exhilarated villagers readied to greet Washington. The old schoolmaster near the common promptly dismissed school. Within minutes, an escort of horsemen formed and rode out. In mid-afternoon, wearing a long coat and officer's hat, the President entered. Though the prosperous merchant, John White, had invited Washington to his elegant Water Street manor, a public house was chosen: Harrod's tavern, at the sign of Freemason's Arms.

Here he received many notable Haverhill citizens and, after resting briefly, set out to see the village. He stopped at Sheriff Bartlett's to thank him for his county escort. (Bartlett, who was away, would be elected to the U.S. Congress in 1796.) The President strolled about one mile along Merrimac Street to Little River bridge (present Washington Square). Washington described Haverhill as standing "at the head of the tide of Merrimack River, and in a beautiful part of the country." From the Merrimack shore, he had an unobstructed, near-pristine picture for miles in either direction. Compared to the stony southern New Hampshire soil, the Virginia planter noticed "the land had a more fertile appearance. The whole were pretty well cultivated, but used (principally) for grass and Indian corn."

Samuel Blodgett recently had established a fabric manufactory on Kent Street where he produced duck which the President described as "upon a small but ingenious scale." These early workshops, more like experimental laboratories, intrigued him. Earlier, he had visited a Boston duck factory; Blodgett's system, however, appeared superior: "At this manufactory, one small person turns a wheel which employs eight spindles, each acting independently of each other, so as to occasion no interruption to the rest if any one of them is stopped."

At dawn, about one hundred militia lined up on the north side of Water Street. Opposite stood Major William Jackson, Col. Tobias Lear—who had joined at Portsmouth—and Washington. The Haverhill troops proudly paraded on review for their commander in chief.

The President spent his closing moments on Israel Bartlett's porch awaiting the ferry, surrounded by nearly the entire neighborhood. Touched by their warmth, he penned: "The inhabit'ts of this small village were well disposed to welcome me to it by every demonstration which could evince their joy." Washington boarded the gondola at the Kent Street landing and bid goodbye. He disembarked at the west village of Bradford.[20]

Washington and entourage traveled through Bradford, within sight of Merrimack waters, toward Andover. They entered at Osgood Street in North Andover and proceeded down present Andover and Elm streets to Deacon Isaac Abbott's tavern. It was a pleasant morning ride, with Washington noting: "The country from Haverhill to Andover is good, and well cultivated. In and about the latter (which stands high) it is beautiful."

He breakfasted at Isaac Abbott's tavern. (Abbott, as a lieutenant in the Revolutionary War, had been wounded at Bunker Hill.) Subsequently, Samuel Phillips, Jr., president of the Senate, rode with Washington in an open carriage to his recently constructed mansion on School Street. Phillips and wife hosted a reception, after which Washington crossed School Street on horseback to the training field and addressed the Phillips Academy students.

Thus concluded the President's Essex County tour. In the company of Phillips and a troop escort, Washington traveled to Lexington, where he "viewed the spot on which the first blood was spilt in the dispute with Great Britain, on the 19th of April, 1775." Already, in fourteen years, the village green had become hallowed ground.[21]

President Washington's journey foreshadowed the dawning of an exhilarating Federalist decade, for the nation and for Essex County. Despite historical suspicions between regions, the renowned Virginian had drawn a throng of well-wishers in Yankee Essex County; indeed, their wholehearted welcome confirmed that admiration for the President was countrywide.

Washington had come to New England seeking first-hand knowledge of the economy and he had visited many towns, including destitute "old" Marblehead, the "Neat Town" of Salem, and Newburyport, where he noticed shipbuilding had begun to "revive again." He found that the region's economy, juxtaposed between the torpor of the war years and the booming Federalist decade, was undergoing a metamorphosis. It would take time, however, to build from a quarter-century of Revolutionary ferment.

ENDNOTE ABBREVIATIONS:

BHS   Beverly Historical Society
DHS   Danvers Historical Society
EI   Essex Institute
EIHC   *Essex Institute Historical Collections*
MHS   Massachusetts Historical Society
NEHGR   New England Historical and Genealogical Register

1. John C. Fitzpatrick, ed., *The Diaries of George Washington* (Boston: Houghton Mifflin, 1925), 4:14.
2. *Salem Mercury*, November 3, 1789; Robert S. Rantoul, "Washington in Essex County," *EIHC*, 58 (1922):1–2.
3. Alonzo Lewis & James R. Newhall, *History of Lynn* (Boston: John L. Shorey, 1865), 353; Fitzpatrick, 39.
4. Fitzpatrick, 39; Samuel Roads, Jr., *The History and Traditions of Marblehead* (Marblehead: N. Allen Lindsey, 1897), 208–09.
5. Fitzpatrick, 39; *The Essex Journal & New-Hampshire Packet* (hereinafter, *Essex Journal*), December 9, 1789; *Salem Mercury*, December 1, 1789.
6. *Salem Mercury*, November 3, 1789; *Essex Journal*, November 11, 1789.
7. Fitzpatrick, 40.
8. For Washington's visit, see: *Salem Mercury*, November 3, 1789; Robert S. Rantoul, "Washington in Essex County," *EIHC*, 58 (1922): 1–19; *The Diary of William Bentley* (Salem: Essex Institute, 1905), 1:130–31.
9. *Salem Mercury*, November 3, 1789; Fitzpatrick, 40–41; *Diary of William Bentley*, 1:131.
10. Fitzpatrick, 41.
11. Thomas Franklin Waters, *Ipswich in the Massachusetts Bay Colony* (Ipswich: Ipswich Historical Society, 1917), 2:370– 71,

12. Newburyport Town Records, October 21, 1789, 1:546.
13. *The Daily Herald*, April 27, 1864.
14. Journal of Alice Tucker, 1784–1791, MS, Private Collection.
15. *Essex Journal*, November 4, 1789.
16. Newburyport Town Records, October 21, 1789, 1:545–46; *Essex Journal*, November 4, 1789; *Salem Mercury*, November 10, 1789.
17. *Salem Mercury*, November 3, 1789.
18. Fitzpatrick, 42; for accounts of visit, see: John J. Currier, *History of Newburyport, Mass. 1764–1905* (Newburyport: John J. Currier, 1906), 1:408–14; Diary of John Quincy Adams, *Life in a New England Town* (Boston: Little, Brown, 1903), 178–79; *Essex Journal*, November 4, 1789; *Salem Mercury*, November 3, 1789.
19. Sara Locke Redford, *History of Amesbury* (Amesbury: Whittier Press, 1968), 69; D. Hamilton Hurd, *History of Essex County* (Philadelphia: J.W. Lewis, 1888), 2:1516; Joseph Merrill, *History of Amesbury* (Haverhill: Franklin P. Stiles, 1880), 304– 05.
20. Fitzpatrick, 46–47; George Wingate Chase, *History of Haverhill* (Haverhill: George Wingate Chase, 1861), 442–49.
21. Fitzpatrick, 47–48; Sarah Loring Bailey, *Historical Sketches of Andover* (Boston: Houghton Mifflin, 1880), 200–02.

CHAPTER TWO

ESSEX COUNTY AT THE DAWNING

At the dawning of the American Revolution, over 150 years had passed since the Dorchester Company had planted its little settlement on Cape Ann; four years later, in 1628, the Puritan-dominated New England Company had sent its first contingent of settlers to Salem. From the beginning, the lure of fisheries and trade and the opportunity for freedom of worship attracted colonists. Essex County continued to grow and to prosper; by the dawning of the Revolution over 50,000 people were living within its 500 square miles. The stage was set for a county already rich in history to write an indelible chapter in its own and the nation's history.

From Coastline to Interior

From coastline to interior, Essex County boasted one of the most beautiful and varied landscapes in the thirteen colonies. Beginning at the New Hampshire boundary, miles of sandy beach stretched along the Salisbury shore to the northern bank of the Merrimack. Salisbury's riverside was composed of tidal marshes, but, on the opposite side, Newburyport enjoyed a long, fairly deep harbor. At the Merrimack's mouth, shifting bars and swift currents—though serious obstacles to unknowing navigators—helped prevent winter freeze-ups, and the northern end of Plum Island protected the narrow estuarial bay from the lash of ocean storms.

The smallest town in the province, 647-acre Newburyport had been a separate town only since 1764. The mercantile-oriented townspeople had been unhappy belonging to agriculturally dominated

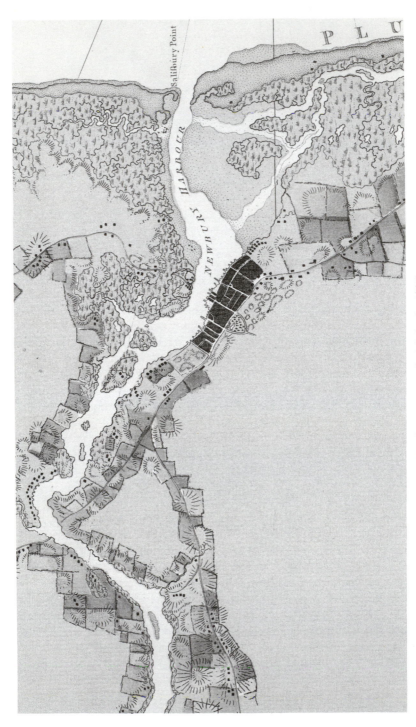

Newburyport and vicinity in 1776.

Newbury and had petitioned to be established as a separate township. The river provided a natural water route for people from the interior to reach Newburyport with their wares to exchange for imported and local items. On several wharves along the river, deck hands and dock workers handled the cargoes of a variety of seagoing vessels. Merrimac and Water streets ran beside the two miles of waterfront and converged at Market Square—the commercial hub of the town. A series of avenues ran at right angles to the river and intersected High Street, several hundred yards up from the waterfront. Tidewaters ran up the Merrrimack more than twenty miles, making the villages of Salisbury Point, Amesbury, Newbury New Town, Bradford, and Haverhill accessible to medium-draft vessels. But Newburyport remained the entrepôt for the upriver valley. Yeomen brought down their surplus goods and returned home with a cask of rum, some tea, imported cloths, and other items. Newburyport's geographic advantages afforded it economic and political eminence in pre-Revolutionary northern Essex County; the town was to continue as a trading and mercantile hub for several generations.

To the south, miles of Plum Island beach protected the ports of Old Newbury, Rowley, and Ipswich. The towns were served by the shallow, navigable Parker, Rowley, and Ipswich rivers, which wound through the tidal salt marshes and flowed into clam-rich Plum Island sound. Past the Ipswich bluffs and the Chebacco (now Essex) and Squam (now Annisquam) rivers, the scene changed abruptly to the craggy granite coastline of Cape Ann. Five hundred inhabitants lived in Squam Parish, where the Squam River nearly divided Cape Ann into two equal parts. A seventeenth-century cut completed the division, permitting easier travel (later, it silted with sand) between Gloucester harbor and Ipswich bay and points east. Several coastal havens indented East Gloucester, including Sandy Bay (Rockport) and Gloucester harbor—both important fishing ports. The Gloucester harbor section had grown over the years to become the central village, with over half the population living in this First Parish. Several narrow dirt roads ran parallel with the waterfront, intersecting others running perpendicular. Fore Street (later Main) ran alongside the wharves; above the waterfront, in the same direction, stretched Middle Street, and still further from the shoreline was Back (later Prospect) Street. From above Harbor Cove near the summit of a rockbound hill, known as Watch House Point, breastworks built thirty years before during a war with the French overlooked the expanse of harbor waters.

Further to the south of Cape Ann, snug coves, picturesque headlands, and sandy beaches dotted the irregular coastline to sheltered Manchester harbor. The port, with many small bays and inlets, was

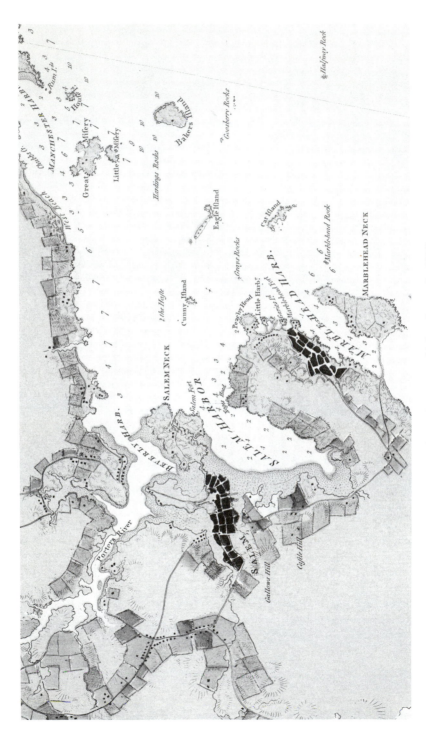

The Beverly—Salem—Marblehead area in 1776.

shallow but spacious and well protected from the open sea. Manchester, a small fishing village, was located at its head.

Further southward still, among sandy beaches and rocky points, was the tri-town cluster of Beverly, Salem, and Marblehead. As a group, they rivaled Boston in size, wealth, and commercial importance. Numerous offshore islands—notably Baker's, Big and Little Misery, House, and Cat—helped protect the towns from the whip of ocean storms, though there was no protecting Marblehead from the pounding of a nor'easter.

Beverly harbor was located at the mouth of the Bass River. New Mills, now Danversport, could be reached by sailing upriver and following Wooliston's, or Porter's, River. Beverly harbor was safe and sufficiently deep for the vessels of the period. A cartway, now called Water Street, which ran along the harbor front from the ferry landing near the present Essex Bridge, was the principal commercial avenue. A dozen or so warehouses had been constructed on both sides. From the warehouses, local merchants conducted a wholesale and retail trade. Fish flakes, or stages, visible in every port town, lined the coastline from Tuck's Point to the Cove. Beverly, like other ports, engaged in the coaster and West Indies market, and ten larger craft plied Atlantic waters, trading particularly with Spain and France. A ferry ran across Bass River between Beverly and Salem. A traveler would cross from Beverly at Ellinwood's wharf, land just north of the present bridge, at Green's Point, follow Ferry lane down present Bridge Street, and round the Common by the training field to the junction of Essex Street, Salem.

Salem was a principle mercantile and trading center in the province—second only to Boston. The town's commercial importance came from its fisheries, its extensive coastal, West Indian, and European trade, and its role as a major marketplace for the countryside.

The settlement was situated between the navigable North and South rivers. While numerous fishing vessels used the northern entry, the South River was the town's principal harbor. Salem Neck and Winter Island, with its ancient fort on the eastern point, overlooked the north side of the harbor entrance. Dozens of wharves lined South River's banks; Long (or Union) and Derby, stretching hundreds of feet, dwarfed the others.

Most of Salem's five thousand inhabitants lived in a compact settlement which covered not more than three hundred acres. About seven hundred shops and homes, nearly all unpainted wooden structures, lined the fifty crisscrossed streets. The only avenue passing through the entire length of the town was King's Street—now Essex—the first thoroughfare to display signs of the town's prosperity. Lined by many elegant homes, 740 feet had been paved recently with cobblestones from Baker's Island. Several lanes ran from Essex Street to the harbor ways. One shoreline avenue, now called Derby Street, extended along the southern side of the Neck. Wharf Street (now Front) was lined with warehouses on one side and wharves on the other. Tierces of rice, hogsheads of molasses, casks of indigo, rum, and wines, bolts of cloth—all were stored here for sale in local markets. Barrels of dried, compacted fish, lumber, and country wares stocked many of the same warehouses, awaiting export.

A single way led out of Salem to Marblehead, following what is now Lafayette Street and over the narrow causeway bridging the Forest River. Great or Marblehead Neck was connected by a narrow isthmus with the mainland to form one of the most excellent, well-protected harbors in New England—one-and-a-half miles long and a half-mile wide. The fort on Gale's Head, built in 1742, overlooked the harbor from a rocky bluff at the northeast entrance. Four hundred and fifty "Generallity Miserable," unpainted, clapboarded houses, "Mostly Close in with the Rocks," dotted the landscape of this rugged 3,700-acre peninsula. In the village above the western harborside, tightly spaced houses and shops lined "narrow, and rugged, and dirty" lanes winding to the coves, wharves, and the deep anchorage along the shoreline.[1]

A road leading from Marblehead southwesterly reached Lynn via what is now Ocean Street, along King's Beach. A second wound further inland following the course of present Humphrey and Tedesco streets. From the hills of Lynn, an observer could see the town's two miles of sandy beach, the jagged cliffs of Nahant, the harbor south of the peninsula, and the Saugus River winding its course to the sea. On a clear day, the view extended straight across Massachusetts Bay to the South Shore.

Landscape

Views of the countryside seen from rural Lynn's hillsides mirrored the remarkable panorama which could be seen from the more than two hundred hills throughout the county. Roads that were "amazingly crooked, to suit the convenience of every man's fields," as Washington observed, wound to peaceful village hamlets in the valleys.[2] Fertile lowlands and lush meadows bordered a network of rambling rivers, which emptied into larger waterways or followed their courses to the sea. Some rivers, notably the Shawsheen of Andover, which discharged into the Merrimack, sprang from crystal-clear ponds several miles inland.

Distant hillsides were dotted with white pines, red oaks, and other hard woods; cows and sheep grazed on their green grassy slopes.

Scores of drumlins—the highest being Holt and Mills in Andover, which rose over four hundred feet—and a few bed-rock protuberances, mostly from Rockport to Lynn—shaped by glaciers 15,000 years earlier—extended over the reaches of the land. From atop the northern coastal hillsides, an observer could see vast expanses of salt marshes and sand dunes stretching seaward. Far off to the north, the foothills of New Hampshire and Maine loomed on the horizon.

The county has grown thirteen-fold over the past two hundred and fifteen years, and much of the landscape has yielded to rows of houses, shopping centers, and factory buildings; yet many inlets and coves, salt marshes, and stretches of sand remain largely untouched. In the northern and western towns, there are still eye-catching glimpses of the same idyllic views which graced the countryside in Revolutionary days.

Cities and Towns

Today, Essex County's population is close to 650,000—thirteen times its number at the beginning of the Revolution. The provincial census of 1776 counted nearly 51,000 people living in the county— over one-sixth the total province population—exclusive of 47,000 living in Maine, then part of Massachusetts. Most were native-born of English ancestry; 2 percent were black, free and slave, most of whom lived in Salem (173), Gloucester (109), Ipswich (100), Marblehead (100), Andover (86), Beverly (79) and Danvers (72).[3]

POPULATION OF ESSEX COUNTY—1776

Amesbury	1,795	Marblehead	4,386
Andover	2,953	Methuen	1,326
Beverly	2,754	Middleton	650
Boxford	989	Newbury	3,239
Bradford	1,240	Newburyport	3,681
Danvers	2,284	Rowley	1,678
Gloucester	4,512	Salem	5,337
Haverhill	2,810	Salisbury	1,666
Ipswich	4,508	Topsfield	773
Lynn	2,755	Wenham	638
Manchester	949	TOTAL:	50,923[4]

Essex County covers nearly 500 square miles—about twenty-three miles on each side. Eight cities (Beverly, Gloucester, Haverhill, Lawrence, Lynn, Newburyport, Peabody, Salem) and twenty-six towns are located in the county, thirteen more than in 1776.

Over the years, many times, when disputes provoked one section to request establishment as a separate township, the General Court approved partition petitions. The division normally was at the parish line. Hamlet Parish of Ipswich was established as the town of Hamilton in 1793; in 1819, the Chebacco Parish was incorporated as the town of Essex. In the same year, the Second and Fourth parishes (New Town section) of Newbury gave rise to the town of West Newbury. To the south of Newbury, in 1838, the West Parish of Rowley was incorporated as Georgetown. Until 1782, when Lynnfield was incorporated first as a district, then, in 1814, as a town, it was known as the Lynn End section. In 1816, Saugus was partitioned from Lynn. Swampscott and Nahant—not separate parishes—were set apart in 1852 and 1853, respectively. There were several other mid-century divisions. Next door to Lynn, Danvers's South Parish became Peabody in 1855. To the northeast, Gloucester's Sandy Bay section was established as Rockport in 1840. Five new interior towns along the banks of the Merrimack River were incorporated: in 1850, the East Parish of Bradford became Groveland, and northeast Boxford (now South Groveland) was annexed in 1856; the remainder of Bradford was joined to Haverhill across the river. During the dawning of the industrial revolution, tiny Lawrence was carved out of both banks of the Merrimack—the northern tip of Andover and the southern end of Methuen—to become a separate town in 1853. Next, in 1855, the North Parish of Andover became the township of North Andover. The final partition occurred in 1876 when South Amesbury was incorporated as the town of Merrimac. Eight towns—Beverly, Manchester, Marblehead, Middleton, Newburyport, Salem, Topsfield, Wenham—have kept largely the same boundaries for the past two hundred years.[5]

Communication by Land and Sea

Passage over water generally was easier than land travel; since the seventeenth century, using relatively uncomplicated water routes that connected seaport towns, coastal merchants and shipmasters had welded important social and economic ties among themselves. The road system that crisscrossed the county remained little more than a series of cartways, which, during the spring thaws, slippery hills and deep muddy ruts made barely passable.

The most important land route was the Boston post road between Portsmouth and Boston, which, by the 1750s, were connected by a stage. The crossing from Salisbury to Newburyport was made via the ferry at Carr's Island. This water route was the oldest of several which connected Merrimack Valley towns. Since there were few important bridges in the county, ferries provided the usual means of crossing. By 1774, Ezra Lunt of Newburyport was advertising weekly runs to and from Boston on his four-horse stagecoach. The stages followed the post road route: over High Street in Newburyport, twelve miles to Ipswich over the old Bay road (present Route 1A), and from Conant Street, Beverly, into Danvers. Continuing on what are now Elm, Ash, and Sylvan streets into South Danvers (Peabody), along Prospect, Summit, County, and Lynn streets, the coaches reached Lynn. They passed Flax Pond and the scattered houses surrounding the unfenced common, ascended Tower Hill, crossed the Saugus River, plied over the Saugus hills to Rumney Marsh (Chelsea), and finally arrived in Boston. In 1770, Benjamin Coats, owner of the Ship tavern in Salem, advertised a second stage, (one was already running), for week-day runs between Salem and Boston. Another stage line left Marblehead, traveling through Lynn to the Winnisimet Ferry (in Chelsea).[6]

Salem did not have a direct land route to Boston. Townspeople were required to turn up Boston Street at the Essex Street intersection and travel as far as the Bell tavern in South Danvers to reach the Boston post road, the main thoroughfare. An alternative was to travel via Marblehead. Passage by sail offered a third option.

Two land routes out of Andover wound toward Boston: one continued into Wilmington; the second, to Tewksbury and Billerica. These roadways, particularly the Wilmington line, were used by Boston-bound travelers in the western part of the county. A Haverhill traveler would take one of three ferries to Bradford, (a fourth crossed at Rocks Village to Newbury), pick up the Boston road in Bradford, and travel southbound through the North and South parishes of Andover, into Wilmington, and then to Medford and Boston.

In addition to the Boston roads, several well-travelled routes wound across the county. Many of today's numbered highways, such as Route 113 (Newburyport to Groveland), Route 133 (Georgetown to Essex), and Route 127 (through Cape Ann to Beverly), follow the course of roadways laid out at the time of the Revolution.

Fisheries and Trade

Originally, settlers were attracted to Essex County by the seemingly endless supply of cod and other bottom fish offshore in the Gulf of Maine and along the vast continental shelf. Rivers also teemed. Ipswich River, winding down from Wilmington, through Middleton, Topsfield, and Ipswich, was filled with bass, shad, and alewives, possibly the best stream in the county. The numerous protected rivers and harbors along the broken coastline offered ideal fishing ports. Virgin forests of oak and pine—ideal boat-building materials—covered the Merrimack Valley and many hills along the coast. By the dawning of the Revolution, the county fisheries were operating at full gear.

Essex County catches found their way to Roman Catholic Europe and to the West Indies. Marblehead, where "the whole Air seem[ed] Tainted" with the smell of fish, exported more cod to Europe than the rest of New England combined.[7] While Marblehead was the fish capital, every port had a fleet of 35- to 65-ton Gloucester-designed fishing schooners. With a wide, square stern and rounded bow, the schooner's low waist and elevated quarterdeck projected the profile of an inverted shoe. Named a "heel-tapper," the first sizable two-masted vessel fitted with a fore-'n-aft rig was the favorite in the coasting and West Indies trade, where England and France restricted trade to vessels of less than 70 tons. In early spring, the schooners were off to the fog-shrouded Grand Banks—about one hundred and fifty Marblehead schooners, seventy-five from Gloucester and another forty-five out of Sandy Bay, forty from Salem, twenty-five from Beverly, another twenty-five from Manchester, eleven from Ipswich, and only ten hailing out of Newburyport. Almost four hundred schooners with nearly three thousand fishermen aboard (not to mention those on smaller craft) were engaged. Raised wooden frames called flakes, on which cod were dried and cured, covered the county shorelines. Seven or eight mariners were employed on each vessel during the eight-month season; an additional number of shoremen, and women, were required for processing and export operations.

During the last half of the eighteenth century, the two-masted schooner was the mainstay of Essex County fisheries and West Indies and coastal trade. From *Encyclopedia Britannica*, 1797. Courtesy, Essex Institute, Salem, Mass.

Early view of Salem harbor. Courtesy, Peabody Museum of Salem.

Every town participated in the export trade, as their catches exceeded local demand.

Ships which set out to Europe loaded with fish returned with cargoes of Bilbao iron, Cadiz or Cape Verde salt, Malaga grapes, Valencia oranges, Madeira or Canary wine, French silks, wines, and olive oil, or English linens, wool, and hardware. There was a ready market for these goods.

Another important county trade route led to the West Indies. Casks of dried, lower quality (summer) cod, mackerel, and alewives were shipped to the West Indies, where fish was a part of the slave diet. Pipe-staves, masts, spars, shingles, and boards, particularly from the Merrimack Valley, were also transported. Gloucester sent fish and lumber as far as Surinam on the South American coast. The vessels returned loaded with coffee, lemons, molasses, rum, sugar, and other tropical products.

A coaster trade from Nova Scotia to the Carolinas had been in process for a century. The trade with the southern colonies was particularly strong. Usually voyages were made in the winter when fishing schooners were available for trading ventures. On board were English imports, rum, woodenware, and barreled beef and pork for barter. On these voyages up the rivers, creeks and inlets of Maryland, Virginia, North and South Carolina, the Yankee traders exchanged their cargoes for bacon, beans, grain, live hogs, rice, and other products. On the eve of the Revolution, Essex County port towns were experiencing an unprecedented prosperity from local fisheries and foreign trade. And the future looked bright.

Trading vessels returned to port towns with a variety of imports. In the trading centers of Salem and Newburyport about twenty shopkeepers offered hundreds of items from other colonies, the West

Shipmaster Benjamin Moses, his wife, Sarah
Carroll, and daughter, Betsey, were among the
fashionable merchant families that shaped
customs and manners in 18th-century Salem.

Indies, England, and southern Europe. Practical items—fishing supplies, duck (canvas), cloth, flour, iron, nails, paper, sugar—were advertised, as well as more expensive luxury items—glass, gloves,
lambskins, port, silks, snuff, spices, tea, wallpaper. A smaller number
of retail stores operated in Beverly, Gloucester, Haverhill, and Marblehead. And general stores even in the smallest towns sold some
imported goods.

Merchant Power

Profits from fisheries and trade bred a mercantile aristocracy in
the port towns. A few merchant princes were at the pinnacle of

These two oil paintings are attributed to Benjamin Blyth (1746–1787), who is best known for his superb pastels. Courtesy, Essex Institute, Salem, Mass.

power. Among them were Jeremiah Lee, John Robie, Benjamin Marston, and Robert "King" Hooper of Marblehead; the Brownes, Crowninshields, Derbys, Gardners, Ornes, and Pickmans of Salem; Moses Brown, Andrew, George, and John Cabot, Joseph Lee, and Israel Thorndike of Beverly; Tristram Dalton and Nathaniel Tracy of Newburyport; and Winthrop Sargent of Gloucester. With a handful of others from these and other ports, they dominated the county's economic, cultural, and political life. The power and prestige of ship masters, often part owners of their vessels, vied with all but the most powerful.

Of nearly equal standing—and allied with the merchants—were lawyers, like Benjamin Greenleaf and John Lowell of Newburyport and William Pynchon of Salem. Those men who held sway over the spiritual life of the communities—clergy such as Rev. Thomas Barnard and Rev. William McGilchrist of Salem—were often closely associated with the powerful merchants. Physicians—such as Salem's E. A. Holyoke, Danvers's Samuel Holten, and Haverhill's James Brickett—shared lower upper-class status with the lawyers and the clergy.

The merchants of Essex County built some of the finest homes in the province: elegant three-story Georgian structures topped by elaborate cupolas, highly decorated and extensively furnished inside, with spacious rooms for dining and entertaining their social equals. The most wealthy owned country homes, like "King" Hooper's Danvers and Tristram Dalton's Newbury residences. Horse-drawn chaises transported families there for the summer months. Many merchants owned slaves, employed as coachmen, household servants, and groundsmen for their well-kept gardens. The wealthy men could always be distinguished by cocked hats, powdered wigs, knee breeches, and silver buckles and were clothed customarily in high-colored blues, scarlets, and purple, rather than in common homespun. The ladies usually were adorned in bonnets, dressed in ankle-length skirts worn over farthingales (hoops), and bodices or jackets over lace-trimmed chemises. During the Revolution, some of the upper class remained with the Crown; others joined the patriot movement. Whichever, they would be found among the leadership.

Shipbuilding

Small ketches, sloops, and schooners were sufficient for fishing and coaster activities, but larger vessels were necessary for the growing European trade. Mechanics had been shipbuilding in Danvers, Gloucester, Ipswich, Lynn, Marblehead and Salem—and especially in the Merrimack Valley—for several generations.

The valley region took an early lead in constructing larger merchantmen. Newburyport's shoreline was dotted with shipyards, from near the Joppa mud flats, at the east end, almost to Carr's ferry. The Navigation Act requirement that vessels engaged in trade with the empire be English or colonial-built was a boon to Newburyport. Large numbers of sturdily-built area vessels, less costly than their English competition, were sold to English merchants. Among the most noted shipwrights were Eleazer Johnson, the Crosses, and the Woodwells. Upriver towns also participated, with Salisbury being particularly renowned. For several miles, its river bank consisted of tidal meadows, unsuitable for shoreline activities. Yet, upstream, on the outer side of a crescent-shaped bend was a mile of higher ground, a strip of shoreline known as Salisbury Point which stretched to the Powow

River. It belonged to Salisbury until 1886, when the West Parish was annexed to Amesbury. Logs cut in the Amesbury, Salisbury, and southeastern New Hampshire woodlands floated down the Powow, where water-powered mills sawed the timbers for shipyard use. The Hackett family was the most noted of local builders, though several others were widely known as outstanding craftsmen. On the river road's northern side stood nearly one hundred dwellings, many of which are standing today. Amesbury's shipbuilding was conducted in the Ferry district, near the mouth of the Powow and adjacent to Salisbury Point. The district became the most populated and prosperous in town. South Amesbury (now Merrimacport), Rocks Village, further upriver in Haverhill, and Bradford also produced ocean-going craft. Upstream, the shallower Merrimack was fit for only thirty-ton vessels, but larger craft were built and floated empty to Newburyport. Adjacent to Amesbury was Haverhill, situated eighteen miles from the river mouth on the northern side across from the Bradford countryside. The Merrimack was navigable up to Haverhill; nearly three miles beyond was Mitchell's Falls, which prevented vessels from going any further. Above the falls, New Hampshire timber was rafted to Swan's ferry, Andover. Local raftsmen took the timber from this point to the shipyards downstream. The compact village of Haverhill was comprised of about two hundred houses and buildings dotted along two principal roads. Narrow Merrimac Street ran close to the river beside three or four warehouses and a number of wharves; Main Street ran perpendicular to it. Many of its two thousand inhabitants lived outside the village on prosperous farms. The valley towns constructed scores of ships each year, earning a reputation for craftsmanship which would endure for generations.

Small Farmers

About half the families in Essex County gained most of their livelihoods from near-subsistence-level farming, with a small surplus for trade. Seven coastal towns—Beverly, Gloucester, Ipswich, Manchester, Marblehead, Newburyport, Salem—were largely fishing and trading communities, and Amesbury and Salisbury were involved heavily in shipbuilding. The other twelve were primarily agricultural villages. In fact, with the exception of Gloucester, Marblehead, Newburyport, and Salem, enough farmers lived in port towns to provide most local basic food needs. On farms usually of less than one hundred acres, yeomen farmers tended their fields, grazed their cattle and sheep, cut their wood lots, and maintained their orchards— thus providing for almost all of their own daily demands. Usually not too far away, alongside a rambling stream, were grist mills to grind corn, saw mills to cut logs, and fulling operations to cleanse, scour, and press woven cloth. Surplus vegetables, barreled beef and pork, and woodenware (buckets, ox-bows, axe helves) hand-crafted over the winter, could be exchanged in the port towns—in Beverly, Newburyport, and Salem—for a few basics, like salt or gunpowder, or an occasional luxury. There was little agricultural produce for export; commercial farming would not come until after the Revolution.

Manufacturing

Importation of molasses from the West Indies prompted a meteoric rise of the rum industry. Distilleries sprang up in Beverly, Haverhill, Ipswich, and Salem, but it was Newburyport that became the center of rum manufacture. Rum was consumed locally and was a staple in the export trade.

Prior to the Revolution, manufacturing was limited largely to artisans and mechanics plying their trades in small shops beside their homes. Ship construction required the talents of various workmen. While shipwrights worked in the yards, skilled tradesmen—caulkers, coopers, sailmakers, ropemakers, riggers, ironworkers—applied their skills in support of the shipbuilding and outfitting operations. Other craftsmen, blacksmiths, cordwainers, cabinet makers, joiners—skills required almost universally—could be found in most villages. Iron and limestone was being mined in Boxford, where a smelting operation had been established. The ancient Saugus River Iron Works had been in production for over a century. Hats were being fashioned in Haverhill and Methuen, while Bradford and Lynn farmers were turning out quantities of shoes in cobbler shops during the winter months. Tanneries were located in several towns, and brick manufacturing had commenced in Danvers. The county already was gaining a manufacturing reputation, which in the next century would be nationwide.

Background to Revolution

In the early years, in accordance with the generous royal charter granted in 1629 to the Massachusetts Bay Company, the province was left to govern itself through popularly controlled town meetings and an elected colonial legislature. Town meetings were open to adult males whose estates were worth twenty pounds, a qualification most could meet. Voters met annually and decided the town's affairs; articles were passed to build bridges, run schools, repair roads, farm out public charges, and elect multitudinous town officers. At the dawning of the Revolution, the democratic town meetings provided a convenient forum in which to discuss common grievances with England. At town meetings, customarily in May, qualifying voters, with personal property worth forty pounds, elected their representatives(s) to the House. The House, in turn, elected the governor's advisory body or upper House, known as the Council. Together, they constituted the General Court, a bicameral legislature. Over one hundred years of largely uninterrupted self-rule nurtured in Massachusetts citizens a fiercely independent belief in their right to govern.

The local unit of church organization was the parish, with from one to five in each town. Every Congregational meetinghouse, one to a parish, governed itself autonomously. The Congregational Church, which was the established religion, attracted the largest membership. Clergy were prominent community leaders and respected for their secular as well as religious views.

Massachusetts' independence extended to the high seas, where colonials traded with whomever they chose. In the mid-seventeenth century, England initiated a policy called mercantilism designed to produce a self-sufficient British Empire. Navigation Acts were passed to strengthen and enrich England. All colonial trade had to be conducted in English or colonial-built, -owned, and -manned vessels. Certain enumerated articles—few from New England—had to be shipped exclusively to England. European imports were required to be shipped first to England for unloading and reloading before going to the colonies. These acts were largely ignored in New England, which caused England to take measures toward strengthening its hand.

New England was consolidated into the Dominion of New England from 1685 to 1688 under the governorship of Sir Edmund Andros. The unpopular, arrogant Andros attempted to remove representative institutions which had evolved under years of independent governance. When Andros tried to impose new taxes, some inhabitants, notably in Ipswich under the leadership of Rev. John Wise, defied his actions and voted to pay no taxes. Wise said taxes could not be levied without consent of the elected Assembly, or House. Over eighty years later, Essex County patriots could take example from these revolutionary stirrings. In England, the Glorious Revolution of 1688–89, a bloodless victory for Protestantism and representative government, brought William and Mary to the throne. During the revolutionary proceedings in England, Massachusetts overthrew the Andros regime. Its representative institutions were restored by the royal family and guaranteed under the new Charter of 1691. They could hardly do otherwise, since events in England closely paralleled those in New England.

Over the next decades Massachusetts was left largely to itself. There were occasional attempts to strengthen enforcement of the Navigation Acts—vice-admiralty trial courts were established, customs officials were sent, writs of assistance (general search warrants) were used—but they met with little success. Poor enforcement and ineptitude contributed to continued evasion and smuggling.

In the early 1750s a new attempt was made to strengthen England's administrative and imperial control of the colonies, but the beginning of the Seven Years' War in 1756 necessitated holding off. After the war, Parliament's decision to initiate a new colonial policy precipitated a chain of events which ended in the War of Independence. This is the story of one county's resistance to these policies and its ultimate decision to sever ties with England and join the "United Colonies of America."

1. George F. Dow, ed., *Two Centuries of Travel in Essex County* (Topsfield: Topsfield Historical Society, 1921), 76, 88.

2. John C. Fitzpatrick, ed., *The Diaries of George Washington* (Boston: Houghton Mifflin, 1925), 4:49–50.

3. *A Century of Population Growth* (Washington: Bureau of the Census, 1909), 158.

4. *Census of Massachusetts 1875 Population and Social Statistics*, 2nd ed. (Boston: Albert J. Wright, 1876), 1:736, 738.

5. The boundary lines of Salem and Danvers were altered, March 17, 1840; part of Salem was annexed to Swampscott, April 3, 1867; part of Beverly to Danvers, April 27, 1857; a parish of Newbury to Newburyport, April 17, 1851.

6. Chelsea consisted of the present communities of Chelsea, Revere, and Winthrop.

7. Dow, 76.

CHAPTER THREE

EARLY REGULATORY DISPUTES

The French and Indian War—or the Seven Years' War, as it was known in Europe—was concluded in 1763. England now had a national debt more excessive than ever before. With taxes in England already high, payment of the interest alone would saddle English taxpayers with an extraordinary burden. As a result of the war, victorious Great Britain acquired the French possessions of Canada and the Mississippi Valley in North America. These acquisitions required stationing of ten thousand troops on the North American continent. The military costs and other administrative expenses triggered a desperate search for additional revenue. Consequently, the feeling began to prevail that the colonies ought to participate in the costs of their own administration and defense.

Writs of Assistance

Some enterprising Massachusetts merchants profited during the French and Indian War by supplying enemy forces with smuggled French West Indies goods. British warships were stationed off the coastline to prevent this illicit trade. Writs of assistance (general search warrants), which were issued by the courts, permitted British customs officers to search private homes and warehouses for contraband goods. Predictably, the merchants protested this long-standing enforcement technique as an illegal invasion of privacy.

The dispute surfaced in November 1760, when James Cockle, collector of customs in Salem, petitioned the superior court for writs in the name of the new king, George III. (Writs lapsed on a sovereign's death. George II had died in October 1760, and twenty-two-year-old George III had acceded to the British throne.) After the fall of Montreal in 1760—the last French stronghold on the continent—a British victory in North America was assured. Since the old writs had been issued to deal with the prohibited American traffic with the enemy, few expected they would be renewed. Cockle's move had surprised almost everyone. Sixty-three merchants from Salem and Boston decided the time was propitious to question the legality of the writs. Two prominent attorneys were hired, James Otis and Oxenbridge Thacher, to argue their case. Though the challenge was unsuccessful, Otis's line of argument was brilliant, advancing broad principles of constitutional rights and rights of Englishmen oft repeated in the struggle toward independence. John Adams noted of the trial fifty years later, *"the child Independence was born."*[1]

Armed with writs, the customs office enforced the trade laws—particularly the one related to dutied foreign rum, sugar, and molasses—with help along the North Shore coming from the British man-of-war *Jamaica*, stationed off the coast. The historically free trade which the merchants had enjoyed was no more. In Salem, Cockle, whose enforcement included several ship and cargo seizures, incurred serious resentment. By September 1764, local political pressures forced his suspension. On September 29, townspeople rejoiced by "firing guns, making bonfires, entertainments, &c." But Cockle would not be Salem's last unpopular customs official. And England's shift toward strengthening imperial power was just beginning.[2]

The Sugar Act

One revenue-raising measure was the reinstitution of the Molasses, or Sugar, Act of 1733, with the duties reduced to more realistic levels. Earlier ones had been prohibitive, resulting in loose enforcement, widespread smuggling, and paltry revenues. The new Revenue Act, or Sugar Act, of 1764 levied fees, with provision for strict enforcement, on imported wines, indigo, coffee, silks, foreign molasses and sugar, the latter aimed especially at the French West Indies. A particularly important enforcement feature permitted customs officials to transfer alleged violators to Halifax for trial by a new admiralty court without a jury. Too often before, local courts seating friendly juries of peers had acquitted smugglers.

The Sugar Act was designed to regulate trade as well as to produce revenue. The primary objective was to encourage trade within and among the members of the British Empire. Smuggling was disliked more because it counteracted British mercantile policy than for revenue losses.

In October, the Massachusetts legislature, after careful study of James Otis's *Rights of the Colonies Asserted and Proved*, sent a carefully worded petition of protest to the king and the House of Commons. The heart of their objection was that the act ran counter to Massachusetts' right to tax itself, as stipulated in the Charter of 1691.

Despite the act's unpopularity (over half of the county's catch of soft and low-quality fish was exchanged in the French West Indies for sugar and molasses), there was little vocal protest from Essex County. Even the merchants were largely silent over these new, strict regulations. Perhaps they expected to evade them as effectively as they had the Molasses Act of 1733. To avoid paying the new duties, American captains purchased counterfeited clearances at St. Eustatius and Anguilla. With the clearances, a vessel laden with sugar and molasses from a French island could enter Salem, Newburyport, or any American port duty-free.

The Stamp Act

It would not be long, however, before town halls in Essex County were filled with hearty protest. In March 1765, Parliament voted the Stamp Act, the first direct, internal tax levied on the colonies. It was to go into effect on November 1, 1765, to defray the expenses of "defending, protecting, and securing" the American colonies. Stamps or stamped paper costing from a halfpenny to twenty shillings were to be affixed to all newspapers, pamphlets, leases, legal documents, bills of lading, tavern licenses, advertisements, and similar papers. Offenses were to be tried in admiralty courts, without benefit of a jury.

Two months later, Parliament passed the Quartering Act. It required colonists to quarter British troops in taverns, inns, barns, and vacant houses, when they could not be accommodated by local military posts. Colonists were expected to supply some provisions and assume part of their transportation costs within the province. The act engendered opposition, colonials suspecting troops were sent more to enforce the Sugar and Stamp Acts than as a defense against Indians or foreign powers. Secondly, the act was viewed as indirect taxation.

Some mutterings and opposition were heard prior to passage of the Stamp Act, but most people in England and the colonies envisioned no real problem. A storm of protest nevertheless was brewing. Since the stamps were to be applied to items in everyday use, the average colonist saw himself directly affected. Those especially hard hit—lawyers, merchants, newspapermen, and shippers—assumed leadership in opposition.

Town Meeting Actions

Each community handled its local affairs through the popular town meeting. At the annual March meeting and at other times during the year, the male freeholders convened to conduct the town's business. With passage of the Stamp Act, vocal protests began to be heard from meeting floors.

The General Court (the legislature), which historically had been left with freedom to manage provincial affairs, did not take kindly to Parliament's new regulatory attitude. The House chamber resounded in protest and debate, with many participants returning home with a raised political consciousness.

Each year, in May, at specially called meetings, residents twenty-one years of age with a freehold valued at forty pounds chose the town's representative(s) to the House. Sometimes, they also received special instructions to carry to the General Court. On October 21, 1765, Salem's representatives, Andrew Oliver and William Browne, were instructed accordingly:

> since we are therein tax'd without our consent, having no Representative in Parliament . . . . And further as we are hereby deprived of another *most valuable right*, that of *trial by juries* . . . . We do hereby request you do every thing you legally and prudently may, towards obtaining a repeal of the STAMP ACT, trusting you will use your whole influence on this important occasion, that the evils we so just dread may be avoided, which this town must largely partake of beyond most others in this government.[3]

Townspeople of mercantile Salem saw themselves subjected to a greater tax burden than most communities. While each town vote was composed differently, many in Essex County voted similar directions.

Instructions often were accompanied by a set of arguments against the Stamp Act. Copies were circulated to other towns and published in newspapers to show the broadbased support for the protest. The same pattern would be repeated to oppose future parliamentary actions during the pre-Revolutionary period. The town-houses were citadels of democracy planted province-wide—a ready-made network from which to launch a revolutionary movement. The first stirrings of revolution were nurtured in these cradles of liberty and spread throughout the countryside.

The commonest objection was that the Stamp Act ran contrary to charter rights of self-government, taxation, and trial by jury. The charter was viewed as a contract between the people and the Crown. It was more than a mere corporate grant. As Boxford voters expressed it, on October 8, 1765:

> By the Royal Charter, granted to our ancestors, the power of making laws for our internal government, and of levying taxes, is vested in the General Assembly. And, by the same charter, the inhabitants of this Province are entitled to all the rights and privileges of natural, free-born subjects of Great Britain. The most essential rights of British subjects are those of being represented in the same body which exercise the power of levying taxes upon them, and of having their property tried by juries.[4]

On October 21, Andover's representative, Samuel Phillips, was instructed not to "assent to any Act of Assembly that shall signify any willingness in your constituents to submit to any Internal Taxes that are under any colour imposed, Otherwise than by the General Court."[5] In northern Essex County, Newburyport was the center of protest. On October 21, its townspeople declared,

> That a People should be taxed at the Will of another, whether of one Man or many, without their own Consent, in Person or by Representative, is Rank Slavery. For if their Superior sees fit, they may be deprived of their whole Property, upon any frivolous Pretext, or without any Pretext at all . . . . for Liberty, or even Life itself, without the Enjoyment of them flowing from Property, are of no Value.[6]

Newburyport's leaders, like most informed Americans, were unmistakably influenced by the teachings of John Locke, a popular English philosopher, who viewed life, liberty, and property as indispensable "natural rights of man."

This was a period of hard times. With the conclusion of the French and Indian War, British wartime contracts and profits from privateering and the illicit trade with the French had concluded. Unemployment had risen, and the cost of living increased. Most people felt the Stamp Act would bring ruin to what was already a bad situation. Gloucester townspeople predicted the Act "would greatly obstruct if not (in Time) totally ruin the Trade & Business of the Province." Rowley argued against the tax, saying Massachusetts also had incurred a big debt from the "late expensive war." Poor harvests over recent years had required sending money "to foreign parts, in exchange for necessary commodities." They were barely able to support themselves, Rowleyites said, and "throw off the yearly load of publick tax." While the specie (cash) drain concerned Rowley, it was of greater alarm to commercial Newburyport. Already, they said, an unfavorable trade balance was causing scarcity of cash. The Stamp Act would drain hard money from circulation, "the Consequence of which is, that our Commerce must Stagnate and our Labourers Starve." At their October 14 meeting, Haverhill townspeople declared that England should realize the Act would "not only ruin their Colonys but greatly affect and distress trade & the manufactories in England." With a drain of specie, Americans would not be able to purchase the goods they normally purchased from British merchants.[7]

Ipswich voters recalled that when their ancestors left England, they came of their "own Accord and att ye own Expence and took Posesion of a Country they were Obliged to Buy or Fight for and to which the Nation [England] had no more Right than the Moon." Ipswichites fought for Massachusetts' charter rights in 1687, when they opposed the administration of Sir Edmund Andros, by refusing to pay their taxes. They saw Andros's policies as inconsistent with charter rights then, and they viewed similarly England's most recent attempt at taxation. The charter was the only reward given Americans for settling at "Infinite Expense of their Own Blood & Treasure their Large Part of New Accession of Empire Wealth & Glory to the British Nation." These recent measures, Ipswich felt, were destructive to their right of self-government.[8]

The various town meeting instructions repeated many concerns: that trial by jury and the right to tax oneself were charter rights of the province and that further taxation would be devastatingly injurious and cause expulsion of all specie. There was also concern that the successful execution of this act would "afford a precedent for the Parliament to tax us in all future time."[9] Some Essex County towns did not participate in this discussion. Amesbury, Bradford, Lynn, Manchester, Methuen, Middleton, Salisbury, and Topsfield were not sufficiently caught up in the protest. They were among the smallest communities, less aware of—and, thus, less affected by—outside events. Normally, Manchester, Methuen, Middleton, and Wenham did not even send representatives to the General Court.

On October 25, the Massachusetts House, consistent with most representatives' instructions, resolved that the Stamp Act was contrary to the British constitution and certain laws of God and nature and common rights of mankind. About the same time, the intercolonial Stamp Act Congress was meeting in New York.

In June 1765, the Massachusetts House had passed a resolution calling a meeting of all colonies to consider a "united, dutiful, loyal and humble Representation of their Condition to His Majesty and the Parliament; and to implore Relief." The Stamp Act Congress convened in New York from October 7 to October 24, with reputable conservative representation from most of the colonies. The Congress adjourned upon approving a "Declaration of Rights and Grievances." Most arguments expressed already had been voted from the floors of Essex County town meetings. Through intercolonial meeting and discussion, the colonies had fostered a common unity and opposition to the Stamp Act crisis.

Violent Tactics

The people of Essex County, future Whigs and Tories alike, seemed to share similar sentiments during the controversy. The terms Whig and Tory—first applied about 1650 to political groups in England—were imported to denote proponents of American economic and political independence versus supporters of royal and parliamentary imperial rule. A minority of people, however, who belonged to the loosely confederated, radical Sons of Liberty (a secret society with upper-class leadership), was intent on more radical forms of protest.

During the month of August 1765, hundreds of angry Bostonians staged effigy hangings, spectacular parades, and the most violent riots in the town's history. Homes of Andrew Oliver, Lieutenant Governor Hutchinson, Benjamin Hallowell (comptroller of customs), and William Story (register of the admiralty court) were extensively damaged by rampaging mobs. A terrified Andrew Oliver resigned as stamp distributor. On September 25, the wild scenes spread to Newburyport. John Boardman had accepted the post of stamp distributor; he was hung in effigy from a large elm tree, subsequently known as the "Liberty Tree,"

> which stood in Mr. Jonathan Greenleaf's yard, at the foot of King Street, [now Federal Street,] a collection of tar barrels [was] set on fire, the rope cut, and the image dropped into the flames. At ten o'clock, P.M., all the bells in town were rung. 'I am sorry to see that substitute,' said a distinguished citizen of Newburyport, 'I wish it had been the original.'[10]

The local Sons of Liberty were determined to prevent compliance with the Stamp Act. On more than one instance, mobs armed with clubs roamed through the streets of Newbury and Newburyport in the nighttime challenging passersby with the question:

> 'Stamp or no Stamp?' The consequences of an affirmative reply, were any thing but pleasant. In one instance, a stranger, having arrived in town, was seized by the mob, at the foot of Green street, and, not knowing what answer to make to the question, stood mute. As the mob allow no neutrals, and as silence with them is a crime, he was severely beaten. The same question was put to another stranger, who replied, with a sagacity worthy of a vicar of Bray, or a Talleyrand, 'I am as you are.' He was immediately cheered and applauded, as a true son of liberty, and permitted to depart in peace, wondering, no doubt, at his own sudden popularity.[11]

The local Sons of Liberty adjourned to William Davenport's Wolfe Tavern, at the corner of State Street and Threadneedle Alley; in the

Wolfe Tavern on Fish (now State) Street was the center of patriot gatherings during the Revolutionary period. Courtesy, Historical Society of Old Newbury.

tap room they celebrated the night's events with double bowls of libation provided by Joseph Stanwood and other supporters.[12]

When the stamp distributors originally had accepted their commissions, the jobs were considered plush political plums. But enjoyment of the fruit of their commissions was not in the cards. By the time November 1 rolled around, every stamp distributor in the colonies had resigned. At the September 30 town meeting, Newburyporters echoed this sentiment: "That it is the Desire of the Town that no Man in it will accept of the Office of distributing the Stamp Papers as he regards the Displeasure of the Town. And that they will deem the Person accepting of such Office an Enemy to this Country."[13] The term "country" suggests Essex County citizenry already thought of themselves living in a distinct, separate society.

Nonviolence

Strongly opposed to compliance with the Stamp Act, Essex County was equally firm in its denunciation of mob disorder. Andover's townspeople were among the first to vent disapproval, voting "utter Detestation and Abhorrence of all Such Violent & Extraordinary proceedings." Selectmen, militia officers, and magistrates were directed to suppress any such disorders. On September 30, Newburyporters voted rejection "of all riotous & tumultuous Assemblies either in the Day or in the Night." Six days earlier, Marbleheaders had directed their representative "to suppress and prevent, all riotous assemblies and unlawful Acts of violence upon the persons or substance of any of His Majesty's Subjects." At their October 21 meeting, Danversites echoed Marblehead's sentiments, almost word for word. On the same day, Salem inhabitants directed their representatives "to pursue all such measures as tend to supp[ress] tumultuous proceedings—to prevent lawless Outrage and Violence." Beverly expressed "abhorance of such Riotous and Mobbish behavior." While favoring noncompliance with the act, the towns showed themselves equally committed to lawful protest.[14]

No Stamps

November 1 arrived with execution of the Stamp Act thwarted before the effective date. The day was celebrated by the ringing of bells and the firing of minute guns, with vessels displaying their flags at half-mast. Every stamp distributor had resigned, and no business requiring stamped paper was being transacted. Fearing a stamp tax on marriage certificates, in October 1765, twenty-two Marblehead couples had announced marriage intentions on a single Sunday before the deadline. Eventually, the colonists simply defied the law and began to accept unstamped paper documents.[15]

Because of the threat of mob disorder, stamps were stored unopened at Castle William (the province fort in Boston's outer harbor). On August 29, 1765, Gov. Francis Bernard requested Col. Richard Saltonstall of Haverhill to raise an independent force to defend the stamps. Sixty men were enlisted to serve four months.

A club-wielding mob of about twenty men from Haverhill's West Parish and Salem, New Hampshire, went to Saltonstall's family mansion—the "Saltonstall Seat," situated below town beside a row of sycamores overlooking the Merrimack—to protest his compliance with Bernard's order. Saltonstall met them at the door, explaining his oath of allegiance to the king required the discharge of his office. Saltonstall invited them to Moors tavern to drink at his expense. The once-ugly crowd departed full of praise for Saltonstall.[16]

Votes of townspeople notwithstanding, Sons of Liberty in Newburyport and Salem continued to coerce non-use of stamped paper. In January, the brigantine *Bradford*, commanded by Capt. John Hathorne and bound for the Grenadines, sailed into Salem harbor. When rumors flew that the captain's papers were stamped, the Sons demanded that customs give up those "Marks of Slavery." The papers were carried to the London Coffee House where a large crowd resolved, "they should be burnt . . . which was accordingly done by a Bonfire prepared for that Purpose, amidst loud Huzzas of the Assembly, and the Ashes scattered in the Air." Former stamp distributor John Boardman of Newburyport was the butt of more misery. Word was he possessed stamped clearance papers for transporting boards, shingles, and horses to the West Indies aboard his schooner *Defiance*. He was forced to surrender them and swear before a justice not to "make use of any again." A large crowd witnessing the event shouted three cheers for Boardman. Nevertheless, next day, he was hanged in effigy for a second time: "the detestable Clearance was fix'd on a Pole with a Chain, carried thro' the Town with Drums beating, and Flag flying, and other Music; at 4 o'clock the Effigie was let down, and that with the Clearance, was burnt under the Tree of Liberty."[17]

Economic Sanctions

The colonists decided to send a message to Parliament that would surely be understood. Because of economic hard times, the importation of British manufactures had slowed. People simply could not afford to buy as much as previously. British shippers and merchants complained. The colonists gradually became aware they possessed the perfect weapon—the boycott. In December 1765, Marblehead, Newburyport, and Salem followed Boston's example and pledged nonimportation of British goods until repeal. Danvers vowed "to be more frugale in our Expences and more Industrious in Supplying ourselves with the Necessarys of Life."[18]

The agreements began to take effect. American colonists found allies in the thousands of English workers thrown out of work. They were joined by a chorus of English shippers, manufacturers, and merchants also demanding repeal.

Repeal

In mid-March 1766, the Stamp Act was repealed by Parliament. At the same time, the molasses duty under the Sugar Act of 1764 was reduced to one penny per gallon. Ironically, the Stamp Act revocation occasioned as much joy and celebration in England as in America.

Essex County, particularly the coastal towns, was jubilant. The county had received the news in mid-May, approximately two months after repeal. On May 21, Salem rejoiced. Church bells rang, and bonfires lighted the skies. Newburyport hastily called a meeting, by "Beat of Drum & word of Mouth," and voted to illuminate the "upper

Part of the Town House" on State Street and to use six half-barrels of gunpowder "in the publick Rejoycings" at the upper and lower long wharfs. Beverly, Gloucester, and Lynn likewise celebrated amid bonfires and illuminations glowing the evening sky.[19]

The Crown demanded restitution for property damage wrecked in Boston; Essex County towns were divided. The question was to be decided by the General Court, and the towns instructed their delegates accordingly. Rowley, contrary to a town committee's recommendations, voted to favor compensation from the province treasury. Andover, Lynn, Newburyport, and Salem also favored payment. Haverhill wanted a law passed to provide that costs of future damages be paid, "by the Town whare permitted to be done & not by the province in general." Beverly, Gloucester, Newbury, and Salisbury opposed remuneration from the treasury, while Ipswich's and Topsfield's representatives were instructed to oppose payment and to "move it to the Court to ask his Excellency our Governor to Recommend . . . to Relieve ye Sufferers Either by Subscription or Contribution as in Cases of Calamities by Fire." The representative from Danvers could do as he "Shall Think most proper." In December, the House finally enacted a law granting compensation and a general pardon to the participants.[20]

Most people presumed that the colonial protest movement had ended, that normality would return. England's intent, however, was to continue on the regulatory road. There still was the act of Parliament, for example, that reserved straight, tall American white pines for masts of the royal navy. If a landowner felled a stand before inspection by the surveyor general of His Majesty's woods, the whole cutting was subject to seizure and forfeit. This was a nagging source of resentment. For parliamentary actions to follow, the Stamp Act protest had defined American opposition tactics: town meeting protestations and resolutions, petitions to the king and Parliament, street demonstrations, ostracism, even terrorism, nonimportation and boycott agreements, intercolonial conventions, and use of the press. On the road to revolution, these tactics would be repeated many times.

1. Catherine Drinker Bowen, *John Adams and the American Revolution* (Boston: Little, Brown, 1950), 217.

2. "Extracts from John Rowe's Diary, 1764–1779" MHS *Proceedings*, 2nd Series, 10 (1895):60.

3. "Newspaper Items Relating to Essex County," *EIHC*, 51 (1915): 136.

4. Sidney Perley, *History of Boxford* (Boxford: Sidney Perley, 1880), 202.

5. Andover Town Records, October 21, 1765.

6. Newburyport Town Records, October 21, 1765, 1:54–55.

7. Gloucester Town Records, October 7, 1765, 87; "Newspaper Items Relating to Essex County," 134; Newburyport Town Records, October 21, 1765, 1:55; George Wingate Chase, *History of Haverhill* (Haverhill: George Wingate Chase, 1861), 363.

8. Ipswich Town Records, October 21, 1765, 4:208.

9. Perley, 203.

10. Joshua Coffin, *A Sketch of the History of*

Newbury, Newburyport, and West Newbury (Boston: Samuel G. Drake, 1845), 231.

11. 231.

12. John J. Currier, *"Ould Newbury": Historical and Biographical Sketches* (Boston: Damrell and Upham, 1896), 499; Newburyport Town Records, September 19, 1768, 1:125.

13. Newburyport Town Records, September 30, 1765, 1:52.

14. Andover Town Records, September 21, 1765; Newburyport Town Records, September 30, 1765, 1:52; Marblehead Town Records, EI, September 24, 1765, 4:65; Danvers Town Records, October 21, 1765, 2:13; Beverly Town Records, October 25, 1765, 5:335; *The Boston Gazette*, March 10, 1766; Salem Town Records, EI, October 21, 1765, 4:544.

15. "Newspaper Items Relating to Essex County," 133.

16. Robert E. Moody, ed., *The Saltonstall Papers, 1607– 1815* (Boston: MHS, 1972), 1:87–89; the Eaton family tradition, in an account less flattering to Saltonstall, says that Timothy Eaton went to the door alone and asked Saltonstall to explain his conduct. In August 1766, Saltonstall was rewarded with the appointment of sheriff of Essex County.

17. "Newspaper Items Relating to Essex County," 292, 294–95.

18. Arthur Meier Schlesinger, *The Colonial Merchants and The American Revolution 1763–1766* (New York: Frederick Ungar, 1966), 80; Danvers Town Records, December 23, 1765, 2:45.

19. *The Holyoke Diaries, 1709–1856* (Salem, MA: Essex Institute, 1911), 65; Newburyport Town Records, May 20, 1766, 1:81; Edwin M. Stone, *History of Beverly* (Boston: James Monroe, 1843), 56; Alonzo Lewis and James F. Newhall, *History of Lynn* (Boston: John L. Shorey, 1865), 334; Joseph E. Garland, *Guns Off Gloucester* (Gloucester: Essex County Newspapers, 1975), 39.

20. Chase, 363–64; Ipswich Town Records, August 18, 1766, 4:213; Danvers Town Records, October 27, 1766, 2:76.

CHAPTER FOUR

THE TOWNSHEND ACTS

Charles Townshend, Britain's chancellor of the exchequer, was charged with preparing the budget of 1767. He convinced his colleagues that duties levied on certain American imports could raise enough money to pay defense costs in the American colonies. The scope of his plan went beyond previous ones, as Townshend expected enough revenue to pay the salaries of certain civil appointees, including governors, judges, and customsmen. The intent was to make them independent of colonial assemblies, which historically had used the "power of the purse" to extract political concessions.

The Acts

The Townshend Revenue Act of June 29, 1767 laid duties upon glass, painters' colors, lead, tea, and paper imported into the colonies. They were added to a list of items already subject to tax by the Sugar Act of 1764. The duties—external ones to be levied at the ports—presumably would not be opposed as was the direct Stamp Act tax. Writs of assistance were specifically authorized to enter and search vessels or private property without warning.

Another Townshend Act established a board of customs commissioners, with Continental headquarters in Boston, charged with reorganizing and tightening the whole American system. Four vice-admiralty courts were established—at Halifax, Boston, Philadelphia, and Charlestown—to try all cases under the acts, without benefit of trial by jury.

Colonists historically had enjoyed extensive freedom of trade. Even when regulation was attempted, poor administration resulted in *de facto* free trade. The Townshend Acts changed this. Soon, customs collections far exceeded costs of administration, and the board in Boston became largely successful in breaking the illicit trade in this and other area ports. In the face of this success, colonial resistance mounted.

Nonconsumption

Just as with the Stamp Act, economic sanctions were used to oppose the Townshend Acts. The whole colonial protest movement took its lead from town meeting activity in Massachusetts. On October 28, 1767, Boston became first to react, voting for nonconsumption of articles imported from England and encouraging local manufactures.

At Boston's behest, several Essex County towns, especially seaports, considered similar resolves. On December 14, 1767, Gloucester voted to "promote industry, Economy & Manufactures among our selves," to prevent "unnecessary Importation of european Commodities, the excessive Use of which threatens the Country with Poverty and Ruin." A subscription was recommended to be signed by the inhabitants, who would agree, beginning March 1, 1768, not to purchase for one year certain enumerated articles from abroad. On the restricted list were a miscellany of items, including anchors, chinaware, coaches, fire engines, glue, house furniture, malt liquors, shoes, snuff, watches.[1] While Cape Ann joined with Boston, conservative Salem rejected this course. Even Newburyport hesitated. At a special town meeting held on March 18, 1768, acting on a committee recommendation, Newburyporters spurned the idea: "This Town has been in a great Measure Supported for many Years past by the building of Ships which have been purchased mostly by the Inhabitants & for the Use of Great Britain: the manner in which we have been paid for our Ships has been mainly by British Manufactures So that the Importation & purchase of these & our Staple Business (if we may so express it) have been almost inseperably united."[2] Later, however, a group of merchants, including Tristram Dalton, Jonathan Jackson, and William Morland, privately agreed to limited nonimportation. Some had been on the earlier committee. Certain articles were excluded, and the agreement would not apply when English goods were exchanged for locally built ships.[3] Most Marblehead and Salem merchants also pledged to nonimportation, provided their counterparts in other colonies did the same. In March 1768, Beverly adopted "the measures of the Town of Boston . . . lately gon into with regard to Divers Sorts of Goods Imported from abroad."[4] Two interior towns, Andover and Boxford, took similar actions at their town meetings. Boxford voters allowed:

> And although this town is but small . . . it would do every thing in its power towards promoting every public good, and discountenancing all vice. Because of the poverty of the town, and its situation, the inhabitants have never been able to go into the use of many articles mentioned . . . yet they cannot wholly excuse themselves from the use of some of the superfluities mentioned in said votes. Therefore, the town would strongly recommend to every householder . . . to lessen in their families the use of all foreign superfluities, and to use such things in the room thereof as shall be of their own manufacture, and to do every thing they can to promote industry, economy, and frugality, and to discountenance all sorts of vice and immorality.[5]

These actions were taken for reasons besides the repugnant Townshend Acts. The province had been experiencing hard times. Exports had fallen off; the heavy importation from abroad had precipitated a trade imbalance, causing specie drain. The effect was compounded by recently increased province taxes, required to pay off the colony's own debt burden from the late war. The Townshend Acts exacerbated an already dismal economic picture, for which frugality, economy, nonconsumption, and home manufacture seemed to be the best medicine. Nevertheless, this early attempt at uniting the towns had met with only limited success.

The Circular Letter and the "Glorious Ninety-Two"

In January 1768, the Massachusetts General Court went into action. Addresses of protest were sent to several members of the ministry and a petition to the king. The following month, the famous Circular Letter was issued and sent to legislatures of other colonies. The letter asserted that only the colonies could tax themselves, encouraged a unified effort toward repeal, and warned against permitting England to pay salaries of colonial appointees.

In June, Governor Francis Bernard was ordered to have the Massachusetts legislature rescind their "flagitious attempt to disturb the public peace"; other governors were commanded to dissolve their assemblies if they voted with Massachusetts. In an act of defiance, the House refused to rescind the vote; only seventeen voted in the affirmative, ninety-two in the negative. The legislators' courageous stand was praised effusively. Toasts to the "glorious ninety-two" became a popular cheer throughout the colonies.[6]

Five Essex County representatives were among the seventeen who favored rescinding: Jacob Fowle of Marblehead, William Browne and Peter Frye of Salem, Dr. John Calef of Ipswich, and Col. Richard

Saltonstall of Haverhill. None were returned to office, and all, except for Fowle, who died a few months later, would remain loyal to the Crown throughout the Revolutionary movement.

Essex County "rescinder" towns promptly took action by meeting and voting to broadcast that their representatives had acted contrary to local opinion. Their votes were published in the *Essex Gazette*. On July 18, Salem thanked the ninety-two "for their Firmness and Resolution shewn in maintaining our just *Rights* and *Liberties*."[7] During the summer, Marblehead, Ipswich, and Haverhill expressed the same sentiments. On August 15, the Sons of Liberty kept the protest movement alive in Boston by staging a big celebration in commemoration of the third anniversary of the first riot against the Stamp Act. Of the multitudinous toasts offered that day, one was to the *"respectable Towns of Salem, Ipswich* and *Marblehead* . . . and their *Constituents*, who have publicly approved of the Vote against *Rescinding*."[8]

Thirty Salem citizens protested, feeling the vote tended "to injure the Gentlemen who represented" the town. A July 30 letter to the *Essex Gazette* expressed concern over the "Spirit of Discord and Faction" in the prosperous port. Indeed, this was the first Revolutionary issue which caused significant division among the Salem population.[9]

Salem's First Newspaper

The Circular Letter controversy was reported in the first issue (August 2, 1768) of Salem's *Essex Gazette*. This four-page weekly was the first newspaper in the province outside of Boston. It was turned out by Samuel Hall, a twenty-eight-year-old native of Medford, who had come to Salem at the urging of Capt. Richard Derby. (At the time, Derby—patriarch of a famous Salem seafaring family—was stirred up over loss of several vessels and their cargoes to British customs.) Hall, a staunch patriot, set his practical printing experience to the task, continuing over the next seven years to highlight America's political disputes with England. Hall himself did not editorialize. Rather, political commentary, usually in line with popular Whig sentiment, was set forth, mostly in letters to the editor with authorship accredited to various pseudonyms. Hall's political bias also was evident in his news coverage. Local events, usually dotted with commentary on Americans' rights as Englishmen—as well as reports from other parts of Massachusetts, outside the province, and "Fresh Advices" from across the Atlantic—appeared in every issue. The *Gazette* continued in operation until shortly after the battles of Lexington and Concord. Its contribution to an informed citizenry and to a communications network that stretched countrywide was priceless to the Revolutionary movement.

Blockade and arrival of British troops in Boston, October 1, 1768. Painting by Christian Remick. Courtesy, Essex Institute, Salem, Mass.

Troops to Boston

There had been several forcible attempts in Boston at landing illicit goods, wresting confiscated cargoes from customs, and attacking revenue officers. Customs commissioners requested a warship and troops for protection. While no troops were sent, the fifty-gun sloop-of-war *Romney* was dispatched.

On June 10, John Hancock's sloop, aptly named *Liberty*, was seized for attempting to smuggle madeira wine into Boston harbor. Hancock, known to be financing much Sons of Liberty activity, had a retributive customs waiting to snare him. The *Liberty* was rescued by a riotous crowd; several customs officers were knocked down and bloodied, and some had their homes damaged. The officers and their families fled to Castle William, the provincial fort in the outer harbor. Once again, Gov. Francis Bernard asked for troops, so that officers could carry out their duty. This time, Bernard's request was approved. Nearly four months later, two regiments (one thousand men) from the Halifax garrison were stationed in Boston.

Boston officials threatened not to quarter the troops when they arrived, requesting that Bernard reconvene the General Assembly to deliberate the matter. When he refused, selectmen proposed a convention of towns at Faneuil Hall on September 22, 1768. The radicals had a popular issue to foster discontent; in alliance with the merchants, whose smuggling had been halted, they pressed for the troops' removal.

Many Essex County towns responded, though some cautioned their delegates to abstain from any disrespect of the Crown. In the years ahead, as the country moved toward independence, many delegates' names would continue to be found among the county's most distinguished leadership.

COUNTY DELEGATES
TO BOSTON CONVENTION

TOWN	DAY CHOSEN	DELEGATE(S)
Beverly	17*	Henry Herrick
Gloucester	19	Capt. Peter Coffin
		Thomas Saunders
Ipswich	19	Michael Farley
Lynn	19	Ebenezer Burrill
Newburyport	19	Benjamin Greenleaf
Danvers	20	Samuel Holten, Jr.
Haverhill	21	Samuel Bachellor
Andover	21	Samuel Phillips
Salisbury	21	Capt. Nathl. Currier
Boxford	22	Aaron Wood
Newbury	22	Joseph Gerrish
Wenham	25	Benjamin Fairfield
Rowley	26	Humphrey Hobson

*September

The response from Lynn and Wenham was their first formal Revolutionary stirring. Several other towns—Amesbury, Bradford, Manchester, Marblehead, Methuen, Middleton, Salem, Topsfield—were silent. Amesburyites actually voted *not* to send anyone. Salem first had chosen two delegates but then decided not to participate.

The convention lasted six days. It was conciliatory in tone, ending with a declaration of loyalty to the governor, a statement of protest against standing armies in peacetime, and a recommendation to restore the General Assembly—a far cry from the flaming rhetoric in store for the years ahead. During the session, much to the indignation of the delegates, warships carrying the 14th and 29th regiments were spotted off Nantasket.

Home Manufacture

Local manufacture was promoted as an alternative, however inferior, to imported British goods. It became fashionable to wear only homespun, rather than imported broadcloth or brocade. Women carded, spun, and wove their own cloth to provide a substitute for British textiles. In Middleton, where only ninety dwellings stood, seventy or eighty looms were operating. The *Essex Gazette* reported that the "*Inhabitants having now tasted the Sweets of the Industry, are determined to prosecute it with the utmost Vigour.*"[10] From January 1769 to January 1770, 20,522 yards of cloth were woven on these looms, amounting to over 40 yards for each man, woman, and child in the community.

Spinning bees became the vogue as women combined the need for homemade goods with the desire for social diversion. Women, young and old alike, gathered at their local parsonage with their spinning wheels and enjoyed each other's company while fulfilling an important political-economic objective. During 1768, 1769, and 1770, mention was made in the *Essex Gazette* of numerous spinning and weaving bees, usually held at Congregational parsonages: one in Byfield Parish in August 1768, two in Gloucester during December, several in Beverly, Wenham, the Linebrook Parish of Ipswich, Salisbury, and Salem over the summer of 1769, and in Rowley the following May. Presumably, others went unreported. Publicity was as important to the boycott effort as homespun; it fostered a unity of spirit and commitment in opposition to the repulsive Townshend duties. The proceedings of a spinning bee in the Chebacco Parish (now Essex) of Ipswich were carefully detailed in the Essex *Gazette* of June 20–27, 1769.

> It gives us a noble Prospect to see what a Spirit of Industry and Frugality prevails, at this Day, in the American young Ladies; and Generosity towards their Gospel Ministers . . . . Yesterday Morning, very early, the young Ladies in that Parish of this Town called *Chebacco*, to the number of 77, assembled at the House of Rev'd Mr. *John Cleaveland*, with their Spinning-Wheels; and though the Weather, that Day, was extremely hot, and divers of the young Ladies were but about 13 Years of Age, yet by six o'Clock, in the Afternoon, they spun . . . all good Yarn, and generously gave their Work, and some bro't Cotton and Flax with them, more than they spun themselves, as a Present.

The day was concluded with a sermon from Rev. John Cleaveland. (This distinguished Ipswich minister agitated throughout the Revolutionary period. When war finally began, he reportedly "preached all the men of his parish into the army, and then went himself.")

> After the Musick of the Wheels was over, Mr. *Cleaveland* entertained them with a Sermon on Prov. 14. 1, *Every wise Woman buildeth her House; but the foolish plucketh it down with her Hands;*—which he concluded by observing How the Women might recover to this Country the full and free Enjoyment of all our Rights, Properties and Priv-

ileges, (which is more than the Men have been able to do): And so have the Honour of building, not only their own, but the Houses of many Thousands, and, perhaps, prevent the Ruin of the whole British Empire, viz. *By living upon, as far as possible*, only *the Produce of this Country*.[11]

Even domestic breeding of sheep was encouraged, so that the whole production cycle could be contained in America. It was reported in May 1769 that Joseph Robinson in Boxford had a ewe that produced four lambs and had produced three the previous year. "If our Sheep should all increase so fast, we should have but little Need of sending Home for our Goods." With a sardonic humor, the *Gazette* queried, "Won't G.B. [Governor Bernard] send Home for another Regiment of Soldiers, in order to have our Rams castrated, or else have a Duty laid upon them."[12]

The Congregational Ministry

During these gloomy, unsettled times, just as pastors inspired the women of their parishes to produce homespun, they also encouraged their whole membership to prayer and reflection. On October 6, 1768, congregations in Newbury and Rowley met for a day of fasting and prayer—a common form of commemoration and protest during the pre-Revolutionary period. Essex County colonials took their religion seriously, and the respected ministry remained in the forefront of agitation. Local pastors sermonized, reminding parishioners of natural law and charter rights, laying the philosophical justification for actions against British encroachments. Not only was town business historically controlled by popular consent, local governing of church affairs was a keystone of Congregationalism. Consequently, British overseas incursions were taken to heart and soul. Minister-preachers were remarkably effective polemicists, stirring their congregations. They provided leadership in the years ahead, calling for fasting and prayer, sermonizing on anniversaries of important events, and, finally, administering the Divine blessing to departing troops the day of the Lexington alarm.

Abstinence from Tea

At church gatherings, women normally would have consumed quantities of black bohea tea, but now they abstained from the foreign herb to support the strategy of nonconsumption. Women attending a spinning bee at Newburyport's Presbyterian parsonage in April 1768 reportedly consumed "Labradore" tea and coffee. Substitute teas were variously called also "Liberty" or "Hyperion" tea. At the

October ordination of Rev. Christopher B. Marsh of the Second Congregational Church of Newburyport, tea brewed from a plant native to Pearson Town, Maine was served. Self-denial of the most widely used imported goods symbolized opposition to all Townshend duties.[13]

Many women found it difficult to give up tea—it had been an everyday custom, part of the daily routine. And some husbands made ingenious attempts to dissuade their wives from sneaking a cup of tea. South Danvers (Peabody) men—suspicious that the large coffee pot ushered to quilting bees contained tea—tried to discourage the ladies by depositing a large toad in that pot. In Beverly, reportedly, one man doctored his wife's tea by adding a Virginia twist (plug of tobacco). At the Jeremiah Page residence in Danvers, tradition tells of Sarah Page inviting her guests to sip tea on the roof. Forbidden to drink tea in her home, she declared that "*upon* a house is not *within* it." It was difficult to abstain from a habit of a lifetime.[14]

Customs Enforcement and Trade Regulation

To enforce the Townshend Acts and collect the duties, several inspectors were required in each major port. Reduction of the molasses duty in March 1766 decreased the profit margin from smuggling. Nevertheless, some shippers continued illicit trafficking and false reporting. In October 1768, a Marblehead vessel carrying unreported molasses was seized and libeled in the court of admiralty. The same month, two molasses-laden vessels entering Newburyport paid the duty, but customs, suspecting the manifest was underestimated, boarded to regauge the cargo.[15] In May 1769, Salem customs cautioned shipowners in the *Essex Gazette* to instruct their seamen not to take on "private Ventures" and for captains to be "punctual" in reporting cargoes. When customs uncovered illegal goods, shipowners often blamed indiscreet crew members or a captain's unintentional error in completing the manifest.[16]

The Townshend duties, with the exception of tea, applied to English manufactured articles, which were still the best available. But the pre-Townshend duty, which applied to wine imported from Madeira or the Azores, made wine-smuggling profitable. Also, the policy of mercantilism required that foreign imports be shipped first to England, where cargoes were unloaded, reloaded, and then shipped to the American colonies on board English (possibly American) vessels. Colonial merchants usually ignored this costly, time-consuming regulation and continued to smuggle Dutch, French, and German manufactures into the colonies.

Ships were examined as they entered and departed. Under the

peril of a one-hundred pound fine, each captain had to swear to the contents. Locals resented customs interlopers (tidesmen, tidewaiters, collectors, searchers, and surveyors), many of whom were hired in England and sent to the towns. Merchants complained of their extraordinary powers and the officers' greedy, high-handed manners. Not only did they receive a share from their seizures, many times customsmen pocketed the fees collected at ports of entry. A "Set of hungry Miscreants" they were called, intent upon enriching themselves "by distressing honest Trade." In the fall of 1768, Captain Grandy of Marblehead had put into Halifax harbor. Though a search turned up no illicit goods, customs abused the crew and "used the Master very scurrilously." Maritime inhabitants were getting fed up.[17]

Mob Violence and Disorder

When informers, who were widely scorned as unpatriotic scoundrels, reported breaches in trade, they risked their own safety. On September 8 or 9, 1768, Thomas Row, a Salem customs employee, was suspected of reporting a vessel moored in the harbor for duties evasion. Mid-morning, he was taken from the wharves to Salem Common, "where his Head, Body and Limbs were covered with warm Tar, and then a large Quantity of Feathers were applied to all Parts." He was "exalted to a Seat on the Front of a Cart" and led down the main street where signs labeling Row "*Informer*" were stuck on his chest and back. Within minutes, hundreds of townspeople thronged around, with Row passing amongst their cheers and shouts. He immediately left town, warned not to return. Once in Boston, Row complained of his brutal treatment, demanding the rioters be brought to justice. One or two days earlier, another informer, Robert Wood, had received a ride, wearing a similar feather coat.[18]

On Saturday, September 10, two alleged informers were submitted to unusually cruel and humiliating punishment by a Newburyport mob. Joshua Vickery, a ship carpenter, was carried to the public stocks, "where he sat from three to five o'Clock in the Afternoon, most of the Time on the sharpest Stone that could be found, which put him to extreme Pain, so that he once fainted." Then, with a rope around his neck and hands tied, Vickery was carted through the streets, pelted by onlookers with eggs, gravel, and stones. At dusk, he was confined to a dark warehouse, handcuffed in irons. Crouched in a room without bedding, so small he could not lie straight, he "made the Edge of a Tar-Pot, serve for a Pillow, so that when he arose the Hair was tore from his Head." On Sunday, only his wife could visit. The following day, a Frenchman, Francis Magno, was seized and feathered. Magno was placed in a horse cart, and Vickery was forced to lead the horse about town. Afterwards, Magno was jailed "for Breach of the Peace."

A few days later Vickery testified Magno had received no information from him concerning Captain John Emery, the alleged runner, or anyone else. Magno confirmed Vickery's innocence, saying he had observed the vessel coming into Newburyport and later reported this intelligence to customs in Portsmouth, while there on business.[19]

To avoid import duties, many captains unloaded foreign goods in Gloucester harbor. The cargo was transferred to pinkies—small two-masted boats—or schooners, used primarily in the coaster trade, and was sailed without suspicion into Boston harbor. Consequently, the merchants avoided duties. Customs, however, eventually got wind of these evasions, and, in 1768, began to station officers on Cape Ann.

First to accept the unpopular post was Capt. Samuel Fellows. He was offered the appointment after having informed Salem customs that undutied molasses had arrived in Gloucester aboard David Plummer's schooner, *Earl of Gloucester*. Joseph Dowse, surveyor and searcher, came to town and seized the cargo. The day after, on September 7, 1768, an angry mob of seventy strong led by several prominent Gloucesterites, including blacksmith Daniel Warner and merchants Joseph Foster and Dudley Sargent, set out after Fellows. They searched the home of Jesse Saville, a local tanner, who was away, where Fellows was suspected to be hiding. Angered by his apparent escape, David Plummer, a local merchant, seized Saville's servant by the collar. Dr. Samuel Rogers, forceps in hand, threatened to yank his teeth unless he disclosed Fellows's whereabouts. The crowd left but returned later. They broke down the door, ransacked the house, and called Saville's wife and mother "all the hoors and all the Dam'd biches and Every Evil name that they Could think of Stricking Down their Clubs on the [floor] Each Side of them." After Saville returned, about ten o'clock, the mob reappeared. They knocked down Saville and searched the house a third time, leaving the terrorized Saville family living in constant fear thereafter.[20]

The Salem, Newburyport, and Gloucester incidents occurred in September 1768—the month of the Boston Convention and shortly before British troops arrived. Passions were high—it was a logical time for excitable, violent malcontents to vent their anger. The secret Sons of Liberty, with a communications network in the maritime towns, fomented most colonial violence. The three incidents probably were a scheme coordinated by the Sons to rid the county of the "Revenue Locusts."

Not intimidated, Jesse Saville accepted a job working for customs. (Several Sons members had been found guilty and fined and the *Earl of Gloucester* and cargo had been forfeited.) Later, the night of March

23, 1770, terrorists disguised as Indians and blacks hauled Saville from bed; they beat and dragged him barefoot four miles to the harbor. Stripped almost naked, the shivering Saville was placed in a cart and, with lantern in hand, driven through the streets. Along the way, Saville's "tormentors" forced him "to declare and publish unto them that he was Jesse Savil[le] the Informer" to each awakened household. "Bestowed a handsome Coat of Tar," he was perched upon the town pumps, where he swore never again to inform on any person. He was released to return home, but the incident left local tensions on tenterhooks.[21]

Lt. Governor Thomas Hutchinson brought the incident to the legislature, but he could raise little sympathy for Saville. From July 1769, when Gov. Francis Bernard left for England, Hutchinson was acting governor until 1771, when his appointment became permanent. The appointment of an American-born, Harvard-educated governor generally was cheered. A euphoria, however, that would be short-lived!

The following November, George Penn, Dr. David Plummer's mulatto servant, was tried and convicted of participating in the Saville assault. In January 1772, he was placed on the Salem gallows for one hour with a rope around his neck. Under the threat of death, he defiantly refused to offer information concerning his collaborators. He received twenty lashes and was jailed. On the same day, in an unrelated matter, a convicted rapist from Marblehead, Bryan Sheehen, was hanged from the gallows, with nearly twelve thousand people congregated to watch the spectacle.[22]

In January 1771, Phillips—"Land-waiter, Gauger and Weigher" for Cape Ann, Salem and Marblehead—was replaced by Richard Sylvester. During September 1772, Cape Ann's selectmen finally had enough of Sylvester's officiousness and ordered him and his family to leave. Courageously and wryly, he responded in the *Boston Weekly News-Letter*, thanking them and prayed leave "to acquaint those Worthies, that he cannot . . . comply with their Request." He added the "next Time they have Occasion to write about [my] Children, to call them by their proper Names."[23]

Whether or not customs officials continued in Gloucester after 1772, smuggling continued. In one instance, a prominent merchant, Col. Joseph Foster, invented an intricate scheme to escape detection. One night, his schooner entered Gloucester with an illicit foreign cargo. The hatches were opened, and unloading began. At daybreak, more than half the cargo still was on board. What was to be done? In the early morning a tidewaiter was expected from Salem. With help from a stout Irishman, John McKean, Foster devised a plan. On the cut, along the post road, was the quarantine station where

McKean was employed. During smallpox alarms, his job was to fu-
migate all strangers entering town. When the customs officer reached
the watch house, McKean kept him there. When he was released in
the evening, he was "purified from all infectious disease, so far as a
thorough smoking could do it."[24]

Customs regulation threatened to unravel the clandestine operations of many local merchants. When peaceful, illegal tactics failed,
some prominent offenders were not adverse to violence. Often, they
were Sons of Liberty leaders, heading ready-made bands composed
of employees and waterfront rowdies. (During these depressed times,
customs regulation crimped the style of dock workers and sailors, as
well as their employers.) This violence disturbed conservative Whigs.
How long could the riotous rabble be kept within bounds? Might
their passions run amuck? Would they forsake their upper-class leadership and turn on all the propertied? Actually, most people disap-
proved of the violence. After the Vickery-Magno incident, Newburyporters voted to appoint watchmen, "to prevent Disorders in the
Night and other Inconveniences." While the majority of people opposed customs regulation and revenue acts, they were unsympathetic
toward rowdy protests that endangered public safety and personal
property.[25]

The First Blood

To enforce mercantile regulations, England deployed several British warships along the American coastline. On April 22, 1769, only
five leagues off Cape Ann, the H.M.S. *Rose*, with twenty guns,
brought to the brigantine *Pitt-Packet*, commanded by Capt. Thomas
Power. The *Pitt-Packet*, owned by Robert Hooper, was bound from
Cadiz carrying a cargo of salt to her home port of Marblehead. Lt.
Henry G. Panton of the *Rose* and a press party boarded. (In emer-
gencies, forcible enlistment of English—not American—sailors for
naval service was permitted. English seamen, however, usually preferred the more pleasant duty of an American merchantman.) Four
crew members ran below and secured themselves in the forepeak.
Despite the lieutenant's "moderate, kind and persuasive Arguments,"
the armed foursome threatened to resist his advances. A pistol shot
blazed at the holed-up sailors, searing the face of one, Michael Corbett, and wounding a second. After an advancing press boarder was
injured, Panton went in to extricate the seamen himself. Corbett
heaved a harpoon, striking the lieutenant's jugular; he died almost
instantly. Even after a marine reinforcement boarded, the besieged
mariners held out. They found a keg of rum and, reportedly, succumbed to temptation and were easily taken, except for Corbett. He

resisted until, finally, demon rum took him, too. They were brought to Boston and kept in irons awaiting trial. Though none of the accused were Americans, mariners along the coastline were in an uproar. James Otis and John Adams volunteered as counsel. Corbett and the others were acquitted, largely because authorities wanted to avoid the legality issue of impressment off Massachusetts waters.[26] The near-riotous protests from Essex County seafarers, and elsewhere, had also influenced the verdict. The *Essex Gazette* hoped "that the shocking Fate which the Lieut. of the *Rose* lately met with" would be a lesson to customs officers and commanders of vessels "not to exert a Power in the Impressing of Seamen or searching of Vessels, which the Laws have never given them."[27]

Common Grievances

In May 1769, the tri-town voters of Beverly, Marblehead, and Salem elected their representatives and sent them to Boston with instructions to deal with their many common grievances against England. Marblehead's representatives were urged to work toward healing "the unhappy Breach with our Mother Country" and "to refute the Misrepresentations, which have been made" about the province, "whereby this People have been treated as if in open Rebellion." They were not to comply with any measure requiring "Reimbursement for any Part of the Charges sustained by the bringing of Troops into this Province," costs the Quartering Act required Massachusetts to assume. Upset with the customs officials' enforcement tactics, they said their rights had been "trampled upon, with Impunity, by highhanded Offenders, thro' their Venality & Corruption." They opposed permitting "any Power on Earth to levy Taxes" except "the General Assembly of the Province." While acknowledging the sovereignty of King George and the British Parliament, representatives were to do whatever possible to "wipe off that Reproach for Disloyalty and Disobedience, which has been so liberally cast upon us by malicious and malevolent Persons." Salem, like Marblehead, wanted removal of "every injurious Impression" on the "Conduct" of Massachusetts, "full and effectual Relief" from the "Revenue Laws" and restoration of "Harmony and Affection" between England and America. In addition, Salem desired Richard Derby, Jr., and John Pickering, Jr., whose election showed Whigs now had the political edge, to work toward confining the courts of admiralty to their "ancient Limits," namely trial by jury.[28] Townspeople voted also for an inquiry into the conduct of the troops in Boston, which had been described earlier in the *Essex Gazette* as "now most wretchedly debauched, & their

Licentiousness daily increasing."[29] Beverly's instructions were more brief and less specific. In Lockean style, its citizens voted that Capt. Henry Herrick use his "best Endeavors that our invaluable Charter Liberties privileges & immunities, dearly Purchased by our Ancestors, & all the rights Derived to us from the invariable Law of God & Nature be transmitted inviolable . . . no man can be safe Either as to his Life, Liberty or Property, if a Contrary Doctrine should prevail."[30] Voters from these North Shore towns were loyal subjects, aspiring to heal wounds and to return to normal empire status, but they resented British troops being quartered in Boston and equally resented being assessed part of their maintenance costs. While steadfastly opposed to taxation for revenue, high-handed customs regulation, and the courts of admiralty, they continued to assert loyalty to king and Parliament.

Nonimportation

In March 1768, Boston merchants agreed to nonimportation, provided the ports of New York and Philadelphia participated. In spite of Philadelphia's failure to accept the boycott, on August 1, 1768, the Boston merchants nevertheless decided not to order any more fall goods and to discontinue all imports from Great Britain, with a few exceptions, for one year beginning January 1, 1769. All but a handful subscribed.

One month later, on September 6, Salem merchants followed suit, unanimously agreeing not to order more goods until January 1770, except coal, salt, and other articles necessary for fishing. Tea, glass, paper, and printers' colors were pledged not to be imported until the acts were repealed.[31]

The embargo was made easier by merchants' overstocked warehouses. Economic hard times had slowed buying and produced high inventories. With the flow of English imports blocked, goods could be sold at higher prices.

On June 30, 1769, Salem traders met at King's Arms tavern to deliberate enforcement difficulties. Several Boston merchants were accused of shipping in English goods, and the merchants resolved to "do all in our Power to discourage" their sale. The public was asked to boycott John Gooll's former shop, presently being managed by John Norris of Salem, and owned and supplied by Boston merchants. These Bostonians were suspected of double-ordering their usual inventory, "*expecting to make their Fortunes*, while others were sinking *theirs* for the Benefit of their Country." To broaden support, help from Marblehead was solicited, and certain local traders, "who (it is well known) have deviated from their Contract" were warned to conform. The names of nonsubscribers and contract breakers would be publicized.[32]

In July and August 1769, Massachusetts heard that the British ministry intended to seek repeal of all Townshend duties at the next session of Parliament, except the duty on tea. Some Boston merchants who had already decided to extend nonimportation were displeased that repeal would be only partial. The remaining tea duty would symbolize England's right to tax the colonies for revenue.

Most major merchants in Essex County seemed to have backed the boycott. Some, however, continued to advertise English imports. Nathan Frazier of Andover and Thomas Lewis of Marblehead specified that they had imported no goods since last year, but John Appleton of Salem, subsequently accused of noncompliance with the merchants' agreement, advertised he "continues to sell, English Goods as usual."[33] Nonetheless, the number of advertisements in the *Essex Gazette* was reduced—a sign at least of perfunctory conformity with the boycott.

On September 4, 1769, Newburyporters voted approval of their merchants' year-old nonimportation agreement; anyone who bought was to be "deemed an Enemy to the Liberties of his Country." The meeting was called at the merchants' request; some suspected that "one or more Persons coming lately into this Town have acted contrary to the Spirit of said Agreement."[34]

On October 16, amid nonimportation discussions, a chest of tea was carted eighteen miles out of Boston to Marblehead. Earlier, a coaster had refused to carry the same cargo. The purchaser, James McCall, was required to return the forbidden tea to the dealer's store—on the "Carriage of a Chair . . . properly decorated, with some patriotic Inscriptions."[35]

It took several meetings at Bunch of Grapes tavern for Marblehead merchants and traders to thrash out an extension to their agreement. On October 26, they concurred not to import until the Revenue Acts were repealed. Excepted were blankets, coal, coarse jerseys, duck, fishing articles, pepper, powder, rugs, salt, and a few other items. Merchandise on order would be stored by the merchants' committee. Fifty or sixty subscribed; the rest were expected to "be convinced that they should prefer the Good of their Country to their private Interest." In December, "the Publick" was acquainted that Jacob Fowle & Son, Thomas Robie, Israel Forster, and John Sparhawk continued to import goods for sale. They defended their actions, claiming that they had ordered fall goods to replenish depleted inventories, though they had subscribed to an earlier nonimportation agreement. They accused some present subscribers of not pledging to the previous one and, consequently, having adequate inventory. They promised to place no further orders, pledging to sell only what was already ordered. Only Thomas Robie, the sole Marblehead renegade in the Stamp Act controversy, flat out opposed nonimportation.[36]

The "Boston Massacre"

The presence of British troops in Boston was the source of constant friction with townspeople. The "lobsterbacks," as their detractors called them, were subjected to continual scorn and ridicule. Epithet shouting, snowballings, and occasional brawls kept the town in an uneasy state.

On the fateful evening of March 5, an incident between a British sentry and a couple of ridiculing wigmakers had escalated to a point where a crowd of ugly, club-wielding rowdies menacingly besieged the solitary soldier. A corporal and six grenadiers were ordered to his rescue. When they reached the scene, the unruly mob swarmed around them blocking their exit. As they closed in, the soldiers brandished their bayonets and tried to make their way out. The jeering pack refused to budge. Someone threw a club, knocking down one of the grenadiers; he got up and fired. Others fired, and five of the crowd fell. Four were mortally wounded; the fifth would die in nine days. In the confusion that followed, a path opened up and the British took their leave.

Unprecedented indignation followed. Sam Adams, the political agitator and master propagandist, and his fellow radicals took advantage of it. A merciless journalistic barrage was launched into the midst of the furor, with the propagandists cleverly coining the phrase "Boston Massacre" to describe the event.

Sparks flew from several Essex County towns. A letter in the *Essex Gazette* described the people as so enraged, "it is thought, if a proper Signal should be given, not less than Fifteen Hundred Men" from Salem and Marblehead were prepared to march "at a Minute's Warning, to revenge the Murders, and support the Rights of the insulted and much abused Inhabitants of Boston." The writer urged each town to pass resolutions expressing "greatest Abhorrence and Detestation." "Never did *Tory Principles*," he declared, "appear in such glaring, odious Colours as at this Time."[37] Communities eloquently expressed indignation. On March 27, Gloucester resolved that the troops had "wantonly spilt the Blood of many of our Brethren which calls for our highest Resentment."[38] In May, Boxford, a small interior farming community, outraged at the violence, noted:

> their most inhuman and barbarous actions since their being quartered in the town of Boston in abusing, wounding, and killing some

of the inhabitants thereof, contrary to the laws of God and man; and the unparalleled patience and prudence of the inhabitants of the said town of Boston, being very desirious of doing all in their power to try and preserve their liberty.[39]

At their May 10 town meeting, Marbleheaders expressed the "highest Indignation and Resentment, that an ignorant, lawless, and bloody Soldiery, should attempt, of its own Authority, to fire upon and destroy so many of our Brethren." "Readiness" was pledged, "with our Lives and Interest, at all Times, to support the civil Authority of this Province, in bringing to Justice all such high-handed Offenders."[40]

Town Meeting Pledges

With rumors that all duties on goods, excepting tea, would be repealed, efforts against importation were stepped up. Removal of *all* duties was vital to the principle that Parliament could not levy revenue taxes. Merchants called for popular support, and the people responded. In the spring of 1770, town meetings in most Essex County towns passed sets of resolutions in support of the merchants of Boston and other maritime towns.

For the first time in the antitax protest, subscription papers were introduced widely. The nonimportation effort had been near collapse; it was hoped popular pledges would sustain it. The threat of publishing the names of nonsigners or offenders, reinforced with financial and social pressures, was expected to control any apathetic or hostile townspeople.

On March 13, 1770, Newbury became the first town in Essex County to approve a popularly subscribed nonimportation agreement "to prevent ye Transportation of Goods from great Britain, & Encourage Industry, [E]conomy & Manufactures amongst ourselves." Fifty townspeople had petitioned, which the town accepted unanimously. Sixteen people were to circulate the papers.

Townspeople agreed to promote local manufacture and to support the "united body of Merchants." Zeroing in on the Newburyport shipbuilders, they promised to cut off any builders taking pay in forbidden British imports. They vowed not to purchase foreign tea or "Suffer it to be us'd in our Families" until repeal of the Revenue Act or return to general importation. Whoever signed and broke the agreement was to be a "Covenant Breaker, an Enemy to his Country, a Friend to Slavery Deserving Contempt." Newbury helped lead the effort, writing to other towns, encouraging them to follow suit.[41]

On the same day, Salisbury voters passed a similar resolve, promising "no Dealings" with anyone importing contrary to the merchants' agreement. Six days after Newbury spoke out, Ipswichites expressed like sentiments.

Several more town meeting votes followed. Newburyport, on March 23, approved continuation of nonimportation and chose a committee to send thanks to the Boston merchants for their "patriotick and noble Spirit." It was agreed the town would not use or buy foreign tea and would "to discourage it in others." Meanwhile, several Boston merchants brought in illicit imports, including a wagonload of tea, which were accepted by local traders. An April 3 meeting appointed a committee of inspection to publicize the violators and to discourage further breaches, "To the intent that they may be known & avoided as ye Pests of Society & Enemies of ye Country & that such Measures may be taken with them as ye Town shall think proper." The committee was charged to investigate all deviations since January 1, 1770, and to take steps to prevent shipbuilders from exchanging imported goods for their ships. A pledge not to buy, sell, or use foreign tea was circulated for signatures. Forty-four men, plus four wives, whose husbands presumably signed, and three widows were reportedly nonsigners. Ninety-four percent of the town's adult males had agreed to comply.[42] On March 27, while approving their resolves, Gloucester voters expressed particular concern that customs enforcement was in the hands of a "lawless and licentious Soldiery, and a Crew of petty Officers." A few months earlier, apparently unimpressed by his September 1768 threat by a mob, the despised Samuel Fellows, commanding a customs patrol cutter off Cape Ann, had come ashore and forcibly removed a prisoner in custody of deputy sheriff Jacob Parsons. Parsons resisted, and several shots were fired, barely missing Parsons and several others. While the underlying circumstances are unknown, Fellows was brought to trial, though he was meted only a ten-pound fine. The town was outraged, not only by his callous act, but by an apparent maladministration of justice.[43] Haverhill scheduled a meeting for April 9 over concern "respecting the importers or the Importing British Goods Contrary to the Agreement of marchents in General." (It was reported that "one G. [possibly John Gooll] is about transporting a large Quantity of late imported Goods from Salem" to Haverhill.) Anyone who sold, transported, or purchased goods contrary to the merchants' agreement was voted "Incapable of being Chosen to any Office of Proffit or Honouer in this Town." Here too, a committee of inspection was appointed, to confiscate and store illicit goods, as well as to publicize violators. Those merchants who had imported since December 1768 pledged to hand over their purchases. Four days later, the committee and "many principal Inhabitants" met at the Sign of the Roebuck, where a general subscription began.[44]

Early in May, other maritime towns voted nonimportation and nonconsumption. On May 1, after a March 12 resolve not to purchase goods contrary to merchants' agreements, Salem voters—amid some opposition—formed a committee of inspection and correspondence and voted a subscription, to discourage trading or purchasing with importers or using foreign tea. Within a week, 360 heads of families had signed compliance. On May 10, Marblehead voted to request reshipment of goods imported contrary to the agreement. If anyone refused or continued to place orders, the violator's name would be published and he would be "looked upon as an Enemy to his Country" and quarantined. Jeremiah Lee, Azor Orne, Benjamin Marston, John Pedrick, Thomas Gerry, Jr., Elbridge Gerry, and Thomas Lewis were appointed committee members. Names of all who did not promise to refrain from tea were to be recorded with the town clerk and printed in the *Essex Gazette*. In mid-May, ten names were published. On May 4, Beverly thanked the "Patriotick merchants" subscribing to nonimportation and pledged not to purchase from noncompliers. Later, on July 3, Beverlyites approved continued nonimportation, discouragement of tea, and popular subscription, to show the inhabitants' "united Sentiments."[45]

Between Andover's May 21 resolves and Topsfield's on June 11, four other communities—Rowley, Boxford, Lynn, Danvers—voted to support the nonimportation effort. The towns adopted similar sets of resolutions, some including popular subscription, others not.

Town actions during the spring of 1770 had several major objectives. One was to provide a second line of defense against British goods imported contrary to the merchants' agreements. (The first line was the merchant boycott.) Town meeting votes secured formal cooperation from the townspeople not to purchase from any merchants ignoring the agreements. This was hoped to discourage recalcitrant merchants. Encouragement of home manufacture, thrift, and frugality continued to be expressed in the resolves. Secondly, the special action taken toward tea was designed to convince Britain that total repeal of the Townshend duties was necessary. If the publicity did not work, impact on sales, it was hoped, would force repeal. Finally, the resolves were intended to raise the spirits of the boycotting merchants and to extend support for their effort province-wide. Consequently, towns usually voted to send a copy of their resolutions to Boston and to publish them. The British ministry and Parliament had to know that the Town of Boston and the House of Representatives were supported by the whole province. When Boston or the General Assembly petitioned, England would know they spoke for a united people. As Marbleheaders said at their May 10 meeting: "That, with equal Approbation, we have beheld the Merchants of

this Place (excepting a few), uniting with those of our spirited metropolis, and the other maritime Towns in this Province, in an Agreement of *Nonimportation*, well calculated to add Weight to the
Proceedings of that Assembly, which has gloriously distinguished
itself as the watchful Guardians of our invaluable Rights and
Liberties."[46]

Votes out of Essex County would "add Weight" to any actions
taken by the General Assembly when it convened. Since Manchester,
Methuen, Middleton, and Wenham continued not to send anyone to
the General Court, they did not formally support the merchants'
agreements. With no representative, no one was present to benefit
from the lively House debate and return to spread his raised political
consciousness. Neither did Amesbury and Bradford take votes. It
would be a while before these small, upriver towns responded to
Revolutionary stirrings.

Enforcement

Town meeting actions formalized what already had been common
practice in most communities. The December 1769 issue of the *Boston
Chronicle* reported that Enoch Bartlett of Haverhill had received imported goods from Boston. Bartlett's excuse was that a Boston merchant had erroneously imported the goods in his name.
"Resentments" from Bartlett's customers and their boycott of his store
had brought a public response.[47] Haverhill apparently was supporting the merchant ban several months before public subscription.

By the spring of 1770, support for nonimportation in Essex
County was near universal. In early May, Jeremiah Lee, chairman of
the Marblehead committee of trade, reported no breaches of sale.
Illicit imports when found were reshipped. John Appleton, Abigail
Eppes, Peter Frye, and Elizabeth Higginson, four of Salem's recalcitrant storekeepers, finally permitted the merchants' committee to
store their goods ordered before February 15 and to reship subsequent orders. This late, reluctant concession came the day after Salem's May 1 endorsement of nonimportation. Public pressures
compelled Thomas Robie to advertise that he possessed no goods
imported since the agreement. Robie requested "All Persons indebted" to pay immediately. Some people must have used a rumor,
coupled with his prominent irascible attitude, as an excuse to withhold payments. Rhode Island had been largely ignoring the nonimportation effort. On June 6, 1770, Capt. Eleazer Trevett, Jr. was
requested to leave Marblehead harbor, as it was "incompatible" to
"hold any commerce" with Rhode Island people. The day before,
there was a similar incident in Salem involving a Newport vessel. The

"infamous" James McMasters of Boston came to Marblehead with his wares. He was ordered to leave. McMasters was one of a handful of Boston merchants who had refused to comply with the original merchants' agreement. McMasters went to Salem "for Countenance and Protection," but was unwelcomed and forced to lodge in a second-rate, obscure tavern. He left the following day. Isaac Wilson from South Danvers, now Peabody, had been selling tea. The Sons of Liberty extracted a public confession in front of the Bell Tavern, forcing Wilson to repeat over his cup of punch, "I, Isaac Wilson a Tory I be, I, Isaac Wilson, I sell tea."[48]

By late spring, enforcement of subscription pledges and nonimportation agreements, particularly in the maritime towns, was becoming difficult. In mid-April, consistent with earlier assurances, the British Parliament repealed all Townshend duties, except tea. In early May, Massachusetts got the word. For a while, the indignation following the "Boston Massacre" sustained the boycott, but the near-total repeal weakened popular resolve. By the end of summer, economic sanctions were breaking down. In August, John Hendy of Salem continued to sell tea, contrary to the agreement, which he refused to sign. The public was asked in the *Essex Gazette* to withdraw patronage from him, as he was favoring "Designs of the Enemies to American Liberty."[49] Also in August, Capt. Samuel Lyon arrived in Marblehead from New York with a cargo of pork; since New Yorkers had broken with nonimportation, Lyons was requested to leave. The same month, committees from Boston visited Haverhill, Marblehead, Newburyport, and Salem to bolster the flagging maritime confederation. These trading towns were suspected of having "departed" from strict compliance. The four members who visited Salem, including the famous patriot William Molineux, stayed at the King's Arms tavern. In the evening, an unexpected visitor, William Luscomb, warned that thirty to forty men had gathered at Long Wharf, intent on tar and feathering them if they did not leave immediately. A local merchant committee member, however, gave assurances that there was no cause for alarm. The Boston delegation met with the committee the next day, then left. To maintain the public perception of a united front, Boston voted their "utmost Satisfaction" that the towns "religiously and steadfastly" were adhering to the agreement.[50]

In late September, four Salem merchants—John Appleton, Abigail Eppes, Peter Frye, and Elizabeth Higginson—fed up with the boycott, broke open the committee storehouse, where their lately arrived cargoes were stored. Accompanied by a sheriff, they removed their goods. Irate townspeople voted to read their names at each annual March meeting for seven years. Inhabitants were asked to shun the boycott breakers and not to employ Benjamin Daland, who assisted in draying the goods. In his defense, Peter Frye stated that glass from Marblehead and Boston was being sold in town, so he saw no sense in respecting the local agreement. The boycott had become an uphill battle in the maritime towns, especially with large commercial towns in other colonies rescinding nonimportation—not to mention the breach among their own membership.[51]

In mid-October, Boston merchants voted to resume importation of British goods, except tea. It was all over. Not only was the agreement hard to enforce at home, it was not having the desired effect in England. Early in September, Capt. Richard Derby of Salem reported that factory workers remained fully employed in London and the American nonimportation effort was attracting little attention.[52] Fortunately for the British, trade elsewhere was expanding during the American cut-off, minimizing any effect of the embargo. Yet, a partial objective had been accomplished; most Townshend duties had been repealed. Repeal had been precipitated, however, by a ministerial policy change designed to make English manufactures more inexpensive abroad—hence, more saleable—not by the colonial protest movement.

1. Gloucester Town Records, December 14, 1767, 104.
2. Newburyport Town Records, March 18, 1768, 1:121.
3. Benjamin W. Labaree, *Patriots and Partisans* (Cambridge: Harvard University Press, 1962), 21; "Thomas Cushing to Dennys DeBerdt," MHS *Collections*, 4th Series, 4 (1858):350–51.
4. Beverly Town Records, March 14, 1768, 5:382.
5. Sidney Perley, *History of Boxford* (Boxford: Sidney Perley, 1880), 205; Andover Town Records, May 23, 1768.
6. *Essex Gazette*, August 16–23, 1768, 15.
7. August 2, 1768.
8. August 9–16, 1768, 11; August 16–23, 1768, 15; August 30–September 6, 23; Haverhill voted on September 1, 1768; George Wingate Chase, *History of Haverhill* (Haverhill: George Wingate Chase, 1861), 365.
9. *Essex Gazette*, August 2, 1768, 3; August 2–9, 1768, 5; Salem Town Records, EI, July 18, 1768, 4:693–94.
10. *Essex Gazette*, February 20–27, 1770, 123.
11. June 20–27, 1769, 193; Robert Crowell, *History of the Town of Essex* (Essex: Town of Essex, 1868), 208.
12. *Essex Gazette*, June 13–20, 1769, 189.
13. John J. Currier, *History of Newburyport, Mass. 1764–1905* (Newburyport: John J. Currier, 1906), 1:46, 48.
14. Harriet Silvester Tapley, *Chronicles of Danvers* (Danvers: Danvers Historical Society,

1923), 60; Edwin M. Stone, *History of Beverly* (Boston: James Munroe, 1843), 54–55; Lucy Larcom, a well-known Beverly poet, wrote a poem, "The Gambrel Roof," about a tea party believed to have been at the Page house.
15. *Essex Gazette*, December 20–27, 1768, 87.
16. May 23–30, 1769, 178.
17. November 8–15, 1768, 65.
18. September 6–13, 1768, 27; Joseph B. Felt, *Annals of Salem*, 2nd ed. (Salem: W. & S. B. Ives, 1849), 2:263; *The Holyoke Diaries, 1709–1856* (Salem: Essex Institute, 1911), 69.
19. *Essex Gazette*, September 20–27, 1768, 37.
20. "Riot at Gloucester in 1768," *EIHC*, 42 (1906):37–38; John J. Babson, *History of the Town of Gloucester* (Gloucester: Procter Bros., 1860), 323–4.
21. *Essex Gazette*, March 20–27, 1770, 139; in mid–1769, Saville, employed as a tidesman in a custom house, was violently seized in Providence. At the time of the Gloucester beating, after having brought suit for damages on September 7, 1768, and lost, Saville appealed the decision and was awaiting a hearing. The March 23 incident apparently persuaded him to drop the matter.
22. January 14–21, 1772, 103.
23. *Boston Weekly News-Letter*, October 15, 1772; the selectmen were Daniel Witham, Samuel Whitamore, Peter Coffin, John Lowe, and Samuel Griffin.
24. Babson, 387.

25. Newburyport Town Records, September 19, 1768, 1:125.
26. *Essex Gazette*, April 18–25, 1769, 157; April 25–May 2, 1769, 161.
27. August 8–15, 1769, 9.
28. May 23–30, 1769, 177.
29. April 25–May 2, 1769, 159.
30. Beverly Town Records, May 22, 1769, 5:418.
31. *Essex Gazette*, August 30–September 6, 1769, 23.
32. June 27–July 4, 1769, 197.
33. November 21–28, 1769, 71.
34. Newburyport Town Records, September 4, 1769, 1:131–2.
35. *Essex Gazette*, October 17–24, 1769, 51.
36. October 24–32, 1769, 55; December 12–19, 1769, 83; December 19–26, 1769, 85.
37. March 6–13, 1770, 131.
38. Gloucester Town Records, March 27, 1770, 120–21.
39. Perley, 207–08.
40. *Essex Gazette*, May 8–15, 1770, 165.
41. Newbury Town Records, March 13, 1770, 225–27.
42. Newburyport Town Records, March 23, 1770, 1:141; April 3, 1770, 142–43; Eben F. Stone Papers, EI, April 3, 1770.
43. Gloucester Town Records, March 27, 1770; *Essex Gazette*, May 16–23, 1769, 173.
44. *Essex Gazette*, April 3–10, 1770, 147; April 17–24, 1770, 155; Chase, 366–67.
45. *Essex Gazette*, March 13–20, 1770, 135; May 1–8, 1770, 163; May 8–15, 1770, 165; Salem Town Records, March 12, 1770, 771; May 1, 1770, 778–81; Beverly Town Records, May 4, 1770, 5:436; July 3, 437.
46. *Essex Gazette*, May 8–15, 1770, 165.
47. January 2–9, 1770, 90.
48. May 8–15, 1770, 165, 167; May 29–June 5, 1770, 179; June 12–19, 1770, 187; June 26–July 3, 1770, 195; Tapley, 60.
49. *Essex Gazette*, August 14–21, 1770, 15.
50. August 7–14, 1770, 11.
51. September 25–October 2, 1770, 38–39.
52. September 4–11, 1770, 27.

CHAPTER FIVE

CALM, AND THEN A STORM

In the three years following collapse of the mercantile alliance, economic good times revived in the wake of relative political calm. After Britain repealed all but the tax on tea, most merchants felt a victory had been won and wished for return to more peaceful times. Many former merchant radicals, notably John Hancock, appeared to have withdrawn from the protest movement. There had been a political turnabout, with the advocates of Crown supremacy now holding the reins of power.

Return of Prosperity

Merchants replenished their inventories, and people rushed to buy what they had abstained from during the embargo. Even the agreement to continue the tea boycott fell by the wayside. William Vans of Salem openly advertised "Bohea Tea" for sale in January 1771. Before the end of the year, John and Andrew Cabot of Beverly were advertising "Choice Bohea Tea," along with John Appleton, George DeBlois, and Nathaniel Sparhawk, Jr., and several other Salem merchants.

Smuggled tea yielded greater profits and could be sold for less than the legally imported herb, so the practice persisted. An illicit trade still continued in wine and molasses, though in smaller volume, because coastal patrols and customs regulation had tightened. In October 1771, the schooner *Pembroke*, owned in Salem, was seized carrying fifty-nine pipes of wine. Shortly afterward, the owner spotted the reputed informer on his dock. Reportedly, after asking him to leave and receiving "repeated Insults," the owner "beat him off the wharf with his own Hands." He was indicted by the grand jury and fined twenty pounds, causing local consternation, since the fine appeared unusually high.[1]

Resentment towards customs reached a high point in June 1772, when the British revenue cutter *Gaspee* ran aground near Providence while chasing a colonial smuggler. A group of revengeful Rhode Islanders waited for darkness, boarded, put the crew ashore, and set the vessel ablaze. Though the perpetrators were known by over one thousand people, no townsperson could be found to testify before the commission of inquiry.

Persistent Sam Adams

During this relatively quiet period, the Whig party seemed to have fallen apart, but Sam Adams never lost his radical fervor. Forever looking for an incendiary issue, Adams had been trying to determine how the governor received his pay. Earlier, when the legislature paid his salary, some measure of control could be exercised over his actions. Adams discovered, however, that the Crown was paying the governor from customs collections. The public reacted angrily, and became angrier still when word reached Boston, in September 1772, that judges of the superior courts would be similarly paid. Adams felt he finally had an issue. The only popular control over these officials was the setting of their salaries. When the autocratic Governor Hutchinson refused to convene the Assembly to discuss this concern, Adams petitioned the Boston selectmen to call a town meeting. The historic meeting was scheduled for October 28 in Faneuil Hall.

Birth of Committees of Correspondence

On November 2, after several town sessions, Adams laid bare his grand scheme, proposing that Boston establish a twenty-one-member committee of correspondence. The plan was approved. The committee was designed to articulate the colonists' rights, particularly in Massachusetts, "with the Infringements and Violations thereof," and to publish and communicate them to towns across the province and beyond. Others were to be encouraged to establish their own committees and to express opinions. On the twentieth of November, Adams and the committee presented Boston voters with a skillfully worded statement of rights and a list of grievances; the report was unanimously approved. Six hundred copies were published, and the pamphlets were distributed to selectmen throughout Massachusetts.

An accompanying circular letter urged discussion of the salient issues: that towns' sentiments be communicated to Boston's committee of correspondence and legislative representatives be instructed accordingly. Radicals in most communities petitioned for town meetings. The response was overwhelming; almost instantaneously, a latent discontent surfaced, as if waiting for the signal.

Fiery Sam Adams had been corresponding with young Elbridge Gerry, legislator and member of a prominent Marblehead shipping family, who had been impressed deeply by his brush with Adams's politics. In May 1772, at twenty-seven years, Gerry had been elected to his first term. Both he and Adams were stirred over the Crown payment of salaries and considered it essential that the English see that the countryside was united with Boston. As Adams said, "If our enemies should see the flame bursting in different parts of the country, and distant from each other, it might discourage their attempts to damp and quench it." Adams saw in Gerry the perfect leader to rally Marblehead and its North Shore neighbors. Three days after Boston's momentous vote, on November 5, Adams wrote and suggested that Marblehead establish a committee of correspondence. On November 10, Gerry replied, "I think the friends of liberty here will be able to hand you something soon, that will give a spring to your proceedings." The "spring" came on December 8, when Marblehead became the first town in Essex County to respond to the Boston invitation. The lengthy protest and succeeding expressions from other towns proved that the appearance of tranquility had been illusory.[2]

Marbleheaders voiced support for a united effort to restore the people's rights. Private possessions (taxes), they said, were being taken without legislative consent. Townspeople objected to the longstanding Navigation Acts requirement that "Lemmons, Wine, Oyl, Feathers, Raisins, and other produce of Spain and Portugal" be transported first to Great Britain for payment of import duties, then shipped to the colonies. Without discussing England's right in this respect, they considered this an "uncommon kind of grievance." It extended the length of the sea voyage, added unnecessary expenses, and subjected lives and property to extraordinary dangers during the most "tempestuous season." They objected to extension of power to the court of admiralty and board of commissioners, to poor treatment by British officials, to dissolution of the legislature and the governor's veto of Assembly council nominations, to the "hostile parade of ships and troops against" Boston, and the "immoralities & debaucheries from" British troops. Marblehead accused the ministry of bribing Parliament to secure their commercial objectives and of keeping colonial petitions from the king. Disapproving of the stipends to superior court judges, they feared this tie to the Crown's purse strings was designed to facilitate future taxes and revenue acts. A committee of grievances was established to correspond with Boston and other communities and to exchange proposals on how to cope with these travails. Appointed to the committee were Azor Orne, Elbridge Gerry, and Joshua and Deacon William Dolliber. Some of Marblehead's protests had been heard before; others were new. Nevertheless, it was evident that the countryside, though prosperous, was not content; that many Essex County provincials had been awaiting an opportune time to vent their grievances.[3]

With the legislature scheduled to meet in January of 1773, county towns convened to consider Boston's actions and prepare instructions for their representatives. On December 28, 1772, Ipswich voted a lengthy response and chose a three-man committee, Major John Baker, Capt. Michael Farley, and Daniel Noyes, to correspond with the towns. On the same day, Salisbury resolved that their representative work for a "redress of these Grievances."[4] At a meeting, on the twenty-eighth, Gloucester chose a seven-member committee of correspondence. Townspeople also protested recent ministerial "innovations" in Lockean style and pledged to oppose all tyranny:

> that when civil Rulers betray their Trust and abuse the Power . . .
> they forfeit the Submission of the Subject and to oppose & resist in
> that Case is not Resistance of Ordinance of Heaven . . . the Town
> of Boston . . . deserve[s] the Thanks . . . of all the english Colonies
> in America and [Gloucester is] ready to join with them and all others
> in exerting ourselves in every legal Way to oppose Tyranny in all
> it's Forms, and to be Stedfast in the Defence of our Rights and
> Liberties which are dearer to us than our Lives.[5]

Newburyport, on December 23, and Newbury, on December 29, chose committees to consider the Boston communications and to make a report. This parliamentary procedure actually was used in most towns. Early in January, the two gatherings recommended formation of committees of correspondence and offered a series of resolutions, which were approved. Newburyport instructed its representative, Jonathan Greenleaf, to join in a petition to Lord Dartmouth "in Behalf of an injured and oppressed People." Joseph Gerrish of Newbury was to "use his most Jealous Endeavours in our General Assembly for the full restoration of our rights & Priveledges." On January 5, Beverly, after hearing a committee report, chose a five-man committee. Next day, Lynn residents signaled their wish to maintain "Constitutional and Charter Rights and Privileges" by forming a seven-man committee. On January 7, Bradfordites expressed "uneasiness at infringements of natural and constitutional rights, particularly taxation & granting of salaries to judges of Superior Court, designed to lay a foundation in time to render property precarious & Introduce a System of Despotism"; voters established a five-man committee.[6]

During February, county towns continued to string a network of committees. Danvers voters resolved unanimously to "Stand Ready (if need be) to Risque our Lives & fortunes in Defence of those Liberties which our forefathers purchased at so Dear a Rate," and established a three-member committee. On February 3, Rowleyites, only one vote away from unanimity, accepted their committee's report, expressing special concern over stationing of British guards and cannon "before our Court-House, and continued them there to the sitting of the General Assembly, and no Remonstrance or Petition of the Hon. House of Representatives could prevail to remove them; the Consequence of which was the Removal of the General Assembly from Boston." In March 1770, Thomas Hutchinson had moved the seat to Cambridge, suffering from the illusion that, save Boston, the province was tranquil. Radicals protested to no avail. Rowley was concerned, too, that Castle William "built and maintained by this Province for our Defence against our own and his Majesty's Enemies is taken from us, and put into the Hands of them who in Conjunction with the Fleet stationed here seem designed to keep us in Awe, and force from us what is generally thought to be an unconstitutional Tax." On February 4, Boxford voters concurred with the November 2 Boston resolutions. Though residents of a small town, voters felt an "indispensable duty" to express their views.

Nearly four months later, on May 31, Andover instructed Rep. Moody Bridges that he "oppose, not with an indifferent coolness . . . every thing that threatens the peaceful and quiet enjoyment of our Liberties."[7] "By a great Majority," Topsfield voted on June 8 to stand ready "to preserve and Defend Our Own Lawfull Rights Libertys and propertys even to the Last Exstremity." By forming a three-member committee, another tie was woven into the county web. The lateness and lack of unanimity of Topsfield's vote suggest the town harbored an important conservative faction.[8]

Unlike in the Stamp Act and Townshend Acts protests, many merchants stayed out of what they viewed as primarily a political dispute. Adams wrote to Gerry in November: "I hear nothing of old Salem; I fear they have had an opiate administered to them." This conservative trading town voted on June 7 that they "see no immediate Necessity" for a committee of correspondence, though selectmen could act as one if the need arose.[9] Not until much later, May 17, 1774, was a committee finally formed. Marblehead also had a prominent, vocal opposition, though a minority. In December 1772, twenty-nine respected citizens and merchants expressed disapproval of the town's actions.[10] Nevertheless, most Essex County inhabitants supported the provincial protest.

The *Gaspee* Inquiry

In 1772, after Rhode Islanders boarded and fired the revenue cutter *Gaspee*, Governor Hutchinson had been appointed to a royal commission whose job it was to locate and arrest the culprits and send them to England for trial. Reaction came quickly. In Andover, voters grieved:

> We have seen a native of this Province invested with power resembling that of a Spanish Inquisition.—To be condemned to dig half starved and chilled in Mines where Hope and Daylight never visit the poor wretches, could not inspire a true Englishman with more resentment and detestation than this newly invented and alarming Tribunal in a sister Province.[11]

Townspeople felt that the commission and its investigatory powers were contrary to rights of Englishmen and likely to destroy the jury system.

While Danvers citizens did not justify burning the *Gaspee*, they argued:

> Yet we Apprehend such methods very Extraordinary as the Constitution had made Provision for the Punishment of such Offenders— by all which it appears to us, that in Consequence of some Unguarded Conduct of particular persons, the Colonies in general, and this Province in Particular, are, for our Loyalty Constantly receiving the Punishment due to Rebellion only.[12]

The *Gaspee* incident was one of the curtain-raising issues that turned the protest into an intercolonial one.

Five Essex County towns did not participate in the recent protests—Amesbury, Manchester, Methuen, Middleton, and Wenham— all small, insular in attitude, and—Amesbury excepted—with no representatives in the General Assembly. Consequently, voting instructions and an accompanying list of grievances would have been superfluous. Hence, there are no lasting memorials to the towns' sentiments. Neither were there representatives returning home, impassioned with legislative oratory, eager to help organize local committees. Not until the Intolerable Acts of 1774 did these towns evince much Revolutionary spirit.

The province-wide unity chilled Hutchinson's optimism. Only months earlier, he had been hopeful that the people had accepted parliamentary authority. Now he was witnessing establishment of a network of intertown committees—ready-made vehicles to spread dissension and rebellion among the inhabitants. The committees of correspondence were, in effect, a separate extralegal branch of government which could function independently in each town to fan the revolutionary fires whenever the opportunity arose.

The Tea Act of 1773

The British East India Company, near bankruptcy and with warehouses brimming with unsold tea, petitioned Parliament for a loan and a change in tea taxes. The Tea Act was passed in May 1773; not until September were its provisions widely known in the colonies. Parliament permitted the British East India Company to be its own exporter, to ship directly to the colonial retailer. In the past, tea went to England, where it was sold at auction and exported to the colonies. At this point, a twelve-pence-per-pound English tax was added, with the tea sold wholesale to American importers. To save middleman costs, the herb could now be shipped directly to colonial dealers, or consignees, chosen by the company. This cut out the English dealer buying at auction and the American merchant-purchaser. The British East India Company could export to the colonies more cheaply than dutied tea imported in the normal manner by private merchants. Former tea importers not among the few chosen as consignees were offended, as well as smugglers whose profitable Dutch tea trade was now endangered. In effect, the company was granted a monopoly to dispose of its surplus tea.

The Tea Act had a double purpose. Left over from the Townshend duties was a three-pence-per-pound tax on tea, which Lord North had wanted to retain. Since East India tea would be lowest priced, North reasoned it would be purchased, whether or not subject to an import duty. Parliament's actions would vindicate its supremacy and its right to tax the colonies. Parliament's actions, however, were the ultimate blunder; members presumed erroneously that the colonists could not see through this veiled attempt to violate their charter rights.

The Prelude to Violence

Sam Adams had his long-sought combination—an important, popular issue and major business support. The radical Adams was intent on inciting the kind of incident that would put the colonies on an irrevocable course of revolution. On October 18, 1773, several ships laden with tea left the English Channel bound for Boston and three other American seaports. Nonimportation merchant agreements would have been ineffective, for the East India Company had its own consignees. Radicals had tried to pressure them to resign, but this failed in Boston. The consignees (several related to His Excellency, including his own sons) would have bowed to the demands. The unyielding, inflexible governor, however, was prepared for a confrontation. Eight years earlier, resignation of the stamp masters had permitted radicals to gain the upper hand early in the crisis. He was determined this would not happen again. Nevertheless, a powerful alliance in Boston and the neighboring towns was determined to stop the shipments.

On November 28, the first of three shipments arrived in Boston harbor on board the *Dartmouth*. Shortly afterward, mass meetings were held opposing the landing of the tea and demanding its return with no duty paid. Meanwhile, the Boston committee of correspondence sent off a circular letter notifying towns that the tea had arrived and requesting their counsel and support. The resolve of Essex County must have been heartening, though most responses arrived after the Tea Party.

Essex County's Responses

On November 10, over two weeks before the tea arrived in Boston, the Beverly committee of correspondence proposed:

> a strict union of all the colonies for a redress of the many grievances the colonies labor under from the acts of parliament imposing duties on certain articles for the express end of raising a revenue on the people of the colonies without their consent, out of which revenue the governor and other great officers are paid, whereby they are independent of this province for their support.

Though committees of correspondence tended to be radical, Beverly members were well in the forefront, advocating the kind of intercolonial union not widely proposed until mid-summer 1774. On the fourth of January, over two weeks after the Tea Party, the committee reiterated hope for "a union amongst ourselves and all our brethren of the several colonies on this continent."[13]

The response from Essex County's merchant community was both spontaneous and supportive. Marbleheaders, meeting informally on December 6, petitioned the selectmen to call a meeting, noting, "if a Sale can be forced in the Colonies *America* is *enslaved*." We "rejoice" at Boston's "Conduct" in opposing the landing of tea, and are ready "to join with them in all their Measures for that Purpose." The next day, freeholders met and pledged their "Lives and Interest to assist" in opposing all measures "tending to enslave our Country."[14]

On December 9, a large gathering in Newburyport of merchants and others pledged to Boston "all the assistance in our power *even at the risque of our lives and fortunes.*" A week later, townspeople voted to "use their utmost Endeavors to prevent the Landing of any Tea sent by the East India Company."[15]

On December 15, Gloucester resolved they "cannot with tame Composure observe this last political Manoevre of the british Ministry in permitting the east India Company to import their Teas into America." Supporting Boston, and other towns' opposition to "this pernicious Innovation," its citizens promised their "strenuous Efforts" to see that no tea is landed and would have "no commerce with any Person . . . buying or selling that detestable Herb." As had Marblehead and Newburyport, Gloucesterites pledged to "defend our Resolutions and Liberties at the Expence of all that is dear to us."[16]

The same day, Rowley freeholders perceived a veiled grand scheme to "draw from the Americans an implicit acknowledgment of the authority of that parliament, to impose a tax upon them without their consent." This was the "pernicious Innovation" referred to by Gloucesterites. Both towns saw the principle of taxation lurking behind cut-rate tea—a ministry trick to get the colonies to accept Parliament's right of taxation.

On December 16, the day of the Tea Party, Lynn citizens unanimously resolved:

> that we highly Disaprove of the Landing & Selling of Such Teas in America & will not Suffer any Teas Subjected to a parliamentary Duty to be Landed or Sold in this town & that we Stand Redy to assist Our Brathren at Boston or Else Where Whenever Our aid Shall be Required.

The choice of words Lynnites used to describe the consignees and the royal appointees in the colonies shows the unusual contempt held for these people:

> Resolved that those Consigneas have Shown a Ready Disposition to become the tules of a vile & corropt Ministrey, Suported by a venal & Tiraniacal Parlement to Oppress & Enslave their native Countrey & Come under the Same Class of infamous Creatures with the Governors, the Commishoners & their Dependants those of Enemies & traitors to their Contrey have manifested the Stupidity to Sacrefise Liberty to averise, & the wickedness when Occasion Shall Serve to Riot on the Spoils of their Brathren & have forfeited their Right to parsonal protection & Secuerity.[17]

The Tea Party

Despite weeks of meetings and protests, inflammatory speeches and resolutions, ominous threats and warnings, the *Dartmouth,* joined

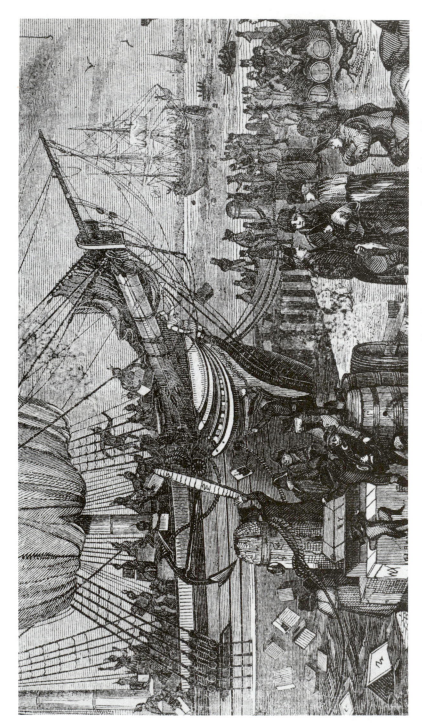

Destruction of tea in Boston harbor, December 16, 1773. Courtesy, Essex Institute, Salem, Mass.

in early December by two more tea ships, continued to lie beside Griffin's wharf. Duties were payable the moment goods hit shore. Haunting the patriots was the specter that twenty days after a ship's arrival, both cargo and vessel were liable to seizure if the duty were unpaid. Midnight, December 16, was the deadline. They expected an attempt by customs to forcefully confiscate and land the tea.

A carefully contrived plan to prevent the landing was set into action. On the appointed day, just a few hours before the deadline, a throng convened at the Old South meetinghouse. They awaited final word on whether the stubborn Governor Hutchinson would permit the ships to leave the harbor. (While the master was willing to cast off, customs at Castle William refused to clear the ships until the cargoes were discharged.) When the answer came in the negative, Sam Adams rose and declared: "This meeting can do nothing more to save the country." This was the signal! "Cloath'd in Blankets with the heads muffled, and copper color'd countenances," a band of hatchet-carrying men disguised as Indians war-whooped at the meetinghouse door and paraded down Milk Street toward Griffin's wharf. Several hundred of the Old South audience poured out following the "Indians" to the waterfront.[18]

Actual Tea Party participants had made their preparations elsewhere in town. One location was Chase & Speakman distillery, where thirty-year-old Dr. Elisha Story of Marblehead—one day to be a surgeon in Col. Moses Little's Essex County regiment—and a number of others donned their Indian guises. A few days earlier Story had stood guard duty on the *Dartmouth* to prevent the tea from being unloaded.

About two thousand onlookers congregated on the wharves, including Tory Dr. John Prince from Salem, physician and son-in-law of Capt. Richard Derby. The British soldiers, who had been removed to Castle William since the Boston Massacre, were unavailable to patrol the wharves. Over one hundred "Mohawks" boarded the vessel, broke open the hatches, hoisted up the chests, cut them open, and threw the contents overboard. Before nine P.M. every chest on board—all 342 of them—was dumped into the harbor.[19]

After the Party

Towns continued to meet in Essex County and voice approval of Boston's actions. It was heartening for the Boston committee to receive their resolutions, to know that the latest measure against ministerial tyranny had met with countryside support. It was usual practice to send Boston copies of these affirmations, to show that a

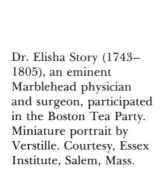

Dr. Elisha Story (1743–1805), an eminent Marblehead physician and surgeon, participated in the Boston Tea Party. Miniature portrait by Verstille. Courtesy, Essex Institute, Salem, Mass.

province-wide united front approved its efforts. On December 20, Newburyporters forwarded their sentiments. It would be bad enough, they said, if the unconstitutionally raised proceeds were to be spent for the benefit of the colonies, but they lost "all patience when . . . Industerous Americans are to be stript of their honest earnings to gratify the Humours of Lawless and ambitious Men, and to support in idleness & Luxury a parcell of worthless Parasites, their creatures & Tools, who are swarming thick upon us and are already become A notorious Burden to the community."[20]

A week after the Party, Ipswich townsmen resolved "real pleasure and Satisfaction . . . of their Brethren of the Town of Boston." Ipswichites saw tea subject to a duty for the "sole Purpose of Raising a Revenue, to Support in Idleness and Extravagance a Set of Miscreants, whose vile Emisaries & Understrappers swarm in the Sea Port Towns, & by their dissolute Lives & evil Practices threaten this Land with a Curse more deplorable than Egyptian Darkness." Anyone offering "any Tea to sale" was resolved "an Enemy to the Town and treated as his superlative Meanness & Baseness deserve."[21]

Boxford voters expressed their determination to do whatever "*is in their power, in a lawful way,*" in unity with others, to assert "*our rights and Charter privileges, not only with our estates but with our lives.*" Tea importers were declared "enemies to their country," to be "treated with contempt." They thanked Boston's committee of correspondence and its inhabitants "for the heroic exertions of themselves in the defence of all our rights and privileges."[22]

On January 4, 1774, committees appointed at meetings held the previous month in Beverly and Newbury reported a series of resolves for approval of their townspeople. Beverly assured Boston they "will allways in Every Salutary meathod Chearfully join . . . in Withstanding every unlawfull measure." Newbury pledged to "stand fast, in the Liberty . . . that neither we, nor our Posterity . . . be intangled with the Yoke of Bondage." Later in January, Salem freeholders approved a series of votes, in which "virtuous and steady Opposition" to the "ministerial Plan" was considered "absolutely necessary." East India tea was not to be imported, Salem resolved, until the duty's repeal.[23]

On January 20, Topsfielders voted not to buy nor sell any tea "that has or may be Exported from Great Britton," approving "every Legal Method the Town of Boston and Others have taken to prevent said Companys Tea being Landed." Merchants continuing to import tea from Great Britain were to be considered "Enimes to all the American Colonys."[24] Topsfield's qualification of "every Legal Method" suggests its uneasiness with violent Tea Party tactics, though many in Essex County saw the tea's destruction as a legitimate political tactic. After all, no one had been injured or killed.

Andover, on February 3, became the last county respondent to Boston's circular letter, the twelfth to voice its support. All the major seaport towns—Beverly, Gloucester, Ipswich, Marblehead, Newbury-port, and Salem—enthusiastically endorsed opposition of the landing; most participated in the subsequent boycott. To gain support of the importers of dutied tea, the boycott applied to all tea, legally imported or smuggled. The difficulty in distinguishing between the two might also have been a consideration. Nevertheless, Lynn limited its boycott only to dutied tea.

County Ceremony and Violence

It was proudly reported in the *Essex Gazette* that a large quantity of the "pernicious stuff was consumed" in Newburyport. In mid-January, residents of varying social rank and political sentiment peacefully imitated the Tea Party "done by FIRE and WATER,"—not on "the wharves and in the public streets," rather with each family destroying its own supply. County vigilante groups, however, resorted to Tea Party tactics to prevent its importation and sale. In Lynn, for example, James Bowler, who owned a bake-house and a shop on Water Hill, was visited by a rampaging group of women who destroyed his inventory, except reportedly for some handfuls stashed in their pockets.[25]

On December 10, a gale along Cape Cod cast ashore the brig *William*, a fourth tea ship bound for Boston. Captain Cook of Salem picked up fifty-eight chests belonging to the consignees and carried them aboard his fishing schooner to Castle William. Cook was rumored to have been employed to retrieve the tea. Salem reviewed the matter and resolved that he had picked up the tea "through mere Inadvertence," after being blown off course by contrary winds and snow and while he was seeking shelter at the Cape. Despite this deliberation, Cook was spared harm by a group disguised as Indians only by being hospitalized for smallpox inoculation.[26]

Resignation of Crown Judges

The turbulent momentum drove patriots to move against the five superior court judges who had accepted pay from the Crown. Judges taking such salaries were accused of consciously helping to subvert the colony's charter rights. Peter Oliver, the sole judge not to disavow his pay, was pressured to resign, and people refused to sit on his juries. Nathaniel Ropes of Salem was one of four who had yielded to popular pressures. In 1772, Ropes, who was chief justice of the Court of Common Pleas, became judge in the Superior Court of the Judicature. Though he had disavowed his salary, Ropes still was targeted for abuse, for continuance as a Crown officer and for his well-known Tory sentiments. During the winter of 1773–74, smallpox had been ravaging Salem; Ropes fell victim to this dreaded disease. On March 17, as he lay in bed feverishly incoherent, ugly crowds massed outside his Essex Street home, breaking windows, defacing the exterior, and threatening to drag Ropes outside. (He actually had resigned his judicial post a few days before.) Ropes died the next day in his forty-eighth year, his death hastened by the violence outside his home.

Punishment of Massachusetts

While protest to the Stamp Act and Townshend Acts brought compromise and repeal by Parliament, Boston's Tea Party produced grave concern, even among English friends of the American colonies. The feeling swept England that the tea-chest-smashing inhabitants of Boston had gone too far, that their actions required discipline and punishment. Authority had been challenged. George III felt time had arrived for Massachusetts to learn a lesson, as an example for other colonies.

Coercive Acts Passed

In the spring, a series of punitive legislative acts, called the Intolerable or Coercive Acts was passed, to become effective in the summer of 1774. On March 31, the Boston Port Bill was enacted, closing the port of Boston, from June 1, to all trade except military stores, and food and fuel arriving from coastal ports. This closing was to continue until restitution for the destroyed tea was made to the British East India Company. For the time, the customs house was to be moved to Marblehead and the capital from Boston to Salem.

A few weeks later, Parliament passed two more acts. One, the Massachusetts Government Act, nearly stripped the province of its cherished self-government. It provided for selection of council members by the Crown, rather than the Assembly. Traditionally, they were elected by the House of Representatives and outgoing councillors, with the governor's consent. The governor was empowered to appoint and to remove judges, sheriffs, and other appointive officials, without approval of the Council. Jurors were to be picked by sheriffs rather than by freeholders. No town meetings could be held, except annual ones, without consent of the governor—an action clearly designed to clip the wings of local committees of correspondence. The moves were conceived to concentrate political power in the hands of the Crown-appointed governor.   The second was the Administration of Justice Act, which permitted a governor to take trials out of local courts when customs collectors, magistrates, or other officers were charged in the conduct of their duty. The trial could be transferred to another colony or to England.

Lastly, a Quartering Act was reenacted in June, requiring local officials to find barracks for British troops, including even unoccupied homes. Troops billeted at Castle William were often too far away; this law permitted them to be stationed anywhere in the colony.

Not until May 10 did Massachusetts learn of the Boston Port Bill, the first Coercive Act. News of the others arrived in the following weeks. The destructive Tea Party had precipitated punitive legislation against Boston's commercial freedom and Massachusetts' charter rights of self-government. With these oppressive moves, Parliament had triggered a chain of events which, in the months to come, steadily escalated emotions and distrust, finally climaxing with the bloody scene at Lexington Green on April 19, 1775. Gen. Thomas Gage had been sent to America to become commander in chief and next governor of Massachusetts. Hutchinson was given a leave of absence. Gage had been commissioned an impossible task. Until the Coercive Acts, many political moderates in Massachusetts had abhorred the destructive Tea Party tactics and favored restitution of the destroyed cargo. But a spiteful, inept Parliament united the whole population— moderate and radical alike, inhabitants of seaport towns and the rural countryside—in opposition to the obnoxious Coercive Acts. The course had been set irrevocably toward revolution.

1. *Essex Gazette*, October 8–15, 1771, 47; November 12–19, 1771, 67.

2. James T. Austin, *The Life of Elbridge Gerry* (Boston: Wells and Lilly, 1828), 17, 18, 20.

3. *Essex Gazette*, December 8–15, 1772, 77.

4. Ipswich Town Records, December 28, 1772, 4:246; Salisbury Town Records, December 28, 1772, 671–72.

5. Gloucester Town Records, December 28, 1772, 137–38.

6. Newburyport Town Records, January 1, 1773, 1:162; Newbury Town Records, January 4, 1773, 260; Beverly Town Records, January 5, 1773, 5:496; *Records of ye Towne Meetings of Lyn 1771–1783*, (Lynn: Lynn Historical Society, 1971), 8; Bradford Town Records, Vol 2, January 7, 1773.

7. Danvers Town Records, February 1, 1773, 2:363; *Essex Gazette*, March 16–23, 1773, 133; Sidney Perley, *History of Boxford* (Boxford: Sidney Perley, 1880), 209–10; Andover Town Records, May 31, 1773.

8. *Town Records of Topsfield*, (Topsfield: Topsfield Historical Society, 1920), 2:319.

9. Austin, 21; *Essex Gazette*, June 8–15, 1773, 182; Salem Town Records, EI, June 7, 1773, 4:944–45.

10. *Essex Gazette*, December 15–22, 1772, 82.

11. Andover Town Records, May 31, 1773.

12. Danvers Town Records, February 1, 1773, 2:363.

13. Edwin M. Stone, *History of Beverly* (Boston: James Munroe, 1843), 58–59.

14. *Essex Gazette*, November 30–December 7, 1773, 75; December 7–14, 1773, 79.

15. Joshua Coffin, *A Sketch of the History of Newbury, Newburyport, and West Newbury* (Boston: Samuel G. Drake, 1845), 242; Newburyport Town Records, December 16, 1773, 1:178.

16. Gloucester Town Records, December 15, 1773, 147.

17. *Records of ye Towne Meetings of Lyn*, 17–18.

18. Catherine Drinker Bowen, *John Adams and the American Revolution* (Boston: Little, Brown, 1950), 435; "Letters of John Andrews," MHS *Proceedings* (1865):326.

19. Francis S. Drake, *Tea Leaves* (Boston: A. O. Crane, 1884), 146, 166.

20. Newburyport Town Records, December 20, 1773, 1:179.

21. Ipswich Town Records, December 23, 1773, 4:253.

22. Perley, 210–11.

23. Beverly Town Records, January 4, 1774, 5:522; Newbury Town Records, January 4, 1774, 278; *Essex Gazette*, January 18–25, 1774, 101.

24. *Town Records of Topsfield*, 2:324.

25. *Essex Gazette*, January 25–February 1, 1774, 106; Alonzo Lewis and James R. Newhall, *History of Lynn* (Boston: John L. Shorey, 1865), 337.

26. *Essex Gazette*, January 11–18, 1774, 99; January 18–25, 1774, 101; Jospeh B. Felt, *Annals of Salem*, 2nd. ed. (Salem: W. & S. B. Ives, 1849), 2:550.

CHAPTER SIX

DEMANDS FOR UNITY

News of the Boston Port Bill reached Massachusetts in mid-May. Boston harbor was to be closed on June 1 to all commercial activity; it was Governor-General Thomas Gage's responsibility to enforce the act. He arrived in Boston on May 17, 1774 to assume the governorship from Hutchinson and to take command of four British regiments. Shortly afterward, a British fleet dropped anchor to help him enforce the embargo.

Arrival of Governor-General Gage

A military governor had replaced a civilian one, but the amiable Thomas Gage's appointment generally was regarded positively. While Hutchinson had been native-born, Gage, married to an American, had been a popular commander in chief of British forces in North America during the French and Indian War. It was widely regarded that he considered the Boston Port Bill improper, justified only under military law. On May 26, Gage addressed the General Court in Boston and punished the town by adjourning the seat of government to conservative Salem. During the Townshend Acts controversy of 1769, the British had considered a similar move if "violence and troubles" had continued in Boston. The *London News* reported in 1769 that "no two towns on the continent of America are more contrasted."[1] Salem contained a powerful, conservative, Loyalist minority, which not until mid–1774 had clearly lost control of local affairs. Gage hoped the move would flatter Salem and be seen in its interest.

One of Gage's first actions was to veto fourteen of twenty-eight councillors proposed by the House of Representatives. Richard Derby, Jr., of Salem, Samuel Phillips of Andover, and Caleb Cushing of Salisbury received approval, but Michael Farley of Ipswich was among the rejected.

Gage came to Salem on June 2 accompanied by some Boston gentlemen in their carriages. "His Excellency was met on the Road by a large Number of the principal Gentlemen" from Salem and Marblehead. Along with a host of civil and military officers, the throng formed a procession and ushered Gage into Salem—to Col. William Browne's stately home, where he received compliments from a large number of prominent area people. On the evening of June 6, a "most brilliant Ball, at the Assembly Room" was held, attended by Gage, celebrating the royal birthday of King George III.[2]

The governor-general established his summer residence and headquarters at "The Lindens," Robert "King" Hooper's house in Danvers, three miles from Salem center. He and his family remained there for the summer, Gage occasionally enjoying a sail on Wenham Lake. On July 21, two companies of the 64th Staffordshire Regiment (from Castle William) arrived at Salem. Next day, they marched to Danvers, encamping opposite the mansion to guard His Excellency. They remained in Danvers until September 5.

Early in August, the 59th Royal Regiment of Welch Fusiliers—light infantry—arrived from Halifax and disembarked on Salem Neck. It was one of four regiments sent to New England. Gage hoped their presence would help restore order.

The Addressors of Hutchinson

Former Governor Hutchinson returned to England, having spent several years enforcing laws with which he had little sympathy, based on a policy that he disliked. He wished that America had been permitted greater control over internal matters by a wiser Parliament, and that the glorious British Empire had continued united, at peace with itself. In accordance with his duty, in pursuit of his dreams, Hutchinson lost his fortune, his reputation, and, finally, his citizenship.

Before he left on June 1, 1774, in deference to his service and in sympathy with his administration, Hutchinson was presented with several addresses. The following address, dated May 25, was signed by thirty-three Marbleheaders:

> Expressing to you our entire Approbation [approval] of your publick Conduct, during the Time you have presided in this Province, and of making you a Return, of our most sincere and hearty Thanks, for the ready Assistance which you have at all Times afforded us,

when applied to in Matters which affected our Navigation and Commerce; we are induced, from former Experience of your Goodness, to believe, that you will freely indulge us in the Pleasure, of giving you this Testimony of our sincere Esteem and Gratitude.[3]

A group of Salem citizens delivered a similar message. It was not published, so the signers were not immediately known.

When the Marblehead address appeared in the *Essex Gazette*, local townsmen voiced outrage and antagonism. On June 2, Marbleheaders assembling in town meeting voted to accept a lengthy report describing Hutchinson as an "inveterate Enemy to the Liberties of the Province" and accusing the signers of trying "to destroy the Harmony of the Town." The address was characterized as "insulting and affrontive" to Marblehead and an "Indignity" to the legislative branch. The thirty-three signers were to be treated "with Neglect and Contempt," and public recantations were called for.[4]

The Addressors of Gage

Local Tories wasted no time expressing satisfaction with Salem being the capital and they pledged loyalty to the governor-general. On June 11, forty-eight "Merchants and others, Inhabitants of the ancient Town of Salem" presented Gage with a welcoming address, noting his "Experience, Wisdom, and Moderation, in these troublesome and difficult Times":

> From that public Spirit and warm Zeal to promote the general Happiness of Men, which mark the Great and Good, we are led to hope under your Excellency's Administration for every Thing that may promote the Peace, Prosperity, & real Welfare of this Province. We beg Leave to commend to your Excellency's Patronage the Trade and Commerce of this Place, which from a full Protection of the Liberties, Persons and Properties of Individuals, cannot but flourish. And we assure your Excellency we will make it our constant Endeavours by Peace, good Order, and a Regard for the Laws, as far as in us lies, to render your Station and Residence easy and happy.[5]

The greeting pleased Gage and he praised "such laudable Sentiments, which cannot fail to encrease your Trade and Commerce, and render you a happy and flourishing People."[6]

The Gage address appeared both in the *Essex Gazette* and a new publication, the *Salem Gazette and Newbury and Marblehead Advertiser*. On June 24, 1774, the first issue—a complimentary copy—was distributed throughout the county. It was published in Salem by Ezekiel Russell, who had earned a pro-Tory reputation from some earlier publishing ventures in other towns. The *Salem Gazette*, however, often reported the news with a Whig bias. It was short-lived, with the last issue published on April 14, 1775.

After the Tory welcome, 125 optimistic Whig "merchants and freeholders" addressed Gage, expressing approval of his example of "wisdom, mildness, and exact regularity" in his previous command. They hoped that Gage would use his "endeavours to prevent a further accumulation of evils on that already sorely distressed people" of Boston and politely noted that closing Boston harbor deprived Salem merchants of a market for most West Indian imports. In a correct, moderate tone, they expressed sincere wishes for a "happy union with Great Britain," praying "that harmony may be restored." The addressors pledged to adopt "every measure compatible with a dignity and safety of British subject," which presumably did not include the Coercive Acts. Their comparatively large number left no doubt these expressions represented popular sentiment. Gage replied that he understood Boston's inconveniences but could not take ameliorative steps "without their Assistance."[7]

In July, Gage was presented an address by the "Justices of the Court of General Sessions of the Peace, and of the Inferior Court of Common Pleas for the County of Essex." The justices expressed their pleasure that "His Majesty" had committed the government to "your Excellency at a time of General Distress, when the Storms of Faction, and the Boilings of Party Rage require the Efforts of the ablest Pilot to save its sinking Constitution." They pledged "to encourage and promote that good order and observance of the Laws which, with but few Exceptions, had hitherto been maintain'd throughout this County; and We take this Opportunity to bear our Testimony against lawless Riots." The welcome was delivered by William Browne, Samuel Curwen, Peter Frye, and Andrew Oliver of Salem and Daniel Farnham of Newburyport—all of whom continued a Loyalist posture during the Revolution. Whether all justices were signatories is unknown. Within their ranks were the likes of Samuel Phillips and Caleb Cushing, who, while conservative, were well-known Whig spokesmen. Nevertheless, the document carried a distinct Tory-like flavor. It was natural that justices—prime bulwarks of law, order, and the status quo and serving at the pleasure of the governor—would issue such an address.[8]

Gage and the Legislature

The two houses met on June 7, and Gage addressed the opening session. A few days later, three appointed members of the Council called on Gage to deliver their colleagues' reply to his address. The communication included some very critical comments of Gage's predecessors. When the spokesmen reached this portion of the text, they were stopped and dismissed. An infuriated Gage said that he refused to hear improper characterizations of previous governors. He described the address as "an insult upon his Majesty and the Lords of his Privy Council, and an Affront to myself."[9]

The House convened at the wooden (albeit painted), two-story Salem Town and Court House on Essex Street. During the ten-day session, resolutions were adopted supporting relief of Boston and opposing use of tea or British manufactured goods. Their most important action was the calling of a general congress (First Continental) of the colonies, to meet at Philadelphia in September. They chose five from their ranks as delegates. Gage had learned of the impending conference and that Massachusetts was planning to be represented. He decided to frustrate their designs by proroguing the session before they took the necessary action. On June 17, he sent his secretary, Thomas Flucker, with a royal order of dissolution. Flucker found the door to the legislative chambers locked. When his demands for admission were ignored, he issued his order from the stairs inside the hall. Meanwhile, the Assembly had elected its delegates, approved their expenses, passed several resolutions, and adjourned. Massachusetts' delegates to the First Continental Congress were chosen in Salem in defiance of the governor. One hundred and twenty-nine members sat behind closed doors; only twelve dissented.[10]

The Relief of Boston

The Coercive Acts struck down practices a century and a half old. No longer was the issue just taxation or trade reform. It was arbitrary usurpation of personal freedoms and constitutional rights. The actions of Parliament were designed to divide Boston from the other towns and Massachusetts from other colonies. What happened was exactly the opposite of the intent.

Punishment of the whole town for the actions of a few made Boston the defender of liberty of all the colonies. Citizens in the Massachusetts countryside as well as in other colonies came to Boston's relief with food, clothing, and money for its poor and unemployed, whom the Port Act had thrown out of work. People in every colony, excepting Delaware, contributed. Donations came from as far as the West Indies and even from Great Britain itself. Several vessels from South Carolina arrived in Salem during July with tierces (casks) of rice. Fairfax County, Virginia, supplied specie, flour, and wheat. Annapolis, Baltimore, Philadelphia, and Wethersfield, Connecticut, sent quantities of bread, corn, flour, and rye. To the north, several New Hampshire towns, Quebec, and Montreal contributed generously. This common interest in the relief of Boston fostered closer ties among the towns and between Massachusetts and other colonies.

Scores of Massachusetts towns contributed toward relief of Boston's poor. The *Essex Journal and Merrimack Packet*, first published in Newburyport on December 4, 1773, reported on June 22, 1774 that the "people were never known to be more thoroughly roused, on any occasion, than they are with the present distresses of our metropolis, they all seem ready to assist, even with the lives and fortunes." The greatest outpouring came from Essex County. In June, twenty-eight Marblehead merchants and traders opened their wharves, warehouses, and stores to Boston merchants, whose business the Port Act had brought to a standstill. On August 3, Newburyport voted to collect £200 in proportion to each person's last province tax, but assessors were not to demand from either the needy or the unwilling. The same month, Newbury inhabitants appropriated an equal amount, followed by £7 in October from Newbury Falls schoolmaster Samuel Moody. Ipswich voted £100 by popular subscription. Salisbury donated some money in July and donated over £40 in September. Gloucester sent 120 sheep in November and forwarded over £117 specie in March 1775. In December, Manchester sent £28, and Wenham also voted contributions. During January, Methuen chose a committee to receive donations, and Rowley voted to send £40, in money. Also, the Salem parishes of Reverends Barnard, Dimon, Dunbar, and Whitaker (and, in December, the Union Fire-Club of Salem) contributed over £300. In January, Haverhill elected to raise £100; none were compelled to pay. Beverly made cash contributions, donated cheeses, coffee, pork, rum, sugar, and other foodstuffs—valued at over £87—even quartering some Boston poor. In January and February, the North Parish congregation of Danvers, plus others from Danvers, Middleton, and Wenham sent over £60 and other donations. In most towns, churches engaged actively. In February, for instance, Newbury parishioners of Reverends Noble, Parsons, and Tucker forwarded more than £65. Next month, Bradford sent thirty-five pairs of shoes and over £18. In March, the committees of inspection for Marblehead and Salem contributed £120 and nearly £110, respectively—proceeds from sales of cargoes imported since December 1, 1774, contrary to the existing Continental Association. The same month, Topsfield voted to collect a donation by subscription. The county's relief effort extended for eleven months—from July 1774, through May 1775. Essex County towns contributed half of all cash contributions from Massachusetts. It was an impressive exhibition of public charity, with the greatest generosity coming from seaports, which stood to gain most from the closure of Boston harbor.

The spirit of unity and charity is reflected in the following letter from Marblehead to Boston, dated July 30, 1774:

> We cannot but express our sincere approbation of the conduct of the Colonies in that beneficence and charity towards the unhappy sufferers at Boston, (by means of that oppressive act,) which has circulated through the whole. The inhabitants of this Town, whose circumstances are at present greatly impaired by a reduction of the fishery, as well as distresses arising from the small-pox beg leave, like the widow, to cast in our mite, which, please to favor by a kind and friendly acceptance of the same. The donation consists of 224 quintals of good eating fish, such as our inhabitants all of them use, except those whose circumstances afford them winter fish.[11]

The "good eating fish" were not judged "victuals" by revenue officers regulating commerce to Boston, so the donation could not be brought coastwise. (These fish normally would have been for export to the West Indies.) Consequently, eleven cartloads of fish and an accompanying load of oil were carried over the road by way of Cambridge to Boston. Haulers gave half their fees. So great grew the traffic of "heavy loaded carriages" from Salem that wagoners could count the ribs on their once-fat horses.[12]

Cargoes of food and fuel headed for Boston first had to be unloaded at Salem or Marblehead for customs inspection. Since early June, a detachment from the 64th Regiment and British patrol vessels had been stationed at Marblehead. Col. Azor Orne and Elbridge Gerry of Marblehead coordinated the relief effort—overseeing cargoes and arranging for their freight to Boston.

Not only did extra handling increase freight cost, but the limited wharf space (forty "woodmen" [vessels] in the harbor on November 3) required carriers to bring additional boats into which to unload the firewood. This inconvenience prompted some captains to threaten discontinuance of the operation. It appeared that the troubles of Boston were daily increasing.[13]

Calling of a County Meeting

In early June, the Bay Colony learned of the Massachusetts Government Act and the Administration of Justice Act, acts which clipped popular prerogatives in Massachusetts law-making and judicial processes while increasing gubernatorial powers. While the Port Act angered people, these statutes bred defiance. Consistent with the provisions of the Government Act, Gage announced cessation of town meetings as of August 1. Ignoring his order and the troops stationed on the Neck, Marbleheaders meeting on August 15 called for a county convention of the delegates from each town, "to deliberate upon all matters that may come under consideration for the publick weal."[14] The committee of correspondence was instructed to address a circular letter, requesting that each town send delegates to a county meeting in Ipswich on September 6. Late in August and early in September, in accordance with Marblehead's August 15 resolve, Essex County towns met to choose their delegates.

Directed by the local committee of correspondence, notices were posted throughout Salem calling voters to a meeting at the Town House at nine o'clock on Wednesday morning, August 24. This call would spark an historic stand-off.

Presuming the meeting was prohibited under the Massachusetts Government Act, which outlawed *special* town meetings, Gage issued a proclamation prohibiting attendance. At eight o'clock in the morning of the appointed day, he sent for the local committee of correspondence to confer with him at Col. William Browne's home—at the time of the Town House meeting. Gage professed to have something important to tell them. The committee met, with young Timothy Pickering (a Salem attorney, more interested in patriot politics than law) as spokesman. The governor said that the town meeting was unlawful and seditious, demanding the inhabitants be dispersed. While admitting responsibility for the notice, the session already had

Essex County delegates to Ipswich convention. Printed in the *Essex Gazette*, September 6–13, 1774.

convened, they said, and, not being magistrates, they had no civil authority to disband a lawful assembly. With "Vehemence of Voice and Gesture," an angry Gage uttered, "I am not going to enter into a Conversation on the Matter; I came to execute the Laws, not to dispute them, and I am determined to execute them. If the People do not disperse, the Sheriff will go first; if he is disobeyed, and needs Support, I will support him."[15]

Meanwhile, troops from the 59th Regiment, encamped on the Neck near the fort under the governor's orders of the previous day, began to march in a pouring rain towards town as though going into battle. The infantrymen marched to the "Neck Gate," where they halted and loaded. At this point, they left their women and children, who had accompanied them from camp. (In the eighteenth century, many families of officers and enlisted men customarily followed along to distant encampments.) A detachment of about eighty men advanced to within one-eighth mile of the Town House, as far as Newbury Street, where the Hawthorne Hotel stands today. While the troops marched and the committee dallied in their deliberations, the town meeting was speedily held, delegates chosen, and adjourned.

The governor ordered the fusiliers returned to camp. Next day, Col. Peter Frye was instructed to arrest the committee "for unlawfully and seditiously causing the People to assemble." Two committee members, Joseph Sprague and Timothy Pickering, posted their bonds for release; the others chose jail. Gage threatened to send the stubborn five to England for trial, if necessary. George Williams, Capt. Richard Derby and the other three members told Gage they would not pay even "if the ninetieth part of a farthing would be taken as bail." Gage was warned that he must suffer the consequences if he chose to jail them. By nightfall, three thousand armed men assembling in adjacent towns had pledged to rescue the arrested members if their torments continued.[16]

On Wednesday, August 31, Boston was astir. The British were preparing two expeditions—one to Quarry Hill, Charlestown, to wrest 250 half-barrels of gunpowder, another Cambridge-bound to seize some field pieces. Both were tactics to limit the rebels' capacity to make war. The activity was suspected to be associated with a larger scheme which included putting the jailed Salem committeemen aboard the *Scarboro* man-of-war, presently sailing from Boston to England. The Boston committee of correspondence sent off an express warning Salem. Townsmen replied they were ready to fend off any move.

Public pressure forced release of the remaining members, and the matter was dropped. Despite Gage's efforts to prevent the Salem meeting, one was held in Danvers "directly under his nose." When he learned of it, Gage reportedly replied, "Damn 'em! I wont do any thing about it unless his Majesty sends me more troops."[17] Gage had failed to enforce a major feature of the Government Act: the outlawing of special town meetings. Apparently, he had little control over the politics of Danvers, Marblehead, and Salem, and no control over the rest of Essex County, let alone the remainder of the province.

John Jenks of Salem writing to Cotton Tufts of Weymouth on August 26 pictured the reigning upheaval:

> The Governor declares they shall be committed and that the Troops shall be brought into Town to guard the Prison. The People say they shall not go and are Arming themselves with Guns and Ammunition as if an Enemy was coming upon them and if they should attempt it God only knows what the Event will be, but Terrible it appears to me it will be for the Women and Children in Town. The Tories seem terribly affrighted. Some have left the Town & some have turn'd Whiggs . . . . The Town seems all confusion. Hope it will be settled soon. If this is the consequence of having the Seat of Government here I hope it will soon be removed back to its ancient place.[18]

Anti-Tory feeling in Salem had heightened to the point where Loyalist views no longer were tolerated.

The Ipswich Convention

The county meeting was held in Ipswich on the sixth and seventh days of September. For the first time, all towns in Essex County deliberated over a dispute with England. The sixty-seven delegates were among the county's most notable radicals—leading merchants, shippers, shipbuilders, yeoman—all prominent in their communities. The delegates represented much of the county's future military leadership. Four convention representatives—James Frye of Andover, Samuel Gerrish of Newbury, John Lee of Manchester, and Timothy Pickering, Jr., of Salem—would be chosen regimental commanders in the upcoming reorganization. Peter Coffin, Michael Farley, Capt. Archelaus Fuller, Dr. Samuel Holten, John Low, John Mansfield, and Samuel Whittemore would become majors and lieutenant colonels in the same regiments. Many patriots, like John Bodwell of Methuen, Joshua Holt of Andover, Moses Little of Newbury, Andrew Marsters of Manchester, Caleb Pillsbury of Amesbury, would lead companies in answer to the Lexington alarm. Within two years, Michael Farley would be a general in the Massachusetts militia, Azor Orne of Marblehead and Daniel Spofford of Rowley, colonels. The list of county delegates meeting in Ipswich was, indeed, an honor roll.

Action against the Massachusetts Government Act was suspended until the Continental Congress then meeting in Philadelphia could make its recommendations. For the moment, the only actions taken were ones necessary to forestall immediate implementation of the act. They urged "Judges, Justices & other civil officers in this county appointed agreeably to the charter and the laws of the province" to continue in their offices. Civil officers were to function as if the law had never been passed. Any officer conforming to the act was to be considered an enemy to his country "and so contribute to involve the colonies in all the horrors of a civil war." Towns were urged to continue calling meetings "agreeably to the laws of the province and the ancient usage of the county." Representatives elected to the October 5 General Assembly were encouraged to form a provincial congress; it was hoped that the towns would instruct their representatives accordingly. While asserting "true allegiance" to George III, they declared their

> liberties too dear to be sported with, and are therefore most seriously determined to defend them . . . . if the despotism and violence of our enemies should finally reduce us to the sad necessity, we, undaunted, are ready to appeal to the last resort of states; and will in support of our rights encounter even death, 'sensible that he can never die too soon who lays down his life in support of the laws and liberties of his country.'[19]

All resolutions were accepted by unanimous vote.

Even conservative Whigs had come to accept defiance of the law. It seemed the only appropriate recourse. If necessary, the county appeared ready to resist forcefully Gage's implementation of the acts.

Unpopular Addressors

The Marblehead and Salem addresses to Hutchinson had aroused the public ire, from as far away as Salisbury, which voted to have no dealings with them. (To a lesser extent, the same was true of the Loyalist addresses to Gage.) Locals had been on tenterhooks since learning of the Port Act, and the addresses insinuated approval of Hutchinson's widely unpopular administration. With news early in June of the Massachusetts Government and the Administration of Justice Acts, the popular temper against Crown Loyalists knew no bounds. The addresses took on a significance beyond their actual importance. Addressors were marked Loyalists, and patriot leaders could not afford to have potential enemies living in their midst. A successful challenge to Parliament's recent denials of self-government would require a united front. It was imperative to secure public pledges of loyalty and renouncements of the addressors' earlier statements. Refusal to recant was viewed as tantamount to being an enemy of the country.

Arrest of the Salem committee of correspondence in late August had caused greater hostility, worsening the division. As men armed themselves to prevent the members' removal for trial, tension and fear took hold. Tories became concerned, and rightfully so, for their own personal safety. A few began to leave town; others became "silent neutrals"; some converted to the Whig majority view. A letter out of Marblehead to the Boston committee of correspondence did not place much stock in the Tory converts, saying "they will take up Arms, if attempts are made to enforce the Acts; but no dependence can be placed in Men who are looking for a safe Retreat to the *strongest* and not *honestest* Side."[20]

An enormous intolerance was focused upon anyone suspected of upholding Crown or parliamentary incursions into domestic American politics. When suspected, the only satisfactory response was a public avowal of the majority opinion. During this unsettled period, freedom of thought and expression came under siege.

These recantations appeared in the *Essex Gazette* and *Salem Gazette* during the next several months. By the first of January 1775, all but ten Marblehead addressers had publicly admitted their indiscretion. Recantations from most Salem addressers took longer. Since their addresses had not been published, it probably took time to establish their identity. William Vans's September recantation was early; most waited several months. In June 1775, after the battles of April 19, twelve conservative Salem citizens publicly recanted. They declared that they had been prompted to address "by the best Intentions," that their actions were not one of "Acquiescence" to the acts of Parliament, but they had hoped to "contribute to their Repeal." The twelve expressed their "Wish to live in Harmony with our Neighbors,"

Local addressers of Governors Gage and Hutchinson were forced to recant publicly. *Salem Gazette*, November 4, 1774.

> **To the PUBLICK.**
>
> WHEN I signed an Address to the late Governor Hutchinson, upon his leaving this Province, I verily thought I was doing right, but was soon convinced of the contrary ; and I declare it was so an Error in Judgment, and not done with Design of injuring the Liberties of my Country, which I ever held sacred, nor with any Design of affronting any Individual within the Circle of my Observation. I hope the Publick will freely forgive their humble Servant,
>
> *Marblehead, October 31, 1774.*   JOHN PRINCE.
>
> WHEREAS I the Subscriber signed an Address to the late Governor Hutchinson---I wish the Devil had had said Address before I had seen it.   J. FOWLE.
> *Marblehead, October 24, 1774.*
>
> WHEREAS I the Subscriber signed an Address to the late Governor Hutchinson---I wish the Devil had had said Address before I had seen it.   JOHN PRENTICE.
> *Marblehead, October 24, 1774.*

and their determination "to promote to the utmost of our Power the Liberty, the Welfare and Happiness of our Country, which is inseparably connected with our own." The Salem committee of safety had accepted the declaration and voted that "said Gentlemen ought to be received and treated as real Friends to the Country." It was signed by Richard Derby, Jr., chairman.[21]

John Lowell, a young Newburyport lawyer, was one of twenty-four signers of a May 30, 1774, address from the "Barristers and Attorneys of Massachusetts" to Gov. Thomas Hutchinson. Their tribute began by saying, "your inviolable attachment to the real interest of this your native country, and your constant readiness . . . to promote its true welfare and prosperity" does not make it improper "to address your Excellency upon your removal from us, with this testimonial of our sincere respect and esteem." The resulting uproar persuaded Lowell to write an open letter of regrets to fellow townsmen, which must have removed any doubts. At the March 1775 town meeting, he was chosen moderator and selectman. Lowell was elected a militia officer in 1776; later, for the 1782–83 term, he was delegate to the Continental Congress under the Articles of Confederation.[22]

Other than Daniel Farnham, Lowell was the only Newburyporter to sign an address. Shortly, both had moderated their views. On March 29, 1775, the renowned patriot leader, John Adams, wrote that Farnham has "grown quite modest and polite," and that Lowell appeared "inclined to be admitted among the liberty men." Leading Newburyport merchants, unlike some in Marblehead and Salem, supported Revolutionary politics early, except, possibly, when exchanging locally built ships for English goods. Located further from Boston, their Crown business and social contacts were fewer; they were less influenced by friendships, lures of position and favors.[23]

The Smallpox Controversy

Smallpox was the scourge of the eighteenth century. During the summer of 1773, the dread disease ravaged Marblehead. Four of Marblehead's merchant prime movers, Elbridge Gerry, John Glover, Jonathan Glover, and Azor Orne, proposed to build a small private hospital on Cat Island in Salem harbor where citizens could be inoculated against the disease.

Treatment was controversial and dangerous. The patient would contract a mild case of the disease through inoculation, but generally gained lifetime immunity. Unfortunately, however, a small percentage contracted serious cases and died. The patients were to be isolated during treatment and convalescence, thereby eliminating the risk of

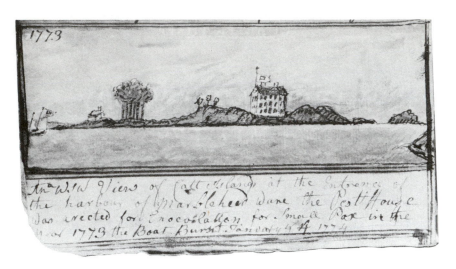

Smallpox hospital on Cat Island off Marblehead. From Marblehead
Historical Society Collections. Courtesy, Peabody Museum of Salem.

contagion. Some denounced the project as a money-making scheme
and argued that inoculation would spread the disease. Construction
of the controversial hospital began in September 1773.

The issue split Marblehead into two factions. A short time after
inoculation began in the fall, new cases of smallpox broke out. Opponents blamed the outbreak on the hospital, and emotions erupted
when a boatload of patients returned to town earlier than prescribed.
In January, the proprietors agreed finally to close the hospital, but
mob frenzy knew no bounds. Proprietors' homes were attacked, and,
in March, incendiaries burned the hospital.

All four owners held important town elective and appointive posts.
Elbridge Gerry, John Glover, and Azor Orne were members of the
committee of correspondence; Jonathan Glover and Orne were selectmen. As members of the radical leadership, their treatment by
former compatriots disgusted them. While Gerry and Orne returned
to the patriot fold shortly after news of the Port Act, the Glover
brothers remained outside until fall. The hospital dispute had cut a
serious cleavage in Marblehead's patriot ranks, but, fortunately, time
healed the wounds.[24]

Demands for Unity

Most of Massachusetts refused to submit to the new acts of Parliament. Meanwhile, the first meetings of mandamus councillors was

held on August 8, 1774. Judges proceeded to hold courts, and sheriffs summoned juries, which were no longer chosen by towns.

The Ipswich convention had sought county-wide unity in opposition to the Coercive Acts. The radical leaders wanted assurances of civil officers and anyone else suspected of harboring Tory sentiments that they would not accept appointments under the Acts, nor assist in their enforcement. If unable to secure a satisfactory public statement from suspected Tories, efforts were made to force resignations.

The Ipswich convention's fourth resolve was directed at Peter Frye of Salem, the well-known magistrate who had issued warrants for arrest of the Salem committee of correspondence. This resolve was omitted from the *Gazette*, because Frye had made a *"frank and generous declaration"* before publication. He had recalled the warrants for arrest of the members and promised further not to accept *"any Commission under said Act of Parliament"* nor to assist in its enforcement. He hoped *"to be restored to that Friendship and Regard with my Fellow-Citizens and Countrymen"* which he had enjoyed. Frye had to choose between making this declaration or he and his family starving. Incensed by his actions, country people refused to sell him provisions. His friends failed to help fearing they, too, would be boycotted.[25]

The Government Act had vested in the governor the power to appoint the Council. Of the thirty-six councillors (increased from twenty-eight) whom Gage chose, twenty-one had resigned or had declined appointment. Accepting mandamus appointments was viewed as tacit recognition of England's authority to pass the recent acts and of conformance with them. Several days after the town meeting incident in Salem, Andrew Oliver reportedly was so scared, that, after having accepted the appointment, he resigned his seat in the Council. The Salem resident was respected as one of the finest legal scholars in his day. Many times sent to the General Court, he was also a common pleas judge. Robert Hooper of Marblehead also declined appointment.[26]

The Ipswich convention had resolved to ask William Browne of Salem to "excuse them from the painful necessity of considering and treating him as an enemy to his country" and to resign as mandamus councillor and as judge. He was visited by a committee of delegates consisting of Jeremiah Lee and Elbridge Gerry of Marblehead and Dr. Samuel Holten of Danvers. He refused to give in to the public outcry by abdicating, saying he *"Cannot consent to defect his Majesty's Intentions and disappoint his Expectations by abandoning a Post to which he has been graciously pleased to appoint me."* Twenty-three officers of Colonel Browne's 1st Regiment met in Danvers on October 4 and unanimously voted to resign their commissions because of his refusal to resign from the "Council Board." Nine Beverly officers voted likewise on the twenty-ninth.[27]

The same month, Col. Richard Saltonstall of Haverhill was "waited on" to resign as sheriff. Several years later, he noted that, having resided in Haverhill "until September 1774, when such were the outrageous and lawless violence of the populace, under the influence of committees of correspondence, and other unconstitutional bodies, that he found himself under the mortifying necessity of repairing to Genl. Gage at Boston, for personal safety."[28] The sheriff and his brother-in-law, Rev. Moses Badger, two of Haverhill's prominent citizens, left in the fall of 1774. Saltonstall had graduated from Harvard with high honors; shortly afterwards, he was commissioned a colonel and served with distinction in the French and Indian War. Later, in 1766, he was appointed sheriff of Essex County. During the patriot siege of Boston in 1775, Saltonstall was commissioned to lead fifty volunteers in the town's defense. He left with Gage's evacuation and sailed for England, where he lived out his life.

Deputy Sheriff Nathan Brown of Salem, who assisted Frye by delivering the warrant to Salem's committeemen, declared late in September before the Newburyport committee of safety that he would not aid or assist "in carrying any of the late tyrannical Act of Parliament into Execution; but will . . . support the Privileges of the People, agreeable to Charter."[29] Brown joined the patriot cause and, later, commanded a company of Salem men during the siege of Boston.

Radical efforts went beyond securing pledges of loyalty or resignations from existing officeholders. Expressions also were secured from those whose Loyalist sentiments made them prime candidates for appointment under the lately passed acts—people either outspoken in favor of British policy or in opposition to rebel activities.

Late in September, John Bayley of Amesbury made public acknowledgment in the *Salem Gazette* of "past Errors." Presumably he had been accused of disloyal actions.[30]

Since June 1768, when Dr. John Calef of Ipswich had voted with the seventeen "rescinders," Calef's sentiments had been known. During much of this period, he was subjected to local enmity. He replied with a declaration that apparently met with the crowd's acceptance:

> I hope and believe I fear God, honour the King, and love my Country . . . . I believe the Constitution of civil Government, as held forth in the Charter of Massachusetts Bay-Province, to be the best in the whole World, and that the Rights and Privileges thereof ought to be highly esteemed, greatly valued and seriously contended for, and that the late Acts of Parliament made against this Province are unconstitutional and unjust, and that I will use all lawful Means to

get the same removed; and that I never have and never will act by a Commission under the new Constitution of Government, and if ever I gave said or done any Thing to enforce said Act, I am heartily sorry for it.[31]

On October 4, twenty-one persons, delegated earlier by a large gathering from area towns, met at Tyler Porter's home in Wenham. With the accused, Nathaniel Brown, present, they inquired into his conduct. "After some Altercation," Brown was charged with "Conduct and Conversation . . . deserving the reproachful Character of a *Tory*." Among the charges was that Brown referred to some newspapermen and ministers as a "publick Nuisance" and to local Whigs as "*Mobbish Fellows*." Unconvinced Massachusetts' rights were threatened by the Coercive Acts, he opposed unlawful actions taken against them. As a result of the meeting, he apologized and agreed not to accept any commission or assist in enforcement of the new acts. A toast was drunk, and the group departed from Porter's home. Brown had been a justice of the peace and moderator of Wenham town meetings for several years. In 1774, Josiah Fairfield was chosen moderator; Brown no longer was in public favor.[32]

A meeting held in Rowley at the home of Solomon Nelson, Jr., formed a committee to draft articles against fellow Rowleyite Thomas Gage. Among the charges were that Gage resisted town meeting actions against the Coercive Acts, criticized Boston's radical leaders, and accused the General Court of acting "like fools." On September 20, Gage declared his willingness to join in opposition of Great Britain's "unconstitutional and arbitrary" actions. The stubborn Benjamin Adams, who apparently had harbored the same sentiments, was unwilling to submit; he was demeaned by being voted "not worthy of any publick Notice."[33]

Nathaniel Brown, John Calef, and Thomas Gage—all justices—numbered among those singled out for public confessions. As addressors of Governor Gage, they were targeted for public queries of loyalty. A submission usually was signed at a specially called public meeting. First, a list of alleged disloyal actions was read, then witnesses were heard, a vote was taken, and finally, the draft was prepared.

Gage and Military to Boston

Gage and his family had returned to Boston on August 27. Later, on September 10, the 59th Regiment (280 officers and rank and file) marched for Boston; they had been stationed on Salem Neck. The officers reportedly behaved with "great Politeness!" and the privates with the "utmost good Order."[34] Earlier in September, the two North

Staffordshire companies that had bivouacked in Danvers had left.
They too, were generally well behaved, though they caused "great
consternation" among the inhabitants. Some from the ranks committed minor infractions, like stealing vegetables, fruit, milk, and
livestock from local farms or visiting women while their husbands
were in the fields. There were several instances during their encampment of transgressors being tied to a nearby white oak and
flogged.[35] Good discipline generally prevailed among the redcoats
stationed in Marblehead; on September 26, however, an incident
ignited between youths and a soldier stationed on Marblehead Neck.
A prominent townsman, Capt. John Merritt, was assaulted and badly
wounded in the arm by a bayonet. The soldier was to be tried, and
reportedly, townspeople were told he would receive five hundred
lashes. The harsh punishment cooled passions and obviated a brewing, potentially nasty confrontation. Even well-disciplined soldiers
camped near civilian centers fast become unwelcome; that the purpose of their presence was enforcement of the unpopular Coercive
Acts was not forgotten.[36]

After the military moved to Boston, popular animosity toward
Loyalists grew more apparent. Encouraged by Whig leadership, unruly Salemites, with sailors as the mainstay, were inspired to frequent
acts of violence and lawlessness: "tarring and feathering," "rocking"
(throwing rocks through) windows, placing hot coals at front doors,
became commonplace. On October 6, at three o'clock in the morning,
a blaze broke out in Peter Frye's store on King Street in Salem. Frye
and his family narrowly escaped. The fire got out of control, destroying eight dwellings, fourteen other buildings—mostly warehouses,
barns and stores—the custom house, and Dr. Whitaker's meetinghouse. The financial losses—buildings, merchandise, and belongings—were considerable. Frye, who lost his home and his store,
offered a reward of three hundred dollars for information leading
to the incendiaries. For some reason, Henry Putnam of Salem felt
compelled to make a public denial. Daniel Bayley, a suspected Loyalist
from Newburyport, wrote an open letter to the *Essex Journal* on
August 3, thanking those who recently had helped extinguish the
fire in his shop. In the same letter, he denied allegations of disloyalty
and, in the future, promised to keep his politics to himself. Often,
the morning-after telltale scorching of a coal left beside a door, no
less than an incendiary fire, was enough to force loyalty and submission from many wavering Tories. By the fall of 1774, Loyalists began
to flee Haverhill, Marblehead, and Salem. Some sailed for England
or Halifax; a number sought refuge with friends or relatives in
Boston under the protection of British troops; others stayed, choosing the anonymity of "silent neutral."[37]

On October 21, the newly formed Provincial Congress demanded assertions of loyalty from all mandamus councillors and any others who had accepted appointments within ten days, or they would be entered in the town records as "*Rebels against the State*."[38] The resolution had little significance in Essex County, where resignations or assertions of loyalty already had been forced from almost everyone. From October 1774, the county was clearly in the control of the rebels. There were still a few hold-outs in Marblehead and Salem, but they no longer retained much political power.

During the final weeks of 1774, in Marblehead, some former Hutchinson addressers persisted in uttering their unpopular views, demonstrating no sign of regret. On December 27, townsmen approved resolutions describing former Governor Hutchinson an "Unnatural, cruel, and perfidious Enemy to his Country." The earlier address was labeled as an "indecent, absurd, and rediculous Instrument" when "good people" were almost "universally incensed." Irreconcilables within town were regarded as "obstinate in refusing to Recede from their principles." It was voted to "break off all Connection in commerce, and in every other way with the persons mentioned, untill they shall manifest Tokens of good Dispositions to joyn their Contry in its just Cause." After February 1, 1775, the names Nathan Bowen, Robert Hooper, Benjamin Marston, John Pedrick, John Prentice, and Thomas Robie were to be published in the *Essex Gazette* if they had not "given the Satisfaction required."[39] Despite immense pressures to recant, a few Marblehead Tories stubbornly refused, believing the radical course would lead to disaster. Since summer, Loyalist murmurs nonetheless had been reduced to a whimper; in Marblehead, as elsewhere in Essex, they soon would silence.

1. *Essex Gazette*, February 6–13, 1770, 114.
2. May 31–June 7, 1774, 176.
3. May 24–31, 1774, 172.
4. May 31–June 7, 1774, 176.
5. June 7–14, 1774, 180; *Salem Gazette*, June 24, 1774, 4.
6. *Essex Gazette*, June 7–14, 1774, 180.
7. June 14–21, 1774, 184.
8. Court of General Sessions 1764 to 1777, 368–70.
9. *Essex Gazette*, June 14–21, 1774, 182; a House delegation also called on Gage and delivered a protest of the removal of the Assembly from Boston.
10. June 14–21, 1774, 183.
11. "Correspondence in 1774 and 1775," MHS *Collections*, 4th Series, 4 (1858):29.
12. *Essex Gazette*, August 2–9, 1774; "Letters of John Andrews," MHS *Proceedings* (1865):344; Philip Chadwick Foster Smith, ed., *The Journals of Ashley Bowen of Marble-head* (Salem: Peabody Museum, 1973), 2:404.
13. Smith, 2:396–97, 415; "Letters of John Andrews," 330.
14. Marblehead Town Records, August 15, 1774, EI, 4:393–94.
15. *Essex Gazette*, August 24–30, 1774.
16. August 30-September 6, 1774; "Letters of John Andrews," 346–48.
17. 348.
18. "John Jenks of Salem to Cotton Tufts of Weymouth," *EIHC* 47 (1911):231–32.
19. *Essex Gazette*, September 6–13, 1774.
20. August 16–23, 1774.
21. June 7–11, 1774, 180; May 25–June 1, 1775.
22. James H. Stark, *The Loyalists of Massachusetts* (Salem: The Salem Press, 1910), 125–26; *Essex Journal and Merrimack Packet* (hereinafter, *Essex Journal*), January 4, 1775; *Essex Gazette*, January 10–17, 1775;

Newburyport Town Records, March 9, 1775, 1:225.

23. George Francis Dow, ed., *Two Centuries of Travel in Essex County Massachusetts* (Topsfield: Topsfield Historical Society, 1921), 95.

24. George Athan Billias, *General John Glover and his Marblehead Mariners* (New York: Henry Holt, 1960), 36–38; *Essex Gazette*, January 11–18, 1773, 99; January 25–February 6, 1774, 107; Smith, 2:369–70.

25. *Essex Gazette*, September 6–13, 1774; "Letters of John Andrews," 357.

26. "John Jenks of Salem to Cotton Tufts of Weymouth," 231.

27. *Essex Gazette*, September 6–13, 1774; October 18–25, 1774; October 25–November 1, 1774.

28. Robert E. Moody, ed., *The Saltonstall Papers, 1607–1815* (Boston: MHS, 1972), 1:521.

29. *Essex Gazette*, September 27–October 4, 1774; *Essex Journal*, October 5, 1774.

30. *Salem Gazette*, September 30, 1774, 58.

31. *Essex Gazette*, October 11–18, 1774.

32. October 4–11, 1774.

33. October 25–November 1, 1774.

34. *Salem Gazette*, September 16, 1774; Smith, 2:409.

35. Harriet Silvester Tapley, *Chronicles of Danvers* (Danvers: Danvers Historical Society, 1923), 66; "The 'King' Hooper House and Its Early Occupants," DHS *Collections* (1913), 1:88.

36. *Salem Gazette*, September 30, 1774, 58; Samuel Roads, Jr., *History and Traditions of Marblehead* (Marblehead: N. Allen Lindsey, 1897), 118; Smith, 2:411–12.

37. *Essex Gazette*, October 4–11, 1774; October 11–18, 1774.

38. October 18–25, 1774.

39. February 17, 1775; Marblehead Town Records, December 27, 1774, 4:419, 421.

CHAPTER SEVEN

TOWARD ECONOMIC AND POLITICAL INDEPENDENCE

Extremists in Boston resisted any thought of making restitution for the damaged tea. Instead, they pressed for a complete commercial embargo, to include no importation or exportation to Great Britain, including the West Indies, both British and foreign. British West Indies planters were influential in Parliament, and inclusion of non-British Caribbean islands would simplify control of the embargo. Never before was trade prohibition attempted on so broad a scale. On May 13, 1774, the Boston town meeting adopted substantially the radicals' resolutions, with the proviso that the embargo take effect when other colonies joined. The committee of correspondence spread news of Boston's vote province-wide and to other colonies.

Revival of Commercial Opposition

A committee of five carried the resolutions to Marblehead and Salem, both likely beneficiaries of Boston harbor's closing. In May, Newburyport merchants had agreed to discontinue trade with British merchants and West Indian planters, provided other Massachusetts ports joined.

> That we will, in Case the other Provinces on the Continent shall join in the Measure, or even if all other Sea Ports in this Province will come into it, lay up all our vessels (as they come in) after the 14th of June next, and that we will neither import or export any one Article of Merchandise or Produce to the Southward of South-Carolina, more especially that we will break off all Trade to and from the West-Indies, or any Part of Great-Britain or Ireland, and that this Resolution we will continue in till the Town and Port of

103

> Boston is again opened and free to go in and out of, or till the
> Disputes between this Continent and Great-Britain are settled upon
> such a Basis as that we and our Children may enjoy all those Priv-
> ileges we are contending and reasonable Men ought to contend for.[1]

Cooperation from Marblehead and Salem was crucial to the success
of any commercial boycott. Fortunately, voters in these towns, along
with Cape Ann's merchants and Salisbury's townspeople, endorsed
Boston's resolutions.

Boston's committee of correspondence letter became famous
throughout the British colonies in North America. The same day, a
letter of concurrence followed from eight neighboring towns of Boston, including Lynn. The committee had invited the towns to a joint
meeting, which climaxed with their support for suspension of trade.

By early June, however, major trading towns outside of Massachusetts appeared not to be joining the embargo. Possibly, it was just as
well; some local merchants were having second thoughts themselves.

Though many Boston merchants withdrew from the conditional
pact, the committee of correspondence nonetheless decided to go
ahead. On June 5, without town authorization, they decided to circulate letters throughout the province accompanied by a "solemn
league and covenant." Inhabitants were expected to sign, pledging
both to suspend trade with Great Britain and not to purchase any of
its imports after October 1. Many of Boston's merchants were enraged, preferring instead to pay for the destroyed tea so the port
could reopen. Most towns, however, approved the committee's intent,
but preferred to wait for recommendations from the Continental
Congress, scheduled to convene in September. On June 23 Newbury
resolved:

> As there is a general Congress of the Colonies proposed to consider
> and Advise on the present distressed State of our Civil and Com-
> mercial Affairs we cannot think it safe, decent, or Suitable to go
> into any decisive binding Engagements previous to that . . . . we can
> with the utmost Freedom and Chearfulness agree to discontinue all
> Commerce with great Britain & with all Importers of Goods from
> thence or those who shall refuse to comply with these or any other
> Measures that shall be determined by the said Congress.[2]

It was expected that the congress would recommend adoption of
some kind of continent-wide nonimportation—nonexportation—
nonconsumption agreement. This was their only weapon, short of
war, to combat British regulatory actions. Whatever the Continental
Congress would recommend, Haverhill, like Newbury, was prepared
to accept. At a July 28 meeting, townspeople:

> 3. *Resolved*, That we will abide by any Determination of the ap-
> proaching Congress which shall be rational & generally adopted; in
> particular, if a nonimportation and nonexportation of Merchandize

to and from Great Britain and Ireland, and a nonconsumption Agreement, shall be their Determination, we will both collectively and individually abide by the Same.[3]

Andover, Marblehead, Newburyport, and Salem passed similar resolves. Gloucester, however, was ready to subscribe, provided other "Seaport Towns generally come into it."[4] By the summer's end, major trading towns in Essex County had replied positively to the Boston letter.

The Continuing Tea Boycott

While a general boycott would wait, news of the Port Act prompted towns to reaffirm their tea pledges. Haverhill voted in July: "That we will not import, purchase, vend or consume any East India Tea, until the Duty imposed upon Importation into the Colonies shall be taken off; & port of Boston opened." The same month, Marblehead residents reaffirmed their disapproval of the sale and use of "any India Tea" and voted violators' names be posted, so the town would know "their Enemies." In July, eighty pounds of tea was taken from a Salem store and "strewed about the Streets."[5] The emptied cask was perched upon the town whipping post—an ominous reminder to violators. Over the summer, school boys, imitating the actions of their fathers, burned two chests of tea on Salem Common.[6] The tea had been found in the chamber closet of David Mason. In mid-August, scuttlebutt in Newburyport reported the forbidden herb was aboard a vessel in the harbor, but a search failed to turn it up, so the agitation subsided.[7] Early in September, the *Julius Caesar* out of London delivered over thirty chests of the *"cursed herb"* at Salem. The consignees, Smith and Atkinson of Boston, said the shipment which came as a "surprise" should not be landed. The committee of correspondence guarded the ship while consignees arranged for the tea to be carried to Halifax. In another instance, a cask brought into town by "a Negro Fellow" was confiscated, and he was "obliged to leave the Town immediately." Early in October, when emotions had reached fever pitch, a small quantity smuggled out of Boston was burned on School Street in Salem, near the Court House. Hundreds observed the spectacle. The Bohea—a high grade of black Chinese tea—had been conveyed to town in a wagon owned by Benjamin Jackson. He claimed that a Negro employed by Mrs. Sheafe of Boston had asked his servants to transport a case, without knowledge of the contents. Jackson had not seen it, he maintained, until it was brought to be burned. Since the committee was storing tea for a public sale, on the day of the burning others known to have sold tea were instructed to deliver all they possessed for storage.[8] In September, Enoch Bartlett of Haverhill was in trouble again. He expressed hope on September 10 that his "future Conduct might atone for past Offences . . . . that I would not buy or sell Tea, or act in any public Office contrary to the Minds of People in general . . . . And in order that my Character (which had lately suffered by false Reports) may stand fair with all good People, I desire you will make these Lines public."[9]

Threat of ostracism teamed with the prospect of vigilante violence minimized violations of the embargo. When infractions were found, offenders usually publicly declared their future cooperation. Impatient, lawless crowds were ever willing to turn tea violations into crowd-pleasing spectacles.

The First Provincial Congress

On September 1, Governor-General Gage called a special meeting of the General Court for October 5. He had summoned the legislature into special session earlier in June, but ended by dissolving the House, after learning of their intentions to call a general congress. The June meeting turned out to be the last convened in Massachusetts by a royal authority. The Ipswich convention, which met on September 6 and 7, had resolved that, on the appointed day (October 5), representatives would transform themselves into an extralegal provincial congress, not under the authority of Gage or his council.

Over the next weeks, towns elected their representatives. Newburyport chose Capt. Jonathan Greenleaf and a committee to draft his instructions. Included was an enumeration of grievances against the Coercive Acts: that the governor's power of appointment makes most civil officers "entirely dependent on his will"; that the manner of choosing juries leaves the defendant "no Assurance, that he shall have a fair and impartial" trial; that the town may not assemble "to procure a redress of our grievances" without it being "deemed seditious, & perhaps treasonable"; that "armed Ships and armed Men" were being used "to compel our obedience." Greenleaf was not to "Acknowledge the Authority" (be sworn in by) the mandamus councillors "who are cruelly and perfidiously assisting to destroy their Country." The committee expected that this snub would provoke Gage into dissolving the House; "if it should, we hereby authorise you to represent this Town in a Convention to be formed of the Members thereof: or any Congress of Deputies appointed by the Several Towns . . . ."[10] Andover instructed its representative, Moody Bridges, to join in establishing a provincial congress if "necessary or expedient,"—also the sentiments of Gloucester, Haverhill, Ipswich, Newbury, and Salem. Beverly already had made up its mind, advising that Capt. Josiah Batchelder, Jr. endeavor to have the membership "form themselves into a Provincial Congress." Manchester, Middleton, and Wenham, having joined the revolutionary protest for the first time at Ipswich, instructed their representatives to associate with the provincial congress if the General Court dissolved. Danvers's representative, Samuel Holten, Jr., was empowered to act similarly and in whatever way would most likely "preserve the Liberties of all America."[11] Other towns, like Boxford, sent representatives without instructions, while Topsfield voted not to send anyone.

On the twenty-eighth of September, Gage concluded it was "highly Inexpedient" to convene the October 5 meeting and discharged the representatives who had been elected. He felt that "many Tumults and Disorders," the "extraordinary Resolves" of the Ipswich convention and other county meetings, and some of the towns' instructions to representatives had indicated cooperation was impossible at this time.[12]

Arguing that the writs already had been issued and could not be recalled, ninety representatives assembled at the court house in Salem at the appointed time, contrary to Gage's orders. Bradford and a few other towns, however, obeyed the governor's proclamation. The first day passed in silence. Neither the governor nor his council appeared to administer the oaths of office. Next day, the representatives proceeded to organize themselves. They resolved that the governor's injurious, unkind statement depicting the Bay Colony as being in a tumultuous, disorderly state, plus recent attempts to annul and supercede constitutional government with a military occupation force, required action to protect freedom and the constitution in Massachusetts.

On October 7, the representatives elected John Hancock as president and adjourned almost immediately, to meet at Concord on October 11. (Towns which had not chosen representatives for Salem hastened to elect them.) With the establishment of the First Provincial Congress, the patriots assumed *pro tem* power and authority to govern Massachusetts. This bloodless act of revolution in Salem marked the emergence of the free, independent state of Massachusetts.

First Continental Congress

Earlier, on June 17, the House of Representatives, voting 120 to 12, had called for a general congress of the colonies to discuss "wise and proper measures" to restore "Union & harmony between Great Britain and the colonies." The resolves were carefully worded, so as not to scare off other colonies from attending. Moderate Whigs knew

Province of
*Massachusetts-
Bay.*

By the Governor.

A PROCLAMATION.

WHEREAS on the first Day of *September* Instant, I thought fit to issue Writs, for calling a Great and General Court or Assembly, to be convened and held at *Salem*, in the County of *Essex*, on the Fifth Day of *October* next : And whereas from the many Tumults and Disorders, which have since taken Place, the extraordinary Resolves which have been passed in many of the Counties, the Instructions given by the Town of *Boston*, and some other Towns, to their Representatives, and the present disordered, and unhappy State of the Province, it appears to me highly Inexpedient, that a Great and General Court, should be convened at the Time aforesaid, but that a Session at some more distant Day, will best tend to promote His Majesty's Service, and the good of the Province :

I HAVE therefore thought fit, to declare my Intention, not to meet the said General Court at *Salem*, on the said Fifth Day of *October* next. And I do hereby excuse and discharge, all such Persons as have been, or may be elected and deputed Representatives, to serve at the same, from giving their Attendance ; any Thing in the aforesaid Writs contained to the contrary notwithstanding.

Whereof, all concerned are to take Notice, and govern themselves accordingly.

And the Sheriffs of the several Counties, their Under-Sheriffs, or Deputies, and the Constables of the several Towns within the same, are commanded to cause this Proclamation, to be forthwith published and posted within their Precincts.

G I V E N at Boston, *the Twenty-eighth Day of* September, 1774, *in the Fourteenth Year of the Reign of our Sovereign Lord,* GEORGE *the Third, by the Grace of* GOD, *of* Great-Britain, France, *and* Ireland, KING, *Defender of the Faith,* &c.

T. GAGE.

By His Excellency's Command,
THO's FLUCKER, Secr'y.

GOD Save the KING.

BOSTON : Printed by M. DRAPER, Printer to His Excellency the Governor, and the Honorable His Majesty's Council, 1774.

Courtesy, Danvers Archival Center, Danvers, Mass.

they could not act irresponsibly. Boston's committee of correspondence actions notwithstanding, any unilateral move by the Bay Colony could spell the death knell to the Revolutionary movement.

Since discussions would center around trade, commercial towns took special interest in the proceedings, though most had indicated they would comply with the congress's recommendations. On August 3, Newburyport appointed a committee to outline the town's attitude toward trade restrictions. Newburyport voted to "stand by" the convention recommendations "even if it be to the Stopping of all Trade." Newburyport had debated on sending a delegate but, on August 10, 1774, settled on sending a letter. In it voters expressed their opinion that any exceptions to a general stoppage ought to apply "Equally or proportionally" to all provinces. Marblehead voted to send a representative and persuaded thirty-year-old Elbridge Gerry to accept. (Gerry would some day become a signer of the Declaration of Independence, a Massachusetts governor, and James Monroe's vice president.) Newburyport and Marblehead took pains to see that their interests would receive a fair hearing.

The First Continental Congress assembled in Philadelphia on September 5, 1774. The Congress was an extralegal assembly with the delegates chosen by provincial legislatures. They were in Philadelphia not to debate independence but to discuss recent parliamentary actions and resolve how to return to their former contented, free status within the empire. All political persuasions were represented; it was clear, however, that the Americans had become restless and anxious for change.

Delegates from towns in Suffolk County, which included Boston, had convened the same day as Essex County delegates had gathered at Ipswich. The Suffolk convention concluded that the Coercive Acts were unconstitutional, urged organization of local militia, encouraged towns not to pay province assessments, recommended formation of a provincial congress, and advised the Continental Congress to adopt economic sanctions. The Suffolk, and presumably the Essex, resolves were rushed to Philadelphia. (Resolves from a Middlesex County meeting had arrived a few days earlier.) The more radical Suffolk declarations, however, received the attention of and were endorsed by the Congress.

The Continental Congress ended on October 20 with approval of a nonimportation, nonconsumption, and nonexportation agreement, known as the Association. The two-thousand-word Continental Association was divided between a preamble and fourteen articles. The agreement expressed Americans' need for relief from the "ruinous" system of colonial administration which had begun after the French and Indian War. It demanded return to conditions in the empire

Col. Jeremiah Lee of Marblehead (left), Col. Timothy Pickering, Jr., of Salem (center), Elbridge Gerry of Marblehead (right). The three leaders held principal positions in the early Revolutionary movement.

before 1763, including the removal of indirect duties on molasses, sugar, wine, and other commodities, which had been in effect since 1764. Congress had outlawed, after December 1, 1774, imports from the British Isles, East Indian tea from everywhere (treating smugglers and importers alike), coffee, molasses, pimento, syrups, or sugar from the British West Indies, wines from Madeira, and any foreign indigo. No goods imported after December 1 could be consumed, except under direction of local inspection committees. Profiteering by raising prices on articles imported prior to December 1 was forbidden. After September 10, 1775, no goods were to be exported to England, Ireland, or the West Indies. It was recommended the Association be enforced by local inspection committees, established and chosen by qualified voters in each community. This strategy, which was designed to paralyze British commercial and mercantile activity, was expected to gain support of the merchant class for political reform in America.

Local Enforcement of the Association

In accordance with the Continental resolves and a similar policy recommended by the Provincial Congress, towns proceeded to adopt the Association. On November 7, Gloucester and Marblehead (and Ipswich, on November 21) chose large committees to carry out resolutions of the congresses. Newburyport, on September 23, had expanded its committee of safety and correspondence to thirty-five

members, including eleven merchants and seventeen lawyers, doctors, shipmasters and builders.[13] On November 10, this committee, with the selectmen, was chosen to seize illegally imported goods and to encourage local economy and thrift. In mid-November, Beverly voters approved the Continental resolves and enlarged the committee of correspondence to thirteen members. Some communities followed Gloucester, Ipswich, and Marblehead and named committees of inspection; others, like Beverly and Newburyport, enlarged existing committees of correspondence, to serve both purposes. These five seaports were the first to approve the proceedings of the Continental Congress. With Boston harbor closed, support from Essex County trading towns was vital to the success of nonimportation and nonexportation.

When the Provincial Congress met on November 23, its first session since adjournment of the Continental Congress, it took up the Philadelphia recommendations. On December 5, the provisions were approved. As a result, committees of inspection were recommended in towns where they did not already exist. Next day, Salem chose a committee of fifteen to enforce the Continental resolves. These inspection teams were to scrutinize incoming merchandise before it hit the retail market, where goods brought in before the December 1 date became indistinguishable from those brought in afterwards. As a check, committees were to take inventories of traders' merchandise. Names of everyone raising prices were to be published. Manchester voted on December 27 to choose a seven-member committee of inspection. A month earlier, Manchesterites had signaled accord with the Continental resolve, which discouraged elaborate mourning dress and ceremony. The Newburyport committee announced, "no giving Gloves to any Person," at funerals.[14] On December 26, Andover adopted the Continental and provincial resolves; later, an inspection committee was chosen. In January, Amesbury, Danvers, Lynn, Middleton, and Salisbury accepted the articles of Congress, choosing five-, seven-, or nine-member committees. Haverhill accepted the resolves in January and approved a covenant for popular subscription. Not until April 4, 1775, however, did Methuen's committee of inspection advise the local committee of safety and correspondence of its policy of nonconsumption of British manufactures.

The Association encouraged domestic agriculture, arts, and manufactures—particularly wool—to relieve reliance on British textiles. Colonists were to increase their sheep herds and improve their breeds, none of which could be exported. When, in December 1774, Captain Hamilton at Salem heard that exportation of sheep was contrary to the Association, he scuttled plans to send thirty sheep to Jamaica.[15]

For nonconsumption to succeed, people would have to live without certain luxuries. Consequently, the Continental Association urged frugality and thrift, disapproving and discouraging "every species of extravagance and dissipation, especially all horse-racing, and all kinds of gaming, cock-fighting, exhibitions of shews, plays, and other expensive diversions and entertainments."[16]

The *Salem Gazette* complimented the "worthy Example" set by Danvers for "discouraging a Number of strolling Vagrants, who live by Idleness and Dissipation." A stranger attempted "to divert the Public in the Way of Horsemanship," and Danvers officials forbade "making any Exhibition of that Kind in the Town." On December 21, Marblehead voters requested Mr. Hilliard to explain why he had refused to stop the use of his billiard table.[17] Next month, their committee of inspection voted, "Parties at Houses of Entertainment, in or out of Town, for the Purposes of Dancing, Feasting, &c. is expressly against the Association."[18] This distinctly stern Protestant provision of the Association undoubtedly pleased Puritan clergy.

Popular subscriptions were circulated in the towns. Though few refused to join the Association, some violations continued.

Violations

Sale of tea persisted. Three or four smuggled chests were found to have been sold to several persons in Newbury; the committee of inspection required profits to be turned over for "*benefit of the Poor*."[19]

Early in 1775, local Sons of Liberty leader Eleazer Johnson—who operated a shipyard at the foot of Ship Street, Newburyport—exhorted his workmen: "knock your adzes from the handles, shoulder the handles and follow me." The band of shipwrights marched to the powderhouse near Frog Pond where the committee of inspection had been storing impounded tea. After smashing down the door, each workman raised a chest to his shoulder and marched to present Market Square, where they burned the contents to ashes. In March, enraged townsmen voted to assist and support the committee's efforts to protect private property, as "the Manner in which the Tea was taken out of their Hands [was] by no means Justifiable & hope nothing of the like kind will take place in time to come."[20] Marblehead's inspection committee caught Thomas Lilly with over a pound of tea, which he had purchased from Simon Tufts, a Boston dealer. Lilly burned the tea before a large crowd and signed a public confession, solemnly promising "not in future be guilty of a like Offence." The committee published that Lilly was *justly intitled to the Esteem and Employ of all Persons as heretofore.*"[21] Those who breached the Association risked unemployment.

Scarcity encouraged profiteering. Nathaniel Carter of Newburyport was caught raising the price of German steel and shipping it to Boston. Carter swore to conform with the Association in the future, suggesting that he had violated it because he misunderstood its provisions.[22]

Owners of goods imported within two months after the December 1, 1774 deadline had three options: (1) to reship the goods immediately; (2) to store them at risk during the term of the nonimportation; (3) to permit the local committee to sell the cargoes. In the last instance, owners would recover costs. Profits would be donated to Boston's needy. The Provincial Congress stipulated that ten days' public notice be given in the newspapers and that goods be sold to the highest bidder. On December 26, Marblehead's inspection committee auctioned part of the *Champion*'s cargo—books, calicoes, hemp, hose, linen, medicines, nails, needles, Russia duck, velvets, and other merchandise—bound from London. The remainder was sold the next month.[23] Also auctioned were contents of the brigantine *Polly* and the schooner *Betsey*, both from Falmouth, England—cargoes of figs, lemons, raisins, and wines. Shipments of similar contents from the schooners *Lynn*, *Britannia*, and *Adventure*, all out of Falmouth, were later sold at innkeeper Benjamin Burdick's.[24] It was rumored that one owner of the auctioned cargoes was planning to land his goods and sell them. The town met on the thirty-first to take "proper Measures," after which the owner apparently changed his mind. (Earlier, on January 10, continued defiance of the Association prompted townspeople to establish a large committee of observation "to attend to the Conduct of Ministerial Tools and Jacobites" and to report their names, so that actions could be taken of "either Silencing or expelling them from this Community.") Profits in excess of £120 were turned over to the Boston committee.[25] During this period, the Salem committee of inspection conducted its own sales. Cargoes of vessels out of Bristol, Dominica, Falmouth, Jamaica, and London were sold at auction, with over £100 contributed to Boston.

One of Marblehead's confiscated cargoes contained boxes of candles consigned to Admiral Graves in Boston, commander of British naval operations on the North American station. When Grave's purser arrived for the candles, the committee upheld the Association and refused, unless Graves paid "1 1/2 per Cent Advance for the Poor of Boston."[26] An indignant Graves responded by instructing Capt. Thomas Bishop of the H.M.S. *Lively*, which was stationed off Marblehead and Salem, to issue press-warrants against local seamen and to inspect incoming vessels for military stores.

During February, on three occasions or possibly more, *Lively* press parties boarded local craft and took off crew members. In one incident, on February 6, the *Lively* barge and yawl pressed two hands out of Capt. "Nick" Bartlett's incoming vessel. "A Number of Marblehead Men observing, mann'd a [whaleboat] with Men and Arms, and putt off after them." Nearing the barge, they bellowed for the pressed men to jump overboard. One leaped, "Boots and all." The "Barge Men" fired at the bobbing mariner, but missed. The sturdy rescuers raised their muzzle-loaders, warning the press gang against any more fire or they would shoot back. The lucky sailor was plucked out unscathed.[27]

Marblehead's selectmen became concerned that the *Lively's* harassment would adversely affect trade. An arrangement was negotiated whereby the candles were released, the seamen returned, and the incident was closed. Nevertheless, strained relations with coastal residents continued. For instance, on March 20, a schooner belonging to Col. John Lee of Manchester was seized at Cape Ann by the *Lively* for "Breach of the Acts of Trade."[28]

In accordance with the Association, cargoes arriving after February 1 were reshipped. On March 2, Capt. Francis Grandy put in to Marblehead laden with Dominica molasses. The owner, Jacob Fowle, agreed to comply, and the vessel put to sea "without breaking Bulk." Early in April, after Captains Andrews and Barker arrived at Marblehead, and Smith at Salem—all from Falmouth—they agreed to return with vessels and cargoes. On April 3, the chronicler Ashley Bowen of Marblehead noted: "at 6 o'clock all our bells began to ring for joy." Ports strictly enforced the Association provisions right up until the beginning of hostilities.[29]

The Slave Trade and Slavery

After December 1, the Association (Article 2) stipulated that the slave trade be discontinued, colony-wide. In January 1774, a similar measure passed in both Massachusetts houses, but Governor Hutchinson refused to approve it. Opposition to slavery was beginning to surface. Perhaps the most vocal opponent was Deacon Benjamin Colman of Newbury. His first article on the subject appeared in the *Essex Journal* on July 20, 1774. Paralleling America's "bondage" with the "yoke on the necks" of Negroes, Colman wrote, "Shall we, my fathers and brethren, or can we lift up our faces with confidence before God, by solemn prayer, that he would remove the yoke of bondage from us and set us at liberty from the bondage that lays upon us, while we keep tenfold heavier yoke on the necks of our brethren, the negroes?" On June 5, 1774, Nathaniel Niles spoke out at the North Church in Newburyport on personal liberty saying: "For shame, let us cease to enslave our fellow men, or else let us cease to complain of those, that would enslave us. Let us either wash our hands from blood, or never hope to escape the avenger." These early abolitionists saw America's freedom irrevocably linked to the freedom of Negroes.[30]

At the time, there were about one thousand blacks, mostly slaves, living in Essex County. They were employed as personal and household servants, on board seagoing craft, and as laborers on some large farms. Finally, in 1783, the Massachusetts Supreme Court outlawed slavery pursuant to the Declaration of Rights provision in the Constitution of 1780 that "all men are born free and equal."

Effects of the Congress

The First Continental Congress had convened to protest arbitrary parliamentary rule, but it had acted more like an extralegal legislative body. It resolved sweeping, continent-wide economic and social policies, and recommended that local supervisory bodies regulate many aspects of the country's life.

The Association permitted ongoing trade, except for certain enumerated items, between non-British ports and the American colonies. In March 1775, the British Parliament retaliated by passing the New England Restraining Act, which forbade colonies from trading with non-British nations, beginning in July 1775. Essex County's vital commerce with Portugal, Spain, and the French and Spanish West Indies would be destroyed. An even a more ominous portent was another provision. Hoping to "starve them into submission," England closed the Grand Banks to New Englanders after July 20, 1775. Fishing was the life line of Beverly, Gloucester, Manchester, Marblehead, and Salem. When Marbleheaders learned of this impending restriction, they sent a circular letter hoping to persuade other ports to harbor all vessels until March 20. Two months of nonexportation might convince Parliament not to enact the proposed measure. But Marblehead could raise little enthusiasm. Even in town, the option was left to each owner and fisherman.[31] Enforcement of the Restraining Act would deal a deadly blow to the colony's economy. The British action gave fishermen and merchants of Essex County one more reason to join the radical political movement.

1. *Essex Gazette*, May 10–17, 1774, 165.
2. Newbury Town Records, June 23, 1774, 285.
3. George Wingate Chase, *History of Haverhill* (Haverhill: George Wingate Chase, 1861), 372.
4. Gloucester Town Records, July 19, 1774, 152.
5. Chase, 372; Marblehead Town Records, EI, July 26, 1774, 4:376–77; *Essex Gazette*, July 12–19, 1774, 200.
6. C. H. Webber, *Old Naumkeag: The City of Salem* (Salem: A. A. Smith, 1877), 121.
7. *Essex Gazette*, August 16–23, 1774.
8. September 6–13, 1774; September 27–October 4, 1774; October 4–11, 1774.
9. September 13–20, 1774.
10. Newburyport Town Records, October 3, 1774, 1:206–09.
11. Andover Town Records, September 15, 1774; Beverly Town Records, September 26, 1774, 6:16; Danvers Town Records, September 27, 1774, 2:426.
12. *Essex Gazette*, September 27–October 4, 1774.
13. Benjamin W. Labaree, *Patriots and Partisans* (Cambridge: Harvard University Press, 1962), 36.
14. *The Essex Journal and Merrimack Packet* (hereinafter, *Essex Journal*), December 28, 1774.
15. *Essex Gazette*, December 6–13, 1774.
16. November 1–8, 1774.
17. *Salem Gazette*, November 18, 1774, 85;

Marblehead Town Records, December 21, 1774, 4:416.
18. *Essex Gazette*, January 10–17, 1775.
19. January 17–24, 1775.
20. Sarah Anna Emery, *Reminiscences of a Nonagenarian* (Newburyport: William H. Huse, 1879), 213–14; Newburyport Town Records, March 9, 1775, 1:226.
21. *Essex Gazette*, March 21–28, 1775.
22. *Essex Journal*, April 12, 1775.
23. *Essex Gazette*, December 13–20, 1774; December 20–27, 1774.
24. December 13–20, 1774, January 3–10, 1775; January 31–February 7, 1775; Philip Chadwick Foster Smith, ed., *The Journals of Ashley Bowen of Marblehead* (Salem: Peabody Museum, 1973), 2:427.
25. Marblehead Town Records, January 31, 1775, 4:428, 447.
26. "Some Letters of 1775," MHS *Proceedings* 59 (1925), 111.
27. 111; William Bell Clark, ed. *Naval Documents of the American Revolution*, 1:93–94; *Salem Gazette*, February 24, 1775; March 24, 1775; Smith, 2:427–29.
28. *Salem Gazette*, March 24, 1775.
29. *Essex Gazette*, March 7–14, 1775; April 4–11, 1775; Smith, 2:434.
30. Joshua Coffin, *The History of Newbury, Newburyport, and West Newbury* (Boston: Samuel G. Drake, 1845), 339–340.
31. Marblehead Town Records, February 13–14, 1775, 4:449–51.

CHAPTER EIGHT

PREPAREDNESS FOR WAR

On August 27, 1774, Governor Gage left Salem and returned to Boston, convinced that the turmoil rupturing the province could lead to war. Time for reason and conciliation appeared to have passed. Without a show of force, Gage felt, disregard for the law would continue. Upon his arrival in Boston, he began to garrison the town and make preparations to seize provincial stores. With supplies kept out of rebel hands, Gage reasoned, they would have limited capacity to attack.

Countryside Forays

On September 1, 260 troops were transported in thirteen boats to Charlestown, where 250 half-barrels of gunpowder were taken from the Quarry Hill powderhouse. Another detachment went to Cambridge and carried off two field pieces belonging to the local militia regiment. These forays occurred shortly after arrest of Salem's incorrigible committee of correspondence. Some Boston radicals, witnessing preparations for Cambridge, suspected the redcoats were Salem bound. An express was sent to warn of an attempt to apprehend the committee and ship them aboard the *Scarboro* for trial in England.

The incidents spun out of control, spawning rumors of imminent attacks from British troops, even actual clashes, including a report that Boston had been cannonaded. In Middlesex County, fears and suspicions magnified, precipitating an alarm and assembly of thousands.

On September 2, Cambridge crowds forced resignations from several council members, including Chief Justice Thomas Oliver. (Gage's actions had been supported by his council—a body viewed as illegitimate by the General Assembly and the people, themselves.) Several days after September 1, as far away as Connecticut, armed men responded and marched. Gage wrote: "The flames of sedition . . . had spread universally throughout the country beyond conception." Little could be effected, Gage felt, except by forcible means.[1]

A Garrison Town

Gage began to fortify Boston Neck, which commanded the causeway, the only land route connecting the capital with the mainland. (Other links were over water. Present-day Back Bay and South Boston were then beneath the sea.) The prospect of living in a garrison was an ominous sign to Bostonians and compounded their bad feelings; the countryside was similarly leery. Gage explained that he intended only to protect His Majesty's troops and Boston's inhabitants—to preserve peace, not to quarantine the town. Nevertheless, erection of the fortification was viewed as a warlike action.

Equally distressing was the arrival of more British reinforcements. Three thousand troops were not necessary for defense, patriots reasoned, so the redcoats' purpose must be to enforce the Coercive Acts and to break up the Association. Salem carpenters were asked to construct more barracks, but, following the lead of Boston compatriots, they refused. In early October 1774, Marblehead appointed a committee of observation to cooperate with other towns in preventing vital services and supplies from reaching British troops. On the restricted list were bricks, labor, lumber, joyce spars, pickets, straw, or any other goods, "except such as humanity requires." On February 7, 1775, the Provincial Congress passed a similar resolve. Some residents, however, ignored the restrictions. During the fall, Michael Coombes of Marblehead shipped building materials to the British, contrary to the resolves. The following spring, in 1775, Samuel Chase of Danvers made a public apology for having helped Samuel Coakly, a New Mills wheelwright, move out of town with his "Goods and Tools." In mid-April, Hugh Mulkoy, a Salem resident, was charged with selling provisions in Boston. Yet, except for a few profiteers, outlying towns were increasingly supportive of Boston and more hostile toward the British presence.[2]

On Thursday, October 14, 1774, twenty-one congressional representatives, including Colonels Lee and Orne and Timothy Pickering, called on Governor Gage to deliver an address. It expressed "utmost Concern" over the "hostile Preparations" that threatened the "Horrors of a Civil War," predicting that execution of the Coercive Acts would reduce Boston to a condition of "Poverty and Ruin" and the whole Colony to a "State of Slavery." Asserting that the "Number of Troops in the Capital" and the "formidable and hostile Preparations" on Boston Neck endangered the "Lives, Liberties and Properties" of the whole province, the Congress appealed for removal of the fortress. Three days later, Gage replied that the patriots' "previous menaces" and "warlike preparations" in the outskirts necessitated the post. Their "open and avowed disobedience" of authority held out little hope of conciliation, "which a more decent and dutiful conduct might effect."[3]

The Final Steps

There was near-unanimous opposition to the Coercive Acts across the province. Most mandamus councillors and Crown-appointed judges had been forced to resign or had retreated into Boston. This was facilitated by the elaborate communications network operating throughout the province, namely, the committees of correspondence. In many towns, committees had been functioning for nearly two years; in others, such as Haverhill, Manchester, and Salem, they had formed more recently; some towns, like Bradford and Middleton, still were without any. The Provincial Congress could count on the committees' help to communicate and enforce their resolves.

Despite Gage's warning to the contrary, representatives wasted no time taking the final steps to insure independence. The Congress could act knowing most towns were in rebel hands. All that remained was to gain control of the purse and the military.

At Concord, on October 14, it was voted to advise local tax collectors not to pay assessments to Harrison Gray, the province treasurer. Monies were to be retained until further notice; two weeks later, the Congress resolved that payments should go to Henry Gardner, the appointed receiver-general. During fall and over the winter, towns voted, first, to instruct constables to turn over provincial taxes to their treasuries; later, treasurers were directed to deposit monies in the Congress's coffers. Having control of provincial purse-strings infused rebels with energy to maintain the independence movement.

The first major step toward military preparedness was taken on October 26 when a committee of safety was established, answerable only to the Provincial Congress, to exercise executive military authority. The committee was authorized: (1) to keep track of potentially troublesome British troops and Tories bent on enforcing the Coercive Acts; (2) to suppress "riots and Tumults"; (3) to purchase ordnance stores, arms, and supplies and stash them in safe havens;

(4) to encourage an effective local militia, headed by patriot officers; (5) "to alarm, muster and cause to be assembled" a "completely armed, accoutred, and supplied" militia, when public safety was endangered. Duties actually were divided between two committees: a nine-member committee of safety and a five-member committee of supplies. Towns soon swung into action making preparations for war.[4]

Marblehead personalities figured prominently. Col. Azor Orne belonged to the committee of safety; Col. Jeremiah Lee and, later, Elbridge Gerry served on the committee of supplies. While their appointments testify to the high regard in which the three were held, they also point to Marblehead's strategic importance as an entry point.

The Supply Buildup

In early November, secret caches of military ordnance and food were being stockpiled miles inland. As early as September, weapons were trickling out of Boston, while guns were hauled off the old battery in Charleston. In December, rebels scaled the walls of Fort William and Mary near Portsmouth, disarmed the garrison, and carried away ninety-seven barrels of powder. To the south, in Newport, forty cannon were similarly seized.

With the rebel buildup, efforts were stepped up to keep gunpowder and arms out of radical hands. After mid-October, sale of gunpowder in the colonies required a special license. In Marblehead, British troops which were withdrawn in January 1775 were replaced the next month by the twenty-gun H.M.S. *Lively*. Anchored off Gale's Head—with Captain Bishop periodically coming ashore to dine with the Fowles, Gallisons, Hoopers—the warship searched incoming vessels for contraband military stores. One vessel discovered carrying a chest of arms was anchored near the *Lively*. A few nights later, a raiding party, led by Samuel R. Trevett, boarded and brought the arms ashore. Never recovered, the muzzle-loaders were used to fully arm Marblehead's regiment.[5]

Towns in Essex County replenished their stocks—flints, gunpowder, and shot. Wenham was set; in August, its selectmen had purchased an adequate supply. Early in October, Salem ordered ten barrels of precious powder, while Haverhill voted eight hundred pounds, plus ball and flint. In mid-November, Beverly selectmen were instructed to procure a "full Complement of Arms and Ammunition." Manchester's were authorized to buy two barrels in December; next month, Amesbury and Bradford took steps to restock. Danvers selectmen were to take "effectual care" to adequately provision the town "with their full stock of arms and ammunition." Salem approved constructing field carriages for two cannon contributed in March 1775 by Richard Derby. By the time of the Lexington alarm, most towns had built up their military stores.[6]

Establishment of Local Militia

One of the October 26 resolves was that towns organize local militia units. Companies were to contain at least fifty privates. One-quarter should be ready to march at a moment's notice. Once companies were established, military drill was to begin forthwith. While the militia system had existed since the earliest days, in most communities it had fallen into disrepair. In many towns, no militia existed whatsoever. Some towns formed committees of safety, to assist overall defense, especially for organization and arming of militia units; others used existing committees of correspondence.

After the privates were enlisted, they chose their own officers. First, all commissioned officers were to resign. Then, elections were held; former officers who had acceptable credentials were reelected. This democratic process assured the purging of Tory officers and their replacement by patriot commanders. Authority to issue military commissions had rested with the royal governor, so Tories had held many high posts.

Indeed, some towns had anticipated the Congress's actions. On September 5, 1774—over seven weeks before the militia resolve—Haverhill citizens, "sensible of the importance of a well regulated Military Discipline," formed an artillery company. Under command of officers they chose, men agreed to meet the first and third Mondays for the "exercise of Arms and Evolutions." Two weeks later, sixty-one Newbury inhabitants organized to "promote the Good of our Country." They agreed to arm themselves, choose their own officers, and obey officers' commands. They had joined "for the purpose of instructing each other in the Military Art"; "all matters acted upon" were to be by majority vote.[7]

Between October 1774 and March 1775, militia countywide were reorganized. Once officers were chosen, the Congress had directed that they elect field commanders of their respective regiments, usually a colonel, first lieutenant colonel, second lieutenant colonel, and a major. Regiments were established in Essex County under the commands of: John Baker of Ipswich, Caleb Cushing of Salisbury, Samuel Gerrish of Newbury, Jeremiah Lee of Marblehead, John Lee of Manchester, James Frye and Samuel Johnson of Andover, Timothy Pickering, Jr., of Salem. Democratically, at the "grass roots," a loosely confederated provincial army had been founded. With loyalty of the military assured, Massachusetts had taken a final step toward independence. Soon, however, they would have to fight to keep it.

In Marblehead, possibly more officers resisted the military purge than in any other town in Essex County. Seven companies comprised its militia. In accordance with the Congress's resolve, Marblehead voted that units meet and choose officers who were "Friend[s] of this country." On October 4, 1774, the *Essex Gazette* reported that the regiment held a field day and that "The military Spirit prevails greatly." While many officers were Whigs, some Tories and their friends resisted the planned reorganization. On December 12, reasoning that no officer with a royal commission could perform his duties "without hostile Designe against the Liberties of America," a town committee called on all officers, Whig and Tory alike, to resign. Their intent was to wipe the slate clean and start anew. Resignations were to be published in the *Essex Gazette* "as soon as may be." Within three weeks most officers had resigned. Several Tories, however, refused to recognize the committee's authority to require resignations from officers commissioned by the royal governor. Townspeople met in early January to take a different tack, warning the recalcitrant minority who had not resigned against mustering their units. In effect, they were left with commissions but without an office or a body of men to command. Shortly, the purge had been completed. There was a general muster. Eight Marblehead companies had formed and chosen their leaders. Officers met and selected regimental staff: Jeremiah Lee, colonel; Azor Orne, first lieutenant colonel; John Glover, second lieutenant colonel; John Gerry, major. Two months had been required for the rebel Marbleheaders to purge their regiment.[8]

The Congress wanted the towns to move quickly to establish minuteman contingents and, in early December, instructed: "that each of the Minute Men not already provided therewith, should be immediately equipped with an effective Fire Arm, Bayonet, Pouch, Knapsack, Thirty Rounds of Cartridges and Ball, and that they be disciplined three Times a Week, and oftener as Opportunity may offer."[9]

In January 1775, companies of minutemen began to form. When an alarm was sounded, they did not have to wait for the regiment, but were authorized to respond immediately. Once Salem had raised its two companies on March 23, every town in the county could boast units. Most did not require companies to drill the prescribed three times per week (in earlier days, militia normally were required to meet only four times a year). Amesbury first stipulated only four hours in a fortnight, but two half-days per week was more common.

In November, some Ipswich townsmen petitioned for land to erect a house to drill in during inclement weather. A plot was provided at the easterly end of the Town House, fifty feet long and twenty-five feet wide. It had been customary for males between sixteen and sixty to serve without pay; but now militia were to be paid. In most towns, pay was a shilling per half-day of drill. On February 15, the Second Provincial Congress convened in Cambridge. Fearing England was readying for the province's "sudden destruction," citizens were warned to prepare for attack. This admonition undoubtedly expedited the formation of minuteman units.

The Congress's October 26 resolve put responsibility for arming and accoutering on the towns. Two days earlier, Newburyporters had voted that its inhabitants should furnish themselves with arms and ammunition and have bayonets fixed to their muskets. Most towns required minutemen to be equipped according to the provincial specifications; many, like Andover, Danvers, Methuen, Rowley, and Newburyport, voted to help the needy by furnishing a gun, bayonet, cartridges, or other trappings. The *Essex Gazette* and *Essex Journal* recommended Indian tomahawks as a "useful and efficacious Weapon" in the "present Contest" for those without bayonets. By the time of the Lexington alarm, organization was largely complete, though some minuteman and regular units were still undermanned and ill equipped.[10]

Local militia often were far from ready. Timothy Pickering, Jr., commented in January 1769, that "not one Officer in five" was well versed "in the most necessary Parts of Military Discipline." Most officers were so untrained, Pickering observed, that a company was fortunate "if an Officer in it was able to give the Words of Command."

Militia often had degenerated, he said, consisting largely of children, apprentices, and "Men of the lowest Rank." Six years later, the unmistakable influence of then-colonel Timothy Pickering was visible in Salem's muster standards. The town voted, in early spring of 1775, "that the men so proposed to be raised should be householders, men of some estate . . . or others whose attachment to the country may be relied upon." In 1775, Pickering published a 150-page volume entitled "An Easy Plan of Discipline for a Militia." On May 1, 1776, the drill manual was officially adopted for the colony.[11]

Salem's militia began drilling on March 14, but without Rev. William McGilchrist of St. Peter's and Rev. Thomas Barnard of the North Church. Other Salem ministers mustered, though some of their pro-Tory parishioners reportedly did not parade to the field, despite what attorney William Pynchon termed threats from "rabble." While Whigs held control, the town still was divided politically.[12]

Marblehead's companies were more prepared than Salem's. Rev.

Moderate voices, like that of Rev. Thomas Barnard, averted violence
at North Bridge, Salem, on February 26, 1775. Painting by Lewis
Jesse Bridgman. Courtesy, Essex Institute, Salem, Mass.

John Barnard of Marblehead reported them in 1766 as well-clad
"vigorous and active men, so well trained in the use of their arms,
and the various motions and marches, that I have heard some Colonels of other regiments, and a Brigadier General say, they never
saw throughout the country . . . so goodly an appearance of spirited
men, and so well exercised a regiment." Readiness of seacoast militia
was imperative. If hostilities were to break out, the British were
expected to strike first at shoreline towns. Early in October 1774, it
was reported that Marbleheaders were turning out, "three or four
times a week, when Col. Lee as well as the Clergymen there are not
asham'd to appear in the ranks, to be taught the manual exercise, in
particular." A Marbleheader predicted in November that with two
months' training American troops could drive out the "inimical
Troops, whenever landed." The boisterous jingoism and revolutionary preparations in Marblehead had reached such a pitch that they
caused James Rivington's Tory New York *Gazette* to comment: "*the mad-
men of Marblehead are preparing for an early campaign against his Majesty's troops.*" Just as the patriots feared a British invasion of the countryside, some pro-Britishers were predicting a rebel siege of Boston.[13]

   Since October, towns had stepped up their military preparations.
The ugly spectacle of British forces encamped in the countryside

enforcing the Coercive Acts and crushing the Continental Association loomed on the horizon. The British were trying to punish Massachusetts as an example to others. Radical leaders had been trying patiently to make the struggle intercolonial. If a major, premature incident were to occur before union had been achieved, the British policy of "divide and conquer" could succeed. As military drilling and reorganization began in the towns, a British march into the environs of Boston would increase risk of a clash with rebel forces. While many moderate radicals viewed military readiness as a defensive precaution, more radical colleagues hoped the buildup was a prelude to a siege of Boston. They would not be satisfied until all British troops on their "infamous errand" were driven out.[14]

No More Nighttime Celebrations

Formation of the committees of safety (consistent with a provincial advice to curb disorderly behavior) was as much an attempt by conservative Whigs to control mob excesses as to oversee establishment of an effective militia system. Early in January 1775, Andover charged its committee to "use their Influence to suppress all unwarrantable Mobs and Riots, and that they promote as much as in them . . . goodwill and Affection one towards another." Earlier in October, amid Newburyport's arming and mustering of able-bodied males, the committee of safety and other local officials were directed to discourage "any Tumult or Disorder taking place at any time in the Evening or Night and that no Effigies be carried about or exhibited on the fifth of November, or other Time only in the Day time." Since the scarce commodity might be needed shortly, townspeople were cautioned against "wasting gunpowder in firing of Crackers, Serpents," on November 5 or any other occasion.[15]

The fifth of November, known as Pope Day or Guy Fawkes Day, commemorated the discovery of a Catholic plot in 1605 to blow up the British Parliament and the royal family. November 5 was a day of public thanksgiving for the uncovering of the scheme. Coffin, in his *History* of Newburyport, reported how during the day:

> Companies of little boys might be seen, in various parts of the town, with their little popes, dressed up in the most grotesque and fantastic manner, which they carried about, some on boards, and some on little carriages, for their own and others' amusement.

Most revelry was reserved for nighttime when young men joined the celebration:

> They first constructed a huge vehicle, varying, at times, from twenty to forty feet long, eight or ten wide, and five or six high, from the lower to the upper platform, on the front of which, they erected a

paper lantern, capacious enough to hold, in addition to the lights, five or six persons. Behind that, as large as life, sat the mimic pope, and several other personages, monks, friars, and so forth. Last, but not least, stood Nick himself, furnished with a pair of huge horns, holding in his hand a pitchfork, and otherwise accoutred, with all the frightful ugliness that their ingenuity could devise.[16]

The platform was mounted on wheels, and ropes were attached to the front. A boy was placed under the platform to manipulate the movable head of the pope as they paraded down the streets. The large procession customarily stopped at the substantial homes in the community to "ring their bell, cause the pope to elevate his head, and look around upon the audience, and repeat the following lines:

When the first king James the sceptre swayed,
This hellish powder plot was laid.
Thirty-six barrels of powder placed down below,
All for old England's overthrow:
Happy the man, and happy the day,
That caught Guy Fawkes in the middle of his play.[17]

After receiving a donation, revelers went on to the next home. Esquires Atkins and Dalton always reportedly gave a dollar apiece. At the end of the evening, the platform was broken up and used to kindle a bonfire. Wash tubs, barrels, stray lumber, and anything else not tacked down, were tossed on. The day's celebration ended with a magnificent bonfire which lit up the Newburyport sky.

During these volatile times, the customary November 5 merry-making was discouraged. With Newburyport's history of rowdyism and violence, few responsible leaders wished to chance wild celebrants turning to destruction and violence. Later, in 1775, Washington suspended celebration of Pope Day in deference to Catholic France, which the Continental Congress was courting in hopes of an alliance. After the war, Pope Day continued to be celebrated in Essex County until 1817.

Another Important Day

March 5 was another important date on the provincial calendar. Until July 4, 1776, the fifth of March was the closest the province came to having a patriotic holiday. Each year, most major towns celebrated the anniversary of the Boston Massacre with an oration delivered by a local revolutionary leader, stirring popular emotions with a vitriolic remembrance. On the fifth anniversary of the massacre, just weeks before Lexington and Concord, Rev. Moses Hale of Newbury, New Town (now West Newbury) noted in his diary for March 8, "Heard Mr. Noble preach on Tyrany—P.M." On that day,

Rev. Oliver Noble had delivered a sermon at North Church in New-buryport commemorating the "Massacre."[18]

Leslie's Retreat

An elaborate spy system kept Gage informed of the secret military buildup in the countryside. Marblehead and Salem participated in these stockpiling operations. Since supplies stored in coastal towns were more susceptible to seizure from the sea, foodstuffs and ord-nance were secreted aboard trading vessels into their harbors and transported to safe hideaways further inland—to Worcester and Con-cord.

A Marblehead-Salem intelligence memorandum of February 21, 1775, reported:

> Horton a Blacksmith at work at Marble Head on Gun Carriages. Went from hence a month since. Gun carriages making at Salem Twelve pieces of Brass Cannon mounted, are at Salem, & lodged near the North River, on the back of Town.

A second report received three days later, on February 24, recom-mended seizure:

> There are eight Field pieces in an old Store, or Barn, near the landing place at Salem, they are to be removed in a few days, the seizure of them wd. greatly disconcert their schemes.[19]

Believing them to be modern brass pieces imported from Holland, the British made plans to seize the ordnance. (Actually, they were old ship cannon which had been purchased from Derby.) The British knew the guns would soon be moved to caches inland. They had to act quickly.

About midnight on Sunday, February 26, favored by fresh breezes and fair weather, the British transport *Sea Venture* slipped out of Castle William for Marblehead, where the *Lively* already was moored. Near noon, she dropped anchor off Homan's Beach on Marblehead Neck. Hidden out of sight, below deck, were about 240 troops of the 64th Regiment, led by Lieutenant Colonel Alexander Leslie. As after-noon worship service began, the troops came topside and prepared to disembark. After landing, with bayonets fixed and guns loaded, the 64th Regiment marched double-time toward Salem, five miles westward.[20]

Some nonchurchgoers, seeing the British troops, ran to the nearest meetinghouse. A general alarm was sounded, as drums beat at the doors of all churches; Marblehead's regiment was mustered. Sus-pecting their mission, Major John Pedrick ran to his stable at Wash-ington and Pickett streets and rode hastily along Dungeons Road toward Salem. Pedrick came upon Leslie at the rear of his troops, as he was about to cross Forest River. The two were acquainted, as the young lieutenant colonel had often visited Pedrick's home. Leslie ordered his troops to file right, so that the Marbleheader could pass, supposedly to visit an ill friend.[21]

View of North Bridge. Here, Col. Alexander Leslie and the 64th British Regiment nearly clashed with Salem residents. Etching by George M. White. Courtesy, Essex Institute, Salem, Mass.

Pedrick continued at breakneck speed until he reached the door of North Church in Salem; bells were struck to alert the town. The congregation emptied, joined in the streets by their fellow neighbors. Meanwhile, the 64th Regiment, carrying lanterns, hatchets, pick-axes, spades, handspikes, and coils of rope, marched into Salem along the old road, presently Lafayette Street, while an advance force proceeded toward Long Wharf, possibly as a diversion. The main body arrived shortly afterward and halted by the Town House, where Leslie conferred quietly with Samuel Porter, a young Tory lawyer; John Sargent joined them. Sargent was a local West Indies merchant and half-brother to Tory Colonel William Browne, a Salem mandamus councillor. (Sargent later was reported atop his roof waving a white flag to direct Leslie's line of march. Hostility toward both Porter and Sargent soon forced them to flee town.) By now, hundreds of curiosity-seekers had poured into the streets. After the Porter-Sargent conference, the troops marched off through Lynde to North

Street, directly toward the North Bridge. Most of the crowd tagged along, including Capt. John Felt, a local shipmaster and owner of coasters. Also, young Rev. Thomas Barnard of the North Church joined the procession.

The resourceful Col. David Mason of Salem, commissioned by the Congress to procure military stores, prepared to convey the guns out of British reach. Mason had hired a local blacksmith, Robert Foster, to shape iron fittings for field carriages. The guns were at Foster's forge, just beyond North Bridge, along a lane which is now North Street. (Secretly, Mason's wife and daughters had been cutting 5,000 flannel cartridges for the cannon.) Assisted by several truckers, including David Boyce, Mason hastily hauled the pieces from Foster's and trundled them toward nearby Danversport.

Colonel Mason and his men, using the draw mechanism on the westerly side, raised the bridge over North River. When Leslie's force reached the opposite bank, surrounded by a throng of townspeople, the commander cursed. He knew that at that very moment the cannon were being hustled westward. Leslie demanded the draw be lowered. Perched atop the upraised draw "like hens at roost" and upon a small wharf jutting from the bridge, jeering rebels hurled coarse epithets at the "lobster coats." They refused Leslie's demand. In the heat of the moment, it looked as though Leslie had turned and ordered one contingent to fire. The tempestuous Capt. John Felt, near Leslie, yelled, "Fire! You had better be damned than fire! You can have no right to fire without further orders! If you do fire, you will all be dead Men." William Northey, a prominent local Quaker, eyeing the armed troops and an officer with drawn sword, moved to restrain Felt. The squad, however, neither faced nor fired.

Meanwhile, Leslie had spotted two large gondolas lying on the bank, which could be used to ferry his men across the river. Some quick-stepping townsmen, however, jumped into the barges and hacked holes in the bottoms. About twenty soldiers charged; scuffling broke out; heated words were exchanged, and one man, Joseph Whicher, foreman of Sprague's distillery, was pricked with a bayonet.

With the crowd aroused, and realizing matters soon could be uncontrollable, the amiable, widely respected, moderate Rev. Thomas Barnard stepped in and persuaded Leslie to restrain his troops from further brandishing their bayonets. The commander told Barnard he was determined to cross the bridge, arguing that he had lawful use of the king's highway. Capt. James Barr, who owned a nearby wharf, was standing alongside. He spoke up, advising the lieutenant colonel that the road was private, that it belonged to the proprietors of North Fields, and that it could be taken forcibly only upon declaration of martial law. Since Gage had not declared martial law, Leslie hesitated. He knew that bloodshed was bound to result.

Colonel Leslie was willing to compromise. If the draw lowered so his troops could cross, he pledged to pass only thirty rods beyond and return forthwith, to prove his right to use the road. By this time, the British had been standing in place for an hour and a half. Through the prudent negotiations of Reverend Barnard, the drawbridge lowered, and the regiment marched over. After they had gone a short distance, Leslie, true to his word, returned to Marblehead, stepping to the old British tune, "The World Turned Upside Down." As the redcoats returned, they passed the Marblehead regiment marching toward Salem.

Immediately after receiving word of the approaching force, Salem riders had posted into the countryside carrying the news to nearby towns. Benjamin Daland, owner of a trucking stable on Summer Street, sounded the cry through Danvers. Capt. Samuel Epes's company responded, arriving in Salem just as the troops had left. Others were marching from Beverly and Lynn. Thousands, from as far away as northern Essex County, would answer the alarm.[22]

It was nighttime before northern Essex County was informed. Militia were marching by sunrise. Word had come up through Haverhill, so Newburyport was last to hear. Companies were trooping from Amesbury, Newbury, and Salisbury, while Newburyport was preparing. Amesbury and Salisbury contingents got as far as Newbury when they learned the threat had passed. They proceeded into Newburyport, where they took refreshment at the invitation of "some gentlemen." Satirist William Gallison of Amesbury, possibly with Tory credentials, wrote a humorous account of their expedition on February 27:

> I saw upwards an hundred men from Various Parts of Merrimack river, moving towards the scene of action. Cyder being exceeding Scarce & the Last Season but an indifferent one for That, they Look'd pale & meagre & seemed to Tremble under the burden of their guns & bread & Cheese, which some ill Natured People attributed to their Fear, but very unjustly: indeed had they really ben Cowards they Would not have had much reason to be afraid, because they knew the Soldiers must have done their Business & returned to Boston, before they could reach Salem, and this they soon Learnt to be the Case on their first Halt, which was at a Tavern, when they meditated a return, which was Performed in martial order. But bloody Minded men as they were . . they valiently attacked and demolished several *Barrels*, whose Precious blood they drew and intirely exhausted. Flushed with Victory they made a much better appearance than when I first saw Them. However such another Victory would have brought them all to the ground, if not

have ruined them, as it was they were scarce able to Crawl home; and most of them haveing disgorged the blood of the slain which they had so plentifully drank, returned as pale and feeble as they set out, and Look'd as Lank as tho' they had been drawn thro' the river instead of Passing over it. So much for this military Expedition.

Your Effectionate Son
WM. GALLISON

Addressed—To
COLL. JOHN GALLISON[23]

Col. Alexander Leslie had shown courage, honor, and restraint as an officer, and cool, sensible Rev. Thomas Barnard and others had kept popular passions within bounds. Otherwise, the Revolutionary War might have begun at North Bridge, Salem, rather than at Lexington Green and North Bridge, Concord. Less than seven weeks later, a peculiarly similar set of circumstances sparked the military phase of the American Revolution. On February 26, the ember had been prevented from igniting the fire, but sooner or later, the conflagration was inevitable.

"Leslie's Raid" had left the North Shore jittery. On February 28, Beverly voted to establish three nighttime watches. The alarm signal was three gun shots and the ringing of the meetinghouse bells. The *Essex Gazette* reported on March 7: "Twenty seven Pieces of Cannon were removed out of this Town, in order to be out of the War of Robbers." In case of a repeat raid, the towns would be better prepared.[24]

1. *Essex Gazette*, August 30–September 6, 1774; September 6–13, 1774; Richard Frothingham, Jr., *History of the Siege of Boston* (Boston: Charles C. Little and James Brown, 1849), 13–14.
2. Marblehead Town Records, EI, October 3, 1774, 4:406; E. Alfred Jones, *The Loyalists of Massachusetts* (London: Saint Catherine Press, 1930), 99; Joseph B. Felt, *Annals of Salem*, 2nd ed. (Boston: James Munroe, 1849), 2:555, *Essex Gazette*, April 4–11, 1775.
3. *Essex Gazette*, October 11–18, 1774; October 18–25, 1774.
4. William Lincoln, *The Journals of Each Provincial Congress of Massachusetts* (Boston: Dutton and Wentworth, 1838), 31–34, 89–90, 96–97.
5. Samuel Roads, Jr., *History and Traditions of Marblehead* (Marblehead: N. Allen Lindsey, 1897), 124.
6. Beverly Town Records, November 17, 1774, 6:20; Danvers Town Records, January 19, 1775, 3:5.
7. George Wingate Chase, *History of Haverhill* (Haverhill: George Wingate Chase, 1861),
373; Organization of Newbury Military Society, 1774, MS, EI.
8. Marblehead Town Records, November 1774–January 1775, 4:408–25; Roads, 118–20.
9. *Essex Gazette*, December 6–13, 1774.
10. March 7–14, 1775; *The Essex Journal and Merrimack Packet* (hereinafter, *Essex Journal*), March 15, 1775.
11. *Essex Gazette*, January 24–31, 1769; Salem Town Records, EI, March 13, 1775, 30.
12. Fitch Edward Oliver, ed., *The Diary of William Pynchon* (Boston: Houghton Mifflin, 1890), 43.
13. "Autobiography of the Rev. John Barnard," MHS *Collections*, 3rd Series, 5(1836):239; "Letters of John Andrews," MHS *Proceedings* (1865):372; *Essex Gazette*, November 22–29, 1774; February 14–21, 1775.
14. November, 1–8, 1774.
15. Andover Town Records, January 2, 1775; on March 13, Salem passed a similar resolve; Newburyport Town Records, October 24, 1774, 1:211–12.
16. Joshua Coffin, *History of Newbury, New-*

buryport and West Newbury (Boston: Samuel G. Drake, 1845), 249–50.

17. 250.

18. Diary of Rev. Moses Hale, Minister of the Second Parish of Newbury, Massachusetts 1775, West Newbury Public Library, 6; *Essex Journal*, March 8, 1775.

19. James Duncan Phillips, "Why Colonel Leslie Came to Salem," *EIHC*, 90 (1954): 313–15.

20. William Bell Clark, ed., *Naval Documents of the American Revolution*, 1:109; Philip Chadwick Foster Smith, ed., *The Journals of Ashley Bowen of Marblehead* (Salem: Peabody Museum, 1973), 2:430.

21. The story of the Pedrick ride was found in old family records. At the time, Pedrick, being one of the recalcitrant addressors, had questionable revolutionary leanings.

He may not have been the messenger who carried the alarm.

22. For accounts of Leslie's Raid, see: *Essex Gazette*, February 21–28, 1775; February 28–March 7, 1775; *Salem Gazette*, March 3, 1775, 145; *Essex Journal*, March 1, 1775; "Leslie's Retreat," Essex Institute *Proceedings*, 1848–1856, 1:104–33; "Leslie's Retreat," *EIHC*, 17 (1880): 190–92; "Boyle's Journal of Occurrences in Boston, 1759–1778," *NEGHR* 85 (1931):6–7; Clark, 1: 123, 125–26; one account suggests that forty armed men led by Col. Timothy Pickering were part of the force gathered across the bridge.

23. "Leslie's Retreat," *EIHC*, 1 (1859):2.

24. Beverly Town Records, February 28, 1775, 6:30; *Essex Gazette*, February 28–March 7, 1775.

CHAPTER NINE

THE LEXINGTON ALARM

B y mid-April 1775, relations between the British in Boston and the Massachusetts rebels had deteriorated to a point where armed conflict was possible at any time. Passage of the Coercive Acts and attempts to enforce them had spun Massachusetts into a state of constant turmoil. The closing of Boston harbor, plus the garrisoning of the town, had caused lasting bitterness. It was only a matter of time, the patriots believed, before troops in Boston would drive into the countryside to execute provisions of the acts. Bad feeling toward British soldiers was worsened by fabricated stories of robbery, rape, and murder, circulated by the radicals.

The Road to Concord

The local Tory population and the British ministry were getting impatient with Governor Gage's reluctance to deal harshly with the principal leaders of the opposition and their rebellious activities. Because of these demands for greater decisiveness, Gage decided to launch a preemptive strike to destroy the provincial military stores in Concord and, it was suspected, to arrest John Hancock and Samuel Adams.

About ten o'clock in the evening of April 18, 1775, eight hundred troops under Col. Francis Smith were ferried across the Charles River to Lechmere Point in East Cambridge to begin an all-night march to Concord. That day, the provincial committee of safety and supplies, which included Marbleheaders Jeremiah Lee, Elbridge Gerry, and Azor Orne, met at Wetherby's Black Horse tavern in the Second 133

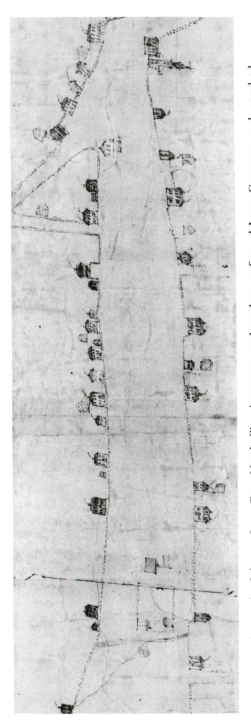

At the crack of dawn, Capt. Ezra Newhall's minutemen gathered on unfenced Lynn Common and marched toward Menotomy—the first company from Essex County to respond to the Lexington alarm. Ink and watercolor sketch of Lynn Common shows Old Tunnel Meetinghouse. Courtesy, Lynn Historical Society, Lynn, Mass.

Parish of Cambridge, known as Menotomy (now Arlington). It was on the road to Lexington. After the meeting, the Marbleheaders chose to remain at Wetherby's. The other committeemen left, including Hancock and Adams. Later in the night, when the main British detachment passed, a file of soldiers broke off to check out the tavern. Half-dressed, the Marbleheaders ran downstairs and hid out in a field of corn stubble nearby. The British searched for more than an hour, but the trio avoided capture, although Colonel Lee contracted a severe fever from exposure and died three weeks later. It was a terrible loss to the patriot cause.

As the eight hundred troops marched in the frosty moonlight toward Concord, church bells and alarm guns sounded in the distance. Colonel Smith realized that, despite his attempt at secrecy, the countryside had learned he was coming. Six companies of light infantry under Major John Pitcairn were detached to press forward and secure two bridges leading out of Concord. Smith sent a messenger to Boston for reinforcements.

At five o'clock the next morning, the advance force under Major Pitcairn reached Lexington Common. Seventy minutemen commanded by Capt. John Parker were waiting there. Pitcairn shouted, *"Disperse you Rebels—Damn you, throw down your Arms and disperse!"*[1] They stood their ground. A shot was fired; no one knows by whom. A series of scattered shots followed, then a general discharge. Eight provincials were killed and ten wounded. Thus began the military phase of the American Revolution.

The troops, joined by the main body under Colonel Smith, proceeded to Concord, six miles away. They confiscated only a small fraction of the supplies; most had been carried off. In the meantime, minutemen from neighboring towns had been gathering on a hillside near North Bridge. Seeing trails of smoke from Concord center, actually caused by burning of confiscated stores, they imagined the British were torching the town. The excited minutemen marched to North Bridge, which had to be crossed to enter Concord, but the British guard resisted their advance. A skirmish ensued, lasting about five minutes, and the British were pushed back. The redcoats regrouped and about noon began the ill-fated twenty-mile withdrawal to Boston.

Meanwhile, thousands of minutemen from the countryside had been converging on Lexington and Concord. Along their return, the British were greeted with fire from behind stone walls and fences, houses and barns, trees and boulders. The troops were saved from annihilation only by the arrival of a twelve-hundred-man rescue column commanded by Brigadier Lord Hugh Percy, which met them as they passed through Lexington. After resting for a half hour, they continued their exhaustive withdrawal. With militia constantly arriving along the line, guerrilla-style harassment persisted until nightfall, when the troops reached the safety of Charlestown. A courageous rag-tag militia, poorly trained and without a command, had chased the "invincible" redcoats out of the countryside.

The Battle at Menotomy

Post riders reached Lynn with the news before sunrise, coming from Malden over the old Boston road through Saugus Parish into Lynn center. Capt. Ezra Newhall's minutemen were the first to leave. From their rallying point on Lynn Common, William Newhall and Samuel Berry, the company's drummer and fifer, called the men to arms. The company's forty-nine men came from every section, including Saugus and Lynnfield. The crack of alarm guns was heard all over, as militia in the other four units rushed to their assembly points. Newhall's minutemen left the Common before eight o'clock, taking the only route to Lexington—over Tower Hill along the County road to Saugus, into Malden and Medford to the Lexington road at Menotomy (Arlington). The British main column had passed this point hours before the alarm had reached Lynn, while the Percy relief force had marched through around noon. Newhall reached Menotomy, a distance of twelve miles, shortly after the reinforcements had passed.

Saugus had been the first Lynn section to receive the alarm. Capt. David Parker's sixty-three Third Parish (Saugus) men soon were under way. Capt. Nathaniel Bancroft's North Parish (Lynnfield) company hooked onto the Boston road after marching through South Reading. Three of Bancroft's thirty-eight men would be killed and several wounded or captured. The Fourth Company of Foot (infantry) was led by Capt. Rufus Mansfield. Most of the forty-six men came from Waterhill and almost all were related—one-third were named Mansfield. The Second Company, led by William Farrington, a local cordwainer, was composed, largely, of fifty-two men, from the eastern and central sections. Abednego Ramsdell did not leave with them; he was duck hunting with his friend Joe Richards, also of the Second Company. They were bagging black duck on the Swampscott shore, too far away to hear the alarm. With their catch in their hands, they sauntered home after sunrise to find the alarm had been sounded. They took off to catch up—Ramsdell was later seen running through town with his stockings falling over his shoes. He would die shortly after reaching the scene. Richards and Ramsdell rushed along old Boston road with scatterings of men from other towns who had likewise missed their muster.[2]

Post riders reached Danvers about nine o'clock. Alarm guns fired, drums rolled, meetinghouse bells in the North and South parishes rang—calling the companies to muster. Over three hundred people marched from Danvers. In such towns as Danvers and Lynn nearly every able-bodied man responded, even inexperienced boys of fifteen and grandfathers who were veterans of earlier wars against the French. Only those too ill to muster or Quakers, whose religious convictions prevented them, remained home.

First to march were the two minuteman companies. Capt. Israel Hutchinson, a housewright, mill owner, and veteran commander of the French and Indian War, led fifty-three minutemen from New Mills (Danversport) and Ryal Side in Beverly. When the alarm bell rang, they assembled near Hutchinson's home and marched toward the South Parish. Capt. Ebenezer Francis, a local businessman who commanded the twenty-five-man Second Beverly Foot Company, had crossed Porter's River at Danversport and combined with Hutchinson's force. Francis and Hutchinson had planned to merge their units and respond mutually in the event of an alarm. Captain Francis also was enrolled as a lieutenant in Hutchinson's company. Regular militia could march only on regimental orders. Minutemen could proceed at their own will. Gideon Foster, a second lieutenant in Capt. Samuel Epes's company, of the South Parish (now Peabody) had become captain of a contingent of minutemen only ten days earlier. The Hutchinson company joined up with about thirty of Foster's minutemen at Francis Symond's Bell tavern on the corner of Main and Washington streets.[3] They moved out in advance at about ten o'clock. All Danvers men killed, wounded, or captured on this day would be from Hutchinson's or Foster's companies. Six more Danvers companies responded to the Lexington alarm. One of the commanders, Samuel Epes of the South Parish, rode to Salem and received permission from Colonel Pickering to march without waiting for the regiment. Epes led fifty-two men toward Lexington on the heels of Danvers's minutemen. (Later, several from Epes's company assisted in the capture of a supply wagon on its way to provision the British expedition. The wagon and its contents were brought back to Danvers, and the prisoners taken to Ipswich jail.) Besides Foster's and Epes's South Parish units, there was a twenty-three-man company commanded by Capt. Caleb Lowe. Capt. Samuel Flint's forty-four man and Capt. Asa Prince's thirty-seven-member force met at the village training ground in the North Parish and marched off together. (Prince's company included eight Middleton men, among them the Revolutionary leader, Maj. Archelaus Fuller.) Jeremiah Page left with thirty-nine men from the Plains. (Both Page's and Flint's companies also belonged to Pickering's regiment.) Edmund Putnam led seventeen men from Putnamville and Beaver Brook, and John Putnam commanded a company of thirty-five from the north part of town. Both Putnams commanded alarm companies, which consisted primarily of over-age men or others who were exempted from regular militia duty—some civil officers, students of Harvard College, and schoolmasters, for example. With the companies' departure, few able-bodied men remained in town.

The South Parish units left from the Bell tavern, located on the then-great thoroughfare leading toward Boston, after receiving the Divine blessing from Rev. Nathan Holt; Reverend Wadsworth gave the benediction to those leaving from the training ground. The Danvers militia marched down what is now Boston Street through Lynn, following the route taken a short while before by the Lynn militia. The six other Danvers companies left shortly after the minutemen, though regimental orders may have delayed them along the way. Joanna Mansfield, a young girl who lived on Boston Street in Lynn, watched the Danvers men passing her house, remembering particularly their homespun gray stockings. Foster's and Hutchinson's minuteman companies, and possibly some others, reached Menotomy by

British redcoats retreat through Menotomy. Henry Cabot Lodge Collection. Courtesy, Beverly Historical Society.

two o'clock, traveling sixteen miles in just four hours! The frantic pace had been too much for sixteen-year-old Amos Putnam; he collapsed and died along the way.[4]

The Danvers forces joined up with Lynn, Dedham, Needham, and Menotomy units already there. The little village of Menotomy was situated on Boston road between Lexington and Cambridge. At quarter to four, the British column left Lexington to begin the hazardous return to Boston—flanking guards running parallel, flushing snipers from their positions. As the troops neared Menotomy close to five o'clock, the minutemen heard the roar of cannon and the rattle of musketry. Percy was attempting to scatter the minutemen along his line of march.

Back in Menotomy, part of Hutchinson's company had taken well-protected cover in the woods above the road. Other Danvers minutemen and some from Lynn took position in the farmyard of Jason Russell, which bordered the road a quarter mile from the village center. They crouched behind a stone wall that lined the road and barricaded a gate opening with bundles of shingles from the barn. About two dozen men anxiously waited in this makeshift fortress. The troops' approach was concealed by a hill to the west, when suddenly, the British column was spotted. Among those waiting in the yard were Samuel Page, Capt. Jeremiah Page's son, and Perley Putnam. Page had fired two volleys when he broke a ramrod while reloading. He turned to borrow Putnam's. At that moment, shots were fired from behind, killing Putnam instantly. A British flanking party, which had been marching along a ridge behind the house, was attacking from their unprotected rear! Page was able to escape to an apple orchard nearby; those unable to find an exit had to stand and fight. The hand-to-hand fighting over the next few moments would be the most savage and costly of the day. Among those killed was Jotham Webb, a brickmaker. Married only twenty days, Webb had left Danvers in his wedding suit saying, "If I die, I must die in my best clothes." Putnam and Webb belonged to Hutchinson's company. Four South Danvers minutemen, Samuel Cook, Benjamin Daland, Ebenezer Goldthwaite, and Henry Jacobs, Jr., also were killed in the Russell yard.[5] Reuben Kennison, from Ryal side in Beverly, was shot in the yard and repeatedly, savagely bayonetted by the angry, distraught troops. Kennison had ridden horseback to New Mills from his Cressy Street farm after hearing the alarm bell toll in Danvers Village. Taking his tricorn, coat, musket and accouterments from his young wife, Apphia, he rode off as she bravely waved good-by to her husband of less than one year. Benjamin Peirce, a Salem baker, was slain moving across a field near the Russell house. He had heard the alarm and rushed to the scene, probably marching alone—his sense

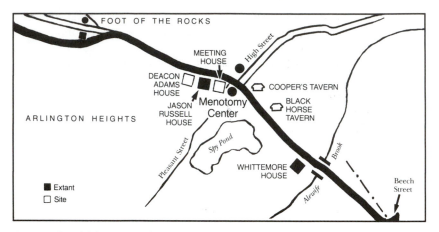

Route of British troops through Menotomy.

of duty his only companion. Russell, old and lame, had refused to follow his family to safety. He was shot at his front door and vengefully bayonetted.[6]

When the flank guard attacked, several militiamen sought refuge inside the Russell house. From behind the home, Daniel Townsend of Lynn had just fired at the main column and yelled, "There is another redcoat down," when he turned to find himself cut off by the flank guard coming through the fields. Townsend and fellow Lynnite Timothy Munroe rushed in through the side door. Futilely seeking protection in the cellar, they could not find the entranceway. With bullets whizzing through the back window, the panicking twosome scrambled for a closet, but with no success. Alonzo Lewis's *History of Lynn* describes the instant death of Townsend and Munroe's miraculous escape:

> Townsend leaped through the end window, carrying the sash and all before him, and instantly fell dead. Munroe followed, and ran for his life. He passed for a long distance between both parties, many of whom discharged their guns at him. As he passed the last soldier, who stopped to fire, he heard the redcoat exclaim, 'Damn the Yankee! he is bullet proof—let him go!' Mr. Munroe had one ball through his leg, and thirty-two bullet holes through his clothes and hat. Even the metal buttons of his waistcoat were shot off.[7]

Several other North Shore militiamen had sought safety in the house. Three Lynn men, Abednego Ramsdell, William Flint, and Thomas Hadley, were trapped and killed there, and Joseph Felt was wounded in the dooryard. Eight men, mostly from Beverly, had managed to find their way to the cellar. One redcoat who opened the door was killed on the stairs, convincing the others to let the rebels

Jason Russell house. Sketched by Edwin Whitefield for
his *Homes of Our Forefathers* (1879).

alone. Dennis Wallis, George Southwick, and Joseph Bell, all Danvers
men, hid upstairs until they thought the British had gone. As they
stepped down, the door burst open, and the British charged in. One
swung his sword and split Southwick's head in two. The others were
taken prisoner.[8]

The bewildered, exhausted British began to shoot their captives.
Wallis broke away. A rattle of musketry followed, and Wallis collapsed
beside a wall. Wounded twelve or thirteen times, he was left for dead
but miraculously survived. Bell was imprisoned for several weeks on
board the frigate *Lively* in Boston harbor. Early in June, he was
released with several others in a prisoner exchange. Another Essex
County man—Josiah Breed of Mansfield's Lynn company—also was
taken prisoner. He was released in mid-May. Breed had been pursuing the British toward Charlestown when he was suddenly surrounded.[9]

Capt. Gideon Foster and the Danvers militia and others from Lynn
and Needham were pushed by the flankers towards Spy Pond, a few
hundred yards east of the Russell house. They were caught in a
precarious spot—the flankers moving toward them, the pond behind
them, and the main column coming down the road. They made a
mad dash for the woods across the highway, directly in front of the
approaching column. They took cover behind a ditch wall and fired
their muzzle-loaders at the oncoming enemy. Foster remarked many
years later, "I discharged my musket at the enemy a number of times
(I think eleven,) with two balls each time, and with well directed aim.
My comrade (Mr. Cleaves of Beverly) who was then standing by my
side, had his finger and ramrod cut away with a shot from the
enemy."[10] Cleaves had traveled from Beverly on horseback. During

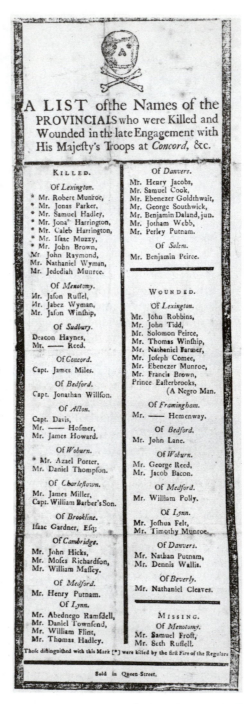

A LIST of the Names of the PROVINCIALS who were Killed and Wounded in the late Engagement with His Majesty's Troops at *Concord*, &c.

KILLED.

Of *Lexington.*
* Mr. Robert Munroe,
* Mr. Jonas Parker,
* Mr. Samuel Hadley,
* Mr. Jonaᵗ Harrington,
* Mr. Caleb Harrington,
* Mr. Isaac Muzzy,
* Mr. John Brown,
Mr. John Raymond,
Mr. Nathaniel Wyman,
Mr. Jedediah Munroe.

Of *Menotomy.*
Mr. Jason Ruffel,
Mr. Jabez Wyman,
Mr. Jason Winship,

Of *Sudbury.*
Deacon Haynes,
Mr. —— Reed.

Of *Concord.*
Capt. James Miles.

Of *Bedford.*
Capt. Jonathan Willson.

Of *Acton.*
Capt. Davis,
Mr. —— Hofmer,
Mr. James Howard.

Of *Woburn.*
* Mr. Azael Porter,
Mr. Daniel Thompson.

Of *Charlestown.*
Mr. James Miller,
Capt. William Barber's Son.

Of *Brookline.*
Isaac Gardner, Esq;

Of *Cambridge.*
Mr. John Hicks,
Mr. Moses Richardson,
Mr. William Maffey.

Of *Medford.*
Mr. Henry Putnam.

Of *Lynn.*
Mr. Abednego Ramfdell,
Mr. Daniel Townfend,
Mr. William Flint,
Mr. Thomas Hadley.

Of *Danvers.*
Mr. Henry Jacobs,
Mr. Samuel Cook,
Mr. Ebenezer Goldthwait,
Mr. George Southwick,
Mr. Benjamin Daland, jun.
Mr. Jotham Webb,
Mr. Perley Putnam.

Of *Salem.*
Mr. Benjamin Peirce.

WOUNDED.

Of *Lexington.*
Mr. John Robbins,
Mr. John Tidd,
Mr. Solomon Peirce,
Mr. Thomas Winship,
Mr. Nathaniel Farmer,
Mr. Joseph Comee,
Mr. Ebenezer Munroe,
Mr. Francis Brown,
Prince Eafterbrooks,
    (A Negro Man.

Of *Framingham.*
Mr. —— Hemenway.

Of *Bedford.*
Mr. John Lane.

Of *Woburn.*
Mr. George Reed,
Mr. Jacob Bacon.

Of *Medford.*
Mr. William Polly.

Of *Lynn.*
Mr. Joshua Felt,
Mr. Timothy Munroe.

Of *Danvers.*
Mr. Nathan Putnam,
Mr. Dennis Wallis.

Of *Beverly.*
Mr. Nathaniel Cleaves.

MISSING.
Of *Menotomy.*
Mr. Samuel Froft,
Mr. Seth Ruffell.

Thofe diftinguifhed with this Mark [*] were killed by the firft Fire of the Regulars

Sold in Queen-Street.

Broadside. Courtesy, Essex Institute, Salem, Mass.

the engagement, he lost both horse and saddle to the enemy. Two other Beverly men were wounded on the British pass through Menotomy: William Dodge, Jr., who belonged to Francis's contingent, and Samuel Woodbury, a member of Shaw's company. Also wounded was Nathan Putnam of Hutchinson's company.

The Battle of Menotomy was a tragic one for several Essex County towns. Most of the casualties were young men in their twenties—with wives at home who had been waiting in desperation for news from the battlefield. Oldest was Daniel Townsend, who was in his later thirties; he left a wife and five young children. Fourteen Essex County men had fallen: eight (including Amos Putnam) from Danvers, four from Lynn, one each from Beverly and Salem. Danvers lost more lives than any other community save Lexington itself.

In the evening, Mrs. Elizabeth Russell returned home to a gruesome, shocking sight. Her beloved husband and eleven others, including men from Lynn and, possibly, some from Danvers, lay dead, side by side in her kitchen, "whare Blud was half over Shoes."[11]

Next morning, Mrs. John Winthrop, like hundreds of others, fled from Cambridge to Andover with her sick husband, where they sought safety until the danger subsided. She noted "passing through the bloody field at Menotomy," strewn with mangled bodies, and meeting "one affectionate father with a cart looking for his murdered son and picking up his neighbor's who had fallen in battle, in order for their burial."[12] Mrs. Winthrop had observed the sorrowful scene of the Danvers militia picking up their dead comrades from the Russell yard. Joanna Mansfield of Lynn saw the ox cart passing her home and recognized the homespun stockings of the dead as belonging to the Danvers men she had observed marching to the scene.

Some grieved and others relieved by the news from Menotomy the night before, Danvers families waited anxiously for their troops' return. Four of the dead were brought to the home of the deceased Samuel Cook on Central Street in the South Parish; the rest were taken to Hutchinson's at New Mills.

On Friday the twenty-first of April, 1775, a funeral service was held at the South Danvers meetinghouse for its dead. The church was crowded with townspeople. Two companies from Salem attended, representing the First Essex Regiment. After the service, they honored their fallen comrades by escorting their bodies, with reserve arms and muffled drums, to the burial ground. On the way, they met Newburyport, Amesbury, and Salisbury militia marching to Cambridge. The northern Essex County companies formed single columns on either side of the road, and the funeral procession passed through the ranks.[13]

Not in Time

By nine in the morning, Timothy Pickering had received word of the Lexington alarm in his office at the Registry of Deeds, but the colonel reasoned there was little point in responding. Cambridge was over twenty miles away; surely, Pickering surmised, the British would have returned to Boston long before Salem troops could get there. Nevertheless, neighboring towns were answering the alarm, and townspeople were urging Col. Timothy Pickering to do the same. A conference was held by the selectmen, the committee of safety, and Pickering at Webb's tavern on School Street (later called Washington). Pickering finally agreed to march. Salem's four companies—nearly three hundred men—set off toward Danvers, two miles away. The road to Cambridge wound through South Danvers, now Peabody, where the troops halted near Bell's tavern. Pickering apparently expected news that the alarm had passed. When no message came, he continued dilatorily, stopping next at Newhall's tavern, the half-way house between Boston and Salem, seven miles from Danvers. After quenching their thirst, the men marched the six miles to Malden and three more to Medford. They passed through Medford and reached the top of Winter Hill—close enough to see Percy's brigade, off in the distant twilight, reach Charlestown.[14] Once on Charlestown peninsula, the redcoats—less 73 dead, over 170 wounded, and 26 missing—reached the protective cover of the sixty-four-gun *Somerset*. Until eight o'clock, the chase had continued, with Lynn, Danvers, and other militia following right up to Charlestown.

Of Pickering's slow deliberation on the nineteenth, Washington wrote on May 21, 1775:

> If the retreat had not been as precipitate as it was,—and God knows it could not well have been more so,—the ministerial troops must have surrendered, or been totally cut off. For they had not arrived in Charlestown, (under cover of their ships,) half an hour, before a powerful body of men from . . . Salem was at their heels, and must, if they had happened to be up one hour sooner, inevitably have intercepted their retreat to Charlestown.[15]

That night, Pickering led his troops back to Medford where they guarded a bridge. William Wait of Malden billeted the Salem militia and supplied them with fourteen buckets of liquor and four quarts of oats—the oats, it is hoped, for a wagon team. Pickering's slow speed toward Cambridge had raised suspicions of his loyalty and courage, but, in August, the General Court absolved the Salem contingent of any neglect of duty.[16] Nevertheless, questions over Pickering's performance continue to this day.

A few Salem men had responded in time to participate in the

battle. As soon as the alarm sounded, they had posted off on horse-back and traveled to Cambridge alone. One of these solitary soldiers was Benjamin Peirce, who was killed at the battle of Menotomy.

To Lexington and Cambridge

Thousands of Essex County militia, while arriving too late to do battle, had eagerly answered the alarm and marched to the scene. Nearly sixty companies from central and northern Essex responded. (For a list, see Appendix A.)

When the drums beat and the bells rang in Andover, Col. James Frye's eldest son was living across the river in Methuen. Frye was out plowing, and his wife knew he would want to leave immediately. She ran out of the house, only to find his plow and ox standing in the field and Frye nowhere in sight. As she ran down the road leading to town, she saw her husband from the top of the hill—running at breakneck speed. She yelled out. He waved and soon was out of sight.[17] Similar scenes were repeated throughout the county—men propelled to battle a tyranny which was threatening their cherished freedom.

The alarm had reached Andover about seven o'clock. Three hours later, the companies began the twenty-five-mile march. Two minute-man units trooped from Andover; Capt. Benjamin Ames's from the South Parish and Capt. Thomas Poor, Jr.'s from the North. James Stevens, a carpenter by trade and a private in Poor's company, kept a journal of this momentous period. It is apparent from his entry of April 19 that Andover forces took a different path to Lexington than those traveling from the Newburyport and North Shore areas.

> April ye 19 1775 this morning a bout seven aclok we had alarum that the Reegerlers was gon to Conkord we getherd to the meting hous & then started for Concord we went throu Tukesbary & in to Bilrica we stopt to Polords & eat some bisket & Ches on the comon. we started & wen into Bedford & we herd that the regerlers was gon back to Boston we went through Bedford. we went in to Lecentown [Lexington]. we went to the metinghous & there we come to the distruction of the Reegerlers thay cild eight of our men & shot a Canon Ball throug the metin hous. we went a long through Lecington & we saw several regerlers ded on the rod & som of our men & three or fore housen was Burnt & som hoses & hogs was cild they plaindered in every hous thay could git in to thay stove in windows & broke in tops of desks we met the men a coming back very fast we went through Notemy [Menotomy] & got into Cambridg we stopt about eight aclock for thay say that the regerlers was got to Chalstown on to Bunkers hil & intrenstion we stopt about two miles back from the college.[18]

Four militia units followed—over three hundred Andoverites having answered the Lexington alarm. To the north, across the river in Methuen, about one hundred and fifty citizen soldiers ferried the Merrimack and stepped out toward Lexington, with John Davis's forty-nine Methuen minutemen leading.

Elsewhere in central and northern Essex County, just as in Andover and Methuen, militiamen flocked to their assembly points. As the day progressed, roads teemed with uneven ranks of militia. The winter had been exceptionally mild and the spring, dry and summerlike, was a month ahead of time. Though dusty and hot, the roads were easily traveled, and messengers posted to the towns with amazing speed. Topsfield, over thirty miles from Boston, received the alarm about ten o'clock. More than one hundred Topsfielders mustered and marched under the commands of Captains Joseph Gould and Stephen Perkins. Three companies from Boxford responded, including Capt. John Cushing, son of pastor John Cushing, with thirty-three West Parish men and Capt. Jacob Gould leading fifty-seven from East Parish, each attached to Samuel Johnson's regiment. The third company was William Perley's fifty-two minutemen, attached to Col. James Frye's regiment.

Earlier, officers of seven minuteman companies from the Merrimack Valley (4th Regiment) region had chosen Frye of Andover as their colonel; Dr. James Brickett of Haverhill, lieutenant colonel; Daniel Hardy of Bradford, adjutant; Dr. Thomas Kittredge, surgeon; Benjamin Foster of Boxford, quartermaster. Col. Samuel Johnson, a respected Andover leader with a distinguished military record, had helped recruit and organize the minuteman regiment which drew from Andover, Boxford, Bradford, Haverhill, Methuen, Salisbury.

Three more Beverly contingents responded. Capt. Larkin Thorndike mustered fifty men from the Lower Parish on the Green. Rev. Joseph Willard, pastor of the First Church, conducted brief services; then the company marched off. (Later, Willard and his neighbor, Manasseh Cutler, pastor of Hamlet—now Hamilton—rode on horseback together toward Cambridge, reaching Winter Hill in time to see the British gain the cover of Charlestown.) When the alarm had reached North Beverly (Upper Parish), Capt. Caleb Dodge carried the news to Wenham and Hamlet. He returned to lead his thirty-two-member horse troop toward Cambridge. (Meanwhile, Capt. Joseph Rea spread the word through the Farms.) A third Beverly company was mustered by Lt. Peter Shaw. The town's first militiamen were marching by three o'clock.[19]

Soon, two Wenham companies and eight from Ipswich were on their way. On the first day, some Ipswich contingents got as far as

Mystic (Medford), a twenty-four-mile trip. On April 20, Salem billeted one Ipswich company, as well as Sawyer's "eastward company," possibly for fear of invasion. The minuteman contingent led by Capt. Thomas Mighill and two other companies marched from Rowley; at least one unit reached Lynn on April 19, arriving at Cambridge headquarters by noon the next day. Some central Essex County companies, like Wenham's, belonged to the regiment commanded by Col. John Baker of Ipswich; others, like Eliphalet Spafford's of Rowley, were attached to Col. Samuel Gerrish's of Newbury.[20]

Probably before nightfall, three companies, a total of 114 men, had left Bradford. Across the river, seven companies—over 200 men—marched from Haverhill and crossed the Merrimack, led by Col. James Brickett.

First rumors of battle had trickled to northern Essex County by mid-afternoon. Newburyport sent off an express to gather reliable information; the messenger traveled as far as Symond's tavern in Danvers to confirm that British troops actually engaged American forces. The messenger returned that evening, and Capt. James Hudson, chairman of the committee of correspondence, rushed the news further eastward:

> NEWBURYPORT, April 19, 1775
> To the Chairman of the Committee of Correspondence in Portsmouth, N. H.
>
> Sir: This Town has been in a continual alarm since mid-day, with reports of the Troops having marched out of *Boston* to make some attack in the country. The reports in general concur, in part, in having been at *Lexington*. And it is very generally said they have been at *Concord*. We sent off an express this afternoon, who went as far as *Symond's* at *Danvers*, before he could get information that he thought might be depended upon. He there met two or three gentlemen who affirmed, the regular Troops and our men had been engaged.[21]

Most likely, the Newburyport force—130 militia under the command of Capt. Moses Nowell—waited until morning and then began the forty-mile trek, probably accompanied by some Amesbury and Salisbury comrades. (Fewer Newburyporters mustered than from towns half its size; many were at sea.) Four companies of Amesburyites marched, 101 of whom belonged to Captain John Currier's and Mathais Hoyt's minuteman contingents. Next door in Salisbury, four companies also mustered, including Jonathan Evans's 43 minutemen.

Of the eight Newbury units responding, among the first was William Rogers's minutemen from the west or New Town section. At the crack of dawn on April 20, the company mustered on the training field that bordered Bradford road, presently known as Main Street. Boards were thrown over an ox cart to prepare a hastily improvised rostrum, from which Rev. David Toppan inspired the men with a few patriotic sentences and invoked the Divine blessing. Shortly after sunrise, the company set out, with their rations and baggage hauled by two ox teams. On the next day, more supplies followed. Everyone in the parish had contributed generously. Baked goods, hams, bacon, flour, medicines, and bandages had been collected by the committee of safety and sent on their way. On the morning of the twentieth and the afternoon of the previous day, the same historic sequences had unfolded in each central and northern Essex County town.[22]

Gloucester and Marblehead—both craggy peninsulas with unprotected, vulnerable shorelines—were the only county towns not to answer the call. With the twenty-gun *Lively* and a sixteen-gun vessel sailing off the harbors, a march could have sparked a retaliatory sea strike. Secondly, both were major fishing ports. While their regiments had been organized for months, many from the ranks were out on the banks or in the Gulf of Maine. A Manchester company attached to the Gloucester regiment did answer the alarm, however. Capt. Andrew Marsters led forty-five men as far as Medford; hearing the British were in retreat, they returned home. Nevertheless, the lure of cod and fear of cannon had kept Cape Ann and Marblehead from marching.[23]

Despite the seaports' poor muster and Salem's slow start, Essex County's reply had been spontaneous and overwhelming. Nearly 3,000 sturdy souls had marched. Especially from many interior towns, nearly all able-bodied males had rushed toward the scene. Most coastal towns would have sent larger contingents save for their people at sea. Some county companies, like Manchester's and Salem's, turned around when they learned the British were back near Boston; others, like Amesbury's, Andover's, and Newbury's minutemen, remained encamped on the hills around Boston for several days. There could be no mistaking the county's commitment to aid its countrymen.

Several days afterward, militia from all over New England continued to pour into the Cambridge area. False alarms had caused them to march before, but there was no ambiguity in the meaning of the Lexington call to arms. James Jeffrey's diary entries on his way toward Boston from Quebec attest to the popular excitement triggered by the battles of April 19. A native of Salem, Jeffrey had been living in Quebec. He saw militia returning from Cambridge and others traveling toward the scene several days after the alarm had been sounded. (Note Jeffrey's casual mention of Hancock and Adams.)

Had here a confirmation of the skirmish, with this addition, that the Regulars were drove back from Lexinton to Boston and that they went out to stop Handcock & Adams from going to the Congress at Philadelphia & to destroy magazines that were formg . . . .

23. Sunday. Rain this morng. Set off abt 8 o'clock with two men who were going to Roxberry or Cambridge to hear the particulars of the engagement. Various reports this day. Lodged near Springfield.

24. Rode abt 2 mile & crossed the ferry & breakfasted at Springfield. A rainy morng. Adams the postman here. He gave us an acct of his mails being taken from the Post Office at Hartford, Genl Gage's letters taken out & burnt with abt 300 of Revington's papers. We set off with 4 men, three from Connecticut & one Docr Bennet from Birkshire county all after news. Met many return'd soldiers & horses & others going down we overtook. The roads very full of travellers. Lodged at Spencer.

25. Clear & very warm weather. At Worcester abt 11 o'clock stopt wth [John] Hancock and Saml Adams. This day we past a great number of Troops going to Cambridge.[24]

The Provincial Congress and its appointed committee of safety had no duly constituted authority to enact and to enforce legislation. They could only advise, resolve, and recommend, but directions were obeyed because Massachusetts citizens believed in their legitimacy. When patriots responded to the Lexington alarm, they were marching to defend their fellow countrymen from British Regulars, who, after the Lexington battle, most Americans believed to be barbarous aggressors. A common unity was shaped against a common tyranny.

1. *Essex Gazette*, April 18–25, 1775.
2. Howard Kendall Sanderson, *Lynn in the Revolution* (Boston: W. B. Clarke, 1903), 1:32–40; Revolutionary Rolls, MA Archives, 11:243; 12:77, 190; 13:27, 45.
3. In 1835, a twenty-two-foot-high granite monument was completed at the intersection of Washington and Main, near where the Bell tavern once stood, in memory of those Danvers men who fell on this day.
4. Anniversary section, *Danvers Herald*, October 15, 1970, 10B–13B; *Report of the Committee appointed to Revise the Soldiers' Record* (Danvers: Town of Danvers, 1895):110–12; Revolutionary Rolls, MA Archives, 12:75, 82, 118, 171; 13:46, 48, 49, 50.
5. Anniversary section, *Danvers Herald*, 10B–13B; J. W. Hanson, *History of Danvers* (Danvers: J. W. Hanson, 1848), 86– 91, 106–07; Daniel P. King, *Address* (Salem: W. & S. B. Ives, 1835), 12–13, 23.
6. Five others, four from Needham and one from Dedham, also died in the yard, and Dr. Joseph Warren, one of the radical leaders, had a near miss when a pin was shot from his hair.
7. Alonzo Lewis, *History of Lynn* (Boston: Samuel N. Dickenson, 1884), 214.
8. Samuel Abbot Smith, *West Cambridge on the Nineteenth of April, 1775* (Boston: Alfred Mudge, 1864), 38–39; John A. Wells, *The Peabody Story* (Salem: Essex Institute, 1972), 219.
9. Peter Force, ed., *American Archives*, 4th Series, 2:921; "Boyle's Journal of Occurrences in Boston, 1759–1778" *NEGHR*, 85 (1931):17; Revolutionary Rolls, MA Archives, 12:190.
10. King, 13, 28.
11. "Amos Farnsworth's Diary," MHS *Proceedings*, 2nd Series, 12 (1898):78.
12. "Letters from Mrs. Winthrop," MHS *Proceedings*, 14 (1875):30; the Lynn dead were buried with Peirce, Russell and five others in a common grave at the Arlington burial ground.
13. King, 16.
14. Octavius Pickering, *The Life of Timothy Pickering* (Boston: Little, Brown, 1867), 2:15–19.
15. Richard Frothingham, Jr., *History of the Siege of Boston* (Boston: Charles C. Little and James Brown, 1849), 78.

16. Salem Town Records, EI, October 2, 1775, 5:65–66.

17. Sarah Loring Bailey, *Historical Sketches of Andover* (Boston: Houghton Mifflin, 1880), 301.

18. "The Revolutionary Journal of James Stevens of Andover, Mass.," *EIHC*, 48 (1912):41–42; also, see: M. V. B. Perley, "Revolutionary War Journal Kept by Phineas Ingalls of Andover, Mass., April 19, 1775–December 8, 1775," *EIHC*, 53 (1917):81.

19. Thomas Franklin Waters, *Ipswich in the Massachusetts Bay Colony* (Boston: James Munroe, 1843), 2:359; Edwin M. Stone, *History of Beverly* (Boston: James Munroe, 1843), 61.

20. Salem Town Records, June 5, 1775, 5:45; Thomas Gage, *History of Rowley* (Boston: Ferdinand Andrews, 1840), 251.

21. Force, 4th Series, 2:359.

22. Sarah Anna Emery, *Reminiscences of a Nonagenarian* (Newburyport: William H. Huse, 1879), 171.

23. Revolutionary Rolls, MA Archives, 12:189; Octavius Pickering, in the biography of his father, mentions that some minutemen did leave Marblehead in the evening, but no record survives in the state archives.

24. "Journal Kept in Quebec in 1775 by James Jeffrey," *EIHC*, 50 (1914):110.

CHAPTER TEN

FEAR, FLIGHT,
AND FIRST DEFENSES

In the midst of the confusion and excitement that followed the battles of April 19, 1775, an incident occurred that caused great distress and anxiety. The episode is usually called the "Ipswich Fright," described as "a curious commingling of the comic, the ludicrous, and the distressing."[1] Whether the event was natural or contrived to agitate the people, those who witnessed it never forgot it.

The "Ipswich Fright"

On the morning of April 20, Capt. Jonathan Burnham and his company of Hampton, New Hampshire, militia were proceeding through Ipswich headed to Cambridge. He saw before him a panic-stricken town, "because, two Men of Wars tenders were in the river full of men and would land and take twenty British soldiers out of a [gaol] that was taken prisoners at Lexington battle and would burn the town, so we stayed that day and night."[2] The previous day, over three hundred Ipswich men had left to answer the Lexington alarm. Captain Burnham was placed in command of two hundred remaining Ipswichites, mostly young boys and old men.

A British landing at Ipswich beach was rumored imminent. Townspeople were hastily concealing their valuables and preparing to leave, to escape the onslaught of vengeful redcoats. Fearful riders dashed in all directions with the cry of "invasion."

On Friday afternoon, the twenty-first day of April, two days after the carnage at Lexington, Concord, and Menotomy, a messenger rode into Newburyport. He rushed up the Town House stairs, where an informal meeting was about to be opened with a prayer from Rev. Thomas Cary. The messenger, Ebenezer Todd of Rowley, breathlessly cried out: "for God's sake, turn out! turn out! or you will all be killed! The regulars are marching this way, and will soon be here. They are now at Ipswich, cutting and slashing all before them!"[3]

Word spread like wildfire, inciting fear most everywhere, as many towns' militia were encamped near Boston. The story was remarkably the same wherever told, from Beverly to Coos County, New Hampshire. In Newbury New Town (now West Newbury), British were rumored to have advanced westward to the Artichoke River. Most able-bodied men and boys left in the parish marched off to confront them.

Sarah Anna Emery of West Newbury wrote an account based on historical fact and family reminiscences:

> It was near sunset when aunt Sarah, (then a girl of sixteen,) on her way to the well, espied a horseman coming at a furious pace up the road, swinging his hat and shouting: 'The regulars are coming! They have landed at Plum Island, have got to Artichoke bridge, are burning and killing all before them!' . . . . The neighbors flocked in, a terror stricken throng, to counsel respecting further measures . . . After the first excitement had passed, doubts of the genuineness of the tidings arose. Neither my grandfather Smith, nor grandsir Little credited the story, and they advised every one . . . to stay quietly at home until further intelligence could be obtained. A few did so, but most, in a perfect frenzy of fright, sought every means of safety.[4]

During the fright, people's actions in the Newbury area reached fantastic proportions. Roads were filled with masses of people riding horses and vehicles of every description and crowds of pedestrians, all fleeing northward as speedily as possible. Some ferried the Merrimack and spent the night in Salisbury and Hampton homes, vacated by owners fleeing still farther north. Others fled inland, away from the coast. Houses on Turkey Hill and elsewhere in New Town were filled with women and children who spent the night trembling in fear. Rev. Moses Hale, at his home in the vicinity of Pipe Stave Hill, noted in his diary: "various Reports—Strangely alarmed here with News that a body of Regulars were Marching to N. Port &c-women & children fled up here in ye Evening more or less in all our House— but soon ye Report contradicted & we lodged 9 women & Children."[5]

While New Town played sanctuary for many coastal evacuees, scores of its inhabitants fled the area, though some went only to more remote, secluded spots within town. Sarah Emery wrote:

> Uncle Thurrel's farm at that time belonged to the family of the late

Dr. Adams. This gentleman had been the first physician to settle in the town . . . . The house was occupied by his grandchildren, and their aged and feeble widowed mother. This household passed the night in the greatest anxiety and alarm. Having hidden their choicest effects, the horse was harnessed to the chaise . . . which was drawn up before the door through the night, while the old lady, wrapped in a coverlet sat through the long hours in her large arm chair, in readiness to be conveyed down 'South End,' a rocky, steep declivity at the southerly side of the hill, a descent from which one might have expected as dire a catastrophe, as from a raid on any number of 'regulars.'

Old Mr. Joshua Bartlett, commonly designated 'Uncle Vun,' yoked his oxen to the cart, and took his family to the Platts place, a lone, unoccupied farm-house, remote from the road. Several families sought the same refuge . . . Hannah Eastman, an old, asthmatic woman, breathed so hard, she was wrapped in a blanket and buried in the leaves under a stone wall, at some distance from the house. After a sleepless night, at sunrise the crowd ventured home.[6]

Joshua Coffin's *History* of Newbury, Newburyport, and West Newbury relates several bizarre stories. In one, a woman had "run four or five miles, in great trepidation, stopped on the steps of the reverend Mr. Noble's meeting-house, to nurse her child, and found, to her great horror, that she brought off the cat."[7]

John Tracy of Marblehead carried the message of an impending killing and pillaging to Haverhill. A panic quickly arose, as townspeople, some by wagon, others on foot, prepared to move into the back country. Homes near the village common and meetinghouse were crowded with rural folk from the outskirts. With a guard posted outside town, scared inhabitants waited out the night. Horses were saddled, ox carts loaded, and children sent to bed fully dressed— ready to evacuate at the crack of dawn.[8] A comparable fright was reported to have spread through parts of Andover.

The night passed without sight of the approaching enemy. With daybreak, the "Ipswich Fright" had passed. On the next day, the eminent Benjamin Greenleaf of Newburyport wrote the following:

We were unhappily thrown into distress yesterday, by false accounts received by two or three persons, and spread abroad, of a number of Soldiers being landed at Ipswich and murdering the inhabitants. We have since heard that it arose in the first place from a discovery of some small vessels near the entrance of their River,—one at least known to be a Cutter,—and it was apprehended that they were come to relieve the captives there in jail.[9]

Imagination, fear, and rumor had combined on April 21 to cause widespread panic of incredible proportions.

The Race to England

After the battles of April 19, the Provincial Congress was resolved to head off possible retaliatory moves by the British ministry or Parliament. They planned to get to England with their version of the incident first, with supporting documentation. A committee of eight, headed by Elbridge Gerry of Marblehead, was appointed to take depositions both from Americans on the scene and from captured redcoats, whose eyewitness accounts would clearly picture the invading British as the aggressors. If English public opinion were convinced, their government would be hard pressed to enact harsh, punitive measures.

The Hon. Richard Derby, a prosperous, retired shipmaster and a Salem member of the Provincial Congress, offered a sixty-ton fast sailer, the schooner-rigged *Quero*, to serve as packet to England. Congress accepted and instructed Derby on the twenty-seventh of April to outfit his vessel. The next day he received sailing orders. Derby was to enter an Irish port, cross over to Scotland or England, and proceed stealthily toward London. The *Quero* slipped out of Salem harbor on April 29 unnoticed by the *Lively*, off shore engaged in searching incoming and outgoing vessels in accordance with the Navigation and Port Acts. Thirty-four-year-old Capt. John Derby, ignoring his secret orders, probably landed on the Isle of Wight and reached London by way of Southampton. The passage extended twenty-nine days, which was considered good time. Derby carried several dispatches, including copies of the April 21 and 25 *Essex Gazette*, which detailed the events of April 19; copies of several sworn statements giving complete battle accounts; also, a masterfully worded letter to the English people written by Dr. Joseph Warren, president of the Congress. On June 1, Derby delivered his dispatches to Benjamin Franklin, Massachusetts' agent in London, with the Congress's expressed desire that they be circulated throughout England, most especially to the sympathetic Lord Mayor of London.

When the 200-ton, heavily laden *Sukey*, carrying Gage's official reports, reached London on June 10, the provincial view of the conflict already had been disseminated and published in the papers. The rebels had gained a decided propaganda advantage. Derby left England with many of its bewildered people sympathetic to Massachusetts' actions in self-defense, convinced British troops had fired without provocation. His mission accomplished, Derby sailed out of Falmouth harbor and headed for home.

Derby may have landed on Ipswich Beach to avoid risk of capture—the *Quero* sailed into Salem without the commander on board. He would have traveled through Beverly along the Boston road, reaching provincial headquarters on July 19. Richard and John Derby charged only their expenses, with John Derby saying that the success of his mission was sufficient reward. Coincidentally, it was a Derby vessel that conveyed news of the Revolution to England, and, eight years later, a Derby ship, the *Astrea*, was the first to bring printed word of peace to America.[10]

Evacuation of the Seacoast

After April 19, communities surrounding Boston and along the coast realized they could be the next scene of a bloody clash with a British invasion force. Their fear was heightened by embellished stories—nevertheless, largely credible—of British barbarity and thievery on their return from Concord. The account published in the *Essex Gazette* horrified many readers:

> They pillaged almost every House they passed by, breaking and destroying Doors, Windows, Glasses, &c. and carrying off cloathing and other valuable Effects. It appeared to be their Design to burn and destroy all before them; and nothing but our vigorous Pursuit prevented their infernal Purposes from being put in Execution. But the savage Barbarity exercised upon the Bodies of our unfortunate Brethren who fell, is almost incredible: Not content with shooting down the unarmed, aged and infirm, they disregarded the Cries of the wounded, killing them without Mercy, and mangling their Bodies in the most shocking Manner.[11]

The large naval force stationed in Boston facilitated launching an invasion anywhere along the shore. Realizing the threat to be real, the Congress, on April 27, ordered inhabitants of the seacoast "to be in readiness to go into the country on the shortest notice." Many already had been convinced to move from the coast and to seek refuge inland.[12]

A Danvers man, pursuing security for his family in New Hampshire, reported widespread evacuation of Marblehead and Salem:

> After this Tragical event we had frequent Alarms, were threatened with haveing our Sea Port Towns burnt down by the King's Ships, the Towns of Marblehead & Salem moveing out into the Country all in confusion & distress. On the First of May I removed with part of my family, part being gone before & part of my goods to New Salem in Hampshire to my Mother's where we remained until the 21st of September.[13]

Ashley Bowen of Marblehead reported on April 25: "Most of our people moving." Three days later, the pro-Tory chronicler noted, "Most of our people gone out of town with their goods. . . . All our countrymen have turned their houses into pawnbroker's shops to

receive the Marblehead men's goods. Glorious times for the country!"
The move was motivated mainly from fear of ravaging by the H.M.S.
Lively, which was blocking the harbor. Nonetheless, amid the chaos,
many Loyalists evacuated to escape spiteful resident looters. Bowen's
steadfastly Loyalist father, Nathan, moved to Andover; his children
were housed at Boxford.[14]

A popular refuge, especially for Salem Loyalists, was the island of
Nantucket, which, many believed, because of its Quaker influence,
would be treated as neutral ground. Fearing an attack on Salem,
William Wetmore noted in his departure for Nantucket: "April 28th.
Mrs. Pynchon, Mrs. Orne, Miss Katy, Sally, John, myself & Mr. Bean's
family, set sail for Nantucket, to avoid ye continual Alarms to wch ye
town is liable by being upon ye sea coast, and exposed to the K . . . s
Ships."[15] Many others sailed. Dr. Edward A. Holyoke, an eminent
Loyalist and Salem physician, sent his family on the twenty-seventh
of April. They remained for three months. An apprehensive Mrs.
Holyoke wrote home, longing to return.

> June 1st, 1775. 'We were alarmed last week with the arrival of a
> Company of Provincials, as they didn't let their business be known
> at first, but it soon appeared they came for flour & whale boats, of
> which they carried off a large number & 750 Barrels of flour, some
> arms, &c.' 'I hear Salem is quite alive. I wish we were all there in
> peace & safety.'[16]

The magnitude of the evacuation (over five hundred families from
Salem, alone) can be imagined by the diary notations of James Jeffrey,
formerly of Salem:

> 26 Breakfasted at Watertown. Went through Cambridge where I
> was detained two or three hours waiting for a pass. At last known
> by Col Dudley Sargent . . . Col Sargent abt 3 o'clock set off with me
> for Salem. He informed me that most of the people from Salem
> were removed into the country. Arriv'd at Salem just at dusk. Found
> all our folks at home excepting Peggy. . . .
> 27 Took a walk round the town. Saw many people, knew but few,
> was not known by many. Great numbers of people leaving Marble-
> head, Cape Ann & Salem.
> 28 Mr. Good[a]le & wife wth Miss Susa Higginson, Mr. [William]
> Pincheon & family, wth several more sailed this morng for Nan-
> tucket.[17]

Late in April, both newspapers in vulnerable Salem closed down.
The town remained without papers for most of the war. Samuel Hall
moved his operation to Stoughton Hall in Cambridge and resumed
publishing a weekly, then called *The New-England Chronicle: or The
Essex Gazette*.

On April 24, the flight from Gloucester started. Families sought refuge in the more protected West Parish or in Ipswich. Many in eastern Manchester took temporary sanctuary in "The Old Garden" settlement (near the former Magnolia railroad station), where they gathered during times of possible peril.

Fear did not stop at coastal town lines. Andover, twenty miles inland, had several false alarms. The town served as haven for some who lived close to Boston or near the sea. Mrs. John Winthrop of Cambridge found Andover "rural and romantically pleasing." "From the profound stillness and security of this woody region," she said, "I can almost persuade myself we are the only human inhabitants of creation."[18]

After the Battle of Bunker Hill on June 17, with the brutal torching of Charlestown, horrors of attack and destruction heightened along the seacoast. Many people heretofore unconvinced to evacuate left in a panic:

> The destruction of Charlestown by fire (for it is all burnt down) has struck our People at Salem with such a panic, that those who before thought our Town perfectly safe, now are all for removing off;— but I cannot be apprehensive of any danger we are peculiarly in.*
> * * As almost every one is moving away, particularly Capt. Williams, Derby, Gardner, Ashton, our neighbour Gardner & Dodge, &c.[19]

After the shocks of April 19 and June 17, people gradually returned. Threat of invasion persisted, but no immediate danger was apparent. Evacuees started to reappear by late summer, though some stayed away for years, and a few for the entire war. Of course, many, unable to afford the expense of seeking shelter inland, never left. In the months to come, the exposed coastlines of Cape Ann, Marblehead, and Salem continued to make their residents nervous.

Early Defense Measures

Towns were kept constantly on their guard. Atop Castle Hill, Ipswich maintained a continual watch—scanning across the sands, eastward toward the sea; tar would be set afire from a beacon for a night alarm or, in the daytime, a flag hoisted. Manchester, on April 21, voted to establish four watches; at Glass Head or Black Cove, in the center of town, at Old Neck, and at Kettle Cove. Lookouts were posted during nighttime in specially constructed watchhouses. During the fall, Negroes were restricted from serving watch. (At the time, some free blacks were threatening to switch sides unless they were permitted to enlist in the American army. Therefore, Manchester was uneasy over blacks standing guard.)[20] Danvers, from May 1, kept a watch at New Mills, and another near Francis Symond's tavern. Its watches were disbanded in July after the Congress provided for a seacoast defense. Andover voted, on May 29, to establish a watch, advising guards to challenge anyone after nine o'clock P.M. Beverly voted sixteen watchmen in four divisions, each with a house. Lynn stationed three. That security was tight is confirmed by James Jeffrey's account of his travels to Portsmouth on May 2:

> I in co with N. S[parhawk] & mother set off for Portsmouth. Dined at Newbury where I was stopt an hour or two by the Committee of Safety, by which means I did not arrive at Portsmouth till after 9 o'clock in the evg. Met by the watch going into town. Examd by some of the Committee at Peggy's just after my arrival. Questioned again abt 12 o'clock this night and had a watch round the house all night and five or six people to examine me in the morng.[21]

Essex County port towns had met at the tavern near Beverly's meetinghouse on April 24 to plan for their mutual defense. Just the day before, Elbridge Gerry reported the British warship *Lively* cruising off Marblehead. With towns defenseless, *Lively* press gangs were able to roam freely, looking for able seamen. On the twenty-seventh, the provincial committee of safety instructed that Col. John Glover "take such effectual methods" to prevent the ship-of-war from receiving intelligence.[22]

Apprehension stretched northward, from the county's southern reaches, around Cape Ann to the Merrimack. On April 26, Newbury voters, feeling threatened by invasion along their "Considerable Sea Coast," requested that their minutemen return from Cambridge.[23] By early summer, Amesbury, Newburyport, and Salisbury worked out a plan to block unwelcome visitors from sailing the Merrimack. They obstructed the channel with rocks and wooden piers at the mouth, near Black Rocks; no one could proceed without local pilots. Town cooperation was crucial to a credible defense.

On May 29, half of all militia was ordered to Roxbury and Cambridge to strengthen the lines against an anticipated British strike. Gloucester requested that forces being raised in Cape Ann and Manchester remain in the towns; a British landing was feared. In early summer, the Provincial Congress voted to raise ten companies of fifty men each for defense of Essex County. A joint committee—one member each from Beverly, Gloucester, Ipswich, Lynn, Manchester, Marblehead, Newbury, Newburyport, Salem, and Salisbury—was to determine where troops would be stationed.

Fear of Harassment and Destruction

Primarily out of fear, Marblehead and Salem were trading with British warships patrolling offshore. The H.M.S. *Lively* and the tender H.M. Brig *Hope* were stationed to prevent supplies from reaching

American forces besieging Boston. In the course of their patrols, Captains Bishop and Dawson had impressed many American seamen from vessels stopped for inspection. Possibly, the towns reasoned, a limited trade would alleviate the harassment.

It would also insure their susceptible shores against the raking of British cannon. After April 19, Capt. Thomas Bishop of the *Lively* cautioned Marblehead against assisting the rebels "upon pain" of the town's destruction. The selectmen submitted, agreeing not to send provisions or men to the army, nor parade under arms. How sincerely they weighed this commitment is questionable. In late May, after fishermen returned from the banks, drummers and a fifer paraded seeking enlistments for Marblehead's regiment. Large numbers obliged. On May 30, when two or three armed vessels were sighted, Ashley Bowen noted that "6 drums beat for an alarm." A British invasion along Salem's shoreline or at the ferry (Naugus Head) in Marblehead was rumored. The Marblehead regiment turned out under Col. John Glover, but it was a false alarm. Troops from Cambridge headed by Col. James Frye of Haverhill marched as far as Middleton before turning back. Capt. William Burnaby of the H.M.S. *Merlin*, which replaced the *Lively* on May 31, reported on June 18, the day after Bunker Hill: "Fired 4 Guns & 4 Swivels at some Rebels who fired at the Ship." Despite a naval threat, many Marbleheaders resolutely opposed the British presence.[24]

Trade continued between the towns and the recently arrived H.M.S. *Merlin*. Captain Burnaby reportedly purchased bread in Salem. Trade with the enemy, however limited, infuriated the countryside. In late May, Vice-Admiral Graves apprised Salem that if his squadron could continue to be provisioned, its "prest" seamen would be returned. As late as early July, patrols were instructed not to impress Marblehead or Salem fishermen, so long as they could land and purchase supplies. Graves also had offered Salem protection from potential attack by angry folk in outlying towns.[25]

Salem allowed some provisions to be carried to British-occupied Boston, maintaining they were for inhabitants. A former Bostonian named Badger captained one craft, shipping in beef and veal and bringing out patriot evacuees. Gage permitted emigration for those wishing to leave and, reciprocally, the Congress allowed passage for those wanting to move to Boston. Criticism from countrymen forced Salem to announce a policy of searching vessels before they cleared, permitting only enough food for their journeys.

Mounting pressure from yeoman Essex County obliged Salem to explain. Granted, there had been sales of fresh meats and some year-old Quebec bread to Captain Bishop and Lieutenant Dawson. "Trifles," Salem called this trade, "as tho' the king's troops had from

Salem a constant supply of fresh meat." Townsmen observed, "we have been branded with every ill name which could be given to traitors . . . & frequently been threatened with the coming of multitudes of armed men from the country to burn our houses." The same feeling was directed toward Marblehead. Diarist Ashley Bowen noted on August 19, "Poor Marblehead is threatened by the Headquarters of a visit from that quarter if we let any of the King's men land or supply them with even water. Only between two stools our ass comes to the grounds,"—one of the colorful Bowen's favorite expressions. On August 23, the Massachusetts General Court absolved Salem of any wrong-doing, realizing that Salem's (and Marblehead's) precarious position, exposed to preying warships offshore, required some conciliatory gestures.[26]

After July, provisioning the enemy became rare. Two Beverly men were caught selling goods and were jailed in mid-November. But most Americans, wanting the British pushed out to sea, realized rupture of their supply line would hasten the departure time.

Battle of Logistics

Not long after April 19, the inhabitants and troops of Boston, cut off from fresh foodstuffs, were subsisting on salt provisions and fish. With Boston encircled and under siege, the British were unable to obtain fresh supplies overland. Provisions could reach Boston by sea, but the Congress had forbidden it. Gage resorted to seizing supplies from American merchant vessels and plundering islands near Boston and along the coast. On May 15, a wary Ipswich requested the committee of safety to permit stationing troops in Ipswich, Newbury, or Newburyport for guard purposes: "Inasmuch as the Scituation of these Towns are such that the Stock will immediately be put to Pasture, where the said Stock will be exposed, and Great Numbers of Chattle & Sheep may be taken by armed Cutters, unless Prevented by our Guards."[27]

To keep them out of British hands, livestock was to be removed from all offshore islands. For years, colonists had used islands for grazing cattle and sheep. Both to deprive foragers and to confuse pilots heading toward Boston, boats, cattle, lamps, and oil were taken from Thatcher's Island, located a short distance from Eastern Point in Gloucester.

In late June, Admiral Graves—intent on keeping supplies from the rebels—noted that Cape Ann, Manchester, and Salem harbors were where supplies could be imported "with most facility" and directed Lt. George Dawson, with one of his schooners, to make the ports "the chief Object of his attention." After July 1, in retaliation against the Continental Association, New England colonies were forbidden to trade with anyone except Britain and its West Indies. On July 17, Admiral Graves—anticipating this policy—instructed Captain Lindzee, commander of H.M. Sloop *Falcon*, to cruise between Cape Cod and Cape Ann and, "to seize and send to Boston all Vessels with Arms, Ammunition, Provisions, Flour, Grain, Salt, Melasses, Wood . . . to deceive and intercept the Trade of the Rebels." During the British blockade of the coastline over the next year, more than a score of Essex County merchantmen were captured plying in and out of the harbors.[28]

Each side was trying to secure certain provisions and to prevent other items from reaching its adversary. The British particularly needed fresh provisions, fuel, and fodder. The American army was in search of muskets, cannon, shot, powder, and other military supplies.

To cut off the British from fresh provisions, on the morning of May 27, an American detachment proceeded to Hog and Noddle's islands in Boston harbor near Chelsea. They were spotted, and the British scrambled to frustrate the plan. Despite British fire from a sloop and schooner, a thirty-man detail of Americans was able to destroy or drive off all livestock on Noddle's. Forty British marines disembarked into barges and headed for the island, forcing the Americans to withdraw to Hog Island—but not before they wounded four invaders, two of whom were killed. With help from the rest of the two- to three-hundred-man detachment, they drove off 350 cows, horses, lambs, and sheep, depriving the British of their last local source of fresh supplies. The patriots crossed to the mainland, taking position on Chelsea Neck while the British raked the mainland. About nine o'clock in the evening, three hundred reinforcements with two field pieces arrived with Gen. Israel Putnam of Connecticut in command. James Stevens, a private in Capt. Thomas Poor's Andover company, was among them. He reported:

> Then the firing Begun on boath sides & fired very worm there come a man & ordered us over a nol rit into the mouths of the canon we got on to the top of the nol & the grap shot & canon bauls com so thik that we retreted back to the rode & then marcht down to the fery the regerlers shouted very much our men got the canon & plast them & gave them two or three guns sids and the firing set in.[29]

After ten o'clock, the schooner ran aground, so the men on board transferred to the sloop. With daylight, facing British fire, the patriots plundered the sails and guns and set the schooner ablaze. During the morning, exchanges renewed between the mainland and the British on Noddle's Island and the sloop. Then the vessel became

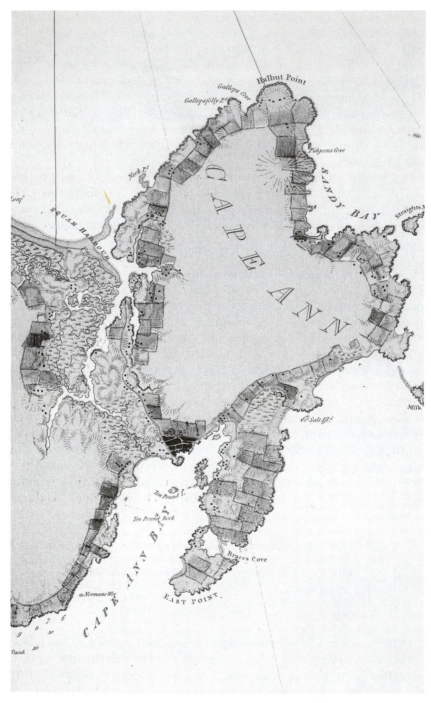

Cape Ann and Gloucester harbor in 1776.

disabled and was towed away, ending the action, after a few parting shots from the island.

> Sunday ye 28 this morning a bout day thay come with thare barjes to bord the sconer Curnal putnum Com & ordered us down the whoife & we fired so that thay retreted back to the sloup our men run down & fired the sconer & it burnt very fast . . . in about three qurters of a our after it was sot on fire the magersene Blod up.[30]

This was the only skirmish of any importance between April 19 and the Battle of Bunker Hill on June 17. Americans reported twenty enemy killed, with only four of their own wounded. The clash was magnified into a battle, with participants praised as heroes—giving the provincial army the psychological boost that news of an early victory gives in time of war.

The Flight of the *Falcon*

On August 5, 1775, the three-masted British sloop-of-war *Falcon*, with a single deck of guns, commanded by John Lindzee, appeared off Ipswich Bay sailing near the mouth of Squam harbor. The *Falcon* had been sailing Massachusetts waters since April. Just two days earlier, Lindzee had impressed John Beckford and John Cook, who had been fishing in Salem, and detained their boat. On this day, Lindzee dispatched a barge carrying fifty men to Coffin's Beach, near the mouth of Squam harbor on the Gloucester side of Ipswich bay, to purloin some sheep grazing on the grassy dunes. Major Peter Coffin—whose prosperous farm was situated nearby—spotted the barge. He hastily rounded up five or six neighbors and farm hands and they rushed to the beach. Positioned behind sand dunes, they fired on the interlopers. The officer in command, believing the fire was coming from a large force, retreated to the *Falcon*. On his return, Lindzee ordered the barge back toward Squam harbor, where a schooner lay close to the water, presumably heavily laden with a West Indies cargo. They boarded—only to find her filled with sand!

Lindzee continued to cruise around Cape Ann, impressing several seamen from vessels out of Gloucester and other North Shore ports. In the morning of August 8, he sighted two schooners bound for Salem. Lindzee captured one, from Hispaniola; the other sought haven inside Gloucester harbor and grounded on the flats between Pearce's Wharf (Vincent's Cove) and Five-Pound Island. Intent on seizing the schooner, Lindzee (piloted by a Gloucester dory fisherman impressed that morning) anchored as closely as possible, given the *Falcon's* draft.

An alarm sounded, bells clanged, and townspeople rushed to the rescue. Two swivel guns mounted on carriages were placed under Captains Joseph Foster and Bradbury Sanders, while men armed with fowling pieces and flintlocks rushed to Pearce's Wharf and to a hill opposite Vincent's Cove. Intent on wrenching the grounded schooner off the flats, two British barges (pinnaces) closed in, past the entrance of Harbor Cove, each armed with swivels and manned with about fifteen musket-toting men—under command of Lt. Edward Thornborough, with six privates in a whale boat. As they approached, gun blasts shot from the schooner's cabin windows, joined by the Cape Ann "Rebels" firing from behind houses, rocks, and schooners grounded at the wharfs. The lieutenant and three of his men were wounded by shots from the shore.

Meanwhile, Lindzee fired several broadsides from his six-pounders (and half-pound swivel shot) into the thickly settled town, with little effect. Then, with the cannonading suspended, he sent in one of the remaining boats to Fort Point, intent on setting the village afire by kindling the wooden fish flakes along the beach. A brisk wind was blowing on shore. The powder fuse, however, ignited early, blowing off the hand of Lindzee's incendiary boatswain. Lindzee resumed firing, hoping to divert pressure from his attack force and permit seizure of the schooner. About four o'clock, he sent in the previously captured schooner accompanied by a small cutter to rescue the trapped contingent.

At about seven o'clock, after six hours of fire, the intruders surrendered. It was a rebel scoop: both schooners, barges, the cutter, plus swivels, small arms and ammunition. About thirty-four prisoners were taken; one was killed. Twenty-four were sent to Cambridge. The others, having been impressed earlier by the British, returned to their North Shore homes. Gloucester lost two men: Benjamin Rowe and Peter Lurvey. Lindzee's three hundred cannon shot did only minor damage to a few houses and the meetinghouse; the sole reported loss was Deacon Kinsman's hog. After the attack, the patriot defenders celebrated at James Prentice's tavern: thirteen buckets of toddy, five suppers, and two quarts of rum were consumed. Next morning, as townspeople breathed easier, the *Falcon* streamed out of the harbor for Nantasket Road. With danger subsided, inhabitants who had fled toward Ipswich with their silver plate and other valuables returned.[31]

1. Joshua Coffin, *A Sketch of the History of Newbury, Newburyport, and West Newbury* (Boston: Samuel G. Drake, 1845), 245.
2. Thomas Franklin Waters, *Ipswich in the Massachusetts Bay Colony* (Ipswich: Ipswich Historical Society, 1917), 2:319.
3. Coffin, 245.
4. Sarah Anna Emery, *Reminiscences of a Nonagenarian* (Newburyport: William H. Huse, 1879), 172.
5. Diary of Rev. Moses Hale, Minister of the Second Parish of Newbury, Massachusetts 1775, West Newbury Public Library, 10.
6. Emery, 172.

7. Coffin, 246.
8. George Wingate Chase, *History of Haverhill* (Haverhill: George Wingate Chase, 1861), 387.
9. Peter Force, ed., *American Archives*, 4th Series, 2:374.
10. Robert S. Rantoul, "The Cruise of the Quero," *EIHC*, 36 (1900):5–6, 17–21.
11. *Essex Gazette*, April 18–25, 1775.
12. William Lincoln, *The Journals of Each Provincial Congress of Massachusetts* (Boston: Dutton and Wentworth, 1838), 160.
13. "Extracts From 'Text Books' of Deacon Joseph Seccomb, 1762–1777," DHS *Collections*, 9 (1921):115.
14. Philip Chadwick Foster Smith, ed., *The Journals of Ashley Bowen of Marblehead* (Salem: Peabody Museum, 1973), 2:436, 437, 439.
15. "Extracts from the Interleaved Almanacs of William Wetmore of Salem, 1774–1778," *EIHC*, 43 (1907):116.
16. William P. Upham, "Extracts from Letters Written at the Time of the Occupation of Boston by the British, 1775–6," *EIHC*, 13 (1876):207.
17. "Journal Kept in Quebec in 1775 by James Jeffrey," *EIHC*, 50 (1914):110–11.
18. "Letters from Mrs. Winthrop," MHS *Proceedings*, 14 (1875):30–31.
19. Upham, 213.
20. *Town Records of Manchester* (Salem: Salem Press, 1891), 2:152–55.
21. "Journal . . . by James Jeffrey," 111.
22. William Bell Clark, ed., *Naval Documents of The American Revolution*, 1:229.
23. Newbury Town Records, April 26, 1775, 310.
24. Clark, 1:202, 210, 585, 713; Smith, 2:441–42; "Revolutionary War Journal Kept by Phineas Ingalls, of Andover, Mass.," *EIHC*, 53 (1917):83–84.
25. Clark, 1:501, 685, 718, 820.
26. Salem Town Records, EI, August 10, 1775, 53–63; MA Archives, 180:88–90; Smith, 2:453; Force, 4th Series, 2:770.
27. Ipswich Town Records, May 15, 1775, 4:268.
28. Clark, 1:768–69, 900.
29. "The Revolutionary Journal of James Stevens of Andover, Mass.," *EIHC*, 48 (1912):46.
30. 46.
31. John J. Babson, *History of the Town of Gloucester* (Gloucester: Procter Bros, 1860), 393–96; Clark, 1:1093, 1110–11, 1114; Robert Crowell, *History of Essex* (Essex: Town of Essex, 1868), 209.

View of peninsula town of Boston and vicinity. From Richard Frothingham's *History of the Siege of Boston*, 1849.

CHAPTER ELEVEN

THE SIEGE OF BOSTON

After the battles of April 19, 1775, the Provincial Congress branded Governor Gage a tool "in the hands of an arbitrary ministry to enslave this people." Since troops under his command had "illegally, wantonly and inhumanly slaughtered" innocent citizens, he was decreed unfit to serve as governor, or in any other capacity. On May 5, the Congress advised no further obedience to Gage's proclamations, calls for assembly, or other of his actions.[1]

A Period of Confusion

On April 20, 10,000 minutemen were encamped in Cambridge environs; two days later, lines of troops encircled Boston. While minutemen continued to pour in from all over New England, many of the first to arrive went home. Some moderate leaders, like Timothy Pickering, Jr., who returned to Salem with his regiment April 20, saw a standing army as unnecessary. But most Massachusetts leadership disagreed. On April 29, the Provincial Congress voted to raise 13,600 men for eight months' service, Massachusetts' share of the 30,000 New England troops estimated to be necessary.

By early May, the number of emergency soldiers manning the lines had dropped to dangerously low levels, seriously weakening defenses. Ranks were so depleted that by May 10 the committee of safety called in all enlistees, whether or not contingents were filled or completely equipped.

The committee had incredible responsibilities and little time to carry them out. It had to recruit soldiers, commission officers, form companies and organize regiments, and (with a companion committee of supplies) provide for their maintenance. In the aftermath of the Lexington alarm, most soldiers had returned home to day-to-day pursuits, but some stayed in the siege lines and enlisted in the provincial army to serve until December 31. Unemployed sailors and fishermen were especially quick to volunteer. At home, in each locality, would-be company and regimental commanders conducted recruiting, receiving commissions for their efforts. Each regiment was to have ten companies, with a captain, two lieutenants, an ensign, and fifty-eight enlisted men. After regimental commanders had enlisted the full complement of companies, they applied to the committee of safety for a commission.

Some militia added to the confusion by switching loyalties from one regimental commander to another. On May 25, Captains John Baker of Topsfield, Abraham Dodge and Nathaniel Wade of Ipswich, Jacob Gerrish of Newbury, Ezra Lunt and Benjamin Perkins of Newburyport, and Nathaniel L. Warner of Gloucester wrote to request Capt. Moses Little of Newbury as their regimental commander and Maj. Isaac Smith of Gloucester as lieutenant colonel. Six companies, however, already had been claimed by Col. Samuel Gerrish of Newbury. Both Gerrish and Little were veteran company commanders of the French and Indian War and early Newbury-area revolutionary leaders. Why the captains preferred Little is unclear, but subsequent actions suggest he was a more able officer. After much discussion, Little was recognized as the regimental commander of eight companies totaling 509 men.

To keep his command, within a few days Gerrish had organized almost an entirely new regiment. It comprised men from Gloucester, Ipswich, Newbury, Rowley, Wenham, and Middlesex County towns. On June 17, though, the regiment was incomplete; some companies were undermanned, others not yet commissioned.[2]

The interlude between April 19 and the Battle of Bunker Hill is depicted by a fictitious west Newbury eyewitness in *Three Generations* by Sarah A. Emery. Published in 1872, the account is based on historical facts and family reminiscences. It recounts the disorganization and disorder of this unsettled period:

> The people were in a state of alarm. Many of the inhabitants of Cambridge had fled from their homes, but the men were threatened with punishment if they injured property. . . . I came home for a few days, then in Gerrish's regiment marched to the seat of war. We began to throw up fortifications . . . army was still in an unorganized state. Officers had not received their commissions, there was want of ordinance, and much confusion everywhere. The army had not become fully organized, when the battle took place . . . .

We had many good officers and privates, old soldiers that had served in the French War; besides all our men were sharp shooters, with plenty of spunk well roused up. Three companies of our regiment formed the left wing of the army at Chelsea; my company was still at Cambridge, when it was decided to fortify Bunker Hill.[3]

Despite a provincial executive-style committee of supplies, the equipping and provisioning of troops fell largely on the towns. Shortly after April 19, wagonloads of supplies trundled toward Cambridge and the American lines. One from Rowley was driven by Sarah Northend Mighill, wife of Capt. Thomas Mighill. All kinds of provisions—beans, beef, bread, fish, pork, vinegar—poured in. Even coffeepots, kettles, and saucepans had to be procured locally. Though fresh fish, meats, and vegetables commanded a premium, plenty of food generally was available. Each man's daily allowance was generous: one pound of bread, a half pound of beef, a half pound of pork, one pint of milk, one quart of beer, and one jill of peas or beans, along with occasional treats like baked apples and chocolate. Wives, neighbors, and soldiers returning from furloughs kept the lines adequately stocked with cider, rum, and wine. A spirited town volunteerism made for a well-fed army.

To Charlestown

By mid-June, 15,000 troops, mostly from Massachusetts, were encamped in an irregular, nine-mile semicircle around Boston, from Roxbury on the south, to Cambridge westward, and northerly to Medford. Gen. William Howe, who arrived in Boston in late May, had a plan to end the siege. On June 18, he intended to launch an amphibious assault on Dorchester Point, a peninsula south of Boston, to secure the heights and move to smash the American army in Roxbury. Another expedition attacking on the north at Willis Creek was to gain the heights at Charlestown. If the end moves succeeded, flanking redcoats would sweep into Cambridge and destroy the provincial organization. Spies alerted the Americans to Howe's strategy. The committee of safety resolved to head off this offensive by erecting a defensive fortification on Bunker Hill (though committee member Elbridge Gerry of Marblehead was opposed, estimating that the powder supply was inadequate). Gen. Artemas Ward, commander in chief of the Massachusetts army, ordered parts of the regiments of Colonels Frye, Bridge, and Prescott—joined by two hundred Connecticut troops led by Gen. Israel Putnam—to march to Bunker Hill. Frye's regiment was comprised of over four hundred Essex County original minutemen under command of Captains John Currier and William H. Ballard of Amesbury, Benjamin Ames and Benjamin

BATTLE OF BUNKER HILL.

Bunker (Breed's) Hill from the perspective of the besieging British. Courtesy, Beverly Historical Society.

Farnum of Andover, William Perley of Boxford, Nathaniel Gage of Bradford, James Sawyer of Haverhill, John Davis of Methuen, and Jonathan Evans of Salisbury. Lt. Colonel James Brickett of Haverhill commanded; Frye was indisposed with the gout. Bridge's regiment included the companies of John Rowe of Gloucester and Charles Furbush of Andover. Nearly 40 percent of the twelve-hundred-man force mustered on Cambridge Green at six o'clock on the evening of June 16 were from Essex County. They waited until dark, then marched two and one-half miles to Charlestown.

After reaching Charlestown Heights at about ten o'clock, Col. William Prescott of Pepperell, who commanded the expeditionary force, was joined on the hillside by Danvers-born-and-bred Gen. Israel Putnam and chief engineer Col. Richard Gridley, a renowned veteran of the siege of Louisburg. After a lengthy exchange among the trio, the plucky leaders decided to fortify seventy-five-foot-high Breed's Hill. While Bunker Hill was thirty-five feet higher and more defensible, they took license and chose a site that would cause more contention. The British would not tolerate a fortification so close to the Charles River. The rebels' site, certain to provoke attack, would force a showdown on ground favoring the patriots.

Construction began about midnight—everyone pick-and-shoveling feverishly and stealthily under the star-studded, clear sky to entrench themselves before daylight. At four o'clock, British on board the *Lively* in Boston harbor were first to awake and see the unbelievable fortification—a 140-foot-square redoubt (little fort) featuring a six-foot wall and projecting angles on its strongest side, which faced south toward town. The *Lively* opened fire without waiting for orders; shortly afterward, General Gage ordered other warships and a battery on Copp's Hill in Boston to join the bombardment.

Guns could not elevate high enough, however, to reach the fort. Undisturbed by the shelling, the defenders worked steadily to strengthen the fortification. Before afternoon, a breastwork had been completed which ran in a line with the eastern side of the redoubt about one hundred yards towards an impassable marsh. In the early afternoon, about two hundred yards from the north end of the breastwork, a rail fence shield—to protect the flank—was established, stretching to the Mystic River. A fence also was built to the right of the redoubt along the cartway. This line of defense was designed to blockade the entire peninsula.

By late morning, the heat had become oppressive. Many, especially men who had neglected to bring provisions, were hungry, thirsty, and exhausted. They wanted Prescott to request a relief force from Gen. Artemas Ward. Prescott held a council of war with his officers and decided to send for fresh provisions and additional troops, but refused to replace the present force. Colonels Brickett and Bridge were moving off the hilltop to seek shelter in some abandoned homes on the northwest slope of Bunker Hill. It was purposeless for Prescott to protest, for, in these democratic times, militia owed their only real allegiance to their regimental colonel.

Only reluctantly had General Ward ordered the original force to Charlestown. He regarded the remaining forces as necessary for the center defenses, to secure Cambridge and provincial headquarters from attack. Therefore, only one-third of Gen. John Stark's New Hampshire regiment marched. Colonels Moses Little, John Mansfield, John Nixon, and two hundred Connecticut troops were scheduled to move at five o'clock. By then, it would be known whether Charlestown would be the primary assault point.

Five hundred men were left on Breed's Hill; only Prescott's regiment was mostly intact. By eleven o'clock, the committee of safety became convinced additional troops were needed; Ward was advised to send them. The remainder of the two New Hampshire regiments and several Massachusetts companies were ordered to Charlestown.

Gen. William Howe, in command of the operation, began ferrying the first of three thousand crack troops: grenadiers, light infantry, line regiments, and marines. Soon, they would be attacking the entrenched Americans. At half past eleven, regiments swung through Boston streets to their embarkation points at North Battery and Long Wharf. An armada of barges set out in double lines for Charlestown. Upon landing after one o'clock, Howe reconnoitered the Americans' formidable works from Morton's Hill. He concluded it would be wise to bring up reinforcements.

Last-Minute Reinforcements

When news of the landing reached Cambridge, Gen. Artemas Ward ordered some reserve Connecticut and Massachusetts troops to Charlestown, withholding his own, Gardner's, Patterson's, and part of Bridge's regiments.

At two o'clock, neither reinforcements nor refreshments had arrived. The boats which had returned to Boston were observed loading a second contingent. The raw recruits entrenched on Breed's Hill grew apprehensive. Prescott, having observed British movements along the Mystic River, had placed a detachment two hundred yards behind the north end of the redoubt. At the base of Bunker Hill, they took cover behind the rail fence; running parallel, four feet in front, another line of fence had been built, with the space between packed with fresh hay. From two to three o'clock, New Hampshire forces and portions of Massachusetts regiments began to arrive; most

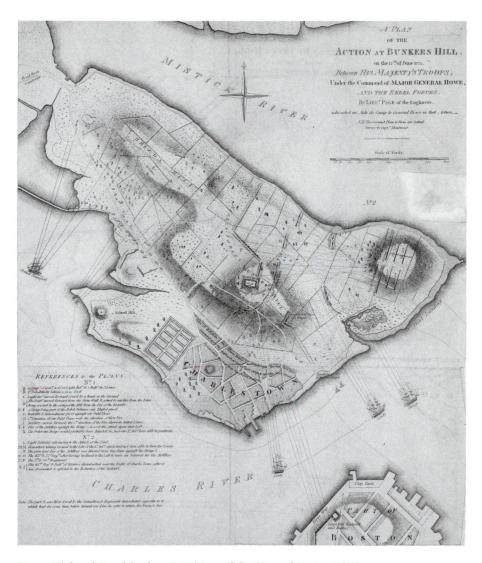

From Richard Frothingham's *History of the Siege of Boston*, 1849.

of Brickett's and Bridge's regiments followed their commanders back to the redoubt and along the lines.

A narrow strip of land connected Charlestown peninsula with the mainland. Several men-of-war and floating batteries pounded the causeway to deter troops marching towards Charlestown. Several forces braved the storm, but others stopped, afraid to make the crossing. Colonel Frye, presumably in better health, met the backed-

up forces as he rode toward the peninsula. Encouraging them on-
ward, he recollected "this day," thirty years ago, when "I was at the
taking of Louisburg . . . it is a fortunate day for America, we shall
certainly beat the enemy."[4]

Col. Moses Little, dressed in his best black velvet clothes, inspired
most of his command to follow across the perilous strip. Capt. Benjamin Perkins, a Newburyport coppersmith, found his wig insuffer-
ably warm; tossing it aside, he led his company in Indian file to the
peninsula.[5] Little's forces reached the front by three o'clock, near
time of the first attack. His command embodied three companies of
mostly intact Essex County troops—Perkins's, Wade's, and Warner's—approximately 125 men. The rest of the regiment was in
Gloucester, Ipswich, Menotomy, and Lechmere Point.

They scattered behind the defense—to the redoubt, behind the
breastworks, to the rail fence and the cartway on the south side.
Wade's Ipswich contingent crouched behind the rail fence. Perkins's
Newburyport company and part of Warner's Gloucester force, under
Lt. John Burnham, lined up along the cartway outside the redoubt's
southwest corner; seventeen of his twenty-three men would be killed
or wounded.[6]

A detachment from Rowe's Gloucester company had carried off
some entrenching tools. On their return Putnam ordered them, including Rowe, to the extreme end of the rail fence on the left near
Mystic River. They helped reinforce the fence and construct a breastwork with stones and dirt at the river bank. This divided the company, as part—under Ensign Ebenezer Cleaveland and Sergeant
William Haskins—had remained in the redoubt.[7]

The First Assault

British reinforcements arrived shortly before three o'clock. The
two-division assault group proceeded forthwith in the face of the
American lines: Howe toward the rebel left at the rail fence; Brig.
General Robert Pigot against the redoubt and breastwork. The American defenders withheld their fire until the troops had advanced well
within musket range (100 yards). Then they let loose a devastating
volley. The red-clad British line was shattered and pushed back in
confusion.

Gerrish and Mansfield

After the first assault, General Putnam rode to the rear of Bunker
Hill to hurry along reinforcements. Some lately arrived forces had

reached the lines, but the murderous cannon fire raking Charlestown Neck had deterred others from crossing.

Among the regiments Ward had hurriedly dispatched were Col. Samuel Gerrish's 38th and Col. John Mansfield's 19th. Gerrish's forces had been stationed at Cambridge, Chelsea, and Malden. Gerrish, obese and unused to such exertion, stopped to rest on Ploughed Hill, just short of the Neck. Succumbing to exhaustion or apprehension, Gerrish dropped beside a haystack. Putnam urged on Gerrish's forces, but they complained of having no officer to lead. A gallant leader named Christian Febiger—possibly America's first foreign continental volunteer officer—took command. Formerly a lieutenant in the Danish army, Febiger had joined in Newburyport on April 28 as Gerrish's adjutant. Febiger, saving the regiment from dishonor, called on Gerrish's men to march to the heights.[8] Thomas Doyl, an Irishman, who had deserted the British months earlier and joined Rogers's Newbury company, helped rally the forces. Part of the force followed.

Gerrish's conduct was severely criticized in testimony taken after the battle. Emery's *Three Generations* described the battle through the eyes of the fictitious eyewitness who had reached the battlefield with Febiger.

> What a sight it was before us! The British were retiring from their first repulse; our men, much elated, stood firm to their post; beyond, the ships and batteries belched forth their destructive missiles. . . . Our colonel, a jolly, portly man, a good officer . . . at this point expressed himself completely used up, and unable to proceed farther, and with a most unwarrior-like air, threw himself beside a haycock. This was not the best example for raw recruits, that had never before smelt gunpowder; but most of the men were rallied, and under the command of our adjutant, a gallant Danish officer.[9]

The account probably is accurate. Thomas Doyl, who had assisted Febiger, was bayonetted to death during the final British assault.

Early in May, Col. Timothy Pickering wrote to the committee of safety recommending John Mansfield of Lynn to command a contemplated Salem-area regiment. Mansfield was Pickering's lieutenant colonel in the First Essex Regiment which had formed in February 1775. Mansfield, with Israel Hutchinson as lieutenant colonel and Ezra Putnam as major, mustered ten full companies: one was commanded by his friend Ezra Newhall of Lynn; three were from Salem under Captains Thomas Barnes, Nathan Brown, and Addison Richardson; three were Danvers companies, headed by Captains Gideon Foster, Asa Prince and Enoch Putnam; two from Beverly, led by Captains Ebenezer Francis and John Low; one out of Manchester, commanded by Capt. Benjamin Kimball. At the time of their commissioning on May 27, the regiment already was stationed in Cambridge.

On the day of battle, Mansfield met Maj. Scarborough Gridley while marching the 19th Regiment toward Charlestown. Gridley, an officer in his father's artillery regiment, was respected largely because of his family's reputation. Inadequate for the job, Gridley succumbed to fear marching to Breed's Hill. Though ordered to advance with a detachment of regimental artillery, Gridley got no further than Cobble Hill, on the mainland side of the Neck. He proceeded to engage in an ineffective artillery duel with the armed vessels *Glasgow* and *Symmetry*, out of range of his 4-pounders. Gridley ordered that Mansfield halt to help defend his position. Gridley, who anticipated a retreat from Charlestown, was preparing to cover the impending withdrawal. Mansfield remained until the battle ended at about five o'clock. Tragically and mistakenly, he had disobeyed Gen. Artemas Ward's orders and taken those of an inferior officer.[10]

Capt. Samuel R. Trevett of Marblehead belonged to Gridley's detachment. Ignoring Gridley, he marched his artillery company with two field pieces to a space between the breastwork and rail fence. Though most deserted, nine men stood by their commander: Marblehead lieutenants Richard Gardner and Joseph Swasey and young Moses Porter, already an accomplished artillerist, and six others. Near the end of the battle, courageously forsaking their own safety, they—helped by some infantrymen—brought off the only gun saved from capture.[11]

Second and Final Assaults

Meanwhile, the British extinguished sniper fire on their flank by setting fire to four hundred homes and other buildings in Charlestown. In the eighteenth century, incendiary acts against civilian centers were not fair game. The provincials would win a decided propaganda advantage from this savage, uncivilized act.

Amid heavy black smoke, the British regrouped and ascended the grassy slope for a second time. An even more devastating fusillade sent them scrambling back in greater disorder than before, leaving scores of dead strewn on the battlefield. The regulars attacked for the third and last time after heavy artillery bombardment. In column formation, rather than in extended order, and with their heavy knapsacks off, the assault force advanced. Concentrating on the redoubt and the breastwork, they soon were attacking from three sides. The grand assault succeeded; Howe's first wave scaled the walls with the exhausted defenders down to their last powder. Amid the savage melee in the redoubt—fought hand-to-hand with gun butts and rocks—having suffered heavy losses, the Americans began to withdraw from the fortification. They fled back toward Bunker Hill and across the peninsula.

At least six Chebacco Parish men from Capt. Abraham Dodge's company engaged in the battle. Francis Burnham wrote an account, including a description of the instant death of Jesse Story:

> Most of our ammunition was gone, and but few of us had bayonets. They did not, however, dare to come up as before. A portion of men took a circuitous route to the south side of our hill, and soon scaled our works. We were now attacked on both sides, and the contest became very hot. Story and I were side by side, when a ball struck his head, his brains flew in my face and he fell back into the ditch, which ran along behind the fence. Another shot gave me a slight wound under the shoulder, which made me stop for a few moments to get breath.[12]

Defenders at the rail fence stood their ground bravely which shielded the retreat from Breed's Hill and prevented their escape route from being cut off. Febiger's contingent from Gerrish's regiment helped by directing a continuous fire on the attackers between Breed and Bunker hills. Sarah Emery's eyewitness related the action at the breastwork: "Here a considerable force maintained their ground with great firmness. They resisted every effort to turn their flank, and prevented the main body, who were retreating in disorder, from being cut off. When we saw that Prescott had left the hill, we commenced a retreat in remarkably good order, considering the circumstances."[13]

Capt. Ezra Lunt's Newburyport company was on guard duty at Lechmere Point. They were unable to get to Charlestown until late in the battle. With some other lately arrived troops, they helped cover the retreat. Caleb Haskell, a private in Lunt's company, stated in his diary:

> The army set out. We found the town in flames, and the Regulars ascending the hill; the ball flying almost as thick as hailstones from the ships and floating batteries, and Corps' Hill and Beacon Hill in Boston, and the ground covered with the wounded and dead. Our people stood the fire some time, until the enemy had almost surrounded us and cut off our retreat.[14]

Back Home

The day was one of anxiety and suspense for families back home. As far away as west Newbury, the distant, muffled sounds of cannon could be heard, helped northeastward by warm southwesterly breezes. From Southend, presumably Crane Neck Hill, a heavy smoke could be seen on the edge of the southern sky.

> The boom of the cannon grew louder and louder, and was heard in many places. Half the town came up to South-end; that is such a sightly place. About noon we began to discern smoke jest on the edge of the southern sky; it grew heavier and heavier; we thought Boston must be burning. Dear sake, what an awful afternoon that was! A'most everybody had some of their family in the army, so you may judge what an anxious time it must have been.[15]

Several miles further north, in Amesbury, the muffled sounds of cannon were clearly heard.

Battle Casualties

The misnamed Battle of Bunker Hill ended with a terrible loss of lives. British casualties exceeded 1,000, with 226 reported killed. Salem Poor, a Negro freedman from Andover of Colonel Frye's regiment, killed one of the highest ranking enemy field officers. He was Lt. Colonel Abercrombie, commander of the Grenadiers. Later, several officers recommended Poor to the General Court for his bravery, "in justice to the Caracter of so Brave a Man that came under our observation."[16]

Essex County blacks served during the entire war. Shortly after Bunker Hill, when the Massachusetts army became part of Continental forces, attempts were made to exclude blacks. On July 10, at Cambridge, Adj. General Horatio Gates ordered regimental commanders: "You are not to Enlist any Deserter from the Ministerial Army, nor any Stroller, Negro or Vagabond, or Person suspected of being an Enemy to the Liberty of America, nor any under Eighteen Years of Age." In December, General Washington permitted free Negroes to enlist, but slaves continued to be excluded. (This concession was prompted by the threat from some free Negroes, "dissatisfied at being discarded," to join the British army.) It was believed victory was unachievable if fighting were left to largely indifferent combatants. Middle-class property owners—with conviction on the issues and a stake in the outcome—had to be the backbone of the army. Nevertheless, blacks continued to be mustered, especially later, when it became difficult to fill local draft quotas. By all accounts, Essex County blacks—at least fifty in the ranks—were good soldiers and fought with bravery.[17]

American losses were about 140 killed, 300 wounded, and 30 captured. Twenty-seven Essex County men were killed, nearly one-fifth the total, with the greatest number coming from Frye's regiment, stationed in the vicinity of the redoubt. (For a list of Essex County patriots who died of their wounds, see Appendix B.) Over 60 Essex County men suffered nonfatal battle injuries, 31 from Frye's and 23 from Little's regiments alone. Lt. Col. Brickett of Frye's regiment, a Haverhill physician, left the field with the first wounded. Seriously hurt himself, he remained on the opposite side of Bunker Hill with other surgeons, attending to the wounded. Daniel Sessions of Andover and Jonathan Norton of Newburyport were made prisoners.

It had been a costly victory for the British. Though the patriots had been pushed off Bunker Hill, they gained strategically. For the first time, the two forces had met face to face on the battlefield. There had been acts of great personal heroism, particularly those of William Prescott, who commanded the redoubt, and Maj. General (Dr.) Joseph Warren, head of the Massachusetts committee of safety. Not yet officially commissioned, he stood, fought, and died as a private in the ranks. The inexperienced patriot militia did not run; they stood their ground and fought with amazing courage.

Cashiering of Gerrish and Mansfield

Col. Samuel Gerrish was commanding a fort on Sewall's Point a few weeks later when a floating battery launched a nighttime attack. Gerrish did not return the fire, observing, "The rascals can do us no harm . . . a mere waste of powder, to fire at them with our 4-pounders." With shore lights extinguished, British fire was wide of the fort. For his fainthearted actions this day and on June 17, Gerrish was arrested and cashiered. On August 19, Lt. Benjamin Craft of Kimball's Manchester company entered in his diary: "It is said that poor little Col. Gerrish is broke! which will make our Col. Mansfield look out sharp."[18]

Three of Col. John Mansfield's officers had gone before General Washington in August, accusing their colonel of cowardice during the battle. A court-martial was ordered. Lieutenant Craft's journal refers to the trial proceedings. A September entry noted:

> 8th. This morning I did not turn out until after breakfast. All the officers went to Cambridge as witnesses in the case of Col. Mansfield. The court was opened, the officers sworn, and the Lieut Col., Major, and all the Captains examined and gave in their evidences and the court adjourned to Wednesday next. Col. Mansfield had a trying time, and I believe he will also find it a breaking time.[19]

Craft's bitterness is evident. On Wednesday, September 13, he reported the conclusion of the proceedings:

> After breakfast went to see the end of Col. Mansfield's court martial. All the lieutenants gave in their evidence much alike, with the

exception of Lieut. Breed,—his evidence being nothing more or less
than Col. Mansfield's own story, which he had learnt from him, he
being, as I suppose, one of the Colonel's own scholars. To me this
was surprising strange. But I suppose neither master or scholar had
any foundation for their support, and I believe what they both said
will fail, and they meet the contempt they justly deserve.[20]

On September 15, Mansfield was ordered cashiered "for remiss-
ness and backwardness in the execution of his duty" on Bunker Hill.
Washington accepted the sentence, which took effect immediately—
to the apparent satisfaction of Mansfield's officers.[21]

Later, the judge advocate remarked that he felt Gerrish had been
treated too severely and that Mansfield's error was largely because of
inexperience. Their trials, and three others, provided General Washington an opportunity to set an example for his raw, poorly disciplined army. Gerrish returned to west Newbury and Mansfield to
Lynn. Still respected and esteemed by their townspeople, they continued to be elected and appointed to offices of trust.

The Continuing Siege

Patriots feared that once the British had caught their breath and
reinforcements had arrived, they would continue their offensive.
Militia, buttressed by enlisted troops, began to entrench on the hills
around Boston. By late June, eight regiments, including Gerrish's,
Little's, and Mansfield's, were encamped on or in the vicinity of
Prospect Hill (Somerville), which commanded a clear view of British
lines.

For several weeks, scattered, occasionally heavy, artillery discharges
continued from Boston, with American riflemen and British sentries
frequently exchanging small arms fire. On June 29, Ebenezer Francis
wrote to his wife, Judith, in Beverly: "I am fully of the mind that
god in his providence is about to work Some—Remarkable Deliver-
ance for us & prevent the further Effusion of Blood. the more
Skirmishes, the more the peopels Spirits Seem to be animated."[22]
Francis's hopes would be dashed by a siege that extended to March
1776, the prologue to over five more years of conflict.

Washington's Arrival

On June 14, the Second Continental Congress assembled at Philadelphia assumed responsibility for the army encircling Boston. Ten
companies of riflemen were voted for its siege lines: six companies
to be raised in Pennsylvania, two each from Maryland and Virginia.
Col. George Washington was selected as commander in chief of all
the Continental forces. Thus, symbolically, the military base was

broadened beyond New England. Washington assumed command in Cambridge on July 3, with Second Maj. Gen. and Chief Deputy Charles Lee, a former lieutenant colonel of the British infantry, who was living in semiretirement in Virginia. (Gen. Artemas Ward was made first major general.) Joseph Hodgkins of Ipswich, in a letter to his, wife, casually noted this historic event:

> I have nothing Remarkebel to rite Except that geaneral Washington & Leas got into Cambridge yesterday and to Day thay are to take a vew of ye Army & that will be atended with a grate deal of grandor there is at this time one & twenty Drummers & as many feffors a Beting and Playing Round the Prayde.[23]

In July, the army was divided into three grand divisions, each with twelve regiments. Major General Ward guarded the southern or right wing at Roxbury; the northern or left wing, including 470 men under Colonel Mansfield (19th Regiment) and 472 men under Colonel Little (17th Regiment), was posted at Prospect and Winter hills under Major General Lee; the center, including 406 men from Colonel Frye's 1st Regiment, 498 from Gerrish's 38th, and 454 from Colonel Glover's 21st (which had marched from Marblehead on June 22), was based at Cambridge, commanded by Major General Putnam.

The siege of Boston—from mid-June 1775 to mid-March 1776—was a tale of false alarms, minor skirmishes, occasional exchanges of shot and shell, and small arms fire. Washington continuously feared that the British were making preparations for an assault against the lines. In fact, on July 3, the day he assumed command, a strike was forecast at Winter Hill.

Conditions in Camp

When Washington took command at Cambridge, about 16,000 able-bodied men were besieging Boston: 11,500 were from twenty-six infantry units in Massachusetts, plus three small armies from Connecticut, New Hampshire, and Rhode Island—poorly trained and inadequately provisioned. They were armed with English military muzzle-loaders left from earlier wars—like the Brown Bess musket—or hunting weapons. Paper for cartridges, gunpowder, and lead balls all were in scarce supply. Late in April, the Massachusetts Congress had resolved that towns provide their men with blankets. In early July, they were required—proportionate with the province tax—to furnish coats for each noncommissioned officer and soldier in the Massachusetts army. The county share ranged from Salem's 380 to 33 from Manchester. Troops dressed in a motley array of clothing colored the lines a hodgepodge of dull greens and browns. With wearing apparel in short supply, however, many men were scantily clad. Townspeople worked to produce shoes, knit socks, and make coats and breeches. Soldiers with peacetime skills as tailors or cobblers were in demand. Nathaniel Cleaves of Beverly was engaged in cutting breeches, coats, and jackets for his comrades, while David How of Methuen crafted pairs of shoes. Men were required to provide their own exchanges of clothing and their laundering. Capt. Ebenezer Francis wrote home to his wife on July 5:

> we Still Live in our Habbitation but Expect to move to Day or to morrow I would have you send my things by Goodridge I spoke to him this morning & he will know where to bring them & tell you where to Leave them for him I Shall want Shurts & other things as Usal I Dont want another Frock at present I have Sold the Horse to Leut Dodge & brother Thomas must make the mare Doo as well as he Can we shall Have very Comfortable accomodations on the Hill & Such as will make me Contented as you write you hope I shall as for Gages fight we fear him not I send by Leut Craft one Shirt one pr of Briches one Jackcoat 2 pr of Stockins.[24]

Francis was moving to new quarters, but Little's regiment, until early October, lingered in tents. It was the last regiment in the brigade to be barracked.

From Prospect Hill, Lt. Joseph Hodgkins, writing to his wife on January 7, 1776, recounted widespread illness in Little's unit:

> It is a good Deal sickly among us we Bured Willeby Nason Last thusday John Sweet is Very sick in Camp & Josiah Persone of Cape ann in our Company is Just moved to the ospittle Capt Parker is a little Bitter Mr. Harden is sick in Camp John Holladay Died Last thusday night there whas five Buried that Day we Bured Mr. Nason from the ospittle Capt Willm Wade has Lost one man he was Burred a friday.[25]

Unfortunately, sickness and death was endemic to the army.

Need for Order and Discipline

Most of the young, untrained troops encircling Boston hailed either from self-sufficient hamlets or seaports, where they labored as mechanics, sailors, and fishermen. Their livelihoods encouraged a free, individualistic outlook; they resisted discipline, authority, or personal restraint. The revolutionary spirit, whereby men gained a sense of equality, furthered their proud, independent style. Washington was an inspiring leader for these young enlisted men. Their indifference to order and obedience, however, hindered the development of an effective military organization.

Indeed, Capt. Thomas Poor of Andover even lacked enough control over his troops to appoint his own subordinates. On May 10, because he objected to his men's choosing their own sergeant, the troops went on strike and paraded in protest. They won! Private James Stevens wrote: "capt Poor come & said that he was mis under stod & the comping [company] setld with him by his making som recantation." On August 7, two hundred of Mansfield's North Shore regiment demonstrated for a month's back pay. However, authority prevailed. Lt. Nathaniel Cleaves of Beverly noted: "This day [August 9] the Major Drumer was put under gard for raising a mutiny in the rigiment Concerning their pay by general Leas order one man spoke and set that he shouldent go under gard general Lea struck him with his cain and orderd him put under gard." An enraged Lt. Benjamin Craft of Benjamin Kimball's Manchester company hoped the drum major "will be punished according to his deserts. I wish every one of those who had a hand in the mutiny, may be punished severely."[26]

Washington and Lee were determined to bring order to the army of the united colonies. Treatment sometimes was harsh. Late in August, Lieutenant Craft reported: "Stephen Stanwood for saucy talk to Gen. Lee had his head broke. The General gave him a dollar and sent for the doctor." Not anyone, however, could strike his men. On August 9, Capt. Timothy Ballard of Amesbury (Frye's regiment) was tried at court martial and fined for "two instances of profane swearing, and of beating one of his men." Each offense cost him four shillings.[27]

Regulations were adopted for strict obedience to regimental orders, which were read every morning after prayers. Daily, thousands worked fortifying and extending the line or engaging in military drill and exercise. Offenses were continual in this raw, inexperienced army. Punishments were handed out by summary action, for lesser offenses, or by courts-martial, for more serious crimes that ranged from betrayal and desertion to disobedience, drunkenness, quarreling, and stealing. Most infractions were punished by fines or lashings, up to a maximum of thirty-nine. Orderly books and journals of the day note the regularity of punishment. Whole regiments were turned out to see lashes to bare backs and men riding the wooden horse. The orderly book of Capt. Enoch Putnam of Danvers describes a typical proceeding:

> Richard Thomson of Corl Weebs Regt on Fine for Disarting the Second time and for every other thing Bad and unbecomeing a Solder tried by a Late Garrison Court Martial and found Guilty therefore Sentence to Receive 20 Stripes on his naked Back Pay the Owner for a Surtute He stole 4 Dollars out of this month of advance pay none Due for the month of Jany and Drumd out of the Armey Likeways John Levate of Capt Coffens Company Tried by the Same

Court for Drunkardness and being absent from Guard Sentances to pay a fine of 10 Shillings but many Elevating Circumstances appearing in his favour induced the Court to Recommend him to the Genl mercey also James Gager of Capt Holland Company in Corl Weeb Regt Tried for threatning and chall[eng]ing to fight, The prisoner Confesd himself Guilty.[28]

Efforts to improve order and discipline started before Washington's arrival. Cleaves noted that on June 3 "the whole army was Mustered on the comon to se 2 theives wiped one 20 stripes Negro 10 one man Drumed out of the army with 36 drums and 40 fifes with the roges march." Later, on September 22, Cleaves mentioned that one of Capt. Nathan Brown's Salem men "rid the wooden hors half in ower for Cusing and swaring and fighting with his Mesmate." He was the first in Mansfield's regiment to be punished since they came to the hill.[29]

In Mansfield's North Shore contingent, court-martial duty among the officers was an excuse for celebration. Cleaves noted on Friday, August 11, "a Dispute who had treated for being on Cort Marshel Capt Low payed one botel of wine . . . for as acting as president Lieut Emonton [Ephraim Emerton of Salem] one bottel for acting as Clark [clerk] Captain Nuel one bottel for not Demanding a treat of them that was on Cort Marshel When he Was president Lieut Craft one Botel for not paying of it when on Cort Marshel the furst time."

Glover's Marblehead marines, courageous, spirited, and independent, were used to the rough and tumble of sea life. Israel Trask of Gloucester, a young boy serving in Mansfield's regiment as cook and messenger, wrote nearly seventy years later that Marbleheaders were "always full of fun and mischief." (For a list of regimental officers, see Appendix C.) When recruits arrived in camp from the backwoods and mountains of Virginia, Glover's men, dressed in round jackets and fishing trousers, ridiculed the Southerners' white linen frock coats. One day, they fought a snowball duel. Within five minutes, over one thousand men were engaged "pellmell with as much rage and bitterness as they would have done with their most deadly enemy." The heavily muscled six-foot-two Washington rode onto the scene and "sprung from his seat," recounted Trask, "rushed into the thicket of the melee, seized two, tall, brawny, athletic, savage-looking riflemen by the throat, keeping them at arm's length, talking to and shaking them at the same time." Both sides scattered, leaving the two terrified riflemen. Such was the awe in which Washington was held by the American troops.[30]

Washington's efforts notwithstanding, lax discipline that allowed furloughs—or even desertions—almost at one's choosing, thinned the ranks. In late June, only days after the Marblehead marines had marched for Cambridge, many deserted and returned home. Those found were sent back. Then, on September 4, they deserted in droves, probably lured by privateering. Next day, a twenty-man contingent trailed them to Marblehead. Some Continental officers, however, often did not set a good example. Joseph Hodgkins wrote on December 3: "But I am something worried with Duty By Reason of so many officers Being absent."[31] Muster roles were being falsified; Washington ordered it stopped. His orders, in the words of Enoch Putnam of Danvers, were that officers were to examine "their Returns before they sign [and] Deliver tham to major of Brigade . . . Negligance will not be over Look't and faile [to] Return punished with the Greatest Severity the Genl Apprehends that more men are absent upon furlough than allowd by Genl Orders."[32]

Officers, as well as enlisted men, needed to recognize their responsibilities. Some officers even employed the "sick" men on their farms. January 1, 1776, marked the inception of the Continental Army, raised and governed by direct authority of the Continental Congress. Washington yearned to begin the year right, but a hint of discouragement is evident from his January 1 orders, as reiterated by Putnam: "Subbordination and Disepline is the life and Soul of an armey which next under providence is to make us Formetable too our Enemys . . . herein is to be Shone the Goodness of the officers.— in Vaine is it for a Genl to Esue orders if orders are not attended too."[33]

In early November, the Congress approved reorganization of the main army into twenty-six infantry regiments totaling about 20,000 men. Each regiment at full strength would number 728, which included eight companies: 4 officers, 2 musicians, 84 noncommissioned officers and privates. Field officers were selected by Washington and his generals. Selection of company-officer ranks was assigned to each brigadier and his field officers.

In mid-November, reenlistment began. Washington sent officer-recruiters into the countryside. Even earlier, however, it had been difficult to maintain full strength. Lt. Benjamin Craft had reported on July 12, 1775: "Lieut. Dodge had gone home to Wenham in order to enlist more men." Massachusetts soon fell behind in meeting its stiff 1776 quota of 11,648 men, divided into sixteen regiments. Lieutenant Hodgkins noted on December 3: "Cape ann men inlist very slow." The sluggish progress was partly because solders were owed months' back pay. Several weeks into 1776, most regiments remained at less than full strength. On January 27, 1776, when the Salem militia mustered, not one man enlisted. Pickering explained that many were at sea, impressed, in the seacoast guard, or already in the army. In most cases, companies from various regiments established in 1775 were merged to form a new battalion. By March, regiments had reached roughly full strength. As the war continued, from one year to the next—with the population increasingly weary—filling quotas became progressively more difficult.[34]

Fun and Vice

When not on fatigue or picket duty, overseeing the building of fortifications, drilling troops, or foraging fresh provisions and military supplies, many young officers enjoyed an active social life. Lt. Nathaniel Cleaves of Beverly, whose diary is a valuable source of information about daily life during the siege, noted dozens of visits from North Shore wives, friends, and relatives. Cleaves was visited, not only by his father and neighbors, but by numerous women. He noted on July 23, "was two gals from wartertown up to our barricks this day"; on August 10, "had 2 gals from lyn to Dine with Me"; September 28, "Mis bouden was haer to day. I had a kiss of her"; October 1, "whe had sum gals down to se us this after noon." This cavorting lifted spirits in the camp before winter snows restricted travel.

Even work details sometimes took pleasurable turns. Cleaves reported on July 14: "Cap nuel [Newhall of Lynn] and Capt Low [Beverly] whent to wartertown after bords to finish our barricks had a very plesent time They fel in Company with avery butiful Lady and toock her into the shay with them the recomp[ence] she gave them is not yet know for Carying of her."

When the quarters of Capt. Enoch Putnam of Danvers were completed, late in September, Cleaves noted that the regimental officers "had a hous warming Whe had 14 botels of Wine Capt putnum . . . moderator. Doctor Welch was the toste Master This Meaten is adjorned til tuesday Night at the Colls New hous."

Lieutenant Cleaves had several "fine frolick[s]" while encamped on Prospect and Winter hills. And July 18 must have been one of the best:

> This morning Warm and Clear I went down to Chelsey with More oficers and one hunderd and thirty Men after a mast for a liberty pole had a fine prospect of the enemy Saw Eighty three horses peradeed and near forty more in the paster I went into a hous got sum [boil]ed cider and kised the old whomans Daughter to pay for it had a fine frolick at the tavern.

Some women in camp were less appreciated by the command. On June 8, Caleb Haskell of Newburyport noted, "a bad woman . . . was doused in the river, and drummed out of town." Later, Cleaves wrote, "A whooman was Drumed of the hill for playing the roge with a

drummer under the wall and bob picket was focksey as the Divel."
David How of Methuen reported in his journal on February 10, 1776:
"There was two women Drumd out of Camp This fore noon." The
besieging lines provided rich territory for these "ladies of the nighttime."[35]

David How chronicled on February 7: "This Day two men In
Cambridge got a bantering Who wodd Drink the most and they
Drinkd So much That one of them Died In About one houre or two
after." Five days later, How noted: "There was a man found Dead in
a room with A. Woman this morning. It's not known what killed
him." While every army has its excess, vice, and corruption, conditions around Boston aroused the disgust of two Ipswich officers.
Lieutenant Hodgkins wrote to his wife: "Wickedness Prevales Verry
much to the astonishment of any that Behold them I have not Time
to Be Pertickler now about maters." Aaron Perkins, Hodgkins's
brother-in-law and also an Ipswich lieutenant, observed he had "nothing to fear of sucksess, but only our sins which seem to prevail heare
very much. We must pray God to give a spirit of repentance and
humiliation."[36]

Hodgkins and Perkins more likely were referring to instances of
gross lasciviousness and drunkenness than to antics of Cleaves and
his fellow officers. The commander in chief had similar concerns,
himself. Washington ordered officers to refrain from "Profane Swaring," noted Enoch Putnam, to set an example, saying: "Unless we
pay a Sacred Regard to the Duty & Sobriety & Virtue we Cannot
Expeects the Blesing of Heaven Nor the Approbation of The Wise
among men."[37]

Consistent with a provision of the Continental Association as well
as the overriding Protestant ethic, officers and soldiers alike were
"possitively forbid Playing Cards and Other Games of Chance at this
Time of Publick Distress. Men may find enough to Do in the Servise
of their God and Country, without Abandoning themselves to Vise
and immorality."[38] Lieutenant Cleaves noted on the twenty-eighth of
September: "I spent the Evening a playing Cards." The previous day,
Cleaves mentioned playing "all Fores til 12 a Clock." Evidently, some
did not take the rules too seriously.

Officers spent some idle time "playing ball," probably stick ball,
which years later was to evolve into a great American pastime. They
also enjoyed "foot ball" and "quait [quoit]," a game where players
throw rings at a fixed peg in the ground. A little grog or cherry rum
often was waged. Cleaves noted, "played quait for 2 mugs of toody."
On another day, "in the after Noon Capt frances and I Chose sides
and played foot Ball. My side Beat threa pichers of grog."[39]

The undisciplined soldiers were unused to the rigors and deprivation they were enduring. Friends' visits, furloughs home, "fine frolicks," and sports—combined with varying degrees of devilishness—helped relieve the loneliness and weariness of camp life. These diversions probably deterred many men from bolting their stations and leaving the lines for good.

Arnold's Wilderness Expedition

In mid-September, a 1,100-man force, consisting of ten companies of New Englanders and three companies of riflemen from Virginia and Pennsylvania, was detached from the army encircling Boston. It was one of two expeditions which the Second Continental Congress had authorized for an attack on Canada.

After Ethan Allen had seized Fort Ticonderoga and Fort Crown Point on Lake Champlain in May 1775, a Connecticut militia officer named Benedict Arnold convinced the Congress to authorize a two-pronged invasion of Quebec. French Canadians were expected to revolt on sight of the Americans and bring in Quebec Province as the fourteenth member of the barely organized confederation. The Congress was attracted also by the huge supply of munitions reportedly stored at Quebec—the strongest garrison in North America. The Canadians, however, would remain surprisingly loyal to the king. Despite some revolutionary stirrings, the British had gone a long way toward ameliorating Canadian relations with the Quebec Act of 1774, which established freedom for Roman Catholics and granted to Canada vast tracts in the Ohio Valley. Anti-Catholic outbursts in northern New England, following the act's passage, cooled thoughts in Quebec of participating in a revolution with its southern neighbors.

On August 31, one expeditionary force, commanded by Gen. Richard Montgomery, launched an invasion with little more than one thousand men. They traveled up between the Hudson and St. Lawrence valleys and moved into Canada, capturing Montreal with ease and proceeding downriver to Quebec.

The second force left Cambridge in mid-September, bound for Newburyport, the port of embarkation. Washington placed Col. Benedict Arnold in command of this force. The group marched in separate contingents. One division, commanded by Maj. Return J. Meigs, proceeded through Malden, Lynn, and Salem on September 14 and encamped at Danvers. In the morning, they breakfasted in Beverly and continued down old Bay road, stopping the second night in Rowley, and reached Newburyport at ten o'clock the morning of September 16. A second detachment got to Malden on the thirteenth, at Beverly on the next day, and marched briskly to reach Newburyport by eight o'clock the following evening. A third unit bivouacked

Nathaniel Tracy and Tristram Dalton were prominent Newburyport merchants. They entertained the officers of Arnold's wilderness expedition before the troops' departure from town. Tracy, courtesy, Newburyport Public Library.

at Salem on the fourteenth, at Ipswich on the next night, and trooped into Newburyport on the sixteenth. The famous Daniel Morgan and his backwoods Virginia riflemen and two Pennsylvania rifle companies possibly traveled with this detachment. Parading through Essex County dressed in fur caps and deerskin frocks, they presented quite a spectacle. The Canada-bound troops marched through the towns to the shrill of fifes and the roll of drums, stirring the patriotism of hundreds along the way. At their pitched tent encampments, throngs visited to wish them well and godspeed.

While they awaited departure, three companies camped on the highland opposite the Green at the corner of Rolfe's Lane and High Road in Newbury. The remainder lodged in the Town House and in two unoccupied ropewalks in Newburyport. On the evenings of September 17 and 18, officers dined at the elegant Fish (now State) Street homes of Nathaniel Tracy and Tristram Dalton. Among the force were twenty Newburyporters who had been detached from Capt. Ezra Lunt's company.[40]

One of the Newburyporters, Caleb Haskell, kept a day-to-day journal of the travails of the disastrous expedition to Quebec:

> September 18th, Monday. This afternoon we embarked on board the transports. We had 1100 men, commanded by Col. Arnold and Lieut. Cols. Green and Enos. Eleven transports.

> September 19th, Tuesday. This day about 9 o'clock weighed our
> anchors, and came to sail with a southwardly wind. After we got
> over the bar, we lay to, waiting for orders from the commodore. At
> 10 o'clock received orders . . . made sail with a fine breeze.[41]

They disembarked at the mouth of the Kennebec; rowing and
sailing against the wind and tide, they ventured on the first leg—an
incredible journey with fantastic hardships through unmapped
northern wilderness. The expeditionary force pushed and pulled
their flat boats up the Kennebec, negotiated several lengthy carries
between small ponds and streams, navigated the treacherous River
Chandiere, and trekked across rough mountains and near impreg-
nable swamps. Only about six hundred of the original force reached
the St. Lawrence. On December 1, tired and weary, the troops joined
with Montgomery outside Quebec. They stationed themselves around
the garrison town. Since many troops' terms of enlistment would
expire at year's end, and since many were unwilling to reenlist, Montgomery and Arnold gambled on a premature attack. It was launched
on the night of December 30 in a blinding snowstorm. Part of Arnold's force broke through into town, but they were unable to hold
out. Montgomery was killed; some of Arnold's men were captured.
Washington sent reinforcements, but the expeditionary force retreated in the spring. Canada remained in British hands.

Knox's Deliverance

A Boston bookseller-soldier, Col. Henry Knox, transported to Boston, three hundred miles from the captured forts of Crown Point
and Ticonderoga, New York, over frozen lakes, the Berkshire mountains, and nearly impassable snows, more than fifty valuable cannon,
mortars, and howitzers and a supply of shells and powder. It was an
extraordinary act of persistence! Delivery of this ordnance in late
January enabled Washington to fortify Dorchester Heights. The guns
towering over Boston would give Washington the capacity to bom-
bard the town and force out the British. To divert attention, cannon
placed at Cobble Hill, Lechmere Point, and Lamb's Dam, Roxbury,
blasted away at Boston. On March 4, David How of Methuen noted,
"Last Night there was Afireing all Night with Cannan and mortars
on both Sides; our people Splet *The Congress* the Third Time that
they fireed it."[42] On the night of March 4, reminiscent of the Breed's
Hill entrenchment, 2,000 men worked stealthily to construct two
fortifications on Dorchester Heights before daybreak. Late at night,
the artillery was brought up to Dorchester Heights, with the British
awaking to see two fortifications looming menacingly above the British fleet and the town. The meaning was very clear—either the British

must evacuate or the patriots must be dislodged. Rain, winds, and high surf, however, frustrated a counterattack. With the army and the fleet at peril, Howe resolved to leave the town. By a mutual understanding, Washington permitted Howe's troops to embark unmolested, and Howe left Boston without destroying it. On Sunday, March 17, 1776, 11,000 British troops and over 1,000 Loyalists evacuated Boston for Halifax.

As Washington prepared to enter Boston, it was suspected that smallpox-infected articles had been left to cause an epidemic among the American army. Only soldiers who had contracted and survived the disease—and now were immune—were chosen for garrison duty. Troops were warned that severe punishments would be meted out for anyone pillaging or abusing inhabitants.

At last, the grand design had been achieved. The British had been pushed out to sea. A few vessels from the fleet lingered for over two months at Nantasket Road, the last indication of a British presence. For the first time in a long while, no British troops were encamped anywhere in New England.

1. William Lincoln, *The Journals of Each Provincial Congress of Massachusetts* (Boston: Dutton and Wentworth, 1838), 193.
2. Richard Frothingham, Jr., *History of the Siege of Boston* (Boston: Charles C. Little and James Brown, 1849), 178; Lincoln, 244, 292–93, 295; Peter Force, ed., *American Archives*, 4th Series, 2:1385–87.
3. Sarah A. Emery, *Three Generations* (Boston: Lee and Shepard, 1872), 48.
4. S. Swett, *Sketch of Bunker Hill Battle* (Boston: 1818), 62–63.
5. Joshua Coffin, *A Sketch of the History of Newbury, Newburyport, and West Newbury* (Boston: Samuel G. Drake, 1845), 406; S. Swett, *History of Bunker Hill Battle* (Boston: Munroe and Francis, 1827), 52.
6. Frothingham, 136, 177; John J. Babson, *History of the Town of Gloucester* (Gloucester: Procter Bros., 1860), 389–90; S. Swett, *Notes to his Sketch of Bunker-Hill Battle* (Boston: Munroe and Francis, 1825), 14, 16–17. Swett places Perkins in an exposed position between the breastwork and rail fence, 55.
7. Babson, 392; Swett, *Notes*, 12.
8. Frothingham, 179; Force, 2:433; Swett, *History of Bunker Hill Battle*, 37, 40; Swett reported that Gerrish's men were led to the front by Capt. Mighill of Rowley, under Febiger's command, and that Capt. Bayley's force was the group which followed and reached the lines, but no commander in Gerrish's regiment was named Bayley.
9. Emery, 49.
10. Frothingham, 183–85.
11. 152; Swett, *Sketch*, 63, 81.
12. Robert Crowell, *History of the Town of Essex* (Essex: Town of Essex, 1868), 208.
13. Emery, 49.
14. Lothrop Withington, ed., *Caleb Haskell's Diary* (Newburyport: William H. Huse, 1881), 6.
15. Emery, 52.
16. MA Archives, 180:241.
17. Broadside, BHS, 1,392; "Negroes as Soldiers," MHS *Proceedings*, 6 (1862), 184–85.
18. Swett, *History of Bunker Hill*, 57; "Craft's Journal of the Siege of Boston," *EIHC*, 3 (1861):134.
19. "Craft's Journal of the Siege," 137; the trial would have been earlier, but Mansfield was "not well enough."
20. 138.
21. "Orderly Book of Col William Henshaw," MHS *Proceedings*, 15 (1876):155.
22. Letters of Colonel Ebenezer Francis Collection, ALS, BHS, 18,175.
23. Herbert T. Wade and Robert A. Lively, *this glorious cause . . .* (Princeton: Princeton University Press, 1958), 171.
24. Letters of Col. Ebenezer Francis Collection, ALS, 18, 176.
25. Wade and Lively, 188.
26. "The Revolutionary Journal of James Stevens of Andover Mass," *EIHC*, 48 (1912):44; Nathaniel Cleaves His Book 1775, MS, BHS; "Craft's Journal of the Siege," 56.
27. 135; "Orderly Book of Col. William Henshaw," 140.
28. "Orderly Book of Capt. Enoch Putnam of Danvers, 1776," *EIHC*, 67 (1931):57.

29. Also, see "Craft's Journal of the Siege," 139.
30. Petition of Israel Trask of Gloucester to the Congress of the United States, February 6, 1844, Cape Ann Historical Society, 81.
31. Philip Chadwick Foster Smith, ed., *The Journals of Ashley Bowen of Marblehead* (Salem: Peabody Museum, 1973), 2:446, 454–55; Wade and Lively, 186.
32. "Orderly Book of Capt. Enoch Putnam," 52.
33. 49.
34. "Craft's Journal of the Siege," 53; Wade and Lively, 186; Fitch Edward Oliver, ed., *The Diary of William Pynchon of Salem* (Boston: Houghton Mifflin, 1890), 3; Octavius Pickering, *The Life of Timothy Pickering* (Boston: Little, Brown, 1817), 1:92.
35. Withington, 6; also, "The Revolutionary Journal of James Stevens," 47; Nathaniel Cleaves His Book, June 30, 1775; Henry B. Dawson, "Diary of David How," *Gleanings from the Harvest-Field of American History* (Morrisania, NY: 1865), 5.
36. 5–6; Wade and Lively, 174; "Revolutionary Letters and Other Documents," *EIHC* 14 (1877):236.
37. "Orderly Book of Capt. Enoch Putnam," 379.
38. 250.
39. Nathaniel Cleaves His Book, July 24, October 3, November 4, 23, 1775.
40. John J. Currier, *History of Newburyport, Mass. 1764–1905* (Newburyport: John J. Currier, 1906), 1:556; "Major Meigs' Journal," MHS *Collections*, 2nd Series, 2 (1814): 227–28; "Journal of Ebenezer Wild," MHS *Proceedings*, 2nd Series, 2 (1886):267; "Journal Kept by Henry Dearborn," 276; Amos Everett Jewett and Emily Mabel Adams Jewett, *Rowley, Massachusetts* (Rowley: Jewett Family of America, 1946), 70–71.
41. Withington, 10.
42. Dawson, 8. The "Congress" was a mortar among the prize munitions cargo on board the transport *Nancy* captured by Capt. Manley of Marblehead in late November 1775.

CHAPTER TWELVE

BIRTH OF THE CONTINENTAL NAVY

The steady stream of British cargo traffic standing toward Massachusetts Bay was ready-made prey for General Washington, who faced a chronic scarcity of munitions and war material. Unable to obtain fresh supplies and fuel locally, the enemy hauled this freight, along with ordnance, from Nova Scotia, the West Indies, and the British Isles. In August 1775, possibly at the suggestion of John Manley or John Glover of Marblehead, Washington decided to send out armed ships with the double purpose of disrupting the British shipping lanes and capturing badly needed materials for his siege lines. Since Boston was occupied, smaller ports to the north and south had to be employed.

The *Hannah*

No American navy existed, so Washington chose the feisty patriot soldier Col. John Glover of the seaworthy Marblehead 21st Regiment to carry out his plan. Glover's trading schooner, the 45-ton *Hannah*, named for his wife, was the earliest vessel leased by the Continental Congress. The Marbleheader conducted a fisheries trade from his own warehouse and cooper's shop in Beverly. At Glover's landing, the *Hannah* was converted into the first armed vessel of the Continental Army. Writing from Winter Hill on August 16 to his wife in Beverly, Ebenezer Francis noted hearing that the schooner was being outfitted. Glover's friend, Nicholson Broughton, an experienced seaman and a captain in the Marblehead regiment, was appointed commander. Eight days later, a volunteer company of Marbleheaders 193

John Glover, owner of the
schooner *Hannah*, the first armed
vessel of the Continental Army.
Lithograph by Fabronius, after
the sketch by John Trumbull.

marched in from Cambridge. On September 5, armed with cannon,
swivels, and about forty officers and crew, the first armed warship
under Continental commission spread her sails from Beverly harbor.[1]

Broughton was to seize all vessels serving the ministerial army
"laden with Soldiers, Arms, Ammunition, or Provisions for or from
sd Army" bound to or from Boston. His objective was to obtain
supplies only. "Engagement with any armed Vessel of the Enemy"
was to be avoided. After proceedings in prize courts, officers and
crew of the *Hannah* would be awarded money (the captain, six shares;
privates, one share each) equaling one-third the value of captured
nonmilitary cargo.[2]

Two days out, Broughton captured the unarmed *Unity* off Cape
Ann, bound from Portsmouth to Boston laden with naval stores and
lumber. He brought the 260-ton ship—the first capture by a Continental Army vessel—into Gloucester harbor and left his prize and
her seven-man crew in custody of the town's committee of safety.
Unfortunately, the *Hannah* had taken a New Hampshire vessel captured earlier, on September 5, by the H.M.S. *Lively* with a prize crew
of British sailors. Because she was an American merchantman, the
Unity did not qualify for prize money. After hearing the news,
Broughton's crew turned mutinous. The thirty-six rebellious members were paraded to Cambridge where they were court-martialed
and found guilty of "Mutiny, Riot and Disobedience of orders." Nathaniel Cleaves of Beverly noted on "Saturday the 23 Day": "this for
Noon over to prospect hill there forteen Marelhead men wiped and
Drumed out of the army. One had 39 stripes and thirteen of them
had 20 stripes the rest of them payed 20 shillings Lawful Money a
peas."[3]

Nicholson Broughton, commander of the schooner *Hannah*. Courtesy, Peabody Museum of Salem.

Broughton, with a new crew, resumed hunting for enemy cargo carriers during the daytime and ducking back to shore at dark. On the morning of October 10, the *Hannah* sailed from Beverly. Later in the day, she was chased back into the harbor by the sixteen-gun British sloop *Nautilus*, which had arrived in bay waters with the *Falcon* in mid-April and had been looking for the "Rebel Schooner."[4] When the *Hannah* got inside the bar, she grounded on mud flats in a cove just outside the harbor. About four o'clock, townspeople boarded and removed her guns, to keep them out of enemy hands.

Capt. John Collins, the *Nautilus*'s captain, anchored outside the bar and ordered grapeshot fired at the stranded *Hannah*, forcing the crew to abandon. Collins hoisted boats and made ready combustibles, intent on setting her afire. But it was ebb tide and the receding waters soon left the schooner high and dry, so the plan was dropped. Firing continued. Irritated that Beverly had been providing safe haven for the *Hannah*, the *Nautilus* directed her retributive broadsides towards town. Aiming for the meetinghouse spire (presently the Unitarian Church on Cabot Street), one shot crashed through the chaise-house of Thomas Stevens; another shattered a house chimney on the other side of the street. Many alarmed townswomen fled beyond range, while men armed with muskets rushed toward the shoreline.

The subsiding tide soon grounded the *Nautilus* also, which lay careened, so no guns could be brought to bear. About two hundred townspeople hurried to Hospital Point (Salem Willows) with two field pieces—a 4- and 6-pounder—and raked the helpless vessel. From behind rocks on the Beverly side, militia fired both from their muskets and from the rescued guns. In the early evening, the battered

Nautilus floated on a rising tide. Shot through her hull, rigging, and sails, and with two wounded, she moved slowly out to sea. William Wetmore, who observed the exchange from Hospital Point, noted: "she got off agn abt 1/2 after 7 P.M.—for 4 hours we fired upon her constantly & tis supposed yt she recd some of our shot—We fired very badly many times."[5]

Washington's Fleet

On October 4, George Washington ordered John Glover and Stephen Moylan to take responsibility for outfitting two more armed vessels. Moylan, who had been a successful merchant in Philadelphia, was mustermaster general of the army and assigned to work with Glover.

Late in September, the Newburyport committee of safety had proposed to the General Court to outfit an "Armed Vessell." If the colony assumed the costs, the committee would procure a local vessel, equip it, and raise the necessary complement. Many vessels, the committee explained, chased by "the Piratical Ships of our Enemies" had sought asylum in Newburyport. But others, loaded with provisions, lumber, and fuel, had been taken before they reached the Merrimack. They maintained that an armed craft stationed in Newburyport would make the whole bay "safe from these depredations." Indeed, the patrol ship would improve security for all harbors between Cape Ann and Cape Elizabeth. The legislature tried to interest Washington, but the general, who planned to engage Continental soldiers, declined the offer.[6]

Glover and Moylan were ordered to procure two vessels "upon the best Terms you can—let them be prime Sailors, put them into the best Order & loose no Time." This was critical, as many transports were "hourly expected at Boston," wrote Col. Joseph Reed, Washington's military secretary.[7] If unsuccessful on the North Shore, they were to proceed to Newburyport. Two schooners, however, were found. Renamed the *Hancock* (formerly the *Speedwell*, belonging to Thomas Grant of Marblehead) and the *Franklin* (formerly the *Eliza*, belonging to Archibald Selman), they were outfitted in Beverly. The 72-ton *Hancock* (six guns) and 60-ton *Franklin* (four guns) were manned with experienced seamen from Glover's 21st Regiment and commanded by Nicholson Broughton and John Selman, respectively, both captains in the regiment.[8]

With Broughton in command, the vessels stood out of Beverly harbor on the morning of October 22 headed toward the Gulf of St. Lawrence in search of two munitions brigs.[9] Earlier, the Continental Congress had received intelligence that the transports had left England on August 11, unescorted and bound for Quebec. On October 5, in the first naval orders of the war, the Congress ordered Washington to intercept them. Broughton and Selman were assigned to the task.[10] Though the vessels were not sighted, in the course of cruising toward St. Lawrence Bay the Marbleheaders learned of several large cannon at St. John's (now Prince Edward Island) and that military recruitment was going on.

After they landed at St. John's on November 17, the intended cargo was found too hefty to move; instead, they carried off Judge Thomas Wright and Commander in Chief Phillip Callbeck! Reinforced by wine, rum, and liquors uncovered during the rampage, the rowdy Marbleheaders recklessly plundered Callbeck's warehouses. Personal belongings and furnishings were taken from his, Governor Patterson's, and others' homes. Callbeck later protested to Washington: "In Mrs Callbeck's bed room they broke open her drawers and Trunks . . . took the Bed and window curtains . . . Rings Braclets Buckles and Trinkets, also some . . . Cloaths."[11] Even the fifty-nine-ounce silver Province seal was stolen! Foolishly, the Marbleheaders presumed their disruption of recruitment would help Arnold and Montgomery, who were preparing to attack Quebec. When the contingent returned to Beverly and reported to Washington in Cambridge, the commander was furious with their unwarranted conduct. The St. John's officials were released, along with ten vessels which had been captured, since Washington feared the incident would hurt relations with the northern provinces and push them toward closer cooperation with England. (At the time, American policy was that the colonies were warring against the British ministry, not against the king and his subjects, and attacking only those vessels in the service of the ministerial army.) Regrettably, the first naval expedition of the American Revolution had been an unqualified failure.[12]

Meanwhile, two more schooners, the 64-ton *Warren* (formerly the *Hawk*, belonging to John Twisden of Marblehead) and the 74-ton *Lee* (formerly the *Two Brothers* belonging to Thomas Stevens of Marblehead) were outfitted at the Beverly naval base. The soon-to-be-renowned John Manley of Marblehead, having recently moved from Boston, was given command of the *Lee*, with an armament of four 4-pounders and ten swivels. His fifty-man crew was detached from the 21st Regiment. On October 28, Manley sailed from Beverly, followed early in November by the *Warren*. The *Warren* was commanded by Capt. Winborn Adams of Col. Enoch Poor's New Hampshire regiment. These vessels were reserved for cruising Boston shipping lanes and permitted to capture all inbound and outbound craft in British service. (The *Hannah*, while officially in service until November 6, had been inactive since mid-October.) The four Beverly and Marblehead Continental schooners commissioned were joined early in November by the schooners *Washington* and *Harrison*, outfitted and manned at Plymouth.[13]

Washington was unhappy at how long it had taken to outfit the schooners. His military secretary, Col. Joseph Reed, wrote to Glover: "The General is much dissatisfied I cannot but think a Desire to secure particular Friends or particular Interests does mingle in the Managment of these Vessels." Washington's suspicions may have been partly justified, but Moylan defended Glover. In a letter to Reed on October 24 Moylan said: "I realy & sincerely believe he has the cause much at heart, & that he had don his best, (in the fitting out these four last vessels), for the publick Service." Moylan blamed the difficulty and delay "in procureing the thousand things necessary for one of these vessels . . . you must Search all over Salem Marblehead Danvers & Beverly for every Little thing that is wanting." And Moylan had little praise for the slow-moving jobbing carpenters whom he termed "the Idlest Scoundrels in nature, If I coud have procured others, I shoud have dismissd the whole Gang of them." He blamed the independent, democratic spirit of the times and the Marbleheaders' reluctance to obey Glover, a man with longer standing as a friend and neighbor than as a commander. Moylan noted that "there is one reason, & I think a Substantial one, why a person born in the same town or neighborhood should not be employed on publick affairs . . . in that town . . . it is that the Spirit of equality which reigns thro' this Country, will make him affraid of exerting . . . authority . . . whereas a few hearty damns from a person who did not Care a damn for them would have a much better effect."[14]

The Capture of the *Nancy*

Washington's besieging army desperately needed gunpowder, shot, mortars, and ordnance of every description. In October, the commander in chief had written to the Congress, "a fortunate Capture of an Ordinance Ship would give new Life to the Camp and an immediate turn to the Issue of this Campaign."[15] The next month Washington heard that an important munitions-laden ordnance brig was overdue to Boston.

On November 26, Washington notified Beverly prize-agent William Bartlett to send out any armed vessels in port "as soon as possible & keep a sharp Look out for this Brigg." Manley, who was in Beverly taking on provisions, set out immediately. Ten miles east of Cape Ann, the 250-ton *Nancy* was sighted, bound for Boston. The captain of the lightly armed transport welcomed aboard eight men who had rowed over from the *Lee*, which he believed to be a pilot boat. The

NEWBURY-PORT, December 8.
The following are the material Articles taken by Capt. Manly, in the Lee privateer, from on board the brig Nancy, bound from London to Boston, which was carried into Cape-Ann last week.

2000 *Musquets with accoutrements compleat*
100,000 *Musquet flints*
  250 *Wall-piece ditto*
 5000 *Carbine ditto*
20,500 *Empty paper cartridges, from three to twelve pounders*
   50 *Camp kettles*
   60 *Reams of cartridge paper*
    3 *Boxes of tin*
   31 *Tons and 500 wt. of musquet shot*
 1200 *Pounds wt. of buck shot*
   61 *Spare spunges and rammer heads, from three to twenty four pounders.*
 3000 *Round shot twelve pounders*
 4000 *Ditto   six pounders*
   10 *Tons of junck*
   11 *Mortar beds 13, 10 and 8 inch*
    7 *Ammunition waggons*
   75 *Carbines with bayonets, and other accoutrements compleat*
  100 *Camp kettles, with frying pan covers*
   50 *Round corcasses, thirteen inch*
  100 *Oblong ditto eight inch*
 4056 *Round shot }*
 2864 *Case ditto } fixed to wood*
 7450 *Caps of cartridge paper, twenty four, twelve and six pounders*
10,800 *Empty flannel cartridges, twenty four, twelve and six pounders*
 8,440 *Fixt fuses, 4 and half inch*
  350 *Eempty shells, 13, 10, 8 and a half inch*
16,000 *Tin tubes, fixt. 6 pounders*
  100 *Bottoms of wood for mortars 13 inch*
20,000 *Iron round shot, 1 pounders, in 200 boxes*
    2 *Barrels of meal'd powder*
  100 *Dozen of port fires*
20,000 *Spikes, 7 and 8 inch*
    2 *Pairs of calipers, the 1 brass the other iron*
    1 *Laboratory kittle*
   36 *Copper ladels*
   11 *Iron melting ladels*
   23 *Lantharns, and 15 dark ditto*
    2 *Perpendiculars, new pattern*
    2 *Iron cannon, 6 pounders, on deck*
    1 *Brass 13 inch mortar, weight 2700 two quarters, sixteen pounds*
    1 *Bed compleat for ditto, weight 2700 two quarters, sixteen pounds.*
Together with a great variety of other articles, viz. Forge and hand bellows, hudge

Among the vital ordnance captured aboard the brig *Nancy* was a thirteen-inch brass cannon, "The Congress." From *The Essex Journal and New-Hampshire Packet*, December 8, 1775. The first issue of this Newburyport weekly was published on December 4, 1773 by Isaiah Thomas and Henry Walter Tinges. During 1775, John Mycall, an Amesbury schoolmaster, had become the sole owner. Courtesy, Essex Institute, Salem, Mass.

boarders drew their weapons and forced the chagrined commander to surrender his brig. Before nightfall on November 28, Manley had brought the *Nancy* into Cape Ann, with a cargo of inestimable value, including 2,000 muskets and bayonets, 100,000 flints, 8,400 fuses, 31 tons of musket shot, and a monstrous, thirteen-inch, modern, brass mortar and other military stores. The mortar, pronounced the "noblest piece of ordnance ever landed in America," was christened "The Congress."[16]

Fearing an attempt might be made to recapture the brig, four companies were sent from Cambridge and about 450 Essex County militia were ordered to Gloucester for guard duty and unloading. Moses Jewett's horse troop galloped from Ipswich. Lt. Abel Kimball and twelve men marched from Andover; Isaac Dodge headed an Ipswich-Topsfield-Wenham contingent. Parts of Moses Brown's and

Joseph Whipple's coastal defense forces came up from Beverly and Manchester. Forty others traveled from Marblehead. The *Nancy* was too valuable to risk losing.[17]

Boxes, kegs, and chests of every description were unloaded in Freshwater and Kettle coves, Magnolia. For days, a continuous stream of wagons trundled the stretch from Magnolia to Beverly, then to Cambridge. Nathaniel Cleaves noted on December 2 the heartening arrival of several Beverly teamsters. "Mr. Jonathan Conant John Woodbery Caleb Balch Sam Conant Came to head quarters With their teams brought a morter and other War Like stores from Cape an." "The huzzas on the occasion," wrote Stephen Moylan, "I dare say were heard through all the territories of our most gracious sovereign in this Province." Capture of the *Nancy* gave a boost to enlistments for the new year and to morale of the munitions-starved army encircling Boston.[18]

John Manley—First Naval Hero

Manley delighted Washington with four repeat performances in December. On December 3, he brought his next important prize into Marblehead harbor: the 300-ton ship *Concord* out of Glasgow with a cargo of dry goods and coal. Six days later, he captured the ship *Jenny*, a 300-ton vessel seven weeks out of London, lightly armed and carrying coal, cheese, porter, and forty live hogs. On the same day, Manley captured the *Little Hannah*, a 150-ton, Boston-bound brig from Antigua with a prize cargo consisting of 131 casks of rum, 98 cases of gin, some cocoa, 123 gallons of "Spirit," and oranges, limes, and lemons.[19] The *New-England Chronicle* noted how the *Little Hannah*, "wanting a pilot, and seeing the ship and privateer together, supposed the latter could help her to one; she accordingly made for them.—She soon came up, when Capt. Manly readily afforded her pilotage, and conducted her, together with the ship, safely into Beverly Harbor."[20]

Manley's fourth December capture was the sloop *Betsey*, fourteen days out of Virginia and carrying Indian corn, oats, and potatoes intended for the British army in Boston. On board were four rebel Virginians, an assemblyman, a militia officer, and two shipmasters, whom Royal Governor Lord Dunmore was sending to Boston for trial. Also on board was a vexed Tory colonel coming to request a commission from William Howe. And Manley had a valuable bonus for Washington: papers and letters which disclosed Lord Dunmore's plans to crush rebel activities in Virginia.[21]

Manley had become America's first Revolutionary War naval hero. For his successes, Washington commissioned him commodore of the fleet. After capture of the *Betsey*, a Beverly citizen wrote that Manley had become so famous that "as many towns contend for the honour of his birth as there did for that of Homer's."[22] His fame spread throughout the colonies, but, unlike other Revolutionary figures, Manley has been since forgotten.

Washington's Navy in 1776

On January 1, 1776, Col. Stephen Moylan came to Beverly to prepare the ships for another cruise, this time authorized by the Continental Congress, then sitting in Philadelphia. A reorganization had taken place, and the armed schooners, although still commanded by Washington, were placed under authority of the newly formed Marine Committee of the Congress.

With the new year, enlistments of the soldiers on board Washington's fleet had expired; officers and men had quit. The sailors were grumbling over not having received all wages from the previous year. Also, because of delays in court condemnation proceedings, prize money had not been distributed. "What a pity," wrote Stephen Moylan, "as vessels are every day arriving: indeed the chance of taking any, is pretty well over, as a man-of-war [*Fowey*] is stationed so as to command the entrance of Beverly, Salem and Marblehead." On January 3, Colonel Glover was in Marblehead to "beat up" for his regiment. Left unemployed by the war, many men returned to the army and privateering. By the twenty-fourth, all North Shore Continental cruisers were manned and plying the coastline.[23]

All vessels had new commanders. Commodore Manley took the fast *Hancock*. Broughton and Selman had resigned, still sore over Washington's reprimand. Capt. Daniel Waters from New Hampshire assumed command of the *Lee*. Samuel Tucker of Marblehead was placed at the helm of the *Franklin*; Charles Dyer captained the *Harrison*, based at Plymouth; William Burke would skipper the *Warren*. The commanders were commissioned captains in the "Army of the Colonies of North America." The *Washington*, which had been captured off Cape Ann in December, was replaced by the *Lynch*, owned by Col. John Lee of Marblehead; in February, she was chopped free in Manchester harbor and brought to Beverly to be outfitted, with John Ayres of Boston appointed commander.[24] The schooners sailed day cruises between Cape Ann and Cape Cod, as the year before, in search of British craft passing in and out of Boston.

Most crew were soldiers in the Continental Army, receiving the same pay as they would receive on land. In addition, they were entitled to one-third the value of every capture, after condemnation proceedings in the courts of admiralty. In early April, Glover was ordered to man the privateers from his regiment, so long as enough men remained on shore to guard the stores and prize vessels at Beverly. Some Essex County blacks served, most of whom were "servants" or slaves whose prize money was expected by their masters. Also on board were a number of British sailors who had been captured aboard Boston-bound transports. Many Negroes and British were probably not Continental soldiers, but were serving solely for prize money.[25]

Prize agents were appointed to libel all captures, that is, claim them in admiralty court actions in their jurisdictions. After legal condemnation, they were to sell the vessels at public auction and apportion the proceeds. On October 10, 1775, Tristram Dalton of Newburyport was appointed first agent in Massachusetts for the united colonies. William Bartlett became Continental prize agent for Beverly. Shortly afterward, John Glover secured the same post in Marblehead for his brother, Jonathan Glover. Bartlett and Glover agreed to handle jointly all prizes taken in Beverly, Marblehead, or Salem. These appointments were valuable "political plums"; commission for their services was set at 2 1/2 percent of sales of condemned cargoes and of local purchases by the armed schooners. Winthrop Sargent, who came from a prominent merchant family, became agent for Gloucester. Cape Ann was not considered a safe place to lay up prizes, and Sargent was instructed to send all captures to Beverly. Evacuation of the British from Boston in March of 1776 reduced activity; no longer was a prize agent warranted in each port. On April 23, John Bradford was appointed Continental agent for entire Massachusetts. But Bradford had trouble getting former agents, particularly Glover, to recognize him. They refused until he could produce a written commission.[26]

In December 1775, Timothy Pickering, Jr., was appointed judge of the admiralty court for the counties of Essex, Middlesex, and Suffolk, the most consequential of the three districts. The Congress had ordered condemnation of prizes in the admiralty courts of each colony, but procedural details had bogged down the actual trials. The first sitting was not until April 16, 1776.[27]

On April 23, the court condemned and decreed that cargoes of seven captured ships, including Manley's five, could be auctioned. The *Jenny*'s lading brought over £3,000, one-third going to Manley and his crew. The *Little Hannah*'s returned almost £4,000. The spirits on board must have been of high quality, as Washington purchased thirty gallons for his personal use. He had his sights set on other goods, also. Shortly after the *Little Hannah*'s capture, on December 10, Col. Stephen Moylan wrote Bartlett:

> Limes, Lemons & Oranges on board, which being perishable, you
> must sell Immediately, the General will want some of each, as well
> as of the sweetmeats & pickles, that are on board; as his Lady will
> be here to day or to morrow you will please to pick up such things
> on board as you think will be acceptable to her & send them as soon
> as possible—he does not mean to receive anything without payment,
> which you will please to attend to—.[28]

Whatever Bartlett sent was of inferior quality, as Manley's crew had
already scooped up the best fruits. Moylan indignantly announced
that the value of all articles taken would be deducted from the crew's
prize money.

The *Little Hannah* was pressed into Continental service, renamed
the *Despatch*, and placed under command of Stephen Cleveland of
Salem. With a load of fish for decoy, Cleveland carried messages for
presentation to the American commissioners in France. He was to
sell his cargo and return with arms and ammunition.[29]

Late in January, Manley captured two transport ships, the *Norfolk*
and *Happy Return*, off Nantasket. They were bound for Boston, laden
with coal and potatoes. Prize crews were put on board and started
for Plymouth harbor, while Manley bravely stood off the eight-gun
sloop *General Gage*. General Washington sent a letter of congratulations for his latest successes.

> I received your agreeable Letter of the 26th instant giveing an
> account of your haveing taken & Carried into Plymouth two of the
> Enemys transports. Your Conduct in engageing the eight gun
> Schooner, with so few hands as you went out with, your attention
> in Securing your prizes, & your general good behaviour since you
> first engaged in the Service, Merits Mine, & your Countrys thanks.

Washington, never especially pleased with his army sea captains,
concluded:

> I wish you Coud inspire the Captains of the other Armed schooners
> under your Command with Some of your activity & Industry—
> Cannot you appoint Such Stations for them, where they May have
> the best Chance of intercepting Supplies going to the enemy.[30]

Manley narrowly missed capture on January 30 when pursued by
the fourteen-gun brig *Hope*. Realizing a challenge would be senseless,
Manley attempted to escape, but grounded near Cohasset. The brig
anchored as close as possible and lobbed four hundred shot at the
disabled *Hancock*, inflicting only minor damage in a five-hour barrage
lasting until seven o'clock in the evening. The next morning, with
Manley's crew ashore, the enemy boarded and attempted unsuccess-

fully to set the vessel afire. Subsequently, the venerable Marblehead captain refloated his schooner and refitted her for another cruise.[31]

A New Command

In April, Commodore Manley was awarded command of the thirty-two-gun frigate *Hancock*, then under construction in Newburyport. The sturdy oaken frigate was one of thirteen that the Continental Congress authorized on December 13, 1775.

Some merchantmen were converted for wartime service, but the Congress required first-class men-of-war. Two of the thirteen were constructed in Massachusetts, and were among the four that got to sea during 1777. Thomas Cushing of Boston, who was a Marine Committee member, wanted both vessels constructed along the Merrimack, which he believed most convenient and having the colony's safest harbor. They were built at the Cross boat yard, near the foot of Federal Street. Jonathan Greenleaf and Stephen Cross, Newburyport's representatives in the General Assembly, working as partners, secured both contracts. Already a successful shipwright, Jonathan Greenleaf had formed in partnership with Stephen and Ralph Cross, Jr., prior to the Revolution. Greenleaf was charged with building the thirty-two-gun frigate *Hancock*, while the Cross brothers were responsible for the twenty-four-gun *Boston*.[32]

Though reputable builders, Greenleaf and Cross had secured the contracts through influence, and some envious Newburyporters denounced Cushing's decision. A Newburyport committee, which included rival shipping interests, sponsored a resolution, which was voted at the February 27, 1776 town meeting, "to remonstrate" Thomas Cushing for "the ill Convenience & unsafety of setting up the aforesaid Ships in the places where the said Messrs. Greenleaf & Cross propose to erect them." Earlier, Elias Hasket Derby of Salem had tried to get one vessel for the Hackett boat yard at Salisbury Point, where he had dealings. Whether Newburyporters were sincerely interested in seeing the frigates constructed in a safer location upriver, or simply engaging in local political banter, is speculation. Neither Greenleaf nor Cross were returned to the legislature nor elected to any major town office in 1776.[33]

On June 3, the *Boston* "was launched in the view of a great number of Spectators" under command of Capt. Hector McNeill. By July 14, eleven days later, the *Hancock* had slid into the Merrimack and was tied up alongside Long Wharf in Newburyport. Cushing boasted of the *Hancock*—which was 136'7" on the lower deck and had a 35'6" breadth of beam—that there was "not one Superior to her on the Continent." Both ships were brought around to Boston for outfitting.

Originally scheduled to sail during the fall, they were delayed many months because ordnance and materials were scarce.[34]

Finally, on May 22, 1777, Commodore Manley sailed out of Boston, leading the two Continental frigates and nine privateers to seek out the enemy frigate *Milford*, which had unleashed havoc along the coast. Within a few days, however, the independent-minded privateersmen had taken separate paths. On June 7, after a damaging fire-fight, the twenty-eight-gun British frigate *Fox* lowered her colors to the Newburyport-built vessels. Homeward bound, off Halifax on July 6, the frigates were chased by three British warships. Manley struck (surrendered) the *Hancock* to the forty-four-gun ship *Rainbow*, while the *Boston* escaped up the Sheepscot River near present Westport Island, Maine, to Wiscasset. Later blamed for not helping the revered Manley avoid capture and for loss of the *Hancock* and her 229 men, McNeill was suspended from his command.[35]

The seriousness of the loss was compounded when the *Hancock* was taken into British service and renamed the *Iris*. Manley wasted in prison until late December 1778, when he returned to assume command of the *Cumberland*, a privateer. He subsequently commanded the eighteen-gun privateer *Jason* and the Continental frigate *Hague*, to complete a naval career surpassed by few men.

Spring Cruises

During the spring of 1776, Washington's privateers routinely hunted in pairs or squadron-style, and with success. On February 1, the *Franklin* and the *Lee*, commanded by Samuel Tucker and Daniel Waters, respectively, captured a large brigantine, the *Henry and Esther*, laden with cords of wood, butts of water, and forty suits of bedding, and sent her into Annisquam harbor. On March 3, four of the schooners engaged the brig *Hope*; during the half-hour exchange the six-gun vessel was only slightly damaged. Toward dark, the schooners, really no match for the brig, sailed off toward Cape Ann. The action had been observed from Marblehead and by people perched atop rooftops and steeples of Salem. Three days later, on March 6, four of the schooners seized the *Susannah* and brought her into Portsmouth. The 300-ton transport contained butts of porter, foodstuffs, and other goods. In mid-March, four privateers captured the 300-ton *Stakesby*, out of London, bound to Boston. The prize—brought in at nighttime—ran up on the rocks at Brace's Cove on the southern end of Cape Ann. Most of the cargo was lost. Early in April, Manley, Ayres, and Waters captured the brig *Elizabeth* off Cape Ann. She had been sailing from Boston to Halifax laden with evacuees' goods and carrying sixty-three passengers, including thirteen of the

"King's Troops."[36] The new year had begun prosperously indeed, for the whole fleet.

Weeks after Gen. William Howe's mid-March evacuation, Boston waters continued to be good hunting grounds. A convoy of over thirty transports carrying 3,000 Highland troops had left Glasgow bound for Boston, not knowing the town had been abandoned. A storm, meanwhile, had scattered the fleet. Most, but not all, arrived before the rearguard British squadron had left Boston harbor. On June 7, the *Lee*, the *Warren*, and the *Lynch* teamed to take the transport ship *Anne* off Cape Cod. She was carrying 110 troops of the 71st Highland Regiment and about 30 sailors. After outsailing her pursuers on the previous day, the *Anne* becalmed when "the Privateers, by Favour of their Oars," wrote Capt. Maxwell aboard the *Anne*, "rowed up, two under her Stern, and one upon her Bow, by which the *Anne*'s Guns could not bear. . . . A Council of War was held, and it was resolved to surrender." The sailors and about one-third of the troops were carried to Marblehead on board the *Lee*, with the *Warren* taking the balance to Plymouth. On June 15, the 180-ton *Annabella* brig and *George*, a 220-ton ship, both transports, "made the land off Cape Ann." Early next morning, sailing near Boston harbor, they were chased and fired upon by four of Washington's schooners. During the afternoon, they were forced to break away and anchored in Plymouth harbor. Once again, about sunset, joined by the Connecticut brig *Defence* and the schooner *Hancock*, the squadron came up. The transports "stood up" toward Nantasket Road, stopped and prepared for action, during which the *Annabella* grounded. The *George* was surrounded. About 11:00 P.M., the *Defence* came about to the *George*'s starboard side and a "hot engagement" ensued. Finally, damaged and hemmed, the enemy ship struck. During the skirmish, the major was killed, seven or eight soldiers and several others wounded. The dead were buried in the sands off Long Island amid the tears of their wives and children, who had accompanied them (which often was the custom) across the Atlantic. Two companies of the 71st Highland Regiment—about 200 troops—were on board. On June 18, the same vessels took the *Lord Howe*, with one hundred more Scottish grenadiers on board. Eventually, more than four hundred of the Highlanders were dispersed into the countryside. Many settled in Essex County, where they found work on farms or in craftsmen's shops.[37]

Supply ships continued to sail towards Boston, unknowing what awaited. Capt. Samuel Tucker of Marblehead was appointed to the *Hancock* when Manley was given the Continental frigate under construction at Newburyport. On May 7, Tucker captured two brigs within sight of four remaining British warships on Nantasket Road.

He brought into "Lynn Haven" the 120-ton *Jane* out of Cork, laden with coal, beef, foodstuffs, and candles, and the 100-ton *William* from Fayal (Western Islands), with a cargo of wines and fruits.[38]

Besides the May 7 captures, Tucker also had joined in spring squadron operations. On July 22, in company of the *Franklin*, now commanded by Capt. John Skimmer, Tucker captured the 230-ton armed ship *Peggy*, bound from Halifax toward New York with a cargo of hose, foodstuffs, beer, wines, and other goods. A native Marblehead sea captain and a lieutenant in Glover's regiment, Tucker came well qualified. During the French and Indian War, at eleven years of age, he left home and shipped out on an English sloop-of-war bound for Louisburg. Having begun early to store a vast naval experience, particularly the art of maneuvering in the face of the enemy, Tucker served through most of the war, chalking up a record of more captures and more sea fights than almost any other Revolutionary commander.[39]

Capture of a Powder Ship

Late in 1775, according to local tradition, Capt. James Mugford, along with other Marbleheaders, was impressed by a gang from the *Lively*, then lying in the harbor opposite "Skinner's Head" on the Neck side. Upon hearing of his capture, Mugford's wife boarded the *Lively* to request his release. She told the captain they had recently married and that she was dependent on his support. The captain permitted Mugford to leave.

Mugford had been serving on board a British sloop-of-war stationed off Marblehead, where he had overheard sailors talking about a "powder ship" expected from England. He communicated this intelligence and requested a commission to capture the ship, which General Artemas Ward, then in Philadelphia, granted. (Ward had taken command of Massachusetts Continental forces when Washington left for New York.) Mugford hastily outfitted the *Franklin*, Tucker's former command, and set out with twenty of Glover's men.[40]

On Friday morning, May 17, 1776, outside Boston, Mugford spotted the 300-ton *Hope*, bound from Cork with seventeen crew and armed with six guns. Mugford and twenty men boarded, within full sight of British men-of-war anchored a few miles away at Nantasket Road; she struck her colors without a fight. In a move of desperation, the captain had ordered the vessel slowed, to give British warships time to reach them. Mugford threatened captain and crew with instant death if the order were executed. The terrified men refused to obey their captain, and the *Hope* fell to Mugford.

The *Hope* had started across the Atlantic in convoy with several

CAPT. JAMES MUGFORD,
OF THE
SCHR. FRANKLIN CONTINENTAL CRUISER 1776.

Lithograph by L. H. Bradford & Co. Published by Glover Broughton
in 1854. Courtesy, Essex Institute, Salem, Mass.

other transports, guarded by a frigate, but got separated. They were
laden with military stores for the British in Boston. After it was
learned the port had been evacuated, the remaining transports sailed
for Halifax.

Capture of the *Hope* possibly was the most valuable of the entire
war. Her cargo consisted of 1,000 carbines with bayonets, carpentry
and entrenching tools, and, most importantly, 1,500 barrels of gunpowder. At the time of her capture, Washington's stock of ammunition was not more than nine rounds per man![41]

It was ebb tide, and the captured vessel grounded passing through
shallow Pulling-Point Gut while being sailed into Boston harbor. She
would lie stuck until nighttime high tide. Taking no risk of losing
her valuable cargo, the American command dispatched a fleet of
boats from Boston to bring up the contents. Henry Hallowell, a Lynn
soldier stationed at Dorchester Point since early April with Israel
Hutchinson's regiment, noted, "ship got aground and for fear of
their barges myself and hundreds saved the ship and cargo and a
Very great prize for us."[42]

On Sunday, May 19, the *Franklin* glided out of Boston joined by a
small privateer, the *Lady Washington*. In the darkness, Mugford ran
aground in the complicated gut channel at Point Shirley, in the same
vicinity as did the *Hope* two days before. With the *Lady Washington*

anchored nearby, the British saw an opportunity to avenge their ignominious loss. About thirteen barges and pinnaces, some outfitted with swivels, carrying about two hundred armed men aboard, shoved off from the *Experiment* and *Renown* to launch a surprise night attack.

At about nine or ten o'clock, Mugford sighted the boats and hailed them to ask where they were from. "Boston," they answered. The astute commander ordered them to keep their distance or else he would fire. They pleaded "for God's sake not to fire," that they wanted to come aboard. Mugford ordered his men to discharge their blunderbusses and muskets.

The canny Marblehead captain cut his cable and brought the *Franklin*'s broadside to bear; cannon blasted musket shot directly into the cluster of boats. Before the guns could be reloaded, two or three boats came alongside and attempted to board. The twenty crew members bravely fought them off, using firearms, cutlasses, and pikes. Several sets of fingers which grabbed the gunwale were chopped off. Two boats were sunk, with many men lost. In the midst of battle, Mugford, gravely wounded in the chest, encouraged his men to continue: "*I am a dead man; don't give up the vessel; you will be able to beat them off.*" A few minutes later, he died. David How of Methuen, on shore with Dudley Sargent's regiment, reported: "She [*Franklin*] fired upon them and Sunk 2 or 3 Boats and its thought killed a grate Many of them so that they soon went off—they killed our Capt and one of the Hands." Eight or nine boats attacked the *Franklin*; the rest converged on the *Lady Washington* and her paltry seven-man crew. After a half-hour engagement with this tiny, valiant band, the British withdrew, with a loss of seventy men. The rising tide floated the *Franklin*, and the crew returned to port safely.[43]

On May 22, Mugford was given a grand Marblehead funeral. Colors at the fort and on board vessels in the harbor flew at half-mast. The hero sailor was carried from his home to the New Meeting House where Rev. Isaac Story conducted the ceremony. A large procession followed Mugford's body to the grave, including seventy men from Glover's regiment in Beverly, Mugford's widow accompanied by the captain's father, relatives, and local citizenry. During the funeral march, the *Franklin*'s minute guns fired, muffled drums rolled, and church bells tolled. At graveside, three volleys fired to salute Mugford, as the valiant commander was put to rest.[44]

Washington's fleet continued yeoman's service into 1777. Several captures had provided Continental forces with vitally needed ordnance. Capture of the *Nancy* was pivotal—second only to Knox's delivery of Ticonderoga's guns—in bringing the siege of Boston to a successful conclusion. The *Hope*'s 1,500 barrels of gunpowder were a godsend to the powder-starved troops. Washington's prowling fleet, with the state-commissioned privateers, forced England to escort her cargo and troop transports; warships performing guard duty were unavailable for offensive operations. The capture of the four troop transports prevented four hundred Highlanders from engaging American forces later in New York and New Jersey. Dozens of transports loaded with food, fuel, and clothing never reached Boston, causing the enemy cold nights and reducing them to a thin menu. Of more than twenty important captures made by Washington's Continental privateers from September 1775 through July 1776, most were executed by craft hailing from Essex County ports. Washington's Continental privateers continued to hunt Massachusetts waters, capturing more prizes, until disbanded by the Marine Committee in 1777. Essex County's exploits on Atlantic waters nevertheless continued and emerged as the county's most valuable wartime contribution.

1. William Bell Clark, ed., *Naval Documents of the American Revolution*, 2:36, Letters of Colonel Ebenezer Francis Collection, ALS, BHS, 18,188; Philip Chadwick Foster Smith, ed., *The Journals of Ashley Bowen of Marblehead* (Salem: Peabody Museum), 2:453, 455.
2. Clark, 1:1287–89.
3. Clark, 2:19, 36, 56–57, 92–93, 169, 175–76; Nathaniel Cleaves His Book 1775, MS, BHS; Ashley Bowen confirmed Cleaves's account; Smith, 2:457. At Washington's suggestion, John Langdon, a prominent New Hampshire merchant and the original owner, rewarded Broughton and Lts. John Glover, Jr., and John Devereaux for the recapture.
4. Clark, 2:362.
5. Clark, 2:386, 416, 417–418; Edwin M. Stone, *History of Beverly* (Boston: James Munroe, 1843), 64–66; "Extracts from the Interleaved Almanacs of William Wetmore of Salem," *EIHC*, 43 (1907):117–118; "Extracts from the Interleaved Almanacs Kept by John White of Salem," *EIHC*, 49 (1913):92; David Newall of Salem had his hand blown off while loading one of the cannon; one of the British crew died a few days later.
6. Clark, 2:218–19, 269, 278, 291–92.
7. 2:289–290.
8. 2:368, 387, 459, 461.
9. 2:565.
10. Coincidentally, the orders came just after Washington already had decided to expand the army's Continental fleet; Clark, 2:307–08, 441–42, 474, 637.
11. Clark, 2:1319–22.
12. 2:899–900, 1125–26, 1216, 1282; 3:289–90; William P. Upham, "A Memoir of Gen. John Glover," *EIHC*, 5 (1863):55.
13. Clark, 2:368–69, 412–13, 637–38.
14. 2:490, 589–90; the same kind of difficulties were experienced in Plymouth.
15. John C. Fitzpatrick, ed., *The Writings of Washington*, 4:24.
16. Clark, 2:1142, 1199, 1247; 3:48, 92; *The Essex Journal & New Hampshire Packet*, December 8, 1775; Manley's only earlier prize had been the firewood carrier *Ranger*, a recapture, after it had been seized and sent into Boston by the H.M.S. *Cerberus*. Subsequently, he was credited with capture of the *Two Sisters*, bound from Ireland laden with beef, pork, and butter, which he had chased into Beverly. The vessel also was claimed by fifteen Beverlyites who, on November 8, had gone out in a boat and brought her ashore. Two other captures were made by Capt. Winborn Adams of the *Warren*. Late in November, he had seized the schooner *Rainbow* bound for Boston laden with 550 bushels of potatoes. Then, on Christmas Eve near Bermuda, Adams recaptured and sent into Marblehead the 70-ton *Sally*, carrying 153 quarter-casks of Lisbon wine.
17. MA Archives, 170:320; Smith, 2:465.
18. Clark, 2:1284; "Diary of Ezekiel Price," MHS *Proceedings*, 7 (1863):218.
19. Clark, 2:1245–46, 1258, 1284; 3:17, 46–48; *Scrapbook Collection*, BHS, Book 12:23.
20. *The New-England Chronicle*, December 7–14, 1775.
21. Clark, 3:145, 147.
22. 3:145.
23. 3:573; by mid-February, they presumably received pay for the last campaign; Orderly Book of Capt. Moses Brown, 14th Regiment, MS, BHS, February 18, 1776.
24. 3: 1077, 1353–65; Orderly Book of Capt. Moses Brown, February 3, 1776.
25. Clark, 3:832–33; 4:694–96; 5:470.
26. 2:384–85, 434, 635, 1019; 3:553–54; 4:1216, 1286; 5:102, 470–71, 1153;

Glover was having other problems. One privateering crew accused him of buying their shares of prize money for one-fourth real value; Clark, 5:849.

27. 3:62, 1193.

28. 3:35.

29. 5:251, 267, 470.

30. 3:1023–24, 1060, 1075–76, 132–33; in December, Washington had written: "The plague, trouble and vexation I have had with the Crews of all the armed Vessels is inexpressible; I do believe there is not on Earth a more disorderly set; every time they come into Port, we hear of nothing but mutinous Complaints"; Fitzpatrick, 4:144.

31. Clark, 3:1078–79, 1169–70; for an account of John Manley's privateering, see: Robert E. Peabody, "The Naval Career of Captain John Manley," *EIHC*, 45 (1909):1–27.

32. Clark, 3:875; 4:124–25; Howard I. Chapelle, *The History of the American Sailing Navy* (W. W. Norton, 1949; New York: Bonanza Books,), 71–72.

33. Newburyport Town Records, February 27, 1776, 1:249; D. Hamilton Hurd, *History of Essex County* (Philadelphia, J. W. Lewis, 1888), 2:1460.

34. Clark, 5:448, 1123; "Extracts From the Diary of Samuel Horton of Newburyport," *EIHC*, 43 (1907):285.

35. Gardner W. Allen, *A Naval History of the American Revolution*, (Boston: Houghton Mifflin, 1913), 1:202–16.

36. 36. Clark, 3:1121–22; 4:82, 147, 257, 296, 307–08, 317, 331, 347, 520, 694, 733, 828–29; some civilian passengers were dropped off at Portsmouth and required to return to Boston on their own hook. One was William Jackson, a well-known Tory merchant. He was forced from his carriage in Newburyport and obliged to walk the entire distance through Salem to Boston, the object of taunts and threats along the way; Fitch Edward Oliver, ed., *The Diary of William Pynchon* (Boston: Houghton Mifflin, 1890), 71.

37. 37. Clark, 5:423, 434–36, 449, 450, 508, 563, 576, 579, 580–82, 583, 596, 618, 619–21, 635–36, 637, 697, 712, 786–87, 853, 908; Colin Campbell, "The 71st. Highlanders in Massachusetts, 1776–1780," NEHGR, 112 (1958), 265–266; John H. Sheppard, *The Life of Samuel Tucker* (Boston: Alfred Mudge, 1868), 59.

38. Clark, 4:1456–57; 5:6, 251–52, 508.

39. 5:1268–69; Sheppard, 14; Samuel Roads, Jr., *The History and Traditions of Marblehead* (Marblehead: N. Allen Lindsey, 1897), 200–15.

40. Upham, 56; Roads, 121; meanwhile, Ward found out something about Mugford which he did not like. He sent a messenger to Beverly to annul the commission, but was too late. Clark, 5:251.

41. Clark, 5:134–35, 141–42, 216–17.

42. Howard Kendall Sanderson, *Lynn in the Revolution* (Boston: W. B. Clarke, 1901), 1:152.

43. Clark, 5:161–62, 217–18, 268, 422; Roads, 122–123; Orderly Book of David How, Methuen Historical Museum.

North Shore coastal defenses helped protect Beverly, Manchester, Salem, and Marblehead waters from British attack. Woodcut of Beverly from Edwin M. Stone's *History of Beverly*, 1843.

CHAPTER THIRTEEN

DEFENSE OF THE COASTLINE

On October 6, 1775, Vice Admiral Samuel Graves, British commander on the American station, instructed Lt. Henry Mowat aboard the armed ship *Canceaux* "to chastize Marblehead, Salem, Newbury Port, Cape Anne Harbour, Portsmouth, Ipswich, Saco, Falmouth in Casco Bay, and particularly Mechias. . . . make the most vigorous Efforts to burn the Towns, and destroy the Shipping in the Harbours."[1] Though inhabitants along the seaboard shuddered at the prospect of attack, it loomed more imminent than most had imagined. Coastal people trembled and general alarms sounded when British sail were sighted. Forsaking a life of trepidation, since April 19 townsfolk had been evacuating the shore. While some coastal Essex County residents eventually returned, others stayed away for the entire war. Ten seacoast militia companies had stood guard since mid-summer, but the parade of hostile ships required a more imposing defense of Essex County shores.

Old Forts, New Forts

Forts erected in earlier eras during conflicts with the French at Gloucester, Marblehead, and Salem languished, slowly deteriorating. In months to come, they would receive a face-lifting, and new earthworks would spring up where none had existed before.

Since late spring, the sixteen-gun *Merlin* had been cruising from Marblehead north to Piscataqua. The *quid pro quo* which had existed with townspeople soon ended. Early in August, the *Merlin* stopped several Marblehead fishing vessels and impressed their seamen. Capt. James Mugford, who had been on friendly terms with *Merlin*'s Capt. William Burnaby, interceded and managed their release. After this incident, the Marblehead committee of safety established coastal watches. With animosities increasing, the town battened down for further harassment and possible attack.[2]

At a September 18 town meeting, Marbleheaders chose persons to oversee repair and reconstruction of the old fort, which was built about 1742 on Gale's Head overlooking the harbor. Three days later, timber was carted to the site, and work began. Major Gen. Charles Lee traveled from Cambridge to view the project, a sign of its significance. Labor came largely from militia ranks. During the month, as British aggressions along the seaboard heightened residents' fears, the work pace quickened. As many as one hundred laborers plugged away, Sundays included.[3] Diarist Ashley Bowen noted acidly on November 5: "At 1/2 past 8 o'clock the old bell rung for laborers at the Fort, and at 10 the drum went about for the Minutemen, and a fine Sabbath this! Whitwell administering the Sacrament and the men at work at the Fort."[4] Finally, on December 6, the fort was completed.

The October 10 clash between the *Nautilus* and Beverly and Salem had kindled action. Next day, men were constructing a fort on Juniper Point, Salem, at the northeast end of the Neck. The town already was defended by old Fort William on Winter Island. Two days after the attack, Beverly voted to construct two breastworks, at Woodberry's Point and Paul's Head, and to procure six cannon (two sixes, four fours) for the redoubts. (Earlier in August, Salem's committee of safety had recommended fortification of Woodberry's Point, so both towns could render a more effective, coordinated defense.) It was the *Nautilus* intrusion, however, that inspired Beverly.[5]

The day Beverly voted, an evil portent occurred only one hundred miles Down East. On October 17, Lt. Henry Mowat on the *Canceaux* gave the inhabitants of Falmouth (now Portland) two hours to vacate, then sacked and shelled the seaport, burning hundreds of stores, homes, and buildings. The message was clear. Each Essex County port could expect the same. A Salem resident wrote, "we are in daily expectation of a Fleet which is sent out to distroy and burn all the seaport towns . . . . What will be the end of these things God only knows."[6] Indeed, Mowat had instructions to burn and lay waste the towns. In addition to the *Canceaux*, his squadron included two converted craft, the transport *Symmetry* and the sloop *Spitfire*, and the schooner *Halifax*.

To revenge the humiliating defeat of the *Falcon* in early August, Mowat's original target had been Cape Ann. Gloucester had expected a revenge match and lost no time preparing. Within two weeks, repairs had been completed to the decaying breastworks on Watch House Point (Old Battery) in the harbor. The day after the *Falcon* flight, Capt. Joseph Foster, Gloucester's representative in the Provincial Congress, petitioned for additional defense forces and ammunition. By August 12, the Congress had directed the committee of supplies to deliver powder and shot to the frightened townspeople, including three hundred rounds for their solitary 9-pounder. Capt. John Lane of Buxton, Maine, stationed with 79 troops in Cambridge—many from Essex County—was ordered to Cape Ann. (They remained for the rest of the year, exemplifying Washington's concern for Gloucester's security.) A few days later, Maj. Robert Magaw and a battalion of 280 riflemen also arrived. Magaw returned to Cambridge after there seemed no immediate danger.

On October 3, however, a secret expedition of two bomb ketches and several armed vessels was reported to have slipped out of Boston to recapture the *Unity* and to free the imprisoned *Falcon* seamen. Five days later, Mowat sailed from Nantasket Road and brought to off Cape Ann. On October 9, a provident northwest gale kept the vessels away from shore. After the wind had shifted, at daybreak on the eleventh, Mowat's artillery officer viewed the town's layout, concluding the houses were too scattered for his fire bombs to have a destructive effect. Cape Ann was saved, but Falmouth was doomed to be reduced to ashes. Those Cape Anners who remained along the eighteen miles of exposed coastline continued to live constantly in fear of attack and invasion.[7]

On October 27, the *Essex Journal* reported that Cape Ann, Beverly, Marblehead, and Newburyport were striving to fortify their towns and harbors. A week earlier, news had arrived that Lieutenant Mowat had destroyed three-fourths of Falmouth. Fearing Salem would be next, townspeople voted to follow Newburyport's example and construct a more formidable defense. A committee was chosen to procure old hulks and timbers to block Salem's northern harbor passage; others were chosen to strengthen coastal defenses. These measures would bolster the town's defenses, which since summer had been guarded by Captains Samuel King and Benjamin Ward, Jr., billeted with their militia at Fort William and on the Neck.[8]

To the north, on October 19, Manchester had voted to construct a breastwork on Glass Head on the northern side of the harbor entrance. Lt. Benjamin Craft noted on October 29, "Manchester people were much engaged in fortifying and intrenching their City!"[9] Additional fortifications were thrown up in Gloucester, near Freshwater Cove, at Duncan's Point, and on a bank near the cut. Late in

October, detachments trooped from Boxford, Ipswich, Rowley, and Topsfield to help with defenses. At an October 20 Gloucester town meeting, William Pearson was chosen captain of Fort Stage Point and Bradbury Sanders of Fort Ann (Watch House Point). Four days later, under command of Col. Jonathan Titcomb, Newburyporters organized four companies of infantry, chose six captains of heavy artillery guns, and named Capt. Joseph Hudson to command Fort Merrimack, provided that Amesbury and Salisbury approved. The battery was on Salisbury's side. The Merrimack River towns of Amesbury, Newburyport, and Salisbury—quick to protect their shores—had laid out and jointly constructed the fort over the summer. Since then, several cannon were mounted, and barracks were erected. During the fall, Newburyport constructed another battery at the northern point of Plum Island, with help coming from Newbury.[10] In November, Salisbury permitted Fort Merrimack cannon to be transferred to Plum Island. An imposing defense was beginning to shape along Essex County's coastline.[11]

Several seaboard towns requested Continental troops for protection. Washington could not oblige, but he worded his refusals politely, so towns would not resort to pulling local contingents from Continental service. The Continental Congress agreed; consequently, the practice was established early of using state militia for local defense.

Dearth of Cannon, Shot, and Powder

Despite the mighty efforts in October, Cape Ann's defenses continued to be undermanned and inadequately equipped. Early in November, the colony permitted two barrels of powder to be purchased on its credit and agreed to assist in locating cannon. But the only find was two 4-pounders in Worcester. In December, after capture of the *Nancy* exposed the cape's vulnerability and the importance of a safe haven, the General Court decided to bolster defenses to four companies and one artillery, totaling two hundred and fifty men. Daniel Warner was chosen captain of the First Company, John Lane, the Second, and Bradbury Sanders and William Pearson, who already had led the seacoast companies, commanders of the Third and Fourth. Col. Joseph Foster was made commanding officer, and, in cases of emergency, he was empowered to call local militia.[12]

Only two 6-pounders projected from Beverly's Woodberry Point fortification, which was designed for seven cannon; even the two were valueless without gunpowder and shot, war commodities in yet shorter supply. Overseas shipments and legislative allotments were insufficient. Saltpeter, the primary ingredient of gunpowder (made up of 12 parts saltpeter, 2.5 parts charcoal, 1.5 parts sulphur) was especially scarce. Late in September, Newburyport voted to start manufacturing near Frog Pond. In Salem on October 27, Rev. Nathaniel Whitaker was leased an acre and a half of the Common for a saltpeter works. The town's stores had become so critical that the General Court instructed the inland towns of Andover, Boxford, Bradford, Danvers, Haverhill, Methuen, Middleton, Rowley, and Topsfield, together, to supply Salem with three hundred and fifty pounds of gunpowder. Throughout the county, efflorescences of nitrous salts were extracted from under barns, houses, sheds, stalls— even meetinghouses. East Boxford parishioners permitted Deacon Symonds to remove the dirt from under their meetinghouse. In Linebrook Parish, Ipswich, Daniel Chapman of Boxford could do the same.[13]

No gunpowder mills were operating in Massachusetts. Samuel Phillips, Jr., of Andover (who was to found Phillips Academy in 1778), proposed to erect a mill at his expense on the Shawsheen River. The Council encouraged Phillips by voting to supply saltpeter and sulphur at cost for a year and to purchase all "Good Merchantable" gunpowder produced from the materials supplied. By March of 1776, Phillips's mill was in operation, and before long was producing more than one thousand pounds per week. But there were quality problems. In April 1777, General Washington complained that the powder was not comparable to grades being manufactured elsewhere. The commander in chief demanded an inquiry; the standards must have improved, as no more complaints were registered. Despite Phillips's operation, supplies continued dangerously low because of rising demands from privateering.[14]

The morning of December 13, Marbleheaders arose to see three of His Majesty's warships, the *Lively*, the *Nautilus*, and the *Hinchinbrook*, threateningly standing near their door. Several times the men-of-war streamed past Gale's Head, at the harbor entrance, with their gun ports up, facing toward town. Fearing another Falmouth, a general alarm was sounded, and a messenger was despatched to notify Washington. Defenders scrambled to their harbor fortification, where twenty cannon recently had been mounted and readied for action. Women and children were quickly evacuated, and neighboring militia, having been warned that a hail of shot was expected momentarily, rushed toward Marblehead. Washington ordered Glover's regiment and a company of artillery forthwith. After maneuvering for over two hours, often within range of the fort on Gale's Head, the warships turned about and sailed out to sea, one by one. It was Marblehead's good fortune; although the town was supplied with cannon and shot, the fort's powder magazine was entirely empty! Until the threat had passed, Glover remained in Marblehead.[15]

Beverly's Continental Importance

When the Congress's marine committee assumed authority over the Continental Navy on January 1, 1776, at least ten captured vessels were in Beverly harbor awaiting condemnation proceedings in the Court of Admiralty. Also moored were thirty-one schooners, ten trading vessels, and three sloops. Washington's fleet was outfitted initially in Beverly because Glover's business was located there. Because of its sheltered harbor, with a complex channel imposing obstacles for unknowing mariners, Beverly was less susceptible to attack. Consequently, the town continued as the base of operations for most Continental vessels, and later, for many private, armed vessels.

As the anchorage for Washington's naval fleet, with valuable prizes also riding in the harbor, the town offered a tempting target to the British. Yet, Beverly was ill prepared to defend itself. On January 1, enlistments expired for Moses Brown's seacoast defense force and crews aboard Continental privateers. Brown's company was temporarily disbanded, and the Continental sailors returned to Marblehead, leaving Beverly largely defenseless. Worse still, Beverly's coastal breastworks lacked guns. After the Beverly committee of correspondence and prize agent William Bartlett appealed to Washington for cannon, shot, and powder on December 11, Beverly had been permitted to borrow surplus cannon and shot from the captured vessels and, if "absolutely wanting," whatever powder was aboard. But defenses improved only slightly.[16]

Conscious that Beverly was valuable but poorly protected, Washington made an exception to his practice of not using Continental soldiers for defense. He despatched the Marblehead regiment. First, Glover came to direct the construction of barracks; then, on January 14, the regiment marched to Beverly. Capt. Moses Brown's seacoast company was reactivated and assigned to the 14th Foot, the new designation for Glover's regiment in Continental service. The troops were stationed to guard vessels that had been captured and were awaiting condemnation proceedings and transfer to the Continental Army. Glover was encamped on both sides of Lothrop Street, including the present Independence Park. In February, Capt. Moses Brown's company erected a sand-bank battery, laid out for four embrasures, at the end of Tuck's Point (which then extended 100 feet further than today) at the harbor entrance. The town had no cannon for the fort, so Glover borrowed two 6-pounders from Marblehead. The committee of safety requested Glover's aid in strengthening Beverly's entire four miles of coastline. In mid-March, the town voted to purchase two cannon borrowed from Capt. George Crowninshield of Salem for the Woodberry Point battery and to procure two more large pieces. By mid–1776, batteries had been erected at Barnard's Point, West Beach, and Thorndike's Point (Paul's Head), so that five forts guarded Beverly.[17]

Moses Brown's guard was comprised of twenty-five Continentals, including one officer. Eight were posted in the outer fort at Woodberry's Point, five on board the ship tied to Captain Bartlett's wharf, and the main guard at Tuck's house on the Point. Sentries were "to challeng & hail all Boats or Vessels coming in or going out of this harbour." Particular notice was to be paid to boats appearing to go or return from the man-of-war—the twenty-gun *Fowey*—anchored "before the harbour." Any vessel refusing "to answer or come on shore after" three hails was to have a musket shot over her; if she "persisted," the sentry was to fire "before her fore foot." If she did not bring to, "fire into her, & alarm the main guard."[18]

Glover's Continental regiment was one of five left in Massachusetts when Washington departed for New York shortly after the British evacuation. Beverly had the distinction of being the only Continental Army post in New England outside of the immediate Boston vicinity. Glover's regiment remained in Beverly until July 19, 1776.

Defenses in '76

On January 1, 1776, coastal defense force enlistments had expired. Ten companies had been prescribed the previous June for Essex County's shoreline. By December 1775, the invasion threat had so subsided in Newbury that the guard stationed there had been dismissed. Not so in Marblehead. In January, in lieu of the earlier force, the General Court provided two new seacoast defense companies, captained by Francis Felton and William Hooper. The next month, a matross (seacoast artillery) company was voted for vulnerable Marblehead, the first to have a matross unit. Before long, these artillery companies would be stationed in each major seaport.[19]

In the spring, when Washington was preparing to march for New York with most of the Continental forces, the General Court ordered two militia companies from Beverly and one each from Salem, Marblehead, and Gloucester to help with Boston's defenses. Also, at Washington's behest, beacons were erected at Cape Ann and Marblehead to warn the capital town if a British fleet were spotted on the horizon. A Continental Congress committee on fortifications saw Cape Ann, being on the eastern approach to Boston, as vital to the whole colony's security. In mid-April, the committee instructed Wash-

Field Officers—Essex County Regiments of Militia

Brigadier General: Michael Farley, Ipswich

First Regiment (Salem, Lynn): Timothy Pickering, Jr., colonel; John Flagg, lt. colonel; Joseph Sprague, first major; David Parker, second major.

Second Regiment (Newburyport, Amesbury, Salisbury): Jonathan Titcomb, colonel; Henry Morrill, lt. colonel; Ralph Cross, Jr., first major; Winthrop Merrill, second major.

Third Regiment (Ipswich, Topsfield, Wenham): Jonathan Cogswell, Jr., colonel; Isaac Dodge, lt. colonel; Charles Smith, first major; Joseph Gould, second major.

Fourth Regiment (Haverhill, Andover, Bradford, Boxford, Methuen): Samuel Johnson, colonel; John Whittier, lt. colonel; Benjamin Gage, first major; Samuel Bodwell, second major.

Fifth Regiment (Marblehead): Jonathan Glover, colonel; Thomas Gerry, lt. colonel; Joshua Orne, first major; Nicholson Broughton, second major.

Sixth Regiment (Gloucester, Manchester): James Collins, colonel; Daniel Warner, lt. colonel; John Rowe, first major; Eleazer Craft, second major.

Seventh Regiment (Newbury, Rowley): Daniel Spafford, colonel; Samuel Moody, lt. colonel; Moses Noyes, first major; Thomas Noyes, second major.

Eighth Regiment (Beverly, Danvers, Middleton): Henry Herrick, colonel; Jeremiah Page, lt. colonel; Archelaus Fuller, first major; Samuel Epes, second major.

February—May 1776[20]

ington to inspect the works and devise a plan for its defense.[21] The next month, on May 22, Isaac Smith of Gloucester stressed, in a letter to committee member John Adams, that a British foothold in Gloucester harbor would raise havoc with the colony's coastal trade:

> but iff C. Ann was well fortifyed which by Nature Is best Able with proper batteries to defend itt self of any I know. Indeed M[arble]

> H[ea]d and Salem are well cituated, and iff properly fortifyed would
> keep Out almost any thing but C. Ann would be the safest harbour
> for them.[22]

Adams concurred. To keep this critical location out of British hands, he committed himself to fortifying it at Continental expense. When Gloucester requested that its company of Continentals remain at home—not march to Boston—permission was granted. The Cape's defenses were deemed too vital. Although the British had evacuated Boston, they were still dangerously close, with their warships based at Nantasket Road and cruising off the coast.[23]

In May, Washington sent Col. Richard Gridley, Congress's eminent chief engineer, to examine Cape Ann's defenses. Gridley's experience superintending fortifications began in 1746 with the Fortress of Louisburg. He reported that the two hundred and fifty men from Squam to Gloucester were too dispersed to afford adequate protection. With four hundred townspeople in military service, though, few able-bodied men remained. Leaving Gloucester, Gridley traveled eight miles south to inspect the small redoubt on Glass Head in Manchester, finding no cannon nor a permanent guard. To improve the cape's precarious condition, "as a fleet is daily expected, and may do mischief," Gridley recommended additional men and cannon.[24]

Attuned to a solid defense line north of Boston, the General Court commissioned its own committee to examine the county coast. In Salem, they found three forts: Fort William on Winter Island; breastworks on Juniper Point at the Willows; and a third, Fort Lee on the Neck (constructed by the poor, working out their taxes), perched upon a summit overlooking Beverly and Salem harbors "in a very advantageous Manner." The latter was named for Gen. Charles Lee, who came to Salem in 1775 with Jonathan Peele, a Salem merchant, and selected the site. "This Fort," the committee members reported, "does Credit to the Gentm of the Town," but they recommended additional "heavy pieces and Ordinance stores."[25]

"The Situation and Importance of the Harbour of Marblehead, with the Strength & Beauty of their Works, are equally conspicuous," wrote the committee. There was the main fort on Gale's Head, two secondary batteries, another being raised on Hewett's Head, and yet another proposed for the "Back Part of the Town." On December 14, one day after the three men-of-war stood menacingly off Marblehead harbor, work had commenced on a fort at Hooper's Head, on the eastern side of the "New Wharf." In May, an eleven-man committee had been appointed to raise added batteries. A third fort—on Bartol's Head—was begun on May 21; in mid-June, a fourth and fifth on Hewett's Head and Twisden's Hill. The fortifications were judged "Sufficient if well manned & supplied with Artillery & ordinance Stores." By August, the forts reportedly were equipped with thirty cannon, including two mammoth 42-pounders, though only one fort was regularly guarded.[26]

The committee was less impressed with defenses between Beverly and Cape Ann. The five Beverly batteries were judged "to demand an immediate Attention." There were only three heavy and four small field pieces, mostly borrowed. Manchester was found "naked & Defenceless," except for a small battery on Glass Head. And Gloucester demanded, the committee said, "a very early and serious Consideration." There was only Fort Anne, two smaller batteries with few serviceable cannon, plus another with no guns.[27]

Newburyport was reported "fortified in such a Manner as to do Honour to the gentlemen concerned." The town could boast of twenty cannon, including ten 9-pounders. On May 8, Newburyporters voted to strengthen defenses by erecting a fort on Plum Island and to purchase two tons of gunpowder and all the cannon recently brought into town by Captain Wilson. Construction was jointly undertaken by Newbury and Newburyport.[28] Upriver, Amesbury, Bradford, and Haverhill had been invited, but they declined, perceiving little danger to themselves.

The committee's June 19, 1776, report recommended more "heavy Pieces," ammunition, and ordnance stores for Beverly, Marblehead, Newburyport, Salem, possibly Manchester, and especially Cape Ann. Also proposed were the "speedy filling" of "Sea Coast" companies in Gloucester and Newburyport, to replace those manning Continental and private, armed vessels. Newburyport also needed ammunition, ordnance stores, and a matross company. With the Essex County coastline so modestly defended, luckily it did not figure in Britain's mid-1776 strategy to win the colonies.[29]

Before the report was officially submitted, the General Court had acted to reinforce Gloucester's coastline. News of the capture, in June, of Newburyport's *Yankee Hero* within sight of Cape Ann, coupled with the valuable prize *Lady Juliana* (taken in the Caribbean by two Pennsylvania privateers) riding in the harbor, inspired the legislature to vote twelve cannon, including four 24-pounders, and to raise a company of matrosses, with William Ellery as captain. Earlier in May, the General Assembly had debated whether even two 18-pounders could be spared.

Later in the month and in early July, a series of resolves strengthened defenses in other towns. Cannon—four for Beverly and Salem, six for Marblehead, and three for Newburyport—were voted, with a supply of gunpowder and shot. Except for some 9-pounders, most were powerful twelves, twenty-fours and forty-twos. In addition to

Gloucester's artillery company, matrosses were to be raised in New-buryport (Edward Wigglesworth, captain) and in Salem (John Sy-monds, captain), as well as a conventional seacoast company (Moses Nowell, captain) in Newburyport. Shortly, Essex County could boast a credible defense system.[30]

On July 19, 1776, the day Glover's regiment headed toward New York, Beverly became the sole provider for its own protection. Col. Henry Herrick was ordered to fill the defenses with sixty men from his militia regiment, while Capt. Joseph Rea occupied the camp and barracks vacated by Glover. Most remaining Continental regiments, including Hutchinson's, were trudging off to New York, leaving mi-litia in entrenchments along the coast to keep vigilant eyes trained on Massachusetts Bay waters.

Though Boston had been evacuated, followed a few weeks later by the departure of enemy warships from Nantasket Road, there was constant apprehension of attack from the sea. His Majesty's armed vessels continued to prowl offshore, frequently patrolling within sight of wary coastal inhabitants. A strategic enemy military base was lo-cated only a few days' sail away, at Halifax. Then, in December 1776, the enemy encroached uncomfortably close when six thousand troops and a large fleet occupied Newport, Rhode Island. Later, to the eastward, in May 1779, three British warships and several transports entered Penobscot Bay to establish a garrison. Consequently, while the major land war pushed south, Essex County had to remain alert. Coastal defenses were supplemented by a handful of state-armed vessels. One was the twenty-gun *Protector*, contracted for in mid-1778 with Jonathan Greenleaf and Stephen and Ralph Cross of Newbury-port. Not until hostilities were nearly concluded did Essex County feel composed enough to drop its guard. Until then, stationed from rocky Marblehead to Pigeon Hill in Sandy Bay, and along the sands of Plum Island, militiamen gazed out over the Atlantic, prepared to sound the alarm on sight of a British sail.

1. William Bell Clark, ed., *Naval Documents of the American Revolution*, 2:324–26.
2. Clark, 1:785, 820, 1177.
3. Marblehead Town Records, EI, Septem-ber 18, 1775, 4:477–78; Philip Chadwick Foster Smith, ed., *The Journals of Ashley Bowen of Marblehead* (Salem: Peabody Mu-seum, 1973), 2:456, 460.
4. Smith, 2:462.
5. "Extracts from the Interleaved Almanacs of William Wetmore of Salem," *EIHC*, 43 (1907):118; Beverly Town Records, Au-gust 25, 1775, 6:63; October 12, 1775, 6:69.
6. "Some Letters of 1775," MHS *Proceedings*, 59 (1925):132.
7. Clark, 2:280, 372, 374, 513–14; MA Ar-chives, 180:288; John J. Babson, *Notes and Additions to the History of Gloucester* (Gloucester: M. V. B. Perley, 1876), 145–46; "Diary of Ezekiel Price," MHS *Proceed-ings*, 7 (1863):204.
8. Salem Town Records, EI, October 23, 1775, 75–77.
9. "Craft's Journal of the Siege of Boston," *EIHC*, 3 (1861):172.
10. Newburyport Town Records, September 13, 1775, 1:241; *The Essex Journal & New Hampshire Packet*, September 29, 1775; Sal-isbury Town Records, November 13–17, 1775, 681; Newbury Town Records, Oc-tober 24, 1775, 321.

11. Gloucester Town Records, October 20, 1775, 165; John J. Babson, *History of the Town of Gloucester* (Gloucester: Procter Bros., 1860), 145–46; Newburyport Town Records, October 24, 1775, 1:244; MA Archives, 180:288; Peter Force, ed., *American Archives*, 4th Series, 4:1254–55.

12. Force, 4th Series, 3:1492, 1500; 4:1230–31, 1246–47, 1317, 1363, 1366–67; Babson, *Notes and Additions*, 147–48.

13. Newburyport Town Records, September 28, 1775, 1:242; Salem Town Records, October 25, 1775, 79–80; Joseph B. Felt, *History of Ipswich, Essex, and Hamilton* (Cambridge: Joseph B. Felt, 1834), 97; Sidney Perley, *History of Boxford* (Boxford: Sidney Perley, 1880), 227; Force, 4th Series, 3:1478–79; 4:1256, 1362.

14. Sarah Loring Bailey, *Historical Sketches of Andover, Massachusetts* (Boston: Houghton Mifflin, 1880), 342–47; *Acts & Resolves*, 19:203–04.

15. Russell W. Knight, "Fire, Smoak & Elbridge Gerry," *EIHC*, 106 (1970):32–45; Clark, 3:80, 95.

16. Clark, 3:44–45, 111; Beverly Town Records, November 6, 1775, 6:71; earlier, on November 7, Wenham had voted to help Beverly with defenses.

17. Beverly Town Records, February 6, 1776, 6:76–78; February 9, 1776, 6:79; March 11, 1776, 6:90; Charles Woodberry, *Independence Park* (Beverly, MA, 1906), 13; for an account of Beverly's defenses, see George A. Billias, "Beverly's Seacoast Defenses During the Revolutionary War," *EIHC*, 94 (1958):119–131.

18. Orderly Book of Capt. Moses Brown, BHS, January 15, 1776.

19. Force, 4th Series, 4:1248, 1299, 1304, 1319–20, 1368, 1443.

20. Revolutionary Rolls, MA Archives, 27:217; Force, 4th Series, 4:1463.

21. Clark, 4:659, 837, 868.

22. 5:198.

23. 5:198, 338; on June 24, the Continental committee recommended that the cape be strengthened with twenty heavy cannon at the Congress's expense, but the recommendation never was executed; 5:713.

24. Force, 4th Series, 6:439–40.

25. Clark, 5:615; William Lewis Welch, "Salem Neck and Winter Island," *EIHC*, 33 (1897):84–88; Salem Town Records, May 18, 1776, 129–130; C. H. Webber and W. S. Nevins, *Old Naumkeag: The City of Salem* (Salem: A. A. Smith, 1877), 224.

26. Clark, 5:615; 6:289; Marblehead Town Records, May 6, 1776, 4:494–95; Smith, 2:467, 487, 489, 491.

27. Clark, 5:616.

28. 5:616; Newburyport Town Records, May 8, 1776, 1:255; May 16, 1776, 1:257.

29. Clark, 5:616–17.

30. Force, 5th Series, 1:265, 268, 271, 273, 277, 296, 297, 303, 307, 308.

CHAPTER FOURTEEN

ESSEX PRIVATEERING: PROFIT AND PATRIOTISM

On November 19, 1775, diarist Ashley Bowen noted: "Raw cold. Came from Boston a sloop and the Salem cruiser took her and carried her into Salem."[1] The "Salem cruiser" was the brigantine *Dolphin*. Earlier, on September 27, the Boston-bound *Dolphin* laden with oxen, sheep, and oatmeal, sent as a gift from the Tory merchants of Quebec to the ministerial troops, was captured off Cape Ann by two boats of Sandy Bay fishermen. Weeks before privateer commissions began to be awarded, the *Dolphin* was outfitted and free-lancing—among the first of several hundred private, armed vessels which made sail from Essex County.

Early Cruising

On June 2, 1775, the armed British schooner *Margaretta* arrived off remote Machias harbor, Maine, to protect two sloops (*Polly* and *Unity*) while they took on lumber for the troops in Boston. Ten days later, the fiery Jeremiah O'Brien and forty Machias compatriots "armed with guns, swords, axes & pick forks" boarded the *Unity*.[2] With O'Brien in command, they pursued the *Margaretta*; after a one-hour bloody skirmish, the four-gun British schooner surrendered. The first naval contest of the war had ended with an American victory! The *Unity*, renamed *Machias Liberty* and armed with the *Margaretta*'s guns, became the first American armed cruiser in the War of Independence. Shortly afterwards, O'Brien seized the six-gun schooner *Diligent* and the tender *Tatamagouche* from Halifax. In late August, the Provincial Congress hired the *Diligent* and the *Machias* 225

Liberty—the first armed vessels taken into Massachusetts service—and appointed O'Brien commander, to help protect the Down East coastline.

On November 1, 1775, Massachusetts declared war on enemy vessels found "infesting" American waters by empowering its council to commission with letters of marque persons who "fix out & equip for the defence of America any Vessell" to "Sail on the Seas, Attack, take and bring into any Port . . . offending [ships] found Making unlawful invasions, Attacks Or depredations on the Sea Coasts" or "carrying Supplies of any kind to the Enemy, or that shall be returning from the Enemy after having carried such Supplies." Courts were to be established "to try & Condemn all Vessells."[3] Bonds were required to insure conformance with instructions and to satisfy claims from an illegal capture. The Council, for example, wanted captured crew brought in—vital for exchanges involving imprisoned Americans—not cast off in a worthless scow or in a nearby port. Later, owners were put under bond to discourage them from enlisting deserters from the Continental Army or noncitizens. The November enactment by Massachusetts—and subsequent ones—and the Continental Congress's March 23, 1776, authorization encouraged enterprising Americans to enter privateering.

The first private, armed vessels commissioned by the Bay province were privateers, rather than ships with letters of marque. Except for its ownership, a privateer resembled a state or Continental warship. A letter of marque licensed a cargo-laden, armed merchantman cleared for a port to take enemy vessels. For craft carrying a letter of marque prizes were incidental, whereas for privateers the captures were their central purpose.

Essex County ship owners soon petitioned for privateering commissions. On November 30, 1775, Salem's committee of safety notified the Massachusetts Council that the formerly-Quebec-owned, 17-ton coaster *Dolphin*, under the command of Richard Masury, had brought in the 70-ton sloop *Success*, bound from Nova Scotia to Boston. The next day, a petition was filed for a commission—the first by a Massachusetts vessel, though no bond was requested until December 15. The *Dolphin*'s captain, Masury, had twenty years experience to become familiar with every stretch of the American coastline. In addition to the *Success*, the "Salem cruiser" chalked up the sloop *Dispatch* (45 tons), the schooner *Friendship* (60 tons), and probably the *Fisher* (50 tons).[4] On December 7, a petition and bond were filed on behalf of the 32-ton *Boston Revenge*, commanded by Stephen E. Mascoll of Salem. The Salem vessels were the first to be commissioned by the Council, to be followed shortly afterwards by two Newburyport vessels. On December 8, owners of the sloop *Game Cock* and the

Early in the war, many privateers were single-masted sloops. From *Encyclopedia Brittanica*, 1797. Courtesy, Essex Institute, Salem. Mass.

schooner *Washington* wrote to Benjamin Greenleaf, Newburyport's representative in the General Assembly, to request his assistance in securing commissions. Three days later, the *Game Cock*, a small, 20-ton sloop with only four swivels (owned by several Newburyporters, including the town's foremost merchant, Nathaniel Tracy) was commissioned under command of Capt. Peter Roberts. The same day, the 50-ton *Washington*, commanded by Newburyporter Offin Boardman, was licensed. On December 19, a fifth vessel was commissioned: the 20-ton schooner *General Ward*, fitted out in Gloucester, commanded by Matthew Kelly.[5] County privateers were awarded the first five petitions granted by the Massachusetts Council. This was the opening salvo of Essex County's preeminent saga in American privateering.

The first privateers were small, former trading or fishing vessels. They were no match in a stand-off with a British man-of-war, but were light and fast, which enabled them to out-sail and out-maneuver most warships and merchantmen. The standard armament on board was light cannon (2-, 4-, and 6-pounders), swivel guns, blunderbusses, and a few muskets and pikes. During the first year, schooners and sloops were the most common craft outfitted. Later, the brigantine, which "carried a large spanker with a square, instead of a gaff, topsail on the main mast," became the favorite.[6]

Like the *Dolphin* before her commissioning, other vessels cruised without legal sanction, hunting down Boston-bound merchantmen or transports. As early as August 1775, a privateer owned by Nathaniel Tracy was sailing—the first fitted out specifically for privateering in the united colonies.[7] *Boyle's Journal* reported on November

24: "A Privateer belonging to Newbury carried into Portsmouth a Schooner of 45 Tons, loaded with Potatoes and Turnips for the Enemy in Boston."[8] Whether the privateer was Tracy's is unknown. On September 27, the 25-ton schooner *Industry*, out of New Providence sailing for Boston, blown off course by a strong southwest wind, sought shelter in Marblehead harbor. It was laden with casks of turtle, lemons, limes, and oranges—luxury foods bound to titillate the palates of British officers stationed in Boston. Capt. Hugh Hill of Beverly, sailing the uncommissioned schooner *Dove*, spotted the *Industry* come to off the fort. He succeeded in capturing her, but Timothy Pickering, prize judge for the middle district, later ordered the *Industry* returned to the owners.[9] Several "illegal" captures were made by open boats rather than sailers. On September 27, the *Dolphin* was grabbed when she sought shelter from the same winds that had pounded the *Industry*. Later, in November, the *North Britain* sloop from Boston, bound for Annapolis Royal, was blown off course and anchored near Misery Island with her sails torn and unable to proceed. Two Beverly men in a small boat took the vessel ashore, and a detachment from Capt. Moses Brown's coastal defense and others brought the vessel safely into Beverly harbor. The *North Britain*, carrying three crew, two passengers, and a small cargo of dry goods, was turned over to Beverly's committee of safety.[10] In December, after commissioning procedures were established, unauthorized roaming largely ended.

More Early Captures

Over the winter of '76, a melange of Essex County privateers in concert with Continental armed schooners wreaked havoc with the British supply lines leading to Boston. Salem's *Boston Revenge* began to match the *Dolphin* catch on January 18 with capture of the 200-ton *Jenny*, bound from England to Boston. When she was taken into Cape Ann, her cargo was found to include 1,500 blankets, 100 casks of oatmeal, shoes, chaldrons (a unit of measure equal to 32–36 bushels) of coal, and 100 bolts of "oznabrigs" (a coarse fabric woven in Germany).[11] On January 15, 1776, Capt. Offin Boardman brought the first prize into Newburyport harbor, the 90-ton *Sukey*, bound for Boston from Cork, full of beef, pork, potatoes, and other foodstuffs.

In the morning of the same day, a ship appeared off Newbury bar flying British colors. Several watched as the vessel, a few miles off shore, tacked often, evidently uncertain of her course. It appeared she had mistaken Ipswich bay for Boston harbor. An ingenious plan was devised. Seventeen men in three whale boats went out to see whether she was actually lost. When movements on board confirmed their suspicions, they rowed within shouting distance. Boardman, who had been chosen commander, hailed the ship and asked her home port and destination. "From London, bound to Boston," was the reply. Boardman responded that they were from Boston and proposed to act as pilot. The offer was accepted, and the ship hove to. Boardman's boat was rowed to the gangway; he boarded and strutted to the quarter deck, shaking hands with Capt. Archibald Bowie, engaging in friendly conversation, and asking of news from London. Meanwhile, three boatloads of men had sprung to the deck. Boardman left the quarterdeck, dropped his masquerade, and ordered the shocked Bowie to strike the English flag, which was instantly executed.

Six hours after the episode started, the 200-ton ship *Friends* was brought into Newburyport and tied up at the wharf. The *Friends*, mounting four guns, carried chaldrons of coal, butts and hogsheads of porter, hogsheads of vinegar, sauerkraut, plus twenty-three squealing hogs, intended for British troops in Boston.[12]

The Council ordered Bowie and Madatt Engs, commander of the *Sukey*, confined to town—jailed, if necessary. For a while, Bowie and Engs boarded at Davenport's tavern. Though Bowie eventually returned to England, Engs remained; later, he was to command a Newburyport privateer.[13] To change loyalties was not uncommon; during the Revolution, hundreds of captured British mariners switched allegiance and fought alongside their former captors.

On January 13, the fourteen-gun, 120-ton brig *Yankee Hero*, commanded by Thomas Thomas, became the third commissioned Newburyport vessel. On February 16, Thomas took the 200-ton snow *Jenny*, carrying coal, flour, and pork to Boston. Four days later, command changed to Capt. James Tracy, but the *Yankee Hero*'s good fortune continued. On February 26, Tracy brought in the 180-ton brig *Nelly*, bound from Whitehaven for Boston with a cargo of coal and cheese. A short time afterwards, the 180-ton snow *James*, also from Whitehaven, was captured. In short succession, three British transports had struck.[14]

During the winter, the *General Ward* had been plying Newburyport waters, manned by only a dozen men carrying muskets and armed with a solitary swivel. On a single cruise, she is reported to have captured two brigs and a schooner. While the brigs were brought safely into Newburyport, the schooner was recaptured. At the time, Capt. William Russell of Newburyport commanded.[15] Later in the war, Russell would stand at the helm of two other armed vessels: the brigantine *Thorn* and the ship *Beacon*, both of Newburyport.

From Newburyport, in February 1776, Jeremiah O'Brien had petitioned the General Court for continuation of his service. O'Brien

Portraits of Capt. Offin
Boardman (1748–1811),
Sarah Greenleaf Boardman
(1747–1796), and their son,
Benjamin (b. 1783).
Boardman was a
Newburyport shipmaster.
Oils on canvas attributed to
Christian Gullager. Courtesy,
Worcester Art Museum,
Worcester, Mass.

and the Newburyport committee of safety, correspondence, and inspection were jointly to outfit the *Diligent* and *Machias Liberty* for
another cruise. The committee, which would be reimbursed by the
state for expenses, found all materials and supplies locally, except for
gunpowder. With the Council's approval, two hundred pounds of
the precious substance was delivered. Each privateer required a complement of fifty men, but because of army demands and competition
from other privateers, only half were available in Newburyport.
O'Brien was confident nonetheless that the deficiency could be made
up in eastward (Maine) seaports. The vessels were outfitted by mid-
March, and the Council reluctantly approved their departure.[16]

Spring Successes

In April 1776, Bartholomew Putnam and Andrew Cabot of Beverly seized the 300-ton ship *Lord Dartmouth* between the high and low
water marks in Danvers. This probably was the vessel constructed by
Samuel Fowler and Simon Pindar, two Danvers shipwrights, and
superintended by Capt. John Lee, who had been sent over from
England. In 1774, Loyalist Doctor John Calef had contracted for her,
as agent for a London merchant. The planking had been framed in,
but the construction phase was still in process when hostilities broke
out. Calef ordered the project halted, but the builders, who wanted
full payment, finished the vessel. The ship was launched at New Mills
on November 10, 1775. Tied to a wharf, she broke away, drifted
downriver, and washed ashore, where she remained until the following April.[17]

With springtime, a flurry of privateering blossomed along the river harbor of Newburyport. In mid-May, Nathaniel Tracy's schooner *Success*—with two guns, eight swivels and fourteen men—was commissioned. On May 28, the fourteen-gun snow *Ranger*, commanded by Patrick Dennis, reportedly brought in two prizes from England. They had been bound for Boston laden with clothing and military supplies, including 11,000 pairs of shoes. On June 4, O'Brien sent in the schooner *Polly* from Barbados and the sloop *Two Friends* from Tortola, taken near St. John's River, Nova Scotia. The captures, however, were deemed illegal and ordered released.[18]

In southern Essex County, most privateering was Salem-based. A 90-ton sloop, *Revenge*, with Joseph White as commander, sailed with sixty crew, armed with twelve 4- and 6-pounders and sixteen swivels. She was owned by Joseph Lee and Capt. Josiah Batchelder, Jr., of Beverly and Miles Greenwood of Salem, all of whom figured prominently in Essex County privateering. (While no state-commissioned privateers sailed from Beverly prior to September 1776, shares were held in several Salem vessels by local investors.) White named the sloop "*Revenge*"; having already lost three vessels to the British, he wanted an identity that would make his objective clear. In June, the Salem commander began to even the score when he sent in the 75-ton brigantine *Fanny*, bound from Antigua laden with 130 hogsheads of rum. Early in the summer, White captured five more merchantmen (the sloop *Betsey*, the sloop *Isabella*, the brig *Harlequin*, the ship *Polly*, and the ship *Anna Maria*) headed for the British Isles with cargoes of West Indies rum and sugar. White became an early leading privateersman.[19]

The Birth of the State Navy

During the war, Massachusetts customarily employed its state war-ships as privateers. Early in 1776, the Bay province ordered construction of five vessels. Richard Derby of Salem and Josiah Batchelder, Jr., of Beverly were appointed to coordinate construction and outfitting of two: the *Tyrannicide* and the *Massachusetts*. They were built by the Hackett family—possibly the most highly regarded shipbuilders in the state—at their boatyard in Salisbury Point village (presently a part of Amesbury) along the Merrimack. The fourteen-gun *Tyrannicide* was first to be completed of the five, while the brigantine *Massachusetts* was sailing under Capt. Daniel Souther by mid-September of 1776.

James K. Hackett was the business head of the partnership, while his cousin, William, was designer and builder. During the Revolution, the Hacketts constructed several other warships, including the famous Continental frigate *Alliance*.

The riverside towns of Newburyport and Salisbury were well protected from enemy intrusion. Wooden piers which obstructed the entrance and the churning estuarine current combined to make the river an imposing obstacle to unfamiliar mariners. More vessels probably were constructed along the banks of the Merrimack during the war than anywhere else in the country.

On March 5, William Hackett contracted the *Tyrannicide* "in Mr John Hackets yard" with twelve shipwrights, to receive half-payment at the start, the balance when finished. In mid-May, an exasperated Derby wrote to the Council that the *Tyrannicide* had been completed for more than three weeks but was not cruising for lack of cannon. Ten more 4- and 6-pound cannon were voted on June 12, and, the following day, Capt. John Fisk, son of the pastor of the First Church, Salem, received his sailing orders, "to Cruise near the Coast of this Colony & from Harbour to Harbour."[20]

With Fisk at the helm, the fourteen-gun sloop *Tyrannicide* carried seventy-five crew, recruited at Cape Ann and Salem. Off Boston, on June 18, she participated with Continental schooners in capturing the Scot Highlander–packed *Lord Howe*.[21] On July 12, with his cruising orders having been extended to Sable Island and the shoals of Nantucket, Fisk took the armed schooner *Dispatch*, while she escorted a fleet from Halifax, bound for New York. The one-and-one-half-hour sea battle left the schooner splintered. Fisk reported to the General Court at Watertown:

> I boarded her, and found on board eight carriage guns and twelve
> swivel guns, twenty small-arms, sixteen pistols, twenty cutlasses,
> some cartridge-boxes and belts for bayonets, nine half-barrels pow-
> der. all the accountrements for said cannon. The commander and

one man were killed, seven others wounded. The crew consisted of thirty men and one boy. I lost one man killed and two wounded, and my vessel was much shattered, which obliged me to return with the prize, which I have at anchor in Salem Harbour and wait your Honours' orders how to proceed with the prisoners.[22]

Fisk's good fortune continued, and he ended the summer by adding four more vessels to his amazing catch: the snow *Anna*, the brigantine *Betsey*, the schooner *Patty*, and the schooner *Three Brothers*.

In 1777, the *Tyrannicide*, now rigged as a brigantine, was commanded by Salem's Jonathan Haraden, with Fisk at the helm of the brig *Massachusetts*. They sailed in March on a prize-taking cruise off the coasts of Ireland, England, and France. Both Fisk and Haraden distinguished themselves and became widely celebrated Revolutionary War commanders.

Mid-Year Privateering

By late spring, privateering was thriving, no doubt spurred on by the Continental Congress's March 23 resolve that all vessels and cargoes taken on the high seas belonging to inhabitants of Great Britain were fair game for commissioned privateers. Several more privateers outfitted by Beverly and Salem merchant entrepreneurs streamed from Salem harbor, which soon became the privateering hub.

In mid-June, the 90-ton schooner *Sturdy Beggar* (carrying six 3-pounders) owned by Elias Hasket Derby and J. & A. Cabot of Beverly was ready, with Peter Lander commander. William Wetmore noted on July 21: "Capt. Lander took a ship with a valuable cargo from Jamaica, put 12 of his men on board . . . she has not yet arrivd."[23] The Salem attorney was reporting the July 10 capture of the *Princess Royal* off Bermuda. Four days after Wetmore's log entry, the H.M.S. *Milford* spotted the capture and gave chase "within about 3 Leagues of Cape Anne, & took her within about 3 Miles of Newbury, & Brought the said ship into the Port of Halifax."[24] In September, the *Sturdy Beggar*'s fortune improved. It was then under command of Capt. Allen Hallet, and it brought the ship *Batchelor* into Newburyport. On November 14, with Capt. Edward Rolland now on the quarterdeck, the *Sturdy Beggar* took four Newfoundland vessels (*Flora*, *Lion*, *Penguin*, *Triton*) laden with fish bound to Spain and, later, two more prizes, the brigantine *Christian* and the ship *Cornwall*.[25]

The *Rover*, owned by Joseph Sprague, Jacob Ashton, and others, sailed in mid-July, commanded by Simon Forrester. The Irish-born captain would soon number among Salem's most prominent and wealthy men. Armed with six guns, eight swivels, two cohorns (mortars) and manned by sixty crew, the 70-ton *Rover* chalked up several scores during the year. In August 1776, she was one of twelve or thirteen Salem-based privateers including nine schooners, three sloops, and possibly a snow. As the war continued, Salem grew increasingly as Essex County's most active privateering port.[26]

Hundreds of men from Cape Ann were serving aboard privateers, but only a few ships were locally owned. First to cruise was the 70-ton fishing schooner *Britannia*, which was purchased for privateering by Joseph Foster, Epes Sargent, Winthrop Sargent, and others. Renamed *Warren*, in honor of Dr. Joseph Warren, she was fitted out during the summer of 1776. Armed with eight aged guns mounted on new carriages, twelve swivels, and four small cohorns, and carrying fifty men, she was commanded by Capt. William Coas. In September, the *Warren* sent three captures into Cape Ann—the ship *Picary*, the brigantine *Swallow*, and the ship *Sarah and Elizabeth*—all sailing from the West Indies bound for London. The captain's wife and other ladies on board the 500-ton *Sarah and Elizabeth* persuaded the captain to surrender, terrified they would be murdered by "savage" Yankees who, by their cries and screams, were presumed to be Indians. At sunrise, when Captain Foot saw his Lilliputian captor, he is said to have broken into tears.[27]

Before long, scores of privateers plied along the coastal seaboard, in the Gulf of St. Lawrence, and in waters off Europe and among the Caribbean isles. While many continued to raid along the seaboard, American armed vessels were venturing increasingly further afield. The dozens of successes inspired more to take the plunge, but the early years were not without casualties. One of the first was the Newburyport brig *Yankee Hero*.

American Losses, 1775–1776

The 120-ton privateer brig *Yankee Hero*, armed with twelve carriage guns and six swivels, sailed out of Newburyport harbor on June 6, 1776, flying her colors, a pine tree on a white field. Manned by only twenty-six officers and crew, with Capt. James Tracy at the helm, she was bound for Boston to fill her 120-man complement.

On her way around Cape Ann, off Halibut Point, the *Hero* was greeted by two or three fishing boats containing about twenty Sandy Bay (Rockport) men. They came alongside and boarded. The excited Cape Anners reported seeing a large merchantman off shore "clumsily worked," as if she had few sailors, and concluded the vessel could be taken. When the ship first appeared, Lt. Mark Pool convinced many of his Sandy Bay neighbors (including Capt. John Rowe, who had served with him in Bridge's regiment at Bunker Hill) to chase the vessel. They had just left their moorings when the *Yankee Hero* was sighted.[28]

Capt. James Tracy eagerly joined. Fourteen Sandy Bay men stayed, and the boats were returned to shore. Still badly undermanned, the *Yankee Hero* made sail for the merchantman. When almost within cannon range, Tracy and the crew became aghast. The mysterious "merchantman" turned out to be the twenty-eight-gun frigate H.M.S. *Milford*! Tracy made for the shore, but the *Milford* took a fresh breeze and in an hour and one-half had come up alongside.

> The ship hawled her wind so close, (which obliged the brig to do the same) that Capt Tracy was unable to fight his lee guns, upon this he backed under her stern, but the ship which sailed much faster, and worked as quick, had the advantage, and brought her broadside again upon him, which he could not evade; and in this manner they lay not a hundred feet from each other, yawing to and fro, for an hour and twenty minutes, the privateers men valiantly maintaining their quarters against such a superior force. About this time the ships foremast guns beginning to slack fire; Capt. Tracy tacked under her stern, and when clear of the smoak and fire, perceived his rigging to be most shockingly cut, yards flying about without braces, some of his principal sails shot to rags and half of his men to appearance dying, and wounded—[29]

During a lull, the wounded were carried below, while crew went aloft to make emergency repairs. Edging closer to shore, Tracy hoped to escape, but the *Milford* ferociously renewed her attack. Shortly afterward, Tracy was wounded in the thigh. Unable to stand, growing faint, he was helped below. But as soon as he came to, the resolute captain ordered that he be taken "up in a chair upon the quarter deck," where he courageously fought on.[30] Weakened from the pain and loss of blood, he was unable to continue. Having spent nearly all ammunition, the battered *Yankee Hero* would either have to surrender or be sunk. After reportedly firing a final charge—pieces of iron, spikes and a crow bar—Tracy ordered the colors struck.[31]

During the two-hour clash, four crew members were killed and about fourteen wounded, including Tracy. The injured were sent to Halifax; the rest were transferred to the *Milford* and other warships in Nantasket Road. A prisoner exchange was negotiated, and the *Hero*'s crew returned in November.[32]

Earlier, on February 25, 1776, the 100-ton *Unity*, carrying molasses and coffee and under the command of Capt. Daniel Lunt, was bound toward Newburyport "about two leagues distant from Cape-Ann" when she was captured by the H.M.S. *Lively*. The prize was brought to Boston, and Lunt was transferred to the *Renown*, a British East

India merchantman. His money was stolen, and he endured, with "all the masters of American vessels who have of late, unfortunately fell into their hands . . . the hardest and most ignominious services on board and were from day to day loaded with curses and reproaches." Lunt escaped on the night of March 20 and published his account in Newburyport's *Essex Journal* of April 19, exposing the harsh conditions that his confined countrymen continued to suffer.

While Massachusetts privateers were combing Atlantic waters looking for ministerial transports, British warships roamed the same seas searching for American ships engaged in foreign trade. Many county carriers had been taken, disrupting normal commerce. The *Unity* was one of more than a score of Essex County craft captured after May 1775, usually traveling inbound laden either with firewood from Maine or West Indies cocoa, molasses, rum, and sugar, or outbound carrying fish or lumber. The extent of losses can be imagined from the captured vessels left behind in the British evacuation of Boston. Tied up to the wharves were at least nine schooners and brigs belonging to Marblehead, Newburyport, and Salem.[33]

Secret Service

At least one local vessel was employed as a spy ship. In the spring of 1776, Robert Haskell of Beverly received permission from the Massachusetts Council to sail his fishing schooner, the *Dove*, from Nova Scotia. Haskell carried a small quantity of foodstuffs, but the real purpose of his voyage was to supply Massachusetts with intelligence of British activity in Nova Scotia. In July, at the recommendation of Josiah Batchelder, Jr., of Beverly, the Council rehired Haskell and the *Dove* for several months' secret service, to furnish intelligence of British naval and troop movements.[34]

There also was enemy eavesdropping. In June 1776, the Boston committee of correspondence urged Newburyport and other ports in the province to restrain fishermen from venturing more than a league offshore. Other vessels should not be allowed out without written permission. The committee had evidence from Halifax that the enemy was trying to gain intelligence through the Newburyport "channel" from sailors in small fishing craft. Too much, they feared, was reaching "our Enemies Ships" in this manner.[35]

Continuation of Trade

In mid-June of 1775, the Massachusetts Provincial Congress clamped an embargo on all foreign exportation. A profusion of provision vessels was being lost to the enemy. Also, most exports were scarce and needed locally. Shortly after the resolve, permission was granted for several vessels to leave Gloucester, Newburyport, and Salem loaded with hogsheads of lower-quality "Jamaican fish" for the West Indies. Others left, however, without authorization. In December, for instance, Benjamin Balch of Newburyport was reported to have exported fish contrary to the resolve. By early 1776, Jamaican and pickled fish were exempted from the trade restriction. Later, with the Council's permission, lumber and captured cargoes could be exported. On April 6, 1776, the Continental Congress permitted import and export of all goods (subject to provincial restrictions), except to and from countries under the domination of Great Britain. While many obeyed Massachusetts' embargo, there was chronic evasion, including a quiet illicit commerce with Nova Scotia.

On October 20, 1774, the First Continental Congress had called for cessation of the export trade with Britain, Ireland, and the English West Indies after September 10, 1775. During their November 1775 Nova Scotia "soirée," Continental privateersmen Broughton and Selman captured the Derby-owned brig *Kingston Packet*, laden with dry fish for Jamaica—weeks after this trade was prohibited. Owned by Richard Derby, Jr., a renowned friend of the Revolutionary movement, the brig was not considered a legitimate prize and released. Provincial headquarters and the Salem committee of safety overlooked the Derby breach of the new regulation, finding his action not clearly contrary to the Continental Association and an activity in which many were engaged.[36] Derby exclaimed, "That if I have by my Conduct in this Voyage, Justly offended any, I am Heartily sorry for it."[37] In December, a legislative committee visited Salem to investigate the allegation that Elias Hasket Derby had imported coffee and other goods from Dominica, contrary to the Association. After the inquiry, Derby was absolved. Instead, Derby's captain, Peter Lander, of the schooner *William*, caught the blame.[38] Business and politics sometimes mixed to compel flexible interpretation of the laws.

While Massachusetts sent its own craft overseas, it also chartered vessels for badly needed material. In mid-June of 1775, the committee of supplies hired the Newburyport schooner *Britannia*. Under command of William Pierce Johnson, the 80-ton vessel returned in October from the West Indies with a godsend: 1,300 pounds of gunpowder and hundreds of arms. The cargo was divided among powder-starved towns up and down the coast, including Marblehead and Salem; twelve swivels went to Newburyport to help reinforce defenses. Two months later, the General Court permitted a vessel owned by Jacob Boardman and others to leave Newburyport for

Europe. When she returned, the agreed price for her cargo of powder was refused, so the General Court authorized its seizure.[39]

Some vital war supplies were shipped quietly out of France before
the 1778 alliance. A vessel would leave a French port with papers
fraudulently cleared for the French West Indies. When nearing the
American coast, she would dash into a convenient port and unload.
On May 29, the frigate *Belleisle* arrived in Newburyport from St.
Maloes, with ninety barrels of gunpowder and some artillery, bombs,
and shells for the provincial army.[40]

Economic Depression

It was not long before coastal towns began to feel the war's economic effects. During the fall, they had to bear most of their own
defense costs. This burden came when town treasuries already were
shrinking, as trade and fishing had come nearly to a standstill. Thousands of craftsmen (housewrights, masons, coopers, etc.), dock workers, fishermen, and sailors were out of work. Traders were left
without goods to sell. Few had savings to fall back on, so the effects
were felt immediately. In Gloucester, Marblehead, and Salem, nearly
the entire economy revolved around fishing or trade. Relief rolls
spiraled. In January, Salem was maintaining 120 people in alms-
houses and workhouses, plus assisting 50 others. Marblehead inves-
tigated "farming out" the workhouse poor as laborers to the country
towns. The staggering wartime costs and narrowed tax base required
many towns to borrow. In 1776, all county ports—Beverly, Gloucester, Manchester, Marblehead, Newburyport, and Salem—were forced
to request an abatement of their annual province tax.

In the port towns, where, customarily, imported grain and flour
had been available, diminished stocks now made bread scarce. Salem
reported no grain after April 19, 1775. Since the town had fewer
than a dozen farmers, only limited produce was home grown. A
committee of five Society of Friends visitors from the Quaker bread-
basket colonies of Pennsylvania and New Jersey came to aid Salem's
poor. On December 29, the town thanked their "charity & kind
relief." The same month, seven Philadelphia Friends had toured
Marblehead, in the company of selectmen, making donations to the
needy. On December 20, four "Quaker gentlemen" visited Gloucester. Early in 1776, Gloucester and Salem were visited for a second
time. In January, two schooners, captained by William Coas and
William Ellery, were sent by Gloucester to Virginia for grain. Ipswich
and Manchester already had voted to do the same. Beverly ordered
selectmen to purchase 1,500 bushels of grain and ten casks of rice
for benefit of the town. With few yeomen in port towns, and large

Newburyport was the privateering hub in northern Essex County. Note ship on stocks and masts of vessels tied to wharves at foot of Fish (now State) Street. Courtesy, Peabody Museum of Salem.

numbers—from seaboard and countryside alike—away in the military, farm produce was sparse; imports from the interior carried a high price tag. Yet, more difficult times would lie ahead.[41]

Continuing Ventures

During the summer, a pod of Newburyport-owned privateers was licensed: the schooner *Hawke*, the brigantine *Civil Usage*, the schooner *Independence*, and the brigantine *Dalton*. While the four met with varying success, the six-gun, 70-ton *Hawke*, owned by the eminent merchant house of Jackson, Tracy & Tracy and under command of the former Marbleheader, Capt. John Lee, earned extraordinary kudos. After being fitted out in mid-August, Lee made five captures during an Atlantic crossing. One was the 200-ton ship *Nancy*, bound from Cork for Quebec laden with provisions (barrels of beef, flour, oatmeal and pork, 68,000 pounds of bread, 1,200 bushels of peas, 200 firkins of butter), 207 casks of nails, and 23 barrels of gunpowder. Another prize was the 180-ton brigantine *Susannah*, from Oporto, Portugal, reportedly carrying a valuable cargo in specie and 300 pipes of port wine. Early in October, the *Hawke* put in to the neutral port of Bilbao, Spain, and was detained while two English captains protested through the British consul, accusing Lee of piracy. Late in October, the sympathetic Spanish permitted Lee to purchase provisions and to proceed home. Furthermore, America was assured that in the future privateers and prizes would be welcomed in Spanish ports. The year ended lamentably, however, when the twenty-gun *Dalton*, owned by Stephen Hooper and Tristram Dalton, sailing from Newburyport in mid-November under Capt. Eleazer Johnson, struck on December 24 to the sixty-four-gun British man-of-war *Raisonnable*. The *Dalton*'s 120 officers and crew (46 from Newburyport) were confined in Mill Prison at Plymouth, England.[42]

The 70-ton brigantine *Retaliation*—first vessel to be both owned by Beverlyites and to sail from Beverly—chose to hunt her prey in the West Indies, a favorite haunt for American privateers. Owned by Josiah Batchelder, Jr., and others, she carried ten guns, nine swivels, and seventy men under command of Eleazer Giles of Beverly. Commissioned on September 4, 1776, the *Retaliation* sailed, loaded with fifty barrels of beef and pork, four quintals (hundredweights) of fish, ten bushels of potatoes, two tons of bread, four hundred cannon shot, twenty-five muskets, thirty cutlasses, and ten lances. On his maiden cruise, Giles fell in with a "Jamaica fleet" and captured four prizes, including the 350-ton, rum-and-sugar-laden *St. Lucie*. On the next sail, with letter of marque papers, the *Retaliation* carried some of the captured sugar, under an export license, to Charleston and returned with rice and naval stores. During the fall of 1777, the *Retaliation* was captured and taken into Halifax. Giles, who became the first Beverly captain to be captured, was released in a prisoner exchange, and later commanded the *Cato* and *Saratoga*.[43] Along the North Shore, the privateering fleet based in well-protected Beverly harbor was second only to Salem's.

August 30, 1776, was commissioning day for the first Marblehead-owned privateer: the New Mills–built, ten-gun schooner *True Blue*, commanded by William Cole and owned by Jonathan Glover & Company. One week later, Marblehead's second privateer, the sloop *Polly*, with Isaac Collyer as commander, was licensed. Owned by William Blacklair, James Mugford & Company, she carried twelve guns, eighteen swivels, and one hundred men. By November 23, two *True Blue* captures were lying in Marblehead harbor. Also, the *Polly* had sent in a 120-ton prize—a brig laden with salt out of Lisbon—followed in mid-December by the ship *Garland*.[44] Before year's end, other Marblehead privateers sailed.

Sure-footed Marblehead seafarers manned scores of privateer decks; about thirty sea hunters were locally owned. But many potential local investors—like Jacob Fowle, Sr., Thomas Gerry, Sr., and Jeremiah Lee—recently had died; some monied men with Loyalist leanings—notably, Robert "King" Hooper, Benjamin Marston, and Thomas Robie—had left town. Still others, like Elbridge Gerry and John Glover, were busily serving their country. So, compared to Beverly, Newburyport, or Salem, privateer venture capitalists in Marblehead were in short supply.

As 1776 progressed, and word of immense profits spread, privateering took on frenzied proportions. During the year, Massachusetts handed out commissions to sixty-nine separate vessels. Amazingly, about half were owned and based in Essex County. Some, after ownership or commands changed, were recommissioned, like the *Dolphin* on August 14. Now under Samuel Waters, within weeks the *Dolphin* brought in three captures: the sloop *Halifax*, the schooner *Prosperity*, the brigantine *Royal George*.[45] On August 15, writing to Samuel Adams, James Warren noted, "The Success of those that have before Engaged in that Business has been sufficient to make a whole Country privateering mad."[46]

By comparison with subsequent years, though, activity was modest. From 1779, annually, Massachusetts issued two to three times more commissions. During 1776, the Continental Congress distributed only thirty-four commissions throughout the colonies; five years later, the number had skyrocketed tenfold to about 350!

A Financial Assist

Privateering offered survival for maritime towns, giving opportunities to thousands who were normally employed in fishing and commerce, as well as to others who flocked in from the countryside. Ships carrying letters of marque paid salaries, and bonuses when a prize was taken, but privateers were all risk—either there was no pay or a bonanza.

In privateering, Salem was preeminent. Its wharves and streets bustled with activity, as swarms of sailors strolled "rolling and rollicking along, with their pockets full of money (hard money), singing songs, chewing tobacco, smoking cigars, drinking at all the public houses, playing tricks upon the country-men, and especially upon the country-women who brought berries into town to sell."[47]

The whole of Essex County embraced privateering. Enemy captures pumped life-saving infusions into the economy, with their cargoes helping to alleviate the wartime scarcity. During 1776, America had taken three hundred and fifty enemy vessels (forty-four were recaptured). At least 25 percent had fallen to Essex County armed vessels, either privately owned or belonging to Washington's fleet! The next year, many more armed privateers would be added to the county flotilla, thirty from Salem alone. In 1777, undaunted, and despite the tight blockade by three British men-of-war in Massachusetts Bay, Essex private warships spread their sails, going on to achieve a record unmatched in the annals of privateering.

1. Philip Chadwick Foster Smith, ed., *The Journals of Ashley Bowen of Marblehead* (Salem: Peabody Museum, 1973), 2:464.
2. William Bell Clark, ed., *Naval Documents of the American Revolution*, 1:677.
3. 2:834–39.
4. 2:1098, 1217, 1316; 4:81, 667; 5:508, 596; Gardner Weld Allen, MHS Coll, Vol 67, *Massachusetts Privateers of the Revolution* (Cambridge: Harvard University Press, 1927), 116; James Duncan Phillips, *Salem in the Eighteenth Century* (Boston: Houghton Mifflin, 1937), 396; Smith, 2:464–65.
5. John J. Currier, *History of Newburyport, Mass. 1764–1905* (Newburyport: John J. Currier, 1906) 1:613–14, 637; Clark, 3:4–5, 49–50, 62–63, 165; Allen, *Mass. Privateers*, 87, 141, 154, 321.
6. Octavius Thorndike Howe, *Beverly Privateers in the American Revolution* (Cambridge: University Press, 1922), 335.
7. E. Vale Smith, *History of Newburyport* (Newburyport: E. Vale Smith, 1854), 106.
8. "Boyle's Journal of Occurrences in Boston, 1759–1778," *NEHGR*, 85 (1931):27.
9. Clark, 2:248–49, 278–79, 300; 5:118–19.
10. 2:879–81, 891–93, 1007.
11. 3:966.
12. 3:810, 855, 1010; Joshua Coffin, *A Sketch of Newbury, Newburyport, and West Newbury*, (Boston: Samuel G. Drake, 1845), 251–52; in addition to the *Sukey* and *Washington* captures, on January 17 William Pynchon of Salem noted that Newbury boats had brought two captures into York harbor, Maine.
13. Clark, 3:876; Coffin, 252.
14. Clark, 3:764; 4:18, 19, 136, 157, 296–97, 389.
15. E. Vale Smith, 109.
16. Clark, 3:1095, 1156; 4:63–64, 389, 609. The powder was delivered by the selectmen of Salem at the request of Richard Devens, commissary general. The town recently had purchased a boatload from Richard Derby, Jr.; 4:405.
17. 6:347–48, 776; "An Historical Trip Through Danvers," DHS *Collections*, 4 (1916), 24–25; Force, 4th Series, 4:1324.
18. Allen, *Mass. Privateers*, 291; Peter Force, ed., *American Archives*, 4th Series, 6:629; Clark, 5:765; 6:347, 358, 817–18.
19. Allen, *Mass. Privateers*, 291; *The Essex Journal & New-Hampshire Packet* (hereinafter, *Essex Journal*), August 9, 1776; Clark, 5:89, 870; 6:192.
20. Clark, 4:177–78; 5:88–89, 140–41, 491, 506.
21. 5:596; Force, 5th Series, 1:274.
22. Clark, 5:1109–10.
23. 5:506; "Extracts from the Interleaved Almanacs of William Wetmore of Salem, 1774–1778," *EIHC*, 43 (1907):118.
24. Clark, 6:92.
25. 6:1114–15; 7:757, 1188; "Auction Sales in Salem, of Shipping and Merchandise, During the Revolution," *EIHC*, 49 (1913):97, 105.
26. Clark, 5:870–71, 1034–35; Phillips, 399–400.
27. Clark, 6:13–14, 899, 952, 1053–55, 1114; John J. Babson, *History of the Town of Gloucester* (Gloucester: Procter Bros., 1860), 409–10.
28. Babson, 399.
29. *Essex Journal*, August 9, 1776.
30. *Essex Journal*.
31. Babson, 399.
32. Clark, 5:447–48, 507–08; 6:128, 373, 1269; 7:83–84.
33. 2:1373–77; 4:812–13.
34. 5:5–6, 1055; Howe, 340–41.
35. "Record of the Boston Committee of Correspondence, Inspection and Safety, May to November, 1776," *NEHGR*, 30 (1876):388–89.
36. Clark, 2:1244, 1284, 1316–17; 3:6.
37. 3:17.
38. Force, 4th Series, 4:1339, 1346, 1437.
39. Clark, 1:678–80; 2:658–59; 839–40; 3:183–84, 714; Currier, 1:562–64.
40. Force, 4th Series, 6:629.
41. Salem Town Records, EI, December 29, 1775, 88, May 18, 1776, 131; MA Archives, 180:120–21; 178, 275–77; Edwin M. Stone, *History of Beverly* (Boston: James Munroe, 1843), 82; Ipswich Town Records, December 4, 1775, 4:270; Babson, 397–98; John J. Babson, *Notes and Additions* (Gloucester: M. V. B. Perley, 1876), 147; Smith, 2:468.
42. Allen, *Mass. Privateers*, 99, 108, 168, 185; Clark, 6:1230–31, 1299, 1411; 7:568, 678–79, 696, 698, 706, 730–31, 8:517.
43. Howe, 336–37; Clark, 6:648–49.
44. Allen, *Mass. Privateers*, 239, 307; Clark, 7:274, 1023; 2:499, 503, 505.
45. Clark, 6:178–79, 1001, 1053, 1114.
46. 6:191.
47. C. H. Webber and W. S. Nevins, *Old Naumkeag: The City of Salem* (Salem: A.A. Smith, 1877), 232.

CHAPTER FIFTEEN

FRIENDS LOYAL
TO ENGLAND

As 1774 drew to a close, it appeared that America's dispute with England would likely lead to bloodshed. More Americans, tinged now with radicalism, were condoning extralegal—even violent—protest. A minority, however, remained obedient to English authority and continued to argue for reform through peaceful, lawful means. When faced with a choice between enduring British rule, admittedly inept and arbitrary, or risking government by what they viewed as a fickle, rebellious mob, the Loyalists opted for Crown rule. They doubted that propertied, respectable leaders in the militant movement could control the direction of the Revolution. A riotous rabble would wrest control, they feared, at the expense of personal liberty and private property. This belief was most common among the cultured, educated elite, whose life experiences and interests nurtured in them a natural conservatism. Indeed, many propertied Whigs were similarly leery of "rabble" excesses. While most Tories, who preferred to be called Loyalists, favored reducing imperial control in the province, they were not prepared to question England's authority to rule the Empire.

Essex County Loyalists

Most Essex County Loyalists belonged to the upper class—refined in culture and manners, prominent and well-to-do. They were important constituents of the landowning, business, and professional community and, until a few years earlier, among the elected political leaders in the county. Their reputations had earned many important 243

Crown-appointed offices. Customarily, they had graduated from Harvard College and had married women of their own social class. While they usually could claim credit for their successes, the family names often had been prominent for generations.

Large numbers lived in Salem, where profits from trade and fisheries had spawned a group of wealthy conservatives. This prosperous elite lived in elegant, stately homes. Leisured, sharing close social and cultural ties, they cultivated mannerisms, tastes, and appearances of an upper class. Salem's cultural, intellectual life flourished, dominated by these distinguished families. Out of this wealthy subculture developed a powerful Loyalist minority, an integral counterforce and an important portent in Salem's Revolutionary politics.

The Loyalist Departure

Those persons whose actions signaled opposition to the popular movement or obedience to imperial regulations were subjected to scurrilous ridicule and attack. More was at stake than reputation. A wave of popular intolerance crested on the heels of Lexington, Concord, and Menotomy. Weeks before April 19, several prominent Salem Tories already had abandoned town. In neighboring Marblehead, shoremen of the fishing fleet reportedly were threatening "that as soon as Gen'l Gage shall begin to execute any of his orders, that every friend of government there is to be immediately seized and destroyed."[1] Only a propitious withdrawal from the county saved many prominent Tories from bodily harm. As the Loyalist Judge Samuel Curwen noted:

> Since the late unhappy affair at Concord, finding the spirit of the people to rise on every fresh alarm which has been almost hourly, and their tempers to grow more and more sour and malevolent against those whom they see fit to reproach as enemies to their Country. . . . I think it a duty I owe myself to seek some secure asylum, if to be found in America.[2]

After blood had spilled on April 19, public sentiment demanded recantation from Tories who still had not disclaimed their addresses of the previous year. To resist was to place one's life in jeopardy. Suspected Loyalists were faced with three choices: to show allegiance to the Revolutionary movement; to risk anonymity as "silent neutrals"; to flee and seek British protection. Scores left the county, finding refuge in British-held Boston, Halifax, neutral Nantucket, and London. Their faithfulness to principle would cost many absent Loyalists their entire personal fortunes.

Judge Samuel Curwen
(1715–1802). Pastel by
Benjamin Blyth, 1772.
Courtesy, Essex Institute,
Salem, Mass.

William Browne had been among Essex County's most confirmed and prominent Loyalists. The son of a wealthy Salem family, Browne was graduated from Harvard third in his class. After college, he prepared for the law and managed his personal fortune, estimated at over 100,000 acres and £5,000. In 1762, he was chosen as Salem's representative in the General Court, and, two years later, was appointed collector of customs for Salem and Marblehead. During the Sugar Act controversy, his actions in opposition won the approval of his constituents, but he lost popularity in 1768 as one of the disdained "rescinders." Browne never was returned to office.

His reputation of loyalty to the Crown merited him two gubernatorial appointments. In 1771, he became colonel of the Essex militia; three years later, upon the death of Nathaniel Ropes, Browne was named to the Superior Court. As one of ten mandamus councillors, his acceptance of the controversial post forced him to leave Salem for Boston in August 1774. When the British evacuated, Browne left with them, arriving in England via Halifax. Two years later, his wife joined him. Browne, an intractable Loyalist, hoped for an eventual English victory. In 1780, he wrote:

> The more then I contemplate the rise and progress of this wretched rebellion, the more I reprobate its motives, and loath its leaders; nor has there been a punctum temporis since I was driven from my inheritance, when I would have exchanged my condition for the most elevated situation of any one of our adversaries.[3]

Benjamin Pickman (1740–1819) went to England in 1775 and left his wife to manage the family estate, which may have saved it from confiscation. Wax bas-relief by John Christian Rauschner. Courtesy, Essex Institute, Salem, Mass.

Expecting to be rewarded for loyalty, Browne finally, in 1781, won appointment as Bermuda's governor. His allegiance had cost him fourteen farms and other property confiscated by Revolutionary regimes in Connecticut and Massachusetts.[4]

When the Revolution surfaced, Judge Samuel Curwen was deputy judge of admiralty, a post he had held for years. He was born in 1715 to a notable Salem family. Curwen resisted pressures to recant his address of Hutchinson; he left for Philadelphia on April 23, 1775, expecting from Quaker officials a warm welcome and an offer of asylum. Meeting with a cool reception, Curwen proceeded to England. While in exile, he kept a journal, the most valuable work extant on the Loyalists living in England.

Curwen noted in his journal, on February 1, 1776, formation of the New England Club at the "Adelphi Tavern where by appointment I met and dined with 21 of my Countrymen who had agreed on a weekly dinner." Samuel Porter, William Cabot, and Benjamin Pickman of Salem were members. Their weekly gathering provided a touch of home for these lonely Americans.[5] With some trepidation, after nine years, Curwen returned to Salem in 1784, where he lived until his death in 1802.

Benjamin Marston, Salem-born and Harvard-educated, had settled in Marblehead, where he owned numerous stores, warehouses, and several large ships in partnership with Robert Hooper and Jeremiah Lee. Widely noted for his integrity, generosity, scholarship, and community-mindedness, Marston had held several important town offices for years. An early member of the committee of inspection, as late as 1772 Marston was elected selectman. He refused to recant the Hutchinson address and was openly critical of local radicalism. Fallout in 1775 resulted in the mobbing and ransacking of Marston's home. With his safety jeopardized, he hid with some friends until he made a hazardous escape to Boston in an open boat in November; he left with the British evacuation.[6]

In 1787, Marston returned to Boston, but left again shortly afterward for London. After several unsuccessful business ventures, he joined a land colonization scheme off the West African coast. In 1792, shortly before his death, he wrote philosophically from Africa to his sister:

> There is not remaining in my mind the least resentment to the Country because the party whose side I took in the late great Revolution, did not succeed, for I am now fully convinced. It is better for the world that they have not. I don't mean by this to pay any complements to the first instigators of our American Revolution, although it has been of such advantage to mankind, I should as soon think of erecting monuments to Judas Iscariot, Pontius Pilate and the Jewish Sanhedrin for betraying and crucifying the Lord of Life, because that event was so importantly and universally beneficial.[7]

Thomas Robie, a successful Marblehead importer and merchant, showed Loyalist colors early. The only Marbleheader not to support the Stamp Act protest, Robie later refused to subscribe to the Non-importation Act and continued to oppose subsequent radical actions. A staunch individualist, his outspoken pro-British stands intensified local animosities as did his defiant attitude, which precipitated a vote, early in 1775, that the town not pay interest on a debt owed him.

A prominent Marblehead Tory, Robert "King" Hooper endured most of the Revolution at his country home in Danvers. Oil painting by John Singleton Copley.

Two years earlier, he had sold the town of Marblehead about twenty half-barrels of gunpowder at a supposedly exorbitant price and contrary to the Association. In May 1775, with their safety threatened, Robie and family left for Nova Scotia. An ugly mob of onlookers crowding the wharf to watch their departure deluged them with insolent and contemptuous epithets. Their ranting provoked Mrs. Robie to explode, "I hope that I shall live to return, find this wicked rebellion crushed and see the streets of Marblehead so deep run with rebel blood that a long boat might be rowed through them." Her taunts enraged the mob further. Had she not been a woman, Mrs. Robie likely would have been harmed. Sailing first for Halifax, the Robies subsequently traveled to London. In 1783, however, they returned to Marblehead.[8]

Dozens of Loyalists left Salem. John Price, in his schooner *Williams*, departed for Halifax; later, in November 1775, Price was labeled a Tory of "first magnitude" and his vessel was detained by the Chatham committee of correspondence.[9] West Indies merchant John Sargent, son of Col. Epes Sargent, was rumored to have assisted Leslie on his Salem incursion. Sargent fled to Boston in March 1775 and sailed for Nova Scotia.[10] Samuel Porter, an attorney and Sargent's half-brother, also was suspected of helping Leslie. He was imprisoned for not joining the army. (Early in May 1775, the Provincial Congress had required all able-bodied men to appear in arms when called upon by their militia officers.) Porter was released late in May, and he accompanied James Jeffrey on his return to Montreal. Along the way, he became apprehensive and turned off for Albany, New York, ultimately ending up in England.[11] Benjamin Pickman, a successful Salem merchant, refused to recant his Gage address. He sailed from Boston for Bristol in mid March 1775; his wife remained behind to manage the family estate. Whether by accident or by design, Mrs. Pickman's occupancy of the home probably had prevented its confiscation. Pickman returned in 1785.[12] Peter Frye, Pickman's son-in-law, was judge of the Inferior Court of Common Pleas, justice of the peace and register of probate. Shortly after the October arson fire, he fled to Ipswich. Frye was searching for peace and security, but threats and harassment forced him out of the country.[13] Capt. Thomas Poynton, a Salem mariner, suffered personal abuse and many broken windows in his home for not recanting his Gage address. Before April 19, he had left for England.[14] English-born George Deblois, Sr., was a merchant and importer of British goods. A supporter of the Stamp Act and an addresser of Hutchinson and Gage, Deblois refused to take up arms. Frequently insulted, his life endangered, Deblois departed for Nova Scotia on April 28, 1775, accompanied by his wife and two children.[15] Widow merchantwomen

Elizabeth and Mehetabel Higginson each left Salem separately for Halifax, but returned several years later.[16] Indeed, Salem lost many Loyalist émigrés only temporarily.

Shopkeepers Andrew Daglish, William Cabot, James Hastie, and Nathaniel Sparhawk, and Doctors P. G. Kast and John Prince (son-in-law of Capt. Richard Derby) left, but Cabot, Hastie, and Prince subsequently came back.[17] Joseph Dowse, surveyor, searcher, and landwaiter for Salem and a Gage addressor, evacuated but later returned.[18] Henry Gardner went to St. Eustatia but reappeared in 1781.[19] Early in May, Nathan Goodale, an addressor of Hutchinson and Gage, fled to Nantucket with his family; he returned and was elected to the General Court in 1781.[20] After years of exile, a surprising number of evacuees returned and were accepted back. This toleration is testimony to the magnanimity and conservatism of Salem's Revolutionary leaders.

Two former Danvers residents were Loyalists: Rev. William Clark of Dedham, minister of St. Paul's, and James Putnam, Sr., who settled in Worcester during 1749. Putnam became a prominent attorney. Both fled Massachusetts.

Attempts to Remain

Born in 1709, Robert Hooper, popularly known as "King Hooper," climbed from poverty to become a major figure in the Marblehead fishing trade. For a while, Hooper bought all fish carried into Marblehead and exported catches to Bilbao and other Spanish ports. Exchanging fish for coin in Spain enabled Hooper to purchase goods in England for resale in America. Hooper possessed vast real estate holdings in Danvers, Marblehead, Salem, and other towns outside Essex County. He occupied a large house in Marblehead and owned a country home in Danvers, where he endured most of the Revolution. One of the most wealthy men in Massachusetts, Hooper rode in a chariot like a king, hence the name, "King." During the summer of 1774, Governor-General Gage occupied Hooper's Danvers residence. An addressor of Hutchinson, shortly afterward Hooper was appointed a mandamus councillor—an appointment he wisely refused. The elderly Hooper was not driven from his home, but he died bankrupt in 1790. Two sons, Robert and Swett, also remained, but a third, Joseph, had to leave, and his property was confiscated. A merchant and rope maker, Joseph Hooper outlasted three failed rebel attempts to burn his elegant home, popularly known as "Tory Hall." Finally, refusing to renounce allegiance to the Crown, Hooper's Tory sympathies forced him to flee. He boarded his father's brig *Nancy* for Bilbao on May 3, 1775 and lay for the forty-two nights of the voyage on a cargo of dried fish. One-third of his vast estate was given to his wife; the rest was confiscated and sold. A fourth son, Stephen, settled in Newburyport. He was brother-in-law to Tristram Dalton, who belonged to one of the leading patriot families.[21]

Unlike his patriot brothers, Colonels John and Jeremiah, Capt. Samuel Lee of Manchester was a prominent Tory. He was a respected merchant and housewright, whose work included the famous Lee mansion of Marblehead. Born in 1714, a former selectman, moderator, and captain of militia, Lee was one of the town's foremost citizens. Though feeling abused and treated unfairly, Lee remained in his native Manchester vigorously fighting punitive taxation. "Turkish Laws," a wrathful Lee explicated, were "Much Preffarable & Juster then the Assessors conduct."[22]

The learned, public-spirited Hon. Benjamin Lynde, Jr., born in 1700, a retired Supreme Court chief justice, remained in Salem environs throughout the Revolution. Lynde's notable reputation and advanced age permitted him to live in relative security. He died in 1781.[23]

Twelve Salem Loyalists who, a year earlier, were addressors of Governor Hutchinson, publicly recanted on May 30, 1775. Although the committee of safety accepted their declarations, four—Andrew Daglish, Nathaniel Dabney, Nathan Goodale, Nathaniel Sparhawk—eventually chose to leave the country.[24] The others—Rev. Thomas Barnard, Francis Cabot, Doctors E. A. Holyoke and Ebenezer Putnam, John Nutting, William and C. Gayton Pickman, William Pynchon—continued to live in Salem. While remaining passively Loyalist, they avoided political controversy by chosing anonymity as "silent neutrals." Like earlier recanters William Vans and Judge Andrew Oliver, they may have even appeared—for survival—to favor the Revolution. There undoubtedly was, however, truth in Oliver's March 1775 statement:

> I readily own that I agree with my countrymen in general . . . if I have had the misfortune in some instances to differ from them in sentiments, it has been only respecting some of the methods which have been pursued for obtaining a redress of our grievances.[25]

Oliver's public declaration apparently satisfied the local committee. Though a Loyalist, his "silent neutrality" permitted him and his family to remain in Salem.

It was a difficult, precarious time for Loyalists. As they walked Salem's streets, they were hissed and sneered at; sometimes, they were snowballed or even tarred and feathered. In mid-November 1775, Timothy Orne barely missed a coat of tar and feathers. A crowd chased him out of his School Street home and forced him to submit, probably for having signed the Hutchinson address.[26] William Pynchon, a prominent attorney and Orne's father-in-law, also narrowly missed a tar-and-feathering, and, months later, in October 1777, had his windows smashed by a mob celebrating Burgoyne's defeat. The celebrants also "rocked" several houses of Pynchon's alleged Tory neighbors. At other times, Loyalist homes were daubed with tar and paint, one of the penalties for continuing to live in Revolutionary Salem.[27]

For some Loyalists, however, the low profile of "silent neutrality" was insufficient to weather the storm. One was Ipswich native Dr. John Calef. On December 30, 1772, Calef went to England as agent for the "Penobscot Associated Loyalists," who had built homes—at Britain's encouragement—along the Penobscot River. For a year Calef remained, in a vain effort to establish Penobscot as boundary for a new, separate territory. Later, in July 1775, the Ipswich surgeon requested permission from the General Court to sail a ship, recently constructed in Danvers, to Penobscot. He proposed to load a cargo of lumber for the West Indies, promising to return laden with locally scarce West Indies commodities. His request was rejected, and the 300-ton vessel was taken. Since the Lexington alarm, Calef had been harassed for refusing to take up arms. On several occasions, in the nighttime, musket shots were fired into his home. Finally, in February 1776, a death threat triggered Calef's departure, with part of his family.[28]

By this time, England had a plan for settling refugee Loyalists at the mouth of the Penobscot and, eventually, for making the region a permanent province. Later in 1779, during the American siege, Calef was engaged as surgeon for a British regiment. Moses Gerrish of Byfield, Newbury, Harvard class of 1762, traveled to Penobscot, where he became a British commissary officer.[29] Refusing to take an oath of fidelity, Michael Coombes was confined to his Marblehead home for eighteen months; in September 1779, he left his family behind and escaped in a small boat to Penobscot. Unable to find employment, he sailed for Halifax the following spring.[30] Many settlers were Down East–bound without political motives. After the war, two hundred and twenty people, largely from Cape Ann and vicinity, settled northwest of Penobscot in the area around the Bay of Passamaquoddy. Only about one in seven, however, were Loyalists.[31]

Many rebels regarded passivity as akin to disloyalty, since there was a scarcity of able-bodied men to fill town quotas. Thomas Buffton, a native of London, had lived in Salem for twenty-three years. In March 1777, rebels tried to coerce him into enlisting. Buffton left town. Nathaniel Dabney owned an apothecary shop and a grocery store in Salem. Fined, intimidated, and insulted for refusing to enlist, he was forced to escape in 1776, leaving his family.[32] Submissive neutrality failed to give the quiet obscurity these Loyalists were seeking.

It was not passivity that jeopardized Jonathan Stickney, Jr., of Rowley; it was his "clamoring in the most impudent and abusive Language" against the Continental Congress, the General Court, and the whole Revolutionary movement. He was arrested and sent to the General Court, which, in April of 1776, ordered him confined to the Ipswich jail. In view of his penitence, the Rowley committee of safety requested that Stickney be conditionally released to his father's house. Freed in June, Stickney left for British-occupied New York, where he probably died. The only other Rowleyite reported to be a Loyalist was young John Hazen, who went to New Brunswick in 1775.[33]

Property of Loyalist evacuees was subject to seizure and sale at public auction. List printed in the *Salem Gazette*, January 31, 1782. Courtesy, Essex Institute, Salem, Mass.

Purfuant to an order of the General Court, there will be fold by us the fubfcribers, at public auction, on the 21ſt day of February, at ten o'clock in the forenoon, at the houfe of Mr. GIDEON PUTNAM, innholder in Danvers, in the county of Effex,

A tract of land in said Danvers, containing about 110 acres of mowing, orcharding, pasturing, and a large quantity of wood and timber, late the eſtate of JOHN LENDALL BORLAND, an abfentee.—Alfo,

About ten acres of upland and ſalt marſh, in Salem, about one mile from north river bridge, fo called, late the eſtate of faid BORLAND.

And on the 22d of February, at one o'clock, P. M. will be fold, by public auction, at Mr. BENJAMIN BURDET's tavern, in the town of Marblehead,

The eſtate late belonging to MICHAEL COOMS, of faid town, an abfentee, confiſting of two dwelling houfes and other buildings, with a large quantity of land for gardening, &c. fituated near the training field, in faid town.—Alfo,

One quarter part of a wharf, with a quarter part of a ſtore thereon.

Likewife, on the 21ſt of February, at one o'clock, P. M. will be fold, by public auction, at the tavern of the abovefaid GIDEON PUTNAM,

A lot of wood land, fituated in the fouth parifh of Danvers, aforefaid, containing about 13 acres, very handy for Salem; faid eſtate was the property of EDWARD GOLDSTON LUTWETCH, of New-Hampſhire State, an abfentee.—

Alfo, will be fold, at public auction, at Mr. GREENLEAF's tavern, at Haverhill, on the 25th of February, at three o'clock, P. M.

A ſtore, &c. late the eſtate of JOHN GOULD, of Haverhill, an abfentee.

The conditions of fale will be made known at time and place; the fale to be continued from day to day, or adjourned to time and place, as the committee ſhall think proper.

LARKIN THORNDIKE,
ISRAEL HUTCHINSON, } Committee.
DUMMER JEWETT,
Danvers, Jan. 16, 1782.

The individualistic mariner Ashley Bowen of Marblehead was among the handful who continued to voice Loyalist sympathies. The colorful diarist and chronicler had been a sailor, rigger, and mender of sails for many years, but his pro-British reputation limited his job opportunities. Shopkeepers, not wanting to anger their patrons, refused to sell him provisions. He was drafted twice and trained for service. When Bowen could find no bondsman, he was assigned to the "Guard Ship" at Boston. In the nick of time, spring of 1778, he met up with an old friend, Capt. Thomas Boyles, and shipped out as mate. The following year, Bowen returned to Marblehead.[34]

Threat of starvation was a weapon used against Col. Epes Sargent also. The prominent Cape Ann merchant had been born in Gloucester in February 1721. His business had grown until he employed ten vessels in fisheries and trade. On March 6, 1775, townspeople voted to investigate residents "Suspected to be Tories." Supposed Loyalists were "to give the Town Satisfaction" of their allegiance. Also among those under committee scrutiny were Dr. David Plummer and Zebulon Lufkin, who complied by declaring support for the proceedings and resolves of the Continental Congress. Only Sargent "refused to comply." Townspeople were forbidden to trade with him. Subjected to abuse and afraid of starving, Sargent moved to Boston, where he decided to sail for Halifax. He could not leave his beloved family, however, so he returned, with some trepidation, to live on Cape Ann. Tragically, he died of smallpox inoculation in 1779, after his request for exemption had been refused.[35]

Of all Essex County Loyalists, Enoch Noyes of Newbury New Town possibly was the most eccentric and colorful. The lanky, long-haired, unkempt Noyes often was seen running barefoot, sometimes brandishing a hatchet. If Noyes were startled, the cause, whether two-legged or four, could be its unlucky target. He had other peculiarities. Noyes occasionally was seen armed with a crossbow shooting robins out of his cherry trees. In one instance, an acquaintance reportedly greeted Noyes with a loud, "How do you do?" Noyes stood up and swung at his unsuspecting greeter and knocked him to the ground. While some considered Noyes erratic and strange, others saw a genius. An avid reader, Noyes could boast the largest library in town. He was among the first in the area to raise fish and to import fruit trees. A free-thinker, Noyes cared little what people thought of him or his political opinions. But he sometimes voiced Tory views too loudly and had to retreat from townsfolk's threats. Noyes built a sub-cellar, with an entrance from the chimney, where he hid for long periods. Each day, he would whittle away on cow horn, shaping buttons and combs. His wife would lower food in a basket tied to a rope. Later in 1777, Col. Moses Little returned to his Turkey Hill farm with ten Hessian mercenaries captured at the Battle of Bennington. One of the prisoners, William Cleland, appeared at Enoch Noyes's door with a knapsack of tools and offered his services as a skilled comb-maker. For nearly twenty years, Noyes had been making combs and selling them in the parish. Now he could apply the techniques of European craftsmanship. From this chance beginning, New Town became the center of a thriving comb industry in the nineteenth century.[36]

Most Difficult Times

The bleak years of 1777 and 1778, when the Revolution was at its low point, were the most difficult for Loyalists. Most who were still living in the county kept their politics to themselves, choosing obscurity through neutrality. In early May 1777, the General Court encouraged towns to report anyone considered an enemy to the Revolutionary movement. On July 8, Rowley voters elected Capt. Thomas Mighill, "being a person firmly attached to the American cause," to proceed against persons believed with "inimical dispositions."[37] Other Essex County communities likewise appointed a trusted townsperson to gather evidence against suspected "internal enemies," but only a few actually were accused. Newburyport voted Daniel Bayley and John Anderson to be tried at a special session. Daniel Farnham would have been tried as well, but he had died the previous year. A prominent Harvard-educated attorney and town moderator, Farnham had openly decried "Whigs and liberty men" as "law-breakers" and "rebels."[38] Marblehead listed seven suspects: Woodward Abraham, Edward Bowen, Capt. Michael Coombes, Richard Coombes, Robert Hooper, Rev. Joshua Wingate Weeks, and John Wormsted.[39] Salem reported eight: Joseph Blaney, Gage addressor and merchant; Peter Frye; Jeremiah Hacker; James Hastie; John Lawless; John Lee; Dr. Ebenezer Putnam; and Nathaniel Sparhawk.[40] Beverly town records for April 1777 noted that Benjamin Ellinwood, Edward Ford, and William Stone had "gone off turned Tory," followed in August by Ezra Ellinwood.[41] With the uncertain course of the war and draft pressures, notwithstanding even silent neutrality, the times were disquieting for Essex County Tories.

At the height of anti-Toryism, Massachusetts passed measures to prevent fugitives from returning and to expropriate their property. The September 1778 Banishment Act forbade return of over three hundred refugees who had left and were believed to have "joined the enemies." Named were William Browne, Benjamin Pickman, Samuel Porter, and John Sargent of Salem; Thomas Robie and Benjamin Marston of Marblehead; Richard Saltonstall and Rev. Moses

Badger of Haverhill. In 1776, a Haverhill committee had seized Badger's house and a half-acre, which it leased. Saltonstall's house was fully mortgaged, so only household possessions were confiscated.[42] Haverhill assumed authority from a January 1776 Provincial Congress resolve which permitted local authorities to manage and lease refugees' real estate and personal property. On April 30, 1779, two confiscation acts passed. One dealt with estates of "notorious conspirators"; of twenty-nine named only William Browne of Salem was from Essex County. The second concerned certain unnamed "absentees" who "hath levied war," given "aid or comfort" to the enemy, or withdrawn to dominions of Great Britain or places under Crown control. The act specified their lands and property shall "escheat, enure and accrue" to the state. Possibly to protect their homes, many refugees, like Benjamin Pickman, endured life without their families, which usually warded off seizure. On June 23, Col. Israel Hutchinson was named to identify Loyalist "Lands and Tenements" in Essex County.[43] An act of November 29, 1780 provided for selling confiscated absentees' "estates and effects" at public auction. For Essex, Capt. Samuel Ward of Salem, Col. Israel Hutchinson of Danvers, and Dummer Jewett of Ipswich were empowered to grant deeds and bills of sale.[44] During 1781 and 1782, auction or confiscation notices published in the *Salem Gazette* named: Moses Badger, John Gould, and Leverett Saltonstall (youngest son of Richard) of Haverhill; Michael Coombes, Joseph Hooper, Benjamin Marston, and Thomas Robie of Marblehead; Nathaniel Dabney and Andrew Daglish of Salem. Also named were John Lendall Borland of Boston; Edward Goldstone Lutwick of Litchfield, New Hampshire; and Abijah Willard of Lancaster, all of whom owned tracts in Danvers, where Hutchinson probably put town property under particular scrutiny.[45] Despite these efforts, many Tories—like Thomas Robie, through influential patriot friends and clever attorneys—later succeeded in reentering the county and regaining much of their property.

In British Service

Some Essex County sons actually joined the British military. Peter Oliver, son of Lt. Gov. Thomas Oliver, was a Harvard-educated Salem physician and surgeon. He fled to Boston, went to Nova Scotia, and eventually became a surgeon to the Royal Regiment of Dragoons.[46] Before the war, Salem surgeon Thomas Boulton authored several articles in which he poignantly argued Crown views. The rebels, who had targeted Boulton, destroyed his home and furniture and robbed him of household possessions. Before April 19, Boulton left Salem and became a British volunteer. William Browne, Jr., fled to England;

soon afterwards, he was appointed ensign in the British 58th Regiment of Foot. Richard Routh, an English-born Salem merchant and deputy collector of customs, left Boston with the British evacuation, went to Halifax and then to New York, where he joined the Associated Loyalists of Massachusetts.[47] Other Salem residents who tried to enter British service were: James Grant, a Gage addressor—who first went to Halifax, then Boston—bound in January 1776 to the promise of a Royal commission; Lt. Francis Cox, of Mansfield's regiment, who defected to the British at Bunker Hill; Peter P. Frye, who deserted to join the enemy, was brought on Boston Common to be shot, "blinded and required to knell," but reprieved at the last moment, "being deemed a lunatic"; John Lawless, who took up arms in 1777 with the Independent Company of Massachusetts Volunteers in defense of New York.[48] In 1782, Daniel Somes of Gloucester, aboard a fourteen-gun brig from Penobscot, lent his knowledge of Gloucester harbor to the enemy to permit a raiding party to "cut out" the fishing vessel *Harriot*.[49] One of Newburyport's few Loyalists was storeowner George Deblois, Jr., who early on left with his family. In 1777, he joined the Massachusetts Volunteers in New York. After the war, he settled in Halifax.[50] Undoubtedly, others fought for the Crown, but their numbers were inconsequential compared to the thousands who served in Revolutionary ranks.

The Americans who fought on the Crown side were honorable, good men. Their love for the British empire was intense and unswerving. Loyalists were convinced that the War of Independence was foolhardy and that England would win.

The Church of England

Popular feeling against the Church of England increased as political antagonisms with the British government escalated. George Whitefield and other evangelists had fostered distrust by their attacks on the church and its teachings. Suspicion toward the church, however, was understandable. Not only the recipient of ecclesiastical direction and financial support from England, the Anglican Church indeed was the established Church of England—irrefutably linked to British political authority. When the Revolution finally arrived, almost all Anglican clergy remained loyal to the Crown.

Avowed Loyalist Rev. Joshua Wingate Weeks publicly advised his Marblehead parishioners to remain outside of the Revolutionary movement. The St. Michael's congregation was divided along political lines; Weeks's words ruptured church unity. During the Revolution, courageously refusing to take an oath of allegiance, Weeks was arrested and imprisoned several times. Early in January, 1778, St.

Michael's closed, and Weeks finally fled to Rhode Island. Most Anglican clergymen in New England had fled long before.[51]

Rev. William McGilchrist of Salem, rector of St. Peter's Church, was highly respected by townspeople and warmly regarded by his parishioners. His popularity suffered early when McGilchrist continued to include in his church service the prescribed liturgy, which embraced an affirmation of loyalty to the Crown. During this period, when enmity was on a personal, as well as a national level, the pastor's character and reputation were assailed. During worship, people demonstrated loudly outside and boys "rock[ed] the tory church," expecting their maliciousness to go unpunished. The congregation lost membership and services were finally suspended in February 1777, when a law was passed forbidding use of the liturgy. McGilchrist died in Salem during 1784, after seeing his life's work and his character destroyed. Dr. E. A. Holyoke wrote that "he was esteemed by all who were really acquainted with his character as a gentleman of learning, integrity, charity, virtue, and purity."[52]

Of the county's Anglican clergy, Rev. Edward Bass, pastor of St. Paul's Church in Newburyport, was the exception. In July 1776, Bass agreed to omit the offensive liturgic portions from his service. He remained in Newburyport throughout the Revolution and, years later, became the first Episcopal Bishop of Massachusetts and Rhode Island.

A Proud Legacy

The Loyalist story is an integral chapter of the War of Independence. The Revolutionary struggle was primarily for political freedom, without the social upheavals that accompanied the French Revolution in the 1790s. Consequently, a reign of terror such as that waged against the French aristocracy and others did not take place. Essex County Tories lost civil liberties, but none came near losing his head. Despite a myriad of tribulations, they stood by the mother country, which was not an easy choice. Choosing the popular side would have made life much less onerous. Ranging from free-thinking individualists like Enoch Noyes and Ashley Bowen to the aristocratic leaders typified by William Browne and Samuel Curwen, Loyalists made abounding contributions to Essex County's history. Fortunately, many remained. Others returned to lend their talents to the creation of a firm foundation for the new Republic.

1. Fitch Edward Oliver, ed., *The Diary of William Pynchon* (Boston: Houghton Mifflin, 1890), 43.

2. Andrew Oliver, ed., *The Journal of Samuel Curwen Loyalist* (Cambridge: Harvard University Press, 1972), 1:1.

3. Letters of William Browne, MHS, January 15, 1780, Section 2:3.

4. E. Alfred Jones, *The Loyalists of Massachusetts* (London: The Saint Catherine Press, 1930), 58–61; "Essex County Loyalists," *EIHC*, 43 (1907):290–302.
5. A. Oliver, 1:111; James H. Stark, *The Loyalists of Massachusetts* (Salem: Salem Press, 1910), 246–54; Jones, 106–07.
6. "Essex County Loyalists," 309–12; Stark, 460–62.
7. Stark, 462.
8. 457–59; Samuel Roads, Jr., *The History and Traditions of Marblehead* (Marblehead: N. Allen Lindsey, 1897), 142–43; "Essex County Loyalists," 313–15; Jones, 243–44.
9. Peter Force, ed., *American Archives*, 4th Series, 3:1513.
10. James Duncan Phillips, *Salem in the Eighteenth Century* (Boston: Houghton Mifflin, 1937), 386.
11. "Journal Kept in Quebec in 1775, by James Jeffrey," *EIHC*, 77 (1914):149; Jones, 237–38.
12. Jones, 236; *The Holyoke Diaries* (Salem: Essex Institute, 1911), 86.
13. Jones, 139.
14. 239; Lorenzo Sabine, *The American Loyalists* (Boston: Charles C. Little and James Brown, 1847), 548.
15. "Essex County Loyalists," 302–04; Jones 114–15.
16. Phillips, 311; "Letters of Mrs. Mehetabel Higginson," MHS *Proceedings*, 2nd Series, 10 (1896):457; *The Holyoke Diaries*, 50, 87.
17. Jones 264, A. Oliver, 1:76, 167; F. Oliver, 23, 25; Sabine, 193, 240, 548; *The Holyoke Diaries*, 87.
18. A. Oliver, 1:331.
19. Phillips, 390.
20. A. Oliver, 1:11; Phillips, 390.
21. Stark, 222–24; "Essex County Loyalists," 305–08; Jones, 165–66. Once, someone shot at "King," narrowly missed and the bullet was imbedded in his front door. (Hooper had objected to stripping large lead-sheathed balls which adorned the tops of posts in the front of his house. The metal was needed for ammunition.)
22. Thomas Amory Lee, "The Lee Family of Marblehead," *EIHC*, 52 (1916): 230–31; D. F. Lamson, *History of the Town of Manchester* (Boston: Town of Manchester, 1895), 329–30.
23. Stark, 463–64.
24. *The New-England Chronicle* or *The Essex Gazette*, May 25–June 1, 1775; Sabine, 329, 340.
25. *Essex Gazette*, March 21–28, 1775.
26. A. Oliver, 1:102; Sabine, 498.
27. F. Oliver, 25, 41–42.
28. *Essex Gazette*, December 29–January 5, 1773; MA Archives, 180:81; Jones 69–74; Thomas Franklin Waters, *Ipswich in the*

Massachusetts Bay Colony (Ipswich: Ipswich Historical Society, 1917), 2:306–11.
29. Wilbur H. Siebert, "The Exodus of the Loyalists," *The Ohio State University Bulletin*, 18 (1914):14–15.
30. Jones, 99–100.
31. Siebert, 32–33.
32. Jones, 62, 108–09.
33. Amos Everett Jewett and Emily Mabel Adams Jewett, *Rowley, Massachusetts* (Rowley, MA: The Jewett Family of America, 1946), 73, 77; Waters, 2:334–35.
34. Roads, 144; Philip Chadwick Foster Smith, ed., *The Journals of Ashley Bowen of Marblehead* (Salem: Peabody Museum, 1973), 2:530.
35. Gloucester Town Records, March 20, 1775, 160; Emma Worcester Sargent, *Epes Sargent of Gloucester and His Descendants* (Boston: Houghton Mifflin, 1923), 10–11; James R. Pringle, *History of Gloucester* (Gloucester: James R. Pringle, 1892), 72.
36. Sarah Anna Emery, *Reminiscences of a Nonagenarian* (Newburyport: William H. Huse, 1879), 71; Bernard W. Doyle, *Comb Making in America* (Boston: Bernard W. Doyle, 1925), 15–18; Moses Little's house still stands located along a section of Turkey Hill Road now belonging to Newburyport.
37. Thomas Gage, *The History of Rowley* (Boston: Ferdinand Andrews, 1840), 256.
38. Newburyport Town Records, June 30, 1777, 1:288.
39. Marblehead Town Records, EI, June 2, 1777, 4:550–51.
40. Salem Town Records, EI, May 27, 1777, 199–201.
41. Beverly Town Records, March 14, 1777, 6:131; August 5, 1777, 6:152.
42. Robert E. Moody, *The Saltonstall Papers, 1607–1815* (Boston: MHS, 1972), 1:471–72.
43. *Acts and Resolves*, 21:82.
44. *Acts and Laws, 1780–81*, November 29, 1780, 183–85.
45. See issues of *Salem Gazette* between March 1781 and January 1782.
46. Jones, 225.
47. 43–44, 61, 249.
48. 188–89; F. Oliver, 38–39; Sabine, 232, 332.
49. John J. Babson, *History of the Town of Gloucester* (Gloucester: Procter Bros., 1860), 443–46.
50. Jones, 115; "Essex County Loyalists," 304–05.
51. Roads, 526–28.
52. Gilbert L. Streeter, "Salem Before the Revolution," *EIHC*, 32 (1896):90–92; F. Oliver, 24; Essex Institute *Proceedings*, 2 (1856–60):131.

CHAPTER SIXTEEN

INDEPENDENCE BORN: THE FLEDGLING MONTHS

Five months after independence was gained all had appeared lost. On December 10, 1776, a melancholy General Washington confided to his nephew: "Our only dependence now is upon the speedy enlistment of a new army. If this fails, I think the game will be pretty well up." A string of defeats beginning in late August with Washington's rout from Long Island had plunged the patriot cause into despair. Then four months later, on December 26, victory in Trenton followed by success at Princeton brought Americans new hope and confidence. Washington's campaign of '76 was the most decisive of the war.[1]

Independence

Since the fall of 1774, Massachusetts had been in rebel hands and, practically speaking, independent of British rule. Throughout the colonies, moderate leaders continued to press for accord, as many still hoped for British recognition of American "rights" and a negotiated agreement. But a spirit of concession and compromise did not prevail. The battles of April 19 and Bunker Hill, as well as minor skirmishes, had dashed hopes of a peaceful settlement. In August of 1775, George III had proclaimed the colonies in open rebellion; the following November, the House of Commons passed the Prohibitory Bill, which authorized seizure of American goods wherever found on the high seas and forcible impressment of American merchant sailors. These actions, plus the winter decision to hire German mercenaries, suggested that Britain had forsaken the olive branch for the sword. In January 1776, Thomas Paine's anonymously written *Common Sense* began to circulate among the colonies. (It was published in Newburyport by John Mycall the following April for distribution and sale by Samuel Phillips, Jr., of Andover.) This powerfully written tract, which argued for complete independence, convinced thousands to accept separation. And acts of British aggression proved even more influential. The burning of Charlestown, the depredation of Falmouth, and Benedict Arnold's defeat at Quebec caused lasting bitterness and fear. Even after General Howe's evacuation of Boston on March 17, 1776, most knowledgeable observers realized that clashes with British troops would continue. Since America stood no chance of winning without foreign assistance, leaders speculated that a formal declaration of independence was needed.

Massachusetts was an early supporter of independence. On May 9, 1776, the Massachusetts House had established a study committee and requested each town to instruct its representatives on how they wished to direct the colony's delegates to the Continental Congress. Between May 21 and May 27, Lynn, Newbury, Rowley, and Salisbury voted assent, in harmony with the sentiments expressed in Newburyport's May 31 vote: "that, if the [Honorable] congress should, for the Safety of the united Colonies, declare Them independent of the Kingdom of Great Britain, this Town will, with their Lives & Fortunes, support Them in the Measure." On June 7, towns which had not instructed their representatives were requested to do so. From Ipswich's vote on June 10 to Amesbury's on July 1, the county was united in its support of the Congress's actions. Some towns, like Bradford, gave absolute support to independence. On June 20, Bradfordites voted, "that our Delegates in General Congress be Instructed to Shake of the Tyranical Yoke of Great Britain, and Declare these United Colonies Independent." England was still trying, they said, to enforce arbitrary rule, "by Spilling our Blood, by burning our towns, by Seizing our Property, and by Instigating the Savages of the Wilderness, and Negroes to take up the cause against us." Gloucester's vote of June 24 was unanimous and cast in a dramatic manner: "125 walked from the east side of the House to the west side by which they Voted in the affirmative"; not one "sole" walked "Eastward."[2]

These deliberations of Massachusetts towns elevated revolution to its highest, finest form. Seldom before or since have the actions of a revolutionary regime been determined by a popular referendum of their countrymen. The Massachusetts General Assembly could instruct the delegates (one of whom was Elbridge Gerry of Marblehead), knowing they were supported by popular sentiment. Town meeting actions of May, June, and July had legitimized the Massachusetts Revolutionary movement.

The Declaration of Independence was officially approved and adopted by Congress on July 4, 1776. Five days later, General Washington was reading the document to his troops in New York. The same day, Capt. Ebenezer Francis of Beverly—who, one year later, would be mortally wounded at Hubbardton, Vermont—recounted the soldiers' exuberant response: "Ye Kings Horse & his Statue that was Set up in this City in ye Bowling Green which together with ye preparations Round Cost £12,000 Currency after Reading ye Independency Declaration they Pulled him Down Horse & all & Cut his head off & yesterday whelled it along in a whell Barrow."[3]

A spirit of exultation filled Essex towns, with bells tolling a new era of popular government and national independence. In accordance with Washington's and Congress's orders, on July 17 Col. John Glover read the proclamation, with his regiment in formation near

In New York, soldiers celebrated independence by pulling down the statue of George III. Henry Cabot Lodge Collection. Courtesy, Beverly Historical Society.

the present Independence Park in Beverly. Afterwards, Glover ordered a thirteen-gun salute from seacoast batteries, joined by ships' cannon in the harbor. Selectmen ordered the ringing of church bells, and a bonfire was kindled on Liberty Hill (now Watch Hill). The declaration was published in Salem's *American Gazette* and Newburyport's *Essex Journal*. It was required to be engrossed in town records; ministers of every denomination were instructed to read the document to their congregations. Congregational ministers, who were among the earliest advocates of independence, cheerfully complied.

Rev. William McGilchrist of St. Peter's Anglican Church in Salem, however, refused to follow Congress's mandate. Their lack of support for the new independence made many Anglicans the butt of popular aggressions. When news of independence reached Marblehead, joyously intoxicated townspeople entered St. Michael's Anglican Church, contemptuously pulled King George's coat of arms from its perch above the chancel, and rang the bell until it cracked.[4]

On July 18, the prominent Newburyport merchant Tristram Dalton wrote to Elbridge Gerry, who was still a delegate in Philadelphia: "I wish you joy on the late full Declaration—an event so ardently desired by your good self and the people you particularly represent. We are no longer to be amused with delusive prospects. The die is cast." Indeed, America had taken the final, momentous step.[5]

To New York

General Washington had anticipated William Howe's next move by shifting most of his army southward to New York. As early as March 20, 1776, Lt. Joseph Hodgkins had discovered that his regiment (Little's 12th Continental) was due to leave for a distant encampment. To serve hundreds of miles away would not be easy. Troops had become used to furloughs at home, and to loved ones and neighbors visiting their lines. Hodgkins wrote to his wife in Ipswich:

> But it is generaly thought that our Regt will March some whare I would not Be understood that I should Chuse to March But as I am ingaged in this glories Cause I am will to go whare I am Called with a Desire to Commit myself & you to the care of him Who is able to Carry through all the Defiltes that we may be Called to.[6]

Devotion to "this glories Cause" ultimately would win freedom for America.

For over a year, since the Lexington alarm, Essex County soldiers' day-to-day household and farm responsibilities had been shouldered by wives and children, but with the aid of occasional visits from

	Field Officers 12th Continental Regiment	
Colonel	Moses Little	Newbury
Lt. Colonel	Isaac Smith	Gloucester
Major	Ezra Putnam	Danvers
Captains	John Baker	Topsfield
	Abraham Dodge	Ipswich
	Jacob Gerrish	Newbury
	Ezra Lunt	Newburyport
	Gideon Parker	Ipswich
	Benjamin Perkins	Newburyport
	Nathaniel Wade	Ipswich
	Nathaniel Warner	Gloucester

husbands and fathers. Now that these Continentals would be stationed over two hundred miles away, their presence would be sorely missed; they too, in distant fields, would long for home and family. In April, Hodgkins wrote to his wife from New York: "My Dear the thought of Being absent from you and my family is the greatest troble that I have at Presant." No matter how urgent a problem arose, a soldier often was powerless to return. Hodgkins knew early in August that his little son was ill and dying, but he could do nothing but agonizingly count the days until a letter arrived—as it did on August 22, with the sad news that his son had died. These were difficult, often cruel times for soldiers and their families.[7]

Col. Moses Little headed the 12th Continental Regiment. Formerly, he had been a surveyor of the King's woods, also an investor in large tracts in Maine, and had been numbered among the brave defenders at Bunker Hill. In early April, he marched his regiment to Providence, and, on April 5, they shared the honor of escorting Washington into that town. Marching from Providence to Norwich, then to New London, they embarked for New York on the fourteenth. The more than 400 present and fit members of the 12th Continental Regiment were nearly all from Essex County.

Loammi Baldwin's 26th Regiment also arrived in New York during April. The Woburn native, later renowned for his "Baldwin" apple, was given Gerrish's Essex County regiment after Bunker Hill. Its ranks included men from Andover, Gloucester, Haverhill, Ipswich, Newbury, Rowley, and Wenham. Five of his companies were commanded by Essex officers: Capt. Ezra Badlam of Andover, Capt. Thomas Cogswell of Haverhill, Capt. Barnabas Dodge of Gloucester,

Capt. Richard Dodge of Wenham, Capt. Thomas Mighill of Rowley. On May 5, Baldwin reported 342 able-bodied officers and enlisted men. Over the summer, others from Essex County would trace the same route to New York.

Only five regiments, including Glover's and Hutchinson's, remained in Massachusetts. Col. Israel Hutchinson's force was directed to improve the fortifications on Dorchester Heights; Col. John Glover's men served aboard Continental vessels based in Beverly or guarded the fleet and captured prize vessels in the harbor.[8]

After reaching New York, the commander in chief posted his nine-thousand-man army mostly in Manhattan, deploying one brigade—which included Col. Moses Little's regiment—across the East River on Long Island, where Brooklyn Heights overlooked lower Manhattan. Josiah Adams of Newbury Falls (Byfield), a member of the brigade, wrote home to his brothers on April 30:

> I am now Engaged in the service, in the defence of every thing that is near and dear to freemen—I trust the Cause that I am now engaged In is Just and good and as it is so order'd that america should be involved in such an Unnatural war . . . [I am] Willing to share Ye fate of it with my fellow Countrymen."[9]

Thousands like Adams, fervently committed to the struggle for independence, provided the army's backbone.

During the spring, Washington's army, with New Englanders its nucleus, threw up breastworks in lower Manhattan. Near Brooklyn village, ground was broken on the heights, which commanded New York City; entrenchments were dug, and redoubts—including Fort Putnam—were raised.

Early in June, the Congress urgently sought militia to build up the army. On June 25, Massachusetts answered the call: two thousand for New York and three thousand for Canada, to be raised from training band and alarm lists.

The British strategy of '76 featured a double-pronged pincers movement. Gen. William Howe was to invade New York City and move up the Hudson, while another army, under Gen. Guy Carleton, streamed southward out of Canada, down Lake Champlain and the Hudson Valley, to cut off rebellious New England from the middle colonies and subdue it.

Expedition to Champlain

Essex County's quota for Canada—actually upstate New York—was 457 troops. On June 29, an order arrived in Haverhill to raise 43 men; by July 23, they were trudging north to Ticonderoga. Haverhill's distinguished physician, James Brickett, who valiantly served at Bunker Hill, was appointed colonel of one battalion; then, in July, he became brigadier of the entire force.

Essex County's Quota					
Danvers	50	Ipswich	10	Newbury	30
Lynn	10	Andover	64	Rowley	20
Salisbury	18	Haverhill	43	Topsfield	30
Amesbury	37	Bradford	43	Wenham	6
Methuen	40	Boxford	38	Middleton	18

With seaports heavily committed, particularly to coastal defense, the burden fell on yeoman towns. Essex County conscriptees were combined with a battalion from York and Cumberland counties, Maine, headed by Col. Edward Wigglesworth of Newburyport. Archelaus Fuller of Middleton was its lieutenant colonel; William Rogers of Newbury would become the major.[10]

In the spring of 1776, with help from reinforcements, Benedict Arnold stubbornly continued the siege of Quebec. His ill-fated effort was doomed, however, when enemy relief troops, arriving in May, pushed the ragged Americans up the St. Lawrence, pursued by thousands of British regulars. By June 1776, the diseased, vermin-infested army remnant finally struggled out of Canada, southward across Lake Champlain. Fearing a British invasion on its heels, the three thousand able-bodied troops remaining in the region occupied Fort Ticonderoga on the southern tip.

With Massachusetts' back door threatened by the Champlain move, the Bay State quickly responded. Over the summer of 1776, Colonel Wigglesworth's militia trooped two hundred miles toward Lake Champlain to head off the pincers movement. Before they were even under way, Massachusetts was asked to equip two additional regiments totaling 1,500 men. On July 10, invasion fears caused every twenty-fifth man to be ordered from training band and alarm lists until December 1.

Since thousands already were serving in coastal defense, among Continental ranks, aboard armed vessels, or in the militia, enlistments came slowly. On July 12, attorney William Wetmore of Salem noted: "A meeting of ye traing band & alarm list to raise men for Canada to make part of ye 1500—this town to raise 20." Eleven days later, church bells summoned townspeople in Marblehead. Diarist Ashley Bowen observed: "This afternoon a grand muster on our Training Hill as there is a call for a draft of men to enlist in the Continental service to guard back settlements &c." A nine-man committee raised bounty money, with one man enlisted and £120 subscribed to hire seven more for the "present Expedition at Canaday." Haverhill divided into classes, a commonly used recruitment method, where two or more able-bodied males shared responsibility to hire a recruit. Some townsmen appeared to have lost their ardor of the year before. Josiah Adams of Newbury was disgusted by those who bought their way out. On July 29, he noted: "I am Inform'd that some have Given 60 dollars to get Clear of Going to Quebeck, (they had money Plenty I presume), If not it is a wonder if they want Cowards." It was impossible for the united colonies, which cherished freedom from restraint, to expect a fervor for military service from its citizen soldiery. Then, as now, Americans have not been favorably disposed to a lengthy war. During 1776, however, thousands from Essex County were serving and would continue the fight—in the field and on the sea—for years to come.[11]

On October 11, 1776, a decisive naval battle was fought at Valcour Island on the west shore of Lake Champlain. Lt. Matthew Fairfield of Wenham wrote home: "I would Inform that Wee are very Formidable on Both sides of the Lake & a grand Fleet on the Lake & are Waiting the Motion of the enemy."[12] Thanks to the makeshift "grand fleet" assembled by Arnold over the summer—a sloop, two schooners, four row-galleys and eight gondolas—the British push down Lake Champlain to Ticonderoga was deferred. The squadron gallantly clashed in a pivotal duel at Valcour Island—with Newburyporter Col. Edward Wigglesworth on board the *Trumbull* galley commanding the left battle line—against a larger British force. Though the "fleet" was lost, the British drive became so delayed that, with winter coming on, General Carleton returned to Canada. An enemy move down the Hudson to Albany would have been catastrophic. The little navy had pushed back the enemy's timetable to 1777, gaining for America a priceless year to prepare for Burgoyne's thrust.[13]

Long Island

Gen. William Howe awaited reinforcements at Halifax, then sallied forth to New York, his springboard for conquering the colonies. He arrived in lower New York bay on June 25 with three warships, a modest foreboding of what was in the offing. On July 6, Col. Moses Little, on Long Island since May, reported: "One Hundred & about Sixty Ships, Transports & other Vessels, are arrived above the Narrows [at Staten Island] with about Ten Thousand Soldiers."[14] Six days later, the general's brother, Admiral Richard Howe, appeared with

150 ships under sail, brimming with troops. By mid-August, an army of 32,000 trained professionals, including 8,000 Hessians, had encamped—Britain's largest-ever expeditionary force.

As enemy sail multiplied, Washington called for reinforcements. On July 18, Colonel Hutchinson's 27th Regiment of about 450 men marched; in two days, Col. John Glover's 14th Continental Regiment of over 300 troops would follow. The North Shore regiments traveled to Norwich and New London, where they embarked aboard transports, arriving in New York by August 2. At this point, four of Massachusetts' eleven regiments in New York were filled with soldiers drawn mostly from Essex County. Additionally, three companies of eight in Col. John Nixon's 4th Regiment were, largely, from the Haverhill and Salem areas. They were led by Captains Thomas Barnes and Ebenezer Winship of Salem and Moses McFarland of Haverhill. Paul Dudley Sargent, who until his recent move to New Hampshire had been a Revolutionary leader in his native Gloucester, raised a fifth regiment which accompanied Hutchinson's to New York. A scattering of men from Essex County were sprinkled among his ranks. Together, Essex County's contingents represented nearly one-tenth of Washington's army.

Field Officers
27th Continental Regiment

Colonel	Israel Hutchinson	Danvers
Lt. Colonel	Benjamin Holden	Princeton
Major	Ezra Putnam	Danvers
Captains	John Baker	Beverly
	Nathan Brown	Salem
	Benjamin Kimball	Middleton
	John Low	Beverly
	Ezra Newhall	Lynn
	Billy Porter	Wenham
	Enoch Putnam	Danvers
	Addison Richardson	Salem.

Unsure where the enemy would strike, Washington had extended his forces among coastal Jersey, southern Manhattan, and Brooklyn Heights. Though numerous Essex Continentals had tasted battle during the siege of Boston, Washington's 19,000 effectives—a majority of whom were militia—looked mostly raw, inexperienced, and untrained.[15]

The undisciplined soldiers continued to show the propensity for mischief they had demonstrated around Boston. On May 18, Ips-wichite Capt. Abraham Dodge recorded a troop romp involving Little's regiment:

> Complaints having been made by the Inhabitants Situated near the mill pond that some of the soldiers Come their to go into swimming in the open view of the Women and they came out of the water and run up to the Houses. Naked with a design to Insult and wound the modesty of Female Decency, 'tis with concern that the General finds himself under the disagreeable Necessity of expressing his disaprobation of such a Beastly Conduct . . . where is the modesty virtue and sobriety of the New England Troops for which they have been so remarkable.[16]

Military courts sat to hear cases of desertion, insubordination, theft, and numerous other offenses punished by fines, lashings, and, sometimes, death.

The urbane Capt. Alexander Graydon of Pennsylvania exhibited a disdain of the unsoldierlike, democratic New Englanders in their motley dress: "There are some, indeed, in the higher ranks; and here and there a young man of decent breeding, in the capacity of an aid-de-camp or brigade major; but any thing above the condition of a clown, in the regiments we came in contact with, was truly a rarity." But the aristocratic young Philadelphian made an exception of Glover's disciplined regiment. While the officers lacked "polish," their aptitude and air of confidence, wrote Graydon, commanded respect. Graydon also objected to Negroes, who commonly served in New England regiments, being in the ranks "which, to persons unaccustomed to such associations, had a disagreeable, degrading effect."[17]

On August 9, Colonel Little wrote to his son Josiah in Newburyport: "It is probable they will make their Attack very soon. God grant . . . that we may be able to give them such a Reception as may make them turn back ashamed."[18]

Speculation ended when at dawn on August 22, protected by British frigates, Howe launched his amphibious move. A procession of flatboats and other craft carried the troops to Long Island shore, and by noon 15,000 scarlet-uniformed troops, forty field pieces, and supplies had been landed off Gravesend, about nine miles from American lines. Three days later, Gen. Philip von Heister's Hessian grenadiers were sent in, raising the invasion force to 19,000.

Encamped on the coastal plain, the British were separated from Brooklyn village by a series of hills, called the Heights of Guan, which ran northeast from nearby Gowanus Cove and stretched almost across the island. Four passes—Gowanus, Flatbush, Bedford, Jamaica—penetrated the densely wooded ridges, natural avenues for an enemy advance. Three routes were guarded, including Flatbush at the center, where Little's regiment was entrenched, but Jamaica, about four miles east, had been left largely undefended.

Since the landing, Washington, who first had underestimated the invaders, had bolstered forces around Brooklyn to 7,000. Under command of the Danvers-born Maj. Gen. Israel Putnam, the still-slim ranks were divided between Brooklyn Heights and an outer perimeter along the hills.

On August 26, at 9:00 P.M. in the evening, Howe sent 10,000 soldiers moving surreptitiously toward Jamaica Pass on the extreme American left, led off by Gen. Henry Clinton with the dragoons and light infantry. By dawn he had pierced the Jamaica artery with a two-mile column, turning west toward the American rear on the Heights of Guan.

Meanwhile, in a diversionary move, Gen. James Grant marched

5,000 soldiers up Gowanus Road on the American right. At daybreak, he confronted 1,700 troops under Gen. Lord Stirling.

Heister's Hessians shelled Flatbush Pass, guarded by three regiments, including Little's. The American center at Bedford and Flatbush passes was commanded by the feisty Gen. John Sullivan of New Hampshire. As Clinton's musket rattle was heard behind them, Heister's jaegers advanced with fixed bayonets. Caught between a German frontal assault and British dragoons and light infantry to their rear, Sullivan's lines collapsed. Two thousand desperate, panic-stricken Americans scrambled toward the Brooklyn lines; many were captured, including Sullivan. Ipswichite Lieutenant Hodgkins of Wade's company in Little's regiment recorded the events of that morning: "After hearing a very hot fire for some time we whare ordered to march for the fire But we found the Enemy whar Endvering to Cut of our Retreet and in a grate measure Did for we whar obliged to go through fire & wharter But through the goodness of god we got cheafly in." The British plan had been perfectly executed.[19]

Only the right held, where General Stirling's 950 brave defenders faced James Grant's over 7,000. Hit from the left and rear, they were nearly surrounded. As 250 Marylanders covered, most of Stirling's men escaped across nearly impenetrable Gowanus Creek to Brooklyn.

By noon on August 27, the last of the shaken defenders, less the 1,500 killed or captured, had reached Brooklyn Heights. From their two-mile-wide and one-mile-deep defensive perimeter, the British were clearly visible one mile away.

Among the August 27 casualties were twenty wounded and three missing from Little's 12th Regiment, including Peter Barthrick of Parker's company, killed; Archelaus Pilsifer of Wade's company, wounded and captured; and Elijah Lewis of Dodge's company, missing. Most, however, had successfully extricated themselves.[20]

Unaware of his precarious position, and determined to hold the heights, early next morning Washington boated three more regiments across from Manhattan to Brooklyn. One was Col. John Glover's, colorfully clad in blue jackets and trousers, trimmed with leather buttons. They were placed at the extreme left near Wallabout Bay. Sight of 1,300 new faces heightened the defenders' spirits.

On August 28, using a series of trenches, Howe opened a classic siege against Fort Putnam on the heights. Col. Moses Little reported that firing "kept up by parties on Both Sides" in front of the fort. About sunset on the twenty-eighth, in a breezy northeasterly rain, they exchanged "in Earnest," as the besiegers tried to drive the Americans from their outworks. "The Fire was very hot," reported Little, "the Enemies party Gave way our people Took that Ground the Fire Ceased, our party retreated to the Fort—but the Enemy Immediately

Took Possession, again." By the morning of August 29, the British had thrown up a breastwork 150 rods away.[21]

Hemmed in, with his back to the river, Washington now sensed impending disaster. It was apparent that William Howe's siege would succeed and, after the northeast blow, that brother Richard's frigates would stand up the East River. By August 29, evacuation had been decided. Maj. Gen. Heath of Massachusetts had combed Kingsbridge and Fort Washington on the Hudson for every available flat-bottomed boat, plus other suitable vessels. They arrived by early evening manned by experienced sailors from Col. Israel Hutchinson's North Shore regiment. From as far as Spuyten Duyvil Creek and Hell Gate, craft floated down the East River. Regimental commanders assembled at seven o'clock, fully armed and accoutered to await further orders. To avoid panic, Washington's troops were told that replacements were arriving for the sick and to relieve some of the regiments. It was a critical moment; if the army had been captured, the war likely would have been lost.[22]

The East River Crossing

Evacuation began at dark, with the ferrying entrusted to experienced hands from John Glover's and Israel Hutchinson's North Shore regiments. It was a race against time, as the crucial crossing had to be completed by daylight. Beginning at about ten o'clock from Brooklyn ferry, men—regiment by regiment—filed to the shore. Back and forth, skilled seafarers from Beverly, Danvers, Lynn, Marblehead, Salem, and other Essex County towns shuttled the "Land Jacks," wrote Capt. Billy Porter of Wenham, across the mile-wide East River. Favorable winds permitted sail until midnight; then, suddenly, the direction shifted. Forced to turn from canvas to oar, and bucking an ebb tide, the evacuation could not have been completed had not—providentially—the wind changed again. Over 9,000 soldiers with their ammunition, baggage, field guns, horses, and provisions—except for a few cannon—were transported safely to Manhattan Island.[23]

It was a brilliant, perfectly executed maneuver. The exit went undetected until about four o'clock in the morning when a British reconnoitering party gawked in astonishment over the breastwork. If the enemy had struck at this point, several rear guard detachments would have been devastated. Miraculously, a thick fog bank abruptly moved in, covering those troops who still awaited departure.

It was the resolute North Shore sailors and fishermen who delivered the army safely from Long Island, thus preserving the country's finest regiments and best officers. For a brief period, American in-

---

Field Officers
14th Continental (Marblehead) Regiment

Colonel	John Glover
Lt. Colonel	Gabriel Johonnot
Major	William R. Lee
Captains	Nathaniel Bond
	Moses Brown (of Beverly)
	William Courtis
	John Glover, Jr.
	Thomas Grant
	Joseph Lee
	Gilbert Warner Speekman
	Joseph Swasey

---

dependence was literally in the hands of a few hundred Essex County Continentals.

Kip's Bay

Washington's army, defeated and disorganized, was physically and morally drained. Troops deserted in droves, particularly militia; Continentals, however, were not immune. Nearly one hundred men, including thirty Marbleheaders, had "gone off" from Hutchinson's 27th Regiment. Lt. Thomas White of Salem rounded up a handful. They were returned to Fort Washington, after being fined five dollars each, but most remained at large. One-quarter of Washington's army was reported unfit, suffering from typhus, dysentery, and fatigue, their condition exacerbated by inadequate clothing, food, and shelter. The Long Island setback was the first of a series which ultimately afflicted the army with a general malaise and threatened its very survival.[24]

Washington now reorganized his troops into three divisions, under Generals Israel Putnam, William Heath, and Nathaniel Greene. Putnam remained in New York with 5,000 men—including Baldwin's and Glover's contingents—who guarded the East River to present 15th Street. On September 4, in the absence of Gen. James Clinton of Rhode Island, and in recognition of his own recent amphibious feat, John Glover was appointed brigade commander of four regiments. General Heath, whose 9,000 troops included Colonel Hutchinson's regiment, held the region from Harlem to Kingsbridge. Nathaniel Greene, with Gen. Joseph Spencer of Connecticut in charge until General Clinton recovered from an illness, occupied the mid-section; excepting a few seasoned units, like Colonel Little's and "Late Nixon's" (Nixon was promoted to brigadier on August 9), his division comprised mainly militia. Washington's army stretched over sixteen miles, the entire length of Manhattan.[25]

The proximity of the powerful British army and navy, though, forced Washington's command to deliberate whether New York City and lower Manhattan were tenable. On September 12, a council of war voted to pull out, and Washington agreed. The complicated withdrawal north toward Kingsbridge would require several days.

Howe, meanwhile, had decided to circumvent southern Manhattan, where American troops were concentrated, and cut off Putnam by smashing thinly manned mid Manhattan. On the fifteenth, while the American evacuation was under way, five frigates lined up along the East River off Kip's Bay, a cove near present 34th Street. Unrelenting broadsides swept the shoreline, as eighty-four flat-bottomed boats brimming with scarlet-coated infantry—4,000 in the first wave—streamed over from Long Island. They jumped ashore without opposition. Under heavy fire, the bankside lines collapsed, with outnumbered, panic-stricken militia streaking inland. Lt. Joseph Hodgkins of Little's regiment [Nixon's brigade], posted at Harlem Point, described the incident: "they Landed . . . 3 or 4 miles nearer york and there whar two Brigades thare But they Being Cheafly Milisha it whas said that Two hundred of the Enemy made them all Run so thay Landed with out much Resistance and marched toward york and Took Posesion of the sitty."[26]

Washington, galloping from Harlem to Kip's Bay, encountered swarms of militia fleeing along the post road. Unable to stop them, an enraged Washington shouted, "Are these the men with whom I am to defend America!" As Glover's regiment—which had withdrawn to Harlem on the fourteenth—rushed eastward, they met the swelling tide of frightened troops, and by their steady presence stemmed the rout.[27]

Though Washington's army in New York City had been nearly flanked, thanks largely to Gen. Israel Putnam's leadership, they were able to escape up the west side of Manhattan. By nightfall, after a rapid, stifling, twelve-mile march, fatigued and parched soldiers joined the forces already at Harlem Heights, leaving lower Manhattan Island in enemy hands. For the next seven years, America's second largest city was enemy-occupied.

Harlem Heights

Washington's army held the narrow neck of upper Manhattan Island, a densely wooded plateau protected on its sides by the Harlem and Hudson rivers, and to the south by the "Hollow Way." Ten thousand Continentals entrenched along three fortified lines extended across Manhattan, with 6,000 more encamped further north around Kingsbridge. The southernmost point, about present 147th Street, was manned by Nathaniel Greene's division of 3,300, including a covey from Essex in John Nixon's brigade.

The British were positioned to the south along heights about two miles distant, below present 100th Street. At dawn on the sixteenth, Boxford-born Lt. Col. Thomas Knowlton with about 120 Connecticut Rangers slipped across the Hollow Way. As they ascended the wooded enemy high ground on reconnaissance, they collided with two pickets. Engrossed in a sharp exchange, the Americans were nearly cut off by kilted Black Watch Highlanders, who had suddenly appeared. With the enemy at their heels, Knowlton's force managed to return safely to American lines.[28]

The enemy light infantry, clearly visible on their hillside, tauntingly "sounded their Bugle Horns as is usual after a Fox Chase."[29] This no doubt strengthened Washington's resolve to snare his arrogant foe. Baited by 150 volunteers from Nixon's brigade led by Lieutenant Colonel Crary of Rhode Island, the British were lured into the open Hollow Way. They dashed down the hillside "with all speed," wrote Ipswichite Lieutenant Hodgkins of Moses Little's regiment, "to a Plain spot of ground then our [Nixon's] Brigade marched out of the woods then a very hot Fire Began on Both sides and Lasted for upward of an hour." Meanwhile, a combined force of Knowlton's rangers and Maj. Andrew Leitch's Virginia riflemen skirted the enemy's right flank.[30]

Premature firing imprudently ordered by unseasoned junior officers foiled Washington's trap, and as Hodgkins noted, "the Enemy Retreeted up the Hill and our People followed them." Though Knowlton, one of America's ablest commanders, and Leitch fell mortally wounded, their troops pushed on. Between noon and two o'clock, thousands of Americans and British surged in, and the skirmish was near full-fledged battle. Finally, the 5,000 exhausted British fell back close to where the morning action had begun. In the late afternoon, with enemy rescuers coming, Washington's forces victoriously "gave a Hurra" and filed off the battlefield.[31]

Enemy losses were about 70 dead and 200 wounded. Hodgkins reported American casualties: "the Loos on our side is about 40 Killed and 60 or 70 wounded there Whas none killed in our Regt and But about 20 wounded." John McLarty of Newburyport was taken prisoner. Thomas Barnes's company, also of Nixon's brigade, suffered several casualties, including James Townshend, killed; Thomas Ryne, made prisoner; and Joshua Winn of Salem, wounded. Harlem

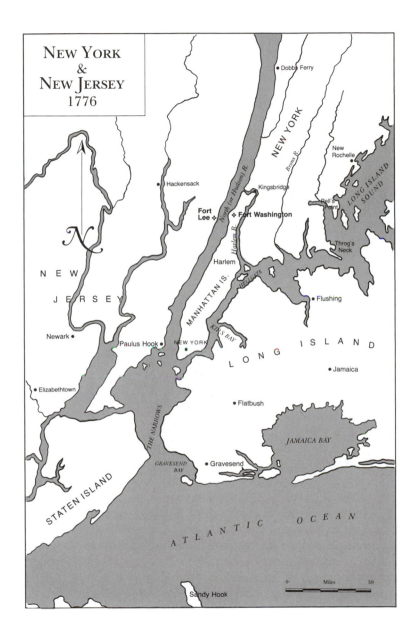

Heights, however, cannot be measured statistically. Though a minor conflict, its timely morale value was of major significance. After enduring major setbacks, the Continental Army had regained its self-respect, and Washington his stature. Before American eyes, British regulars had retreated, proving Continental soldiers could better the best.[32]

Pelham Bay

For twenty-six days, Manhattan was quiet, while Sir William Howe deliberated his next move. Meanwhile, to guard both front and flank, Washington shifted forces. Deploying General Greene across the Hudson in Jersey with 5,000 men, he kept 10,000 on the heights; an equal number would hold the Kingsbridge vicinity under Heath, to the north. In mid-October, Heath's command went to Maj. Gen. Charles Lee, who had rejoined the army. Of the 25,000 troops on paper, though, only 16,000 were actually present and fit for duty.

Avoiding a direct assault against Harlem Heights, Howe chose to flank at Throg's Neck, a peninsula jutting into Long Island Sound. Once landed, he planned to press northwest toward the American left at Kingsbridge, hoping to push Washington off Manhattan, or, better yet, to force a pitched battle. On October 12, his main army boarded eighty vessels for a thirteen-mile sail through tempestuous Hell Gate up the East River. By day's end, most of Howe's army had disembarked.

Col. Edward Hand with his Pennsylvania riflemen had been stationed near Throg's Neck; when Howe landed, reinforcements were rushed up. The Neck, separated from the mainland by a creek and adjacent marshland, with only a plankless narrow bridge connecting, proved a poor invasion site; with Americans dug in, a crossing would be perilous. Thus, six days later, Howe reembarked his troops for Pell's Point in Eastchester, a peninsula three miles east which adjoined the coastline south of Pelham Bay.

By the sixteenth, with Howe threatening his rear, Washington had decided to vacate Harlem Heights. Two days later, the first contingent of 13,000 troops slowly trudged over Kingsbridge, which spanned the Harlem River along the west bank of the Bronx River toward White Plains. Moses Little's regiment, which had crossed the Hudson from Fort Lee, was posted west of Williamsbridge at the Bronx River to help cover the movement. Incredibly, 2,000 men were kept behind Fort Washington on the Hudson; soon they would be isolated amid a sea of enemies.

On the first day of the northward withdrawal, a combined advance party of 4,000 redcoats and Hessians landed near Pelham Bay. Led by Sir Henry Clinton and Lord Cornwallis, they soon had moved a mile and a half toward the mainland.

Col. John Glover had been sent eastward to guard the road leading from Pelham, and was posted in front of Pell's Point. That morning, as he gazed through his glass from a nearby hilltop, he sighted "upwards of two hundred sail, all manned and formed in four grand divisions." The stocky, veteran campaigner commanded four under-sized regiments—Col. Loammi Baldwin's, Col. Joseph Read's, Col. William Shepard's and his own 14th—about 850 men—and three field pieces. Brigade Maj. William Lee was despatched to inform General Lee three miles away, but an immediate action was needed. Holding his 170 Marbleheaders with cannon in reserve on a hillside behind Hutchinson's Creek, Glover had gone only half way before he spotted a thirty-man enemy advance guard strutting up the road. A company of forty from Read's regiment was sent to delay the patrol while Glover deployed his men.

He placed his regiments strategically behind stone walls along narrow Split Rock Road. Each was to delay the enemy, then withdraw, as the next contingent took over. Furthermost on the left was Col. Joseph Read's 13th, with about 226 men. To the right and the rear was Col. William Shepard's 3rd Regiment with over 200 men. Further back on the right was Col. Loammi Baldwin's 26th, with 234 troops, largely from Essex County. Glover would "have given a thousand worlds," he later wrote, for a more experienced field officer, but the responsibility was his to shoulder.

With his troops placed, Glover rode ahead and ordered the advance guard to proceed. They got within fifty yards when the enemy fired. No ball found its mark; Read's men returned a volley which leveled four British. The Americans stood their ground as five rounds were exchanged. With two lost and several wounded, their mission accomplished, the advance was recalled, with the reinforced enemy vanguard "not more than thirty yards distant."

When Read's company pulled back, the enemy advance force, believing they had routed all resistance, "gave a shout" and rushed up Split Rock Road. Behind their cover, Read's regiment waited for the proper moment. When the enemy was less than 100 feet away, they jumped to their feet, leveled their muskets, and gave the invaders "the whole charge." The enemy broke and withdrew to await "the main body."

After an hour-and-a-half lull, the strengthened enemy—chasseurs, grenadiers, and light infantry—pressed forward under cover of artillery. From behind the stone walls, Read's regiment waited apprehensively until the British were within fifty yards, then rose and delivered a withering fusillade, halting the attackers. Read's men exchanged seven rounds before they were ordered to move behind Shepard's men. Once again assuming that all resistance had been swept away, the shouting enemy pushed on. Then Shepard's regiment rose from "behind a fine double stone wall." Firing by platoon, they kept up a constant rattle, spending seventeen rounds and beating back several fierce enemy assaults. With British and Hessian forces steadily increasing, Shepard's and Read's regiments finally had to be withdrawn as Baldwin's covered.

About noon, Cornwallis led a second contingent toward Hutchinson's Creek bridge, where the Americans had crossed that morning. To avoid being outflanked, Glover's troops forded the creek and ascended the hill toward the Marblehead regiment and the artillery position. For the remainder of the day, both sides engaged in an inconsequential artillery duel.

At dark, leaving most of their baggage, Glover's brigade hastily withdrew three miles toward Dobb's Ferry. That night, the exhausted soldiers rested, expecting an enemy raid at any time. Glover recollected: "after fighting all day without vituals or drink, laying as a picket all night, the heavens over us and the earth under us, which was all we had, having left our baggage." Actually, the enemy had moved north along the coast to New Rochelle.[33]

Americans losses of eight killed and thirteen wounded were slight compared to the astounding enemy losses, particularly among the Hessians: about two hundred killed and many wounded. More importantly, by delaying the British advance Glover's brigade had bought Washington precious time to withdraw the patriot army. Lee thanked the brigade not only for their heroics but "for their prudent, cool and orderly and soldierlike conduct in all respects."[34] On the twenty-first, Washington thanked the brigade for "their merit and good behaviour" and urged others to follow their example.[35] Glover's plucky initiative and his men's gallantry may well have averted catastrophe for Washington's army.

White Plains

Glover's brigade rejoined Lee to help cover Washington's retreat toward White Plains, no easy task with the scarcity of draft animals and wagons. Howe's dilatory actions had gifted Washington with invaluable time, and, by the twenty-second, his main army of 14,500 effectives reached White Plains.

Earlier, September 20, Lee had ordered Glover to retrieve 200 or 300 barrels of pork and flour left behind at East Chester. At night, the brigade, with fifteen wagons, moved "so nigh the enemy we heard their musick and talk," wrote Glover. His foray was a success; the brigade returned at 2:00 A.M. with all supplies.[36]

American lines occupied several hills overlooking the plains, with Washington holding the center, White Plains village. Another 2,000 defenders remained to the southwest in upper Manhattan at Fort Washington, including part of Hutchinson's North Shore regiment. The others were across the Hudson with the 3,500 troops occupying Fort Lee. The fort, formerly Fort Constitution, was newly named for Gen. Charles Lee, in recognition of his magnificent defense of Charleston, South Carolina.

On the twenty-fifth, Lee's rear guard of 8,000, which included Glover's brigade and Little's regiment, marched from Miles Square to join Washington's consolidated position at White Plains. Three miles out, they were nearly cut off by the enemy right advancing toward a crossroad less than a mile away. Lee, the former British officer, outdistanced the column by turning westerly along Dobb's Ferry road. However, three men from Little's regiment—Ezekiel Woodward and John McDarmitt of Warner's company and Francis Cogswell of Wade's company—were among those captured. At ten o'clock the following morning, Lee's fatigued troops finally reached White Plains.[37]

Howe took ten days to move the seventeen miles to approach White Plains. Finally, on September 28, after crossing the Bronx River, his forces stormed and captured weakly defended Chatterton's Hill on the American extreme right. The British, led by Gen. Alexander Leslie of Salem North Bridge fame, and Col. Rall's Hessian regiment (assisted by horsemen of the 17th Light Dragoons), had won the day.

Three days later, Washington slipped north to nearby North Castle Heights, a more defensible position, keeping his New England supply line intact. Howe advanced to the former lines, waited a week, then bewildered the Americans by withdrawing southwesterly toward Dobb's Ferry, where his army was resupplied by ships which had run the gauntlet at Fort Washington.

Forts Washington and Lee

Washington speculated that Howe would move next against Fort Washington in upper Manhattan, which was perched on "Mount Washington," a mile-long hill rising 230 feet above the Hudson. This four-acre pentagonal open earthwork stood opposite Fort Lee on the New Jersey shore, separated by a line of sunken hulks and submerged timber frames where the Hudson narrowed to 3,600 feet. This shield, which Israel Hutchinson's regiment helped construct, was intended to stop enemy travel upriver. It soon proved useless. On October 9, after a deserter revealed a breach, three British warships using a flood tide and a brisk southerly wind passed up the Hudson through the opening. Though heavy cannonading from Forts Washington and Lee wreaked minor damage and inflicted twenty-seven casualties,

Washington observed: "to our surprise and mortification, they ran thro without the least difficulty."[38]

Several row galleys, each mounting a gun on the prow, had been standing before the *chevaux-de-frise* which barricaded the Hudson. As the H.M.S. *Tartar* breezed upriver with bow-chasers blazing, she forced the galley *Independence*—crewed by Hutchinson's North Shore men and commanded by Lieutenants Putnam of Salem and Cleaves of Beverly—plus another galley, ashore at Dobb's Ferry, where they fell into enemy hands.[39]

One month later, with the enemy closing in, a deluded American command still occupied Fort Washington, believing it tenable, but, if necessary, quickly evacuable over the Hudson. Recent additions had increased Commandant Robert Magaw's force of mostly Marylanders, Pennsylvanians, and Virginians to nearly 3,000.

On November 16, Howe's 11,000 men hit Mount Washington's outer defenses from three sides. Three hours later the outgunned and outnumbered American lines collapsed, driving troops back to the inner fort, which was designed to hold only a thousand. Colonel Magaw, seeing the futility of further bloodshed, surrendered. Though casualties were comparably light—59 men killed and 96 wounded—nearly 2,900 were captured, including over 130 members of Col. Israel Hutchinson's North Shore regiment. Each of his eight companies lost men, which included Salem Capt. Addison Richardson's entire company of about 50. (Earlier, in October, the 27th Continental had been split between Forts Lee and Washington. So part survived.)[40]

Long columns of prisoners were marched fourteen miles through Manhattan to New York City. Enlisted men and noncommissioned officers crowded poorly ventilated, unheated sugar houses, churches, and jails, without seats and blankets, with only straw bedding, and given little to eat. In mid-January 1777, thanks to Washington's December 26 victory at Trenton, most survivors would be exchanged. During the brief span of their imprisonment, hundreds died from disease, exposure, and starvation—carted away each morning by carmen for burial. Officers, who first were paroled to deserted houses in the city, survived better, though their exchange came later. They were transferred to Long Island and billeted two to a house, mostly with Whig families. Those from Hutchinson's 27th included Lt. Col. Benjamin Holden of Princeton, Lt. Nathaniel Cleaves of Beverly, Ens. Gibson Clough of Salem, Lt. David Poor of Winchendon, Capt. Enoch Putnam of Danvers, Ens. Jeremiah Putnam of Salem, and Capt. Addison Richardson of Salem. Most finally were exchanged during February 1778.

Howe's next logical step was to enter New Jersey. Four days from the capture of Fort Washington, the 27th's remaining members were among the evacuees hastily abandoning Fort Lee. British and Hessian light infantry, having crossed six miles above, almost trapped the entire garrison. Camp kettles were left cooking over fires as columns of men flew out the back; one hundred stragglers, including some from the North Shore, were captured. Henry Hallowell of Lynn noted their speedy departure: "The same day the British took the fort [Washington] they moved up the river to cut general Washington and his men off. Then we at fort Lee had in great haste to flee and left cannon, a mortar, some clothes and some money, etc."[41]

Loss of the forts was devastating. In addition to nearly 3,000 Americans, 150 cannon, 2,800 muskets and 12,000 shot and shell, invaluable blankets, tents, and other supplies fell into British hands. Now, the enemy controlled Manhattan Island, along with Long Island waters, the East River, and the Hudson, and had a foothold in Jersey.

Through New Jersey

Washington had divided the army into three commands. Uncertain of Howe's target, General Lee had remained at New Castle with three divisions of 5,500, while Gen. William Heath commanded four brigades of 3,200 able-bodied men at Peekskill on the Hudson's east bank. During November 9 and 10, Washington had crossed into New Jersey from Peekskill with 2,000 troops to meet a possible southern drive. On September 21, he was joined at Hackensack by 1,000 disorganized troops routed from Fort Lee.

The army crossed the Hackensack and Passaic rivers and continued their retreat through Newark, New Brunswick (where Stirling's brigade attached), Princeton, and, finally, Trenton beside the Delaware, which they reached on December 3. The dispirited, weary army had trudged southward with British and Hessian columns in hot pursuit; when the enemy reached Trenton on December 8, Washington already had streamed across the Delaware to Pennsylvania. By taking or destroying all boats close by, he had checked Howe's forward motion for the moment.

The succession of catastrophic defeats, particularly at Forts Washington and Lee, plummeted patriot morale; Washington's 14,000 dropped in numbers steadily, especially because of desertions. On December 1, many enlistments had expired; within one month almost the entire army would be detached. Since much valuable equipment and supplies had been left behind, Washington's shivering army was left unprotected and ill prepared for the oncoming winter. Already New York City and environs had fallen; in December, Newport followed. Ten thousand victorious British and Hessian troops were encamped near the Delaware, only thirty miles from the congressional seat at Philadelphia, the country's largest city. On December 12, an apprehensive Continental Congress transferred complete military control to Washington and adjourned to Baltimore. The commander in chief, who saw no way to prevent an eventual enemy crossing, was close to admitting defeat. In mid-December, pamphleteer Thomas Paine wrote his now famous words in *The Crisis*: "These are the times that try men's souls: The summer soldier and the sunshine patriot will, in the crisis, shrink from the service of his country; but he that stands it Now, deserves the love and thanks of man and woman." December of 1776 would be recalled as the war's bleakest period.

On December 13, the widely acclaimed Gen. Charles Lee, second in command under Washington, was captured. While his loss was viewed as another link in a calamitous chain, it proved to be a boon; Washington was fortunate to be free of the intractable Englishman. After Fort Washington had fallen, and Howe's intentions had been made clear, Washington had requested Lee to join him. Instead, the arrogant, ambitious former British army colonel followed his own instincts, which told him that Howe planned to invade New England. When he finally crossed the Hudson on December 2, Lee dallied in northern Jersey. On the evening of the twelfth, he left Gen. John Sullivan of New Hampshire in command and rode off to a tavern in Basking Ridge, where an enemy patrol captured him the following morning.

Sullivan promptly marched Lee's force, shrunken now to 2,000, to Washington's camp. One regimental commander, Moses Little, was confined with fever and stayed at Peekskill with about 100 of his "naked convalescents and sick."[42] (From Peekskill, Major Hugh Hughes, assistant quartermaster general, wrote of the Newbury colonel: "He is, in my opinion, a most excellent man, but, unhappily . . . unable to go through the duties of the post."[43]) Slashed by captures, casualties, desertion, and sickness (20 died during the year), 16 officers and 134 homesick remnants from the 12th regiment, now commanded by Lt. Col. Henshaw, plodded on. They had been consolidated into a "New England Brigade," under the Rhode Islander Daniel Hitchcock, with four other undersized units from Massachusetts and Rhode Island, including Essex County men in the 4th Continental now commanded by Lt. Col. Thomas Nixon. The brigade marched in front, with Glover's, in the center of Sullivan's column, which included 177 effectives from the Marblehead regiment. In case of frontal attack, both Hitchcock and Glover were to form the first line.[44] On December 20, Ipswichite Joseph Hodgkins wrote: "we are Very Much fatagued with a long march we have Ben on the march ever since ye 29 of Last month and we are not within 10 or 12 miles of general Washingtons Army."[45] Two days later, Sullivan crossed to the Pennsylvania side of the Delaware, bolstering Washington's army to 10,000 men fit for duty. This was only temporary, however; on December 31, most enlistments would expire.

Trenton

In mid-December, with cold coming, Sir William Howe suspended operations and took most of his army to winter in New York. Earlier, Gen. Henry Clinton, with 6,000 troops, had left New York for Rhode Island, where they occupied Loyalist Newport. This foothold was expected to annoy mercantile New England so greatly as to obscure the struggle going on elsewhere. A string of posts, mostly garrisoned by Hessians, was left in New Jersey, at Perth Amboy, New Brunswick, Princeton, and along the Delaware at Trenton and Bordentown–Mount Holly. The river garrisons, about six miles apart, held 42nd Scot Highlanders and 3,000 Hessians under Colonels Rall and von Donop. With New Jersey protected, Howe intended to wait until spring to launch an offensive.

Sensing a vulnerability in the isolated riverside bases of the enemy, Washington planned a multi-pronged, Christmas night surprise crossing into New Jersey. The plan was risky. While a successful expedition would lift public spirits, failure could sound the war's death knell. Half of his forces were to be deployed. They would land at three sites, hit the posts, and recross to the west side of the river. Trenton was the main objective. Downstream, Lt. Col. John Cadwalader's detachment, which included the New England brigade, was to divert by hitting Donop at Mount Holly. To help bottle up the Hessians, a second contingent, commanded by Gen. James Ewing, would land at Trenton Ferry to seize the bridge south of town over Assunpink Creek. Crossing nine miles above at McKonkey's Ferry, a third division under Washington—2,400 men in seven brigades, which included Glover's—was to converge on the garrison in Trenton.

Washington entrusted the vital crossing to Glover's seafaring army mariners. Black-painted Durham boats, cargo-hauling vessels unique to the Delaware, were used. Displaying keels and pointed at both ends, the maneuverable, canoe-shaped craft were poled upstream or rowed downstream using eighteen-foot oars. Forty to sixty feet long and eight feet wide, the boats had a capacity load of fifteen tons and drew only about two feet. Their shallow drafts permitted Washington's men, plus their field pieces, baggage, and horses, to be disembarked close to the opposite bank. Again, as he had in late August

1776 at Long Island, Washington depended upon the seasoned amphibious Marblehead regiment.

The men pushed off about dusk. In bitter cold and darkness, Glover's seasoned hands navigated the swift, churning waters of the ice-clogged Delaware. The boat captained by Marbleheader William Blackler had the honor of ferrying Washington. About eleven o'clock, northeast winds swept in sleet, which whipped against the mighty Marbleheaders as they pushed, rowed, and steered ten regiments, with a cargo which included two hundred horses and eighteen heavy howitzers and guns, across the treacherous 1,000-foot-wide Delaware waters. It was not until after three o'clock in the morning, three hours past schedule, that the last troops forged ashore. Washington's assault force was successfully landed, assuring the expedition a chance for success.[46]

Ice had impeded Cadwalader's and Ewing's crossings. As Lt. Joseph Hodgkins, who belonged to Cadwalader's detachment, wrote, "on Christmas night we marched with about 2,000 Men to a ferry about 7 miles from Camp in order to Pass over to the Jersey side . . . But the Ise Prevented our crossing."[47] The Pennsylvania colonel managed to ferry 600 troops, but withdrew them when artillery could not land.

After five miles, Washington's force split into two divisions, each

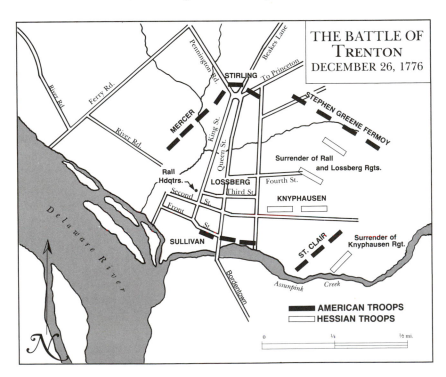

THE BATTLE OF
TRENTON
DECEMBER 26, 1776

■ AMERICAN TROOPS
☐ HESSIAN TROOPS

taking one of two roads that led to Trenton. Gen. John Sullivan, with
Arthur St. Clair's, Paul Dudley Sargent's, and John Glover's brigades,
followed the River Road running parallel to the Delaware. Glover
commanded five regiments—115 officers and 858 men—plus a battery of artillery led by Winthrop Sargent of Gloucester. Washington
and Major Gen. Nathaniel Greene, leading deFermoy's, Mercer's,
Stirling's, and Stephen's brigades, took the northern route, Penning-
ton Road. One-seventh of Gen. Hugh Mercer's 800-member brigade
belonged to the 27th Continental North Shore Regiment, now led by
Major Ezra Putnam of Danvers. The plan called for two concurrent
strikes at opposite sides of Trenton.[48]

The garrison was manned by Knyphausen's, Lossberg's and Rall's
German regiments, fifty Hessian jaegers, and twenty light dragoons
of the 10th British Regiment; about 1,400 troops altogether. The
Hessians had celebrated Christmas in customary German fashion
with revelry lasting well into the night. Dozing sentries guarded
outposts as the groggy garrison slept, ill prepared for attack.

The operation's countersign, "Victory or Death," poignantly manifested Washington's determination to succeed. The troops, thinly
clad and ill shod, plodded on amid the driving sleet with bayonets
fixed and with rags tied to protect their firing pans. By dawn, in a
perfectly coordinated approach, on the heels of enemy pickets sound-
ing alarms, the detachments entered Trenton from two directions.

Greene's division drove in from the north. Mercer's brigade
pushed west of town, while the main body continued straight to upper
King and Queen streets. Col. Henry Knox's artillery raked these main
thoroughfares, and Fermoy's and Stephen's brigades rushed easterly
to block a retreat toward Princeton, leaving Assunpink Creek Bridge
as the only escape.

Sullivan attacked from the northwest. A lead company drove in
the picket guard, who were pursued by Glover's brigade. The River
Road, which turned into lower Trenton, steered the Massachusetts
Continentals first down Front Street, and then to Queen, where they
nearly severed the southern exit. From behind a red board fence, an
advance party of Glover's peppered some of Rall's men, who fled
toward the bridge leading to Bordentown.

To the north, Rall fell back to the east fringe of town with his
remaining troops and most of Lossberg's. The determined colonel
drummed together his ranks and led them back with fixed bayonets
to regain the village. By now, Trenton was swarming with Americans.
Along Queen Street, from cellars, doorways, and windows, deadly
shots poured on the returning enemy. With visibility cut by gunpowder smoke and by sleet, soldiers—singly, in groups, and by company
and regiment—clashed headlong. The Americans, having dry pow-

der, discharged their muskets, while the Germans, with their firearms immobilized, resorted to bayonet, sword, and spontoon (a spear).

Meanwhile, Sullivan's troops were expanding their foothold to the south. Famed Indian fighter Col. John Stark of New Hampshire spiritedly shouted as he led St. Clair's right wing along Second Street toward Knyphausen's regiment. Glover's troops crossed the Assunpink Bridge, turned left, and ascended a ridge, where Winthrop Sargent erected a two-piece artillery battery.

Knyphausen's troops, pushed by Stark toward the southeast near the creek, fled toward the bridge, but found Glover's soldiers had plugged the last escape. The desperate Germans, racing along a path above the Assunpink in search of a fording point, became mired down with their field pieces, while from across the creek Sargent's guns blasted away. With no way out, the enemy surrendered to St. Clair's brigade, though a few brave souls waded across the neck-deep, rushing, icy waters. Shortly before, to the north, Rall's and Lossberg's encircled regiments had surrendered. By nine o'clock, hostilities were over. While about 500 had escaped, including the British light infantry early in the battle, 22 had been killed, 92 wounded, and nearly 950 taken prisoner; also, 1,000 muskets and other valuable supplies were seized. And not a single American life was lost![49]

That afternoon, the Continentals marched off with their prisoners toward McConkey's Ferry. Not until the following day did the weary soldiers reach camp. As David How of Methuen, in Sargent's brigade, reported, "we Toock 1000 of them besides killed Some Then we marched back And got to the River at Night And got over all the Hushing. 27 This morning we Crossed the River and Come to our Camp At Noon. 28 This Day we have been washing Our things."[50]

Years later when he was a Massachusetts legislator, Henry Knox described the perilous crossing:

> The powerful current bearing onward the floating masses of ice . . . threatened destruction to whosoever should venture upon its bosom. I wish, that when this occurence threatened to defeat the enterprise, they could have heard that distinguished warrier demand, 'Who will lead us on?' . . . *There, sir, went the fishermen of Marblehead, alike at home upon land or water, alike ardent, patriotic, and unflinching, whenever they unfurled the flag of the country.*[51]

Princeton

Washington's desperate gamble had won; his crucial victory across the ice-clogged Delaware raised public spirits and renewed confidence in his military leadership. Persuaded by patriotic appeals, plus a ten-dollar bounty, many New Englanders, whose enlistments were expiring, extended them an additional six weeks, including about 150 from Baldwin's mostly Essex regiment. But not Glover's men. They rendered their arms, trudged to Philadelphia looking for more familiar service aboard a Continental warship, and finally returned home on January 20.[52]

Three days after the crossing, intent on holding part of New Jersey, Washington crossed over once more, going directly to Trenton. He had intended to move against Princeton, only twelve miles away, but Generals Cornwallis and Grant had reached the town with 8,000 troops. Washington had 5,000 men, but many were ill-equipped, raw, locally recruited militia; and the backbone of his army was still exhausted from the Christmas night campaign.

The youthful, energetic Cornwallis, who had been recalled after the Trenton debacle, pushed out on January 2 with 5,500 fresh troops. Three regiments, 1,200 men, were left behind to guard Princeton under Lt. Col. Charles Mawhood; an equal number guarded Maidenhead to the south.

An American guard that Washington had sent forward near Maidenhead was compelled to slowly retreat before a hard-driving 1,500-man, enemy advance force. The Americans withdrew through Trenton to Washington's main lines along a ridge on the south bank of Assunpink Creek. Covered by Hitchcock's New Englanders, the fatigued defenders filed safely across the narrow stone bridge.

Near dusk, the enemy made three unsuccessful attempts to force the bridge. Meanwhile, a Hessian contingent pressed a fording point upstream, only to be repulsed by Hitchcock's New Englanders firing from a makeshift breastwork beside the creek. With Washington's back to the Delaware, Cornwallis put off his major assault until daylight.[53]

During the night, leaving their campfires burning and using muffled artillery wheels, the American army stealthily skirted Cornwallis's left and slipped away. Avoiding Maidenhead, they pushed to capture weakly defended Princeton, ten miles away. Along Quaker Road at Stony Brook, about two miles from their objective, the army split. Mercer's troops, followed by Cadwalader's brigade, swung left to hold a bridge on the post road, while Sullivan with three brigades continued toward town.

Two rear-guard regiments, the 17th Leicesters and 55th Borderers, had left Princeton and traveled along the post road under Mawhood to join the impending assault at Trenton. The 40th Regiment had stayed behind to protect stores. Shortly after Mawhood crossed over Stony Brook, he caught a glint from musket barrels of Mercer's advance party headed toward the bridge off to his left.

Mawhood faced about his troops, recrossed the bridge, and rushed toward a high ground, William Clark's orchard. But Mercer, who was closer, occupied the position first. His men formed, facing the British in an open field below. With battle lines drawn, each side fired a volley; then, with bayonets fixed, the British charged and routed the Americans.

Mercer fell mortally wounded while trying to rally his brigade. As the enemy pursuit continued, suddenly Cadwalader's Philadelphia militia appeared, forcing Mawhood to withdraw. As the Pennsylvanians followed to within fifty yards of Mawhood's line, the tables turned, and they were pushed back. Cadwalader's brigade merged with Mercer's and fled frenzied, while Washington rode among the broken men, in the face of enemy fire, desperately trying to rally his troops.

Hitchcock's New England brigade and Hand's Pennsylvania riflemen were brought up against the enemy left. While Hand's tried to turn Mawhood's flank, Hitchcock's veterans were to attack head-on. Meanwhile, parts of Cadwalader's and Mercer's brigades returned to the field, as a two-gun battery and a detachment led by Capt. Thomas Rodney of Delaware on Clark's ridge continued to rake the enemy with grapeshot and musket balls. Hitchcock's five undersized regiments—only 500 strong, riddled with Essex County Continentals—lined up within 200 yards of the enemy between Nixon's regiment on the right and Henshaw's on the left. The New Englanders advanced one hundred yards, stopped, fired a volley, reloaded and, firing by platoons, drove forward and charged. As they lunged, Hand's Pennsylvanians joined, and the enemy gave way.[54]

With bayonets fixed, Mawhood's men cut a swath down the main road, crossed the bridge, and withdrew toward Trenton. The enemy soon broke; many tossed their muskets and accouterments aside as they scurried down the post road in wild confusion.

Washington led his triumphant troops into Princeton, where the 40th South Lancashires had been encamped. Joined by part of the 55th, which had withdrawn to Princeton, many already had fled north toward Brunswick. The rest—including nearly two hundred holed up in Nassau Hall—soon surrendered. With Cornwallis's reinforcements undoubtedly advancing from Trenton, Washington's fatigued army pushed off toward winter quarters in the western New Jersey highlands. On his way out of Princeton, Washington expressed thanks to Colonel Hitchcock and the New England Brigade for their gallant conduct. In the meantime, on January 6, American troops captured Hackensack and Elizabethtown, leaving New Jersey largely British-free.[55]

Recounting the battle of Assunpink Bridge and the skirmish before Princeton, on January 6 the renowned Dr. Benjamin Rush wrote:

"Much credit is due to a brigade of New England men commanded by Col. Hitchcock in both actions, they sustained a heavy fire from musketry and artillery for a long time without moving, they are entitled to a great share of the honor."[56] Once again, in the thick of fighting, Essex County troops had played a memorable, pivotal role.

The Princeton victory, like the success at Trenton, lifted America's spirits and buttressed faith in its military leader. Washington's defensive strategy through New York and New Jersey had repeatedly saved his army from what seemed like inevitable defeat. He had proven himself an able commander, earning wider respect both from his countrymen and from leaders abroad. Six months after independence, America had arisen from despair to greet the promise of a new year.

1. John C. Fitzpatrick, ed., *The Writings of George Washington*, 6:347.
2. Newburyport Town Records, May 31, 1776, 1:259; Bradford Town Records, June 30, 1776; Gloucester Town Records, June 24, 1776, 178; Manchester and Methuen did not vote, presumably because neither sent representatives to the legislature.
3. Letters of Ebenezer Francis Collection, July 9, 1776, ALS, BHS, 18,200.
4. Charles Woodberry, *Independence Park* (Beverly, 1906), 24; Harriet Silvester Tapley, *Salem Imprints 1758–1885* (Salem: Essex Institute, 1927), 36–40; in June 1776, Ezekiel Russell, publisher of the *Salem Gazette*, started another paper called *The American Gazette: or The Constitutional Journal* in partnership with John Rogers. The operaton dissolved shortly afterwards on account of personal differences; Samuel Roads, Jr., *The History and Traditions of Marblehead* (Marblehead: N. Allen Lindsey, 1897), 141.
5. Peter Force, ed., *American Archives*, 5th Series, 1:461.
6. Herbert T. Wade and Robert A. Lively, *this glorious cause . . .* (Princeton, N.J.: Princeton University Press, 1958), 195.
7. 199, 216.
8. During the winter, Hutchinson's regiment had moved from Winter Hill to Cambridge. On April 2, they had marched to Dorchester Point; on the 16th, twenty members of the regiment were found guilty of "mutinying and disobedience of orders, assaulting and entering the main guard." Their sentences ranged from death to a week's imprisonment in the provost's dungeon and from fifteen to thirty-nine lashes. MHS *Proceedings*, 16 (1878): 343–44.
9. "Letters Written by Josiah Adams of Newbury During Service in the Revolution," *EIHC*, 77 (1941):147.
10. *Acts and Resolves*, 19:462–466, 510; Force, 5th Series, 1:287–292, 314, 320; George Wingate Chase, *History of Haverhill* (Haverhill: George Wingate Chase, 1861), 394–395, 623.
11. "Extracts from the Interleaved Almanacs of William Wetmore," *EIHC*, 43 (1907):119; Force, 5th Series, 1:317–319, 778–779; Philip Chadwick Foster Smith, ed., *The Journals of Ashley Bowen of Marblehead* (Salem: Peabody Museum, 1973), 2:495; Marblehead *Town Records*, EI, July 23, 1776, 4:508; Chase, 394; "Letters Written by Josiah Adams of Newbury," 152; MA Archives, 180:402–403.
12. Letters of Ebenezer Francis Collection, ALS, 18, 233.
13. William Bell Clark, ed., *Naval Documents of the American Revolution*, 6:708.
14. Moses Little to Josiah Little, ALS, Little Family Papers, EI.
15. Force, 5th Series, 1:514, 638; "Heath Papers," MHS *Collections*, 7th Series, 4, Part 2 (1904):43; Smith, 2:495; Howard Kendall Sanderson, *Lynn in the Revolution* (Boston: W.B. Clarke, 1903), 1:153; Henry P. Johnston, *The Campaign of 1776* (Brooklyn, NY: Long Island Historical Society, 1878), Part 1:116–17, 124–25.
16. "Orderly Book Kept by Capt. Abraham Dodge," *EIHC*, 80 (1944): 120–21.
17. [Alexander Graydon], *Memoirs of a Life* (Harrisburg, PA: 1811), 131, 138.
18. Moses Little to Josiah Little.
19. Johnston, *The Campaign of 1776*, Part 2:43; Wade and Lively, 215.
20. Moses Little to Josiah Little, September 1, 1776; Force, 5th Series, 3:722; Wade and Lively, 215.
21. Washington Irving, *Life of George Washington* (New York: G.P. Putnam, 1855),

2:328–29; Moses Little to Josiah Little, September 1, 1776. In recounting the siege, Little appears to be a day ahead.

22. Force, 5th Series, 1:1211; Johnston, *The Campaign of 1776*, Part 1:218–220; Heath, 49.

23. Johnston, *The Campaign of 1776*, Part 1:221–22; Letters of Colonel Ebenezer Francis Collection, September 8, 1776, ALS, 18,226.

24. Fitzpatrick, 6:1; Orderly Book of Israel Hutchinson, MHS.

25. Henry P. Johnston, *The Battle of Harlem Heights* (New York: Macmillan, 1897), 28–29; Johnston, *The Campaign of 1776*, Part 1:228; Fitzpatrick, 6:17; Christopher Ward, *The War of Independence* (New York: MacMillan, 1952), 1:239.

26. Wade and Lively, 221.

27. Irving, 2:353; George Athan Billias, *General John Glover and His Marblehead Mariners* (New York: Henry Holt, 1960), 108–09; during Glover's move to Harlem, two men were lost: Wormsted Trefry of Marblehead and Benjamin Bowden of Lynn.

28. Johnston, *Harlem Heights*, 47–50.

29. 135.

30. Wade and Lively, 222; Ward, 1:247–48.

31. Wade and Lively, 222; Johnston, *Harlem Heights*, 177; for an account of the battle, see Henry P. Johnston's *The Battle of Harlem Heights* (New York: Macmillan, 1897).

32. Wade and Lively, 222; Force, 5th Series, 3:722; Joseph B. Felt, *Annals of Salem*, 2nd ed., (Salem: W. & S.B. Ives, 1849), 2:521.

33. Preceding quotations describing Pelham Bay encounter are extracts from a letter written later by Glover; Force, 5th Series, 2:1188–89; Billias, 119; Henry B. Dawson, *Westchester County, New York During the American Revolution* (Morrisiana, NYC: 1886), 241–45.

34. Force, 5th Series, 2:1240.

35. Fitzpatrick, 6:221.

36. Force, 5th Series, 2:1189; Diary of Moses Brown, MS, BHS.

37. 2:1189; 3:722; Diary of Moses Brown.

38. Clark, 6:1185.

39. 6:1180–87.

40. Sanderson, 1:154–55.

41. 155.

42. Moses Little to Josiah Little, November 16, 1776; "Letters Written by Josiah Adams of Newbury," 158–59; "Heath Papers," 46.

43. Force, 5th Series, 3:1366.

44. 3:1401–02; Otis G. Hammond, ed., *Letters and Papers of General John Sullivan* (Concord, NH: New Hampshire Historical Society, 1930), 1:302.

45. Wade and Lively, 227.

46. William S. Stryker, *The Battles of Trenton and Princeton* (Boston: Houghton Mifflin, 1898) 113–15; Roads, 154–56.

47. Wade and Lively, 229.

48. Stryker, 352–53, 355–56; Force, 5th Series, 3:1401–02.

49. Stryker, 150–85.

50. Henry B. Dawson, ed., *Diary of David How* (Cambridge: H. O. Houghton, 1865), 41.

51. Lorenzo Sabine, *The Principal Fisheries of the American Seas.* (Washington, D.C.: Dept. of Treasury, 1853), 1853), 202.

52. Diary of Moses Brown; Smith, 2:510.

53. Stryker, 264–266.

54. Alfred H. Bill, *The Campaign of Princeton* (Princeton, NJ, 1948), 105–10; Stryker, 280–85; Johnston, *The Campaign of 1776*, 294–95.

55. Stryker, 297.

56. 298.

CHAPTER SEVENTEEN

A MORE PERFECT ARMY

Washington rested his exhausted army in winter quarters around Morristown village in northwest New Jersey. After an arduous, lengthy campaign, most seasoned veterans, including Glover's Marbleheaders, had given up army life. By mid-March discharges and lagging enlistments had thinned the destitute ranks to less than 3,000—only one-third Continentals, plus a contingent under General Putnam at Princeton and a few hundred at Peekskill guarding the Highlands. Fortunately, General Howe preferred the comforts of New York City to an offensive against rebel Americans. Nonetheless, with 27,000 British professionals cantoned in New York and New Jersey, Washington faced the grim prospect of one day withstanding their relentless onslaught. During the winter of 1777, the flame of independence barely shone.

Reorganization

During December 1776, Col. Timothy Pickering called a meeting at Salem's First Church to recruit a company of volunteers. Massachusetts was raising four regiments for three months' duty, reinforcing Continental forces in New York under the command of Gen. Benjamin Lincoln. One regiment was to march from Essex County. In a dramatic moment, the colonel spoke from the pulpit, exhorting the congregation. Ninety-two men—more than Salem's quota—arose and followed the eloquent Pickering from the church.

One in four eligible males was called to form ten companies of sixty-eight troops each. On December 24, Pickering left Salem in command of the Essex County regiment and reached the rendezvous point at Danbury, Connecticut, on January 2. Ten days later, he was ordered to proceed twenty-seven miles toward North Castle. By now, most companies had arrived, except for those from Danvers and Marblehead. In New York, the regiment was kept on the move, while Gen. William Heath ineffectually maneuvered to storm Fort Independence. In mid-February, the Essex County troops crossed the Hudson into the Jerseys, where they remained encamped before returning home on April 1. Washington's lean Continental ranks would compel the calling of state militia during each successive crisis.[1]

Enlistment prospects, languid earlier, improved with the Trenton and Princeton victories. In September 1776, the Continental Congress had called upon the states to raise eighty-eight battalions, or regiments, of 726 men each. Fifteen were expected from Massachusetts. Later, on December 27, Washington was authorized to form an additional sixteen battalions, 3,000 light horse, three artillery regiments, and a corps of engineers—under direct Continental authority. Three infantry units were to be raised in Massachusetts; one by Col. David Henley of Charlestown, a second by Henry Jackson of Boston, and a third by Col. William R. Lee of Marblehead—though none met with much success. No more than 35,000 of the needed 75,000 would be enrolled during 1777, the year of highest enlistment. Of this number, about 7,800 of 10,200 requisitions were from Massachusetts Bay, over one-fifth of the whole Continental Army.

On January 26, 1777, the General Court resolved that militia officers muster their commands and enlist one-seventh of the male inhabitants sixteen years and older in each town. Efforts to comply with the Congress's September call actually had begun earlier, on October 19, when appointed committees visited the armies in the field to select officers for raising seven battalions. Captains and subalterns, officers of lower rank, were to receive six shillings for each enlistee that passed muster. But the real push came with the new year. In the weeks following, militia companies mustered to raise volunteers for the newly organized army. Only Quakers were exempted. An enlistee was promised a Continental bonus of twenty dollars cash and a suit of clothes, which Massachusetts augmented with twenty pounds in scrip. Because the war effort had been handicapped by short-term enlistments, men were engaged either for three years or for the entire war.[2]

Despite Continental and state incentives, "further encouragement" was required. Topsfield, for example, voted a bonus of eight pounds on February 13; this proved inadequate, so on March 25 it was more than doubled, to eighteen. The recruitment committee in neighboring Boxford had discretion to determine amounts needed to meet its quota. Militia officers customarily served on these committees. In Boxford, Lt. Benjamin Perley, when he was unable to enlist enough willing souls, went to Boston. On May 13, though the quota was deficient by two men, the town approved the committee's transactions, with bonuses ranging from eighteen to thirty pounds. Only thirteen soldiers were from Boxford; sixteen were Boston residents, one was from Wenham, and three were Down Easterners, from Scarboro and Bridgton. The Boston men actually enlisted in John Crane's Boston artillery regiment, but were credited to Boxford.

Distant hires commonly served in military units close to home. For example, many Falmouth, Maine, inductees—counted for Andover, Bradford, and Haverhill quotas—enrolled in Capt. Nicholas Blaisdell's Falmouth company, attached to Wigglesworth's regiment. Impoverished Down Easterners enrolled in large numbers, motivated by a blend of patriotism and the need for money. It was not unusual

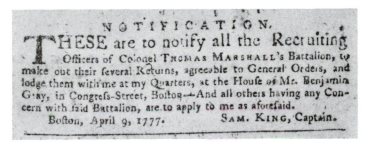

NOTIFICATION.

THESE are to notify all the Recruiting Officers of Colonel THOMAS MARSHALL's Battalion, to make out their several Returns, agreeable to General Orders, and lodge them with me at my Quarters, at the House of Mr. Benjamin Gray, in Congress-Street, Boston—And all others having any Concern with said Battalion, are to apply to me as aforesaid.

Boston, April 9, 1777.   SAM. KING, Captain.

Capt. Samuel King advertised for recruits in the *Independent Chronicle* of Boston, April 10, 1777. Courtesy, Essex Institute, Salem, Mass.

to hire out-of-towners to meet quotas. For example, during early 1777, the 4th Essex Regiment towns of Andover, Boxford, Bradford, Haverhill, and Methuen enlisted 287 men, more than 30 percent outside Essex County.[3]

Essex County's muster master, John Cushing of Boxford, traveled weekly between Salem, Ipswich, Newburyport, and his home town, enrolling soldiers into various regiments. As long as an enlistee arrived armed, properly accoutered, and under direction of an officer, the recruit received Continental and state bounties.[4] Local committees, with Continental recruitment officers searching to fill their companies, competed among a dwindling pool of likely prospects. They looked far and wide and were frequently forced to engage young boys, the infirm, and tippling transients occasionally found at local taverns.

Lucrative enlistment opportunities spawned a new phenomenon:

bonus jumping. The practice became so pervasive that on April 6 Washington proclaimed a "free pardon" for anyone returning to his unit by May 15. Capt. Moses Greenleaf of Newburyport, of the 11th Massachusetts Regiment, reported seven men as "Deserted before Joined." Capt. Samuel Page of Danvers, of the same regiment, published a reward in the *Independent Chronicle* of Boston for twenty-two deserters. Greenleaf and Capt. Billy Porter of Wenham, also of the 11th Regiment, placed similar advertisements.[5]

> DESERTED from Captain *Greenleaf's* Company, in Col. *Francis's* Regiment, the following Persons, viz. *Daniel Price*, aged 29, about 5 Feet 6 Inches high, dark Complexion, short black Hair; *James Summers*, aged 21, 5 Feet 8 Inches high, short sandy Hair; *James Donnoly*, aged 23, 5 Feet 9 Inches high, black strait Hair; *John Gardner*, aged 32, 5 Feet 9 Inches high, brown curled Wig, well set; *John Brown*, aged 27, 5 Feet 5 Inches high. Whoever will take up all or either of said Deserters, and convey them to Goal, shall be intitled to SEVEN DOLLARS each, and all necessary Charges paid.
> MOSES GREENLEAF.

Bonus jumpers and deserters were common problems during the formation of the Continental Army in 1777. *Independent Chronicle* of Boston, April 17, 1777. Boston Athenaeum.

By the end of February, although all regiments were needed desperately by Washington, most were undersized and unready. After May 15, the General Court instructed towns either to have enlistments mustered or to draft the necessary men for eight months. Recalcitrant draftees could locate a substitute or pay a fine. On June 5, to enable regiments to march, it was further resolved to commission officers when their units were two-thirds complete. Nonetheless, summer would arrive before several scant units had left.[6]

Writing home from Peekskill on June 17, Gen. John Glover echoed Washington's sense of urgency:

> Had people of Interest & influence attended to the public Interest, we might have had an Army now in the Field that would bid Defiance to Howe & his whole Force but Privateering & Stockjobbing (I am sorry to say it) had been the sole Object of their Attention . . . Rouse my fellow Countrymen from your Sleepy Lethargy, & Come forth into the Field & Assist your brethren who are jeopard[iz]ing their Lives for you, your wives & Children, as well as for themselves.[7]

In mid-February, Washington had called on Massachusetts to march seven regiments hastily northward to Fort Ticonderoga, on the shore of Lake Champlain, where an enemy move was feared.

Field and Staff Officers 11th Massachusetts Regiment		
Lieutenant Colonel	Noah M. Littlefield	Andover
Major	William Lithgow	Andover
Quartermaster	Aaron Francis	Beverly
Adjutant	John Francis	Beverly
Chaplain	Enos Hitchcock	Beverly

The fort, which commanded the lake, controlled the waterways that linked Canada with New York harbor.

Among the first to march was the 11th Massachusetts Regiment of the Continental line, commanded by Col. Ebenezer Francis. The former Beverly businessman had led a militia regiment on Dorchester Heights since August 1776. In mid-November, he was commissioned and authorized by the Massachusetts Council to form a new regiment. All his field and staff officers hailed from Essex County. Aaron and John Francis were brothers of the commander. Essex men also headed four of eight companies: Capt. Benjamin Farnum of Andover, Capt. Moses Greenleaf of Newburyport, Capt. Samuel Page of Danvers, and Capt. Billy Porter of Wenham. Farnum's men were almost entirely from Andover; Greenleaf's forty-four were from Newburyport, with a handful from Haverhill, Newbury, elsewhere in Essex County, and Chelsea. Twelve of Page's forty-three men were fellow Danversites, with the rest from several Essex County towns. Page's lieutenant, John Foster of Gloucester, had recruited eight Cape Ann men. There were also Beverlyites, including three blacks: Scipio Herrick, Scipio Bartlett, and Caesar Raymond. It was not uncommon for owners to enroll their slaves, nor for free blacks to enlist. Billy Porter's sixty-two troops came mostly from Beverly. Francis's regiment would play a central role in the upcoming campaign.[8]

After four months of organizing and recruiting, in late March each company, traveling separately, trudged about 230 miles to the upper Hudson Valley, scene of the expected onslaught. Moses Greenleaf's journal, which provides a valuable chronicle of events, noted: "23rd of April 1777 Arrived at Ticonderoga the Sun half an hour high. P.M. found all the officers & men in good Spirits." The twenty-two-year-old shipwright, son of the renowned Newburyport builder, Jonathan Greenleaf, ended the day with Adjutant Francis savoring fried fish and pigeons and "turned in" at the old French barracks.[9] On March 28, Lt. Stephen Abbot left Andover with about forty enlistees; North Parish yeoman Captain Farnum, who probably

---

Field and Staff Officers
13th Massachusetts Regiment

Lieutenant Colonel	Dudley Colman	Newbury
Major	John Porter, Jr.	Wenham
Adjutant	Thomas Smart	Danvers
Quartermaster	Job Winchell	Berwick
Surgeon	John Wingate	Haverhill

---

stayed to recruit, followed on April 15 with a small contingent, via Bennington to Fort Edward, where the Hudson becomes navigable. Capt. Page's detachment did not arrive until June 16. By late May, however, 359 of Francis's regiment were encamped in upstate New York.[10]

The remaining eight Bay State regiments were directed to Peekskill in the Highlands, primarily to protect the lower Hudson Valley. Washington expected Howe, in concert with a southward thrust from Canada, to attempt a breakthrough up the Hudson Highlands.

Col. Edward Wigglesworth of Newburyport, formerly a ship master for the merchant house of Jackson, Tracy and Tracy, had returned from Lake Champlain late in 1776 after helping stop Gen. Guy Carleton's Canada push. On November 9, the Massachusetts Council awarded his new commission. During the winter, he organized the 13th Massachusetts Regiment, recruited in York, Cumberland, and Essex counties. Most field and staff officers were from Essex. Two of eight companies were from Essex, led by Capt. Daniel Pilsbury of Newbury and Capt. Matthew Fairfield of Wenham. And county representation—including Lt. William Greenleaf of Haverhill in Joseph McNall's company—was noticeable in others.

Wigglesworth, who arrived at Peekskill in early June, was assigned to John Glover's brigade. Though he had at first refused, the reluctant Marbleheader accepted a brigadier's commission. Washington wrote to Glover: "I know of no man better qualified than you to conduct a Brigade." In mid-June, the new brigadier returned to active duty at Peekskill.[11]

Others from Essex County were officers in regiments led by men from outside the county. In February, Capt. Joseph Hodgkins of Ipswich left Morristown and journeyed home to muster a company. A few members were recruited in Ipswich and Topsfield; most hailed from the Worcester vicinity, however, home of Col. Timothy Bigelow of the 15th Massachusetts Regiment, Hodgkins's regimental commander. In mid-July, the detachment would march two hundred miles to the mouth of the Mohawk on the Hudson, just above Albany.[12]

As with Francis's and Wigglesworth's regiments, Continental recruiters usually concentrated their efforts close to home. Therefore, though more extended than in 1776, most county enlistees were clustered in units led by local line officers: in Joseph Vose's 1st Regiment, Maj. Thomas Cogswell of Haverhill; in Rufus Putnam's 5th, Lt. Col. Ezra Newhall of Lynn, Captains Job Whipple of Danvers, Haffield White of Wenham, and Ebenezer Winship of Salem; in Thomas Nixon's 6th, Capt. Thomas Barnes of Salem; in Ichabod Alden's 7th, Capt. William H. Ballard of Amesbury; in Michael Jackson's 8th, Captains Ebenezer Cleaveland of Gloucester and John Burnham of Ipswich; in James Wesson's 9th, Captains Samuel Carr of Newbury and Amos Cogswell of Haverhill; in Thomas Marshall's 10th, Capt. Samuel King of Salem; in David Henley's Additional Regiment, Capt. Ezra Lunt of Newburyport; and in William Lee's Additional Regiment, Captains Joshua Orne and Stephen Sewall of Marblehead. Also, dozens of Essex lieutenants and ensigns held commissions in these and other Bay State regiments. So well distributed were officers that enlisted men, likewise, circulated throughout most of the Massachusetts line. Indeed, by the summer of 1777, over one thousand Continental soldiers from the four corners of Essex County were standing tall, dispersed among distant encampments near Peekskill or Ticonderoga.

Occupation of Philadelphia

In January, Gen. William Howe brought in his troops from their outlying posts; they wintered at New Brunswick and Perth Amboy, New Jersey, while he enjoyed the amenities of New York City. The dilatory general wasted the cold months and the following spring in quarters while Washington's army grew stronger. Late in May, the Continentals marched out of Morristown to Middlebrook, near New Brunswick, and positioned to head off an expected British advance toward Philadelphia.

Finally, in mid-June, Howe undertook a series of maneuvers in northern New Jersey. If the Americans could be engaged on an open field, he reasoned, his British professionals would whip them handily. After three faltering attempts Sir William withdrew his forces to New York.

On July 23, Howe cleared Sandy Hook with a vast fleet carrying 15,000 troops headed for the seat of the Continental Congress. Earlier, at embarkation, it had seemed the warships and transports would be navigating up the Hudson to join General Burgoyne, who had taken Ticonderoga and was headed south toward Saratoga. Howe had his own agenda: the seizure of Philadelphia. His troops were sailed into Chesapeake Bay and landed at Head of Elk, Maryland, fifty miles from the patriot capital.

On August 23, Washington was bound southward to intercept Howe, and, on September 11, 1777, the armies met at Chad's Ford on Brandywine Creek. As on Long Island, Howe turned the American flank, while Gen. Knyphausen's German mercenaries pressed the center. By dark, confused and disorganized, the beaten Americans retreated toward Chester.

Ten days later, the British successfully thrust their bayonets against Gen. Anthony Wayne's detachment at Paoli. On September 26, Howe took Philadelphia. (The Congress already had fled.) A week later, Washington counterattacked at Germantown, five miles to the northwest, where the main army was encamped. Initially, the British gave ground, but an overcomplicated four-column battle plan and a dense morning fog doomed the operation. By ten o'clock, the action was over, and the Americans, who had fought gallantly, were forced to withdraw.

Although Howe's force would occupy fashionable Philadelphia that winter while Washington endured the elements at Valley Forge, capture of the Quaker City marked Britain's high point. Several days later, the British suffered a humiliating defeat at Saratoga that would transform the War of Independence into a world war, signaling the final chapter in England's fight to retain its colonies.

Burgoyne's Invasion

On June 17, Lt. Gen. John Burgoyne, who had arrived in Canada six weeks earlier to take command, initiated the first phase of a three-cornered plan to isolate New England. He left St. Johns, Canada, on the Richelieu River and moved upstream with a combined force of about 8,000, including British, Germans, four hundred Indians, and a few Tories and Canadians. Burgoyne's plan was to cross Lake Champlain and capture Ticonderoga, then proceed south to the Hudson as far as Albany. The second stage required Lt. Col. Barry St. Leger to lead an expedition eastward from Oswego down the Mohawk River and join Burgoyne at Albany. The united force would meet Sir William Howe, who was headquartered in New York City, as he moved up the Hudson. Burgoyne believed that by controlling the strategic waterways between New York harbor and the St. Lawrence, New England would be divided from the other colonies and the rebellion soon crushed.

Three days later, on June 20, the historic expedition set out from the head of Lake Champlain and landed at deserted Crown Point. Twelve miles south was Fort Ticonderoga, which was commanded by Maj. Gen. Arthur St. Clair, a former British army officer who had settled in America after the French and Indian War. Ticonderoga rested on the west bank, high on a rocky promontory. At its foot, the outlet waters of Lake George flowed into Champlain. Across the lake on the Vermont shore, a quarter mile away, a new secondary fortification, Mount Independence, perched on a rocky bluff.

The optimistic Burgoyne launched a full-scale siege, intent on taking the forts and capturing the defenders, who comprised the nucleus of the northern army. On July 1, the expedition embarked from Crown Point headed southward. The main British army landed on the west side of the lake, three miles above the fort, while the distinguished Maj. Gen. Baron von Riedesel, twenty years a soldier, led the German division ashore on the opposite bank. Wading through a mosquito-infested primeval forest, the Hessian and Brunswicker mercenaries plodded toward Mount Independence.

A siege, however, turned out to be unnecessary. A short distance to the southwest of Ticonderoga the British occupied a 750-foot peak, Mount Defiance (or Sugar Loaf Hill), which had been left undefended. Less than a mile away, St. Clair mistakenly believed that its precipitous slopes were unassailable. On July 5, the dismayed general spied enemy guns on the summit, which towered over both forts. He knew at once his position was untenable. First, under cover of darkness, he loaded five vessels of Arnold's former Valcour fleet, two hundred bateaux, and several smaller craft with sick troops, artillery, and supplies. Once the transfer was completed, the mini-flotilla was sent up the lake, south-bound for Skenesboro, now Whitehall. Then St. Clair abandoned Ticonderoga and crossed the bridge to Independence. With both garrisons, 2,600 in all, the general marched along a cart path, which ran southeasterly to Hubbardton, then around Lake Bomoseen, six miles to Castleton, and westerly fourteen miles to Skenesboro. About daybreak, Gen. Simon Fraser, commander of the British advance corps, reported the forts deserted; he was ordered in pursuit.

The Battle of Hubbardton

St. Clair warily withdrew towards Skenesboro, chased by an 850-man British advance party that was tailed, in turn, by a contingent of Riedesel's Germans. Col. Seth Warner of Vermont, with 150 men, had been left at Hubbardton to await St. Clair's rear guard: soldiers of the 11th Massachusetts, commanded by Col. Ebenezer Francis. That night, Warner's Green Mountain Boys, along with Francis's troops and Col. Nathan Hale's 2nd New Hampshire, encamped in the Vermont hamlet. Fraser's men rested upon their arms a short distance away.

Early next morning—at about five o'clock—the British first encountered Hale's surprised troops. His New Hampshire men fled into the woods; most would be captured later. At 7:20 A.M., Fraser came upon Warner's and Francis's regiments. Just moments before, an express had arrived from St. Clair warning that they should march. The British pushed back the Continentals in utter pandemonium, but they were rallied by Colonel Francis. Lined behind trees, rocks, and bushes, the embattled troops blazed away, felling twenty-one enemy and halting their advance.

This marked the beginning of a bloody skirmish lasting until nearly nine o'clock. Warner's force faced the enemy right; Colonel Francis's largely Essex County 11th Massachusetts confronted the left. Crouched on a rise, along a half mile front, opposing forces skirmished pell mell. To Warner's left was a steep incline, Zion Hill. Intent on flanking the Vermonters, Fraser reinforced his wing with grenadiers from the left and sent them scurrying up on all fours. Eyeing the weakened British line, Col. Ebenezer Francis initiated his own end move. From the edge of a clearing, with their gallant colonel in the lead, the 11th came near defeating Fraser. At a vital moment, General Riedesel arrived with the fire power of about eighty jaegers and grenadiers.

A ball pierced Francis's right arm; still, he led on until dropped by a German bullet through his right breast. Greenleaf noted: "Numbers fell on both sides, among ours the Brave & ever to be Lamented Col Francis, who fought bravely to the Last."[13]

Two Essex County men from Capt. Billy Porter's company were killed: Philip Grush of Marblehead and William Collins of Beverly. Undoubtedly others fell, possibly including Job Cressy, William Peirce, and Jonathan Standley of Beverly. In an era that did not carefully record losses of privates and noncommissioned officers, their names were lost.[14]

Riedesel's reinforcements, combined with Francis's death, broke the 11th Regiment, then Warner's, scattering rank and file in several directions. "Our people being overpowered by numbers," wrote Greenleaf, "was oblig'd to retreat, over the Mountains, [Pittsford] Such as I never saw before." In the confusion, only one wounded sergeant and six men escaped with Greenleaf. At least 17 in the company were missing or captured, though four escaped. In all, 324 were casualties killed or wounded, including over 200 captured. In late September, captives not sent on to Quebec would be rescued at Ticonderoga. By noontime, the Newburyport captain reached Rutland, where he "join'd the Main Body," including St. Clair.[15] At Castleton, after the general had learned that Skenesboro was in British hands, he had turned east. By July 12, leading some of his fatigued troops, St. Clair had moved south to Fort Edward, a vintage French and Indian War garrison.[16]

Meanwhile, Fraser and Riedesel moved west toward Skenesboro, where they rejoined Burgoyne's army. "Gentleman Johnny," as his men affectionately called him, had sailed up Champlain. The vast stores sent to Skenesboro by the retreating Americans fell into his hands.

An angry Congress heaped blame for the catastrophic loss of Ticonderoga on both St. Clair and Schuyler, commander of the Northern Department, for not putting up a defense. In command only three weeks, St. Clair was suspended; Schuyler would be replaced in August by Maj. Gen. Horatio Gates, a retired British officer turned Virginia squire. George Williams of Salem, writing to brother-in-law Adj. Gen. Timothy Pickering, expressed the popular belief: "I rejoice with Others that there is a New Commander, and by Some Letters I have Seen & hear'd of, the Sean is changed, & now I hope there will be Sum Stop to the retreating of the continental troops, in the Northern Department."[17] Brig. Gen. John Glover, in a letter written from Stillwater to James Warren, paymaster general of the Continental Army, noted: "The Clamour of the People runs very high against Genl. Schuyler & St. Clair." He felt the criticism was unwarranted: "I have not the least Charge against either of them," he wrote. The Marbleheader considered St. Clair and Schuyler "exceeding good officers," who had acted appropriately, complaining that the people attribute "every misfortune, or Accident that happens [to] either the Cowardice, Negligence, or Treachery of the Officers commanding."[18]

Down the Hudson

From Skenesboro, where Burgoyne had paused, it was twenty-three miles to Fort Edward on the Hudson—forty more downriver to Albany, the rendezvous point. The colorful general could have returned to Ticonderoga, put his boats into Lake George, and moved southward along a good highway on the left shore. From the end of Lake George, a ten-mile, well-constructed road led to the Hudson near Fort Edward. Astonishingly, Burgoyne was persuaded instead to hack and bridge through a wet, rough cart road overgrown by dense forest, which crossed narrow, meandering Wood Creek forty times between Skenesboro and Fort Anne. Fort Edward was fourteen miles further. The route was nearly impassable for wagon trains and heavy artillery. (Larger cannon and baggage were sent by the alternate route.) To further delay the advance, one thousand Americans slipped north close to Skenesboro and obliterated the British path. They felled trees, dammed streams with large boles and rolled boulders, flooded causeways, and destroyed bridges spanning deep rav-

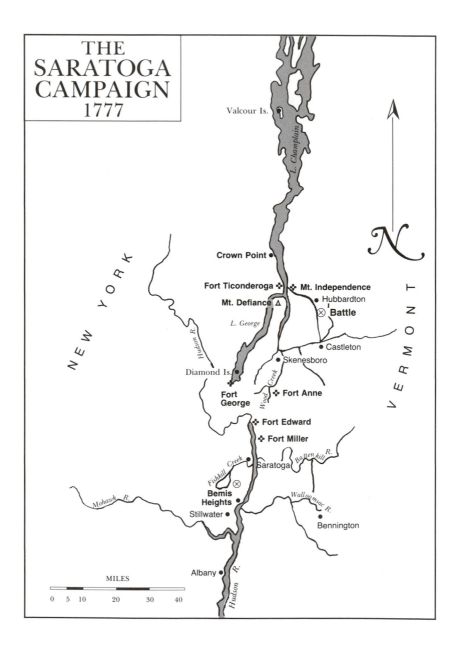

THE SARATOGA CAMPAIGN 1777

NEW YORK

VERMONT

Valcour Is.

L. Champlain

Crown Point

Fort Ticonderoga   Mt. Independence
Mt. Defiance   Hubbardton
                ⊗ Battle

L. George

Hudson R.

Castleton

Diamond Is.   Skenesboro

Wood Creek

Fort George   Fort Anne

Fort Edward

Fort Miller

Batten kill R.

Fishkill Creek   Saratoga

Mohawk R.

⊗
Bemis Heights
Stillwater   Walloomsac R.

Bennington

Albany

Hudson R.

MILES

0 5 10   20   30   40

ines. Burgoyne bivouacked until July 25, while hundreds toiled to open the way, including imported, skilled Canadian axemen. On the twenty-ninth, three long weeks after landing at Skenesboro, the British finally reached Fort Edward.

Gen. Philip Schuyler had come from Albany headquarters to Fort Edward, where a small contingent, including Farnum's Andover company, had been garrisoned. Schuyler's thin army, bolstered by remnants of St. Clair's Ticonderoga troops and 600 led by Brig. Gen. John Nixon of Framingham, grew to about 2,900 regular army and 1,600 militia. (Included was part of Colonel Long's New Hampshire regiment that survived capture in a delay action at Fort Anne.) A more imposing force would have been required to repulse Burgoyne. So Fort Edward was abandoned. The Americans withdrew twenty-four miles past Fort Miller down the Hudson to Stillwater, on the opposite bank twelve miles below Saratoga. In mid-August, Schuyler moved further south, near to the mouth of the Mohawk, only nine miles from Albany. Morale was low. Many New Englanders deserted rather than serve under the aristocratic New Yorker. Equally disdained by eastern congressmen, Schuyler soon was replaced with the favored Maj. Gen. Horatio Gates.

The Murder of Jenny McCrea

On July 27, Capt. Benjamin Farnum of Andover noted: "Nuse that the Wider McNeall & a young Woman that was with hir at hir house are taken out of the seller & carried of by the Enemy aboute a Mile and barbarously treated then kiled and skulped."[19] Only two days earlier, the rampaging Iroquois band, led by the half-breed LeLoup, had killed nine people—the entire John Allen family—near Fort Edward. At the time, the American army was moving five miles below Edward at Moses' Creek. The tragic death of Jenny McCrea, who had been staying near Fort Edward as guest of Mrs. McNeil, an elderly widow and cousin of General Fraser, inflamed the countryside. She had been the fiancee of Lt. David Jones, a Tory volunteer with Burgoyne. The drunken Indians, scouts for Burgoyne, brought McCrea's scalp and the unharmed Mrs. McNeil to the British camp at Fort Anne, where Jones is said to have identified McCrea's tresses. Lynn diarist Henry Hallowell, of Rufus Putnam's regiment, noted he and several "hundred attended the funeral and soleum time it was."[20]

Burgoyne, fearing defection of his scouts—his eyes and ears—left the culprits undisciplined. Though Indian atrocities were relatively common, the widely publicized murder of innocent young Jenny McCrea, coupled with the fact that the perpetrators got off, incensed the countryside. The previously neutral population saw the British presence with their Indian allies as endangering their lives and property. Indeed, Burgoyne, embarrassed by indiscriminate Indian ravaging, called a conference to channel native violence from civilian noncombatants toward enemy soldiers.

Schuyler's army had been continually harassed along their southerly withdrawal by Burgoyne's howling Indians. On August 1, Glover's brigade, which included Wigglesworth's regiment, arrived in camp. This was one of several units rushed north to reinforce Schuyler. Five days later, writing from Stillwater, Gen. John Glover reported that the Indians had killed and scalped twenty-five to thirty soldiers and had captured "as many more." "This strikes a Panic on our Men," he noted, "which is not to be wonder'd at . . . to hear the Cursed War hoop which makes the Woods ring for miles."[21]

Discouraging News

Burgoyne set up headquarters at Fort Edward, left in ruins by the retreating Americans. The wilderness Wood Creek route had depleted his animals, already in short supply, as well as foodstuffs, and cost him irreplaceable days. The British commander remained at Edward awaiting artillery and supplies from Fort George, a welcome respite for his men, but one which gave the American army vital time to strengthen its ranks. Meanwhile, on August 3, a courier had arrived with congratulations from Sir William Howe on the Ticonderoga victory. The indolent Sir William informed Burgoyne that he was going south to Pennsylvania, not north to Albany. This was a terrible surprise, for Burgoyne had counted on being bolstered by Howe's force. However, he quickly continued with his own southward move. To prepare for the journey ahead, superfluous baggage went back to Ticonderoga; this did not include thirty carts of luxury goods—clothes, food, wines—for high living "Gentleman Johnny" and his mistress, Mrs. Commissary.

In need of cattle, carts, horses for Riedesel's mountless Brunswick dragoons, as well as draft animals to haul artillery and wagons, Burgoyne proposed a foraging expedition across the Battenkill into the Vermont (or Hampshire Grants) hillside. On August 11, the foray set out from Fort Miller, seven miles below Fort Edward, with Lt. Col. Friedrich Baum in command of about 650 British, Canadians, Germans, Tories, and Indians. Soon, Indian scouts were reported shooting horses, slaughtering cows for bells, and wantonly terrifying Tory and rebel alike. Baum nevertheless continued. On the sixteenth, near Bennington village on a hill overlooking the Walloomsac River, his entrenched forces were surrounded by 2,000 militia led by the renowned Gen. John Stark of New Hampshire. Eager to avenge the immortalized Jenny McCrea, they surrounded Baum and overran his position, killing or capturing nearly the entire expedition. The same day, Stark, with help from Seth Warner's Green Mountain Boys, drove back a relief column of 650 Germans led by Lt. Col. Heinrich von Breymann, cutting their ranks by one-third. It was a shattering setback for Burgoyne.

A few days later, the general received word that Lt. Col. Barry St. Leger had lifted his siege of Fort Stanwix in the Mohawk Valley. On July 20, he had left Oswego on Lake Ontario with an army of 850, mostly British and Tories, plus nearly 1,000 Iroquois. They besieged Fort Stanwix, where the 750 defenders put up a stiff resistance. An American relief column headed by General Herkimer was ambushed on August 6 at Oriskany, but the 800 militia fought back courageously, inflicting heavy casualties and pushing back the Tory and Indian attackers. When General Arnold, who had been sent by Schuyler, was rumored to be leading an American relief column up the Mohawk, the panicked Indians and Tories abandoned St. Leger. The British commander withdrew toward Oswego, leaving Burgoyne isolated in an expansive, inhospitable wilderness.

By mid-August, Burgoyne had moved his command to Fort Miller, four miles above Saratoga. Despite his recent setbacks, between September 13 and 15 he crossed a bridge of boats to the Hudson's west bank at Saratoga. Since he had only one month's supplies and cold weather was coming on, he was forced to move. Return to Ticonderoga had remained an option; instead, Burgoyne severed his link with Canada and risked everything by pressing on toward Albany.

In the early morning of September 8, the American army, now over 7,000 men, struck their tents and marched north to engage the enemy. General Gates, in command since mid-August, stopped at Bemis Heights, three miles above Stillwater. A fortified line was constructed, extending from Bemis's tavern on the Hudson's west bank across the river road, which squeezed between the river and the eastern slope, to the heights. A three-sided breastworks on the steep two-hundred-foot plateau towered over the road and the Hudson. Glover's, Nixon's and Patterson's Massachusetts brigades occupied the right wing, closest to the river.

Battle of Freeman's Farm

Burgoyne marched his entire force southward toward Bemis Heights, only ten miles away. Knowing that one of the densely wooded adjacent hillsides teemed with Americans eager to spoil the British drive, they moved cautiously in three columns along the narrow river plain. When, on the eighteenth, an American patrol attacked a foraging party in an abandoned potato field, Burgoyne located the rebel position, then prepared for battle.

On September 19 at ten o'clock in the morning, three wings went forward, according to plan. Led by Fraser, the right wing—2,000 advance corps—moved westward to take the high ground and press the Americans against the river. Meanwhile, Brig. Gen. James Hamilton, accompanied by Burgoyne, led the center column of 1,100, which comprised four regiments and six field pieces. Under Generals Phillips and Riedesel, an equal number in the left wing—embracing three regiments and eight field pieces—advanced down the river road. Baggage and boat guards included, Burgoyne's army had dwindled to 6,000 rank and file.

The Americans awaited the advancing enemy behind their breastworks. At the urging of Benedict Arnold, who had come in July, Gen. Horatio Gates sent out Daniel Morgan's riflemen and Henry Dearborn's light infantry to face the British drive from the right. A majority of Arnold's division followed—including Bailey's, Wesson's and Jackson's Massachusetts regiments—moving against the enemy center. They clashed at Freeman's Farm, about one mile north of the American zone, where furious fighting ensued, concentrated in a twenty-acre clearing. Hamilton's wing held the northern edge, while Arnold's formed along the southern fringe. Each side skirmished; they broke across several times, only to be swept back. British bodies piled up in the fields and woods, as Hamilton's 62nd Wiltshires lost heavily. At a crucial moment, Arnold called for reinforcements, but Gates, unwilling to weaken his lines, refused. Late in the battle, Riedesel came up from the river and saved the three British regiments. Attacked on their flank, Arnold's forces withdrew. Although the British held the field, it cost them dearly—600 casualties, with no hope of reinforcements.

Hundreds of Essex County men had helped stop Burgoyne. At least three died: Joseph Burnham of Ipswich, in Capt. John Burnham's company, Jackson's 8th; Reuben Dunnell of Lynn, in Putnam's 5th; James Clements, Jr., of Haverhill, in Capt. Moses Greenleaf's company, Francis's 11th. In all, about 100 American lives were lost.

The two armies rested, spaced a mile apart. They were separated by woods and ravines, and raiding parties were sent out almost nightly by each side. On the twenty-seventh, Glover led 100 against a picket of about 60 posted a half mile away. Near daybreak, they attacked "like so many Tygers," driving back the enemy with three killed, one captured, and many wounded. Such raids were especially disconcerting to the British, who were forced to remain constantly on their guard.[22]

On September 19, Gates, who had originally anticipated that the British would push along the river plain, had built up his right wing. The general believed that Arnold's unauthorized heroics had ignited a general engagement in a disadvantageous location. Consequently, Arnold was relieved of his command.

Two days after the Bemis Heights battle, Burgoyne received hopeful news from Gen. Henry Clinton in New York. Clinton had promised a diversionary push toward Albany. Burgoyne buttressed his camp with a line of entrenchments, including several strong redoubts, and waited. On October 3, Clinton finally despatched 3,000 men, who attacked and captured Forts Montgomery and Clinton, forty miles above the city. The force went no farther, however, dashing any possibility of rescue.

Behind the Lines

Evacuation of Ticonderoga, Washington wrote, on July 18, "opened a door for the Enemy."[23] He called upon militia from Massachusetts, New Hampshire, and New York to help close the portal. During August, Maj. Gen. Benjamin Lincoln of Hingham, Massachusetts, whom Washington sent north from New York, arrived at Manchester, Vermont. He was charged with command of several thousand "Eastern" militia soon to be streaming toward this staging point in the upper Hudson Valley.

New Englanders, vulnerable to a southward lunge since the loss of "Fort Ty," responded promptly. On August 9, the Massachusetts legislature resolved that one-sixth of able-bodied Bay State militia in seven counties, including Essex, should reinforce the northern army against "our cruel & inveterate Enemies" until November 30, unless sooner discharged.[24]

The distinguished and eloquent Revolutionary leader, Samuel Johnson of Andover, colonel of the 4th Essex Regiment, was designated to lead a regiment drawn from seven regiments of the Essex Brigade. Only Cape Ann's contingent, needed at home to defend its exposed coastline, was exempt. In late August, nine companies—more than five hundred citizen-soldiers—traveled their separate ways to Bennington and formed into a regiment. (Marbleheaders, presumably gone privateering, were noticeably absent.) Encamped with comrades from nearby counties, they awaited Maj. Gen. Lincoln's instructions. Hopes ran high at home for this back-door push.[25] On

September 4, Gen. Michael Farley of Ipswich, Essex County's brigadier, writing to Johnson, relished "that the Militia of these States With
the Continental Troops May Defeat Burgon and all his Infernal
Banditti that Peace May once More be."[26]

On September 4, Lt. Col. Ralph Cross of Newburyport, who preceded Johnson, was ordered by Lincoln to lead those Essex County
contingents already encamped to Manchester carrying only one day's
provisions and "one Shift of Cloaths."[27]Four days later, Colonel Johnson and companies from Andover, Newbury, and Salem joined them.
Next day, they arrived at Pawlet and bivouacked with 2,000 troops.
On September 12, Gen. Benjamin Lincoln gave marching orders. An
expeditionary force was sent out comprised of three 500-man detachments, to "annoy, distract, and divide the enemy" bases at Ticonderoga and Mount Independence. Provided it were not too risky, the
fortresses were to be stormed. A regiment under Col. John Brown
of Pittsfield was ordered toward the north end of Lake George, near
stone-walled Ticonderoga and its outposts. Col. Ruggles Woodbridge
of South Hadley was sent to Skenesboro, since abandoned by the
British, to cover Brown's possible withdrawal. The third contingent,
led by Colonel Johnson, included over 300 from his Essex County
regiment, a contingent of Continentals under Lt. Col. Samuel Safford
of Vermont, and some Middlesex County militia. Their objective was
Mount Independence, opposite Ticonderoga.[28]

The Andover colonel proceeded to Castleton, and waited for
Brown to reach his position. Then, on September 15, he divided his
unit into three parties: (1) leading, Safford's Continentals and Zad-
dock Buffington's Salem company; (2) in the center, the prominent
shipwright Lt. Col. Ralph Cross heading "Essex men"; (3) bringing
up the rear, Col. James Barret and Col. Samuel Bullard, with Middlesex County militia.[29] On the sixteenth, they marched all day, arriving at eight o'clock within two miles of Independence.

Next day, two messengers swam Lake George, bringing the word
that Brown was positioned on the western side of Mount Defiance.
As the Pittsfield colonel readied to assail Ticonderoga early the following morning, he counted on a concurrent attack against Independence, "with vigour." Meanwhile, Johnson's divisions had advanced
and exchanged fire with the enemy picket. Cross wrote: "The Centuries fired upon us but Sustained no Damage the Enemy Kept upon
us a Heavy fire all day to no purpos."[30] Worcester County's Brig.
Gen. Jonathan Warner, who was in overall command, arrived and
held a council of war with Johnson. They concluded that the fort,
protected by a steep bluff and defended by 700 Brunswickers, was
too strong to be stormed. Instead, Johnson's force would "make a
feint," so Brown's moves across the lake would go unnoticed.[31]

Essex Regiment in Service of the United States[32]

Regimental Officers

Colonel	Samuel Johnson	Andover
Lieutenant Colonel	Ralph Cross	Newburyport
Major	Eleazer Crafts	Manchester
Adjutant	Bimsley Stevens	Andover
Quartermaster	Caleb Cushing	Haverhill
Surgeon	William Bacheller	Haverhill
Surgeon's Mate	George Osgood	Andover

Company Officers

Captain	Joseph Eaton	Haverhill
First Lieutenant	Thomas Stickney	Bradford
Second Lieutenant	Nathaniel Plumer	Bradford
Captain	Samuel Flint	Danvers
First Lieutenant	Joseph Herrick	Beverly
Second Lieutenant	Joseph Porter	Danvers
Captain	Jonathan Evans	Salisbury
First Lieutenant	Robert Rogers	Newburyport
Second Lieutenant	Daniel Bayley	Newburyport
Captain	Benjamin Adams	Rowley
First Lieutenant	Edward Thompson	
Second Lieutenant	Thomas Green	Rowley
Captain	Robert Dodge	Ipswich
First Lieutenant	Benjamin Gould	Topsfield
Second Lieutenant	John Safford	Ipswich
Captain	Samuel Johnson, Jr.	Andover
First Lieutenant	James Mallone	Methuen
Second Lieutenant	John Frye	Andover
Captain	Zaddock Buffington	Salem
First Lieutenant	Thomas Cox	Lynn
Second Lieutenant	John Berry	Salem
Captain	Stephen Perkins	Newburyport
First Lieutenant	Amos Pearson	Newburyport
Second Lieutenant	Benjamin Newman	Newburyport
Captain	John Noyes	Newbury
First Lieutenant	Samuel Pilsbury	Newburyport
Second Lieutenant	Stephen Brown	Newbury

At daybreak on the eighteenth, the mainly Essex County force advanced on Independence; their war whoops and musket fire drove in the picket (outer guard). The fort's batteries replied, and gunboats raked the shoreline with grapeshot. The Americans, concealed in the woods and out of range, kept the enemy preoccupied. Firing continued intermittantly all day.[33]

On September 18, Brown's troops overran the British camp near the portage landing between Lakes George and Champlain. They also took a blockhouse near the sawmills, a small garrison on Mount Defiance, and the old French lines behind the fortress on the western shore. Along the way, they captured 293 British and Canadians, cannon and ammunition, baggage, 200 bateaux, a sloop, and 17 gunboats. Also, they released 118 fatigued, elated Americans captured at Fort Anne and Hubbardton, including part of Francis's corps. After laying siege to the old stone fort—the only position still in British hands—Brown withdrew, finding that its walls, manned by the 53rd British Regiment, were too imposing.[34]

On September 22, reinforced by 200 of Johnson's men, Brown's force boarded the three-gun sloop, two gunboats, and a number of bateaux, all captured earlier. Before embarking, they destroyed remaining bateaux and plunder they were unable to carry. The troops—420 strong—headed up Lake George for a daybreak attack against the British garrison on Diamond Island, twenty-five miles south near old Fort George. An alerted enemy, however, had prepared a "warm Reception."[35]

The assault was not launched until September 24. After Brown's craft were "shot through" and disabled—except for one commanded by Capt. Samuel Johnson, Jr.—the effort was abandoned. All boats, plus nonportable stores, were burned. The Americans forged through the woods to Skenesboro; with the rest of Johnson's contingent going by way of Castleton, both forces returned victoriously to Pawlet by September 27.[36]

Earlier, on the twenty-first, Burgoyne's troops had heard three great cheers coming from Bemis Heights, followed by thirteen cannon salutes. Gates's army was celebrating news of Brown's and Johnson's successes. With minor casualties, the militia had wreacked havoc along Burgoyne's possible line of retreat.

Meanwhile, militia by the thousands from New York and New England were converging toward Bemis Heights. Colonel Johnson's Essex County regiment joined the main camp on October 5 and climbed the heights for the upcoming battle.[37] Two days later, Gates counted an effective force over 11,000—2,700 Continentals, the rest militia.

Second Battle of Freeman's Farm

Burgoyne's position stretched between Freeman's Farm on the right and the river bluffs. His once-polished army of nearly 8,000—before Ticonderoga—now was a slimmed down, tattered 5,000, surviving on two-thirds rations of salt pork and flour. Desertions ran high, particularly among the Germans. With no forage, the already-depleted supply of horses was starving. As colder weather set in, with the extra gear back at Ticonderoga, most rank and file were exposed to the chilly elements. Many were sick and wounded. With few transports available, Burgoyne had become largely immobile; retreat was unfeasible.

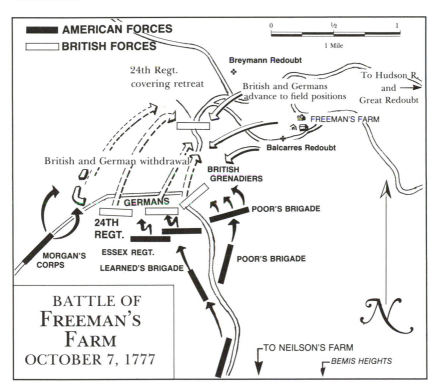

That the British were stalled in their southerly drive was long-sought, encouraging news. It appeared possible that, with reinforcements, the Americans could destroy Burgoyne's army. On September 22, reinforcements from five Bay State counties streamed northward, including half of the 3rd and 4th Essex regiments. At a rally of militia mustered in Andover, Samuel Phillips, Jr., rendered an appeal that stirred a "goodly number" to step out to the sounds of fife and drum.

Next morning, Andoverite Capt. John Adams rode out on horseback leading a company from North Parish, Boxford, and Bradford, along with Capt. John Abbot's company from South Parish and other towns. After the first day, the horses were returned and the men "footed on." The regiment, with Maj. Benjamin Gage of Bradford as commander, contained companies led by Capt. Nathaniel Marsh and Capt. Samuel Merrill of Haverhill, Capt. Nathaniel Gage of Bradford, and Capt. John Robinson of Boxford. The 3rd Essex County regiment, commanded by Maj. Charles Smith, marched from Ipswich. Capt. Robert Perkins led a thirty-six-man horse troop; seventy others trudged behind Capt. David Low of Ipswich and Capt. Richard Dodge of Wenham. However, the county's reinforcements arrived too late to do battle.[38]

On October 7, realizing relief from Clinton was unlikely, Burgoyne primed for a final push. Rashly, he moved to test the American left wing by sending a heavy reconnaissance force of 1,650 troops in three columns: Lord Balcarres led the right, with Brigadier Simon Fraser; the center was commanded by Baron von Riedesel leading Lt. Col. Breymann's grenadiers; the left was headed by Maj. John Acland, supported by ten field pieces. After one-half mile, they reached two clearings flanked by woods, and deployed along a 1,000-yard line, amidst wheat stubble on a low ridge. The troops sat down in double ranks and waited for an hour and a half.

In mid-afternoon, the Americans opened a three-pronged, concurrent attack. Newbury native Enoch Poor moved his New Hampshire and New York brigade up a slope toward the ridge held by the left column of embattled, fur-hatted British grenadiers, forcing the outnumbered enemy to retreat. To the west, Morgan's Virginia riflemen arched around through the woods and hit Balcarres's flank, followed by a frontal withering volley from Dearborn's light infantry. As the fighting began, Nixon's brigade and some of Patterson's—including the partly–Essex County 11th—advanced. The British right was driven back; Balcarres vainly tried to re-form, then finally retreated.

Ebenezer Learned's brigade, counting scores of Essex Continentals among Jackson's and Wesson's ranks, pushed toward the center. Now the whole line was engaged, with the enemy taking the brunt at midpoint. Defended by three hundred Brunswickers and the cannons of Hesse-Hanau, Riedesel's gallant men, strengthened by the Rhetz and Hesse-Hanau infantry, repelled the assault. "The smoke was very dense and no movements could be seen," recalled Lt. Ebenezer Mattoon of the Continental artillery, "but as it soon arose, our infantry appeared to be slowly retreating and the Hessians advancing, their officers urging them on with their hangers[swords]." Col. Johnson was leading half his regiment; Lt. Colonel Cross and Major Crafts commanded the rest. At the critical moment, Mattoon wrote: "The troops continuing warmly engaged, Col. Johnson's regiment coming up, threw in a heavy fire and compelled the Hessians to retreat. Upon this we advanced with a shout of victory." The Essex contingent swept through the German position, driving past several brass cannon, where bloodied dead and dying men were strewn about. Suddenly, they encountered the 24th British Regiment, commanded by Brig. Gen. Simon Fraser, hurrying to support the disintegrating German ranks. The Essex County militia fought bravely, but the skirmish "proved very fatal to one of Col. Johnson's companies," Mattoon wrote.[39]

General Arnold, who had stayed on without a command, rode onto the field. He joined Brookes's regiment of his former brigade. Boosted by his example, cheering troops along the line followed the intrepid general.

Shortly afterward, Gen. Simon Fraser fell, mortally wounded, and resistance faded. As the British withdrew toward their forts, Americans gained the field. Arnold pushed forward leading an unsuccessful assault on Balcarres's redoubt, a bastion held by 1,500 light infantry. Then, facing enemy crossfire, with amazing courage Arnold galloped across the battlefield to lead Learned's troops against two fortified cabins near the Breymann redoubt. Around dusk, after an enemy bullet had fractured Arnold's leg, the battle ended.

The valor of the Essex County regiment was pivotal to the historic October 7 victory, a glorious success for which they paid dearly. Lt. Col. Ralph Cross, who chronicled the campaign, reported ten killed and thirty-four wounded. The county's dead included: Capt. Samuel Flint of Danvers; his lieutenant, Joseph Herrick of Beverly; Benjamin Mains, Samuel Fowler, and Samuel Gould of John Noyes's company; Jonathan Stevens of Johnson's company; Ezekiel Eastman of Evans's company; Jeremiah Chaplin, Adams's company.[40]

Essex County losses were also felt in Continental ranks: from Learned's brigade, Lt. Ezekiel Goodridge of Amesbury in Jackson's 8th regiment and Lt. Wadleigh Noyes of Newbury in Wesson's 9th; from Patterson's brigade, John Louger of Haverhill and Luke Roundy of Beverly in Tupper's (formerly Francis's) 11th.[41]

On October 9, writing to Gen. William Heath, John Glover assessed American losses at "not more than 30 killd, nor more than 100 wounded." On October 13, six days after the battle, Rev. Enos Hitchcock's accounting was: "[Americans] killed, wounded & missing not exceeding 150." Incredibly, soldiers from Essex County suffered over 25 percent of the total number killed and wounded. The Second Battle of Freeman's Farm, generally acknowledged as marking the turning point, exacted an uncommon and painful sacrifice from Essex County sons.[42]

Victory

During the night of that momentous October 7, Burgoyne quit Freeman's Farm and withdrew behind the "Great redoubt" on the river bluffs; the following evening he retreated slowly north with his exhausted, dispirited army, leaving three hundred sick and wounded. The troops forded the Fishkill and dug in at Saratoga Heights, which he had fortified on September 13 and 14.

Amid dense early morning fog, on October 11, Gates's army moved up, mistakenly believing Burgoyne had gone on toward Fort Edward. Nearly a mile upstream, Morgan's riflemen forded the kill, followed on the right by Learned, leading two brigades. Nixon's and Glover's commands crossed easterly nearer the mouth, drifting unwittingly toward the barrels of twenty-seven enemy guns mounted from behind a strong barricade.

During the crossing, the trap was disclosed to Glover by a British deserter; he pulled back and quickly alerted Nixon. His force already had forded the river; before they could backtrack, the fog lifted. Enemy cannon fire ripped through Nixon's ranks. Several fell, but most waded to safety. Upriver, braving British fire, Learned's troops moved back unscathed. Glover's timely discovery saved Gates's army from almost certain defeat.[43]

By afternoon, artillery entrenched on the south bank was bombarding the British position; next day, batteries from across the Hudson joined in. On October 13, the British army was encircled by 14,000 Americans. Knowing a breakout attempt would have been futile, Burgoyne entered talks which led to surrender four days later. The accord, known as the Convention of Saratoga, called for the British to lay down their arms, march to Boston, and board transports for Europe, pledged to not take up arms again. Canadians could return home.

On Friday, October 17, 1777, regiment by regiment, scarlet- coated British and Germans dressed in blue or green paraded, grounded their arms, and marched away, as fifes and drums played the English tune, "The World Turned Upside Down." The army was permitted to come out under their own command, screened from Americans' view, though sounds of music reverberated across the Fishkill. Altogether, 5,000 troops, women and children, headed by Burgoyne in his plumed helmet and followed by twenty-seven field pieces and dozens of carts carrying munitions, including 5,000 small arms, were surrendered.

Gen. John Glover was assigned to escort the captive army, its entourage of wives, children, and wagonloads of baggage to Boston. Lt. Col. James Brickett of Haverhill, who had gone north with the volunteers, was appointed a brigadier and commanded 500 militia detached to accompany the captured troops to Boston. Several Essex County companies that had marched toward Saratoga numbered among the escort.[44]

On October 18, the British were rafted across the Hudson at Stillwater, with the Germans following the next day. Rather than oversee the ferrying operation, Glover, accompanied by his former adversary, Baron von Riedesel, rode south twenty-five miles to Albany to attend a lavish dinner party at the Schuyler mansion. General Burgoyne and Major General Phillips were also among the invited guests. Such was the military custom of the eighteenth century.

On October 20, the overland journey commenced, with the British taking two routes: a northerly course and a more central one through Northampton. The almost all-Brunswicker Germans traveled by a southerly path through Great Barrington and Springfield. Riedesel, riding with his family, met up with his troops at Kinderhook, about fifty miles south of Stillwater.

Glover escorted Burgoyne and Phillips well behind the columns, apparently more pleasurable duty. It was a task, however, already assigned to Gen. William Whipple of New Hampshire. By Glover's negligence, and because of his absence, many accompanying American troops, particularly along the southern route, largely ignored their responsibilities. They dallied, sometimes for several days, enabling thieves to rob the defenseless German captives of their knapsacks and horses. Their billeting not attended to, the weary German soldiers sometimes slept exposed to the icy elements. Also, food and supplies were inadequate. Riedesel took charge and generally arranged shelter and provisions for his troops. At Worcester, on November 4, the Germans and Glover connected, and the Marbleheader was persuaded to see that adequate quarters were provided.

According to the Convention of Saratoga, Burgoyne was required to pay hard money for the subsistence of his army. Though a pile of bills accumulated due to German pilfering and property damage—including uprooted fences burned for warmth—townspeople were compensated. First, however, Glover convinced the General Court to appoint a committee to audit the often-inflated charges.

A large crowd gathered, bells were rung, and cannon saluted to greet the Americans' November 7 arrival in Cambridge. Glover entered on horseback, escorting Burgoyne, with the bedraggled army following. At this juncture, Col. William R. Lee took charge. (Coincidentally, he was Glover's former brigade major, whose undersized regiment of less than one hundred had come to Boston on September 19.)[45]

The Germans were paraded to Winter Hill in Somerville, the British to Prospect Hill in Medford, where both forces occupied huts constructed by the Americans besieging Boston two years earlier. Generals enjoyed the quarters of private Cambridge homes. During the year following, about 500 Essex County men stood guard on Winter Hill in Jacob Gerrish's regiment, under overall command of Lee. Some ex-mercenaries, with approval—others without—journeyed into outlying towns where they were employed as farm hands or in their crafts. Samuel Phillips, Jr., and Moses Little were among Essex County employers who had Council permits to hire captive Germans. More than a dozen others worked in Boxford and lived with Capt. William Perley and other residents. Although the Convention terms provided for the army to embark for England, only Burgoyne and his staff were permitted to return. Congress repudiated Gates's pledge, suspecting the troops would have been redeployed in America, not sent to Europe. A year later, for security reasons, the enemy troops were marched to Virginia; in 1781, they were transferred to Pennsylvania and remained there until peace returned.

Up and down the seaboard, following news of victory, much-relieved coastal residents at Boston, Gloucester, Marblehead, Newburyport, Portsmouth, and Salem engaged in "rejoicings." Newburyporters reportedly fired "great numbers of cannon." Over-exhilarated Salem revelers "rocked" several windows in the Summer Street home of attorney William Pynchon, a suspected Tory, and other nearby residences. At town meeting, conservative Salem voted that the rioters must repair or pay for the damage.[46] The surrender, today generally regarded as the turning point of the war, raised spirits of officeholders, soldiers, and citizens throughout the colonies. It became a major factor in France's decision to ally itself with America in February 1778.

Valley Forge

From Saratoga, Glover's, Learned's and Patterson's brigades marched south, as ordered, to reinforce Washington's army. From Albany, Ipswichite Capt. Joseph Hodgkins wrote the disconcerting news to his wife:

> I wish I Could inform you that I thought our fartague was over for this year But to the Contray I Expect we shall march to Morrow Morning Down the River to wards the Pakskills & I Expect we shall Be ordered towards Philledalpha to Take another winters Camppain in the Jerseys Soldiers must not Complain.[47]

General Washington's army endured a winter of outrageous deprivation at Valley Forge. Henry Cabot Lodge Collection. Courtesy, Beverly Historical Society.

On December 19, after several skirmishes, Washington's cold, ragged, exhausted army struggled into winter quarters at Valley Forge, eighteen miles northwest of the Quaker City. It was a good choice for an encampment because its natural barriers made it defensible—Mount Joy and Mount Misery to the west, the Schuylkill River to the north, and the high ridge to the south. Also, General Washington was close enough to watch the British occupying Philadelphia.

With additions from the north, on January 1, 1778, Washington's army numbered about 12,000 fit for duty. Without provisions, ill-clothed and shod, haggard from the past campaign, they huddled in their new encampment. In the blustery air, they prepared for winter's fury. Huts—fourteen by sixteen feet, though actual dimensions varied—were to be constructed of logs, each designed to house twelve men. Valley Forge was a carefully laid out military town with prescribed locations for each unit.

It was a winter of outrageous deprivation: lack of shoes, stockings, clothes, blankets, meat, bread. On January 25, Moses Greenleaf showed nine men "unfit for Duty for want of Clothes"; fifteen of Farnum's men were equally pitiful.[48] At one point, 4,000 in the tattered army were listed unfit for duty. Hodgkins wrote home in late February: "I must just inform you that what our soldiers have suffred this Winter is Beyond Expression as one half has Ben Bare foot & all most Naked all winter the other half Very Badly on it for Clothes of all sorts." In March, with public stores depleted, towns were urged to collect donations of shirts, shoes, and stockings. Col. Israel Hutchinson of Danvers was Essex County agent. Massachusetts' Continentals, however, were among the last reclothed. Hodgkins charged seaport townspeople particularly for having "Lost all Bowles of Compassion if they Ever had any."[49] In mid-May, Rev. Enos Hitchcock, now chaplain for Patterson's entire brigade, wrote to his friend, Capt. Josiah Batchelder, Jr., in Beverly: "Numbers of our brigade are destitute even of a shirt, and have nothing but the ragged remains of some loose garments as a partial covering." Reassured by reports that relief was coming, the Beverly pastor hoped "the shame of our nakedness will not long appear."[50] Eking out on short rations, the famished Continentals often resorted to eating "firecake," a thin bread of flour and water. Inept quartermaster and commissary departments, nearly nonexistent wagons, and farmers who favored British coin at nearby Philadelphia to Continental scrip were to blame. By spring, food arrived, with increasing quantities of other supplies, allowing each soldier a daily food allowance of bread, meat or fish, and a gill of whiskey.

In the depths of winter, ranks were reduced about one-half. Among the killer diseases were dysentery, pneumonia, typhoid, and typhus, which felled about 2,000 troops. Large numbers deserted or went home. Capt. Moses Greenleaf logged thirteen of his men on "furlough," possibly a euphemism for desertion.[51]

In late February, the Prussian Baron Friedrich von Steuben came to camp and volunteered to drill the awkward, under-trained troops.

Tirelessly, the popular taskmaster drilled the regiments into an effective fighting force, including practice in how to thrust the lethal bayonet. Most importantly, the army learned to march compactly, four abreast. By mid-May, it had undergone a dramatic change. Hitchcock was able to write: "Great improvements are making in the discipline of the army—several hours every day being devoted to that purpose. Our strength increases faster in this way than by the addition of numbers."[52]

On December 31, 1777, possibly 500 rank and file and an estimated 70 officers from Essex County were billeted at Valley Forge, particularly Wigglesworth's 13th and Bigelow's 15th regiments, of Glover's brigade; Marshall's 10th and Tupper's 11th, of Patterson's; Michael Jackson's 8th and James Wesson's 9th, of Learned's. Attached to Col. John Crane's Continental Artillery were five Essex County officers, including Capt. Winthrop Sargent of Gloucester, and dozens of enlisted men. Many hand-picked Essex County men served in Caleb Gibbs's hundred-man Life Guard or in Lt. George Lewis's mounted cavalry, the commander in chief's guard. John and Lemuel Coffin of Newbury and Michael and Zebulon Titcomb of Newburyport, among others, numbered in the elite corps. Hundreds of steadfast Essex County Continentals, hardened by the winter privation and honed into fighting shape by Baron von Steuben, could claim proud membership in a transformed first-rate American army. Through the courage, sacrifice, and suffering of these men—and that of thousands from throughout Massachusetts and most other states—Valley Forge lives as a symbol in the struggle to achieve independence.[53]

Evacuation of Philadelphia

Sir William Howe and his officers, ensconced for the winter in Philadelphia, spent the time enjoying the fashionable city's lavish social life. With 20,000 troops at his command, the lax general intended to wait until spring to attack Washington at nearby Valley Forge. By then, however, he had been replaced by Sir Henry Clinton. With British armies linked solely by sea and expecting a superior French fleet to arrive, Clinton brought secret orders to evacuate Philadelphia and return to New York. This forced consolidation was the first dividend reaped by the new Franco-American alliance. Sir Henry chose the land route, across the rebel-held Jerseys toward Sandy Hook.

On June 19, six months after his arrival, Washington finally broke winter camp in pursuit of the 10,000 British troops and their twelve-mile-long supply train. Now leading a well-trained, disciplined army—bolstered by newly arrived troops—the commander in chief emerged, hopeful of success. Gen. Charles Lee, recently released in a prisoner exchange, was sent on June 28 to engage the enemy rear at Monmouth Court House. The eccentric general led 5,000 men into battle without a formal line to face 2,000 British. Consequently, no major pitched battle ensued, but rather, several uncoordinated skirmishes. In spite of oppressive, nearly 100-degree heat, the Americans fought spiritedly and well. Lee, however, convinced that British reinforcements were on the way, ordered a retreat toward Englishtown.

Only Washington's timely arrival prevented a complete rout. Decisively, the commander organized a line, behind which the embattled Continentals repulsed successive enemy assaults. Capt. Samuel Page of Danvers recalled the day as the most exhausting he had ever experienced. While Americans fought in shirt sleeves, conforming to military code, the British wore their suffocating, thick uniforms and heavy accouterments.[54] On both sides, more died of fatigue than at each other's hands. By evening, the British pulled back and renewed their march toward New York. The day, which had begun with all the earmarks of an American victory, had ended in a draw. Nonetheless, Baron von Steuben's training had paid off; Washington's troops, exhibiting a martial composure and a fighting skill, had engaged in a formidable defense against the professional British army.

As Clinton continued safely to New York City, Washington led his army to northern New Jersey, crossed the Hudson, and, by the end of July, had established a new encampment at White Plains. The Battle of Monmouth was the last important engagement in the north; after Clinton was directed to conquer the Carolinas, the major theater of action shifted south.

Brighter Hopes

The Americans' near win at the battle of Germantown, linked with news of the victory at Saratoga, convinced France to ally with the fledgling United States. France's entry changed the entire picture; the War of Independence was transformed into a world conflict, diverting England's attention to her own shores and to the West Indies. Now the British faced two formidable adversaries. One and a half years earlier, the Continentals encamped around Morristown had been pitiably weak. Von Steuben's painstaking drilling had helped them become a well trained, disciplined standing army of 12,000. No longer, either, could England rely upon its dominance of the seas. The Comte d'Estaing had sailed from Toulon with an imposing French fleet and 4,000 troops. During July, he arrived off Sandy Hook, heartening Washington. Word of his cruise had prompted the evacuation of Philadelphia. Military victory still was years away, but with thanks to the blossoming Franco-American alliance, coupled with Washington's strengthened army, the flame of liberty glowed brighter.

1. *Province Laws*, 5:595–600; Octavius Pickering, *The Life of Timothy Pickering* (Boston: Little, Brown, 1867), 1:94–128; "Extracts from the Interleaved Almanacs of William Wetmore," *EIHC*, 43 (1907):120.

2. *Acts and Resolves*, 19:605–06; 675–76, 681, 781–82.

3. *Town Records of Topsfield* (Topsfield: Topsfield Historical Society, 1920), 2:371–72; Sidney Perley, *History of Boxford* (Boxford: Sidney Perley, 1880), 235; Boxford Town Records, May 13, 1777, 150; Military Manuscripts, Fourth Regiment, Regimental Papers, 1776–1781. Essex County Militia Records, EI.

4. *Acts and Resolves*, 19:736–37; *Independent Chronicle*, January 25, 30, 1777.

5. John C. Fitzpatrick, ed., *The Writings of George Washington*, 7:364; *Independent Chronicle*, April–May, 1777, Revolutionary Rolls, MA Archives, 11:71.

6. *Acts and Resolves*, 20:12, 102–03.

7. Russell W. Knight, ed., *General John Glover's Letterbook 1776–1777* (Salem: Essex Institute, 1976), 13.

8. Revolutionary Rolls, MA Archives, 19:129, 130; 22:96, 99, 100.

9. Diary of Capt. Moses Greenleaf, Moses Greenleaf Military Papers 1776–1780, MS Volume, MHS.

10. Diary of Capt. Greenleaf; Sarah Loring Bailey, ed., The Diary of Capt. Benjamin Farnum 1775 to 1778, MS, MHS; Revolutionary Rolls, MA Archives, 2:35.

11. Fitzpatrick, 7:472.

12. Herbert T. Wade and Robert A. Lively, *this glorious cause . . .* (Princeton, NJ: Princeton University Press, 1958), 108–11.

13. Diary of Capt. Greenleaf; accounts of the skirmish are contradictory; Greenleaf has Francis's regiment facing the enemy right, though it may have been at the outset of the conflict.

14. Frank C. Damon, "Fell at Hubbardton Philip Grush and William Collins," *The Salem Evening News*, February 1, 1929.

15. Diary of Capt. Greenleaf; Moses Greenleaf Military Papers, 87, 109.

16. For accounts, in addition to Moses Greenleaf's diary, see: "Capt. Enos Stone's Journal," *NEHGR*, 15 (1861):301, 303; Edwin M. Stone, *History of Beverly* (Boston: James Munroe, 1843), 76–78; Benson J. Lossing, *The Pictorial Field-Book of the Revolution* (New York: Harper, 1855), 1:145–46; Christopher Ward, *The War of the Revolution* (New York: Macmillan, 1952), 1:412–14; Lieut. James M. Hadden, *A Journal Kept in Canada and Upon Burgoyne's Campaign*, (Albany, NY: Joel Munsell's Sons, 1884), Appendix No. 15. Hale was widely censured for his conduct and was arrested, but died in prison before his trial.

17. George Williams, "Revolutionary Letters Written To Colonel Timothy Pickering," *EIHC*, 42 (1906):316.

18. Knight, 27.

19. Bailey, Diary of Benjamin Farnum.

20. Howard Kendall Sanderson, *Lynn in the Revolution* (Boston: W.B. Clarke, 1903), 1:160–61.

21. Knight, 26.

22. 44–45.

23. Fitzpatrick, 8:429.

24. *Acts and Resolves*, 20:88–90.

25. Revolutionary Rolls, MA Archives, 17:19, 21, 43, 65; 18:146, 249, 254; 19:8 1/2, 41, 69, 84; 20:102, 106; 21:139, 171.

26. Michael Farley to Samuel Johnson, ALS, Fourth Regiment, Regimental Papers, 1776–1781. Essex County Militia Records, EI.

27. "The Journal of Ralph Cross, of Newburyport, Who Commanded the Essex Regiment, at the Surrender of Burgoyne, in 1777," *The Historical Magazine*, 7 (1870):9.

28. Revolution Letters—1777–78, MA Archives, 198:176–178; Richard P. Northey, "The Letters of Colonel Samuel Johnson of Andover Relating to an Expedition in September 1777 to Recapture Fort Ticonderoga," *EIHC*, 123 (1987):290.

29. "The Journal of Ralph Cross," 9; Cross's report of the line of march differs somewhat from Johnson's.

30. "The Journal of Ralph Cross," 9.

31. Northey, 290–93.

32. Revolutionary Rolls, MA Archives, 17:209.

33. "The Journal of Ralph Cross," 10.

34. Northey, 293–95; Revolution Letters—1777–78, 198:179–80; "Col. John Brown's Expedition Against Ticonderoga and Diamond Island, 1777," *NEHGR*, 74 (1920):285, 286, 292.

35. "Col. John Brown's Expedition," 286, 289; Northey, 293.

36. "Col. John Brown's Expedition," 289, 293; Northey, 293–94; Revolution Letters—1777, 198:191.

37. "The Journal of Ralph Cross," 9.

38. Revolutionary Rolls, MA Archives, 17:13; 18:152; 19:139, 143; 20:225, 226; 21:44, 71; 22:57, 58, 168; M. M. Quaife, ed., "A Boy Soldier under Washington: The

Memoir of Daniel Granger," *The Missis-sippi Valley Historical Review*, 16, (1930): 543–44.

39. William L. Stone, *Visits to the Saratoga Battle-Grounds* (Albany, NY: Joel Munsell's Sons, 1895), 244, 246; for an account of the battle, see Rupert Furneaux's *The Battle of Saratoga* (New York: Stein and Day, 1971).

40. "The Journal of Ralph Cross," 10; Revolutionary Rolls, MA Archives, 17:19, 21; 18:249, 254; 19:69; Mass. *Soldiers and Sailors*, 14:972; *EIHC*, 45 (1909):86. Among the more seriously wounded were Adjutant John Francis of Beverly and Samuel Lacount of Haverhill in Eaton's company, and William Stone of Middleton, Flint's company.

41. Revolutionary Rolls, MA Archives, 11:71, 72; *Mass. Soldiers and Sailors*, 6:599; 11:558; Moses Greenleaf Military Papers, 110.

42. "The Heath Papers," MHS *Collections*, 7th Series, 4 (1904):163; "Diary of Enos Hitchcock, D.D.," *Rhode Island Historical Society Publ.*, New Series, 7, (1899):157.

43. George Athan Billias, *General John Glover and His Marblehead Mariners* (New York: Henry Holt, 1960), 147, 149.

44. *The Massachusetts Magazine*, 3 (1910):195–96.

45. *Letters from America 1776–1779* (Boston: Houghton Mifflin, 1924), 114–30; William L. Stone, *Memoirs of Major General Riedesel* (Albany: J. Munsell, 1868), 1:191, 214–22; for an account, see: Billias, 150–62.

46. Fitch Edward Oliver, ed., *The Diary of William Pynchon* (Boston: Houghton Mifflin, 1890), 41, 44; Joshua Coffin, *A Sketch of Newbury, Newburyport, and West Newbury* (Boston: Samuel G. Drake, 1845), 254.

47. Wade and Lively, 232.

48. Revolutionary Rolls, MA Archives, 11:71, 76.

49. Wade and Lively, 235.

50. Edwin M. Stone, 275.

51. Revolutionary Rolls, MA Archives, 11:71.

52. Edwin M. Stone, 275.

53. Charles H. Lesser, ed., *The Sinews of Independence* (Chicago: University of Chicago, 1976), 54–56; "Massachusetts Soldiers Who Served at Valley Forge Under His Excellency, General George Washington," Military MSS, EI.

54. J. W. Hanson, *History of the Town of Danvers* (Danvers: J. W. Hanson, 1848), 213.

CHAPTER EIGHTEEN

TOWARD POLITICAL AND ECONOMIC STABILITY

While war was being waged, the people of Massachusetts Bay were embroiled in their own political and economic struggles. When independence was declared, Massachusetts literally abandoned its basis of government: the Charter of 1691. Debates over the province's new political foundation stimulated years of wrangling. Neither did financial freedom unleash the expected prosperity; rather, war's disruptions foreclosed more economic opportunities than were opened. Financial despair invaded thousands of Essex County homes. Amid the worsening conditions specie disappeared, while overworked presses turned out near-worthless scrip. In town meetings, county conventions, and state assemblies, debates raged, bringing to light such brilliant figures as Newburyport's Theophilus Parsons. Finally, in 1780, a state constitution was ratified; continuing economic instability, however, ultimately would ignite civil strife.

No Constitution

The Provincial Assembly convened at Watertown during July 1776 and elected a new council with executive and legislative powers. James Bowdoin was chosen its president. During the next four years—until October 25, 1780, House and Council managed Massachusetts affairs without a governor.

The belief that sovereign Massachusetts should be guided by a constitution gained public acceptance. On September 17, 1776, towns were asked whether House and Council ought to meet jointly to frame a new government. Beverly was the only Essex County town

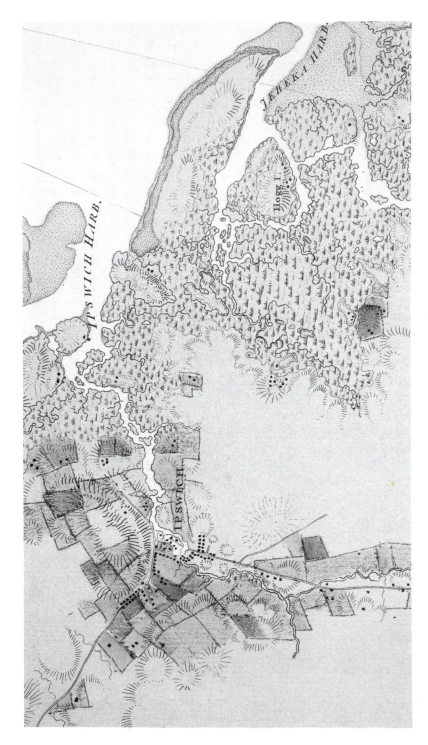

In 1778, the Essex County constitutional convention was held in Ipswich, a major seaport and farming town.

opposed. Bradford and Newburyport supported the idea, but, mindful of checks and balances, wanted each house to proceed separately. Topsfield voted yea, subject to ratification by the next House. By then, New Meadows hoped the "ancient rule of Representation" would return. (Until 1776, when apportionment changed, most towns, except for such larger communities as Marblehead and Salem, had been entitled to only one representative.) Members thus chosen, Topsfielders hoped, would see "their duty, not only to Represent particular parties, nor their own town only, but the whole State in general." Essex County towns nevertheless generally cast approval for the constitution provided that, as Lynn voters said, it "be Published and Laid befour the Several Towns" before ratification.[1]

Accordingly, on May 5, 1777, townspeople were requested to instruct their House members to combine with the Council in a constitutional convention. In some communities, however, people were having second thoughts. Gloucester and Haverhill joined Beverly in opposition. So did Topsfield. The town reasoned that "Valuable men" were in the army and thus unable to participate. There was no rush: "ancient Laws and usages of this State are in full force and practise."[2] Though most Essex towns, either by implied consent or actual vote, responded positively, it was not a clear mandate.

By February 28, 1778, meeting in convention, the General Court approved a draft and submitted it to the towns. On March 26, Newburyport led the opposition when voters lambasted the proposed "unequal and unjust" method of representation. To reduce the House from its unwieldy 260 members, an incremental formula successively raised the mean number by 20 for each additional town representative. This method worked against populous Newburyport. Other provisions, Newburyporters believed, were not based on "Natural rights of mankind and the true Principles of Government." They called for a county convention and instructed their selectmen to distribute circular letters.[3]

The historic convention met on April 29, 1778 at Treadwell's tavern on the Bay road (North Main Street) in Ipswich. Present were delegates from Boxford, Danvers, Gloucester, Ipswich, Lynn, Manchester, Methuen, Newburyport, Salem, Salisbury, Topsfield, and Wenham. Newburyport sent five prominent citizens: Stephen Cross, Tristram Dalton, Jonathan Greenleaf, Jonathan Jackson, Theophilus Parsons. The proposed constitution was read paragraph by paragraph and debated; afterwards, eighteen qualifications were noted. The first was to postpone ratification to a "more peaceable and settled condition" when there would be time for deliberation. The second was to provide a bill of rights "clearly ascertaining and defining the rights of conscience, and that security of person and property, which every member in the State hath a right to expect." Other exceptions mostly concerned representation and election matters, as well as sep-aration of powers. Delegates adjourned until May 12. Meanwhile, a committee was chosen—Theophilus Parsons, Nathan Goodale of Salem, and Gideon Putnam of Danvers—to outline the "true principles of government" and an acceptable framework. When the convention reconvened, chaired by Peter Coffin of Gloucester, the committee's report was read and accepted—a remarkable success, considering the wide spectrum of interests that extended from agrarian, populist Boxford, Methuen, and Topsfield to mercantile Gloucester, Newburyport, and Salem.[4]

Printed and sold by John Mycall in Newburyport, the pamphlet containing the report was circulated statewide. Known as the "Essex Result," it was authored by twenty-seven-year-old Theophilus Parsons, a promising attorney on the threshold of a brilliant, distinguished career. In 1806, Parsons would become chief justice of the Massachusetts Supreme Court.

Parsons penned what he perceived as the embodiment of a constitution—natural rights, popular government, separation of powers, checks and balances—with frequent references to ancient Greece and Rome, as well as to contemporary Europe. Objections to thirteen proposed articles were elaborated. Though the young politician-scholar was recommending a new plan, his "Essex Result" is best remembered as a treatise on fundamental libertarian, conservative, republican principles of government.

The proposed constitution had been perused too briefly, Parsons wrote, by people busily engaged in conducting the war and affairs of state. Special groups were suspected to have been accommodated. "Let all ambitions and interested views be discarded," Parsons said, "and let regard be had only to the good of the whole." That a politically pressured General Court had prepared the draft, rather than specially elected delegates, contributed to popular misgivings.[5]

The "Essex Result" reiterated principles indispensable to political liberty. "A republican [representative] form is the only one consonant to the feelings of the generous and brave Americans," observed Parsons. But all republics were not free. Concentration of power, which breeds political injustice, is inconsistent with free republican government. Mindful of Locke's and Montesquieu's teachings, Parsons stated that government needed to be separated into branches embodying checks and balances to limit powers. "All men are born equally free: the [natural] rights they possess at their birth are equal, and of the same kind." Some are "unalienable" or "rights of conscience": "We have duties, for the discharge of which we are accountable to our Creator and benefactor, which no human power can cancel." Others are "alienable": when men establish "a body politic or State," they are "as one moral whole, which is in possession of the supreme power of the State." Individuals enter into a social contract whereby alienable rights are given up for the common good. In exchange, they obtain political liberty: "the right every man in the state has, to do whatever is not prohibited by laws, to which he has given his consent." Unalienable rights, which can not be infringed upon, must "be clearly defined and ascertained in a Bill of Rights," previous to ratification.[6]

Parsons believed a bicameral legislature would promote checks and balances: a senate chosen by propertied men and a house of representatives elected by freemen.

> That among gentlemen of education, fortune and leisure, we shall find the largest number of men, possessed of wisdom, learning, and a firmness and consistency of character. That among the bulk of the people, we shall find the greatest share of political honesty, probity, and a regard to the interest of the whole, of which they compose the majority.

"Crude and hasty determinations of the house," Parsons believed, "will be revised or controuled by the senate; and those views of the senate which may arise from ambition or a disregard to civil liberty will be frustrated." Each body would have "a negative" over the other.[7]

Executive power, as embodied in a governor, Parsons said, "is to martial and command her militia and armies for her defence, to enforce the law, and to carry into execution all the orders of the legislative powers." The privy council, to advise the governor, would be chosen by the house out of the senate. To balance the executive branch with the legislative, the governor, with consent of the privy council, should have veto power.[8]

Parsons proposed an independent judiciary. "Let the judges of the common law courts, of the admiralty, and probate, and the register of probate, be appointed by the Governor and privy council; let the stipends of these judges be fixed; and let all those officers be removeable only for misbehaviour." The house would impeach; the senate would then judge.[9]

When the convention accepted the "Essex Result," it called for unanimous disapproval of the state constitution in town meeting. To a voter, Danvers, Gloucester, Manchester, Marblehead, Methuen, and Newburyport were unified in opposition. Indeed, most Essex County towns were near unanimous. Rowley, however, was divided; after several adjournments, a decision was postponed. In Essex County, only Andover voted approval and by the slimmest margin: 33 in favor, 32 opposed, 23 abstaining. Statewide, the constitution was rejected decisively, 9,972 nays to 2,083 yeas—five-to-one opposed. Parsons's "Essex Result" had been a major influence. Later, many of its principles would become embodied in the Massachusetts Constitution of 1780.[10]

A Convention of Delegates

Uncertain of popular sentiment, on February 20, 1779, the House quizzed towns as to whether they wanted a constitution. If so, would they empower next year's representatives to call a state convention?

While only 60 percent replied, towns that responded generally assented. Essex, though, continued to see no urgency; only Amesbury, Gloucester, Lynn, Marblehead, and Salisbury voted approval. Countywide, in a low turnout, nays outnumbered yeas 400 to 164. Based on the statewide returns, with support from 70 percent of the voters, in June 1779 the General Court instructed towns to elect delegates to a constitutional convention, beginning September 1.[11] It recommended that any draft be submitted to the towns for ratification by at least two-thirds, and that all freemen twenty-one years or older be able to vote.

Delegates convened at the old meeting house of the First Church in Cambridge. After the convention was called, Essex County joined wholeheartedly. Among the 293 delegates present on opening day were some of Massachusetts' leading citizens: John Adams, Samuel Adams, James Bowdoin, John Hancock, Samuel Otis. Forty-six were from Essex County. Key to the county delegation was the Newburyport-centered "Essex Junto": George Cabot of Beverly; Daniel Noyes of Ipswich; Benjamin Greenleaf, Jonathan Greenleaf, Jonathan Jackson, Theophilus Parsons, and Nathaniel Tracy of Newburyport; Benjamin Goodhue and John Pickering of Salem; and Newburyport native John Lowell, who had recently moved to Boston. Mostly well-to-do lawyers and merchants, the leaders' shared political conservatism would have an extraordinary bearing on convention proceedings. The celebrated array of delegates from counties across the state were luminaries perfectly cast for the historic occasion.[12]

James Bowdoin was chosen president of the convention. A committee of thirty-one, named by each county delegation, with four delegates chosen at large, was to draft "a Declaration of Rights, and the form of Government" to be brought before all the delegates. Jackson, Parsons, and Samuel Phillips, Jr., of Andover represented

Essex County, with John Pickering as delegate at large. On September 7, conventioneers adjourned to await the committee design. Young attorney politician John Adams, already an acknowledged authority on constitutional law, would write nearly the entire document.

When the convention reconvened on October 28, the draft was presented. (At this time, a Marblehead delegation—Thomas Gerry, Jonathan Glover, Azor Orne, and Joshua Orne—presented their credentials; a delegation chosen earlier had refused to attend.) Most discussion revolved around the Declaration of Rights, particularly Article III, on religion. By adjournment on November 11, all but four provisions had been adopted, though much of the frame of government remained to be discussed.[13]

The convention reconvened on January 27, 1780—delayed twenty-two days by the coldest winter in nearly forty years. Boston harbor froze to Nantasket Road; most routes were impassable, except for part of the Boston-Hartford highway. Snow packed so deep and hard that loaded teams could be driven over walls and fences. Only forty-seven towns were represented by sixty delegates, including nine Essex towns: Amesbury, Andover, Beverly, Danvers, Ipswich, Newbury, Newburyport, Salem, and Salisbury. Since no more than eighty-two members were present at any time, dealing with the most controversial provisions fell to a handful of delegates. Cabot, Jackson, Parsons, and Pickering were especially influential.

Once the draft was completed, members adjourned until early June. Meanwhile, 1,800 copies were distributed. Each town was to vote on the constitution, article by article. Whenever two-thirds margin was not achieved, substitute wording was to be suggested, so the document would be consonant with popular opinion. Massachusetts was taking an epochal step: popular participation in constitution making.[14]

The Constitution of 1780

A preamble set forth the purpose of government: "to secure the existence of the body-politic, to protect it, to furnish the individuals who compose it, with the power of enjoying in safety and tranquility their natural rights, and the blessing of life." The "body-politic" was a "voluntary association of individuals," who form a social compact, whereby each citizen agrees to be governed for the common good.

An unprecedented "Declaration of Rights" followed. In the spirit of Parsons's "Result," Article I declared: "All men are born free and equal, and have certain natural, essential, and unalienable rights." Thirty articles cited the rights: to freedom of worship, to limited government, to life, liberty, and property, to assembly, to trial by jury, and to freedom of petition. These guarantees to individual freedom preserved the essence of the Revolution.

Article III was the most controversial. Until this time, towns had been required to support the Congregational Church by providing a minister with a meetinghouse and a salary. Excepting affiliates of another recognized faith, the church received tax revenues from everyone, including nonbelievers, nonchurchgoers, and sects too small to maintain a pastor. In effect, Article III perpetuated this system: monies "paid by the Subject" for public worship and teachers "shall, if he require it, be uniformly applied to the support of the public teacher or teachers of his own religious sect or denomination, provided there be any of whose instructions he attends: otherwise it may be paid towards the support of . . . teachers of the parish . . . in which the monies are raised." Baptists were among the most vehement in denouncing this church-state provision. While some were calling for more religious freedom, many orthodox Congregationalists were annoyed that all Christians were "equally under protection of the Law: And no subordination of any one sect or denomination to another shall ever be established by law." Some dissenters saw an issue of conscience, others perceived simply a case of majority rule, as no one was compelled to accept any religious belief. These differences, however, made Article III the battleground between religious toleration and Puritan orthodoxy.[15]

Last was the frame of government which covered making, executing, and interpreting the laws. A clear separation of powers was provided for, with checks and balances among the three branches. The General Court was composed of two annually elected houses: Senate and House of Representatives. Forty senators were to be elected from the counties—the number was based on taxes paid, which favored eastern Massachusetts. Essex and Suffolk counties were entitled to six each. Towns with 150 rateable polls (males over sixteen with certain exemptions) or less were permitted one representative. Every additional 225 rateable polls allowed another, a compromise struck between small hamlets wanting equality and large towns calling for proportional representation. While many delegates preferred a unicameral legislature, John Adams and "the Essex Junto" (Cabot, Jackson, Lowell, Parsons, etc.) prevailed. Parsons's call for a balance between propertied and popular representations prevailed; property ownership requirements for senators were three times greater than for House members. Most adult males were qualified by the voter franchise: a freehold estate with an annual income of three pounds or any estate worth sixty pounds. The legislature, no longer supreme, would share power with a relatively strong, annually elected executive. An introductory address noted: "The Governor is emphatically the Representative of the whole People, being chosen not by one Town or County, but by the People at large."[16] Thus, he was given legislative oversight and made commander in chief of the state militia. Some delegates, including Parsons, also envisioned strong executive powers to check popular excesses. The governor had veto power over legislation, which could be overridden by a two-thirds vote. A nine-member executive council, chosen among the forty senators elected in joint session by the General Court, was to advise the governor. Judges were appointed by the governor subject to the Council's advice and consent. While courts were unaffected, the legislature was empowered to make changes later. Though during the last two hundred years the Massachusetts Constitution has been amended more than 115 times, the basic structure, with its inherent principles, has endured.

Ratification

Time for tactful persuasion had arrived. A carefully written introductory address—prepared by a committee which included Parsons and signed by Bowdoin—was distributed statewide. In a state where home rule was cherished, the address emphasized: "It is your *interest* to revise it with the greatest Care and Circumspection, and it is your undoubted *Right*, either to propose such Alterations and Amendments as you shall judge proper, or, to give it your own Sanction in its present Form, or, totally to reject it." Throughout the state, citizens put aside their everyday concerns and thoughtfully deliberated. William Pynchon of Salem noted on May 22: "The town meeting was full, and the whole day was spent upon the constitution; many objections and several amendments were made."[17]

Spring of 1780 was a melancholy time. Unemployment, scarcity of goods, hyperinflation, and indebtedness were endemic. The war was going badly. Nine months earlier, Massachusetts had been humiliated at Penobscot, suffering loss of untold lives and eight valuable Essex County privateers. The South was being overrun by the British. Washington was encamped on the Hudson, destitute of men, money, and supplies. Despite the uncertain times, undaunted, Essex County townspeople joined their fellow citizens statewide to deliberate the constitutional future of their beloved Massachusetts.

The "Dark Day"

During the constitutional debate, the memorable "dark day" of Friday, May 19, cast its shadow, symbolic of the dreary times. Morning was overcast, with light sprinkles; by ten o'clock, it had become unusually overcast. Suddenly, a light southwest breeze swept in a stratum of very black clouds. At noontime, candlelight was required for dinner. "Could not read a word in large print close to the window. Dined with two candles on the table," wrote Hamlet pastor Manasseh Cutler; some Lynn people forsook their meal, convinced Judgment Day had arrived. Between eleven o'clock and one o'clock, there was nearly total darkness. It turned dark, lighter, then dark, intermittently throughout the day. The clouds carried a "brassy hue," which glazed the landscape "with so enchanting a verdure," recalled Samuel Tenny of Rowley. Eerily, fowl retired to their roosts; cattle gathered at barns; cocks crowed as at daybreak; frogs peeped; birds became silent. Pynchon noted: "People in the streets grew melancholy, and fear seized on all except sailors; they were hallooing and frolicking through the streets." In Beverly, an elderly gentleman, dressed in his finest suit, grasped his silver-headed cane and walked out in an open field to await judgment. Dr. Whitaker's Salem congregation flocked to the meetinghouse and listened to the pastor preach from Amos 8:9: "and I will cause the sun to go down at noon, and I will darken the earth in the clear day." Whitaker's fear of the supernatural contrasted with Rev. Willard's reaction in neighboring Beverly. He, surrounded by his parishioners, methodically set up instruments on the common and studied the phenomenon. As he was pursuing his investigations, an excited man rushed from the shore nearby shouting frantically that the tide had stopped flowing. Taking out his watch, Willard calmly observed, "For it is just high water."[18]

During late afternoon, the air smelled like "burning turf." Though it had become lighter, evening began in "pitchy darkness"; finally, about midnight, the clouds disappeared, and the moon and stars shone. Darkness had been greatest over Essex County, southern New Hampshire, and Maine, but extended southward over Rhode Island and Connecticut, even into New York and New Jersey. It was attributed later to thick smoke from large tracts burning in northern New England, where settlements were being carved out of the wilderness. The air had been thick and heavy for a week, with little breeze, which made the sun blush unusually red. Occurring during a gloomy month of May, when God's purpose was in question, the curious "dark day" would be long remembered.[19]

The Vote

A comprehensive examination of Essex County's vote on the constitution is not possible, as most county returns are missing from the Massachusetts Archives. For some towns, such as Boxford, Danvers,

Middleton, Rowley, and Salem, detailed tabulations survive in town records. In other instances, town clerks recorded only summaries. Some towns did not vote on each article, as asked. For example, on May 22, Gloucester voted only once: those "for Accepting the Constitution were desir'd to walk round the meeting house to the Eastward and forty Eight Walk'd they that were against it were desir'd to walk the other way and none Walk'd."[20]

Boxford, with two common threads—suspicion of central government and preference for a more democratic House—objected to several provisions. A committee chosen at Boxford's May 16 meeting composed eleven reservations. They concluded that the Declaration of Rights was unclear and ambiguous; all freemen, regardless of property, should be permitted to choose House members; the House quorum of eighty was too small. They feared that representatives from merchant towns within easy reach of Boston would enact special-interest legislation at sparsely attended sessions. At least monthly, House members should be required to disclose their voting, so "that the people may be able to judge who are friends of their country"; towns should be able to recall their representatives, with promise-breakers subject to trial by jury; the General Court should not be permitted to alter qualifications of civil officers without constitutional amendment. Based on the report, Boxford voters, in whom revolutionary times had nurtured a hearty democratic spirit, opposed six articles. Though near ninety articles passed overwhelmingly, delegate Aaron Wood opposed the constitution.[21]

In each town hall, procedures were generally the same. After pondering a committee report, near-unanimous approval was voted on most articles. A handful of provisions often was hotly debated, with some being altered. Most changes, however, had been debated already at the convention, and lost. Newburyport, Salem, and Salisbury, for example, wanted to limit suspension of habeas corpus to cases of war, invasion, or rebellion, rather than "upon the most urgent and pressing occasions." This motion had been defeated in convention. Boxford did not want ministers of the gospel to serve in the House, Senate, or Council. This exemption had been proposed, but lost. At least seven Essex County towns favored qualifying only Protestants for governor, to provide, as Newbury voters expressed, "effectual a security as possible against Domination of Papists." In fact, Andover wanted this proviso extended to all elected offices. These motions also had been debated. Newbury thought military service should be limited to six months, to check abuse of power and provide for sharing of burdens. Wenham modified the article on freedom of press, so that no person could "be allowed to Publish any Defama-mortory or Libel against any person without his Signature." Though none of these alterations was incorporated into the original draft, they pointed to the careful deliberation of Essex County citizens, who were acutely aware they were building a political foundation for future generations.[22]

Religious freedom (Article III) and constitutional revision (Chapter VI, Article X) were the most controversial subjects. Salem, Salisbury, and Wenham accepted Article III with minor changes, but several towns—including Amesbury, Bradford, Danvers, and Methuen—voted opposition (most likely, they were resistant to freedom for Catholics). Article X stipulated a constitutional convention in 1795, if favored by two-thirds of the voters. For many, this was unsatisfactory, especially for skeptics leery of aristocratic, mercantile intentions, who wanted sooner, more frequent opportunities to remedy unforeseen issues. Andover, Boxford, and Salisbury were among the towns that favored conventions at fixed intervals in the future.

On June 7, 1780, assembled delegates at Boston's Brattle Street Church chose a committee to examine the more than two hundred returns. Clearly, the complexities and enormousness of the task were unanticipated. Unraveling the hodgepodge became a tabulating nightmare. When an article was objected to, for example, many towns recorded only the vote as amended, omitting the number who favored the original wording. Some towns, like Gloucester, recorded only a grand total, not article by article as specified. To cope with the confusion, the committee of returns was enlarged twice. In some instances, two sets of votes were tabulated: yeas and nays on each article as proposed, plus yeas and nays as amended. In the end, though, votes favoring the article as amended were counted with yeas of the original article. At other times, amendments went uncounted entirely. (This was interpreted by historian Samuel Eliot Morison as deliberate chicanery to assure passage.)

Substantial opposition arose against only two provisions, Article III and Chapter VI, Article X. Disagreements over Article III varied; some people preferred greater religious freedom while others favored a more orthodox stance. Sometimes, those tallied as opposed wanted only minor changes. Acceptable substitute language would have been impossible; as written, it was a compromise. Also, many towns with proposed changes to various provisions—such as Andover, Marblehead, and Newburyport—favored overall adoption and instructed their delegates specifically to ratify the entire document, if amendments failed. Counting was conducted in full view, and some spectator delegates were vehemently opposed to passage. Yet there is no record of anyone questioning the tabulation.[23]

On June 15, article by article, totals were read. After each, the delegates were asked: "Is it your opinion that the people have accepted this article?" Each passed by a "very great majority." Finally, the convention voted that the constitution had been accepted by a "very great majority" as it stood.[24]

Next day, President James Bowdoin proclaimed that more than two-thirds of the voters had signified approval. The constitution would go into effect the last Wednesday in October. Following the October 25, 1780 election, John Hancock was inaugurated as first governor under the Constitution of the Commonwealth of Massachusetts.

Massachusetts had legitimatized the Revolution by adopting a popularly approved, representative government. Essex County sons Cabot, Parsons, and Pickering deserve special credit. Among the constitutions of the thirteen states, Massachusetts' best delineated the relationship between the individual and the state, embodying the principles of natural rights, inalienable rights, limited government, representative government, separation of powers, and checks and balances. It was the first written by a specially chosen convention of elected delegates. Furthermore, it set the precedent of drafting a constitution subject to ratification by the voters. It would be an important model in shaping the United States Constitution of 1787. The Massachusetts Constitution of 1780—in effect for over two centuries—has held sway longer than any other in the world.

Financial Hurdles

The four-year constitutional struggle, however, paled beside Massachusetts' seemingly interminable financial burdens. Trouble signs first appeared in May 1775, just weeks after the Lexington alarm, when the legislature authorized a loan of 100,000 pounds at 6 percent interest for one year; the Bay Colony thus incurred its initial wartime indebtedness. Since many notes were in small denominations, they passed as currency. Also £26,000 circulated, issued to soldiers in bills of credit. Another emission was printed in August 1775. Though modest by comparison with some states, Massachusetts emitted almost four million dollars between 1775 and 1779. Borrowing seemed the only course available to meet financial obligations.

The Continental Congress, unable to contract foreign loans, without taxing authority, and generally unsuccessful in convincing states to pay requisitions, also resorted to printing bills. On June 23, 1775, the Congress approved distribution of two million Spanish-milled dollars in Continental currency, which were dispersed throughout the provinces according to population. While the thirteen colonies generally continued to transact business in pounds, shillings, and pence, from that time on, accounts of the federal government have been kept in dollars. Between 1775 and 1779, over two hundred and forty million dollars were issued!

For a while, Massachusetts bills were on a par with specie, but, with Continental issues soon circulating alongside, public confidence waned. Attempts nevertheless were made to stabilize value. Anyone refusing paper currency as legal tender could be penalized, including creditors owed private debt. Sometimes punishment was vigilante-style. On July 26, 1777, William Pynchon of Salem reported: "A countrymen beat for not taking paper for his meat." As issuance of scrip escalated, value plummeted, with doubts mounting whether paper ever would be redeemed.[25]

Wage and Price Controls

Wage and price controls seemed a plausible solution. On January 25, 1777, after attending a conference of New England states, Massachusetts representatives joined in enacting "An Act to Prevent Monopoly and Oppression." Maximum labor wages were established for farmers, mechanics, and tradesmen, and prices were set for more than fifty articles, including wheat, rye, fleece, wool, linen, tanned hides, fresh pork, beef, cheese, homespun cotton, and rum.[26]

On April 22, a county convention held in Ipswich, with representatives from nearly every Essex County town, supported the act. Every two months, selectmen and committees of correspondence and safety were to set prices of merchandise and wages that had not been legislated. Broadsides, called "Price Acts," were posted. Violation of the committee-enforced regulations was viewed as bordering on subversion. On April 14, Ipswichites unanimously voted:

> Whereas some Persons from an inimical Disposition to the Glorious Cause . . . & Others from a Selfish Spirit, have for some Time past been practising every vile and wicked Act, to hinder the Operation . . . Voted. That we the Inhabitants of this Town will not only strictly adhere to & Observe the aforesaid Act, but also use our utmost Endeavours to detect and bring to punishment those unfriendly, selfish Persons, who at this important Crisis, Shall have the Effrontery to Counteract the good & wholsom Laws of this State.[27]

In mid-October, with the money supply ballooning, Massachusetts rescinded its short-lived attempts at wage and price controls.

The year 1777 was a period of scarcity. On April 28, Pynchon reported: "The Marblehead people and Salem people quarrel for bread at the bakers, and . . . scramble at the wharf in weighing out and selling Capt. Derby's coffee." In May, the Salem attorney noted that buying an imported half-cord made him "richer in woods than

In Purſuance of an Act from the Great and General Court, of the State of Maſſachuſetts-Bay, entitled an " *Act to prevent Monopoly and Oppreſſion*," the Selectmen and Committee of the Town of *NEWBURY*, have ſet and affixed the following PRICES to the Articles herein after enumerated, which are to be taken and deemed to be the Prices of all ſuch Goods and Articles, in the ſaid Town of NEWBURY, and all other Articles not herein after particularly enumerated, to be in proportion thereunto, according to the Uſages and Cuſtoms which have heretofore been practiſed in ſaid Town.

WHEAT. Good merchantable Wheat, at 7s. 6d. a buſhel.
RYE. Good merchantable Rye, at 5s. a buſhel.
INDIAN CORN. Good Indian Corn, at 4s. a buſhel.
SHEEPS WOOL. Good merchantable Sheeps Wool, at 2s. a lb.
PORK. Freſh Pork well fatted, of a good quality, under 200 wt. 4d. a lb. between 2 and 300 wt. at 5d. a lb. and above 300 wt. at 6d. a lb.
BEEF. Good well fatted Graſs fed Beef, at 3d. a lb.

STOCKINGS. Men's soft yarn Stockings, at 6s. a pair, and in that proportion for an inferior quality.
SHOES. Men's Shoes made of Neat's Leather of the beſt common ſort, 6s. a pair, and for others the like price according to their ſize and quality.
SALTED PORK. Good Salted Pork of 220 wt. or upwards, at 6d. a lb. by the barrel.
BEEF. Good Salted Beef of 240 wt. or upwards, at 3d.½ a lb. by the barrel.
OATS. Good Oats, at 2s. a buſhel.
BARLEY. Good Barley, at 4s. a buſhel.

TURKEYS, Dunghill Fowls, and Ducks, at 6d. a lb.
GEESE, at 4d. a lb.
MILK, at 2d.½ a quart.
Good REFINED IRON, at 50s. cwt.
BLOOMERY IRON, at 30s. cwt. at the place of manufactory, and the ſame allowance to be made for tranſportation of Iron by land as is ſtated for other articles.
LIVER OYL by the barrel, 4s. a gallon.
BLUBBER Rained, 30s. a barrel.

In an attempt to control wages and prices, towns posted broadsides called Price Acts. Broadside. Courtesy, Essex Institute, Salem, Mass.

39/40 of the whole town, having part of 2 loads by me! We crawl about and exist, but cannot be said to live."[28]

Merchants who held back goods rather than accept depreciated scrip risked sparking an uprising. On July 23, Pynchon observed: "The ladies rise and mob for coffee; cart it and the owner, Boylston." Later, on a crisp November morning about sixty Beverly women wearing lambskin cloaks and riding hoods strutted down Main (now Cabot) and Bartlett streets with two ox carts. They marched to the distillery of Stephen Cabot, recently deceased, where locked gates and a foreman obstructed the entrance. Not to be thwarted, the persevering women bolstered their ranks with some men nearby and cut through the barricade. The guard resisted.

> His fair assailants, nothing daunted, pressed vigorously to the onset, and seizing him by the hair which was not of nature's growth, were proceeding to executive summary vengeance, when he eluded their grasp by leaving his artificial covering in their hands—and fleeing all but scalpless to the counting room, locked himself for safe-keeping.

After the doors were broken down, the crowd loaded and carted off two hogsheads of sugar. Rather than chance a similar attack, several merchant bystanders each readily exchanged one barrel of sugar for scrip. The spoils were carted to the woman leader's shop, and divided.[29]

As currency depreciated, many congressmen believed wage and price controls would work if applied over a wide region. Early in 1778, a multi-state conference at New Haven recommended a scale of prices, but Massachusetts did not enact them. The long-term solution seemed to be reduction of the money supply, though temporary measures could be taken.

On February 8, 1779, "An Act Against Monopoly and Forestalling" was passed. It forbade buying grains, meal, flour, "dead meat," or livestock in excess of family needs. Forestalling, that is, buying goods before they reached market, was outlawed. Merchants who were not town residents could sell only directly imported goods or products and wares manufactured in the state. Wholesalers could not resell at wholesale, only at retail. These measures, it was hoped, would increase supplies and minimize price rises. No wage and price controls were enacted, though, since legislators believed they would discourage incentive and cause further economic stagnation.[30]

While Haverhill and Salem were taking steps to enforce the act, pressures for more stringent controls were building. A statewide convention of 176 delegates from committees of correspondence, inspection, and safety was called by Boston, and on July 14 met at Concord. Thirteen Essex County towns—Andover, Beverly, Boxford, Bradford, Danvers, Haverhill, Ipswich, Lynn, Marblehead, Newburyport, Rowley, Salisbury, Topsfield—sent a total of nineteen delegates. A scale of prices was recommended for country produce and merchandise, including home manufactures and West Indies goods, as well as rates for innholders, various types of labor, and for teaming. Each trading town was encouraged to set prices on European goods. Loans of specie and payment of taxes, rather than an increase in the supply of scrip, were recommended as long-term measures to achieve stronger currency. President Azor Orne of Marblehead reported, wishfully, that the *unanimity* and *brotherly love* of the proceedings demonstrated that the rift between seaport and country had been largely imagined, kindled by enemies of the country. The convention adjourned until October.[31]

Beginning with Salem on July 29, 1779, Essex County towns promptly lined up in support of the popular resolves. On August 2, Danvers voted to encourage subscriptions from everyone over twenty-one years of age. Marblehead accepted the proceedings on the same date. The following day, Salisbury approved unanimously measures for putting "our Currency upon a more Respectable footing." Meanwhile, as more towns voted approval, even the village towns of Manchester, Middleton, and Wenham, which usually did not even send representatives to the House, participated. Prices affected everyone's pockets.[32]

To achieve further unity, Danvers asked prestigious Salem to call a county convention. It met at Ipswich on August 19 with eighteen Essex towns represented. Nathaniel Mighill of Rowley chaired, with

Miles Greenwood of Salem as clerk. They resolved to "fully approve of the Proceedings" at Concord. A scale of prices was fixed, using ratios for county (20:1) and West India (25 1/3:1) produce, with 1774 as the base year. Furthermore, it was recommended that "trading towns" regulate prices for European manufactures in their communities. County towns were urged "to carry their produce to the seaports, and sell the same at prices not exceeding what they are set at" and "the inhabitants of the sea-ports" were urged to observe "the same rate in disposing of their imports." Delegates underscored the need of mutual cooperation to assuage growing tensions between coastal and yeoman Essex County.[33]

Towns met to endorse the county resolutions, with those that had not done so also accepting the earlier Concord resolves. An intimidating spy system was designed, to insure compliance. On August 25, for example, Beverly voted to have their thirteen-member committee prepare a price list of over one hundred items, and handbills were circulated. Townspeople agreed "to watch carefully over the conduct of Each other." Names of persons knowingly and intentionally violating the regulations were to be printed in the newspapers. Possibly, they would be transported to the enemy (expelled from their country, as co-conspirators) "according to the nature and degree of the crime." The need for large committees—forty members in Marblehead—was testimony to the enormity, indeed, the impossibility, of the task.[34]

Distrustful country farmers and coastal merchants alike suspected each other of profiteering. Dudley Carlton, Bradford's delegate at Concord, had been advised to agree to lower farm prices only in proportion to the decreases made by merchants. Salem merchant George Williams labeled farmers "allmost as cruel as the enemy." Cut off from southern foodstuffs by an enemy naval blockade and, Down East, by the Penobscot garrison, ports depended on inland produce and wood supplies. "Thay dont consider the suffring sea ports," Williams complained, "I believe in General thay have no feeling for us." Writing to Rev. Enos Hitchcock of Beverly on September 20, Manasseh Cutler faulted yeomen: "Many of ye stupidly ignorant, avaricious Farmers are determined if possible to break over ye regulations. But ye Merchants & Sea Ports to their honour, strictly adhere to them & appear to be determined."[35]

To reduce scarcity, an embargo had been tried earlier for a brief period. Again, on June 21, 1779, a ban was imposed on outward-bound vessels carrying country produce, including wheat, flour, bread, beef, pork, and other provisions. Later, on September 23, the list was lengthened, with shipment forbidden by either land or water. It continued in force until June 15, 1780.[36]

Overcharging was risky business. On September 13, Danvers voted to publish the name of innholder William Gideon Putnam as an "Enemy to his Country" for selling cheese at nine shillings. Several names of nonsubscribers also were to be printed. On October 3, Salem chastised Josiah Dewing for selling "dead meat—Viz. Pork" at an "exorbitant price."[37]

On October 6, as prices continued to rise inexorably, delegates reconvened at Concord. Many from Essex County attended; later, towns adopted the convention resolves. The futility, however, soon became obvious. Neither embargoes nor wage and price controls could shackle the laws of supply and demand. Oversupply of paper currency, exacerbated by an unsettled war, and scarcity determined price. Soon, enforcement efforts were abandoned.

Early in 1779, scrip had less than one-sixth the buying power of two years earlier. During the year, value depreciated over threefold. The only long-term solution was reduction of paper; spending had to be financed by taxation and loans, not printing presses.

Reducing Currency Supply

By 1779, Massachusetts had replaced its bills of credit with treasurer's notes redeemable in 1781 at 6 percent annual interest. Earlier bills became unacceptable, even for taxes, while the notes circulated as legal tender.

Early in 1780, the Continental Congress confronted the vortex depreciation by recommending substitution of Continental currency with state-issued notes. On May 5, 1780, Massachusetts called in its share, issuing "new emission" bills of credit which yielded 5 percent interest annually, payable in specie on December 31, 1786. Old bills were to be redeemed and replaced at a 40:1 ratio. Amounts emitted could not exceed one-twentieth of old currency. New emission was legal tender, apportioned 1:1 with specie and 1:40 with "old emission." An annual tax of £72,000 payable in specie provided for redemption and interest charges.

Though unlikely to be redeemed ever, millions of Continental notes continued to circulate. By late 1780, value had plummeted to 75:1. On December 19, 1780, for example, Beverly voted to raise 50,000 pounds. One silver dollar would be accepted in lieu of seventy-five Continentals, one dollar new emission for forty old. In mid–1781, towns stopped accepting the nearly valueless scrip for taxes. "The continental currency, old emission, passeth no more here," noted William Pynchon on May 18, 1781. "Not worth a Continental" became a common expression.[38]

Depreciation gave debtors the advantage of paying loans contracted years earlier with cheaper money. Thus, on September 29, 1780, Massachusetts repealed the Tender Act of 1776. A scale of depreciation was drawn to settle all creditor-debtor contracts. Between January 1777 and April 1780, bills of credit were determined to have dropped forty times in proportion to specie dollars. New emission, though limited, also was suspect, and depreciating. In January of 1781, its tender provisions were repealed, leaving courts to determine value. Debtors no longer had the advantage of paying with cheaper dollars.[39]

Repeal opponents were in small agrarian towns, especially those west of Worcester. They persuaded the House to reinstate "new emission" as legal tender, but the propertied, inflation-conscious Senate would not consent. On December 25, fiscally conservative Danvers instructed its representative, Col. Israel Hutchinson, to resist, while populist Boxford in March 1781 petitioned for renewal. Paper continued to circulate, but creditors refused it, although new emission still was acceptable for taxes.[40]

Counterfeiting

Finances were further confused by the introduction of counterfeit notes, which Britain and her Tory allies used as a form of economic warfare. Printed in America and Europe, phony money flowed freely to whomever would pass it. On May 19, 1779, Ipswich voted that selectmen "make Such Allowance to the Several Constables that have taken Counterfeit money for taxes in time past." In March of 1782, Middleton voted to pay Jeremiah Flint and Francis Peabody, Jr., constables for 1780, "agreeable to the Exchange for 245 Dollars of the old Emission they Recvd for taxes which was Counterfeit." The next month, Salem credited Benjamin Ward with £150 of old currency for counterfeit money. Indeed, these few examples illustrate that bogus currency circulated county-wide.[41]

Taxes

By 1777, Massachusetts had become serious about revenue raising, levying over $1,400,000. In 1780, town taxes had increased to $37,670,000—on a par with war costs, though largely offset by currency depreciation. In October of 1781, Essex County's tax was largest in the state: £46,280. One-seventh (£6,660) was Salem's; only Boston's levy was higher. Andover, Beverly, Ipswich, Newbury, and Newburyport each were assessed more than £3,000, placing six Essex County towns among the top ten taxpayers.[42]

Town Constable

Usually town constables also were tax collectors, an especially unpopular task during lean times. In small towns, one person held the job; in larger ones, several were chosen. Fines could be imposed for refusing the office, and many paid rather than serve. On November 3, 1777, for example, Danvers chose two constables to replace Daniel Purington and Daniel Osborn, both of whom were fined for declining the post. On March 6, 1780, Manchester voters elected Malachi Allen, but he "Refused to take the Oath," and instead accepted a penalty of over thirty-seven pounds. When William Hooper was chosen, he too rejected the offer and paid. Then Capt. William Tuck was named, who, refusing, likewise was fined. In 1779, Danvers paid constables three pence per pound for collecting the Continental tax. But collectors were personally liable for deficiencies. The state treasurer could give sheriffs execution orders against constables who did not collect taxes committed. It was hardly a responsibility many would savor.[43]

Hard Times

As the war lengthened, an increasingly painful economic toll was exacted. Towns that traditionally pursued fisheries and trade were the first to suffer. Scores of county vessels manned by thousands of Essex mariners were captured or lost, their once-proud fleets nearly destroyed. Coastal people customarily had relied on imported food and fuel, but, with languishing trade, prices skyrocketed. For hundreds of the impoverished, it became a question of survival. Early in 1777, Gloucester voters expressed thanks to Capt. Andrew Giddings, who generously donated molasses and flour for poor relief. By September, state stores were opened to provide "Bread Corn" for the poor in Beverly, Gloucester, Marblehead, and Salem. In October, Gloucester, Manchester, and Marblehead were three of only nine towns throughout the state whose taxes were abated. Ocean-dependent North Shore residents were enduring terrible economic anguish.[44]

Faced with burgeoning war costs, by 1777 Massachusetts was levying taxes on towns' rateable polls and estates. Not only were communities assessed state and Continental expenses, such as soldiers' salaries, they were assigned beef and clothing quotas. In 1780 alone, Essex County towns were expected to supply over 379,970 pounds of beef; 1,161 shirts, pairs of shoes, and stockings; and 580 blankets. An October 10, 1777 act also saddled towns with up to half pay for families of Continental Army enlisted men, eventually to be repaid by the state. On top of normal, peace-time expenditures, these burdens were overwhelming, particularly along the destitute North Shore.[45]

By spring of 1780, Cape Ann's fisheries, trade, and privateering had hit rock bottom. Since March of 1779, nearly 700 tons of merchant ships with cargoes had been lost: brigs *George* and *Shark*; schooners *Dolphin, Hannah, Hawke, Orient, Rogers, Speedwell*; ship *Starks*. It was catastrophic. Before hostilities erupted, Gloucester had harbored eighty fishing schooners averaging 50 tons each, plus 1,000 tons in "foreign Merchantmen—Coasters & Fishing Boats." Only 2,040 tons survived, "improv'd or not." The merchant fleet had plummeted to half-ownership in one small transport; left privateering was one lonely ship, which had sent in "two provision Vessels." In 1779, the number of rateable polls (males sixteen and older) was down from 1,053 to about 692—a 10 percent annual drop in four years. "In 1775, When the General Alarm of War sounded in the Ears of All," townspeople bemoaned, in an August 17, 1779 appeal for lower taxes, that "our most active, wealthy Inhabitants" had fled the vulnerable, rocky promontory, depriving it of their taxes and talents. As the economy worsened, "most Industrious Men," skilled dock laborers, mechanics and mariners, followed. Left were, largely, the indigent or soldiers' families. In January 1780, a profusion of worthy poor, 291 widowed women and 437 fatherless children, over 80 percent of whom needed support—one sixth the total population—drained town coffers. Another 305 needy families were "not taxable." Gloucester's 856 "Arable, Orcharding—and Mowing" acres produced enough food for only two months. Since in recent years Cape Ann had imported grains, neglected grist mills had fallen into disrepair. In addition to the economic disaster, beginning early in 1779, Gloucester was ravaged by a smallpox epidemic. Inoculation, new and controversial, was at first opposed, but eventually townspeople submitted to it. Hospitals were opened around town for convalescing inoculees, whose treatment occasionally proved fatal. In May, 1780, twenty-one of the Gloucester poor were brought to Beverly. Reminiscent of Beverly's 1777 sugar raid, twenty desperate Gloucester women trooped to Col. Joseph Foster's warehouse on his Beaver Dam farm, demanding groceries and provisions which the patriotic Foster generously supplied. Indeed, Cape Anners had reached desperate straits.[46]

With Gloucester seeking tax relief, in December 1779, the House sent a three-man delegation. They witnessed the miserable huts that housed Gloucester's "half starved miserable women & naked children," without wood for fuel nor food "but what they Beg." They observed deteriorating wharfs, dockside warehouses, and sheds, where years earlier a bustling trade had centered. Impressed by

Gloucester's plight, in May 1780, the last two state and Continental assessments were halved, until further notice.[47]

Manchester and Marblehead were in the same foundering boat. Tucked between Beverly and Gloucester, Manchester was home to eighty brokenhearted widows with over one hundred fatherless children. Fifty men died in 1777 alone! In 1776, about one thousand residents lived in Manchester; in three years, captures, deaths, and emigration had divided the number in half. Besieged by demands of their own families, as well as the town poor, taxpayers revolted. They refused to pay earlier fines, and assessors were instructed not "to make the Tax." Like Gloucester, Marblehead depended on fisheries and trade. In 1780, nearly 60 percent of its workforce—477 out of 831 men—was unemployed. On December 2, 1780, two-thirds of beef, currency, and specie taxes were remitted, as well as two-thirds of future taxes and requisitions until a new appraised valuation.[48]

Grain and firewood had become scarce, particularly in import-dependent Gloucester, Marblehead, and Salem. Unable either to obtain or to afford precious Down East firewood, fuel-hungry, shivering Marbleheaders resorted to demolishing houses, stores, fences, and fish flakes. In April 1779, the state resolved that people "in this and neighboring States" permit Salem's Overseers of the Poor to purchase a shipment of grain or flour. The following spring, Salem petitioned for an extension on the previous year's tax collections and for an abatement. Even this once-thriving epicenter was feeling the pinch. By 1779, feeding the hungry had become an imperative state priority. Flour, Indian corn, rice, rye, and wheat were to be imported, with Azor Orne of Marblehead, Tristram Dalton of Newburyport, and George Williams of Salem among a committee of five to oversee the relief operation.[49]

Fewer Taxes

On December 10, 1781, an excise tax was imposed on wines, liquors, teas, coaches, chaises, and carriages, with the income earmarked to pay interest on state securities. To sell wine, liquor or tea, innholders and other retailers had to obtain licenses. More than thirty-five were issued in Salem alone.[50] While wealthy folk would be most affected, several Essex towns, including Bradford, Gloucester, Ipswich, and Salem, worked for repeal.

In 1782, the General Court did not burden towns with new state tax levies. It assessed only £200,000, the Massachusetts Continental war quota. In 1783, the same amount was assessed. In the first year, commodities or money was accepted; in the second, only specie or banknotes. For some towns, though, already in arrears for 1780 and

1781, even these modest assessments were backbreaking. On May 27, 1782, for example, Boxford asked for more time to pay its October 1781 tax. When in August 1783 the state treasurer published names of towns that had not procured their beef quotas, seven in Essex County were listed: Gloucester, Lynn, Manchester, Marblehead, Methuen, Newburyport, Salem. With the exception of Methuen, which owed only a small amount, each delinquent was a coastal town.[51]

To encourage prompt tax payments, in mid-1781 new emission was pegged at 17/8:1 for one silver dollar when fair market value was 4:1 or 5:1. Purchases by French commissaries and privateering successes had increased the specie in circulation. Coupled with actions by the General Court, new emission actually appreciated, and Massachusetts paid its first annual interest payment in silver, as promised. Consequently, state monetary and taxing policies created a more stable currency.

Peacetime

The tumultuous war years had brought scarcity of goods, instability of currency, costly borrowing, high taxes, and widespread unemployment. Massachusetts expected the winning of independence would harbinger a return to prosperous, stable times. The dislocation caused by the Revolution, however, would take years to correct, and ultimately conditions were normalized only by the formation of a new nation. Meanwhile, new economic and political struggles emerged.

1. Beverly Town Records, October 7, 1776, 6:110; Bradford Town Records, September 17, 1776; *Town Records of Topsfield*, (Topsfield, MA: Topsfield Historical Society, 1920), 2:368–69; *Records of ye Towne Meetings of Lyn 1771–1783*, (Lynn: Lynn Historical Society, 1971), October 8, 1776, 42.
2. *Town Records of Topsfield*, 378.
3. Newburyport Town Records, 1:299.
4. [Theophilus Parsons], *Result of the Convention of Delegates Holden at Ipswich* (Newburyport, MA: 1778), 3–6.
5. 12.
6. 12–15.
7. 20, 56–57.
8. 24, 58–60.
9. 65–66.
10. Thomas F. Gage, *The History of Rowley* (Boston: Ferdinand Andrews, 1840), 260; Andover Town Records, June 1, 1778.
11. MA Archives 160:32–123.
12. *Journal of the Convention for Framing a Constitution of Government*, (Boston: 1832), 9–11.
13. 24–30, 34–35.
14. 55–57, 168–69.
15. *Constitution of the Commonwealth of Massachusetts* (Boston: Secretary of State).
16. *An Address of the Constitution* (Boston: 1780).
17. *An Address of the Constitution*; Fitch Edward Oliver, ed., *The Diary of William Pynchon* (Boston: Houghton Mifflin, 1890), 64.
18. William Parker Cutler and Julia Perkins Cutler, *Life, Journal, and Correspondence of Rev. Manasseh Cutler* (Cincinnati: Robert Clark, 1903), 1:77; Alonzo Lewis and James R. Newhall, *History of Lynn* (Boston: John L. Shorey, 1865), 343–44; "Dr. Tenny's Letter on the Dark Day," MHS *Collections*, 1 (1806):95; Oliver, 63; Edwin M. Stone, *History of Beverly* (Boston: James Munroe, 1843), 86–87.
19. For accounts, see Joshua Coffin's *A Sketch of the History of Newbury, Newburyport, and West Newbury* (Boston: Samuel G. Drake, 1845), 257; also, Sarah Loring Bailey's *Historical Sketches of Andover, Massachusetts* (Boston: Houghton Mifflin, 1880), 387.

20. Gloucester Town Records, 227.
21. Sidney Perley, *History of Boxford* (Boxford: Sidney Perley, 1880), 249–50.
22. Newbury Town Records, March 29, 1780; *Wenham Town Records*, (Wenham: Wenham Historical Society, 1959), 4:39.
23. Samuel Eliot Morison, "The Struggle over the Adoption of the Constitution of Massachusetts, 1780," MHS *Proceedings*, 50 (1917): 398–401; *Journal of the Convention*, 172–79.
24. *Journal of the Convention*, 180.
25. Oliver, 35.
26. *Acts and Resolves*, 5:583–89, 642–47.
27. Ipswich Town Records, 4:280.
28. Oliver, 29, 31.
29. Oliver, 34; Stone, 83–84.
30. *Acts and Resolves*, 5:924–26.
31. Concord Convention, Broadside, EI.
32. Salem Town Records, EI, 5:331–32; Danvers Town Records, 3:121; Salisbury Town Records, 112.
33. Salem Town Records, August 10, 1779, 5:335; Proceedings of a Convention, Broadside, EI.
34. Beverly Town Records, 6:263–68; Marblehead Town Records, EI, August 2, 1779, 4:641–42; November 1, 1779, 4:665.
35. Bradford Town Records, June 12, 1779; George Williams, "Revolutionary Letters Written to Colonel Timothy Pickering," 44 *EIHC* (1908):313; Manasseh Cutler to Enos Hitchcock, ALS, EI.
36. *Acts and Resolves*, 5:1114–15, 1254–55; 21:71.
37. Danvers Town Records, September 13, 1779, 3:123; Salem Town Records, 5:342–43.
38. *Acts and Resolves*, 5:1178–83; Beverly Town Records, 6:334; Oliver, 95.
39. *Acts and Resolves*, 5:1412–16.
40. Danvers Town Records, 3:153; Boxford Town Records, March, 1781, 193.
41. Ipswich Town Records, 4:293; Middleton Town Records, March 5, 1782, 258–59; Salem Town Records, April 1, 1782, 5:506.
42. *Acts and Laws, 1780–81*, 503–24.
43. Danvers Town Records, 3:71; *Town Records of Manchester* (Salem: 1889), 175.
44. John C. Babson, *History of the Town of Gloucester* (Gloucester: Procter Bros., 1860), 412; *Acts and Resolves*, 20:119, 126.
45. *Acts and Resolves*, 20:159–60; 21:488–90, 621–23.
46. Babson, 409, 416, 418, 440–41; Beverly Town Records, October 9, 1780, 6:321; MA Archives, 185:251–54; 228:2, 4.
47. MA Archives, 228:3, 4; *Acts and Resolves*, 5:1309–10.
48. D. Hamilton Hurd, *History of Essex County* (Philadelphia: J.W. Lewis, 1888), 1266; *Town Records of Manchester*, 171; Marblehead Town Records, November 27, 1780, 4:756; *Acts and Resolves*, 5:1044–45; *Acts and Laws, 1780–81*, 202.
49. *Acts and Resolves*, 20:569, 674; Marblehead Town Records, December 11, 1780, 4:761; Salem Town Records, March 13, 1780, 5:368.
50. *Acts and Laws, 1780–81*, 525–33; see Salem Town Records, January 12–March 23, 1782, 5:478–96.
51. Boxford Town Records, 204; *Independent Chronicle*, August 21, 1783.

CHAPTER NINETEEN

VICTORY IN AMERICA: NEWPORT TO YORKTOWN

The Salem attorney William Pynchon, with his Tory leanings, must have lamented the news. His journal entry of September 30, 1781: "Various are the rumors concerning the English and French fleets at the southwestward, and of their engagements, and of the return of part of the English fleet into N. York, all tattered and torn."[1] Twenty-four French warships had pounded the pride of Admiral Graves's navy off Chesapeake Capes, in the precursor to a momentous allied victory at Yorktown peninsula. British visions of success took an historic setback—to the chagrin of New England Loyalists—as America's alliance with France finally blossomed.

Between August 1778 and October 1781, France and the United States joined in four land and sea operations. Three—Newport, Savannah, and New York—were failures. The fourth, the Yorktown campaign, was decisive to the winning of American independence. It was the perfect capstone to years of Gallic military assistance.

During the period between the Newport and Yorktown campaigns, Essex County soldiers persevered in the Continental ranks. During the Newport operation, they rendered important service. Then, the land war shifted south. A handful from Essex County were in Virginia and witnessed the Yorktown victory. Most soldiers, however, stayed in the north—like other New Englanders—completing uneventful tours at West Point, or nearby in the Hudson Highlands.

Assault on Newport

The first combined assault by newly allied France and United States was against British-occupied Newport. The Comte d'Estaing,   347 who had cruised north from Delaware Capes in mid-July 1778, was off Sandy Hook weighing a move against New York. When the venture appeared too hazardous, the cautious Frenchman and General Washington chose an alternative objective: the garrison based at Newport, then under the command of Sir Robert Pigot with 6,000 men.

The port with its fine harbor had been British-held since December 1776. In 1777, an uneasy Massachusetts—fearing invasion of the Bay State—organized the so-called Secret Expedition to wrest control from the British. Three thousand militia and an artillery company were sent, including over 300 men from Essex County. Others marched from Rhode Island and Connecticut. But the expedition was called off when it appeared unlikely to succeed.

Since mid-April 1778, Maj. Gen. John Sullivan of New Hampshire had been headquartered near Providence with 1,000 Continentals. He was responsible for protecting Rhode Island's 120 miles of coastline, from Point Judith to Sakonnet Point. When he arrived, Sullivan found Rhode Island undefended. Under a 1777 New England pact, Massachusetts was committed to supply 1,500 men, but enlistments had expired. In early March of 1778, Nathaniel Wade of Ipswich—stationed in Rhode Island during 1777 as a lieutenant colonel in Danforth Keyes's regiment—was chosen to command one of two new regiments. The second was placed under Col. John Jacobs. To make Rhode Island duty more palatable, Massachusetts counted it as service in the Continental Army. Recruitment nonetheless went slowly. On June 12, sensing trouble was brewing, Massachusetts called up 1,800 reinforcements from county brigades (260 from Essex), partly to fill up Wade's and Jacobs's regiments. Four days later, amid fears of imminent attack by the British, Massachusetts resolved that 554 more men be detached from militia units. Still, by mid-July, General Sullivan's total command comprised only 1,500 troops.[2]

Essex County provided no exception to the prevailing enlistment problems. Jonathan Titcomb, a prominent Newburyport merchant, was the county brigadier. Formerly colonel of the 2nd Essex Regiment, he had held his new command since 1777. On July 19, Titcomb assured the Council that he and his colonels were trying to recruit enlistees. The "Scarcity of Men" was blamed on two unrelenting obstacles: the lure of privateering in the "Seaport Towns" and demands brought on by the farming season in the "Country Towns."[3]

The time had arrived to revive an expedition against Newport. On July 17, from his Haverstraw headquarters, Washington ordered Sullivan to raise 5,000 troops, inclusive of those he had already, from Massachusetts, Rhode Island, and Connecticut, along with boats and pilots for an amphibious crossing to Newport. By late July, Massachusetts had offered to raise 3,000 men for fifteen days' tour upon arrival in Rhode Island. Meanwhile, Wade's ranks had been filling. Three of his eight companies were commanded by Essex County Captains Simeon Brown of Danvers, Jonathan Evans of Salisbury, and Jeremiah Putnam of Danvers. Finally, an army was taking shape.[4]

To Rhode Island

Brigadiers Jonathan Titcomb of Newburyport and Solomon Lovell of Weymouth were appointed to lead Massachusetts militia in Rhode Island. About one-third of Titcomb's 900 men belonged to an Essex County regiment headed by Col. Larkin Thorndike of Beverly. The balance were Bristol County troops under Col. Josiah Whitney. By mid-August, 1,386 of Massachusetts' promised 3,000 troops had arrived.[5]

Washington sent two of his best brigades—John Glover's and Rhode Islander James Varnum's—from White Plains under the young French nobleman Marquis de Lafayette. Gen. Nathaniel Greene of Rhode Island followed. By early August, more than ten thousand Continentals and militia had poured into little Rhode Island. Two New England militia brigades were to be commanded by Brig. Gen. Cornell and Col. Christopher Greene; Wade's regiment was attached to Greene. Later, Maj. Gen. John Hancock would arrive to command Titcomb's and Lovell's Massachusetts regiments. On August 5, the army was directed to Tiverton.

Eighty-six flat-bottomed boats were needed to cross to the island where Newport was situated. Skilled hands to navigate them, however, were in short supply. On August 1, Sullivan ordered Glover to Boston, Marblehead, and "such other places [he] may think proper" to enlist two or three hundred experienced boatmen. Though Glover actually remained in Rhode Island, Sullivan soon received the essential crews.[6]

Inspired by the example of many leading citizens, eighty-one volunteers from Salem, including twenty-five boatmen, enlisted. Among them were Jacob Ashton, Francis Cabot, Capt. Jonathan Felt, Capt. Benjamin Goodhue, Capt. Jonathan Haraden, Capt. Samuel Tucker, Samuel Ward, Jr., George Williams, and others of the trading town's notable mariners, merchants, and ship owners. Commanded by Capt. Samuel Flagg, the volunteer company marched to Flynt's tavern in Danvers about seven o'clock on the morning of August 4, where they mounted horses and carriages for Rhode Island. Boatmen were also enlisted from other ports: one hundred from Marblehead, sixty from Newburyport, eighty Bostonians, mariners from as far away as New Hampshire. So long as strategic Newport was held by the British, Bay State coastal towns and their ocean-going traffic were threatened.

Thus ready hands rushed south to drive the enemy from their only New England base.[7]

Franco-American Action

Since July 29, the French commander, Estaing, had been anchored, waiting, near Narragansett Bay. After a joint plan was agreed upon, on August 8 the fleet sailed up the Middle Passage toward Newport.

The American troops were to be transported from Howland's ferry near Tiverton, westerly across the East Channel, to disembark on the northeastern side. Concurrently, the French were to boat four thousand soldiers from Conanicut and strike the northwest shore. The combined attack was planned for August 10.

Americans parading near Howland's ferry practiced their amphibious maneuver, with the crucial crossing entrusted to Essex County and Boston seafarers. A day before the planned invasion, Sullivan found that Gen. Robert Pigot had abandoned Butts Hill to the north and had gone southward toward Newport. Despite his prearranged plan with Estaing, Sullivan could not resist the opportunity of an unopposed landing. His troops boarded flat-bottomed boats and were ferried across the narrow waterway. They landed and promptly occupied the vacated fort.

Though Sullivan's premature move had irked Estaing, the next day he proceeded to disembark his troops. But when, about mid-day, a fleet commanded by Adm. Richard Howe was sighted off Point Judith, the Frenchman changed plans. Though he could have completed his landing, soldiers were reboarded and—over Sullivan's protests—he sailed to engage Howe. For two days, the fleets maneuvered for advantage.

On August 11, on the island—from shore to shore—Americans formed in an order of battle. Out front, four miles forward, was an advance party of light troops, independent companies, and fifty men from each brigade. In the first line, Varnum was stationed on the right; Glover on the left; Cornell left of center; Greene, with Wade's regiment, right of center. Titcomb's brigade manned the second line on the left, with Lovell's on the right; both militia were headed by Maj. Gen. John Hancock. The Marquis de Lafayette led the left wing; Maj. Gen. Nathaniel Greene commanded the right.[8]

Meanwhile, on August 12, Col. Larkin Thorndike of Beverly, pleading "his inability & inexperience in Military Affairs," requested to be relieved from his command. Peleg Wadsworth of Duxbury was made commander, with two new field officers: Lt. Col. Eleazer Crafts of Manchester and Maj. Joseph Hiller, a Salem volunteer. The reason for Thorndike's sudden resignation is uncertain. In his orders, the resolute Gen. John Sullivan expressed hope that "this Example might deter Men who have neither firmness or Knowledge for a Military Life from accepting offices which they cannot discharge." A week later, however, he noted that Titcomb's original report had not fully explained Thorndike's "Motives" for resigning. The Beverly colonel, who was staying on, had given up command voluntarily; he was not induced by "a Spirit of timidity," rather for "the good of the Service." Sullivan wished to "wipe off any unfavorable Impressions" implied by the earlier orders.[9]

The army's scheduled move on August 12 was interrupted by a full-fledged nor'easter. The day before, a gale began to blow, and during the night it gathered momentum. Violent, unabated rain squalls toppled nearly all tents, drowned horses, and ruined cartridges, powder, and provisions. The drenched army was left exposed for two days.

By August 15 operations resumed. Sullivan's army advanced six miles south toward Newport, stopping within sight of British lines two miles away on Tonomy Hill. The Americans entrenched on the eastern side to await Estaing's promised return. Meanwhile, heavy cannon fire erupted. The prominent Salem merchant George Williams noted on August 20: "The Last 48 hours past thay Sent us about 600 Shot, & yesterday we return'd them about 60 18lb shot in exchange."[10] On the same day, Estaing's fleet was sighted.

Abandoned

The French commander—in no mood to help the Americans— had resolved to go to Boston for provisions and repairs. Both fleets were battered and scattered by the northeaster, foreclosing any Anglo-French naval engagement. Stunned by Estaing's decision, American army officers, including John Glover, despatched a protest. The fleet nevertheless sailed, leaving bitterness and recriminations in its wake. As George Williams wrote on September 12: "This I can say, never was greater Spirit seen in America for the expidision, and greater disappointment, when Mr Frenchman Left us on a Island in the Lurch."[11] With help from Estaing, Newport would have fallen.

Without Estaing, the American position was tenuous. Any serious idea of attacking Newport had been dashed. Withdrawal of the French fleet "cast a universal gloom on the army, and threw us all into consternation," wrote Hamlet pastor Rev. Manasseh Cutler, Titcomb's brigade chaplain. Estaing's defection spread gloom among militia and volunteers, whose enlistments were near expiring, swaying thousands to return home. Though most Essex County troops stayed, Sullivan's invasion force shrunk to 5,400. On August 23, the commander invited opinions from his field commanders: without reinforcements, both Glover and Titcomb recommended withdrawal. Hearing that more British were on their way, Sullivan abandoned the siege and moved north to the fortified hills.[12]

Withdrawal

On the evening of the twenty-eighth, the American force struck their tents. By two o'clock in the morning, they were repositioned twelve miles north, near Butt's Hill. A line was established the entire breadth of the island. About two miles from Newport, a road leading out of town forked into two roadways extending on either side of the island, roughly north and south. The American right ran to the west road; the left stretched to the east road, with both flanks towards the water covered. Rear guards were placed a few miles south along both routes. Behind Col. Henry B. Livingston's guard of light corps on the east road, Col. Nathaniel Wade led a picket of ninety-one men.

Shortly after daybreak on August 29, Sir Robert Pigot sent several units along the two roads in pursuit of the retreating Americans. Four British regiments under Brig. Gen. Smith took the east road toward Quaker Hill; Hessian light infantry and two Anspach battalions under Maj. Gen. Lossberg traveled the west road. About five miles north, the two thoroughfares were connected by a crossroad. From this nexus, another roadway ran northerly and parallel with the nearby east road. An open field enclosed by stone walls bordered the three roads. One account places part of Wade's picket crouched behind a fieldstone barricade awaiting the approaching enemy. At the crossroad, the 22nd British Regiment divided, with one column continuing along the east road. The second contingent turned westerly. Wade's men rose from their cover. They poured out two deadly volleys on the advancing detachment, inflicting casualties on one-fourth of the British regiment. Two Hessian regiments bounded up the road to their aid, but the Americans fled north toward the main line beyond Quaker and Turkey hills. They stopped sporadically to fire at the oncoming enemy.[13]

During the withdrawal, about one mile from the rear guard, John Glover was headquartered in a house east of Quaker Hill, on the American left. The general and several officers were at breakfast. Young Rufus King of Newburyport, his aide-de-camp, had just stood up, with Maj. John Sherburne of New Hampshire taking his chair. Suddenly, a spent cannon ball bounced through an open window narrowly missing Glover; it fell to the floor, rolled, and crushed Sherburne's foot.[14]

Col. Edward Wigglesworth leading the 13th Massachusetts Regi-

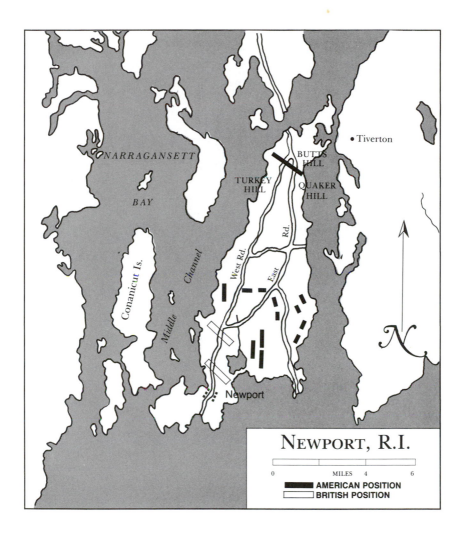

NEWPORT, R.I.

0   MILES   4   6

AMERICAN POSITION
BRITISH POSITION

ment in Glover's brigade, part of the left-wing rear guard, withdrew
slowly north along the east road, checking the enemy advance. The
Newburyport colonel had planned to entrench on Quaker Hill, but
heavy artillery fire thwarted this plan. A more immediate danger,
however, posed on his right. Unknown to him, he had become outflanked by the German column marching up West Road. When Gen.
John Sullivan from Butt's Hill sighted a regiment forging east toward
Wigglesworth, he despatched aide-de-camp John Trumbull (later a
renowned artist) to warn him. Trumbull shouted: "Do you see those
troops crossing . . . towards your rear?" "Yes," Wigglesworth replied,
"Americans, coming to our support"—he had mistaken the Germans
for American reinforcements because their uniforms were similar.

Trumbull yelled, "No, Sir, those are Germans . . . moving to fall into your rear, and intercept your retreat. Retire instantly—don't lose a moment, or you will be cut off."[15]

The Continentals scurried down the north slope chased by the British; American reinforcements racing to the scene faced a torrent of stampeding soldiers, friend and foe. The would-be rescuers "took to their heels," joining Wigglesworth's regiment in retreat. They made a mad dash toward a crossroads guarded by Glover's troops, who stood fast from behind stone wall defenses. Four-pounders from their artillery redoubt and others along the line raked the approaching enemy. Later, Gen. John Sullivan gave much of the credit to Glover's brigade, noting: "The Enemy made a Show of attacking our Left. General Glover advanced to meet them upon which they halted on Quaker Hill about a mile in our Front." From atop Quaker Hill and Turkey Hill, His Majesty's troops proceeded to cannonade the American lines.[16]

The first American line was drawn south of the abandoned British works on Butts Hill. The second was to the rear, with a reserve still further back. The enemy was situated on high ground running northward from Quaker Hill. Butts Hill and Quaker Hill were separated by about a mile of marsh, meadows, and woodland.

From 9:00 A.M., British field guns had peppered the American right, a prelude to assault. Their fire was returned "with double force," General Sullivan later reported. As advance parties skirmished, armed enemy vessels, including the twenty-two-gun *Vigilant*, came up the passage and fired toward the American right flank. During the day, enemy pressure was concentrated against General Greene's command. Two deadly assaults—the attackers trying to turn the American right—were handily repulsed. After a third, the Americans streamed forward, bolstered by the second line: Lovell's brigade. Thanks to uncommon heroics from this Massachusetts unit and Rhode Islander Christopher Greene's black regiment, the enemy was routed, in utter chaos, back toward the chain of hills. On the left, Titcomb's brigade was exposed to little action. Next day, Gen. John Sullivan, after hearing enemy reinforcements had sailed, withdrew from the island.[17]

Earlier, on August 24, Sullivan had made contingency plans for evacuation. Salem's volunteers were sent to Howland's ferry, where they were placed under Glover's former brigade major, Col. William R. Lee of Marblehead. A veteran of many campaigns, Lee recently had resigned from the army, but reenlisted for the Newport campaign. Just four days earlier, Sullivan had thanked "the truly Spirited Citizens of Salem, M'head etc who so Chearfully turn'd out to take Charge of the Boats." Despite their expiring enlistments, they were

Col. William Raymond Lee, who was engaged in Marblehead commerce before the Revolution, served in the Newport campaign. Miniature by Nathaniel Hancock. Courtesy, Essex Institute, Salem, Mass.

staying on. Capt. Samuel Flagg and the Salem Independents were to secure the boats and be prepared to crew them when required.[18]

On August 30, Col. Thomas Sears, Major Rogers, and Maj. Joseph Hiller—a leader of the Essex County regiment—were ordered to Howland's ferry to "assist Capt. Flagg in the Department of the Boats." In the late afternoon, the amphibious retreat got under way, beginning with the militia. At night, Capt. Frederick MacKenzie of the Royal Welch Fusiliers reported: "we could plainly hear the noise of their Oars, much talking, and many boats in motion towards Howland's ferry." By midnight, thanks to ready hands, many from Essex County, the entire army, all artillery, and most baggage had been transported safely to the mainland.[19]

The last page was being written of the frustrating Newport campaign. On September 3, at Pawtucket, General Titcomb jotted the final entry in his orderly book. The brigade was warned not to pillage or destroy local gardens, hay, or fences—and "no profane Cursing or Swearing!" Nathaniel Wade's regiment finished the year encamped near East Greenwich. Glover's brigade bivouacked nearby until June 30, 1779, when it rejoined the main army. Thus ended inauspiciously the first operation of the Franco-American alliance.[20]

Coastal Fears

On August 29, one day before the island retreat, cannon salutes greeted the damaged French fleet as it entered Boston harbor. When Bostonians found Estaing had abandoned the besieging Americans, however, tempers flared. Several nasty brawls erupted on Boston streets between townsmen and the French.

With Newport remaining in enemy hands, concerns arose that an invasion of Boston or a North Shore port loomed on the horizon. Already, New Bedford and Fairhaven had been burned; with the French fleet in for repairs, Boston presented a tempting target. Militia were ordered to be detached for its defenses. Beverlyites, alarmed over their own "Exposed Situation," wanted "men now Called for" to remain. Lynn, likewise, with a seacoast "very convenient for the landing of troops," wished to keep its militia "unless necessarily called to some of the neighboring towns on an alarm." Indeed, the Massachusetts Council, concerned for the entire North Shore, rescinded marching orders for Beverly, Danvers, Gloucester, Ipswich, Marblehead, and Salem. Early in November, though, after the refitted French fleet had sailed for the West Indies, fear of attack abated.[21]

Southern Action

After the Newport operation, the scene of action shifted south. On December 29, 1779, the British took Savannah. The following May, Sir George Collier's devastating raid against the Chesapeake cost America over one hundred vessels and vast amounts of supplies. But the scales tipped momentarily in September when Estaing appeared unexpectedly off Savannah with a huge fleet and 4,000 troops.

He had sailed from the West Indies where France had been warring with England over the valued Caribbean isles. Learning the French fleet was moving toward the American coast and unsure of its intentions, Lt. Gen. Sir Henry Clinton, commander of British forces in North America, took the defensive. Newport—the allied objective a year earlier—was evacuated to shore up weakly protected New York. But Savannah was the target.

In mid-September, Gen. Benjamin Lincoln left Charleston to join Estaing and American advance units in a lengthy siege—rather than an immediate assault—against the Georgian port. Under pressure from his officers—the hurricane season was approaching, his fleet needed repairs, and men were dying of scurvy—a restive Estaing demanded that the siege be broken off and that the allies attack enemy defenses. After a series of misfortunes the joint assault was repulsed, with heavy allied casualties. Although Lincoln urged Estaing to stay and continue the siege, the Frenchman returned to his ships on October 20. He hastily quit America. The admiral's actions, reminiscent of his abrupt departure from Newport, once more soured feelings toward the French. Many Americans began to question the value of the French alliance.

After Estaing had cleared American waters, leaving Georgia safely

British, General Clinton initiated his southern strategy. In late December 1779, he embarked from New York with ninety transports brimming with 8,500 of His Majesty's troops bound for Charleston. In May 1780, the vital harbor of America's fourth largest city fell, with a loss of 5,000 Americans and four Continental warships—a disastrous defeat. The victory was Clinton's curtain-raiser to the winning of the southern colonies.

Timely Reinforcements

For Americans, the spring of 1780 was fraught with blue devils. Not since December 1776 had northern morale been so low. Less than 4,000 ragged effectives remained with General Washington at Morristown. Three-year enlistments had expired, and replacements dribbled in slowly. Pay in nearly valueless Continental scrip was five months overdue. Inadequately provisioned and reduced to half rations, many disgruntled soldiers were near mutiny. Not a few informed Americans believed that victory was impossible.

The outlook quickly changed, however, after Washington learned that France was sending him a powerful force. Now he could launch his long-sought attack against New York City! On May 2, the transports left Brest, carrying 5,500 troops under the Comte de Rochambeau, a French and Indian War veteran. Twelve warships under Chevalier de Ternay provided escort.

To assure that the "intended co-operation" was successful, Washington emphasized "the absolute necessity of every possible exertion to draw out the resources of the Country." States were to fill their undermanned Continental regiments. During June, towns in the Bay State were called upon to raise nearly 4,000 troops for six-month duty—by draft, lot, or voluntary enlistment. Essex County's share was 565 men.[22]

The pool of able-bodied men, however, had nearly dried up. For every battlefield casualty, several already had fallen to disease, exposure, or noncombat injuries. Many potential enlistees had emigrated from exposed coastal towns such as Gloucester and Marblehead; hundreds more had been lost at sea or were languishing in British prisons. The war-torn years had caused spirits to flag. And the scourge of inflation continued to gnaw at soldiers' pay.

Towns had to sweeten their bounties. Gloucesterites voted to borrow $60,000 on the credit of the town to hire thirty-two Continentals. Three men were hired, however, at a cost of $6,000 each, so this was made the standard offer. Continental currency—depreciated more than forty times—required the raising of enormous sums. Though Cape Ann voted a second $60,000 on June 30, it ended mustering only two men and was fined £152. Newburyport offered recruits "hard money or provisions," an option available only to fiscally liquid towns. Rowley first tried hiring men out of state but wound up dividing residents into thirteen classes, with each class responsible for hiring one man. The choice of bounty was $1,000 up front or two bushels of Indian corn and three pounds in hard money upon return. The seaport of Marblehead—a shrunken specter of its former self— had a quota of twenty-four, equal to Rowley's. By August 15, Marbleheaders were near giving up; most able-bodied men were in the service already, or away privateering. On June 12, Beverly countered the depreciation of currency by offering a bundle of staples: 100 pounds of beef, coffee, and sugar, 10 bushels of corn, 50 pounds of cotton, or £1,370 in scrip. A few days later, it fattened the bounty, but still found only seven recruits. Despite these difficulties, Essex County towns mustered, collectively, nearly 400 six-months men, 70 percent of the quota. John Glover was sent to meet the Massachusetts arrivals at Springfield, New Jersey.[23]

Washington believed a second line was essential to assure success of the contemplated campaign. On June 2, over 17,000 militia were called, 4,725 from Massachusetts. After they arrived at Claverack, New York, near the Hudson, their three-month tour was to begin, long enough for the anticipated operation. One of nine Bay State regiments was raised in Essex County. Col. Nathaniel Wade of Ipswich was charged with command of seven companies. About half of the requisitioned 677 men were mustered. Contingents were led by John Abbot of Andover, Nathan Ayer of Haverhill, Benjamin Gould of Topsfield, Thomas Mighill of Rowley, Benjamin Peabody of Middleton, Addison Richardson of Salem, and Richard Titcomb of Newburyport. No militia marched, however, from depopulated and privateer-committed coastal Manchester, Marblehead, or Salem. The rendezvous point of the regiment was at Great Barrington—the staging place for the Massachusetts brigade. By early August, they reached West Point—America's strongest military post—fifty miles north of New York City and high above the Hudson Highlands, where the commander in chief expected an enemy thrust. A series of forts still under construction overlooked the Hudson, where a huge chain spanned the river to block the enemy. Washington's army, meanwhile, had vacated Jersey and moved to nearby Tappan.[24]

During mid-July 1780, the French fleet had dropped anchor off Newport. New England militia, including Capt. Andrew Woodbury of Cape Ann, arrived to help the Comte de Rochambeau rebuild the former British fortifications, while de Ternay's squadron of warships guarded the harbor. For the first time British naval superiority had been challenged in American waters, and Lt. Gen. Clinton had been forced to return north. In September, Washington and Rochambeau met at Hartford to discuss a joint land-sea assault against New York. Their plans were scrapped, however, when Adm. Sir George Rodney, sailing from the Indies, arrived at Sandy Hook with ten warships. The British, now enjoying undisputed naval control, bottled the French in Newport harbor. Thus ended the abortive campaign of 1780.

Arnold's Treason

During late September, America was shocked by a treasonous conspiracy: the esteemed Gen. Benedict Arnold had been discovered plotting the delivery of West Point to the enemy. The aggrieved commander in chief felt especially betrayed. A disillusioned Washington asked: "Whom can we trust now?"

After the British had evacuated Philadelphia, Arnold had been made military governor of the fashionable city. While in command, he and his young bride, Peggy Shippen, who was from a prominent Tory family, enjoyed such a lavish lifestyle that Arnold was soon short of money. The hero of Bemis Heights also had become embittered, believing his prior services to his country had merited greater recognition than he had received. Then, early in 1780, Washington reprimanded him for improper administration verging on corruption. The combined effect of these factors, it is believed, influenced Arnold to sell out his country.

The turncoat American opened communications with Gen. Henry Clinton in New York City, and they corresponded. Meanwhile, in August 1780, Arnold convinced Washington to give him command of vital West Point. His plan was to hand over this stronghold to the British in exchange for a brigadier's commission in His Majesty's army, plus gold. By now, most outposts along the Hudson, like Verplank's and Stony Point, were in American hands. They were manned largely by New Englanders; Continentals and three-month militia.

On September 21, Maj. John Andre, the respected British adjutant and friend of Sir Henry Clinton, came up the Hudson aboard the sloop-of-war *Vulture* to rendezvous with Arnold. Four miles below Stony Point on the Hudson shore, they conferred. Arnold gave the young major plans of West Point, estimates of troop strengths, and other classified documents.

Meanwhile, a shore battery had forced the *Vulture* downriver, requiring Andre to return toward headquarters by land. The major was proceeding in civilian clothes—having forsaken his regimentals—when he was stopped by three patrolling militiamen near Tarrytown. The fatal papers were discovered hidden in his stockings.

Unaware that Arnold was involved, the militia commander informed West Point. Benedict Arnold, knowing his name would be implicated, bid good-by to his wife and hastily rode to his military barge. Eight boatmen tacked and rowed the general eighteen miles downstream to the *Vulture*. Unwittingly, they aided his escape. (Among the eight were John Brown and Samuel Pilsbury of Newbury, Stephen Pearson of Ipswich—all three-month men—and coxswain James Lurvey of Gloucester, in Rufus Putnam's regiment.) Once aboard, Arnold coaxed the crew to desert with promises of promotion in His Majesty's service. Lurvey indignantly replied: "No sir, one coat is enough for me to wear at a time."[25]

As Arnold set foot on British-occupied Manhattan, unsure of what to expect, Washington was preparing for any eventuality. In the absence of the commandant, Col. John Lamb, Col. Nathaniel Wade was placed in temporary command of West Point. On September 25, Washington instructed Wade: "I request you will be as vigilant as possible, and as the Enemy may have it in contemplation to attempt some enterprise, even to night, against these Posts, I wish you to make immediately after receipt of this, the best disposition you can of your force." The commander in chief feared that a sally on the strategic fortress was imminent.[26]

Andre was tried by a fourteen-man military court of inquiry, which included Gen. John Glover, that found the British major to be a spy. He was sentenced to death by hanging, at high noon on October 2. The solemn procession set out from the village of Tappan along a narrow lane to a grassy hilltop, widely visible to regiments encamped on surrounding hillsides. Benjamin Abbot of Andover and Isaac Organ of Lynn tapped the dead march on muffled drums as the cortege ascended to a makeshift gibbet. A composed Andre stood atop a horse-drawn wagon as a noose was placed around his neck. The hangman cracked a whip across the horses' hides. The wagon lurched forward, instantly hanging Andre. The gruesome sight was witnessed by scores from Essex County, who were among the crowds of civilian and military onlookers.[27]

A New Year

The militia returned home in mid-October 1780, leaving Washington's undersized army quiescent on the highlands. Short of money, his men scantily clothed, ill fed, and sickly, the commander in chief questioned how long the struggle could go on. On November 27, he instructed Glover "to discharge every Mouth that can be dispensed with . . . dismissing those first who are most in want of Cloaths or who are unhealthy." Washington's situation had become barely tenable.[28]

On December 12, William Pynchon noted: "The drum is beat to raise a martial spirit for town meeting to-day, at which 73 men are to be raised for the Continental Army." Once more, with six-month enlistments expiring, Massachusetts was trying to fill its Continental deficiency: over 4,000 soldiers "for three years or during the war." The state offered each enlistee fifty dollars new currency, but local bounties also were required. A series of interrelated circumstances— widespread indigence, public apathy, manpower shortages, unstable currency, war fatigue—impeded enlistments. This was especially true along the North Shore and Cape Ann, where recruiters continually competed with privateering.[29]

Since for years the worth of currency had been sinking, the value of future salaries had to be weighed. Wenham, for example, promised one hundred dollars hard money annually to enlistees or the going exchange rate in paper when due. On January 11, Boxford gave enlistees "surety" for their bounty each year. They would receive 120 Spanish silver dollars (160 the third year) or the equivalent in paper currency. Incredibly, £20,624 in old emission was raised—an exchange rate of 170 to 1—to settle accounts! Mustering was going so slowly, that, in order to fill vacancies, on February 26, 1781, towns were instructed to divide their inhabitants into classes and to require each class to procure a man. On March 15, Newburyporters agreed "to comply." Later, they voted to class "according to their property." Not until July 10, however, were forty-three classes organized, after still another call for enlistees (for reinforcements at West Point). Destitute Marblehead resorted to selling town-owned real estate— near Bubier's Plain—to pay for its quota. The money was sent to John Glover for hiring at West Point, though the general was not successful. To raise monies for recruits, on April 24 no-nonsense Salem told its collectors "to take the goods" from delinquent taxpayers or "carry" them before the assessors for possible jailing. Poverty-stricken Gloucester, severely deficient, was scheduled for heavy penalties. The town petitioned for abatement; a year later, on March 4, 1782, an empathetic legislature abated ten men (one quarter of its quota) and granted an extension to April 1, 1783! The victory at Yorktown, only a few months away, could not, of course, be foreseen. During the spring of 1781, the American spirit was near despair.[30]

In February, Washington's French-speaking aide, Col. John Laurens, crossed the Atlantic to France with an urgent appeal. The French came through, not only with additional money and supplies, but with manpower. A large fleet under the Comte de Grasse was readying for the Caribbean; when the hurricane season neared, the French admiral would leave the Indies and steer for America.

The World Turned Upside Down

When General Clinton departed from Charleston, the promising young Lord Cornwallis was left in command. In the following July-August 1780 Camden campaign, he led a brilliant action against Horatio Gates's army. Cornwallis subsequently moved away from the coast, out of upper South Carolina into North Carolina's hilly back country. Then, in March 1781, the tenacious Gen. Nathaniel Greene delivered him a setback at Guilford Court House, inflicting casualties on one-fourth of Cornwallis's army.

Earlier in December, Brig. Gen. Benedict Arnold, now dressed in scarlet, had been sent to Virginia with 1,600 men. During March, Gen. William Phillips arrived, infusing British ranks with 2,000 more troops. Their major opposition was a brigade under Marquis de Lafayette. It was composed of three special, temporary, light infantry regiments led by Col. Joseph Vose of Massachusetts; Lt. Col. Jean Joseph Gimat, a French officer and aide to Lafayette; and Lt. Col. Francis Barber of New Jersey. The British were encamped at Petersburg, south of Richmond. In late April, Cornwallis pushed from North Carolina into Virginia. On May 20, 1781, he assumed command of British forces. Though the combined redcoat army now tallying 7,000 outnumbered the Americans, the young Lafayette, with help from von Steuben and Anthony Wayne, slowed their advance. The campaign ended in July when Cornwallis occupied Yorktown, on an isolated peninsula in Chesapeake Bay, where he awaited supplies and reinforcements.

In May, upon learning that Admiral de Grasse soon would be sailing north, Washington and Rochambeau conferred. While America's commander in chief favored attacking New York, the French commander preferred Virginia. A decision was held in abeyance until de Grasse arrived. Meanwhile 4,000 French marched from Newport to join Washington's 4,500 Continentals at White Plains. Gen. Henry Clinton in New York, observing the movements, prepared to fend off a land-sea attack.

By August 18, French and American armies were southbound. Four days earlier, they had learned that Admiral de Grasse had left the Caribbean, bearing for the Chesapeake with an imposing battle fleet. The time had ripened for a southern offensive. The complicated campaign would require proper timing and coordination between land and sea forces.

Most Essex County Continentals remained with General Heath to guard the highlands. Since the remaining northern army consisted of less than 2,500 rank and file—including ten lean Massachusetts regiments—they would be powerless to stave off attack from 17,000 nearby enemy troops. The allies planned their campaign in secrecy, while diversionary moves were undertaken to convince Clinton that New York was the target.

By August 30, de Grasse arrived off Hampton Roads. After routing Admiral Thomas Graves in a brief battle, the French commander gained control of Chesapeake Bay. The British were thereby blocked from relieving Cornwallis, which doomed his command. Allied land forces near Williamsburg, across from the peninsula, hemmed in the enemy. On September 28, the force of 17,000 French and Americans closed to within the Yorktown environs to begin a siege.

It was a classic approach that required shovelling parallel trenches successively closer to the enemy. By October 9, batteries mounted in the first parallel opened bombardment. Within five days, a second parallel had been completed, except for an area exposed to fire from two British redoubts. The French were to assault one, while American light infantry under Lafayette was assigned the second, by the river bank. Lt. Col. Alexander Hamilton of New York had overall command of the four hundred American troops, drawn from several corps: Gimat's, Hamilton's, and Laurens's. Lieutenant Colonel Gimat's command—a regiment composed of New England troops—included a company led by the venerable Capt. John Burnham of Chebacco, Ipswich. Some soldiers from Essex County would take part; others would stand in reserve with Colonel Vose's 1st Massachusetts Regiment. On the night of October 14, the Americans advanced stealthily, carrying unloaded muskets with fixed bayonets. Nearing the abatis, they charged and overwhelmed all resistance.[31]

Without reinforcements, General Cornwallis was helpless. The end was inevitable. On October 17, four years exactly since the British surrender at Saratoga, a drummer boy atop the parapet beat Cornwallis's request to discuss terms and a cease-fire. Two days later, at two o'clock in the afternoon, the British garrison paraded out of their lines with colors cased to the beat of the old British march, "The World Turned Upside Down." On the surrender field, company after company of solemn troops grounded their muskets and colors. Yorktown—the last major battle of the war—had been a brilliantly conceived and executed army-navy campaign. The British will to continue had been shattered.[32]

As news of the victory was broadcast through the country, joyous crowds spontaneously celebrated. On October 26, despite the overcast, rainy weather in Salem, William Pynchon reported wild jubilation: "Cannon, small arms, mortars, bells, and all kinds of arms, sounds, reports, clamours, noises, and rumours through the town make the diversions and employments of this day."[33]

Cornwallis's surrender concluded the last major conflict in America. Except for the west, the military phase was over. The British would soon abandon their land war in America to concentrate their energies at sea and against France and Spain, which had joined the war in 1779.

Washington's army, however, returned to the Hudson Highlands and resumed their watch over General Clinton in New York. It was not until April 18, 1783, three days after Congress's approval of the peace treaty, that Gen. George Washington proclaimed hostilities actually closed. By June, the army had mostly disbanded.

Essex County soldiers—steadfast to the last—finally returned to their homes and families. Indeed, some had persevered for seven fatiguing years—the entire war—serving their country. Among them were several officers of the Continental line: Capt. Stephen Abbot of Andover, Capt. John Burnham of Ipswich, Capt. Matthew Chambers of Marblehead, Lt. William Greenleaf of Haverhill, Col. Ezra Newhall of Lynn, Maj. Billy Porter of Wenham, Maj. Winthrop Sargent of Gloucester. They were but a few of the thousands of Essex County men whose indefatigable service in the Continental Army and state militia helped win independence for America.

1. Fitch Edward Oliver, ed., *The Diary of William Pynchon of Salem* (Boston: Houghton Mifflin, 1890), 107.
2. *Acts and Resolves*, 20:218–19, 299, 311, 341, 441–44, 450.
3. MA Archives, 199:311.
4. Otis G. Hammond, ed., *Letters and Papers of Major-General John Sullivan* (Concord, NH: New Hampshire Historical Society, 1930), 2:89, 111, 132.
5. Titcomb's Orderly Book, MA Archives, 327:5.
6. William P. Upham, "A Memoir of Gen. John Glover," *EIHC*, 5 (1863):107.
7. "Expedition to Rhode Island in 1778," *EIHC*, 1 (1859):112–13; George Williams, "Revolutionary Letters Written to Colonel Timothy Pickering,"*EIHC*, 43 (1907):15–16; Oliver, 55.
8. "Heath Papers," MHS *Collections*, 7th Series, 4, Part 2 (1904):245–46.
9. Titcomb's Orderly Book, 327:10, 26; Glover's Orderly Book, August 12, 19, 1778, Vol. 4, Family MSS, EI; also, "Orderly Book of Capt. Simeon Brown, Colonel Wade's Regiment," DHS *Collections*, 11 (1923):69–70.
10. Williams, 15.
11. 199.
12. William Parker Cutler and Julia Perkins Cutler, *Life, Journal, and Correspondence of*

Rev. Manassah Cutler (Cincinnati: Robert Clark, 1903), 1:71; Hammond, 2:261–62; 281–82.
13. Samuel Greene Arnold, *History of the State of Rhode Island* (New York: D. Appleton, 1860), 2:425–26; Hammond, 2:282; Herbert T. Wade, "Col. Wade and the Massachusetts State Troops in Rhode Island," *EIHC*, 89 (1953):372–73; *Diary of Frederick MacKenzie* (Cambridge: Harvard University Press, 1930), 2:381–82.
14. *Autobiography, Reminiscences and Letters of John Trumbull*, (New Haven: B. L. Hamlen, 1841), 53–54.
15. 53, 305.
16. 305; *Diary of Frederick MacKenzie*, 2:382–83; Hammond, 2:274.
17. Arnold, 427–28; Hammond, 2:274–75.
18. Glover's Orderly Book, August 20, 1778.
19. Glover's Orderly Book, August 30, 1778; also, Titcomb's Orderly Book, 327:47; *Diary of Frederick MacKenzie*, 2:387.
20. Titcomb's Orderly Book, 327:54.
21. Beverly Town Records, September 23, 1778, 6:212–13; Howard Kendall Sanderson, *Lynn in the Revolution* (Boston: W. B. Clarke, 1903), 1:123–24; Council Records, MA Archives, 38:657.
22. John C. Fitzpatrick, ed., *The Writings of George Washington*, 18:416, 483; *Acts and Resolves*, 21:519–24.

23. Gloucester Town Records, June 19–30, 1780, 228–29; *Acts and Resolves, 1780–81*, 92; Newburyport Town Records, June 19, 1780, 1:336; Thomas Gage, *History of Rowley* (Boston: Ferdinand Andrews, 1840), 274–75; Marblehead Town Records, EI, August 7–September 5, 1780, 4:728–34; Beverly Town Records, June 12, 1780, 5:308; Revolutionary Rolls, MA Archives, 27:5–10; Fitzpatrick, 19:39, 43.

24. Fitzpatrick, 18:468, 470; 19:39; *Acts and Resolves*, 21:568–72; *Acts and Laws, 1780–81*, 92–93; Herbert T. Wade, "The Massachusetts Brigade on the Hudson, 1780," *EIHC*, 90 (1954):84–92; "Orderly Book Kept by Benjamin Peabody of Middleton While at West Point in 1780," DHS *Collections*, 18 (1930): 105–06.

25. William Eustis, "Anecdote of the Soldiers of Arnold," MHS *Collections*, 2nd Series, 4 (1816):51; William Abbatt, *The Crisis of the Revolution* (New York: William Abbatt, 1899), 42; for a varying account, see: Winthrop Sargent, *Life and Career of Major John Andre* (Boston: Ticknor and Fields, 1861), 330.

26. Fitzpatrick, 20:85.

27. Sargent, 393–400; James Thacher, *Military Journal of the American Revolution* (Hartford, Conn.: Hurlburt, Williams, 1862), 221–29.

28. Fitzpatrick, 20:403.

29. Oliver, 81; *Acts and Resolves, 1780–81*, 190–201.

30. *Wenham Town Records* (Wenham: Wenham Historical Society, 1959), 4:41–42; Boxford Town Records, January 4–11, 1781, 189–91; Newburyport Town Records, 1:350, 357, 360; Marblehead Town Records, December 26, 1780–March 3, 1781, 4:769–95; Salem Town Records, EI, April 24, 1781, 5:447–48; *Acts and Resolves, 1780–81*, 894–95.

31. Henry P. Johnstone, *The Yorktown Campaign and the Surrender of Cornwallis 1781* (New York: Harper, 1881), 144–47.

32. 151–57.

33. Oliver, 109.

Ships with bowsprits and three or more sails were the major ocean-going cargo carriers of the eighteenth century. During the War of Independence, these sturdy craft also served America as letters of marque and as privateers. From *Encyclopedia Britannica*, 1797. Courtesy, Essex Institute, Salem, Mass.

CHAPTER TWENTY

DISASTER AT PENOBSCOT

"**E**mbargo is Taking place," wrote Salem merchant George Williams to Timothy Pickering, Jr. "The reason is the enemy is got into the river of Penobscot." Massachusetts Bay officials were in the throes of assembling an expeditionary force to wrest from the enemy their only foothold in New England. Williams went on to predict: "When our Littel Fleet & Troops Arrives I make no doubt but we shall be able to Take them—all we have to fear the enemy will send a reinforcement of havey Ships. In that case they will block us all in and may Take the whole of us—."[1] Tragically, Williams's worst fear materialized, sinking the battered spirit of Massachusetts to new depths.

On June 12, 1779, eight British vessels—a frigate, three sloops-of-war and four transports—made sail from Halifax headed for Penobscot Bay, 270 miles south. About twenty-five miles up the vast bay on the eastern side was Bagaduce, now Castine, a peninsula protruding at the confluence of the Penobscot and Bagaduce rivers. Off this promontory, on June 16 and 17, Brig. Gen. Francis McLean anchored and disembarked with a detachment of 700 troops from the 74th and 22nd Scottish regiments. During the following weeks, they proceeded to clear the land and erect fortifications. The main garrison, later named Fort George, was built on a high, wooded bluff commanding approaches to Penobscot River to the north. The frigate left, but the sloops-of-war and transports remained, under command of Capt. Henry Mowat. In 1775, Mowat had incurred New Englanders' wrath by burning Falmouth Neck (Portland). Having been stationed for years along this craggy shore, he was charged with protecting McLean's force.

Shock Waves

News of the invasion sent reverberating waves to coastal Essex County and Massachusetts Bay. The British had implanted themselves uncomfortably close—only 150 miles away, just two days' sail—well positioned for a future southerly drive. They extended their control over Maine's long stretch of coastline, disrupting its vital trade in firewood, lumber, cod, and river fish. Now, under protection by their garrison, the scarce, tall virgin pines would be cut for His Majesty's ships. British merchantmen could sail offshore shielded from roving privateers. In the future, Penobscot could become a permanent settlement for dispossessed Loyalist refugees from New England living in Nova Scotia. The incursion incited alarm, and garnered widespread support in northeastern New England for removing the enemy.

Over the years, an ongoing trade had nurtured close friendships between Newburyporters and their Down East neighbors. On June 23, prominent 'port merchants met, probably at Michael Hodge's Market Square insurance office. This was their customary location. Nine of them, Jonathan Jackson, Jacob Boardman, Thomas Thomas, and six others, all shipowners, "ever zealous to promote the public good," rushed a proposal to the General Court offering four privateers—the ships *Vengeance, Monmouth, Sky Rocket*, and the brig *Pallas*—and three prize vessels lying in the harbor for an expedition "to reduce the enemy." The owners would assume the risks of losing their vessels, provided they were manned, supplied, and equipped at public expense.[2]

Expedition Eastward

On June 24, the Board of War, an agency appointed by the General Court to equip the army and navy, was instructed to outfit a combined fleet of state warships and privateers. The day before, Massachusetts Council member Aaron Wood of Boxford had brought into the House a letter from Brig. Gen. Charles Cushing of Pownalborough, Maine, urging that a force be raised "to expel" the British. A special House committee—Gen. Michael Farley of Ipswich, Gen. Solomon Lovell of Weymouth, and Col. Samuel Gerrish of Newbury—concurred.[3]

Newburyport's four armed vessels were accepted. They, the General Court noted, with Continental and state vessels "and others taken up here, will be sufficient to compleat the Design." Board of War President Samuel Phips Savage wrote to Tristram Dalton, one of the owners, complimenting "the Spirited Exertions of the Gentlemen in Newbury Port, which have given animation to all who wish to promote the present important Expedition."[4]

With only three vessels in the puny Massachusetts navy ready to sail, the legislature called upon "Owners of private armed Vessels now in Port of Boston, and in the Ports of Salem, Marblehead, Beverly and Newburyport." While Newburyport had responded, others were holding back. On June 24, chronicler Ashley Bowen noted: "The Masons of Salem and Marblehead had a meeting at the [Second Congregational] New Meeting House. Doctor [Isaac] Story gave the oration." They were celebrating the Feast of St. John the Baptist, a special Masonic day. Since most notable Essex County merchants and ship captains were brother Masons, the two-day-old news out of Penobscot Bay must have dominated their conversations. The North Shore stalwarts, however, shared no general sense of urgency.[5]

On July 2, Suffolk County's sheriff was instructed to impress the *General Putnam*, a fast-sailing privateer out of New London lying in Boston harbor. The following day, commander Dudley Saltonstall reported that his crew had gone home; and furthermore, he and his officers were unwilling to join the expedition. Saltonstall's lack of enthusiasm reflected the prevailing privateer sentiment—a proclivity to expend their energies hunting prizes on potentially lucrative sea lanes.[6]

On June 29, the Board of War had written to Capt. George Williams. Noting Newburyport's example, they said: "We are assured Salem will never be behind her in exertions in so glorious a Cause." On July 3, when no cooperation seemed forthcoming, the Essex County sheriff was empowered and commanded to take the ships *Hector*, *Black Prince*, and *Hunter*, moored in Salem harbor. This, however, became unnecessary. A two-member council delegation conferred with Capt. Elias Hasket Derby, Capt. Thomas Mason, and Capt. George Williams, all agents, stressing the mission's importance. Indemnification already had been promised; meanwhile, captured prizes were resolved to be private booty. These decisions, along with notice that their vessels would be impressed, brought concurrence from the trio. In addition to the three ships at Salem, the Beverly brigantine *Defence* was offered.[7]

Three Continental warships—the frigate *Warren*, the brig *Diligent*, and the sloop *Providence*—lay in Boston harbor. Massachusetts had requested them for the expedition, and the marine committee approved their sailing. Negotiations included installing the hitherto recalcitrant Dudley Saltonstall, brother-in-law of committee member

Silas Deane, commander of the thirty-two-gun *Warren*. The politically connected Saltonstall, now a willing participant, became commodore of the fleet assembling at Nantasket Road.[8]

Newburyporters' fervor ran high. At a July 6 town meeting, "support" was voted for "the Merchants & Traders of this Town in their Resolves of the twenty third day of June last." There were plenty of enlistees. Thirty ship masters volunteered as common seamen rather than be left out. At the town's expense, an armed spy boat sailed to gather intelligence of enemy movements. Earlier, on July 2, the Council had voted that Newburyport's naval officer clear out the four privateers.[9]

Success depended on speed, secrecy, and volunteer mariners, many of whom preferred privateering to heading Down East. Sentries were stationed at the "several Ferries" and "other Outlets" to press "escaping" seamen. Three guard boats patrolled the mouth of Boston harbor to block nighttime travel. The intention was to be under way in six days, before the enemy was firmly entrenched or reinforcements arrived. To this end, work was permitted on the Sabbath. First a twenty-, then a forty-day embargo was imposed, with the purposes of promoting secrecy and keeping in port those men whose services were essential.[10]

Not six days but, rather, nearly four long weeks elapsed. Scarcity of supplies presented a problem; time was needed to gather clothes, food, arms, ammunition, and a host of other equipment. Beginning July 8, Beverly and Salem privateers were scooting in and out of Marblehead, looking to round out their complement, voluntary or otherwise. They were "obliged at Last to press men for them," wrote George Williams, "which was very disagreeable work." Meanwhile, the *Black Prince* and *Defence* lay at the mouth of Marblehead harbor awaiting the fleet.[11]

Obtaining full complements of able-bodied sailors was the foremost obstacle to a prompt departure. On July 11, the sheriff of Essex County, his deputies—or any constable—were ordered to prevent ordinary seamen or marines "from escaping out of the Town of Marblehead or such other Town" until privateers were manned. Those adverse to enlisting were to be impressed into service. Suffolk County officials had similar orders. Colonels Lee and Orne were informed the *General Putnam* needed at least sixty seamen to replace her Connecticut crew. Capt. Daniel Waters, the *Putnam*'s new commander, was to sail for Marblehead and, if called upon, help press. Sailors were to be assigned to the *Putnam*, and wherever else required. The Continental Navy's undermanned *Warren* was permitted to take thirty seamen from the fleet. By July 17, though preparations were completed, northeasterly breezes and rain delayed departure.[12]

Two days later, favored with fair skies and southwest winds, the expeditionary force weighed anchor with the members confident of success. As they passed Marblehead, the *Black Prince* and *Defence* also sailed. The fleet stopped off Rye beach to wait for the frigate *Hampden* of Portsmouth, loaned by New Hampshire, but she already had sailed.

The General Court had called for 1,500 militia recruits from Cumberland, Lincoln, and York counties, Maine, where enthusiasm appeared far-reaching. As it turned out, however, after four years of war, willing and able citizen soldiers were in short supply. Only 873 enlistees were mustered, one-fourth young boys or old men, poorly equipped, and with little training. Earlier, on July 10, ten transports had gone to Falmouth, a staging point for part of the militia, escorted by the Massachusetts brig *Active* and the Newburyport privateer *Pallas*. On July 22, they joined the fleet at Townsend (now Boothbay), the rendezvous point.

Earlier, on June 26, legislator Solomon Lovell was appointed brigadier general and given command of the land forces, with Peleg Wadsworth of Duxbury second in command. A detachment of state artillery was led by Lt. Col. Paul Revere. Their commands, together with the marines on board, were to conduct an amphibious landing and assault the garrison.

By the twenty-first, the Nantasket fleet had reached Townsend, where the ship *Hampden* was waiting. Next day, the Falmouth vessels stood in, also the ship *Charming Sally*, the brig *Defence*, and the sloop *Providence*. The largest naval expedition to sail during the war— eighteen armed vessels, twenty-four transports and victualers— cleared Townsend on July 22 headed for Penobscot.[13]

The privately armed portion of the fleet was two-thirds Essex County owned—a huge stake—including some fine local vessels. The *Black Prince*, Salisbury-built by William Swett, for example, was designed to be Massachusetts' "largest, fastest, and most heavily armed privateer." Owned by a syndicate of Beverly and Salem shareholders and commanded by Capt. Nathaniel West of Salem, the 220-ton *Black Prince* carried eighteen guns and 130 crew. The ship had just returned from a lengthy, uneventful cruise and was being outfitted for another when she joined the expedition. Also owned by Beverly and Salem men—including investors Moses Brown and Andrew Cabot— was the brigantine *Defence*. The spanking new privateer commanded by John Edmonds of Beverly had been recently fitted out and carried sixteen 6-pounders and 100 men. Most privateers were valued at about £100,000 each. Construction and outfitting of these vessels had taken substantial time and money; their loss would be grievous.[15]

NAME	GUNS	COMMANDER	OWNERSHIP
Armed Vessels in Penobscot Expedition			

Armed Vessels in Penobscot Expedition

NAME	GUNS	COMMANDER	OWNERSHIP
Ships			
Warren	32	Dudley Saltonstall	Continental
Hampden	20	Titus Salter	New Hampshire
Hector	20	John Carnes	Salem
General Putnam	20	Daniel Waters	Connecticut
Vengeance	20	Thomas Thomas	Newburyport
Monmouth	20	Alexander Ross	Newburyport
Charming Sally	20	Alexander Holmes	Boston*
Black Prince	18	Nathaniel West	Beverly/Salem
Hunter	18	Nathaniel Brown	Salem
Sky Rocket	16	William Burke	Newburyport
Brigs			
Hazard	16	Jonathan F. Williams	Massachusetts
Pallas	16	James Johnson	Newburyport
*Active***	16	Allen Hallet	Massachusetts
Tyrannicide	16	John Cathcart	Massachusetts
Defence	16	John Edmonds	Beverly/Salem
*Diligent****	12	Philip Brown	Continental
Sloops			
Providence	12	Holsted Hacker	Continental
Charming Polly	6	John Palmer	Boston*[14]

*Owned by William Erskine and others from Boston.
**Captured by the *Hazard* in March 1779 while sailing from Antigua and enlisted into the Massachusetts Navy.
***Taken from the British.

Siege

Despite precautions, by July 18 the British got wind of the impending siege. They doubled their efforts to brace fortifications; all hands worked around the clock. About one hundred residents labored; some did so willingly, but others had to be forced. The largely uninhabited region had attracted some Loyalists from Portland, Boston, and elsewhere. Most notable was Dr. John Calef, General McLean's volunteer surgeon and chaplain. Unpopular in his native Ipswich, Calef had gone to London, but became homesick for America and returned to settle in Penobscot. The Tory doctor kept a journal of the siege and drafted a map of the naval action, both valuable records.

On the afternoon of the twenty-fourth, the American fleet was spied entering Penobscot Bay. McLean's force dug in behind their largely incomplete earthworks. Captain Mowat positioned his warships at the harbor mouth, chained in line, so their broadsides faced the oncoming fleet.

On Sunday, July 25, Saltonstall maneuvered near the narrow harbor entrance between Dyce's Head and Nautilus Island, while the transports streamed past, anchoring one-half mile up the Penobscot River. Nine ships in three divisions hove to and, for two hours, exchanged gunfire with Mowat's armed sloops. Only minor damage to enemy riggings was inflicted. If Saltonstall had entered the harbor, almost certainly he could have captured or destroyed the enemy sloops and transports. Without naval protection, McLean would have surrendered his weakly defended garrison. In the following days, several times the American vessels bore up, exchanged fire, and returned to their anchor. Despite his superior force, Saltonstall made no attempt to enter.

Meanwhile, on the twenty-fifth, General Lovell undertook a landing on Bagaduce, but high winds and rough seas scuttled his plans; the first contingent was recalled before the second went. Next day, two hundred marines landed on wooded Nautilus Island, where a secondary battery shielded the harbor entrance. They drove off the enemy, occupied their station, and landed heavy artillery. During the night, to move out of range, Mowat pulled into the harbor.

Well-directed fire from American guns on Nautilus Island forced Mowat further into the harbor. It seemed propitious, with the entrance open, for Saltonstall to attack. But he took no action. On July 27, thirty-two exasperated officers aboard the warships and transports petitioned the commodore "to go immediately into the Harbour, & attack the Enemy's ships." They believed delays "extremely dangerous: as our Enemies are daily Fortifying and Strengthening . . . in daily Expectation of a Reinforcement." As days passed, the garrison grew stronger, especially when cannon were brought in from the sloops. And Saltonstall's indecisiveness grew more perplexing.[16]

Near dawn, on the twenty-eighth, under cover of naval bombardment, a combined American force—over four hundred militia and two hundred marines—stormed ashore on Dyce's Head, the island's rocky southwest extremity. Landing below the steep precipice, daringly, they grappled up the rock-strewn, brush-covered hillside to the heights. They gained control of the entire west side, including a small battery. If Lovell had followed up with an assault on the "Grand

Fort," McLean would have surrendered; instead, the Americans dug in and strengthened their siege line. Cannon were hauled ashore, and a battery was erected one-quarter mile from the fort.[17]

The siege became a stand-off. Each side exchanged cannon fire, sent out sorties, and occasionally skirmished. On August 1, at 2:00 A.M., a combined force of three hundred militia, sailors, and marines assailed the enemy's half-moon battery, which commanded the harbor. They stormed the picket, but reinforcements from the fort drove them back. Among the casualties was Newburyporter Lt. William Dennis of the *Vengeance*, commander of the naval contingent. General Lovell wrote to Jeremiah Powell, president of the Council, requesting "a few regular disciplined troops" and additional munitions. To take the fort by storm, with the present raw troops, he wrote, would be impossible; the only choice was a lengthy siege.[18]

Councils of war—between Lovell and his field officers and Saltonstall and his naval commanders—became almost daily occurrences. Lovell, while eager to attack, wanted Saltonstall to enter the harbor first and destroy the sloops-of-war. With the garrison deprived of naval protection, land forces would launch a frontal assault. Otherwise, Lovell deemed the troops incapable of the task. Conversely, Saltonstall and most of his captains refused to sail their fleet into the harbor until Lovell had stormed the fort.

With precious days fleeting, Lovell became increasingly annoyed. Assuring his "ardent desire to co-operate," on August 11 he posed two options to the commodore: "The alternative now remains," he said, "to destroy the ships, or raise the siege." Morale was low, desertions were rising, and British naval reinforcements were expected. Some privateer commanders were apprehensive; there was talk of leaving. Lovell, though, could not employ his dispirited, poorly trained militia until Saltonstall eliminated Mowat. On August 12, an increasingly impatient Council in Boston urged Lovell to move. Similarly, the Navy Board wrote Saltonstall: "We think it your Duty to Direct you to attack & take or Destroy them without Delay."[19]

Friday, August 13, a council of war voted 14–10 in favor of continuing the siege. Saltonstall, Colonels Revere and McCobb, of Maine, and most privateer captains wanted to abandon Penobscot, but Lovell, other army officers, and six naval commanders voted continuation.[20]

They finally agreed that, upon a favorable tide late in the day, they should make a coordinated attack. At noontime, the five ships leading—with the *General Putnam* headmost—came to anchor in line at the harbor entrance. While they awaited high tide, Mowat readied. A condition to Saltonstall's thrust was that Lovell should march nearly half his army, four hundred men, to a position behind the fort. Once he held the ground between McLean and Mowat, cutting their contact, he sent word. This was the cue for Saltonstall.

About two o'clock, cruising near the harbor entrance on picket, the *Active* and *Diligent* spotted a cluster of unknown sail standing into the bay. Capt. Philip Brown on board the *Diligent* broke off to warn Saltonstall; Capt. Allen Hallet of the *Active* continued watch.

In late afternoon, with flood tide, the attack commenced. As American warships proceeded, the *Diligent* relayed the unsettling news of the approaching sail. Saltonstall ordered a halt, and the American vessels dropped anchor. When Lovell was notified, his force fell back.

Closing to four miles, Hallet confirmed seven enemy sails, then bore away to deliver the grave word. (In an August 4 letter to the Massachusetts Council, Washington had warned that an enemy fleet was headed north, possibly toward Penobscot.) The oncoming enemy vessels were led by the sixty-four-gun *Raisonnable*, under command of Sir George Collier. The heavily armed squadron carried more than 200 guns and 1,500 men. Only the *Warren* could boast 12- and 18-pound carriage guns; the rest of the American fleet—*Hector*, *Putnam*, and *Vengeance*—had 9-pounders; others, light sixes.

Ignoble Retreat

About midnight, with the ships identified, Lovell ordered the peninsula evacuated. By eight o'clock next morning—an amazingly short time—the army, ammunition, and supplies were all aboard the transports headed toward the Penobscot River. After sailing only two leagues, they becalmed, facing an ebb tide. They anchored to await more favorable conditions.

Formed into a huge crescent, Saltonstall's armed vessels readied to fend off His Majesty's ships, which were moving menacingly up the bay. American transports thus would be given vital time to seek refuge upriver, where the waters narrowed, and large enemy craft could be held at bay. About noon, however, Saltonstall suddenly turned about-face, called off his defense, and signaled the commanders to shift for themselves. A southward breeze had picked up, helping the oncoming enemy to narrow the gap. As the fresh winds rolled up the bay, the American warships made sail.

The defenseless transports, towed by rowboats and proceeding slowly upriver, were last to catch the draft. As crews looked aft, a horrifying spectacle confronted them: armed vessels, their supposed protectors, coming up crowded with sail. Three British ships were chasing close to their sterns. Lovell, who had counted on Saltonstall, watched aghast as the armed American craft, rigged with larger sails, fled past. By sunset, bucking the downrushing tide, the troop carriers made little headway. Four got beyond Odom's Ledge, where the river

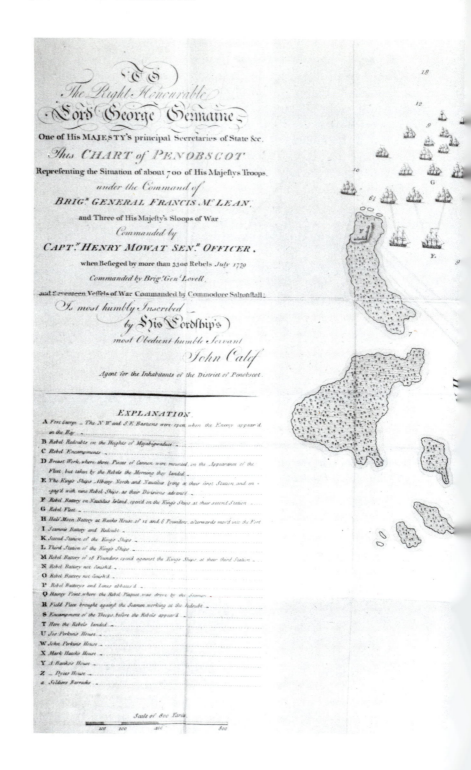

To

The Right Honourable

Lord George Germaine

One of His MAJESTY'S principal Secretaries of State &c.

This CHART *of* PENOBSCOT

Reprefenting the Situation of about 700 of His Majeftys Troops,

under the Command of

BRIG. GENERAL FRANCIS Mc LEAN,

and Three of His Majefty's Sloops of War

Commanded by

CAPT. HENRY MOWAT SEN. OFFICER,

when Befieged by more than 3300 Rebels *July 1779*

Commanded by Brig. Gen. Lovell,

and Seventeen Veffels of War Commanded by Commodore Saltonftall.

Is moſt humbly Inſcribed

by His Lordſhip's

moſt Obedient humble Servant

John Calef

Agent for the Inhabitants of the Diſtrict of Penobscot.

EXPLANATION.

A *Fort George – The N.W and S.E Baſtions were open when the Enemy appear'd in the Bay*

B *Rebel Redoubts on the Heights of Majabigwaduce*

C *Rebel Encampments*

D *Breaſt Work, where three Pieces of Cannon were mounted, on the Appearance of the Fleet, but taken by the Rebels the Morning they landed*

E *The Kings Ships Albany North and Nautilus lying at their firſt Station, and engag'd with nine Rebel Ships, as their Diviſions advanc'd*

F *Rebel Battery on Nautilus Iſland, open'd on the Kings Ships at their ſecond Station*

G *Rebel Fleet*

H *Half-Moon Battery at Banks Houſe of 12 and 8 Pounders, afterwards mov'd into the Fort*

I *Seamens Battery and Redoubt*

K *Second Station of the Kings Ships*

L *Third Station of the Kings Ships*

M *Rebel Battery of 18 Pounders erected againſt the Kings Ships at their third Station*

N *Rebel Battery not finiſh'd*

O *Rebel Battery not finiſh'd*

P *Rebel Batterys and Lines abbatis'd*

Q *Haney Point where the Rebel Piquet was drove by the Seamen*

R *Field Piece brought againſt the Seamen working at the Redoubt*

S *Encampment of the Troops before the Rebels appear'd*

T *Here the Rebels landed*

U *Joe Perkins Houſe*

W *John Perkins Houſe*

X *Mark Hawks Houſe*

Y *A Banks's Houſe*

Z *Dyces Houſe*

a *Soldiers Barracks*

Scale of 800 Yards.
100   200   400   800

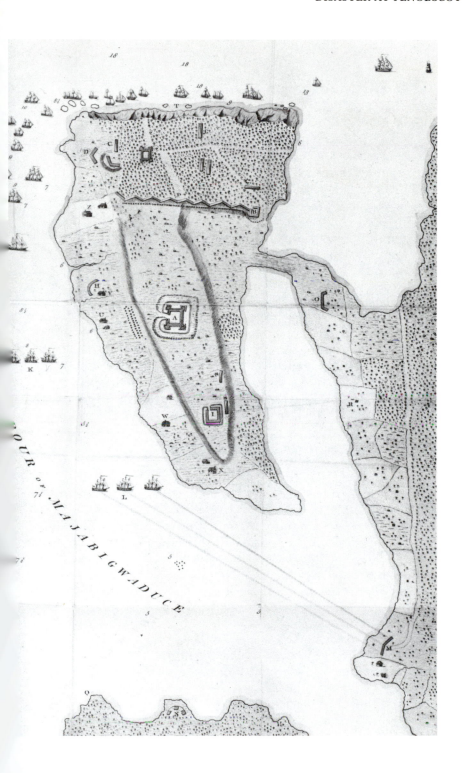

narrowed. Three had been swept down and fell in enemy hands. For the rest, seizure seemed imminent. The enemy lay nearly abreast. With no option, the transports were grounded; after troops and crew had splashed ashore, they set the transports afire to prevent the enemy from taking them.

Three privateers, however, had taken alternate courses. The brigantine *Defence* of Beverly ran into a nearby inlet on the western side of the bay, beached, and was set afire. The *Hunter* and the *Hampden* tried to escape via a passage between Long Island (now Isleborough) and Belfast, but were headed off. The *Hampden*, sails torn after clashing with the thirty-two-gun *Blonde*, was surrendered. The twenty-gun *Hunter* of Salem was run up "all standing." Her crew escaped, but the enemy freed the privateer on a rising tide.[21]

The rest of the American fleet navigated up the Penobscot toward a point where the river narrowed to less than one hundred yards. Furthest back was the *Sky Rocket* of Newburyport. Sensing no chance of escape, Capt. William Burke put ashore at Fort Point Ledge on the west side. That evening, after the crew disembarked, the *Sky Rocket* was fired. Shortly, three more warships were burned; when flames hit their magazines, the bellowing explosions were deafening. Others, including the *Hector, Black Prince,* and *Monmouth,* traveled upstream, several nearly twenty miles to the falls near Bangor. In the late evening of August 14, a sickened Lovell reported seeing

> four Ships pursuing seventeen Sail of Armed Vessells nine of which we[re] stout Ships, Transports on fire, Men of War blowing up, Provision of all kinds, & every kind of Stores on Shore . . . and as much confusion as can possibly be conceived.[22]

During the night, troops and crews scattered into the woods; the following day, most were nowhere to be found.

On Sunday morning, August 15, Lovell traveled down the Penobscot to gather those forces still in the vicinity, to make a stand further upstream. He found Commodore Saltonstall on the *Warren* seven miles from the river mouth. The pitiable flagship was towed several miles further upriver. Then, intending to burn the *Warren*, Saltonstall began to disembark his 220 men. Lovell persuaded Saltonstall to hold off. The army general, however, was having trouble maintaining his command. Earlier, he had unsuccessfully commanded Colonel Revere to erect a battery near the falls. The silversmith, who, during the siege had appeared preoccupied with his personal comfort, chose instead to start for home. By nightfall, nevertheless, seven ships had reached the head.

Lamentably, there would be no final defense. Downriver, at about 4:00 A.M., two officers stood on the deck of the scuttled *Vengeance*, already abandoned by 130 crew. They were preparing to ignite the Newburyport vessel. Four hours later, near the falls, Captain Brown of the Continental brig *Diligent* gazed in dismay as sheets of fire devoured the Salem ships *Hector* and *Black Prince*. The blaze jumped to the nearby *Monmouth* of Newburyport. Then a fourth and a fifth vessel burst in flames. The end was near. Downriver, the *Warren* lay charred and smoldering, while her fainthearted commodore hiked home through the woods. As Capt. Hallet of the brig *Active* testified on September 25:

> On the 16 Inst. Nine A.M. recd Intelligence that the *Warren, Vengeance, Putnam & Sky Rocket* were Consumed, the Militia Scattered the Private arm'd Ships around us on Fire, I landed my men in Company with Capts Hacker Williams, Cathcart, Brown & Holmes and with them Committed my Vessell to the Flames.[23]

The *Pallas* of Newburyport was the only armed vessel not captured or destroyed. Since Capt. James Johnson, a Maine native, had been sent to patrol along the coast, the *Pallas* probably was out of the bay.

Tattered and poorly supplied, the retreating Americans made their way through the wilderness southwesterly toward the settlements along the Kennebec. The schooner *Shark*, sent out of Newburyport and commanded by David Coates, put in at Falmouth loaded with relief provisions: beef, bread, coffee, pork, rum, and sugar, for the weary survivors.[24]

Earlier, Gen. Horatio Gates had heeded an August 8 appeal for reinforcements and released Michael Jackson's 8th Continental Regiment at Newport. The relief expedition that was assembling at Nantasket Road needed escorts. The Massachusetts Council asked committee of correspondence member John Gerry to send the 180-ton, twelve-gun privateer *Terrible*, which was lying in Marblehead harbor. Transports were "ready & waiting," but no *Terrible* arrived. On August 14, the chronicler Ashley Bowen noted: "The brig *Terrible* bent her sails but could not get her men together &c." Gerry explained that "certain disaffected people" had dissuaded the crew from sailing. The Council nonetheless ordered her out; on August 17, the *Terrible* left port with a scanty crew. Next day, Jackson's regiment was Penobscot-bound, with the transports warily hugging the shore escorted by brigs *Renown* and *Terrible*. The relief flotilla was to be provisioned by Capt. Samuel Laha of the six-gun *Hannah*. Off the Isle of Shoals on August 19, Captain Spooner overtook them in a whaleboat sent out by Newburyport's committee of safety with news of the disaster. Ashley Bowen of Marblehead heard the news on the same day, noting: "worse and worse from Penobscot. The Devil to pay! The Devil to pay!" Earlier, on August 8, the Council had despatched couriers to Marblehead, Newburyport, and Salem, urging enlistments. Two days later, Salem voters offered sixty-pound bounties to each enlistee mustered by Major Joseph Hiller. Regrettably, however, the opportunity to stave off defeat had passed.[25]

Investigation

The disaster triggered "universal uneasiness." On August 16, Marbleheaders, already concerned over the "alarming movements of the Enemy," voted that seven persons should oversee repair and refurbishing of three forts: "Great Fort," Bartol's Head, and Twisden's Hill. Fear mixed with public outrage. "Never was ye popular cry raised higher against Commanders, than against Lovel & Saltonstall," wrote Rev. Manasseh Cutler of Ipswich to Rev. Enos Hitchcock.[26]

On September 9, the General Court appointed an investigatory committee: five Board of War members and four others, chaired by Gen. Artemas Ward. Four seats were held by Essex County legislators who held high ranks in the militia: Maj. Gen. Michael Farley of Ipswich, Col. Moses Little of Newbury, Maj. Samuel Osgood of Andover, and Brig. Gen. Jonathan Titcomb of Newburyport. Testimony was heard from more than thirty army and navy men. Saltonstall argued that he was exempted by his Continental rank. Though Lovell was not faultless, his fellow legislators exonerated both him and his second in command, Wadsworth. "Each and every" naval commander in state service, reported the committee, was found to have "behaved like brave experienced good officers." The principle reason for failure, they wrote, was Saltonstall's "Want of proper Spirit & Energy." Destruction of the fleet was due to his "not exerting himself at all" to oppose the enemy during retreat. Saltonstall faced a United States court-martial and was cashiered from the Continental Navy. The expedition's late start out of Nantasket and "deficient" numbers of troops were cited as contributing factors. Nonetheless, the primary blame was placed squarely on Saltonstall's conduct.[27]

Capt. Thomas J. Carnes, marine commandant on the *Putnam*, was among several who criticized Paul Revere's conduct. Carnes lodged a formal complaint charging the lieutenant colonel with disobedience, neglect of duty, and unsoldierlike behavior. Revere was censured for his actions, but he protested and demanded a court-martial from the General Court. Finally, Gov. John Hancock interceded; a court-martial was held which cleared Revere of any wrongdoing.

For twenty-one days, a small garrison and three sloops-of-war had held off a powerful invasion force. The disaster was a tremendous blow to Massachusetts pride and resulted in great human and monetary losses. On August 21, Ashley Bowen reported a small schooner arriving home with thirty "escaped" Marbleheaders. Weeks passed, however, before many soldiers and sailors, by boat and on foot—barefoot, bloodstained, and exhausted—reached home. No accounting ever has been made of those lost along the way. With the treasury empty, it would be years before private losses, which exceeded one million pounds, would be compensated—a heavy burden for the mercantile shareholders of Beverly, Newburyport, and Salem. A saddened George Williams wrote to his brother-in-law Timothy Pickering, Jr.: "All most every body Laments the Loss of Interest, and more so the Loss of the hour when thay might have Took the enemy. Allso The great disgrace which Layes on the Massachusetts."[28]

It was tragic. An expedition so popular and so likely to succeed had ended in abject failure. The British continued to occupy Bagaduce until December 1783, after the Treaty of Paris. Years afterward, bitter debate continued to rage among survivors of land and naval forces over the humiliating retreat at Penobscot.

1. George Williams, "Revolutionary Letters Written to Colonel Timothy Pickering," *EIHC*, 64 (1908):313.
2. MA Archives, 185:225–27; Eben F. Stone, "Newburyport in the Penobscot Expedition," *Newburyport Daily Herald*, January 9, 1879.
3. *Acts and Resolves*, 21:90–91; *Journal of the House*, (Boston: House of Representatives, 1779), 61.
4. *Acts and Resolves*, 21:100; MA Archives, 151:296.
5. *Acts and Resolves*, 21:91; Philip Chadwick Foster Smith, ed., *The Journals of Ashley Bowen of Marblehead* (Salem: Peabody Museum, 1973), 2:536.
6. Council Records, MA Archives, 24:9; Penobscot Expedition, MA Archives, 37:208; MA Archives, 145:8.
7. Council Records, 24:10; Penobscot Expedition, 37:178, 194; MA Archives, 151:295; *Acts and Resolves*, 21:93.
8. Penobscot Expedition, 37:224.
9. Newburyport Town Records, July 6, 1779, 1:317; Stone; James Thacher, *Military Journal of the American Revolution* (Hartford, Conn.: Hurlburt, Williams, 1862)), 170; Council Records, 24:8.
10. Council Records, 23:397, 24:12, 27; MA Archives, 37:231, 240, 244; *Acts and Resolves*, 5:1255; 21:101.
11. Williams, 315; Smith, 2:537.
12. Council Records, 24:11, 35, 36; Penobscot Expedition, 37:177, 193, 242; MA Archives, 145:33–34.
13. Williams, 313; Smith, 2:538–39; MA Archives, 145:207; *Acts and Resolves*, 21:104–05; "The Heath Papers," MHS *Collections*, 7th Series, 4 (1904):319.
14. Penobscot Expedition, 37:186, 280; "Heath Papers," 310–11; [John Calef], *The Siege of Penobscot by the Rebels* (London: 1781), 25; Smith, 2:538.
15. Octavius Thorndike Howe, *Beverly Privateers in the American Revolution* (Cambridge: John Wilson, 1922), 347–48, 407.
16. Calef, 8–9; MA Archives, 145:50–51.
17. Letter of Solomon Lovell to Jeremiah Powell, July 28, 1779, Boston Athenaeum; Calef, 8.
18. Calef, 12–14; "Operations in Maine in 1779," *The Historical Magazine*, 8 (1864):52–53; "The Heath Papers," 322; MA Archives, 145:63.
19. George Augustus Wheeler, *History of Castine* (Bangor: Burr & Robinson, 1875), 310–11; MA Archives, 145:95, 98–98a.
20. 145:107–09.
21. Calef, 22–23.
22. "The Original Journal of General Solomon Lovell," [No. 1.] (Weymouth Historical Society: 1881), 105.
23. MA Archives, 145:209, 245.
24. Stone.
25. MA Archives, 145:87, 110, 132, 139, 420, 423; Council Records, 24:128; Smith, 2:541; Thacher, 171–72; Salem Town Records, EI, August, 10, 1779, 5:333–34.
26. Marblehead Town Records, EI, 4:646, 652, 653; Manasseh Cutler to Enos Hitchcock, September 20, 1779, ALS, EI.
27. *Acts and Resolves*, 21:125; *Boston Gazette*, December 27, 1779; also, "Proceedings of the General Assembly and of the Council Relating to the Penobscot Expedition," (Boston: General Assembly, 1780), 28.
28. Smith, 2:541; Williams, 317–18.

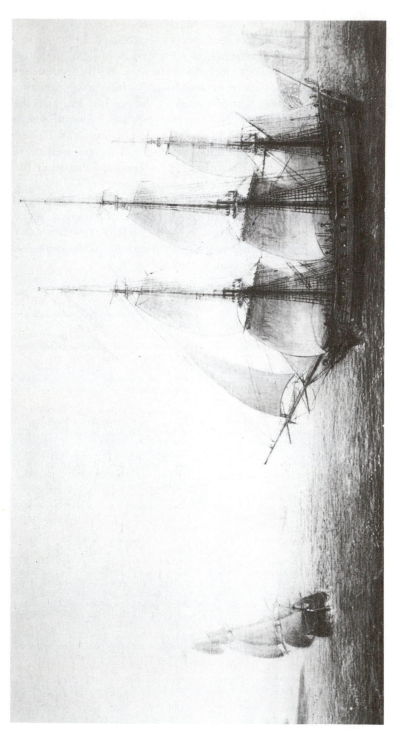

The frigate U.S.S. *Alliance*, built at the Hackett shipyard on Salisbury Point, was the American Navy's fastest sailing warship. Courtesy, Peabody Museum of Salem.

CHAPTER TWENTY - ONE

ESSEX AT SEA:
THE TIDE OF VICTORY

"Titus Cabot, Mrs. Cabot's negro, has made more profits as agent for privateersmen than Ansil Alcock or Dr. Whitaker," scoffed William Pynchon, Salem's Loyalist attorney on August 13, 1781. "[He] wears cloth shoes, ruffled shirts, silk breeches and stockings." Indeed, 1781 was a banner year. Prizes were streaming into port; the fortunes of almost anyone touched by privateering seemed to be waxing on the prodigious returns.[1]

About two months after Pynchon's observations, Cornwallis surrendered; shortly afterwards, America's seemingly interminable ground war was over. But the extended conflict at sea continued and intensified until Congress proclaimed hostilities ended on April 11, 1783. Essex County's naval contribution—to shipbuilding, Continental and state service, and especially privateering—was unmatched.

During the war, particularly in later years, county energies were concentrated at sea. Local seafarers manned Continental and state vessels, trimming sails to orders lustily bellowed from quarterdecks by the likes of Essex County commanders Henry Lunt, John Manley, and Samuel Tucker. Thousands of others chose the more pleasing and potentially lucrative life aboard an Essex County privateer. Privateering became so alluring it handicapped efforts to keep the Continental Navy at sea. A correspondent writing to John Adams from Boston on December 17, 1778, complained: "The infamous practice of seducing our Men to leave their ships . . will make it impossible ever to get our ships ready to Sail in force, or perhaps otherwise than single Ships."[2]

The Continental Navy

In January of 1779, most of the surviving Continental naval vessels—six warships—were at Boston: the *Alliance, Boston, Deane, Providence, Queen of France,* and *Warren.* Thanks to privateering, most were lacking in crews; only the *Deane* was ready for sea. Two—the *Boston* and *Alliance*—were Essex County vessels.

The twenty-four-gun *Boston* had been built in Newburyport during 1777 by Stephen and Ralph Cross. The next year she had transported John Adams to France, to become one of three American commissioners there. Her skipper, ruddy-faced, heavy-set Samuel Tucker, a feisty Marbleheader whose wartime experience began as captain in Washington's navy, returned in October richer by several prizes captured off France and on the homeward passage. On April 13, 1779, he was once again at sea, steering a Down East course.[3]

Newest of the vessels was the *Alliance*; in April 1778 she had cleared the Merrimack and come around to Boston. Rated as carrying thirty-six guns, but usually toting forty, she measured 151 feet on the lower deck and boasted a 36-foot beam. Built at the Hackett boat yard on Salisbury Point by shipwrights William Hackett and his cousin John, and fitted out in Newburyport, this sleek Continental frigate was reputed to be the navy's fastest sailing warship, once reported to have cruised at fifteen knots when the wind cooperated.[4]

European Waters

One vessel not in Boston was the eighteen-gun *Ranger*. Earlier, in November 1777, John Paul Jones had left Portsmouth and steered the newly built Hackett sloop across the Atlantic. On April 10, 1778, the bantam Scotsman sailed from Brest, standing toward Whitehaven and intent on torching all ships in the English seaport. The raid caused minimal damage but struck panic along the coast, which elicited the deploying of several men-of-war. On April 24, after a one-hour engagement that Jones described as "warm, close, and obstinate," the large sloop-of-war, twenty-gun *Drake*, was captured. Her sails and rigging shot away, the first British warship taken in European waters was towed toward Brest with two hundred prisoners holed below deck.[5]

These captives would become Franklin's ransom. For some time, the colorful American commissioner in France had been working to free Americans held in English prisons. In March 1779, thanks to Franklin's negotiations, ninety-seven Americans were released from Old Mill prison near Plymouth to a cartel—a vessel sent to bring out prisoners, usually after a negotiated exchange—sailing for Nantes, the first prisoner transfer of its kind.

In mid-January of 1779, the *Alliance* left Boston on her maiden cruise, sailing for Lorient, France, under the erratic French captain Pierre Landais. There she joined a squadron headed by John Paul Jones, who was commanding a former East Indiaman purchased by the French government. He had rechristened the ship *Bonhomme Richard* in honor of Benjamin Franklin and his *Poor Richard's Almanack*. They were accompanied by three French vessels flying American colors.

Twelve Newburyporters shipped aboard the *Alliance*; five crewed among *Bonhomme Richard*'s hodgepodge of nationalities, all signed on for a year. They had arrived on the first cartel from Old Mill, having been aboard the captured home-town brig *Dalton* in December 1776. Committed to prison, they had languished until the exchange.[6]

Jones's squadron got under way August 14, 1779, headed toward the British Isles on what was to become an historic cruise. Two Newburyport "Mill-mates" officered on the *Alliance*: Second Lieutenant Henry Lunt and Third Lieutenant Cutting Lunt. Among the crew who had sailed from Boston were John Carrisco of Beverly and Francis Perkins and Jonathan Wells of Ipswich.[7]

On September 23, off Flamborough Head on England's east coast, the *Richard* tangled with the new forty-five-gun British frigate *Serapis*. At dusk a battle raged "with unremitting fury," Jones reported: "Every method was practised on both sides to gain an advantage, and rake each other."[8] Tenaciously, Jones closed in. The *Richard*, leaking badly, with most cannon silenced and fires on the lower deck—with Jonathan Wells standing fast amid the dead and Francis Perkins mortally wounded—had grappled hold of the *Serapis* and fought on.[9] In the midst of battle, after nine o'clock, the *Alliance* suddenly appeared out of the moonlit darkness; unexplainedly, a broadside was fired, then another, not at the enemy, but into the *Richard*! Jones believed Landais's actions were deliberate; later, he would bring charges.

Having suffered heavy casualties, many to musketry fired from *Richard*'s tops, and on fire after a deadly, searing grenade explosion, the *Serapis* struck her colors. Another vessel in the squadron took the sloop-of-war *Countess of Scarborough*. Two days later, despite Jones's efforts, the battered *Bonhomme Richard* went to the bottom. The intrepid captain took command of the *Serapis* and headed east toward Holland. Jones's victory, which brought him immortal fame and glory, was joyous news in what was otherwise a dismal year.

A Shrinking Navy

By mid-1780, the Continental Navy had lost its punch. Three of the fleet had been burned during the humiliating retreat at Penobscot: the brig *Diligent*, the sloop *Providence*, the ship *Warren*. Four more went at Charleston: the frigates *Boston*, *Providence*, *Queen of France*, and the sloop *Ranger*. Only five ships remained, one of which was the *Alliance*.

The Salisbury-built frigate had been made Jones's flagship, with Henry Lunt as first lieutenant. By July of 1780, however, commands changed, and she embarked for America under her old commander, the quarrelsome Frenchman Pierre Landais. During the crossing, he became so unstable—endangering everyone aboard—that he was forcibly relieved of command. After the *Alliance* stood in to Boston on August 19, the experienced Philadelphian, Capt. John Barry, was appointed commander.[10]

In February 1781, the *Alliance* left for Lorient. So short was she of able hands that British prisoners at Boston had to be enlisted. Among the passengers was Washington's aide, Colonel Laurens, traveling on a special mission for French assistance. Shortly after reaching France, the *Alliance* returned with military supplies. John Gill's *Continental Journal* of Boston reported that when Captain Barry was homeward-bound off Cape Sable on May 21, two sloops-of-war "belonging to George the Tyrant," the *Atalanta* and *Trepassey*, headed toward him. The wind had died, leaving Barry a sitting target. The lighter enemy sloops used their sweeps (long oars) to maneuver astern; safe from most guns, they mercilessly raked the frigate with grapeshot. Suddenly a fortuitous light breeze puffed up *Alliance*'s sails; she brought her broadsides to bear, and after a few blasts both sloops struck. On June 6, the victorious *Alliance* entered Boston.[11]

Jones returned to America early in 1781 to assume command of the seventy-four-gun *America* under construction at Portsmouth. When in August he went to oversee construction, Jones found the navy's largest warship only partly completed. The builder was James K. Hackett; his cousin, William, was master shipwright. The keel had been laid in mid-1777, but inadequate funding and scarce materials, combined with the challenge of constructing so large a vessel, had slowed work. Jones never got his command. In September 1782, lacking resources to outfit her, Congress presented the ship to France.[12]

In May 1781, the Bay State's twenty-gun *Protector* was lost, captured by His Majesty's Ship *Roebuck* and the frigate *Medea*. She was the Massachusetts navy's finest warship. Constructed by Jonathan Greenleaf and Stephen and Ralph Cross, the frigate was launched in mid-

1779 from the Cross shipyard below King [Federal] Street in New-buryport. She had been in active service less than a year.[13]

By September, the Continental Navy had been nearly dissolved. Only two frigates remained: *Alliance* and *Deane*. The two vessels lay idle in Boston, unable to recruit crews. Finally, while the *Deane* stayed in port, the *Alliance* left on a cruise. That year a frigate purchased from France and recapture of the *General Washington* increased the Continental fleet to four.

On September 26, 1782, after Silas Deane—America's diplomat in France—had been suspected of treason, of profiteering and double-dealing, the frigate that was his namesake was renamed the *Hague*. The renowned Marbleheader Capt. John Manley, who had been released in an exchange after two years in Old Mill prison, was put in command. Shortly he sailed south for the West Indies, where he took several prizes. In January 1783, chased by the large enemy frigate *Dolphin* off Guadeloupe, Manley ran between two reefs and grounded. Three more British warships arrived and for two days joined in cannonading the immobile *Hague*. Finally, Manley freed the vessel: "A Continental salute was fired as the topsails were sheeting home, in defiance." The French governor of Guadeloupe had high praise for Manley's conduct:

> It is with the greatest pleasure I heard of your good conduct, courage and bravery, that you showed in defending a frigate trusted to your care. You have perfectly fulfilled the duty of a brave officer, and it is with the utmost satisfaction that I pay the tribute to your valour.[14]

Honors for parting shots, however, belong to the Salisbury-built *Alliance*. Sailing off Florida on March 10, 1783, Captain Barry closed in to engage the British frigate *Sybil*; within pistol range, he let loose his cannon and sent her sheering off wounded with tattered sails and rigging . . . the last engagement by a Continental warship in the War of Independence.[15]

While the Continental Navy never threatened British control of the seas, some excellent vessels nonetheless flew the United States ensign. They included the *Alliance*, *Boston*, and *Hancock*, all constructed along the Merrimack. Essex County contributed hundreds of able-bodied seamen and dozens of Continental and state officers; most famous were Jonathan Haraden, John Manley, and Samuel Tucker. Though successes against His Majesty's ships were few, the Navy impeded delivery of enemy supplies by capturing nearly two hundred British merchantmen. The undersized Continental fleet—proudly helping keep independence alive—recorded the first chapter in the lustrous annals of the United States Navy.

Essex Privateering

The war years saw growing numbers of privateers and letters of marque cruising the Atlantic, particularly after French and Spanish ports opened. Massachusetts commissions nearly doubled between 1777 (with 98) and 1781 (with 174). Licensed to take enemy shipping, private vessels crowded Britain's sea lanes, where a lush, steady traffic of merchantmen presented opportunities for immense profits. England needed not only to maintain its normal trade but to keep supplies flowing unimpeded to His Majesty's forces overseas. Consequently, British warships expended valuable energies escorting merchantmen rather than engaging in offensive operations. Also, Britain stepped up its patrols in the Caribbean and on the North American station. The enemy also had its pod of privately owned commerce raiders preying on cargo-laden American, French, Spanish, and—later—Dutch merchantmen. Thus, rising numbers of Yankee armed vessels faced a galaxy of adversaries, both Royal Navy vessels and British privateers, including over one hundred based at New York.

To insure greater protection, American privateersmen used fewer sloops and schooners and started building larger, faster vessels fitted out more heavily. They were looking for booty, not a fight, but needed to improve their odds in case of a stand-off. During 1779, for example, the naval district of Beverly, Danvers, and Salem sent

An early model of a Revolutionary War brig. During the later years, privateersmen relied increasingly on more formidable brigs and brigantines than on the lighter sloops and schooners. Courtesy, Peabody Museum of Salem.

out at least fifty-five different vessels; on the average, they carried more guns and crew than in 1778. Thirty-four—more than twice the previous year's number—were brigantines, brigs, and ships. By 1780, the fleet, which exceeded sixty sail, counted forty-two of the larger classes.[16]

Many Essex privateers hunted the fertile Gulf of St. Lawrence, which teemed with fishing and trading vessels that trafficked particularly with Halifax, Quebec, and St. Johns. Sometimes, they tracked their quarry in "wolf pack" or squadron-style. In July 1780, eight Salem privateers prowling "on the Newfound Land Station" for the Quebec fleet took about fourteen prizes loaded mostly with dried fish, madeira, molasses, and salt. The ship *America*, reportedly Newburyport-owned and under the command of John Somes of Gloucester, captured three more vessels. Off Cape Breton, the Gloucester ship *General Starks* took another three carrying valuable cargoes: assorted dry goods, iron and steel, madeira, rum, sugar. That summer, Essex privateers made lucrative scoops seldom matched during the war.[17]

On her next cruise, the Cape Ann–owned *General Starks* met with misfortune; she was captured by the ship *Chatham* and brought into Halifax. The 400-ton vessel, owned primarily by David Pearce, a major Gloucester merchant, had been built specifically for privateering. She carried 135 men and boys, mostly from Cape Ann environs, and sported eighteen guns. Although her two initial cruises in 1778 had met with little success, she embarked for a third try on April 5, 1779 under Capt. William Coas. This time, after ten days cruising "to the eastward," the ship took a brig from Limerick laden with beef, pork, and butter—a welcome arrival in hungry Gloucester. Before the cruise ended, on September 15, eight more enemy fell, including an eight-gun "Guernsey privateer" schooner which had been prowling around the Spanish coast and menacing Bilbao Bay. (Bilbao officials had offered Coas one thousand dollars to take the menacing warship.) One prize, a fish brig out of Newfoundland bound for Lisbon, showed fourteen guns, though ten were "Quakers," dummy wooden guns to fool attackers. The next two cruises, under James Pearson, were uneventful, but followed by the productive mid-1780 venture to the fog-shrouded Gulf of St. Lawrence. The *General Starks*'s ventures proved to be the most fruitful of all Cape Ann privateers.[18]

Overseas waters became a popular hunting ground. Ships based in France or Spain would seek their prey upon Continental waves, as well as around the British Isles. Early in 1779, the Cabot-owned, eighteen-gun 200-ton *Pilgrim*, commanded by Irish-born Hugh Hill, glided along the Emerald Isle, English Channel, and Bay of Biscay.

Gloucester-born Capt. Jonathan Haraden (1744–1803), who commanded the *General Pickering* of Salem, and, later, the ship *Julius Caesar*, went on to seize enemy warships carrying a total of a thousand guns. Courtesy, Peabody Museum of Salem.

In six weeks, Hill took eight prizes; on the entire cruise, more than twenty. One, the *Success*, a letter of marque brig carrying eighteen guns and thirty men, struck after a brisk fight in which most of her officers were killed or wounded. On March 24, when Hill resigned to command the *Cicero*, Joseph Robinson of Salem took the helm of the *Pilgrim* and continued to pile up impressive successes.[19]

Letters of marque set their course on trade; privateering was incidental. Staple goods as well as luxury items made scarce by dislocation of peacetime trade could bring huge profits at home. The ship-rigged *General Pickering*, commanded by Gloucester-born Capt. Jonathan Haraden, reached Salem in April 1780 chock full of West Indies cocoa, coffee, cotton, rum, and sugar, causing the Salem merchant George Williams to note with satisfaction, "a much better Cruise than priverteering."[20]

On May 1, the eighteen-gun *Pickering*, carrying forty-five men, set out with sugar for Bilbao. At dusk, outside the Bay of Biscay, Capt. Haraden, who had been schooled in fighting aboard the Massachusetts *Tyrannicide*, spotted a more heavily gunned British privateer, the *Golden Eagle*. During the night, the mild-mannered Salem master came alongside; using bravado and bluff, he pretended to be sailing a larger vessel and boldly persuaded the British skipper to surrender. Next day, standing toward Bilbao, Haraden spotted a "large lugger," the forty-two gun *Achilles*, beside which the Salem vessel seemed "little larger than a long boat." A sea fight followed in which Haraden respectfully kept his distance. Low on ammunition, the resolute commander fired a broadside of crowbars, which tattered *Achilles'* sails and chased her out to sea. The spectacle was enjoyed by many thousands of cheering Bilbaoans lined up along the shore. They greeted Haraden as a hero, carried him triumphantly through the streets at the head of a parade, and dined him festively. Described in Boston's *Continental Journal* as a "man of undaunted courage," Haraden returned to Salem in September with three prize brigantines loaded with dry fish. "Capt. Harraden's name rings all over Spain & France for his Brave deffence of his ship," wrote Williams. The valiant Salem captain went on to compile an incredible war record: the seizure of enemy warships carrying a total of 1,000 guns.[21]

Another favorite privateer target was West Indies traffic, south to the Caribbean or along the rich trade routes linking the sugar islands with England or North America. Writing to Quartermaster General Timothy Pickering on October 24, 1780, George Williams reported extensive activity between Salem and the Indies: "Last night the Ship *Rodes* [*Rhodes*] arrive from a Cruise off of Charleston and she fell in with the sd ship *Brutus*. Thay Took 4 Jamaca Vessels . . . Ship *Pickering* Sailes in a few dayes on a voyage to West Indies . . . a small schooner gone to West Indies, a New Brig called the *Salem* . . . will go to Bilbao or West Indies, soone."[22]

In January 5, 1781, Caribbean waters provided the backdrop for a dramatic duel: Beverly's most famous privateer, the *Pilgrim*, captained by Joseph Robinson, versus the English ship, letter-of-marque *Mary*, with twenty-two guns, bound from Cork. For five hours, both "lay yard arm to yard arm," exchanging broadsides and musket fire; finally, the British letter of marque, after suffering twenty-two casualties and taking on three feet of water, lowered her colors. On course to port, British prisoners conspired to overwhelm the prize crew and retake the ship. When the plot was uncovered, the officers and crew were set adrift one hundred leagues west of Barbados in a long boat adequately fitted out to reach land. Between the time when he assumed command and war's end, Robinson sent twelve prizes into Beverly, and many others to France, Spain, and Martinique.[23]

The *Pilgrim* was manned by one hundred and forty mostly Scottish and Irish crew. This was not unusual. In the later war years, British deserters and captives were increasingly employed to man ships as there were not enough able-bodied American seamen to supply the growing privateer fleet. In America, people of many occupations, including artisans, shopkeepers, and yeomen, signed on to taste adventure and share in profits. With the dearth of experienced hands, they were welcomed.

In the Caribbean, as elsewhere, merchantmen sought mutual safety by sailing whenever possible in convoy escorted by privateersmen. On April 17, 1781, the *Salem Gazette* noted a fleet of eighty-eight merchantmen and privateers; fifty-six were bound for France, the others for American ports. Fourteen American merchant carriers also reportedly had left the Indies for Europe "under convoy of Capt. Hill, in an armed Ship [new Cabot-owned *Cicero*] belonging to Beverly." In a hostile open sea, there was strength in numbers.

On Balance

While Essex County's contributions to the Continental and state navies were noteworthy, its awesome, enthusiastic embrace of privateering was truly historic. It suited the speculative spirit of merchants and ship owners, who risked astronomical amounts that otherwise would not have been invested. Privateering was also more agreeable to the individualistic mariner whose temperament was incompatible with the discipline demanded of the Continental military. Once their army enlistments had expired, thousands of Essex men chose life aboard a privateer or letter of marque. Some, more impetuous, began sea life before their army duty was over. In June 1779, for instance, Continental frigates, privateers, and letters of marque in Boston harbor were ordered searched for deserters from Glover's brigade, who, it was rumored, were aboard. In addition to *Dalton* captives, an early-1779 count at Old Mill prison showed that more than 100 out of the total inmate population of about 250 hailed from Haverhill, Ipswich, Manchester, Marblehead, Newburyport, and Salem—a measure of Essex County privateering involvement. The government could not have raised through taxes and quotas what voluntary investment and initiative bestowed to independence.[24]

"Prizes daily come in," noted Salem attorney William Pynchon in August 1781. During the year, Newburyport and Salem newspapers reported a parade of captured enemy merchantmen arriving in port. Auction and sales notices for scores of prizes were published. Many people prospered, with the rich proceeds usually divided fifty-fifty between owners and ships' crews.[25]

Yet privateering was becoming more hazardous and costly. English merchant vessels began either to sail as well-armed letters of marque or to travel in escorted convoys. Easy pickings had dwindled. At the same time, scarcity of labor and materials multiplied expenses for outfitting privateers. Rising risks and costs, coupled with chances for fewer prizes, turned merchants increasingly to trade.

In January 1781, J. & A. Cabot was selling imports at Beverly and sending letters-of-marque ships *Rambler*—with sixteen 6-pounders and fifty men—and *Defence*—with sixteen 4-pounders and fifty men—to Bilbao. "Goods on Freight will be taken from hence and from thence to this Port," was advertised. During spring, the Tracys were readying ships *Minerva* and *Post-Packet* for "freight or passage" to

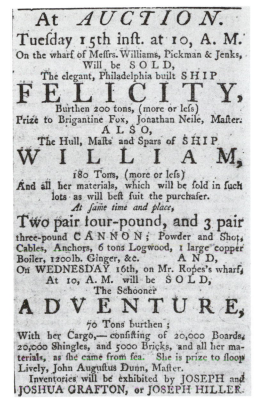

At *AUCTION.*

Tuesday 15th inst. at 10, A. M.
On the wharf of Messrs. Williams, Pickman & Jenks,
Will be SOLD,
The elegant, Philadelphia built SHIP
FELICITY,
Burthen 200 tons, (more or less)
Prize to Brigantine Fox, Jonathan Neile, Master.
ALSO,
The Hull, Masts and Spars of SHIP
WILLIAM,
180 Tons, (more or less)
And all her materials, which will be sold in such
lots as will best suit the purchaser.
At same time and place,
Two pair four-pound, and 3 pair
three-pound CANNON; Powder and Shot,
Cables, Anchors, 6 tons Logwood, 1 large copper
Boiler, 1200lb. Ginger, &c. AND,
On WEDNESDAY 16th, on Mr. Ropes's wharf,
At 10, A. M. will be SOLD,
The Schooner
ADVENTURE,
50 Tons burthen;
With her Cargo,—consisting of 20,000 Boards,
20,000 Shingles, and 5000 Bricks, and all her ma-
terials, as she came from sea. She is prize to sloop
Lively, John Augustus Dunn, Master.
Inventories will be exhibited by JOSEPH and
JOSHUA GRAFTON, or JOSEPH HILLER.

During 1781, a parade of prize vessels was brought into Essex County ports and auctioned. *Salem Gazette,* January 10, 1782. Courtesy, American Antiquarian Society.

Amsterdam and Bilbao. In April, a Derby sailer also traveled to Holland, while the twelve-gun *Salem Packet* prepared for Bilbao. Increased trade helped satisfy a home market, stimulated transatlantic traffic, and made for healthy profits.[26]

Again, reminiscent of prewar days, stores and warehouses were crammed with imported stock. Cargoes from scores of prize vessels brought into port and returning letters of marque made available an array of imports. Specie, introduced by privateering gains and by purchases of French forces stationed in Rhode Island, circulated in the ports. In November 1781, William Vans of Salem was advertising good raisins and Bilbao handkerchiefs. During February 1782, William Stearns offered imports galore from his Salem shop: raisins by the cask and jar, figs by the basket, currants and prunes by the cask, lemons and oranges by the box, spices, and many varieties of drugs and medicines. Moses Brown, who moved to Beverly in 1772, with his partner and brother-in-law, Israel Thorndike, were marketing at wholesale: broadcloth, baize, shalloons, napkins, sewing silk, linens, calicos, dimities, lutestrings, catgut, lace, and wine glasses. In stores

Late in the Revolution, successful letter-of-marque ventures could reap tremendous profits for the owners. *Continental Journal* of Boston, January 25, 1781. Boston Athenaeum.

of other merchants, including Appleton & Ropes, John Fisk, John Norris, and J. Ward, infusions from overseas burgeoned both wholesale and retail markets.[27]

The imports, however, came at a high price. Both letter of marque and privateer faced the heightened presence of armed vessels in enemy home waters, in the Caribbean, and along the North American coast. During 1781, Elias Hasket Derby alone lost six vessels: the brig *Flying Fish*; the schooner *Nancy*; ships *Commerce*, *Hersey*, *Oliver Cromwell*, *Rover*. At least fourteen other Essex County armed vessels were taken: the brigantines *Active*, *Defence*, *Dispatch*, *Fanny*, *Hero*, *New Adventure* of Beverly and/or Salem; the brigantine *Ranger* of Gloucester; the schooners *Rambler* of Newburyport, *Comet* of Salem; the sloop *Fish Hawk*, the snow *Diana*, of Beverly; the ships *Congress* of Salem, *Essex* of Beverly, and *General Starks* of Gloucester. In 1782, losses were higher still. Immense profits to be gained from successful cruises, however, seemingly continued to outweigh the risk of capture.[28]

Increased losses resulted in thousands of Essex County mariners wasting at Halifax, Quebec, and St. Johns prisons, and in England at Forton and Old Mill. Or worse, rotting aboard the dismantled sixty-four-gun prison ship *Jersey* or another dungeon hulk moored in Wallabout Bay, Brooklyn, where thousands of Americans died. On the notorious *Jersey*, up to 1,100 moribund prisoners, many almost naked, were sunk in filth with no berths or benches. In 1782, a Salem privateer officer formerly imprisoned aboard the *Jersey* wrote: "The deplorable situation I am in cannot be expressed. . . . I am left here with about 700 miserable objects, eaten up with lice, and daily taking fevers, which carry them off fast."[29]

The British taken aboard prize vessels brought into Essex County ports and Boston were ready-made for prisoner exchanges. In practice, exchanges had been conducted for years. Parliament formally consented to them early in 1782, when jailed Americans came to be regarded as prisoners of war rather than treasonous rebels. Thousands were exchanged, the flood beginning on October 27, 1781, when 38 prisoners were brought from Halifax aboard a cartel to Salem. Four days later, a prison ship out of Newfoundland stood in to Salem carrying 400 captives, the crews of five Salem privateers. At about the turn of the year, a second boatload of homeward-bound sailors from Halifax, which included some of the *General Starks*'s crew, landed in the Harbor Cove at Cape Ann. Most were sick, some were unable to walk. On January 17, 1782, 100 more arrived at Salem from Halifax; another 76 came the following August, plus a cartel with 170 from London. On August 22, the *Salem Gazette* noted that a third cartel bound from England sailed into Marblehead bringing 116 Americans formerly confined at Mill Prison. A cartel from Halifax arrived at Marblehead on September 4. On October 7, 62 more prisoners reached Salem from Bermuda; on the sixteenth, a Newfoundland cartel brought in 292 former Salem privateersmen, including *Junius Brutus*'s crew. Later in October, another cargo reportedly arrived. A shipload of 230 reached Marblehead from Halifax on November 24. Next, a prison ship from Quebec touched Salem, with 130. The parade of weary, repatriated Essex County sailors disembarked upon Cape Ann, Marblehead, and Salem landings, often lined with hundreds of wives and family members hoping

Capt. James Barr of Salem (1754–1848), who was English-born, commanded the privateer ships *Oliver Cromwell* and *Rover* and the brigantine *Montgomery*. Courtesy, Peabody Museum of Salem.

to catch sight of missing loved ones. For many, the fall of 1782 brought a joyous reunion.[30]

Of the more than 1,100 United States merchantmen and 200 privateers captured by Britain, over 10 percent had Essex County owners. Salem had lost nearly one-third (at least 54) of its armed vessels. Still other ports, notably Gloucester, Marblehead, and Newburyport, suffered worse. Gloucester's entire fleet—twenty-four armed vessels—was nearly wiped out. Marblehead began with 12,313 tons of shipping; it wound up harboring only 1,509, one-eighth the prewar total! Newburyport's foremost shipowner, Nathaniel Tracy, reportedly held shares in 110 merchantmen—23 being letters marque—but ended with 13; only one of his 24 privateers survived![31]

George Williams wrote in January 1783 of the terrible losses suffered along the North Shore by privateering:

> I have with sons Labour'd hard this Two years past and have Lost by the enemy a goodeal of money. . . . The English ships of war has Keept cruising in our Bay & have Taking a great many of our privateers & marchant Vessels which cost their owners a very Large Sum. I have but part of Two ships Left. . . . The Town of Marblehead is Lost all but 2 or 3 Vessels, the Town of Beverly is all most in the same order except John & Andrew Cabbets.[32]

There were exceptions, including Essex County privateers that flew French ensigns and operated out of French ports, especially Dunkirk. But the prosperity of coastal Essex County linked to fisheries, privateering, and trade would need years to recover.

The losses were more than economic. Thousands of Essex County mariners were killed in action, captured, or lost at sea. All hands— over 1,000 sailors—were lost on twenty-two Newburyport vessels alone. One-third of Cape Ann's adult male population—more than 350—died, mostly at sea. In the hamlet seaport of Manchester, the proportion was even higher. During 1780, Marblehead counted 166 men in captivity and 121 missing. After the war, its rateable polls (males of sixteen years and older) numbered 544, less than half of the prewar totals. Beverly granted hundreds of abatements to absent mariners—town records graphically testify to the tragic price: "Dyed abroad," "absent if alive," "long absent Supposed to be lost," "missing at sea," "in the Hands of the Enemy," "in Captivity," "being Taken long absent," "Taken if alive," "long Missing if alive," "being Taken and Sick," "Lost at Sea Supposed." Possibly two-thirds of Beverly's adult male population between the ages of eighteen and sixty were taken prisoner. Because of frequent prisoner exchanges, some Beverlyites were captured two or three times.[33]

The impact at home was catastrophic. In Gloucester, almost 300 impoverished widows and more than 350 children were dependent on town support. Manchester had nearly 100 widows and over 100 fatherless children. Over one-third of Marblehead women—378 out of 1,069—were made widows; 672 out of 2,242 children were fatherless! The grief and suffering experienced by Essex County are inestimable.[34]

A charmed few, however, made fortunes through privateering. Before the war, the importing firm of J. & A. Cabot was of no special importance. It entered privateering cautiously, but left it as the most prosperous mercantile enterprise in Massachusetts. John Cabot and Andrew Cabot, teamed with their brother, George, and brother-in-law, Joseph Lee—a noted expert in ship architecture—owned shares in about forty vessels They were shrewd judges of men and chose excellent commanders—John Buffington, John Edmonds, Hugh Hill, Benjamin Lovett, Joseph Robinson, and others—who shared in J. & A.'s financial successes. In 1780, the partnership controlled two-thirds of the total tonnage in Beverly.[35]

Elias Hasket Derby of neighboring Salem also attained great wealth. An early Revolutionary leader and a leading merchant, Derby outfitted 85 vessels for over 110 cruises, an astounding 50 percent of Salem's entire privateering effort. Over 8,000 seafarers shipped out on these vessels. Salem's largest privateer, Derby's 300-ton *Grand Turk*, which was launched in May 1781, accounted for 17 of Elias Hasket's 21 prizes during 1781–82. While losing only 19 sail, Derby's adept commanders captured 144 of the enemy: 29 ships, 58 brigs, 10 snows, 25 sloops and 22 schooners. Derby became the most affluent man in Salem, probably a millionaire.[36]

Despite the county's heavy losses, North Shore, Cape Ann, and Merrimack mariners had succeeded in capturing hundreds of British vessels, 445 out of the Salem District alone. Privateers owned by the Tracys of Newburyport are said to have captured 120 enemy sail: 23,360 tons of ships with their cargoes. American privateers took and kept from recapture a grand total of over 2,200 British merchantmen and about 71 enemy privateers, a large percentage of which were captured by Essex County ships. As Yankee vessels racked up their successes, English insurance rates spiraled, and enemy losses ultimately totaled $66,000,000.[37]

The Salem District, which included Beverly, Danvers, and Salem, kept more craft at sea than any jurisdiction in the country. On the average, fifty vessels were cruising with about 2,000 men. An estimated one-half of Massachusetts' armed vessels sailed from Essex County ports. More than 350 private armed vessels sailed: 55 from Beverly; 24 from Gloucester; 5 from Ipswich; 30 from Marblehead;

80 from Newburyport; 180 from Salem. (Duplicate commissions of the same vessels have been eliminated, but because of major, multiple shareholders and sales between merchants living in different ports, perhaps thirty armed craft have been assigned twice. In many instances, attribution is difficult.) Most private armed vessels were owned by several investors in order to hedge high-risk investments by spreading costs. Cruises lasted only a few weeks or months, after which owners changed commanders or sold their interests, particularly if no prizes had been taken. Ships were officered locally and manned at least partly by Essex County seamen, but not necessarily based in the owner's port(s).[38]

Of 1,697 vessels commissioned by Continental authorities, 626 were from Massachusetts. With five other states, the Bay State also issued its own commissions. Taking Continental and state numbers into account, over 2,000 different armed vessels, carrying 18,000 guns and 70,000 men, were issued licenses. While estimates vary, up to 20 percent of the entire United States privateering fleet embarked from Essex County. From Newburyport to Cape Ann to Marblehead, the valorous and adventurous seamen embarking from Essex County seaports combined patriotism with profit to produce a seafaring effort unparalleled in United States history.

Peace Negotiations

In late February 1782, Parliament ended further military operations in America. The new Whig ministry headed by Lord Rockingham set out to negotiate a peace. Racked by tremendous losses, British merchants were among those who called loudest for cessation of hostilities. In April, negotiations began in Paris to end the war. Meanwhile, from Salem to Salisbury, the fishing towns of Essex County voted to urge Congress "to make the right of the United States to the Fisheries an indispensable article of treaty." Thanks largely to John Adams's skillful diplomacy, the right to fish off the Grand Banks and onshore privileges were secured. The preliminary articles were signed on November 30, 1782, with Britain formally ending hostilities on February 4, 1783. John Derby of Salem, on board the 20-gun letter-of-marque ship *Astrea*, received the news at Nantes. He sailed on March 12 and arrived at Salem twenty-one days later carrying a handbill which contained the first printed word of peace to reach America. Later, in April, further confirmations set off wild rejoicing. Cannons roared in Beverly, Cape Ann, Salem, and elsewhere in Essex, as the Bay State joined in celebrating this historic event.[39]

The final Treaty of Paris was signed on September 3, 1783. Eng-

SALEM, April 8.
By the ship *Astrea*, Captain *John Derby*, who arrived here yesterday, in 22 days from France, we have received a printed copy of a Declaration of the American Ministers, as follows:

By the MINISTERS PLENIPOTENTIARY of the United States of America, for making Peace with Great-Britain.

A DECLARATION

Of the Cessation of Arms, as well by Sea, as Land, agreed upon between His Majesty the King of Great-Britain and the United States of America.

WHEREAS Preliminary Articles were signed, at Paris, on the thirtieth day of November last, between the Plenipotentiaries of his said Majesty, the King of Great-Britain, and of the said States, to be inserted in, and to ~~....~~ the ... ty of Peace. to be

five months in all other parts of the World, without any exception, or any other more particular Description of Time or Place.

AND WHEREAS the Ratifications of the said Preliminary Articles, between his M... ... ... his said

Broadside. Courtesy, Essex Institute, Salem, Mass.

land recognized the independence of the thirteen united states, with a boundary that stretched north to Canada, westward to the Mississippi, and south to Florida. Congress agreed to recommend to the states that no obstacles be put in the way of Loyalist attempts to collect prewar debts, that restitution be made of confiscated Loyalist property, and that Loyalists be permitted to return for as long as twelve months to recover their property. Too much bitterness had been engendered for Massachusetts to accept the last provision. On April 24, 1783, Marblehead voters warned all refugees "to leave the Town within Six hours after notice is given, and in Case of neglect, to take them into Custody, Ship them to the nearest port of Great Britain." Sentiments echoing in the House chamber were similar to Danvers's June 9, 1783 instructions to representative Col. Israel Hutchinson: "You are to use your endeavour that no Absentee or Conspirator against the United States, Whether they have taken up arms against these States or not be admitted to Return." Popular pressures precipitated the July 2, 1783 resolve that the governor banish returning Loyalists without a trial. With time, however, passions subsided; by March 1784, the governor could grant licenses which permitted absentees the right to return.[40]

The next year, Benjamin Pickman, after ten years of exile, returned to his native Salem. In February 1783, an unrepentant Pickman had written to his wife, Polly: "Upon a Review of my Conduct during the late war I have Nothing to tax myself with; I was influenced by the purest Principles of Loyalty to my late Sovereign and affection to my Country; and when I return to America shall enjoy what Fortune I have left from the ruin of War in undisturbed Tranquility."[41]

Epilogue

Thousands of seafarers hailing from Essex County had joined with their army brethren to win the war. Now, with independence gained, came new challenges: sustaining stable domestic politics, keeping the peace with England, restoring wealth and prosperity. To accomplish these common goals would require support from all Americans, even returning refugees like Benjamin Pickman. As the newly independent union evolved, however, the courageous sons of Revolution would be foremost in the shaping of the new Republic.

1. Fitch Edward Oliver, ed., *The Diary of William Pynchon of Salem* (Boston: Houghton Mifflin, 1890), 103.
2. *Rhode Island Historical Society Publ.*, New Series, 8 (1901): 255–56.
3. Philip Chadwick Foster Smith, ed., *Captain Samuel Tucker* (Salem: Essex Institute, 1976), 39–58.
4. Howard I. Chapelle, *The History of the American Sailing Navy* (W. W. Norton, 1949; New York: Bonanza Books), 85; *Independent Chronicle*, April 13, 1778.
5. John H. Sherburne, *Life and Character of the Chevalier John Paul Jones* (Washington: Wilder & Campbell, 1825), 43–49.
6. Gardner W. Allen, *A Naval History of the American Revolution* (Boston: Houghton Mifflin, 1913), 2:371, 441–50; John J. Currier, *History of Newburyport, Mass. 1764–1905* (Newburyport: John J. Currier, 1906), 1:603; R. Livesey, ed., *The Prisoners of 1776* (Boston: George C. Rand, 1854), 249–50.
7. Currier, 1:603; Octavius Thorndike Howe, *Beverly Privateers in the American Revolution* (Cambridge: John Wilson, 1922), 300; Thomas Franklin Waters, *Ipswich in the Massachusetts Bay Colony* (Ipswich: Ipswich Historical Society, 1917), 2:342–44; Sherburne, 140–45.
8. Sherburne, 119.
9. 141, 145.
10. Allen, 2:527–29.
11. *The Continental Journal and Weekly Advertiser*, June 14, 1781 (hereinafter, *Continental Journal*); Allen, 2:546–54.
12. Allen, 2:609–11.
13. Currier, 1:587–89.
14. Isaac J. Greenwood, *Captain John Manley* (Boston: C. E. Goodspeed, 1915), 127–34; Allen, 2:608–09.
15. Allen, 2:605–08.
16. James Duncan Phillips, *Salem in the Eigh-*

teenth Century (Boston: Houghton Mifflin, 1937), 419, 426.
17. George Williams, "Revolutionary Letters Written To Colonel Timothy Pickering," *EIHC*, 45 (1909):122–23; John J. Babson, *History of the Town of Gloucester* (Gloucester: Procter Brothers, 1860), 422.
18. Babson, 416–23.
19. Howe, 349–50.
20. Williams, 44 (1908):322.
21. 45:124–25; *Continental Journal*, August 17, 1780; Freeman Hunt, *Lives of American Merchants* (New York: Derby & Jackson, 1858), 2:36–41.
22. Williams, 45 (1909), 126.
23. Howe, 349–50.
24. Council Records, MA Archives, June 15, 1779, 23:422–23; Livesey, 249–63.
25. Oliver, 103.
26. *Salem Gazette*, January 9–30, 1781; May 1, 1781; *Continental Journal*, January 11, 18, 25, April 26, May 4, 1781.
27. See *Salem Gazette* between early 1781 and spring 1782.
28. Richard H. McKey, "Elias Hasket Derby and The American Revolution," *EIHC*, 97 (1961): 191; Howe, 354, 355, 405, 408; "Records of the Vice-Admiralty Court at Halifax, Nova Scotia," *EIHC*, 45 (1909): 47, 48, 168, 175, 180, 239; James Duncan Phillips, "Privateers Condemned at Jamaica," *EIHC*, 76 (1940): 53; Joseph B. Felt, *Annals of Salem*, 2nd ed. (Salem: W. & S.B. Ives, 1849), 2:270, 272; *Continental Journal*, July 19, 1781; *Salem Gazette*, August 7, 1781; August 21, 1781.
29. *Salem Gazette*, December 5, 1782.
30. See *Salem Gazette* between November, 1781 and November, 1782; Felt, 2:282, 284; Babson, 423.
31. Samuel Roads, Jr., *The History and Traditions of Marblehead* (Marblehead: N. Allen Lindsey, 1897), 134; E. Vale Smith, *History*

of Newburyport (Newburyport: E. Vale Smith, 1854), 106–07.

32. Williams, 45 (1909):291.

33. E. V. Smith, 105; Babson, 440; Marblehead Town Records, EI, November 27, 1780; 4:756; Beverly Town Records, 6, 1779–81; Howe, 404–05.

34. Marblehead Town Records, November 27, 1780, 4:756.

35. Howe, 421–22.

36. McKey, 189–96.

37. Hunt, 2:48–49; E. V. Smith, 107.

38. Gardner Weld Allen, "Massachusetts Privateers," MHS *Proceedings*, 64 (1930–32):45; this article, which credits the county with over 100 additional armed vessels, seems generous; Babson, 409–11, 423–26; Currier, 1:637–47; Howe, 400–421; Hunt, 2:48–50; Ralph D. Paine, *The Ships and Sailors of Old Salem* (Boston: Charles E. Lauriat, 1923), 454–60; Phillips, 396; Waters, 352–57. Essex, particularly Gloucester, must have had a surplus of experienced mariners as dozens were employed out of the county commanding, primarily, Boston-owned vessels,

39. A Declaration, Broadside, EI; Oliver, 148–49, 151; Babson, 351.

40. Marblehead Town Records, 4:935; Danvers Town Records, 3:240.

41. Benjamin Pickman to Polly Pickman, ALS, Benjamin Pickman Papers, EI.

At a Meeting of the Directors and Agents of the OHIO COMPANY, *held at the Bunch of Grapes Tavern in* Boston, *the following Report was received from the Rev.* MENASSAH CUTLER.

THAT in consequence of resolves of Congress, of the 23d and 27th of July last, he agreed on the conditions of a contract with the Board of Treasury of the United States, for a particular tract of land, containing in the whole as much as the Company's funds will pay for, should the subscriptions amount to one million of dollars, agreeably to the articles of association, at one dollar per acre,—from which price is to be deducted one-third of a dollar for bad lands, and defraying the expences of surveying, &c.

That those lands be bounded on the east by the western boundary of the seventh range of townships ; south, by the Ohio ; west, by a meridian line drawn through the western Cape of the Great Kanhawa-River, and extending so far north, that a due east and west line from the seventh range of townships to the said meridian line, shall include the whole.

This tract to be extended so far northerly as to comprehend within its limits, exclusively of the above purchase, one lot of six hundred and forty acres, in each township, for the purposes of religion—an equal quantity for the support of schools, and two townships of twenty-three thousand and forty acres each, for an university, to be as near the centre of the whole tract as may be ; which lots and townships are given by Congress and appropriated to the above uses forever. Also three lots, of six hundred and forty acres each, in every township, reserved for the future disposition of Congress ; and the bounty lands of the military associators to be comprised within the whole tract : provided they do not exceed one seventh part thereof.

That five hundred thousand dollars, be paid to the Board of Treasury upon closing the contract.—In consideration of which, a right of entry and occupancy for a quantity of land equal to this sum, at the price stipulated, be given—and that as soon as the Geographer, or some proper officer of the United States, shall have surveyed and ascertained the quantity of the whole, the sum of five hundred thousand dollars more be paid, amounting in the total, to one million of dollars, for which the Company are to be put in possession of the other moiety of the lands above described, and receive a deed of the whole from the said Board of Treasury.

Whereupon *Resolved*, That the above report be received, and the proceedings of Mr. CUTLER be fully approved, ratified and confirmed.

Adjourned till to-morrow morning, eight o'clock, to convene at Mr. Brackett's tavern

AUGUST 30.

Met according to adjournment, and continued until the first of September ; during which time, the following resolutions were agreed to.

THAT five thousand seven hundred and sixty acres of land, near the confluence of the Muskingum and Ohio Rivers, be reserved for a City and Commons.

That within the said tract, and in the most eligible situation, there be appropriated for a City, sixty squares, of three hundred and sixty feet by three hundred and sixty feet each, in an oblong form, of ten squares in front, and six in depth, with streets of one hundred feet in width through each range.

That four of said squares, be reserved for public uses, and the remaining fifty-six divided into house-lots. That each square contain twelve house-lots of sixty feet front, and one hundred feet depth, and six lots of fifty-three and three tenths feet by one hundred and eighty feet, amounting in the total to one thousand and eight lots.—And that this plan be pursued as nearly as the situation of the ground will admit ; and when the same is completed, a plat thereof, with the lots numbered thereon, be transmitted to the Secretary, who shall notify a meeting of the Agents for the purpose of drawing the said city lots—one of which shall be annexed to, and become a part of each proprietary share. That contiguous to, and in the vicinity of the above tract, there be laid off one thousand lots, of sixty-four acres each, as equal as possible in quality and situation ; one of which, as the city lots, shall be considered a part of each proprietary share, and drawn for in the same manner ; and that a complete survey and return of these lots be made by the 1st of March next, to the Secretary's office.

That, for the reception and protection of settlers, one hundred houses, of thirty-six by sixteen feet, be erected, in the course of the ensuing autumn and winter, on three sides of the before mentioned oblong square, and connected by a stockade.

That, in order to carry into execution the above purposes, it is absolutely necessary that the subscribers pay into the hands of their several Agents the monies subscribed, that the same may be paid into the hands of the Treasurer by the 4th of October next ; which payment the Agents are to make to the Treasurer accordingly.

That, as saw-mills and corn-mills will be necessary, in forwarding the settlement, proposals from any of the subscribers for erecting one or more of each kind, without expence to the proprietors, will be received by either of the Directors, the Treasurer, or at the Secretary's office ; and such proposals will be decided upon, as soon as may be, after the completion of the contract with the Treasury Board.

And,

That the manner of removing the first settlers, and superintending their operations, will be agreed upon as soon as practicable.

Resolved, That General JAMES M. VARNUM, be one of the Directors of the OHIO COMPANY, and that Col. RICHARD PLATT be the Treasurer.

A true copy from the journals.

WINTHROP SARGENT, Sec'y.

CHAPTER TWENTY - TWO

CONFEDERATION POLITICS AND THE "WESTERN COUNTRY"

After peace arrived in 1783, the government, under the recently ratified Articles of Confederation, faced an array of challenges. Public finances were a shambles, unpaid Continental Army personnel were restless, and the country was plagued by severe economic depression which would fester for years. One vexatious domestic issue was western lands, particularly in the Northwest. With notable help from Essex County leaders, Congress produced viable plans for its disposal and administration, thus enabling this vast wilderness to be opened for settlement. Many "western country" pioneers were indomitable adventurers who hailed from Essex County.

The Articles of Confederation

Since May 1775, delegates to the Second Continental Congress had been conducting the war effort, but without duly constituted authority. In November 1777, after much debate and compromise, Congress adopted the thirteen Articles of Confederation and Perpetual Union, wherein each state would retain "its sovereignty, freedom, and independence, and every power, jurisdiction, and right, which is not . . . expressly delegated to the United States, in Congress assembled." The union was to be a "firm league of friendship . . . for their common defense, the security of their liberties, and their mutual and general welfare." Congress could declare war, regulate currency, make treaties, and borrow money, but it could not regulate trade, raise taxes, nor raise an army. Since no executive or judiciary branch was provided for, government was to be conducted by multiple committees. The articles were given to the states for ratification.

Local Opinion

When Massachusetts submitted the proposed articles of confederation, sentiment in Essex County towns was generally favorable. After hearing a committee report on January 19, 1778, Ipswich townspeople, for example, voted unanimously that representatives Michael Farley and Stephen Choate authorize the delegates of Massachusetts to ratify and confirm the articles.[1] Some towns were less directive; Beverly voted on February 4, 1778 that representative Captain Josiah Batchelder, Jr., act as his "wisdom Shall Judge it to be most for the Publick good."[2] Once Batchelder was privy to discussion and debate, voters reasoned, presumably he would make an intelligent decision.

Surprisingly, the articles gave rise to only limited local debate, with only two towns, Haverhill and Amesbury, expressing reservations. Viewing the confederation of "greatest importance for the defense and protection of this, and the other American States," Haverhill voters supported the articles, with two exceptions: Firstly, states should have votes in proportion to taxes paid for the common defense, a view expressed during congressional debate. Secondly, there should be some way to compel delinquent states to raise their prescribed share of taxes for common defense.[3] The new Congress, without power of taxation, could only requisition assessments; in time, this would prove a major weakness. Amesbury's reservations were more general. On January 26, the town chose seven men—the three selectmen, plus Thomas Rowell, Col. Jonathan Bagley, Stephen Kelly, and Capt. John Currier—to draft instructions for their representative, Caleb Pilsbury. The draft was accepted unanimously on February 3. Taxes should be apportioned according to personal income and wealth as well as real estate, Amesbury voters believed, a view shared by many northern agrarians. Congress should be required to consult state legislatures on war-and-peace issues, with consent from nine law-making bodies required. In regard to financial matters, Amesbury indicated that states were entitled to an accounting of monies borrowed and emitted. Noting the articles were "perpetual" once ratified, with unanimous consent required for amendment, townspeople wisely concluded it "highly behoves" everyone to "see their way clear before they bind themselves and thousand and ten thousands yet unborn."[4] These agrarian populists were cautious about relinquishing state prerogatives, however limited, to a faraway central government. Despite the qualifications of Haverhill and Amesbury, however, Essex County towns unanimously supported the notion of confederation.

First Federal Constitution

With instructions from their towns in hand, Massachusetts legislators sat to debate the proposed Articles of Confederation. Some espoused reservations similar to those raised by Haverhill and Amesbury, but consensus was achieved. On March 10, the day prescribed by Congress, the General Court assented to the articles as submitted, unless certain alterations "can be received and adopted without endangering the Union proposed."[5] Three more years would elapse, however, before the articles went into effect.

On July 9, 1778, Massachusetts and seven other states ratified the proposed government; within a year, all remaining states had acted similarly, except Maryland. Approval of every state was required, but Maryland refused to make it unanimous until states with territorial claims beyond the mountains relinquished them to the central government. When, in 1781, Virginia voted to cede its claims and Maryland became convinced others would soon follow, it ratified the articles. On March 2, 1781, the Articles of Confederation and Perpetual Union—America's first federal constitution—took effect.

Though Essex County held one-seventh of the Bay State's population, the county contributed about one-third of the delegates to Congress. Under the confederation, states were represented by delegations chosen annually of not less than two nor more than seven, with each state having one vote.

Six delegates came from Essex County; they were among the county's most celebrated, esteemed, patriotic leaders. Samuel Osgood, Andover-born, a graduate of Harvard College in the class of 1770, was engaged in retail trade on a farm in Andover with his elder brother, Peter. After serving as officer and aide-de-camp to Gen. Artemas Ward, in 1776 he left the army. Elected to the House several times, Osgood was chosen senator in 1781, the first Andover citizen to hold this office. For one year he attended the Continental Congress, and from 1781 to 1784 sat as delegate under the Confederation. When, the following year, he became one of three treasury commissioners, Osgood moved to New York. Elbridge Gerry of Marblehead, son of a prosperous merchant family, graduated in 1762 from Harvard. After having engaged in successful commercial pursuits, in 1772 Gerry was elected to the Massachusetts House. A four-term veteran, he was appointed to the Continental Congress (1776–

1781). A drafter of the articles, Gerry served as delegate from 1782 to 1785. Dr. Samuel Holten, Jr., of Danvers, a dedicated and highly respected physician, was first elected to the House in 1767. In subsequent years, Doctor Holten held many offices, including delegate to the Provincial Congress, member of the Governor's Council, and state senator. At sacrifice to himself and his family, he served as delegate from 1782 to 1787. Two representatives were from Newburyport. Jonathan Jackson, Boston-born, who graduated from Harvard in 1761, became a prominent merchant in Newburyport. He was elected to the House in 1776 and also chosen a Board of War member. Jackson was delegate in 1782. Second was Rufus King, who served from 1784 to 1787. After graduating from Harvard in 1777, Maine-born King studied law under the eminent Theophilus Parsons. He went on to serve as captain and aide-de-camp to General Glover. After the war, he was elected to the House, where he was appointed confederal delegate. The Ipswich-born Nathan Dane graduated from Harvard in 1778; he moved to Beverly and taught school while studying in the Salem law office of William Wetmore. In 1782, at age thirty, he was admitted to the bar and elected to his first of four House terms. Dane was a member of Congress from 1785 to 1788. Each Essex County delegate to Congress was remarkably qualified. All had entered politics early, and, by age thirty, had been entrusted to represent their towns in the House, where they soon gained the esteem of their colleagues. During the crucial 1780s, as the congressional representation suggests, many Bay State leaders were drawn from Essex County. Also, several Essex County confederal delegates were prominent in the expansion of the northwest.[6]

Northwest Territory

One major concern of the new government was western land cessions, a subject which was especially meaningful to many soil-hungry Revolutionary War veterans. In 1776, the Continental Congress had promised bounty lands for three-year enlistments in Continental service. With hostilities nearly concluded, discontented, unpaid veterans clamored for their lands. The highly esteemed Timothy Pickering of Salem, quartermaster-general of the army, sympathized; in April 1783, he drafted a proposal on their behalf. Called the "Pickering Plan," it advocated establishing a new state—in which slavery was prohibited—northwest of the Ohio River to Lake Erie and extending thirty miles west of the Scioto River (part of the present state of Ohio). Pickering proposed that the territory would be settled by those entitled to acreage, with the remaining land to be sold. Former brigadier-general Rufus Putnam of Rutland, Massachusetts, whose family roots extended to Danvers, was acquainted with the plan and may have helped draft it. Two months later, from Newburgh, New York, headquarters, Putnam petitioned Washington on behalf of 288 officers—more than 150 from Massachusetts—for bounty lands in the territory. Putnam had his own sights set on migrating westward, motivated partially by prospects of profiting from land promotion.[7] Though Congress was not yet inclined toward land grants, Putnam and other signers continued their unflagging efforts.

When states relinquished their claims to western lands, the United States took possession of an enormous domain east of the Mississippi, south of Canada, and northwest of the Ohio River. [In April 1785, delegates Dr. Samuel Holten, Jr., and Rufus King finally executed a deed in which Massachusetts gave up its land claims.] The war had left the central government a huge debt, and the states were unable to agree how to apportion it. The problem was compounded by economic hard times, which made it difficult for states to pay their assessments. There was a sense of urgency; bankruptcy was knocking on the confederal door. But revenue from land sales could reduce the federal debt.

Once Congress adopted the Ordinance of 1785 to provide for orderly migration, the first surveys of the Northwest Territory were begun. Lands were to be carved out in ranges six miles in width, the northernmost base line beginning where the Ohio River crossed Pennsylvania. Seven ranges were to be established south of this line to the Ohio. The New England system was adopted, whereby each township, prior to settlement, was to be surveyed into thirty-six one-mile-square sections, to be sold for a minimum of one dollar per acre. One-seventh of the Seven Ranges was to be set aside for bounties promised to soldiers. Passage of the ordinance was notable, as it also addressed the bounty lands pledge and the government indebtedness problem.

The Ohio Company

Rufus Putnam continued to champion the settling of Ohio. He devised a plan for purchasing public lands with Continental certificates (promissory notes) issued to soldiers at discharge. Since notes had been depreciated, they could be bought for one-eighth face value, then used instead of cash at full face value. Putnam formed a partnership with his friend Gen. Benjamin Tupper of Stoughton, who had been employed by the government to survey the Seven

Ranges. Using Tupper's knowledge of the area, they soon chose for their venture the region along the Muskingum and Ohio rivers, bordering the western boundary of the Seven Ranges.

In January 1786, the partners advertised in several Bay State newspapers inviting Revolutionary War officers and soldiers and "all other good Citizens" to become "adventurers" in a "delightful region" known as the Ohio Country. Interested persons were to meet in each county on February 15 to choose delegates, who were then to convene at Boston's Bunch of Grapes tavern on March 1 and form an association. The designated location in Essex County was Benjamin Webb's tavern in Salem, where the Connecticut-born, Yale-educated Rev. Manasseh Cutler, pastor of the Congregational Church in Hamlet Parish, Ipswich, was elected. For some time, the genial, portly pastor had been looking to improve his fortune. The inflationary war years had been difficult, and Cutler had become disenchanted when his Hamlet parishioners did not raise his salary; thus, the western land venture presented an appealing opportunity. Eleven representatives attended the Boston meeting, including five Newburgh petitioners. Major Winthrop Sargent was a Suffolk County delegate. Son of a wealthy merchant family and a former artillery officer, Sargent was born in Gloucester; he returned to Cape Ann after the war. Sargent, Benjamin Tupper's future son-in-law, had been surveying the Seven Ranges and had become enamoured with Ohio. Both Cutler and Sargent were appointed to a committee to prepare a plan of association. It was adopted, and the subscription books were opened.[8]

At the time, Massachusetts was promoting land in Maine. Shortly after the meeting, Cutler wrote to Sargent suggesting that "authentic accounts" of Ohio be circulated in the newspapers to inform the public. "They are constantly emigrating into the northern frozen deserts" he wrote, "but were they made sensible of the fertility & temperature of ye climate in the Ohio Country, they would turn their faces to the southward." When popular commotions stirred emotions—the prelude to Shays's insurgency—Cutler saw Ohio as the beneficiary. Writing to Sargent on October 6, 1786, the Hamlet pastor envisioned "well disposed persons" leaving the Bay State and becoming "adventurers for who would wish to live under a government subject to such tumults & convulsions."[9]

Though 1786 appeared to be an opportune time, a year passed before stockholders met and fully organized under "the Ohio Company." Former brigadier-general Samuel Holden Parsons of Connecticut, Rufus Putnam, and Manasseh Cutler were appointed directors. Winthrop Sargent was made clerk. They set out to raise one million dollars in certificates—one thousand shares—each costing one thousand dollars in scrip and ten dollars in coin. When the promotion ended, Cutler and Sargent had solicited the most shares. Although shares were offered first in Massachusetts, the company advertised elsewhere, attracting investors from Connecticut, New York, and Rhode Island, especially among former Newburgh petitioners. Ex-officers, who had developed wartime friendships, webbed a close, powerful network. A majority, including Winthrop Sargent, were brother Freemasons, who had belonged to the American Union Lodge, which traveled with the army as it moved. Some from Essex County were members of Washington Lodge No. 10, another traveling lodge. Masonry, based on moral truths, goodwill, and charity, fostered a continuing association between war veterans. A majority of investors also belonged to the Society of the Cincinnati, which had been formed by officers in 1783 to perpetuate their friendship.[10] New Englanders of the former Continental line, united by economics, friendship, and fraternity, and intent on settling and improving their fortunes in the west, became the backbone of the Ohio Company.

The company proposal was skillfully packaged for Congress. One-seventh of the territory was to be reserved for military associates holding bounty warrants, which would be honored. Reminiscent of the Land Ordinance, the proposal offered the prospect of fulfilling a long standing promise while paying off a debt. These were two good reasons for a favorable congressional reception.

Cutler and Congress

The Ohio Company, after reaching only one-quarter of its goal, applied to Congress for a private land purchase. Parsons was the lobbyist. When he appeared to be ineffectual, the forty-five-year-old Cutler replaced him. The pastor was an excellent choice. An eminent scientist, he was widely known for his scholarly writings on botany and the general sciences. With his wide circle of friends, courtly manners, and charming personality, the renowned Cutler would prove persuasive and skillful in dealing with the machinations of New York politics. On June 24, 1787, Cutler left his Ipswich home in a one-horse sulky, headed toward New York. (His journal provides an invaluable record of his transactions there.)[11]

Cutler reached New York on July 5, his satchel packed with letters of introduction accumulated in transit from influential friends. The following morning he set out, intent on striking a successful deal for the Ohio Company. After delivering his introductory letters, the pastor was taken to the floor of Congress, where he presented his proposal. To replace the current practice of selling small parcels, which had been going slowly, he petitioned Congress to dispose of an immense tract at less than the minimum one dollar per acre. A congressional committee was formed which included Nathan Dane of Beverly. Dane and Cutler dined on the first day; they would confer on several occasions, though Cutler mistrusted Dane. He theorized that since Dane was heavily invested in Massachusetts' own land promotion of 30,000 square miles in Maine, he could not be expected to cooperate in establishing a competing enterprise. An intense, often frustrating, three weeks was in store, during which numerous dinners, visits, meetings, and negotiations took place. Cutler did, however, manage to get away on a sojourn to Philadelphia where he visited the "venerable sage" Benjamin Franklin.[12]

At the time of Cutler's mission, Congress was in the process of working out a government for the Northwest Territory which would encourage settlement. Cutler was given for review a final draft of the proposed ordinance, in which territorial rule and land sale were intertwined. The astute pastor suggested several changes and proudly noted, on July 19, that all but one were accepted. The Northwest Ordinance of 1787, which passed unanimously on July 13, 1787, provided for three stages of republican government, leading eventually to statehood. Nathan Dane had been the prime mover. Serving on the government committee, he drafted the wording and reported the ordinance to Congress. Included in his draft were bill-of-rights provisions taken from the Massachusetts Constitution. Earlier, in 1784, Thomas Jefferson had headed a committee to devise a government for the territory; their work later became the basis for the ordinance. Since March 1785, Rufus King, at Timothy Pickering's urging, had pushed Congress in vain to prohibit slavery in the Northwest Territory. (Slavery—inimical to the principles of the Declaration of Independence—was opposed because it encouraged a plantation system rather than wide land ownership.) Also at the behest of Pickering, King made other suggestions, including freedom to navigate rivers leading to the Mississippi and St. Lawrence, which would promote interstate trade. (In July 1787, King was sitting as delegate to the Constitutional Convention at Philadelphia.) The final draft encompassed protection of personal liberties, abolition of slavery, and right of navigation; measures originally proposed by Dane or King. After several years' discussion and debate, the Northwest Ordinance evolved as the confederation's most significant accomplishment. The Ohio Company proposal had been the catalyst needed for passage. Tribute belongs to Quartermaster-General Timothy Pickering, delegates Rufus King and Nathan Dane, and agent Manasseh Cutler— all Essex County sons.[13]

After several sessions with Cutler, on July 20 Congress proposed a contract. Cutler immediately rejected it, countering that several states were offering land on better terms. To move discussions forward, Cutler threatened to end negotiations and return home. At this juncture, he was approached by the influential Col. William Duer, secretary of the Board of Treasury, who was charged with disposal of public lands. Duer had a proposal. A syndicate of unidentified government officials—some of them members of Congress—plus a number of wealthy merchants were organizing a company for speculation in western lands, the Scioto Company. Their objective was to obtain an option to purchase 5,000,000 acres. Since these influential people could not openly lobby, if Cutler were willing to do their bidding, Duer would see that the Ohio Company got 1,500,000 acres for one million dollars. So long as payment could be made in soldiers' certificates, Cutler was agreeable. The pastor meanwhile strengthened his position with another congressional faction by shifting his support for governor of the new territory from Samuel H. Parsons to Pennsylvanian Gen. Arthur St. Clair, president of Congress. Duer's friends, as well as the well-connected Winthrop Sargent, who was in New York to help, pressured Congress. Not only could support be counted on because some members might profit financially, the government did need revenue. The congressmen viewed this proposal—now considerably greater in magnitude—favorably. When Cutler renewed negotiations, he stressed that the sale would significantly reduce the country's indebtedness and increase the value of abutting federal lands. He noted also that the territory would be settled by "men strongly attached to the Federal government."

Within a few days, Congress was to approve the sale. Samuel Osgood, head of the Board of Treasury and a former resident of Andover, Massachusetts, was a principal behind-the-scenes player with Duer. Cutler observed of Osgood: "No gentleman had a higher character for planning and calculating." The "solicitous" Osgood promised to push for Cutler's plan, and General St. Clair similarly assured the pastor of his support. Every possible "machine in the city" was "set to work," as there were still members to be persuaded. Although the outcome continued uncertain, an impatient, discouraged Cutler could take solace from Dr. Samuel Holten's July 26 reassurance that, given Congress's usual pace, his accomplishments had been astonishing. On July 27, negotiations looked stalled. Cutler, seemingly exasperated, packed his bags and once again expressed his intention to leave; before departing, however, he would await Congress's decision. Cutler's "air of perfect indifference" paid off; Congress passed the agreement as proposed, the largest public contract yet to be consummated in the United States. Without the Scioto alliance, which included many "principle characters in America," Cutler noted, the Ohio Company could not have obtained its favorable terms.[14]

Settling Ohio

Once negotiations were completed, the Ohio Company turned its attention to settling the Muskingum Valley. After Cutler returned home, he reported to the directors and agents at an August 29, 1787 meeting and explained the terms: one dollar per acre (in soldiers' certificates), reduced one-third as an allowance for marginal or bad lands and survey expenses. One section (640 acres) in each township was to be reserved exclusively for religious use and a second for free schools, with two entire townships set aside for the establishment of a university.

Cutler continued to be immersed in company business, noting in several journal entries during September that his home was "full of Ohio people." An astonished Cutler reported in late September that Ohio was now the "rage," although scarcity of money prevented many people from becoming "adventurers." In mid-October, he boarded a packet for New York to finalize the contract. On October 27, Cutler and Major Winthrop Sargent signed, as agents, one contract for the Ohio Company and another for the Scioto Company, with Treasury Board members Samuel Osgood and Arthur Lee signing on behalf of the United States. For their efforts, Cutler and Sargent were issued thirteen shares in the Scioto land option. Two days later, Cutler boarded a stage and returned home, though much fatigued, in time to preach on Sunday. Again, Ohio business consumed his energies "over head and ears," Boston's Rev. Jeremy Belknap wrote, meeting with directors and making preparations generally for the "western country."[15]

At a meeting on November 21 and 22 to prepare for the spring migration, the directors resolved to reserve four thousand acres near the confluence of the Ohio and Muskingum rivers for a city, to divide contiguous land into one thousand eight-acre parcels, and to further divide the land in the countryside. The acreage was to be allocated by drawing lots and divided in proportion to each person's stock holdings. No one could own more than five shares, which promoted a sense of equality. While the directors' motives were speculative, they shared an ideal: the shaping of a secure, orderly, harmonious society, a model community, out of the Ohio wilderness.[16]

Under company employ, two advance parties were sent out to make preparations. They were supplied with tools and provisions and paid four dollars per month in cash or land. Each man had to furnish his own musket, bayonet, flints, powder, and shot. The first contingent—of about twenty-three men, including six boat builders, four house carpenters, a blacksmith, nine common workmen, and others traveling at their own expense—set forth from Hamlet Parish in Ipswich and Danvers.

About dawn on December 3, a group assembled in front of Manasseh Cutler's home on the Bay road. After a brief, spirited address and best wishes from the pastor, the energized band fired three volleys. The pioneers, including Cutler's nineteen-year-old son Jervis, set out amid cheers from a crowd of bystanders. Cutler accompanied them as far as Danvers, where they joined with others. The entire expedition was placed under the command of "thick set and robust" Major Haffield White of Danvers, a former Revolutionary War officer and member of the Society of the Cincinnati. Leading the way was a "long ark-like looking wagon," pulled by oxen driven by another Danvers resident, William Gray. The wagon was covered with black canvas; on each side in large, white letters was the slogan, *"For the Ohio at the Muskingum,"* painted by none other than Cutler himself.[17]

The contingent starting out from Ipswich and Danvers was made up of mostly Essex County people. The leader, Major Haffield White, had begun his military career when he answered the Lexington alarm as a private in Capt. Billy Porter's company (at the time, White resided in Wenham). Shortly afterwards, he became a lieutenant in Capt. Ebenezer Francis's company and was present at Trenton, Hubbardton, and Saratoga. Later promoted to captain, he served as quartermaster under Col. Rufus Putnam at West Point and was commissioned major in 1781. White was accompanied to Ohio by his sons, Josiah and Peletiah. Other former Continental Army officers were Lt. Benjamin Shaw of Beverly, a Freemason of traveling Washington Lodge No. 10, and Capt. Ezekiel Cooper of Rowley, a Society of the Cincinnati member. Oldest was sixty-seven-year-old William Moulton, a Newburyport goldsmith, traveling with his son Enoch. The majority were younger men, who, with the economy in the doldrums, were Ohio-bound, seeking greater opportunity. Isaac (twenty-two years of age) and Oliver Dodge (twenty-one years) were from Wenham; Amos Porter, Jr., Allen Putnam, Capt. Jethro Putnam, and Josiah Wittredge came from Danvers. Simeon Martin, David Wallis, and Joseph Wells, all in their early twenties, probably hailed from Ipswich. The party also included young John Gardner, a Middleton native, whose family had moved to Marblehead in 1783; Hezekiah Flint, carpenter and farmer, and his sixteen-year-old son, Hezekiah, Jr., of North Reading in neighboring Middlesex County; and Capt. Jonathan Devol and his nephew, Gilbert Devol, Jr., from Tiverton, Rhode Island. Seasoned veterans, skilled craftsmen, and young hands—hearty adventurers all—left Essex County, bound westward to lay a groundwork for the Ohio Company.[18]

Eight weeks later, after a sometimes difficult journey, the group arrived at Sumrill's Ferry on the Youghiogheny River in western Pennsylvania (presently West Newton, Westmoreland County) across the Allegheny Mountains. On February 14, 1788, they were joined by a second group—four surveyors and about twenty-two attendants—under command of General Rufus Putnam, superintendent for the entire expedition, who had started out in early January from Hartford, Connecticut. For the final stretch, by river, the parties combined.

Captain Devol, master boat builder, supervised all hands in constructing a fleet to travel the remaining expanse. A fifty-ton galley, the *Mayflower*, was the mainstay—forty-five feet long, with a twelve-foot beam and covered deck. She was supplemented by a hefty three-ton flatboat and three large pirogues (log canoes). By April 1, they were set. The combined expedition—forty-eight men, horses, wagons, tools, baggage, and provisions aboard—shoved off from Sumrill's Ferry. Floating the Youghiogheny and Ohio rivers, two hundred miles downstream from Pittsburgh, they reached the northeast bank at the confluence of the Ohio and Muskingum rivers on April 7. Their historic landing marked the beginning of the first permanent settlement in Ohio.[19]

To prepare for the anticipated spring migration, the party promptly turned to erecting temporary shelter, clearing land, and laying out the town. They also built a large garrison—named, in true classical style, *Campus Martius*—overlooking the Muskingum. It was a formidable structure—one hundred and eighty feet long with timber blockhouses at each corner—and was designed to afford protection for the little community in case of Indian raids.

Gov. Arthur St. Clair and Gloucester native Winthrop Sargent, first territorial secretary and second in command, were among the settlers who arrived during spring. On May 3, an ebullient Cutler wrote to Gen. Henry Knox, of Revolutionary War fame: "The spirit of emigration to the western country is dayly increasing in the N. England States." With unbounded enthusiasm, Cutler estimated that over one thousand families would reach the Muskingum during the year.[20] The *Salem Mercury*, which consistently reported the venture, stated on May 22 that not less than eight hundred families already had left New England for the Ohio country. A June 22 account announced that the Ohio Company had surveyed four thousand acres for a city and one thousand eight-acre lots. It noted that "a large quantity of ground was sowed and planted, and the people were beginning to erect houses."

The first directors' and agents' meeting west of the Alleghenies was held in the settlement on July 2. Mindful of France's contribution to America's independence, it was resolved that the city be called Marietta, in honor of Marie Antoinette. During that year, eighty-four additional men and fifteen families joined the first settlers. Many were from Essex County.

Maj. John Burnham departed from Chebacco Parish, Ipswich, bound for Marietta in 1788. Burnham was a distinguished former Continental Army officer, an original Society of the Cincinnati member, and a Freemason. Maj. Andrew Story, his wife and family also left Chebacco, accompanied by pioneers from Hamlet Parish, Beverly, and Salem. During the first year, Capt. John Dodge and his family set out from Beverly. Capt. Ezra Lunt, a former Continental Army officer and a Freemason, and William P. Lunt left Newburyport. Boxford-born and Harvard-educated Dean Tyler migrated in 1788 or 1789. Portrayed as brilliant, agreeable, and refined, Tyler headed for Ohio possibly on the rebound from the death of his sweetheart. Among Danvers families was Maj. Ezra Putnam (also a Freemason), his wife, and three sons. Sons David and Ezra arrived first, in 1789. Capt. William Bartlett—presumably the former Continental prize agent—of Beverly and his family sailed to Philadelphia and proceeded toward Ohio, but stopped in July 1788 at Sumrill's Ferry.[21]

Two families from Cutler's parish—Ebenezer Porter of Ipswich and his son-in-law, Nathaniel Sawyer, with their wives and children—started out in September 1787 ahead of the advance party. They were going to "*Indian Heaven*," wrote Rev. Jeremy Belknap, who observed their departure from Boston: "Some people pitied them, as sheep going to the slaughter; others wished themselves in company." They stopped in Westmoreland County, Pennsylvania, where they took up temporary residence, and finally moved to Mariettta in 1789.[22]

Various turns in the pioneers' lives would lead some to remain and make lasting contributions to Ohio's history, others to return East eventually. Most of the first settlers stayed. In the months following, some were joined by their families; others returned East to accompany their wives and children westward. A letter from Marietta, dated July 20 and printed in the *Salem Mercury*, gave a glowing account of the territory, no doubt intended to promote further migration. A "beautiful passage down the Ohio from Pittsburgh" was described, and a Fourth of July celebration which included a "fine dinner . . . among other things there were on the table perch that weighed 24 pounds—pickeral of 22 pounds—roast pig, venison, &c." Another account, dated September 30, reported that ten thousand emigrants had passed Marietta on their way "to Kentucky and other parts on the Ohio and Mississippi rivers." If preparations had been further along, it was speculated many would have settled on Ohio Company land. George Washington, whose interest in Ohio had been longstanding, observed: "No colony in America was ever settled under such favorable auspices. . . . I know many of the settlers personally and . . . there never were men better calculated to promote the welfare of such a community."[23]

In subsequent years, difficulties surfaced. *Campus Martius* proved to be a wise investment, when, in January 1791, relations between the settlers and the Indians worsened and hostilities broke out. Settlers were forced to seek refuge in the garrison, unable to cultivate their fields and threatened by starvation. Settlement of Marietta slowed down; the Ohio Company's finances were exhausted. The company was unable to fulfill its contract for the entire purchase and had to negotiate a settlement with Congress. But the movement west, once begun, was irrevocable. In 1795, the Treaty of Greenville brought peace; once again, settlers streamed down the Ohio, the gateway to the West. Many were New Englanders, adventurers from Essex County and other parts, transporting their cultural heritage to forge an indelible imprint on the history of the Northwest Territory.

1. Ipswich Town Records, 4:285.
2. Beverly Town Records, 6:165.
3. Haverhill Town Records, 1010.
4. Amesbury Town Records, 398–400.
5. *Acts and Resolves*, 20:324–25.
6. See *Biographical Dictionary of the American Congress* (Washington, D.C.: United States Government Printing Office, 1950) and Clifford K. Shipton Sibley's *Harvard Graduates* (Boston: Massachusetts Historical Society).
7. Archer Butler Hulbert, ed. *The Records of the Original Proceedings of the Ohio Company* (Marietta, Ohio: Marietta Historical Commission, 1917–1918), 1:xiv-xxxiii; 3:xxii-xxvi; Octavius Pickering, *The Life of Timothy Pickering* (Boston: Little, Brown, 1817), 1:546–49.
8. Hulbert, 1:xlv-xlviii, 1–7.
9. Manesseh Cutler to Winthrop Sargent, Winthrop Sargent Papers, ALS, MHS, 2:616, 647.
10. Hulbert, 1:xl-xlix.
11. Hulbert, 1:l-lvii.
12. William Parker Cutler and Julia Perkins Cutler, eds., *Life, Journal, and Correspondence of Rev. Manasseh Cutler* (Cincinnati: Robert Clark, 1888), 1:225–85; "The Part Taken By Essex County in the Organization and Settlement of the Northwest Territory," *EIHC*, 25 (1888):203–04; Winthrop Sargent Papers, MS, MHS, 1:38.

13. Hulbert, 1:xcii-xcvi; "Essex County in the Northwest Territory," 174, 190–93, 196–219; Charles R. King, ed., *The Life and Correspondence of Rufus King* (New York: G. P. Putnam, 1894), 38–47, 268–92; Cutler and Cutler, 1:293, 335–73.
14. Hulbert, 1:lxx-lxxx; quotations are from Cutler's journal entries printed in Cutler and Cutler, 1:294–305.
15. Hulbert, 1:13–18; 29–37; Cutler, 1:327–29, 332–33; *Salem Mercury*, December 11, 1787; "Belknap to Hazard," MHS *Collections*, 2, 5th Series, 2:488.
16. Hulbert, 1:18–21; Andrew R. L. Cayton, "A Quiet Independence: The Western Vision of the Ohio Company," *Ohio History*, 90:1 (1981):5–32.
17. Hulbert, 1:24–26; Cutler, 1:329–30; S. P. Hildreth, *Memoirs of the Early Pioneer Settlers of Ohio* (Cincinnati: H. W. Derby, 1852), 397, 399–400, 414.
18. Almira Larkin White, *Genealogy of the Descendants of John White* (Haverhill: 1900), 1:347–49; E. J. V. Huiginn, *Centennial History of Liberty Lodge* (Beverly: 1924), 15–16; Membership File, Grand Lodge of Massachusetts, Boston; Henry W. Moulton, *Moulton Annals* (Chicago: Edward A. Claypool, 1906), 270; Joseph Thompson Dodge, *Genealogy of the Dodge Family* (Madison, WI: 1894), 121; *Salem Mercury*, June 17, 1788; Eben Putnam, *The Porter Family*

(Danvers: Eben Putnam, 1895), 40–42; Births, Marriages, and Deaths, Vol. 4, Town of Danvers; *Danvers Mirror*, August 6, 1881; Danvers, Ipswich, Rowley, Wenham *Vital Records to 1850*; Frank Augustine Gardner, *Gardner Memorial* (Salem: 1933), 3; "Danvers People and Their Homes," DHS *Collections* (1913): 1:3–4; John Flint and John H. Stone, *Descendants of Thomas Flint* (Andover: Warren F. Draper, 1860), 38–39, 74; David Wallis contracted smallpox on reaching the Muskingum. To prevent the disease from spreading, he withdrew from camp, got well, and walked home to Ipswich; "Essex County in the Northwest Territory," 176; the account lists John Porter and William and Edmund Knowlton as members of the expedition. The reference may refer to Ebenezer Porter's son, John, thirteen years old. William and Edmund Knowlton probably were William and Enoch Moulton of Newburyport. The December 19, 1787 issue of the *Essex Journal* noted that: "30 men employed by the directors of the Ohio Company set out for the western country," rather than the twenty-two or three believed to have reached the Muskingum. Several travelers were Ohio Company proprietors: Ezekiel Cooper (1/2 share), Jonathan Devol (1 share), Isaac Dodge (1/2 share), Oliver Dodge (1/2 share), Simeon Martin (1/2 share), William Moulton (1 share), Amos Porter, Jr. (1/2

share), Allen Putnam (1/2 share), Jethro Putnam (1/2 share), and Haffield White (2 1/2 shares). Some shares may have been in lieu of wages. Hulbert, 2:235–42. Across the Muskingum, on the opposite bank, was Fort Harmar, which Congress established in 1785 primarily to ward off squatters.

19. See copy of Rufus Putnam's journal: Mary Cone, *Life of Rufus Putnam* (Cleveland: William W. Williams, 1886), 61–65.

20. Knox Papers, MS, MHS, 22:32.

21. Cone, 65; Robert Crowell, *History of the Town of Essex* (Essex: Town of Essex, 1868), 239; Dodge, 154–55; Hulbert, 1:61; 2:235–42; William A. Tyler, *The Tyler Genealogy* (Tylerville, CT: Rollin U. Tyler, 1912), 73; "Danvers People and Their Homes," 6–8; *Salem Mercury*, November 20, 1787; May 27, 1788; Winthrop Sargent Papers, 843. Bartlett (1 share), Burnham (4 shares), Dodge (2 shares), Ezra Lunt (4 shares), and Putnam (1 share) were major proprietors; Hulbert, 2:235–42.

22. "Belknap to Hazard," 493; Joseph W. Porter, *A Genealogy of Richard Porter and John Porter* (Bangor: Burr & Robinson, 1878), 263–64; Herbert L. Roush, Sr., *The Unknown Settlement* (Parsons, West Virginia: Herbert L. Roush, 1983), 14–16; Cutler and Cutler, 1:374, 407, 426.

23. John C. Fitzpatrick, ed., *The Writings of George Washington*, 29:521.

GENERAL ORDERS

FOR THE

Second Division of the Maſſachuſetts' Militia.

THE Major-General, impelled by a ſincere regard for the honor of his Diviſion, as well as by the repeated public calls of his Excellency the Commander in Chief, finds it his duty, notwithſtanding his having already iſſued to the different towns of this Diviſion, his Orders for the organizing of their reſpective companies, in this public manner, again to call on the Select-men of the ſeveral towns forthwith to aſſemble the Train-band and Alarm-liſt, on due notice, at ſome convenient place in their ſeveral diſtricts, for the purpoſe of electing their Officers, according to law.

HE preſumes that elections in many towns *have* taken place, of which he expects an immediate return.

To thoſe who have not made ſuch elections, he cannot but obſerve, that, if they neglect to improve the valuable privilege in this reſpect reſerved to them by our excellent Conſtitution, the mode of appointment, directed by the militia-act, muſt be adopted.————With this view, the Adjutant-General of this Diviſion will, without delay, wait on the Select-men of the different towns, that are yet unorganized, and make return of ſuch as refuſe. He will alſo promote the election of Field-officers, who will, as ſoon as may be, after they are qualified, be directed to elect a Brigadier-General, according to law.

THE Adjutant-General will alſo uſe his endeavours to eſtabliſh a Company of Artillery in each of the towns of Marblehead, Beverly and Gloceſter, and a Company of Horſe in the Regiment commanded by Colonel Bricket.

THE Major-General recommends to the Militia of the whole Diviſion, as ſoon as they are formed, to uſe their beſt endeavours to perfect themſelves in the Art Military, and ſuggeſts to them that the leiſure of the winter ſeaſon will afford to them an happy opportunity for improvement. Nothing can give him more ſatisfaction, than to find them, at the opening of the ſpring, well diſciplined, and expert in the manual exerciſe and the manœuvres of the Field : as in the courſe of the next ſeaſon the Adjutant-General will inſpect the ſeveral Regiments.

THE Major-General expects a return of all the organized Regiments, and of the Companies of Artillery and Cavalry, by the twentieth of December, and returns his hearty thanks to the Officers and Soldiers of thoſe reſpective Corps, for their great attention to diſcipline and improvement in military ſkill, and particularly for their ſpirit and activity on receiving the late Orders from the Captain-General, when an Inſurrection was expected in a neighbouring County.

HE feels no ſmall pleaſure in reflecting, that while, in various parts of the Commonwealth, the good Citizens have been ſubject to frequent alarms, from the indecent attempts of diſcontented, or miſinformed Bodies of men, on the officers of Government, while, in ſome parts, the adminiſtration of civil Juſtice has been entirely ſtopped—the worthy and reſpectable Yeomen of the County of Eſſex have manifeſted an uniform attachment to the Government ſo happily eſtabliſhed among us——He ſincerely hopes that the candid attention of the honorable Legiſlature to every Petition and Complaint offered to them, and the generous Indemnity proffered to thoſe who had imprudently expoſed themſelves to juſt puniſhment, will have their intended effect in informing the ignorant, quieting the minds of the diſcontented, and deterring the guilty from future attempts of the like kind.

HE freely indulges the pleaſing expectation, that the Inhabitants of the county of Eſſex will ſtill maintain that manly ſubmiſſion to ſuch Government, and that the zeal and activity in its ſupport, which have ſo long diſtinguiſhed them, and which have procured them the reſpect of their fellow-citizens, through the Commonwealth ; that their worthy example will have an extenſive effect, and that by a zealous attention to military diſcipline, and to every virtue which can adorn the good ſoldier ; and the good citizen, they may aſſiſt in preſerving to us and our poſterity the invaluable bleſſings of Freedom.

Given under my hand in Newbury-port, this firſt day of December, Anno Domini, 1786.

JONATHAN TITCOMB, *Major-General.*

During the tumult and disorder, Maj. Gen. Jonathan Titcomb, in accordance with Governor Bowdoin's orders, activated the Essex County militia. Broadside.

CHAPTER TWENTY - THREE

SHAYS'S INSURGENCY: ESSEX COUNTY RESPONDS

During the sultry summer of 1786, mob violence erupted. By October 6, Rev. Manasseh Cutler wrote to Winthrop Sargent: "We are in this Commonwealth on ye very border of complete anarchy. A most infamous insurrection has taken place, within a few weeks, in ye western and one of southern counties, viz. Worcester, Middlesex, Hampshire, Berkshire, & Bristol. The minds of ye people are thrown into a most violent ferment."[1] The opposition was centered in Hampshire and Berkshire counties, where the Regulators, or Shaysites, soon became organized into military companies led by former Revolutionary officers. Burdened with debt, besieged with foreclosures, and taxed beyond their limits, thousands of grieved country folk threatened to topple Massachusetts' fledgling constitutional system.

Before Shays

During the war, and for years afterward, Massachusetts was plagued by economic depression. With many prewar export markets shattered, income from commerce and fisheries had ebbed significantly since colonial days. At first, farmers had profited by supplying armies in nearby fields, but, as the war shifted south, demand softened; after hostilities were concluded, commodity prices continued downward. Earlier, in 1780, after Massachusetts called in its "old emission," paper currency contracted; then, in January of 1781, "new emission" ceased to be legal tender, frustrating debtors who wanted cheap money. New emission, however, was acceptable for taxes. Be-   419 ginning in 1779, spiraling war costs forced the Bay State to raise the tax; one-third was levied on polls and two-thirds applied to real and personal property. A new revenue-raiser, the excise tax, followed in November. A rising taxpayers' revolt, however, persuaded legislators to suspend future state levies. Almost everyone—artisan, fisherman, merchant, professional, sailor, and yeoman—suffered from the stagnated economy, exacerbated by scarcity of money, huge indebtedness, both public and private, falling prices, and higher taxes.

Western Massachusetts farmers were desperate—most living at nearly subsistence level. They saw the market for their goods declining and they held little hard cash. Though the economic solutions were complex, their remedies were simple: emission of paper, so debts could be paid with cheap currency; less expensive government, in particular the lowering of taxes by trimming the costly, squeaky judicial machinery and reducing officeholders' salaries; a personal property–legal tender law, so a debtor could pay in commodities if he had no cash, thus eliminating property seizures and cut-rate auctions; and suspension of civil court suits, through which defaulters often had been imprisoned.

During the early 1780s, as county conventions met, the General Court was deluged with scores of petitions; occasionally, angry mobs tried to obstruct court proceedings. In April 1782, an impassioned itinerant preacher, Samuel Ely, so inflamed emotions that a crowd rose up and obstructed the Northampton courts. Ely was jailed. When, two months later, a mob freed the firebrand, ensuing commotions nearly exploded into civil strife.

The General Court had responded with both resolution and compassion. A confession act passed on May 3, permitting a debtor to appear before a justice, admit his debt, and agree on a payment date. Since a formal suit was avoided, there were no court costs. On June 27, in response to tensions in Hampshire County, habeas corpus was suspended for six months; however, a week later, a personal property tender law passed, making livestock, flour, grain, pine boards, and other commodities acceptable tender. Furthermore, a grievance committee went to Hampshire County for an investigation of the Ely riots. Except for habeas corpus, the measures were generally well accepted, though some objections remained.

Protests over taxes and spending were not confined to western Massachusetts. Though taxes for state operations had been suspended, in March 1782 and again in 1783, £200,000 was assessed for carrying on the war effort. The first year's tax was payable in commodities, but not the second. Hard-pressed, debt-riddled towns objected. Many also opposed Massachusetts' new tariff law, adopted in November 1782, which would raise prices. While opposition was concentrated in western sections, seeds of discontent had spread throughout the Bay State.

War's legacy brought new costs. During hostilities, Congress had encouraged enlistments by pledging Revolutionary officers half-pay for life, later commuted to full pay for five years. Now, with hostilities over, many towns protested. In January 1784, for instance, Rowley instructed Rep. Thomas Mighill to "use his utmost Influence in order to have the General Court repeal their act Respecting giving the Officers of the Continental Army half pay during life. Or five years whole pay after the war was over." Though confederal delegate Samuel Holten of Danvers believed Congress had "made a good bargain," support for commutation cost him his seat.[2] After the Ely incitement, county conventions still met; occasionally, mobs threatened violence, though no riots ignited until Shays's. To a large extent, opposition was being nurtured by the ingrained distrust that had fostered the fight for independence. Political conservatives, however, including eastern merchants, viewed the conventions—not to mention direct political action—as unjustified and illegal. Many believed they were Tory-inspired. Radical tactics had been required in pre-Revolutionary times, but the popularly ratified Constitution of 1780 provided civil liberties and republican government, including annual popular elections of an assembly. Extralegal conventions—often by self-appointed delegates—court blocking, and mob actions were unwarranted; an orderly airing of grievances was called for through duly elected representatives.

No political conventions were held in western Massachusetts during 1784 and 1785. Crop harvests improved and taxes came down. Since the excise tax was used for interest payments, towns were assessed only £140,000; the following year, no tax was levied. Yet, the economy still was depressed. Common pleas cases increased; specie remained scarce; farm prices continued flat. Despite some judicial reforms, the machinery of government remained essentially untouched. With peace, most open discontent quieted, though murmurs continued as emotions simmered. All that was needed was a catalyst to cause an eruption.

Old and New Grievances

Gov. John Hancock resigned from office in February 1785, due, he said, to ill health. The governor's detractors, however, contended that his departure was a shrewd sidestep of the approaching political storm clouds. In either case, Hancock avoided confronting the impending civil strife, which allowed him to capitalize on the resulting political turmoil later. In May, James Bowdoin, a respected, conservative Boston merchant, assumed the gubernatorial office.

During early 1786, many old grievances revived: judicial process, public indebtedness, tax burdens, money supply. The popular rumblings were magnified by innate suspicion of central government, coupled with common misunderstandings of state administration, finance, and taxation. The General Court's inaction on the plethora of protests and recommendations exacerbated the people's dissatisfactions.

Increasing numbers of suits and subsequent judicial decisions renewed calls for revised fee schedules and court restructuring, particularly the four-judge, county inferior court of common pleas. Since its jurisdiction was limited to civil cases, debtor suits usually crowded the docket. Essex County's judges were widely esteemed gentlemen with years of extensive public service: Benjamin Greenleaf of Newburyport, Samuel Holten, Jr., of Danvers, Samuel Phillips, Jr., of Andover, and John Pickering of Salem. Though court fees were the sole source of compensation for the judges, quarterly sessions alternating between Salem, Ipswich, and Newburyport which averaged about four hundred entries must have provided ample compensation. Notwithstanding their repute, they undoubtedly incurred the wrath of some defendants.[3] Litigation often was not settled at common pleas court, but, upon a hearing, bounced on appeal to superior court. This seemingly inefficient practice caused delay, expense, and duplication, leading to calls for abolition of common pleas.

Some circles also called for elimination of county general sessions of the peace, which had original jurisdiction in criminal cases, such as fornication, profanity, and theft. In addition, general sessions had administrative responsibilities, such as assessing and spending county taxes, approving new bridges, laying out highways, and licensing innkeepers. This vast county control led to accusations of improper administration and abuse of powers.

Antilawyer sentiment was extensive. Many attorneys who held public office were convenient scapegoats for malcontents. They were particularly scorned by debtors who were beleaguered by court and legal fees, a disdain exacerbated by attorney speculators who bought defaulted notes and forced collection in court. When Lynn voters chose John Carnes as representative on May 8, in addition to investigating "grants of public salaries and other monies," he was instructed "to bring about another mode of proceeding in our law matters and to put it out of the power of the gentlemen of the law to take advantage of their clients as they have often done, and to put them to so much needless trouble and expense."[4] On June 1, 1786,

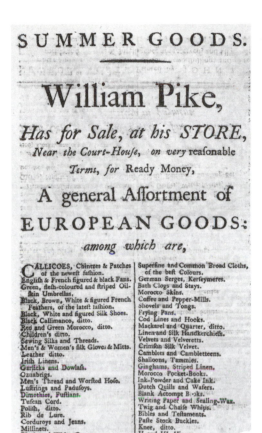

SUMMER GOODS.

William Pike,

Has for Sale, at his STORE,

Near the Court-House, on very reasonable

Terms, for Ready Money,

A general Assortment of

EUROPEAN GOODS:

among which are,

CALLICOES, Chintzes & Patches of the newest fashion.
English & French figured & black Fans.
Green, flesh-coloured and striped Oil-skin Umbrellas.
Black, Brown, White & figured French Feathers, of the latest fashion.
Black, White and figured Silk Shoes.
Black Callimanco, ditto.
Red and Green Morocco, ditto.
Children's ditto.
Sewing Silks and Threads.
Men's & Women's silk Gloves & Mitts.
Leather ditto.
Irish Linens.
Garlicks and Dowlass.
Oznabrigs.
Men's Thread and Worsted Hose.
Lustrings and Padusoys.
Dimothies, Fustians.
Tuscan Cord.
Polish, ditto.
Rib de Lure.
Corduroys and Jeans.
Millinets.
Black and White Gauzes.

Superfine and Common Broad Cloths, of the best Colours.
German Serges, Kerseymeres.
Bath Clogs and Stays.
Morocco Skins.
Coffee and Pepper-Mills.
Shovels and Tongs.
Frying Pans.
Cod Lines and Hooks.
Mackarel and Quarter, ditto.
Linen and Silk Handkerchiefs.
Velvets and Velveretts.
Crimson Silk Velvet.
Camblets and Cambleteens.
Shalloons, Tammies.
Ginghams, Striped Linen.
Morocco Pocket-Books.
Ink-Powder and Cake Ink.
Dutch Quills and Wafers.
Blank Accompt Books.
Writing Paper and Sealing Wax.
Twig and Chaise Whips.
Bibles and Testaments.
Paste Stock Buckles.
Knee, ditto.
H and HL Hinges.
Sad-Irons.

The wide array of goods available after the war tempted people to buy. A great many became overburdened with debt. The *Essex Journal and the Massachusetts and New-Hampshire General Advertiser,* July 27, 1785. Courtesy, Essex Institute, Salem, Mass.

attorney William Pynchon of Salem noted: "The Lawyers are, most of them, turned out or left out of the General Assembly, and are vilified in the public prints."[5]

State liabilities intensified clashes between debtor and creditor. The major state indebtedness, other than Continental obligations, was £1,300,000 in securities. Also, principal and interest was owed on wartime notes issued to soldiers. Hard-pressed veterans subsequently sold IOU's at discounts to eastern speculators, such as Timothy Dexter of Newburyport, hoping for full redemption. The 6 percent annual specie interest had been paid from tariff and excise revenues; many legislators, especially those from the western counties, wanted revenues sent to Congress instead. By the end of 1786, all army notes and one-third of securities were scheduled for redemption. Veterans and other former note holders, already disgruntled over interest payments, joined the chorus, demanding debt relief by redemption at fair market value, rather than face. But Danvers voters disagreed, noting in their August 2 instructions to Rep. Israel Hutchinson that a creditor "did not hesitate to accept the solemn pledge of his country's faith, as his only security; and most confidently relying on her justice, resolved to stake his all on her ability and success." Whether or not first holders had parted with their securities "for a valuable or a vile consideration," Danvers townspeople saw the obligations "unchangeable, and ought to be inviolable."[6] Earlier, on May 22, mercantile Newburyport had voiced a similar opinion.

By omitting taxes in 1785, the General Court was forced to raise the next year's assessments to over £300,000, the highest since 1781. One-third was earmarked to redeem army notes; £29,000 was tagged to securities interest. Still, indebtedness maturing in 1785 and 1786 had not been budgeted. The poll tax rose to 40 percent of revenues, which, unlike property levies, was not geared to ability to pay. Howls were heard, particularly from western Massachusetts, denouncing legislators for exacting an inequitable burden from cash-poor farmers.

The General Court prorogued July 8, 1786, after passing only two minor reforms. After lengthy debate and several close votes, proposals to divert excise income to Congress and to redeem debt at market value were dealt death blows. Sound currency advocates also defeated paper money and voted down a tender law. Government salaries, which agrarians branded excessive, were unchanged. As news of legislative inaction filtered into the countryside, the simmering passions of embittered westerners came to full boil.

Summer Passions

During July and August, State House intransigence triggered a string of conventions in Berkshire, Bristol, Hampshire, Middlesex, and Worcester counties, all of which approved long-standing reformist demands. Some were sparsely attended rump affairs; others were crowded and popularly representative. Hampshire County yeomen published their convention proceedings, hoping to gain more adherents. The conventions' proposals, however, were not uniformly supported among counties nor within member towns. Established trading centers like Hadley, Hatfield, Northampton, and Springfield opposed many resolutions, particularly radical notions such as issuing paper money and forcing constitutional revision nine years before it was provided for in the Massachusetts constitution. Eastern critics stridently labeled the conventions treasonable and British-inspired.

Westerners wanted to move the government seat away from the seaboard. Boston, they complained, was too distant, too expensive, and inordinately dominated by the merchants clustered along the seaboard. While residents in major Essex County seaports relished Boston's proximity, others, in Amesbury, Andover, Boxford, Rowley, and Salisbury, backed the move.

To decrease costs and diminish the power of commercial interests, reformers sought to amend the six-year-old constitution. Popular mistrust of the executive, reminiscent of pre-Revolutionary days, inspired efforts to curtail the governor's patronage and his ability to fix salaries. Western hamlet inhabitants resurrected the ancient concept of apportioning representatives by town, rather than by population. The propertied Senate, suspect as obstructionist and believed to be an unnecessary expense, was targeted for elimination. The proposals were intended to enhance agrarian, village power at the expense of the commercial elite.[7]

By late summer, peaceful conventions had been abandoned by many yeomen, who resorted instead to focusing public attention through mob violence. The rebellion phase started on August 29 when fifteen hundred insurgents—led by Capt. Luke Day of West Springfield, among others—suddenly attacked the Northampton courthouse—the symbol of debtor frustration—and prevented the judges from sitting. Court closings were similarly forced in Bristol, Middlesex, and Worcester counties. When militia were summoned, they usually showed half-hearted enthusiasm toward restraining their zealous neighbors. In Berkshire County, when armed insurgents seized the courthouse, most militia deserted to the crowd; debtors in Great Barrington jail were released. In the disquieting interim between late August and mid-October, no courts sat in five counties.

The fall session of Essex County's court of common pleas was scheduled to open September 26 in Newburyport. Attorney William Pynchon, traveling to court down Bay road, ominously noted "a great uneasiness" at Rowley. But no raucous mobs gathered. Justices Greenleaf, Holten, and Phillips, joined by special justice Ebenezer March of Newbury, opened court. To deter rabble-rousers, the merchant-dominated Newburyport artillery company paraded conspicuously about Newburyport streets to sounds of fifes and drums.[8]

Emergency Session

Gov. James Bowdoin called an emergency session for September 27. On the day before, 1,100 club-wielding, musket-rattling agitators had confronted the Springfield Supreme Judicial Court. The scarlet-robed jurists sat protected by Major General Shepard, who, expecting trouble, had occupied the courthouse, braced by 800 disciplined militia. After a day-long stand-off, with the former Revolutionary officer Daniel Shays prominent in negotiations, an agreement was struck. After adjournment, Shepard surrendered the courthouse and moved his men to the vital federal arsenal, permitting each side to claim victory.[9] This dire threat to Massachusetts' fledgling government underscored the importance of the upcoming special session.

The town of Salisbury—neither strictly agrarian nor mercantile nor debtor-creditor—had a mixed economy. Its people made their livings in a variety of ways: fisheries, husbandry, trades in hat- and shoemaking and, of course, shipbuilding. A moderate committee chosen by Salisbury voters on September 19 prepared a report on what they considered salient issues for Rep. Joseph March.

While favoring change, the committee stressed that March "pay the most sacred regard to our Constitution . . . the Basis or Foundation of all Security to every Individual for his Life, Liberty, Property, and Character." They endorsed moving the General Court from expensive Boston to Andover or Concord; either being, they wrote, "most central" and "convenient for the purpose." Because many common pleas and general sessions cases were "sent up to the Supreme Judicial Court," which became "tedious & expensive," they favored "enlarging the authority of the Justices of the Peace and empowering them to issue Rules binding upon the parties." They opposed the "Multiplicity of attorneys," and their buying "a great part of the Property of the Country." They indicated that impost and excise revenues would serve "a more necessary and important purpose" were Congress permitted to apply them toward Massachusetts' interest on the foreign debt. They advised the General Court to allow outstanding taxes and debts due prior to 1784 "to be paid in State Securities at a certain rate," which would expedite collections and reduce state indebtedness. Emission of paper money was considered "a vain & dangerous Expedient" which increased "Confusion, Fraud & Injustice." An act "to prevent excessive Usury," however, was favored. With a decrease in "circulating cash," many principal officeholders' salaries were judged "disproportionate to the ability of the People to pay." And every government department was admonished to practice "Frugality & Economy." The committee concluded that popular acceptance of these virtues "with those of Temperance & Industry throughout the State," and of manufacturing "amon[g]st ourselves" were the "surest & safest method of extricating us from our present disagreeable & embarassed situation."[10]

On October 6, Hamlet pastor Manasseh Cutler reported to Winthrop Sargent:

> I am happy to inform you that ye County of Essex has remained perfectly quiet, & ye several town meetings that have been held here

in consequence of those insurrections, have afforded an opportunity for ascertaining ye dispositions of ye people, who, universally, appear determined to support Govt & ye present Constitution at every hazard.[11]

Though the extent of support for the proposed reforms varied throughout the towns of Essex County, paper money schemes and armed mob scenes were vehemently opposed by all.

Gov. James Bowdoin opened the special legislative session calling on both houses "to enact measures required to secure the safety of the state."[12] While the Senate was primed, many House members reacted cautiously, wanting to study the grievances. On October 6, William Pynchon observed: "We hear from Boston of the debates in General Court; some for vigorous measures and for suspension of the *Habeas Corpus* Act; others for a redress of grievances, and for all mild, soothing measures first."[13]

House members soon became persuaded that firmness was required. On October 24, a measure passed that provided for punishment of attempts by soldiers or officers to "begin, excite, cause, or join in any mutiny or sedition." Four days later, a riot act was enacted, requiring armed groups and riotous crowds to disperse within one hour after so ordered by sheriffs or justices of the peace. In November, because insurgents were arming, the writ of habeas corpus was suspended, and state warrants were provided for permitting the arrest and imprisonment of anyone believed to be endangering state security. There were, however, some misgivings. Yeomen of Rowley, for example, led by pastor Ebenezer Bradford of the First Church, had instructed Rep. Thomas Mighill to oppose suspension of this long-standing civil liberty.[14] Legislators, however, committed to combating the threatened anarchy, went further and voted to assume costs of the county militia.

While enacting countermeasures, legislators concurrently studied debtor grievances. On November 8, they voted that pre-1784 taxes could be paid in goods—beef, butter, grains, nails, pine boards, pearl ash, pork, and other commodities—rather than specie. Also, a tender law was passed, permitting debtors to pay their debts with real and personal property. In line with the thinking in Salisbury, court reform was adopted: most civil suits would be heard before justices of the peace; to avoid court costs, after issuing writs, justices were to urge use of referees. If necessary, plaintiffs still could go to the court of common pleas. After lengthy debate, the governor's £1,100 annual salary remained uncut. The issue of whether the seat should be moved was delayed to the next session. One-third of excise revenues was to be spent on general expenses, with the balance going toward interest on securities. To ease tensions, an indemnity act extended clemency to such persons as would renounce their earlier illegal actions by taking a loyalty oath before January 1, 1787. By the time of adjournment on November 18, although far from soothing all passions, legislative actions had alleviated some tensions.[15]

Before proroguing, the General Court crafted a candid, conciliatory address designed to quiet popular rumblings. In a lengthy, persuasive style, it explained the perplexing entanglement of indebtedness and expenditure. Noting the wartime "injuries and frauds" of paper currency, legislators warned that emissions "may seem to refresh us for a moment; but they will serve to fan the flame, that must eventually consume us." Personal indebtedness was blamed on frivolous indulgence in imported "gewgaws" and "fantastical and expensive fashions and intemperate living," during a spree begun in 1781 when luxury imports flooded the market. With specie "exported," the address noted, "Government is complained of, as if *they* had devoured them, and the cry of many persons now is, make us paper money." Ruin could be averted by restoring "the principles of integrity, and public spirit, and the practice of industry, sobriety, economy and fidelity in contracts."[16] Bemoaning the demise of republican wartime austerity, Bay State Puritan clergy echoed these sentiments.

Salisbury's committee had proposed that "a System of Laws" be adopted to encourage these "virtues." Earlier, on May 22, 1786, Newburyporters' instructions to representatives Stephen Cross and Jonathan Titcomb included: "We need not describe to you the discouraging embarrassments of our commerce; they so universally affect the interests of all classes of the community, as to excite the most anxious apprehensions. There are two ways of obtaining relief: By lessening the Consumption of foreign manufactures, and encouraging our own."[17] The buying frenzy had been real; indeed, belt-tightening was required, and domestic manufacturing was an admirable goal, but these practices would not remedy the immediate indebtedness and taxation quandary.

Rebellion

Some tempers had been mollified, but many people remained disgruntled. Enraged by the antiinsurgency measures, many farmers were ripe targets for demagogues. Just three days after adjournment, two hundred armed rebels from outlying towns wrested control of the Worcester courthouse at the point of bayonets. Benjamin Page, Oliver Parker, and John Shattuck of Groton became inspired to try a takeover in Middlesex County; however, because support from

Worcester and Bristol counties failed to arrive, the takeover was cancelled. On November 30, the mutinous leaders were apprehended on state warrants, with the resisting Shattuck broadsworded across his knee. Salem's William Pynchon noted: "P.M. comes the news that the troop of about 80 horse, under Colo. Hitchborn, go from Boston to Middlesex and take Shattuck and . . . bring them, on charge of traitorous conduct, to prison to Boston; this, 't is supposed, must soon bring our publick disturbances to a crisis." The conservative *Salem Mercury* reported its satisfaction that the mutineers were "now resting from their labours in Boston jail, waiting, we ardently hope, an *adequate* reward for all the toils."[18]

Repercussions were felt beyond the western counties. The uproar, fed by false rumors of government brutality, spread to Rowley. On January 30, a town meeting was held to consider calling for an investigation "into the conduct of a number of men that we have been informed went from the County of Suffolk into one of the [western] Counties and made Prisoners of one Shattock and two other men and brought them to Boston" where they were jailed. These actions, some townspeople believed, were "contrary to our Constitution." The *Salem Mercury* played down the reverberations, reporting that only three townspeople—Capt. Benjamin Adams, Lt. Rufus Wheeler, both former Revolutionary officers, and one other—favored the measure. (A second provision favored suspending the "hostile measures"—recalling the army sent in January to repress the insurgency—until a new General Court would sit.) A *Mercury* correspondent noted later, however, that "a respectable number" had requested the meeting. The articles were defeated handily; it was clear, though, many impassioned Rowleyites believed the imprisoned Middlesex Shaysites had been treated improperly.[19]

Disruptions recurred in Worcester on December 5; insurgents marched on the courthouse, but the forewarned judges already had adjourned. Four days later, in Hampshire County, a "Committee of Seventeen" organized themselves into six military regiments. Daniel Shays of Pelham, who had become a major participant, was captain in the 4th Regiment. On November 25, the *Salem Mercury* had published a western correspondent's letter in which he reckoned a majority of Springfield inhabitants "were now ready to follow Shays, and his infamous banditti" and that several towns were choosing Shaysite military officers. The protest had entered an ominous radical phase. Militants, estimated at one-quarter of western county males, mostly from rural towns, were forming to overthrow the commonwealth government.

On December 26, three hundred Regulators—as the Shaysites preferred to be called—identified by sprigs of pine in their hats, marched into Springfield and presented a petition listing their demands. They were bent on closing the courts. The petition was signed by Capt. Daniel Shays, a five-year war veteran, Luke Day, and Thomas Grover; Shays is believed to have been in command. This show of force persuaded the justices not to open court.

In 1777, after two years of war service, Shays had been promoted to captain in Col. Rufus Putnam's Continental regiment. The disgruntled Hampshire County "gentleman" land owner—once a debtor himself in two uncontested civil lawsuits—had joined the dissident leadership early in 1786. Though Shays steadily gained public recognition as overall commander within the diffused Regulator infrastructure and would lead the largest assembled armed force, he had no formal command over other leaders. Later accounts, however, have made his name synonymous with the rebellion.

A Call to Arms

On December 1, 1786, a "fine, moderate day," Maj. Gen. Jonathan Titcomb, responding to Governor Bowdoin's readiness alert, primed his 2nd (Essex) Division of Massachusetts Militia. Selectmen were ordered "to assemble the Train-band and Alarm-list" for election of officers. Within twelve days, Titcomb wanted a roster of reporting militia from all organized regiments, artillery, and cavalry companies. He had "no small pleasure in reflecting, that while, in various parts of the Commonwealth, the good Citizens have been subject to frequent alarms, from the indecent attempts of discontented, or misinformed Bodies of men . . . the worthy and respectable Yeomen of the County of Essex have manifested a uniform attachment to the Government so happily established among us."[20]

Four days later, a violent snowstorm roared through the North Shore, raising the highest tide in recent memory. It was followed by a second blizzard. The piling snow suspending most travel "was uncommon & very much drifted," wrote diarist Rev. William Bentley of Salem.[21] As the month advanced, political turmoil also raged, with increasing numbers of disgruntled farmers choosing the radical path of Daniel Shays. For months, angry, armed mobs had shut down courts. Now, the mood had turned uglier. Anarchy threatened.

During the fall, Salem already had taken the precaution of forming two military companies. One named the Independent Cadets was commanded by Capt. Stephen Abbott. The second, an artillery company, was headed by Zadock Buffington. On January 5, 1787, John Hodges of Salem wrote to Nathan Ward: "It is the opinion of most people that [the insurgents] are a pack of ruffi[a]ns & that they will easily be dispersed."[22]

By early January 1787, both Bowdoin and the Council concluded that a state-wide militia army was required to suppress the growing insurgency. The rebellion had gone beyond control of county sheriffs and local militia. A force of 4,400 volunteer Bay Staters was called for thirty days, to be assembled from five county militia—Essex, Hampshire, Middlesex, Suffolk, Worcester—under command of Maj. Gen. Benjamin Lincoln, an able, experienced former Revolutionary War officer. His orders were to protect the courts, particularly in Worcester, and to assist magistrates in executing the laws. Should hostilities erupt, Lincoln was to repel and apprehend all persons engaged in "the destruction, detriment or annoyance of this Commonwealth." Except when facing armed resistance, he was subject to civil authority. Though state funds and supplies were lacking, £5,000 was subscribed by about 130 "patriotic gentlemen" from Boston and Salem to call out the army. They were guaranteed reimbursement.[23]

Masssachusetts looked for support from the Congress meeting in Philadelphia. The federal arsenal in Springfield, housing 7,000 muskets plus other valuable military stores, was imperiled. Furthermore, agrarian disorders were spreading to neighboring states. On September 21, diarist Stephen Chase reported from Exeter, New Hampshire: "The mob went to see general court at Exeter drove home by militia 40 taken prisoner."[24] Gov. John Sullivan's mettle had averted a takeover. In October 1786, a vexed Congress resolved to raise 1,340 troops, ostensibly to fight Indians, but lack of funds delayed fielding the federal troops; thus, Massachusetts faced the peril alone.

On January 10, former Revolutionary War officer Col. Nathaniel Wade of Ipswich was called to command a 500-man Essex County regiment. Between January 8 and 17, more that 400 men (nearly 90 short of quota) were mustered in six companies from the four corners of Essex County under Capt. John Francis of Beverly (68 men), Capt. Samuel Johnson of Andover (73 men), Capt. John Rowe of Gloucester (61 men), Capt. Ezra Lunt of Newburyport (72 men), Capt. Nehemiah Ramsdell of Lynn (66 men), Capt. John Baker of Ipswich (75 men). Towns augmented the Bay State's pay of two pounds for thirty days' service with their own bounties: Amesbury's sixteen men received one dollar; Lynn's twenty-three, one pound; Bradford's eighteen, two dollars plus camp utensils. Several Danvers citizens advanced bounty monies on behalf of the town. County mercantile and yeoman towns alike rallied to suppress the invidious western rebellion.

When Colonel Wade reported to General Lincoln in Boston, he received orders to form his Essex County regiment ten miles northwest, at Woburn. On January 15, volunteers from the Ipswich area were enlivened by a rousing speech from Hamlet pastor Manasseh

Officers in Col. Nathaniel Wade's
Essex Regiment[26]

Colonel	Nathaniel Wade	Ipswich
Lieut. Colonel	Jonathan Evans	Salisbury
Major	John Robinson	Boxford
Adjutant	Robert Farley	Ipswich
Quartermaster	John How Boardman	Ipswich
Surgeon	Elisha Whitney	Ipswich
Surgeon's Mate	Thomas Farley	Ipswich
Captain	Samuel Johnson	Andover
Lieutenant	Peter Carlton	Andover
Ensign	Nathaniel Thurston	Bradford

from Andover, Bradford, Haverhill, Methuen

Captain	John Rowe	Gloucester
Lieutenant	William Kinsman	Gloucester
Ensign	William Tuck	Manchester

from Gloucester, Manchester

Captain	Ezra Lunt	Newburyport
Lieutenant	Moses Pike	Newburyport
Ensign	Aaron Colby	Amesbury

from Amesbury, Newburyport, Salisbury

Captain	Nehemiah Ramsdell	Lynn
Lieutenant	Benjamin Moses	Salem
Ensign	John Pynchon	Salem

from Lynn, Salem

Captain	John Baker	Ipswich
Lieutenant	Aaron Perkins	Ipswich
Ensign	Ephraim Smith	Danvers

from Ipswich, Rowley, Topsfield

Captain	John Francis	Beverly
Lieutenant	Ezekiel Sawyer	Rowley
Lieutenant	Daniel Needham	Danvers
Ensign	Aaron Francis	Beverly

from Beverly, Danvers, Ipswich, Rowley

Cutler, in which he exhorted them to crush the insurgency; on the following day, they marched. In northern Essex County, troops assembled at the head of Market Street, Newburyport; they heeded Capt. Ezra Lunt's stirring patriotic appeal, shouted "in loud and cheerful huzzas," and streamed out of town. Further south, on January 18, young Ensign John Pynchon led the Salem contingent; after stopping to refresh themselves at Bell tavern, they stepped off "in high spirits" to three cheers from a crowd of Danvers and Salem people. Two days later, Capt. Rowe's Cape Ann company strode through Salem "with fife and drum." A correspondent to the *Massachusetts Gazette* bragged "that the people of the respectable and loyal county of Essex, upon the late call . . . manifested the warmest zeal and patriotism, and that five times the number of men, that were required, might have been enlisted with the greatest ease." Six companies of volunteer militia, led by former Revolutionary officers from mercantile and yeoman Essex County converged on Woburn.[25]

Local Opposition

Nicolas Pike of Newburyport, a respected justice of the peace and grammar school teacher (and soon to be author of America's first arithmetic book), wrote to Gov. James Bowdoin: "There are many enemies to Government in these parts, who are very impudent & constantly endeavoring to inflame the minds of people." Though Newburyport had none "of any note," he reported several from yeoman Newbury: John Atkinson, Nathaniel Emery, Silas Little, Samuel Noyes, and Deacon Silas Pearson. Among Pike's complaints were: Atkinson's berating of the General Court for believing "they had all Power in heaven & earth"; Emery's effort to delay raising Newbury troops; Little's branding of Masssachusetts as "much oppressed"; Noyes's rebuking of enlistees and expressing the hope "every one who went to Worcester would die there"; and Pearson's discrediting of the November legislative address as "a pack of Lies to deceive the People." Tied by family and friendship, they were among Newbury's prominent, well-to-do, principal elected officials—Atkinson and Emery were selectmen—and militia officers (Adams and Emery). Sixty-two-year-old country squire Silas Pearson was a major land holder and owned several mills. These were not stereotypical Shaysites; their opposition was more philosophical and libertarian-based, fed by historic contentions between Newbury yeomen and Newburyport merchants and shipbuilders, rather than strictly by current debtor-creditor worries. In Rowley, Pike singled out Capt. Benjamin Adams, who had called Rowley's recent meeting, and Rufus Wheeler, whose "constant Practice is to wish & drink Confusion to our Army

& Success to Shays." Pike wished the government would take measures to "silent these impious wretches."[27]

Despite notable examples, anti-Shaysites were firmly in control, with one important exception: impoverished Marblehead. Its quota of fifty-one men never marched. Due to pressures from Titcomb and others, on February 1 the November legislative address was read in town meeting. Six days later, lip service to the militia request was voted: "That this Town do most heartily Concur in the measures Adopted by Government for the Suppression of the Rebellion." Marbleheaders pledged to raise their quota and appointed a committee to receive subscriptions of ammunition, arms, clothing, money, and provisions. But little was done. Seeking to defuse concerns and rumors, the *Salem Mercury* published the vote; Marblehead's inaction, though, confirmed the presence of a powerful pro-Shaysite faction.[28]

To Worcester and Springfield

On Saturday, January 20, the Essex regiment left Woburn to march to Concord; the following day, they merged with the Middlesex and Suffolk regiments in Marlborough. On January 22, Lincoln's army entered Worcester; combined with loyal area militia, his total strength exceeded 3,000. Courts proceeded without interruption. Two days later, leaving behind one regiment and an artillery company, Lincoln's force trooped toward Springfield.

The Regulators, meanwhile, had withdrawn from Worcester, with their sights set on Springfield's federal arsenal. The vital stockpile was defended by Gen. William Shepard and 1,100 Hampshire County militia. Over 1,000 rebels from Middlesex and Worcester counties converged on Palmer, a staging point east of town, while insurgents from Berkshire County congregated four miles north. On January 25, Daniel Shays was to lead the assault with 1,200 attackers, joined by Luke Day and 400 men from across the river in West Springfield. Once they had armed from the well-stocked magazine, the rebel insurgents planned to march on Boston.

An intercepted message, however, scuttled the scheme, and Shays advanced alone. When his agrarian army marching in twelve-man platoons reached within 250 yards of the arsenal, Shepard forbade Shays to cross "over a certain line, which was described." Shays laughed, brazenly ignored the warning, and proceeded, seemingly unswayed by two artillery rounds whistling overhead. As the platoons advanced menacingly close, a round of grapeshot burst into the rebel ranks, instantly killing three, mortally injuring a fourth, and wounding twenty. The insurgents broke and retreated up the east side of the Connecticut River toward Amherst, where they regrouped.[29]

On Saturday, January 27, General Lincoln entered Springfield with four regiments—2,000 men, including the Essex County regiment—and four companies of artillery. Shortly afterward, they crossed the ice-covered Connecticut to disperse Luke Day's rebel band. When Day's picket spotted Lincoln's advance force, they "ran like foxes, leaving their guns behind," reported Ipswich surgeon Dr. Elisha Whitney.[30] Pursuing cavalry brought about fifty back to headquarters. Upon taking an oath, they were freed by a compassionate commander. Day, however, escaped toward Northampton.

Back home, on the day Essex County troops arrived in Springfield, penurious Methuen voted *not* to provision "the men gone to Wooster."[31] Whether this stemmed from local opposition or meager resources is not known. Later, though, supplies were sent. Times were difficult for about one hundred tax-delinquent families in this Merrimack Valley hamlet. Despite local adversity, however, Essex County responded with sleigh-loads of provisions—beans, beef, bread, pork, New England rum—oxen-teamed out of most towns destined for Worcester and Springfield.

Meanwhile, Eli Parsons's insurgents had joined Shays's; together, they moved to South Hadley. By Monday morning, January 29, Lincoln's army was on their tail, forcing the embattled Shaysites first north to Hadley, then on to Pelham. From Hadley, General Lincoln sent word that pardons would be recommended for enlisted men who gave up their arms and took the oath of allegiance. The morning of February 3, holding out for a general pardon, Shays quit Pelham with about 1,500 men for Petersham, thirty miles away.[32]

That evening, Lincoln's army trudged in pursuit. Halfway, howling north winds blew in a sudden, blinding, nearly impassable snowstorm. But they plodded on in the face of biting cold and knee-high snow. Finally, at nine o'clock in the morning, the army arrived, taking the rebels by complete surprise. More than one hundred and fifty were captured, including forty taken by twelve Salem militiamen. Shays, Parsons, and the remaining rank and file scattered into the countryside.[33] Lincoln left the Shaysite army splintered and no longer an organized threat.

Back in Session

In January, Amesbury had chosen a committee to prepare instructions for Rep. Peleg Challis. Their report, which bore close resemblance to neighboring Salisbury's September draft, expressed the hope that this "dangerous" and "critical" situation would be "brought to a happy conclusion without the shedding of blood . . . our fellow citizens in arms in a most tumultuous manner which we fear may be our ruin."[34] Amesbury, like other towns near the seaboard, was concerned that the insurgency could topple Massachusetts' infant constitutional government.

Meanwhile, on the day Shays had left Pelham with Lincoln's army on his heels, Governor Bowdoin addressed the General Court, observing that government's "*lenity and forbearance*" had been treated with contempt and interpreted as weakness and calling for "vigour, decision, energy" to prevent the rebellion from being transformed into civil war. Annoyed that earlier "lenient and merciful" actions had been scorned, legislators approved Gen. William Shepard's decisive action and depicted insurrectionist leadership as guided by "a settled determination to subvert the Constitution." On February 4, they declared "*that a horrid and unnatural* Rebellion and War, has been openly and traiterously raised and levied against this Commonwealth" and equipped Governor Bowdoin with martial law powers. Distinguishing between leaders and followers, they conciliated by resolving that the governor could pardon private soldiers and noncommissioned officers who would surrender their arms and take an oath of allegiance.[35]

Legacy of Shays

After dispersing the Hampshire County Shaysites, General Lincoln left a regiment at Northampton under General Shepard and marched to Pittsfield in Berkshire County. When he arrived on February 11, up to forty insurgents a day were laying down their arms and swearing oaths of allegiance. On February 22, with the storm subsiding, Lincoln's army, including the Essex regiment, was ordered home.

Skirmishes flared sporadically among recalcitrant bands of holdouts until March. Daniel Shays, Luke Day, Eli Parsons, and other leaders, with their intractable bands, sought refuge in the friendly Green Mountains and in neighboring states. An Essex County company originally headed by Ezra Lunt, which helped replace militia dismissed in late February, remained in service until late June–early July, under Col. Timothy Newell.[36] Border raids persisted until May, when, with help from neighboring governments (except for Rhode Island, which was in sympathy with the Shaysites), these incursions were brought under control. Not until September, however, were the last state troops disbanded.

A disqualifying act passed in Massachusetts on February 16 made pardoned rebels ineligible to serve as jurors or in public office. Neither could they exercise "the employments of School-Masters, Innkeepers or Retailers of spirituous liquors," occupations which were considered seedbeds for nurturing social discontent. Moreover, they could not vote "for any officer, civil or military, within this Commonwealth." Within three years, however, full citizenship would be restored.[37]

The commonwealth prescribed that assessors, collectors, constables, selectmen, town clerks, and treasurers take an oath that noted their "true faith and allegiance" and willingness to defend the commonwealth "against traitorous conspiracies and all hostile attempts whatsoever," renouncing "all allegiance, subjection, and obedience to the King, Queen, or Government of Great Britain." At Beverly's March 12 town meeting, "as the laws direct," the address from the General Court was read, along with the riot act and the disqualifying act.[38] County-wide, town officers signified their loyalty by taking and subscribing to the oath of allegiance.

As quickly as resistance faded, sympathy arose for the rebels. In March, the General Court appointed a pardoning commission for cases not covered by the disqualifying act; that is, for people who had openly sympathized but who had not taken up arms. Eventually, 790 were pardoned. Finally, in June, a new General Court repealed the disqualifying act, and Gov. John Hancock proclaimed indemnification for everyone who took an oath of allegiance. Only nine leaders were excluded; later, even Daniel Shays, Luke Day, and the others received pardons.

New political winds were blowing in the gubernatorial election of April 2, 1787. With support from all classes, former governor John Hancock was elected three to one over his political rival, Governor James Bowdoin. Less ominous times produced a backlash sympathetic to the western rebels, who had been tracked down, captured, and dispossessed of their citizen rights. A capricious public censured Bowdoin's firm, vigorous handling of the insurgency and viewed the popular, more informal Hancock as compassionate toward debtor and taxpayer grievances. In an unprecedented turnout, the electorate gave Hancock over 18,000 votes to 6,000 for Bowdoin. In Essex County, Gloucester voted overwhelmingly for Bowdoin; also, Salem delivered a slim Bowdoin majority. All other Essex County towns voted for Hancock; agrarian towns did so, decisively.

Rebels and supporters of reform held high hopes for the new May 1787 General Court. In the House, 160 of 222 representatives were freshmen; about half the Senate had been replaced. Most from Essex County were anti-Shayites, though Newbury sent Nathaniel Emery.

Instructions from Boxford and Rowley to their representatives for the upcoming session were barometric measures of Essex County agrarian sentiment. Both wanted state officeholders' salaries reduced, the court of common pleas abolished, and former insurgents pardoned, so long as they "behave as good subjects." Rowley wanted to stop specie interest payments on depreciated securities and favored a new "circulating medium," while Boxford sought to extend the tender act, to dismiss the army "as an armed force is dangerous to the Liberties of a People in time of peace," and to coin a "large Bank of Silver and Copper Money," already authorized by the General Court in October 1786. The two towns, most Shaysite of any in Essex County, favored *only* the moderate, long-standing debtor-taxation demands.[39]

Partial Gubernatorial Returns, Essex County		
TOWN	HANCOCK	BOWDOIN
Amesbury*	45	4
Andover	138	65
Beverly	77	48
Boxford	89	12
Danvers	94	19
Gloucester	4	109
Ipswich	194	55
Marblehead	64	38
Methuen	27	5
Middleton	61	3
Newbury	189	96
Newburyport	214	107
Rowley	136	18
Salisbury	68	5
Salem	120	131
Wenham	31	6
*16 votes for Benjamin Lincoln.		

Andover's March 5 instructions for Rep. Peter Osgood, Jr., to exert his "influence to retrieve & preserve the Public Credit" and to strongly oppose the emission of a "paper medium" demonstrated the commercial orientation of this inland market town. The General Court could be moved, Andover agreed, though not "into any county where there has been an open Insurrection." "A speedy collection of all Taxes granted" prior to 1786 was called for, so as not to discourage those heretofore "punctual." So far as feasible, revenues were to come from import and excise, rather than from polls. Though Andover's conservativism was clear, there was modest support for some agrarian reforms.[40]

Despite its promise, the new court failed to effect any substantial change, a disappointment to former insurgents and their coterie of sympathizers. While the tender law was extended for six months, the provision to issue paper money failed by a wide margin. To address money scarcity, a mint was established; copper cents and half-cents began to be minted—the first conformance with the 1786 acts of Congress that proposed a federal decimal coinage. During the fall, the poor law was changed, permitting debtors' release from prison when they took an oath of penuriousness. Furthermore, the 1788 tax bill imposed only modest levies on polls and estates. These mild reforms held intact Massachusetts' credit, which more radical measures would have jeopardized.

Essex County did not split into warring, dissident factions. Even in the most agrarian towns—Boxford, Bradford, Methuen, Rowley, Topsfield—wide majorities opposed the armed insurgency. Despite their endemic indebtedness, they did not gravitate toward radical demands or violence. Yeoman Essex County, plus communities with mixed economies, such as Amesbury, Lynn, and Salisbury, rejected extremism and limited their support to moderate reforms. Had Essex County been more agrarian or less tied to port markets, conditions might have been different. Instead, the prevailing influences were the values of temperance and frugality and the shaping of a lasting, strong economy through commerce and manufacturing. In short, the county heeded the message of its creditor- and trade-oriented towns: Andover, Beverly, Danvers, Newburyport, and Salem.

By year's end, signs augered well for the future. In the East, soon, increased trade would stimulate fisheries and improve demand for farm products, both of which put more specie into circulation. Westward, vast, fertile, uninhabited lands in the Ohio Valley would open for settlement—an economic safety valve for impoverished toilers. To the south, a new constitution was being crafted: one eventual result would be federal assumption of state debts, relaxing tax pressures on the member states. Thus a most unsettling chapter in Massachusetts history was brought to a happy conclusion.

1. Manasseh Cutler to Winthrop Sargent, October 6, 1786, ALS, Winthrop Sargent Collection, MHS.
2. Rowley Town Records, January 19, 1784, 103; "Letter from Samuel Holten to Rev. Benjamin Wadsworth," DHS *Collections*, 26 (1938):93.
3. Court of Common Pleas Docket, September 1785–September 1786, EI.
4. Alonzo Lewis and James R. Newhall, *History of Lynn* (Boston: John L. Shorey, 1865), 352.
5. Fitch Edward Oliver, ed., *The Diary of William Pynchon* (Boston: Houghton Mifflin, 1890), 240.
6. 6. Danvers Town Records, August 2, 1786, 3:329.
7. Robert J. Taylor, *Western Massachusetts in the Revolution* (1954; Millwood, NY: Kraus, 1974), 139–40.
8. Oliver, 249, 251.
9. Taylor, 145–146; *The Essex Journal & New-Hampshire Packet* (hereinafter, *Essex Journal*), October 11, 1786.

10. Salisbury Town Records, September 25, 1786, 158–60.
11. Manasseh Cutler to Winthrop Sargent, MHS.
12. MA Archives 190:275.
13. Oliver, 252.
14. Rowley Town Records, October 9, 1786, 126–27.
15. Taylor, 150–53.
16. *Essex Journal*, December 20, 1786.
17. Newburyport Town Records, May 22, 1786, 1:468.
18. Oliver, 257; *Salem Mercury*, December 2, 1786.
19. Rowley Town Records, January 30, 1787, 130–31; *Salem Mercury*, February 10, 24, 1787.
20. Oliver, 257; General Orders, Broadside, EI.
21. *The Diary of William Bentley*, (Gloucester: Peter Smith, 1962), 1:48.
22. John Hodges to Nathan Ward, ALS, Ward Family Papers, EI.
23. *Salem Mercury*, January 6, 1787.
24. Diary of Stephen Chase, MS., NEHGS.
25. Herbert T. Wade, "The Essex Regiment in Shays' Rebellion—1787," *EIHC*, 90 (1954):329; William Parker Cutler and Julia Perkins Cutler, eds., *Life, Journal, and Correspondence of Rev. Manasseh Cutler* (Cincinnati: Robert Clark, 1888), 1:197; E. Vale Smith, *History of Newburyport* (Newburyport: E. Vale Smith, 1854), 127;

Oliver 264–265; Massachusetts *Gazette*, January 19, 1787.
26. MA Archives 191:84, 225, 289, 320; 192:47, 66, 167.
27. Nicolas Pike to James Bowdoin, February 12, 1787, ALS, Bowdoin—Temple Papers, MHS.
28. Marblehead Town Records, EI, February 7, 1787, 4:1073–76; *Salem Mercury*, March 3, 1787; few militia marched from Newbury, and there is no record that volunteers were raised in agrarian Middleton; possibly, the hamlet was dominated by pro-Shaysites.
29. *Essex Journal*, January 31, 1787; *Salem Mercury*, February 3, 1787.
30. Cutler and Cutler, 1:197.
31. Methuen Town Records, January 27, 1787, 121.
32. *Essex Journal*, February 7, 1787.
33. Oliver, 268.
34. Amesbury Town Records, January 30, 1787, 494–95.
35. *Essex Journal*, February 7, 1787; *Salem Mercury*, February 10, 1787.
36. MA Archives 191:319.
37. *Salem Mercury*, February 24, 1787.
38. Beverly Town Records, 7:255.
39. Boxford Town Records, February 22, 1787, 239; May 24, 1787, 245–46; Rowley Town Records, May 28, 1787, 138.
40. Andover Town Records, March 5, 1787.

CHAPTER TWENTY - FOUR

CONTEST FOR
A NEW REPUBLIC

In February 1788, after Bay Staters concluded the momentous debate in Boston over the United States Constitution, delegates from Essex County towns cast the largest, most lopsided proadoption vote of any county. Without this sweeping mandate, the crucial ratification in Massachusetts might have been defeated. The consequent reverberations could have relegated the Constitution of 1787 to a forsaken footnote in American history. Indeed, throughout months of contest, Essex County leaders played principal roles within Federalist and Antifederalist ranks alike. A sympathetic popular groundswell, coupled with adroit maneuvering by the Federalists, however, positioned pro-Constitution forces solidly in control.

Calling a Convention

After the Articles of Confederation were adopted, many nationalist leaders gradually became convinced that America's first constitution required amendment. Gov. James Bowdoin was acutely aware of its deficiencies, particularly of Congress's inability to protect American commerce. In his inaugural address of 1785, the governor suggested calling a federal convention to revise the articles. With shipbuilding foundering at one-quarter the volume of prewar years, Newburyport voters expressed their gratitude to Bowdoin on July 7, noting: "The critical state of our Commerce and the weight of Publick debt that presses us, demand the strictest attention to every commercial & economical principle, that may extricate us from our embarrassed situation."[1] These sentiments were shared by all mercantile towns.   441

The legislature lent Bowdoin their support and instructed its con-federal representatives, Elbridge Gerry, Samuel Holten, and Rufus King, to raise the question of revision. The delegates refused, believ-ing the time was "premature." The three states-rightists—all of Essex County—suspected the call for stronger national powers was a veiled attempt to establish an aristocracy that "will afford lucrative Employ-ments, civil and military," require a standing army, and hordes of "pensioners, and placemen to prop and support its exalted Admin-istration."[2]

The following year, Virginia invited the states to Annapolis to discuss trade regulations. Although nine states appointed commis-sioners, four delegations, including one from Massachusetts, failed to attend. The convention in September 1786 called for another meeting in Philadelphia—the second Monday in May 1787—for gen-eral revision of the articles. After several months' delay, Congress endorsed the May convention on February 21, 1787, "for the sole and express purpose of revising the Articles of Confederation, and reporting to Congress and the several legislatures, such alterations and provisions therein." But nationalist government forces intended to go further—which their opponents had suspected. Shays's uprising had sent a wave that had reverberated disquietingly throughout the states. That the Confederation had neither the resources nor the authority to suppress the insurgency swayed many states to favor a convention. When it came time, all but radical Rhode Island would send delegations.

Massachusetts' confederal delegates continued in opposition, be-lieving amendments should emanate from Congress, as provided. Sensing the drift of public opinion and wanting to join the talks, Rufus King revised his view. Before the Philadelphia convention concluded, he would become a foremost nationalist.

The Philadelphia Convention

Four Massachusetts delegates numbered among the fifty-five "demi-gods" attending the convention. Supreme Court Justice Fran-cis Dana was chosen, but he did not attend. Caleb Strong, a North-ampton attorney, traveled to Philadelphia and participated in the proceedings, but, on account of family illness, returned home by late August. Those remaining were Nathaniel Gorham, a prominent Charlestown merchant; Marblehead native Elbridge Gerry, who had moved to Cambridge in 1787; and Maine-born Newburyport attorney Rufus King. All three had attained impressive records of public service, including years in the General Court and the confederal Congress. Successful in their private lives, steeped in practical politics, the delegates would ably represent Massachusetts. Gerry and King would be active on the floor and in committee. The ex-Marbleheader would chair the Grand Committee, designed to reconcile differences between large and small states, while King, at only thirty-two years, would serve on the committee "of Style and Arrangement," to shape the final draft.

By May 25, with a quorum of seven states, the convention convened. From the onset, it was agreed to replace the articles with a new constitution. Nearly four months of debate—often heated—would be held, amid a sweltering Philadelphia summer. A multitude of compromises was required to accommodate the diverse, often-conflicting interests in the states. The outcome was the shaping of a new federal constitution that provided a national government with three separate branches: legislative, executive, and judicial. It included a bicameral legislature, a House of Representatives apportioned by population, and a Senate with equal votes for each state. One person, the president, constituted the executive. He would serve four years and be chosen by electors selected by the states. Delegate Gerry, who considered the proposed government too centrist, sought to make several changes and to attach a bill of rights. Furthermore, he believed the constitution should not go into effect until the confederal Congress and all the states had approved it. When his efforts failed, he refused to sign. Nonetheless, on September 17, thirty-nine of the forty-two delegates present, including Gorham and King, lined up to affix their signatures to the new "Constitution of the United States of America."

The proposed constitution, while limiting the powers of the states, provided for a national government, stronger than under the articles, with full sovereign powers. It alone could levy duties on foreign commerce. States were prohibited from issuing paper currency or passing laws to impair contracts, two elements favored by creditors and investors. Should "domestic violence" erupt—another Shays's insurrection, for example—and a state request military assistance, the national government would be required to give it. If deemed necessary, national officials were empowered unilaterally to call the state militia to "suppress insurrections." To preserve American independence, the national government, without asking for money or personnel, could declare war, make the peace, form alliances, and decide treaties.

On September 28, reminiscent of the procedure adopted by Massachusetts in 1780, Congress voted to submit the draft to the states for approval in special conventions. Congressmen Nathan Dane of Beverly and Richard Henry Lee of Virginia, believing the articles were being subverted, tried to block submission; when they failed,

444 THE WORLD TURNED UPSIDE DOWN

Dane and Lee tried to amend the document, without success.[3] Upon ratification by nine state conventions, the constitution would take effect.

Contrasting Views

Bay Staters speculated nervously over what the proposed frame of government contained. Curiosity peaked as a copy of the draft reached Boston on September 25. Within a few days, the text was published across the state; it appeared in the *Salem Gazette* on October 2 and, the next day, in Newburyport's *Essex Journal*. Shortly afterward, pamphlet editions circulated, including an official one ordered by the General Court. The contents, which soon became generally known, were the chief source of conversation throughout the Bay State.

During the 1780s, no story, except possibly Shays's revolt, received comparable coverage in Newburyport and Salem newspapers. Extracts of letters, pamphlets, and speeches, and also "progress" reports on the "Federal Constitution" in other states, were printed in each weekly edition. During October, a series of articles by "An American Citizen" praising the new constitution appeared in the *Salem Mercury*. A proadoption speech delivered by James Wilson, the brilliant nationalist Pennsylvania delegate, was covered in the *Essex Journal*, where it was noted that Wilson "was frequently interrupted with loud and unanimous testimonies of approbation."[4] Later, on November 28, the Newburyport *Journal* ran a powerful Federalist appeal authored by "Cato," which vilified anticonstitutionalists. Extracts taken from Boston and out-of-state weeklies often were published, particularly from the Federalist *Massachusetts Centinel*. On December 12 and 19, for example, the *Journal* carried the *Centinel's* "observations" that argued for adoption. Though Antifederalist prose was scantily reported, a commentary authored by "Cincinnatus" was printed in the December 11 *Salem Mercury*; the *Essex Journal* devoted its front page to Virginia delegate George Mason's objections. (He was one of three who refused to sign.)[5] On January 2, 1788, a Federalist critique followed, which had originated in the *Connecticut Courant*. One of Mason's reservations, popular among export-conscious southerners, fueled ratification in commercial Newburyport. Navigation laws, Mason believed, should require two-thirds approval; otherwise, "foreign bottoms" would be excluded from "carrying American produce to market, and throw a monopoly . . . into the hands of the eastern states." A most welcome event in Newburyport and other maritime centers! Newburyport's reliance on shipbuilding and trade caused a correspondent to ask if "there is not a town in the Union, perhaps,

To return to their defcendants who lately emigrated to America, *Fœderalift*, who inherits all the republican virtues, and has drawn all his maxims of national policy from his glorious Progenitor, concludes every addrefs he makes to the public with the following laconic injunction, UNITE AND BE HAPPY—while the preachments of *Antifœderalift*, who retains all the perfidious, villainous, bafe, traitorous and anti-republican principles of *Antifœdus* his great grandfire, when ftripped of their fophifm and falfe colourings amount to this : The peoples' happinefs is incompatible with the aggrandizement of ME and MINE, therefore, IF YOU UNITE I FALL.

                          C A T O.

During the ratification debates, "Cato" vilified the Antifederalists in the *Essex Journal & New-Hampshire Packet*, November 28, 1787. Courtesy, American Antiquarian Society.

which suffers more severely on this account." Under the proposed constitution, America could retaliate with uniform tariffs against other countries' trade restrictions. This would result, the author predicted, in the Merrimack shore "lined as heretofore with new ships."[6] The unabashed Federalist stance of the Newburyport and Salem papers is not surprising. The economic future of these mercantile entrepôts—along with other seaboard towns—hinged, it was believed, on ratification.

Early in November, both Essex County newspapers copied Elbridge Gerry's objections. Originally, they were composed in a letter to the Massachusetts legislature and reprinted in the *Massachusetts Centinel*. The people were inadequately provided with representation, Gerry wrote, and had "no security for the right of election." The powers of Congress were sometimes "ambiguous," he said, and "others indefinite and dangerous." He predicted that the executive would have "undue influence over the Legislature," and that the judiciary "will be oppressive." Only two-thirds of a Senate quorum could confirm treaties, and Gerry contended no bill of rights was provided to protect personal liberties. The proposed constitution, Gerry warned, was a "system of *national* government," rather than federal. He conceded that "in many respects," the constitution had "great merit," but amendments were required. The *Salem Mercury* noted editorially that thirty-nine out of forty-two members had signed and commented: "To suffer ourselves to be influenced, on this momentous subject, by the opinion of an individual, in opposition to so large a majority of enlightened, distinguished, decided Patriots, would be sacrificing the rights of the People, and adopting the wishes of, perhaps, an interested minority."[7] Later, the *Essex Journal* carried a rebuttal to Gerry's remarks. As a respected delegate to the Philadelphia convention, however, Gerry carried considerable weight with an already wary public. The Marblehead republican had delivered an important setback to ratification momentum.

Another Antifederalist commentary was penned by William Symmes, a twenty-seven-year-old North Andover attorney. Son of North Parish pastor Rev. William Symmes and a graduate of Harvard College, young Symmes became a student in the law office of Theophilus Parsons. After being admitted to the bar, he opened his own practice—the first in town—in an office attached to the home of Peter Osgood, Jr. In a lengthy, fervent letter to Osgood on November 15, 1787, Symmes shared his sentiments on the constitution. His intense rhetoric suggests the message may have been a political statement intended for the public. Symmes, together with Osgood, would be elected to represent Andover in the upcoming Massachusetts convention.

Apportionment of taxes, Symmes believed, would work against the North because only three-fifths of the slave population was counted for taxation. He objected to equal representation in the Senate, calling it "quite ridiculous" that "little Delaware" should have equal weight with Massachusetts. The young attorney protested Congress's control over "times, places and manner of holding elections" and its power to withhold parts of journals which, "*in their judgment* require secrecy." Quipped Symmes, "A very wise Congress!" He particularly opposed the legislature's sweeping revenue-raising powers: "A more general . . . surrender of all ye property in the United States could not perhaps have been framed." Despite his personal antipathy toward paper money, Symmes believed states should have the option to issue scrip, and to enact tender laws. He was disturbed by the Congress's wide discretion to raise and support armies, with "no bar against a standing army in time of peace," wrote Symmes.

He objected that the president and ten senators (two-thirds of a quorum—a majority) could make treaties and that only eight senators (majority of a quorum) were needed to confirm executive appointments. The president—"or elected King?"—was vested with too much power, which, he believed, should be shared, as in Massachusetts, with a council. Disputes between citizens of different states, subject to federal jurisdiction, Symmes predicted, "will carry men 600 miles, and cause them more expense than the matter in dispute may be worth." He viewed this "grievous" and "quite unnecessary," and also objected to the Supreme Court's appellate jurisdiction. Finally, the guarantee of republican government to every state, Symmes felt, "meddles too much" with states' rights. He allowed the constitution "would make us formidable abroad, and keep us very *peaceable* at home." The price, however, was loss of state sovereignty: to be "contented to become citizens of America, and confuse the thirteen stripes, and change the stars into one glorious sun." Symmes admonished: "Let us equally shun a hasty acceptance or a precipitate rejection of this all-important scheme."[8]

In contrast to Symmes's Antifederalism, in 1788 the conservative Newburyport merchant Jonathan Jackson published an abstruse political tract intended to "excite" the reader "to a national exertion and conformity of sentiments" that is "very necessary to our political system." Jackson's *Thoughts upon the Political Situation . . .* was printed during the ratification struggle under the pseudonym, "A Native of Boston."

Unless we form "one efficient government," Jackson asked, "how are we to support the independence we have claimed?" The separate states were "puny governments" needing to be "cemented by one common interest." He attacked "sly, artful politicians" in the states trying to "save power and importance to their own states, and consequently to themselves." Jackson warned that another state could have a Shays-type uprising, which it may "not so soon be able to suppress." A handful of elitists would always be bent on forming an aristocracy inimical to liberty, but they presented little danger, Jackson believed, in contrast to those prone "to a highly democratical government." There is "no rule but their own will and caprice, or the interested wishes of a very few persons, who *affect* to speak the sentiments of the people." The best opportunity for free government, he theorized, depended on "obtaining the wisest and best general will of the community" and enforcing conformance. Jackson called for a natural aristocracy "who by nature, education, and good dispositions, are qualified for government," whether they be "taken from the plough, from the mechanick's bench, or from behind the counter." He rejected two popularly touted safeguards: rotation in office and frequent elections. The Newburyporter wrote: "to part with a good man . . . appears to be contrary to common sense"; also, he objected to submitting office holders to the "whim and caprice of the people." Once "tranquility and industry" were established "under a mild but steady government," Jackson prophesied that within a century the progress of the United States would compare favorably with Europe's. Since the war, there had been "immense importations" that had drained currency from the country. If imports were limited to necessary and useful items, and people gave up "gewgaws and trifles," the country would become free of debt to Europe. Though he had reservations, Jackson saw the proposed constitution as "much more perfect than any plan of government." The lengthy, disjointed tract included a fanciful plan of national union, whereby Jackson proposed a complex election process, which would have made obsolete state boundaries and traditional town government. To begin, a ward of ten voters would choose a delegate and, after several levels of selection, would end with election of a congress. The unitary scheme must have appalled states-rights Antifederalists, but Jackson's confidence seemed unbounded. How many readers he persuaded, however, is an open question.[9]

Contest for Delegates

On October 20, two days after convening, the Massachusetts Senate approved the calling of a convention. When the House took up the matter, Dr. Daniel Kilham, who operated an apothecary on State Street, and was Newburyport's only prominent Antifederalist, arose to argue "upon the impropriety of being in a hurry" with a measure of this importance. Kilham questioned the "right of either convention or people" to dismantle the Confederation. Should only nine states approve, he warned, the resulting disunion could precipitate civil strife and suffering. Kilham's views were widely criticized, with a correspondent to the *Massachusetts Gazette* recommending a coat of tar and feathers. Henceforth, the outspoken doctor was out of political favor in Federalist Newburyport.[10]

Others spoke against the convention. Some representatives favored a popular referendum on the constitution, which likely would have defeated it. To take the convention out of Boston and to delay the meeting date were both suggested. With amendments which moved the date to the second Wednesday in January and provided for three copies of the draft, rather than one, to be distributed to towns, the motion passed on October 24. Next day, the Senate concurred, and the call was issued.

Voters converged on town halls during November and December to select delegates. Towns were entitled to the same number of delegates as they had representatives in the House. Newburyport sent four prominent conservatives: Benjamin Greenleaf (141 votes), Theophilus Parsons (92 votes), Jonathan Titcomb (87 votes), and Rufus King (80 votes). The highly esteemed Judge Greenleaf, Parsons's father-in-law, was the overwhelming choice, while King received fewest votes, though enough to be chosen. After becoming a

Massachusetts delegate to Congress in 1784, King had been residing in New York, where he married into the prominent Alsop family. Some locals resented his continued nonresidence and viewed him as an outsider. King was in town for the vote, but, shortly afterwards, left for New York. The *Journal* noted the good fortune of having this gentleman's "great political knowledge, abilities and integrity in deciding upon the great national question." Federalist leadership, statewide, knew that this eloquent spokesman—one of thirty-nine signers—would be crucial to the outcome. One of Beverly's three delegates was the prosperous merchant George Cabot. Although Cabot had served as state senator, he had not held office recently. Nathan Dane, a seasoned confederal delegate, would have been a logical choice. However, Dane had originally fought the proposed constitution in Congress; he returned home nonplussed to find his political friends were proadoption. He became silent and, gradually, changed his opinion. Beverly voters, leaving nothing to chance, chose Cabot.[11]

Unlike in the seaports of Beverly, Gloucester, Marblehead, Newburyport, and Salem, in some Essex County communities delegate selection became intense and controversial. Town records show only the names of delegates chosen—not their accompanying instructions. Presumably, their stances were known. The *Essex Journal* reported that an "Anti-federal Junto" in Newbury—likely the pro-Shaysite leaders of a year earlier—"highly disgusted" with the choice of delegates, called a meeting weeks afterward to issue instructions. On the appointed day, voters did not pick a moderator and, by three to one, dissolved the meeting. On December 25, Ipswich Antifederalists tried a similar belated move, but voters were 61 to 102 against taking up the constitution, hearing Elbridge Gerry's objections, or giving delegates instructions.[12] Throughout the contest, the proadoption politicians, skillful leaders with superior communications, organization, and resources, consistently outmaneuvered their opponents. For several months, the ratification question remained the single major political issue. It split many towns into two contentious factions, Federalists and Antifederalists, laying the seedbed for the American party system.

County Profile

Forty-five among the 364 seated delegates hailed from Essex County. Generally mature and experienced, several from the region had reached their sixtieth year: John Carnes, Michael Farley, Israel Hutchinson, Isaac Mansfield, Thomas Mighill, Enoch Sawyer, Daniel Thurston, and Jonathan Titcomb had all launched their business and political careers years earlier, during colonial times. There were also youthful members who aspired to greater distinction and accomplishment: thirty-year-old Salem merchant Francis Cabot, the young attorney William Symmes, and Rufus King, wise at thirty-two years. In addition to men who were successful in their private lives, the ranks would produce two congressmen, three United States senators, one state supreme court chief justice, and a contender for the presidency of the United States.

During the War of Independence, many Essex County delegates served their country in civilian and military capacities. Willis Patten of Amesbury, Joseph Wood of Beverly, Jonathan Cogswell of Ipswich and several others held membership in Revolutionary committees of correspondence, inspection, and safety. John Glover, Israel Hutchinson, and Thomas Mighill were famed Continental Army officers, while John Burnham, Ebenezer Carlton, Jonathan Cogswell, Michael Farley, Nathaniel Marsh, Daniel Thurston, and Jonathan Titcomb had held commissions—ranging from lieutenant to major general— in the Massachusetts militia. There were former privateer owners— including George Cabot, Tristram Dalton, Jonathan Glover, John Glover, Azor Orne, William Pearson, Israel Thorndike, Jonathan Titcomb—who had held investments in scores of vessels; Benjamin Lurvey of Amesbury had captained the privateer *Betsey*. The distinguished Thomas Kittredge of Andover, surgeon in Col. James Frye's regiment, cared for the wounded on bloody Bunker Hill. Another surgeon, Dr. Samuel Nye of Salisbury, served aboard the *Vengeance* and the *America*, while Rev. John Carnes of Lynn was a regimental chaplain. With independence achieved, but the course uncertain, these veteran patriots were called upon to help determine the direction of America's history.

Delegates reflected varied backgrounds, experiences, and talents. There was major representation among the professions. Four were physicians: Kittredge, Nye, the venerable Holten, and Enoch Sawyer of Newbury. King, Parsons, Symmes, and Lurvey were lawyers. Benjamin Lurvey of Amesbury was a self-styled lawyer without formal training; he made his living writing deeds, wills, and settling estates. Several men held judicial or county offices. Former schoolmaster Daniel Noyes of Ipswich was register of probate; the renowned Benjamin Greenleaf, a probate and common pleas judge. Since 1775, Samuel Holten had been a justice of the court of common pleas. Michael Farley was sheriff and county treasurer; one-third of the delegates were justices of the peace. Major commercial centers sent large representations of merchant traders and shipmasters: Tristram Dalton of Newbury, Jonathan Titcomb of Newburyport, Cabot and Thorndike of Beverly, and nearly the entire delegations of Glouces-

Salem, Richard Manning, Efq.
Edward Pulling, Efq. Mr Wm.
Gray, jun. Mr Francis Cabot.
Danvers, Hon. Samuel Holten,
                    I. Hutchinfon, Efq'rs
Newbury, Hon. Triftram Dalton,
EnochSawyer, E. March, Efq'rs
Newbury-port, Hon. Rufus King,
Hon. B. Greenleaf, T. Parfons,
Hon. JonathanTitcomb, Efq'rs.
Beverly, Hon. G. Cabot, Efq. Mr.
J. Wood, Capt IfraelThorndike.
Ipfwich, Hon. Michael Farley,
J. Chote, Daniel Noyes, Efqrs.
Col. Jonathan Coggefwell.
Marblehead, Ifaac Mansfield, J.
Glover, Hon. Azor Orne, John
Glover, Efq'rs.
Gloucefter, Daniel Rogers, John
Low, Efq'rs. Capt W. Pearfons.
Lynn & Lynnfields, John Carnes,
Efq. Capt John Burnham.
Andover, Capt PeterOfgood, jun.
Dr T. Kittridge, Mr William
Symmes, jun.
Rowley. Capt Thos. Mighill
Haverhill, Bailey Bartlett, Efq.
Capthain Nathaniel Marfh.
Topsfield, Mr Ifrael Clark.
Salifbury, Dr Samuel Nye, Mr
Enoch Jackman.
Almfbury, Capt Benj. Lurvey,
Mr Willis Patten.
Boxford, Hon. Aaron Wood, Efq.
Bradford, Daniel Thurfton, Efq.
Methuen, Capt Eben. Carlton.
Wenham, Mr Jacob Herrick.

Delegates to the Massachusetts
constitutional convention from
Essex County. From the *Essex
Journal & New-Hampshire Packet* of
Newburyport, January 23, 1788.
Courtesy, American Antiquarian
Society.

ter, Marblehead, and Salem. From interior towns came retail merchants Bailey Bartlett of Haverhill and Peter Osgood, Jr., of Andover. Several were skilled artisans and tradesmen: John Burnham, housewright; Jonathan Glover, hatter and merchant; Enoch Jackman, cordwainer; Nathaniel Marsh, feltmaker and hatter; Willis Patten, brickmaker; Daniel Thurston, architect and housewright. Israel Hutchinson, also a housewright, owned a grist and saw mill in the New Mills section of Danvers. Some craftsmen and tradesmen doubled as farmers; a handful were primarily yeomen: Ebenezer Carlton of Methuen, John Choate and Jonathan Cogswell of Ipswich, Israel Clark of Topsfield, Thomas Mighill of Rowley.

Several delegates, including Cabot, Thorndike, Daniel Rogers of Gloucester, and William Gray of Salem, were among the county's most affluent men. In addition to Tristram Dalton's imposing residence on State Street in Newburyport, he owned a magnificent two-hundred-acre farm situated on Pipe Stave Hill in Newbury New Town. Thomas Kittredge's home was reputed to be the finest in North Andover; Daniel Thurston of Bradford owned one of Essex County's best farms.

The delegation represented men of all ranks and occupations: professionals, judicial and county office holders, business and commercial classes, artisans and mechanics, yeomen. The United States was a meritocracy, and voters customarily selected their leaders from doers—the achievers, the learned, the prominent and prosperous.

Delegates mostly were chosen because of local distinction earned by their public-service records. Over the years, the vast majority had held numerous appointed and elected positions. Nearly one in four had been delegates to the Bay State constitutional convention of 1779–1780, an appropriate measure of suitability for the job ahead. Joseph Wood had been Beverly's town clerk since 1771; Thomas Mighill had served Rowley from 1773, one year excepted, and, since 1783, had been representative to the House. Six of the last seven years, John Choate had been an Ipswich representative. Indeed, in January 1788, sixteen delegates held elected state office.

The stakes in the outcome were high. Differences abounded—heated debate and impassioned controversy were inevitable. The people nonetheless could take comfort in having chosen delegates from among their most eminent, experienced, and talented citizens, and, as importantly, those worthy of the public trust.

Two delegate selections defy easy explanation. One was Manchester's seat, occupied by Simeon Miller, a Universalist preacher and Yale graduate. Town records disclose no exemplary public service by Miller, nor even that he was *elected* delegate; further, his name does not appear in the January 23, 1788 *Essex Journal*. Though the process remains an enigma, Miller, however, was officially seated. Secondly, in Wenham, on December 26, Jacob Herrick was elected delegate. A Beverly native and member of the Harvard class of 1777, he probably did not reside in Wenham. Why was the relatively anonymous Herrick elected? For years, neither town chose representatives to the General Court or sent delegates to the Massachusetts Convention of 1779–80. Signs seem to indicate that a well-oiled Federalist machine quietly selected and seated two proadoption delegates whose spaces would have gone unfilled.[13]

Convention Proceedings

The convention was convened on January 9, 1788, at the old State House in Boston, but the quarters were inadequate for 364 delegates.

Next day, they moved temporarily to the Brattle Street meetinghouse, while a committee chaired by Tristram Dalton searched for a more "convenient" location. Rev. Jeremy Belknap's Congregational meetinghouse on Long Lane, which extended between Milk and Purchase streets, was suggested. There were pews on the ground floor to seat the delegates and galleries for spectators. The recommendation was accepted; on the seventeenth, the convention adjourned to meet at Long Lane, which, after ratification, the delegates renamed Federal Street.

At the outset, if a vote had been taken on the constitution, the Federalists would have lost. They nonetheless enjoyed several strengths, which proved decisive. Their leaders were from the proppertied and educated class, men with established reputations and recognized abilities. Three of the four delegates who sat at Philadelphia—Nathaniel Gorham, Rufus King, and Caleb Strong—were counted in their ranks. Former governor James Bowdoin and Generals William Heath and Benjamin Lincoln were staunch Federalists. The leadership also included the able and experienced Fisher Ames, George Cabot, Tristram Dalton, Francis Dana, Theophilus Parsons, and Theodore Sedgwick. The only Antifederalist of comparable reputation was Dr. Samuel Holten of Danvers, who was in poor health. Holten would attend for only eleven days and would be absent during the final vote.[14] Gov. John Hancock, who had been elected president of the convention, was noncommittal; Sam Adams was opposed. Neither, however, labored hard against the constitution. Two days before the convention, the Federalists cleverly orchestrated a political gathering by four hundred Boston shipwrights and other tradesmen at the Green Dragon tavern. At the meeting, resolutions urging passage were voted. With his old artisan and mechanic allies strongly in favor, Adams was silenced. So the job of heading off the formidable Federalist leadership fell upon heretofore obscure delegates, largely from Maine and small towns in central and western Massachusetts.

During December, it was doubtful whether King would be leaving New York. Imploring King to travel, Gorham wrote, "You can have no idea how much depends on your presence." On December 30, writing from Boston, Christopher Gore reminded King: "You can do great good." To the relief of Gore, Gorham, Parsons, and other Federalists, King arrived on Friday, January 11.[15] His knowledge of the Philadelphia proceedings, bolstered by his impressive oratorical powers, would be critical.

In a tactical ploy, Antifederalists moved that Elbridge Gerry be invited to take a seat and to answer questions which might arise. A resident of strongly Federalist Cambridge, Gerry was not a delegate. The resolution passed, but, within a few days, contention arose. Gerry insisted upon taking the floor to clarify a point—actually a ruse to expound on his Antifederalist views—but was ruled out of order. When the dispute ensued, Gerry stalked out, never to return. For a time, the ensuing turmoil imperiled the entire proceedings.

The Gerry episode weakened the Federalists. More than ever, a tactful, conciliatory approach was demanded. They resolved to let opponents speak for as long as they wished, then to thoughtfully answer every objection, again and again. The convention voted to discuss the constitution, paragraph by paragraph, to give every member an opportunity to express his sentiments. When the Antifederalists tried to hurry the session and move to the final question, Federalists found an ally in Sam Adams, president of the Senate. He rose to say that delegates ought not be "stingy of our time, or the public money, when so important an object demanded them."[16] The Federalists had bought some time. They knew, no matter how convincing their arguments, most opponents would not be won. Instead, sights were set on a few wavering souls. Inside and outside the hall they lobbied, and sometimes they pressured. The *Boston Gazette*, on January 21, alleged that bribes had been paid; an investigation that was ordered repudiated the charge. Superior organization and excellent leadership—with some intrigue and chicanery—paid dividends and eventually led to Federalist triumph.

Actual debate commenced January 14 with discussion of a two-year-term provision for House of Representatives members, which many delegates opposed. During the proceedings, delegates would often drift from subject to subject, only to return to them later. Dr. John Taylor of Worcester County favored annual elections, as well as right of recall and rotation in office, all provided under the Articles of Confederation as safeguards. On the fifteenth, Rufus King countered that two years was not too long for representatives concerned with the entire thirteen states, "where the complicated interests of united America are mingled with those of foreign nations, and where the great duties of national sovereignty will require constant attention." During the nearly month-long session, King would take the floor many times, articulating eloquent rejoinders to Antifederalist objections. Several days later, Theophilus Parsons, addressing recall and rotation, asserted that representatives "will lose all ideas of the general good, and will dwindle to a servile agent." Furthermore, he stated, the people may be deprived "at critical seasons, of the services of the most important characters in the nation."[17] When Gen. Samuel Thompson of Maine objected to having no property qualifications for House members, King replied that he "never knew that property was an index to abilities." On apportionment, complaints were heard that Massachusetts had only eight House seats to Georgia's three.

This young state, it was explained, was growing from recent migrations. Furthermore, Tristram Dalton of Newbury saw it as "a great deal"; under the articles, there was to be one state, one vote, without regard to population.[18]

Col. William Jones of Maine questioned the six-year term for senators, suspecting they would move to the capital and forget their own states. King observed that senators would be checked by others "who wish for their seats," and, furthermore, would always be subject to instructions from state legislatures, which elected them. With vital obligations which included confirming executive appointments and treaty making, they needed time "to mature their judgment" and to become "acquainted with the rights and interests of nations."[19]

Congress's authority to alter state election regulations became a major battleground. If they could change the "Time, places and Manner of holding Elections for senators and representatives," it was argued that Congress would soon restrict the franchise and ultimately control elections. On January 16, George Cabot explained he viewed "the *democratic* branch" as a "*check* on the *federal* branch." (Under the constitution, senators were originally chosen by state legislatures.) If state legislators were permitted "to regulate conclusively the elections of the democratic branch," they might "first weaken, and at last destroy, that check." Theophilus Parsons expanded on Cabot's points, noting that "the sovereignty of the States is represented in the Senate." The Senate's power is balanced and checked by the House of Representatives, the people's branch. The two houses "have different constituents," he said, and "there will be frequent struggles and contentions between them." If state legislatures had exclusive control over election regulations, Parsons warned, "the Representatives will very soon be reduced to an undue dependence upon the Senate." Echoing Cabot's admonitions, he predicted that a "State legislature, under the influence of their Senators . . . would introduce such regulations as would render the rights of the people insecure, and of little value."[20]

Objections were leveled at several of Congress's delegated powers (Article I, Section 8), particularly with regard to revenue raising. The objection was not so much to Congress laying and collecting duties, imposts, and excises, but, rather, to the word "taxes," that is, direct taxes. Mindful of the powerful merchants in Massachusetts and their opposition to duties and imposts, many delegates feared this commercial class would control national politics, making direct taxes the rule. The ineffectiveness of the confederal requisition system was noted by King, who remarked that several states had failed to contribute their share. "The history of our own country is a melancholy proof," he said, that requisitions are not workable. For laws "to be effective," King argued, taxes "must not be laid on States, but upon individuals." The following day, Tristram Dalton warned that the inability to tax "will in time ruin us." "The danger of accepting this Constitution," Dalton said, "is not equal to the danger of refusing it." The Newbury delegate anticipated that direct taxes would be levied only in wartime; at other times, imposts and excises would be sufficient.[21] Opponent William Symmes spoke at length against an unlimited taxing power, fearing a time when "true patriots" in Congress would be outnumbered by "men of less and selfish principles." Symmes observed that sooner or later "all governments have degenerated, and consequently have abused" their powers. Delegating Congress the "power to collect," he predicted, would give rise to "a standing army of ravenous collectors." John Choate of Ipswich, however, saw taxation providing Congress the means to "defend us abroad, and preserve to us peace at home." Otherwise, people would be deprived of "defense and self-preservation," unable to regulate commerce and protect trade. Most county delegates supported the taxing power, lack of which had been a major confederal deficiency.[22]

Slavery in the South stimulated several debates. To some, the institution was strictly a representation, taxation matter; to others, it was a religious and moral issue, permitting little compromise. Thompson of Maine believed the southern states should be required to abandon slavery as a condition to union. "No gentleman within these walls detests every idea of slavery more than I do," rebutted Gen. William Heath, but states are "sovereign and independent to a certain degree, and they have a right, and will regulate their own internal affairs, as to themselves appears proper."[23] The apportionment of three-fifths of the slave population for purposes of taxation and representation in the House came under fire. Some believed the representation formula would give slavemasters too much political influence, while others viewed the taxation arithmetic unfair to New England. But the framers intended, King said, for representation and taxation to "go hand in hand." The Antifederalist Dr. Samuel Holten, a former member of Congress, understood the widely diverse sectional interests that needed to be accommodated. Should the constitution prevail, Holten favored the three-fifths compromise, the best he believed that could be negotiated.[24] To present a favorable comparison, Rufus King offered the awkward analogy that five Negro children from South Carolina would pay the same tax as the three governors of New Hampshire, Massachusetts, and Connecticut. Some delegates were incensed that Congress would be prohibited from abolishing the slave trade for twenty years. Cabot and Dalton, however, defended the provision, asserting, as Dalton observed on the twenty-fifth, "we gain a right in time to abolish the slave trade," whereas under the articles, there was no chance.[25]

Several delegates' anxieties about "judiciary power" were manifested in a speech delivered January 28 by Abraham Holmes of Plymouth County. No provision required that grand jury indictment precede issuance of a warrant and imprisonment, for instance, nor were other civil rights protected, such as the right to obtain the benefit of council, to face one's accuser, to cross-examine witnesses, or to be protected against self-incrimination. Congress could institute courts, Holmes believed, with powers "little less inauspicious than . . . that diabolical institution, the *Inquisition*," and establish the "most cruel and unheard of punishments." Mr. Christopher Gore of Boston rejoined that one should not presume "that wherever Congress may possibly abuse power, that they certainly will." Nonetheless, several delegates demanded judicial protections and other civil liberties. Nearly ten years earlier, in his "Essex Result," Theophilus Parsons had championed a bill of rights for the Massachusetts Constitution. Parsons saw this as impractical on the national level, noting on February 5 that "no power was given to Congress to infringe on any one of the natural rights." Many delegates remained unconvinced and continued to press until a bill of rights was amended.[26]

Only a few people were active debaters, most preferring to listen and leave the oratory to others. Federalists who made memorable contributions were Ames, Dana, Gorham, Sedgwick, and Newburyporters King and Parsons. Rev. Jeremy Belknap wrote on January 25: "Rufus King shines among the Feds with a superior lustre. His speeches are clear, cool, nervous, pointed and conclusive. Parsons distinguishes accurately and reasons forcibly."[27]

Federalists sensed that little hope existed for passage without some conciliatory gesture. King wrote to James Madison on January 23: "We are now thinking of amendments to be submitted not as a condition of our assent & Ratification, but as the opinion of the Convention, subjoined to their ratification."[28] By packaging the constitution with recommendations for amendments to be considered by the future Congress, they hoped to mollify enough delegates to gain approval. This way, the constitution would remain intact, without absolutely obligating the new government to pass a bill of rights.

Supporters believed the proposal would be received better if it were presented by a heretofore neutral or uncommitted delegate and, preferably, one who was widely trusted and respected. Such a person was Gov. John Hancock, president of the convention, who, until this time, had avoided a public position. Not until January 30, in fact, had Hancock taken his seat, having been indisposed with the gout, supposedly. Not for the first time detractors labeled Hancock's ailment a convenient excuse while he tested the political winds. Rufus King wrote on January 20: "Hancock is still confined, or rather he has not yet taken his Seat; as soon as the majority is exhibited on either Side I think his Health will suffice him to be abroad." Within ten days, a deal had been struck. King wrote to Madison: "Our hopes are increasing. If Mr. Hancock does not disappoint our present expectations, our wishes will be gratified." Writing confidentially on January 30 to friend and ally Michael Hodge in Newburyport, Tristram Dalton predicted that the ambitious governor "will give countenance to the proposed constitution, which will carry a large majority in favor of it." Sam Adams "will come out in favor," he wrote, which "will settle the matter favorably. All this is scarcely known out of our caucus, wherein we work as hard as in Convention." When Adams was told of the proposed amendments, he had promised to support them. The bargain struck with Hancock included "universal" help from Bowdoin's friends in the next gubernatorial election. His Excellency was further influenced by the alluring prospect of the vice presidency, or even the presidency. As King explained to General Knox, *"we told him, that, if Virginia does not unite, which is problematical, he is considered as the only fair candidate for President.*[29]

On the following day, Thursday, January 31, Hancock arose to present the plan of conciliation, the Constitution with nine recommended amendments. Sam Adams seconded it. Penned by Theophilus Parsons, who was deftly and continually maneuvering behind the scenes, the resolutions included what ultimately would be the Tenth Amendment, that all powers not expressly delegated to the federal government be reserved for the states. Other amendments would have restricted Congress's power to regulate elections, made direct taxes only a last recourse, and outlawed commercial monopolies. In judicial matters, criminal trials would be preceded by grand jury indictment, and civil actions between citizens of different states would allow for jury trials. While many Antifederalist objections were addressed, what they actually wanted was a prefatory bill of rights.[30]

Meanwhile, Federalist efforts were unrelenting. Their caucus, in the words of Tristram Dalton, was "not idle by Night or Day—and sacrifice everything but moral Honesty to carry our point." Their determination was rewarded when several rank-and-file delegates, heretofore opposed to ratification, announced support. One who gave his "unreserved assent" was William Symmes, no doubt after some convincing by caucus leader Theophilus Parsons, his former mentor.[31]

On the day of Hancock's proposal, a record number of townspeople turned out at the North Parish meetinghouse in Andover, where a town meeting had been called "for the purpose of expressing sentiments of the inhabitants on the Subject of the Federal Constitution." Symmes's change of heart must have prompted the meeting. When the vote was taken, 115 favored adoption and 124 were opposed. Afterwards, however, the town voted unanimously not to give instructions. The deep divisions and bitterness engendered would last for years. So strong was the antipathy toward Symmes that soon afterwards he relocated to Portland, Maine.[32]

The motion to ratify came on February 6 and narrowly passed, 187 in favor to 168 opposed. The vote from Essex County was overwhelming—thirty-eight yeas and only six nays—the widest margin enjoyed in any county. The four coastal counties of Essex, Suffolk, Barnstable, and Plymouth voted strongly in favor, while majorities from the five interior counties were opposed. Maine was about evenly divided. Ten votes could have changed the outcome, but, in a month's time, a shrewd Federalist stratagem had effected an amazing comeback, turning likely defeat into victory.

Essex County's formidable vote reflected popular sentiment. With news of passage, many townspeople were jubilant. Mercantile-oriented inhabitants, anticipating economic rejuvenation under the new government, had supported ratification near unanimously. Small coastal communities and the Merrimack Valley towns below the falls also assented. They too had their commercially oriented citizens: fishermen, merchants, shipwrights, and yeomen with surpluses to trade. Furthermore, much of the populace were nationalists who believed that domestic and foreign interests of the United States required a stronger central union. And Shays's insurgency, widely unpopular, highlighted the weakness of the Confederation. Editorial support for ratification out of Newburyport and Salem, plus the fervor of leading citizens, had laid a proadoption base county-wide.

There was, however, some local organized opposition. While almost everyone agreed the Confederation needed an overhaul, a vocal minority believed that the proposed government was too national; they perceived certain features as aristocratic and monarchical, posing a threat to state sovereignty and personal liberties. These views, for example, were reflected by the five Andover and Danvers delegates—Dr. Samuel Holten, Jr., Israel Hutchinson, Peter Osgood, Jr., Dr. Thomas Kittredge, and William Symmes—educated, patriotic, well-to-do, prominent citizens. Their skepticism was grounded partly on an abiding faith in town-meeting democracy, with its popular, ever-vigilant management of government. Often suspicious of political machinations in the General Court at nearby Boston, these opponents believed activities hundreds of miles away would be nearly impossible to control. In addition to reservations among the propertied and learned class, a geographic, class-based resistance had evolved. Inland "plough joggers" and a few coastal folk alike manifested their longstanding suspicion of propertied, educated classes, particularly merchants, lawyers, and judges—and, also, the clergy.[33] Writing to James Madison on January 20, Rufus King noted "a distrust of men of property or education" has "a more powerful effect upon the minds of our opponents than any specific objections against the Constitution."[34] This explains the Antifederalism of agrarian Boxford, Methuen, and Rowley, whose delegates—Aaron Wood, Ebenezer Carlton and Thomas Mighill—voted against the Constitution. Opposition from Andover and Danvers, however, was composed more of a mixture of democratic populism and political theory.

When the vote was declared—Massachusetts was the sixth state to ratify—cheers burst from "a very large concourse of spectators," as the "*whole* Convention" was invited to a banquet held in the Senate chamber. The toasts were "truly conciliatory . . . all appeared willing to bury the hatchet of animosity, and to smoke the calumet of union and love," reported the *Essex Journal* and *Salem Mercury*. Spontaneous demonstrations, firing of cannons, and ringing of church bells erupted around Boston. Friday, February 8, provided "an exhibition, to which America has never before witnessed an equal." A spectacular procession wound through the streets. Hundreds of mechanics and artisans—blacksmiths, shipwrights, painters, riggers, tailors, hatters,

On February, 8, 1788, after Massachusetts ratified the Constitution, Boston celebrants provided "an exhibition, to which America has never before witnessed an equal," reported the *Essex Journal & New-Hampshire Packet.* Courtesy, American Antiquarian Society.

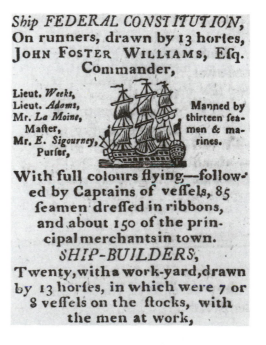

Ship FEDERAL CONSTITUTION, On runners, drawn by 13 horses, JOHN FOSTER WILLIAMS, Esq. Commander,

Lieut. *Weeks,*
Lieut. *Adams,*
Mr. *La Moine,*
  Master,
Mr. *E. Sigourney,*
  Purser,

Manned by
thirteen sea-
men & ma-
rines.

With full colours flying—followed by Captains of vessels, 85 seamen dressed in ribbons, and about 150 of the principal merchants in town.
SHIP-BUILDERS,
Twenty, with a work-yard, drawn by 13 horses, in which were 7 or 8 vessels on the stocks, with the men at work,

and other tradesmen—joyously marched in the "Grand Procession." The parade ended at Faneuil Hall, "where refreshment was liberally provided." A capacity crowd of fifteen hundred celebrants squeezed in, but two-thirds of the marchers were left outside.[35]

A celebration at Capt. Benjamin Somes's tavern in Gloucester was hosted by the "principal inhabitants" to congratulate Cape Ann's delegates.[36] The *Essex Journal* reported a "general joy" throughout Newburyport, where the news met with "almost universal" approval. Returning Newbury and Newburyport delegates were welcomed at the Newbury Green by a reception committee, which included the "gentlemen of the Trade and Officers of the militia." Young John Quincy Adams, then a student in the office of Theophilus Parsons, described the thrilling event: "A number of very respectable citizens,

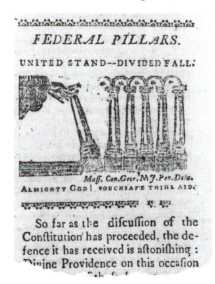

The pillar of Massachusetts rises symbolically to support the Federal edifice. The *Essex Journal & New-Hampshire Packet*, January 23, 1788. Courtesy, American Antiquarian Society.

and a number who were not very respectable, went out on horseback to meet the members and escort them into town; as they came along the bells at the different churches were set to ringing, and the noisy expression of joy was continued with some intermissions till eight o'clock in the evening." A grateful, enthusiastic throng applauded, celebrating into the night the brighter days that lay ahead.[37]

Once the Constitution won approval, opposition gradually melted. There was surprisingly little rancor; most accepted the outcome and confidently envisioned better times. Manasseh Cutler wrote on May 3: "Antifederalism is become very unpopular in this part of Ye State. Those who have been leaders are totally silent, or have changed sides." Rufus King writing to Alexander Hamilton on June 12, noted: "I have made a business of conversing with men from all parts of the

State, and am completely satisfied that the Constitution is highly popular; that its opponents are now very few, and those few hourly diminishing."[38] The Antifederalists held to their belief in limited national government, but they redirected their energies to competing for political office and promoting views later known as "Jeffersonian Republicanism." Bay Staters avidly followed ratification in the remaining states, faithfully reported by the Essex County newspapers. Upon approval by the ninth state, the new national government would go into effect.

Contest in April

Antifederalist forces in central and western Massachusetts enlisted Elbridge Gerry to challenge John Hancock's bid for reelection. Gerry's running mate, James Warren, speaker of the House, also had opposed the Constitution. In early April, county Federalist leaders caucused in Ipswich and agreed to fulfill the convention pledge to Hancock.[39] With support of Bowdoin people—bitter rivals just one year earlier—Hancock won an easy victory on April 7, by four to one.

The old Revolutionary republican, Sam Adams, was a candidate for lieutenant governor. Though he eventually advocated adopting the Constitution, Federalist leadership preferred their staunch ally Benjamin Lincoln, whose margin of victory in Essex County nearly matched Hancock's. Since no candidate received a majority in the three-way statewide contest, however, the decision rested with the General Court. And they chose Lincoln.

Governor Hancock gained a landslide mandate, more than 90 percent out of every mercantile town, with totals reaching an astonishing 99 to 100 percent in Gloucester, Lynn, Lynnfield, Newburyport, and Salem. Gerry managed respectable percentages in the anti-Constitution towns of Methuen (58), Danvers (54), Boxford (48), Andover (42), and Rowley (39). Added support came from Middleton (which did not send a delegate, 50), Wenham (43), and Ipswich (38), all basically yeoman towns. Coming only two months after the convention, the election was a referendum on the Constitution, confirming Essex County delegates' overwhelming endorsement.[40]

On the same day that gubernatorial contests were held, state senators were also elected. Essex County was entitled to six seats, to be chosen at large. The state's constitution provided that senators be elected by a majority of votes cast, but only five candidates, all Federalists (Stephen Choate, Tristram Dalton, Benjamin Goodhue, Azor Orne, Samuel Phillips, Jr.), got the prescribed number. The General Court was required to fill the "deficiency" from the two top runners-up. While the Antifederalist Dr. Holten received more votes than Jonathan Greenleaf of Newburyport (1,157 out of 2,595), the legislature settled on Greenleaf, making the entire Federalist ticket victorious. Subsequently, the two houses voted Greenleaf and Azor Orne of Marblehead to the Governor's Council. In 1787, Israel Hutchinson had sat on the Governor's Council; Aaron Wood of Boxford and Capt. Peter Coffin of Gloucester were senators; Doctors Samuel Holten, Daniel Kilham, and John Manning of Ipswich, and Capt. Richard Ward of Salem were House members. In 1788, not one held state office. The seven—four unequivocal Antifederalists, three surmised to be—were senate candidates; with anti-Constitutional views out of favor, all were defeated. (When towns chose House members later in May, none was elected.) Statewide, particularly in the seaboard counties, results were comparable, giving Federalists a decisive Senate mandate. This had important implications in the upcoming United States Senate contest.[41]

Congressional Elections

Soon, the Federalist alliance with Hancock, fragile from the onset, started to totter. Bowdoinite Federalists never cared much for the governor, sizing him up as a capricious crowd pleaser. Some broke ranks, including Essex leaders George Cabot and Theophilus Parsons, preferring the conservative, respected Lt. Gov. Benjamin Lincoln. But other leading county Federalists—Jackson, King, and others—remained with Hancock. Factionalism arose, both ideological and personal, which became apparent in the upcoming congressional elections.[42]

Massachusetts, the sixth state, had generated the first close contest. On June 21, when New Hampshire voted approval, becoming the ninth state, the new government was assured. The confederal Congress sitting in New York declared the Constitution duly ratified; congressional and presidential elections were called. By election day, only North Carolina and Rhode Island remained outside the union.

The General Court met in November to choose Massachusetts' United States senators. Federalist Caleb Strong was quickly agreed upon; the second contest, however, became bitter. The politically moderate House suggested Hancock's ally, Charles Jarvis, whom the Senate rejected. Rufus King was favored by several Boston Federalists, but his nonresidency, especially annoying to Parsons, disqualified him. (Later, King would become one of New York's first two United States senators.) The Senate countered with Federalist John Lowell, formerly of Newburyport, now living in Boston. Voted down by the House, Jarvis's name was sent up again, but the Senate would not concur. This time, they "returned" state Senate veteran Azor Orne of Marblehead. A third time, the House "put up" Jarvis. Refusing Jarvis, the Senate "sent down" the name of Tristram Dalton. The House responded by proposing moderate Nathan Dane, by a majority of one. The former Beverly congressman had the support of several Essex County senators—the Parsons faction—including Samuel Phillips, Jr., whom Boston Federalist Christopher Gore observed as exerting "himself most warmly" for Dane. Now strongly pro-Constitution, many Essex County Federalists accepted Dane into the fold, but others were mistrustful and held misgivings. The Senate "repeated" the Newburyport merchant; finally, the House agreed.[43]

A four-way contest developed among Dane, Goodhue, Holten, and Jackson for the Essex County congressional seat, one of eight in Massachusetts. Holten was the Antifederalist candidate. Before adjournment, caucusing county legislative leaders—Parsons, Phillips, and others—agreed on Dane. Goodhue and Jackson were stalwart Federalists. On election day, December 18, no candidate received a majority: Dane received 296 votes, Goodhue, 567, Holten, 229, Jackson, 391.

The two top vote getters, Goodhue and Jackson, would face off on January 29, 1789. Jackson's candidacy was endorsed in the January 21 *Journal* by a correspondent who described him as "a man whose integrity and abilities are indisputable, and whose conduct will doubtless be such as to justify the choice, and do honour to those who appoint him their Representative." It was also noted in the January 20 *Salem Mercury*. The week following, "An Elector of Essex" reminded voters that Jackson had "pledged his life and fortune in his country's cause" during the war. As to Jackson's pamphlet written under a pseudonym, which had come under attack, "whoever he be" was praised as "a staunch friend to the liberty & union of these states." The *Salem Mercury* of January 26 carried a lengthy letter in support of Goodhue, noting his "long and faithful services in publick life, both as Representative for this town and a Senator [since 1784] for the county—his firmness and experience as a politician—his integrity and fidelity as a man." With trade regulation a likely first calendar item, the writer believed "it may be of the utmost consequence to this town, to have one of its merchants in the cabinet, who is well versed in trade and commerce." Benjamin Goodhue, a forty-year-old Salem native, had graduated from Harvard to become one of Salem's most successful merchants. The Boston-born Jonathan Jackson, also a Harvard graduate, had moved to Newburyport and likewise became a prosperous trader. During the war, he suffered severe financial losses from which he never recovered while heavily engaged in privateering with the prominent firm of Jackson, Tracy and Tracy. Jackson served several terms in the Massachusetts House and as delegate to Congress. Originally, Jackson wanted to be collector of customs for the port of Boston, but withdrew when he found his friend Benjamin Lincoln wanted the job. The campaign became nasty at times, including the allegation that Jackson was propertyless and, consequently, unfit for the office. Though Jackson's credentials were bedrock conservative, the Parsons faction opposed his candidacy. Jackson was further damaged by his nationalist pamphlet, which steered small town and Antifederalist voters toward the more temperate Goodhue. Though he lost Marblehead (by a lopsided vote of 421 to 3), Beverly, Manchester, and Jackson's Newburyport, the Salem merchant carried other towns, winning countywide by a comfortable two to one margin. Goodhue traveled to New York in April and took his seat in the historic First Congress.[44]

The First Congress

The presidential electors, including Samuel Phillips, Jr., of Andover, met and cast their ballots on February 4, 1789. By early April, enough congressmen had assembled in New York, the temporary capital, to commence business. The electoral ballots were counted on April 6, with George Washington the unanimous choice. John Adams of Massachusetts won the vice presidency. On April 30, Washington took the oath of office. The ship of state was launched!

1. Newburyport Town Records, July 7, 1785, 1:450.
2. Edmund C. Burnett, ed., *Letters of Members of the Continental Congress* (Washington: Carnegie Institution, 1936), 8:206–09.
3. Burnett, 650, 662.
4. *The Essex Journal & New-Hampshire Packet* (hereinafter, *Essex Journal*), November 7, 1787.
5. *Essex Journal*, December 12, 1787.
6. October 21, 1787.
7. *Salem Mercury*, November 6, 1787; *Essex Journal*, November 7, 1787.
8. N. W. Hazen, "A Memorial Discourse on William Symmes, Esq.," *EIHC*, 4 (1862):194–97, 211–17; Sarah Loring Bailey, *Historical Sketches of Andover* (Boston: Houghton Mifflin, 1880), 197–200.
9. A Native of Boston [Jonathan Jackson], *Thoughts upon the Political Situation on the United States of America* (Worcester: Isaiah Thomas, 1788), 4, 45, 47, 51, 55, 57, 58, 71, 77, 79, 96–97, 120–21, 186–87.
10. *Debates and Proceedings in the Convention of the Commonwealth of Massachusetts, 1788* (Boston: 1856), 19–21; *Salem Mercury*, October 30, 1787; *Essex Journal*, October 31, 1787; Anson Ely Morse, *The Federalist*

Party in Massachusetts (Princeton: University Library, 1909), 52.
11. *Essex Journal*, November 21, 1787; Newburyport Town Records, 1:500, 501; Charles R. King, ed., *The Life and Correspondence of Rufus King* (New York: G. P. Putnam's Sons, 1894), 1:263, 265–67; George Bancroft, *History of the Constitution of the United States* (New York: D. Appleton, 1882), 260.
12. *Essex Journal*, January 2, 1788; Ipswich Town Records, December 25, 1787, 5:140; King, 312.
13. Delegate information was derived from biographical files in the Massachusetts State House Library, family genealogies, the Essex South Registry of Deeds, the Massachusetts Archives, local published histories, and town meeting records.
14. King, 257; Pay Roll, MA Archives, reel 278.
15. King, 263, 266, 267.
16. *Debates and Proceedings*, 196.
17. 101–02, 116, 191.
18. 133–34, 144.
19. 146.
20. 123, 124–25.
21. 155–56, *Essex Journal*, February 13, 1788.

22. *Debates and Proceedings*, 171–73, 313.
23. 217, 320.
24. 134, 302.
25. 135, 304, 319.
26. 211–13, 215, 265.
27. "The Belknap Papers," MHS *Collections*, 5th Series, 3:11.
28. King, 316.
29. "The Thatcher Papers," *The Historical Magazine*, 2nd Series (1869): 6:266; King, 317–19; Eben F. Stone, "Parsons and the Constitutional Convention of 1788," *EIHC*, 35 (1899):94; John C. Miller, *Sam Adams* (Boston: Little, Brown, 1936), 381–82; see also William Pynchon's journal entry of January 31; Fitch Edward Oliver, ed., *The Diary of William Pynchon* (Boston: Houghton Mifflin, 1890).
30. *Debates and Proceedings*, 80, 84.
31. Stone, 94; *Debates and Proceedings*, 278.
32. Andover Town Records, January 31, 1788; Bailey, 199–200.
33. King, 316–17; Samuel B. Harding, *The Contest Over the Ratification of the Federal Constitution in the State of Massachusetts* (New York: Longmans, Green, 1903), 8–10, 74–79.
34. King, 314.
35. *Salem Mercury*, February 12, 1788; *Essex Journal*, February 13, 1788.
36. *Salem Mercury*, February 12, 1788.
37. *Essex Journal*, February 13, 1788; Diary of John Quincy Adams, *Life in a New England Town* (Boston: Little, Brown, 1903), 94.
38. Knox Papers, MHS, 22:32; King, 333.
39. Morse, 58.
40. Votes for Governor & Lieutenant Governor, MA Archives, 9th choice, 1788.
41. *Salem Mercury*, June 3, 1788; Council Records, MA Archives, 30:1786–1789.
42. Benjamin W. Labaree, *Patriots and Partisans* (Cambridge: Harvard University Press, 1962), 79–80.
43. King, 345–46; Labaree, 80; Van Bech Hall, *Politics Without Parties* (Univ. of Pittsburg Press, 1972), 306–08.
44. *Essex Journal*, January 28, 1789; Labaree, 80–81; Abstract of Votes for Member of Congress, 1788, MA Archives; Hall, 310.

CHAPTER TWENTY - FIVE

ESSEX COUNTY IN 1790: A NEW DAWNING

On the eve of the last decade of the eighteenth century, Essex County was grappling with chronic financial depression. Yeomen plodded behind their plows, hoping for higher crop prices, while merchants, sailors, and tradesmen focused their efforts on mainstay industries and already established trade routes. An enterprising few, however, with penchants for venturing onto untrodden territory, set out toward new, exciting frontiers.

Old Routes

After the war, Essex County was mired in its worst economic depression in history. Most of the local ships had been captured or lay rotted at wharves and in dry dock. Many ship owners, like Jonathan Jackson, Joseph Marquand, Nathaniel Tracy of Newburyport, Azor Orne of Marblehead, and Winthrop Sargent of Gloucester, had suffered major losses. On June 25, 1787, Alice Tucker wrote of Nathaniel Tracy's downfall: "He shone for a while and attracted the notice of the admiring multitude but now is overshadowed and sunk into obscurity, many are disposed to compassionate him, but the World in general are too ill natured to bestow such a soothing consolation."[1] The county's economic backbone had been shattered; there was little cash or credit to rebuild and refit a new fleet.

With ocean trade nearly standing still, farmers were unable to sell goods and wares. English exporters revived their business connections after the war and offered American merchants plenty of credit. Stores and warehouses stocked goods heretofore scarce or unobtain-   467 able for more than five years. Eager buyers indulged in a spree, including luxury trifles. American producers could not compete. As specie dissipated and indebtedness escalated, the economic picture worsened.

A few fortunate privateersmen, notably J. & A. Cabot and the Derbys and their accomplished captains, had accumulated enormous profits. During this uncertain period, these patriots-turned-entrepreneurs ventured their capital in commerce and manufacturing. Their risk-taking would prime the pump of economic revitalization in Essex County.

Merchants sought to restore the traditional prewar trade routes, leading to England, France, Portugal, Spain, the West Indies and southern coastal ports. Eager to reestablish its overseas manufactures market, England encouraged a reciprocal trade by opening its home ports to American raw materials, though its West Indies remained closed. Meanwhile, English vessels were dumping goods on American shores and making inroads among the southern states' export market. For a while, American vessels also were shut out of French and Spanish colonies. Schooled in the art of evasion, Essex County Yankee traders sought to revive the British Indies trade by using false Nova Scotian clearances. Fortunately, the Danish, Dutch, and Swedish Caribbean Islands remained open, so that St. Croix, St. Eustatia, St. Maarten, and St. Bartholomew gradually harbored a large number of American vessels that were trading illicitly with the entire Caribbean basin. The ultimate solution, however, required building new trade routes.

During colonial times, Essex County merchants customarily exchanged West Indies goods for southern staples. Years would pass, however, before the Caribbean trade recovered. Meanwhile, local schooners embarked for Chesapeake Bay and points south laden with mostly local commodities: bricks, earthenware, cheese and other farm produce, fish, hats, molasses, New England rum, shoes, and woodenware. As the Caribbean trade revived, more Indies items were listed in the manifests of southbound vessels.

By 1790, the vast majority of merchant vessels were clearing for the Indies—Danish, Dutch, and Swedish ports—and also to French islands—Guadeloupe, Hispaniola (Cape François, Aux Cayes, Port au Prince), Martinique, and St. Martin—now open to American commerce. Sale of an entire cargo—low-quality dried cod, pickled mackerel and herring, earthen- and ironware, foodstuffs, including salted meats, lumber, shingles, staves—often required several stops. Payment sometimes was in coin; more often, contents were exchanged for brown sugar, crude cocoa, coffee, quantities of molasses and West Indies rum, along with cotton, gineva, indigo and salt. Although volume stayed below prewar levels, the Caribbean trade developed into Essex County's most lucrative market.[2]

Increased Indies sales strengthened ties with southern ports. Sometimes the route was triangular; ships left the islands and put into tidewater towns. Most local brigantines and schooners, however, returned before embarking on the coasting trade to New York, Philadelphia, Baltimore, and Virginia for beans, corn, flour, peas, rye, leaf tobacco, wheat; to North Carolina's inlets for pitch, tar, tobacco, and turpentine; to Charleston and Savannah for rice.

In 1787, twenty-eight vessels comprised the Beverly trading fleet: one ship, five brigs, seventeen schooners, and five sloops. Most belonged to former privateer owners or their captains: Moses Brown, Andrew Cabot, John Dyson, Hugh Hill, Benjamin, James and John Lovett, Joseph Lee, and Israel Thorndike. During two and a half years—from February 1787 to July 1789—105 mostly locally owned sail entered Beverly harbor. Over 90 percent had cleared West Indies or southern coastal ports. These were vital markets to Beverly—in fact, to all seaports of Essex County.[3]

On July 4, 1789, the first tariff law for the United States went into effect. It levied a 5 percent import duty on products. Also, extra tonnage duties placed on foreign-flagged vessels effectively reserved the coastwise trade for American shipping. Essex merchants and traders gained, particularly in southern markets.

Benefits from the ocean commerce extended to the interior of the country; wagons trundled from the back country as far away as New Hampshire, filled with livestock, produce, and wares. Hordes of yeomen converged on Newburyport and Salem. Their docksides were transformed to bustling marketplaces, with bushels of corn and potatoes, bunches of onions, barrels of cranberries, casks of flaxseed (or linseed oil), firkins of butter and cheese, hams and other salted meats, livestock (cows, hogs, oxen, poultry, and sheep), potash and pearl ash, staves, tow cloth, and woodenware arriving in the brimming wharfside warehouses to be exchanged for imports and kegs of New England rum. Some Merrimack Valley farmers stopped at Haverhill; merchants, such as James Duncan, Jr., Isaac Osgood, John White, and Benjamin Willis, stocked English and West Indies imports. Haverhill, an upriver town, could be reached by shallow-draft vessels; most traders docked at Newburyport, which rivaled Salem as a major entrepôt.

Newburyport, America's ninth largest town, boasted an array of vessels: six ships, forty-five brigs, thirty-nine schooners, and twenty-three sloops, fishing boats included. With ten rum distilleries in town, its merchants concentrated on importing molasses. Trade with Nova Scotia, as with some other ports, had roots that extended to colonial days and continued during the Revolution. William Bartlett, Moses Brown, Timothy Dexter, and William P. Johnson numbered among the up-and-coming merchant traders. Dexter began as a leather-dresser, but later became wealthy buying devalued Continental notes. Famous for his eccentricities, Dexter made a far-fetched specula-tion—both literally and figuratively—when he sent a cargo of warm-ing pans and mittens to the Caribbean. The pans found a market on sugar plantations as ladles, while the mittens were sold to an out-bound Baltic trader, turning a handsome profit for the shrewd Dex-ter.[4]

Trade made Salem the sixth largest town in the United States. Though its smaller schooners and sloops worked the coastwise com-merce, the majority were West Indiamen. Since the war, over five hundred cargo-laden sail had cleared for the West Indies, usually after the hurricane season. Salem harbored the county's most for-midable assembly of merchant traders: five ships, forty-one brigs, eighty-eight schooners, and ten sloops. Many former privateersmen, including the Derbys, George Dodge, Simon Forrester, William Gray, Jr., Thomas Mason, John Norris, Jonathan Peele, Jr., and George Williams, were among the notable merchants and ship owners. Though the Derbys were in a class by themselves, all, presumably, had saved profits from their wartime successes to engage in com-merce.[5]

Gloucester, while active throughout the Caribbean, enjoyed an especially strong trade with Surinam, exchanging fish for molasses. David and William Pearce and Daniel Rogers were Cape Ann's most affluent merchants. David Pearce, the largest ship owner, owned a wharf on Front Street. His vessels cleared in many directions: the smaller, toward the Caribbean; larger brigs and ships to Europe, and later, East Asia. Gloucesterites owned more than forty traders: four ships, nine brigs, twenty-three schooners, and seven sloops. In the next decade, the town would join Newburyport and Salem as a thriv-ing Federalist seaport.[6]

Across the Atlantic

Most southern coastal imports were reexported to Europe mixed with a cargo of West Indies goods, hogsheads of cod, and other commodities from New England. For the five years 1786 to 1790, New England shipped 142,050 quintals of dried cod and other scale fish to the West Indies for plantation slaves—30 percent more than to Europe; however, the higher-quality grade of cod exported to Europe grossed 15 percent more (a total of $325,800). All ports participated, but Salem was foremost, clearing two ships per month by 1787. Usual routes were the established pre-Revolutionary courses: to Bristol for manufactures, such as hardware, glass, paint; to Lorient for wine and brandy; to Bilbao and Cadiz for scarce specie, feathers, lemons, raisins, salt, soap, and more wine. Trade routes extended south toward Africa for Portuguese madeira wine and Cape Verde salt. During the spring of 1789 alone, eight Beverly schooners returned brimming with Cape Verde hogsheads.[7]

On the West African Gold Coast, local ship owners joined in the increasingly controversial slave trade with the Ashanti and other tribes. Joseph and Joshua Grafton of Salem, owners of the *Africa* and the *Gambia*, were among the traffickers. In 1784, the brigantine *Gambia* embarked on a triangular route; from Salem to Africa, across the Atlantic to Charleston, South Carolina, and back to Salem. The slave trade—disdained by most ship owners—was risky and fraught with danger. In 1787, the brig *Favorite* of Salem embarked from Guinea with a human cargo; by the time they reached Martinique, however, many of the crew and the Africans had died from disease. On September 23, 1788, when Capt. William Fairfield of the *Felicity* cleared for Cape Verde, Rev. William Bentley, pastor of Salem's Congregational East Church, suspected the actual destination was West Africa. He noted disgustedly in his diary: "The event in its probable consequences gives great pain to thinking men" and betrays "signs of the greatest moral depravity." In fact, the destination *was* Africa, where thirty-five slaves boarded. While Indies-bound, a black uprising erupted, in which Captain Fairfield was killed. Undoubtedly, other ship owners quietly engaged in this nefarious traffic.[8]

New Routes

Despite the reassuring increase in trade during the 1780s, to return to prewar volume required opening new trade routes. In 1783, the Cabot-owned *Buccanier* of Beverly was the first vessel to northern Europe; the following spring, Capt. William Tuck sailed the J. & A. Cabot ex-privateer *Commerce* to St. Petersburg. She was followed by the ship *Sebastian*. A few years later, Elias Hasket Derby began to cultivate the Baltic trade; his ships most often visited Gottenburg and St. Petersburg and hauled home bar iron, canvas, duck, and hemp. The imports were either utilized by the New England shipping industry or exported, particularly to East Asia. For years, the Baltic was a mainstay of Essex County commerce.[9]

Elias Hasket Derby, Salem's renowned privateersman, then set his sights on yet newer horizons. On December 3, 1785, after an earlier trailblazing voyage to the Cape of Good Hope, the ex-privateer *Grand Turk*, with Ebenezer West as master, made sail for the Isle of France,

In late 1785, Capt. Benjamin Carpenter of Salem sailed the schooner *Benjamin* to Cape Town, becoming one of the first New England traders to reach the Cape of Good Hope. Courtesy, Peabody Museum, Salem.

five hundred miles east of Madagascar. From there West continued to Batavia (Java) and Canton, sailing the first New England vessel to East Asia. On May 22, 1787, eighteen months after her departure, the *Turk* returned to Salem with a precious cargo of chinaware, skins, silks, and an array of teas, substantially enriching Derby's coffers. Instead of sailing toward the Strait of Magellan, the Derby flag had headed easterly around Cape of Good Hope into the Indian Ocean and the China seas. This new route became the customary Salem course to Asia; the fabulous success of Derby's pioneering venture had ensured that others soon would follow.

Six months later, on December 7, 1787, the *Grand Turk* sailed to Isle of France (now Mauritius) with Derby's eldest son, Elias Hasket, Jr., in charge. After selling her cargo, Derby received a generous offer for the *Grand Turk*, which he accepted. Next summer, two Derby-owned barques, the *Atlantic* and the *Light Horse*, were cleared on the same course. When they arrived in late 1788, young Derby was waiting. Once the cargoes were sold, the ships were sent to Bombay, where blackwood and cotton could be procured for the Canton market. From the *Turk* monies, Elias Hasket, Jr., purchased a smaller merchantman; after sailing to Madras and Calcutta, he finally returned to Salem in January 1791.

A third and fourth Derby vessel were dispatched straight to Batavia and Canton: the *Three Sisters* (in December 1788) and the former letter of marque *Astrea* (in February 1789). The *Astrea* was filled with a huge, diverse cargo: barrels of flour and tar from the coasting trade, boxes of Nantucket spermaceti candles, hogsheads of Philadelphia beer, Russian bar iron, pipes of Portuguese madeira and French port, plus New England beef, butter, chocolate (made from Caribbean cocoa), rum, salmon, and women's shoes. And not the least to be included were hogsheads of ginseng, an aromatic North American root valued by the Chinese for its medical uses, and nine kegs of Newbury snuff.

The *Astrea* had reached Canton and anchored at Whampoa; out of the blue, on October 5, 1789, the *Atlantic* and *Light Horse* loomed, arriving from Bombay, followed two days later by the *Three Sisters*. The *Atlantic* and *Three Sisters* were sold, with their proceeds invested primarily in teas. Loaded to the gills, the *Astrea* and *Light Horse* made sail, reaching Salem in June 1790.

During 1789, fifteen American vessels had visited Canton. Five hailed from Salem: the four owned by Derby and the *William and Henry*, which belonged to William Gray, Jr., and William Orne. The latter had returned safely to Salem with a manifest of teas.[10]

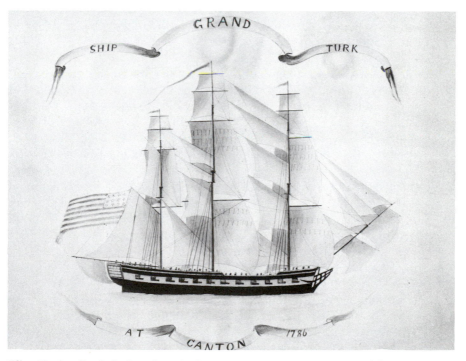

Elias Hasket Derby's *Grand Turk* of Salem, pictured at Canton in 1786, was the first New England vessel to visit China. Watercolor. Courtesy, Beverly Historical Society.

Fisheries

War, like the shipping trade, devastated county fisheries, leaving few seaworthy schooners. When peace came, the British West Indies, formerly New England's largest codfish market, was closed to American traders. In addition, both England and France gave bounties to their own nationals and prohibited foreign fish imports. Consequently, Essex County fishermen continued in bleak straits after hostilities ended.

Thanks to John Adams's negotiations, remnants of the fleet could return to prewar fishing grounds off Canada. They ventured first to the teeming Grand Banks off Newfoundland and gradually expanded their fishing grounds into the Bay, or Gulf, of St. Lawrence and to the waters off Labrador. The Treaty of Paris permitted American fishermen to dry their catches on Nova Scotia, the Magdelen Islands, and Labrador. Nonetheless, women and children continued to spread out most fish for curing on home-port beaches, flakes, and ledges. The fishing fleets, carrying nine or ten mariners each, made two or three trips (fares) each season. For these longer hauls, fishermen usually boarded a maneuverable schooner, rigged with fore-and-aft sails. During winters, the same schooners often plied West Indies and southern coastal waters.

Before the war, Marblehead was preeminent in fisheries and rivaled neighboring Salem, only three miles away, in foreign commerce. In 1790, its dilapidated private homes and fish sheds and neglected town property graphically testified to its infirmity. War and fishing casualties had taken a ghastly toll: 459 widows and 865 orphans, most needing public assistance. In 1790, so desperate was the town's plight that the Massachusetts legislature sanctioned a lottery for relief. Gambling fever spread, and 8,000 tickets quickly sold out.[11]

Though twenty-seven trading vessels registered in 1789, in an effort to revive the European and West Indies routes, the town's future was in fisheries. In 1787, there had been a turn of good fortune; not one of Marblehead's 800 fishermen was lost at sea. That year, gross earnings per vessel amounted to $483; two years later, however, income tumbled to $273.[12]

By 1790, Marblehead's fleet comprised ninety vessels, each averaging sixty tons—one-fourth the entire Massachusetts tonnage. With its catch exported mostly to Spain, Portugal, and the West Indies, New England's largest and finest-built fleet soon returned good times to craggy Marblehead. But the free-wheeling, independent townies— a breed unto themselves—usually engaged in high spending over the winter months and continued in debt to their schooner creditors.

View of the town of Marblehead. From *Gleason's Pictorial Drawing-Room Companion* (1854). Courtesy, Peabody Museum of Salem.

Once again foremost in fisheries, Marblehead's glory days of afflu-ence, however, were gone forever.[13]

Since the seventeenth century, coastal Essex County with its prox-imity to lush ocean fishing—in the Gulf of Maine, on George's Bank, the Grand Bank, and other offshore grounds—had been predomi-nant in ocean fisheries. In Lynn, a handful of dory men ventured off Swampscott to earn their livelihoods. Around Marblehead Neck to Salem, twenty or more Grand Banks vessels moored in the North and South rivers. Between Salem and Beverly, five bankers and a pod of small two-mast boats sailed out of New Mills, Danvers. Across the bay from Salem, at least nineteen sailers, mostly schooners, were based at Beverly. In 1790, only Beverly's catch exceeded that of pre-Revolutionary days. Neighboring Manchester was home to fifteen schooners, averaging sixty tons and employing 120 men, a major segment of the male population. Along Cape Ann, fishing had de-clined, compared to prewar years; the fleet nonetheless numbered 160—more than any other Massachusetts town—which included about fifty banks and bay vessels with tonnage second only to Mar-blehead's. While larger ketches were operated, Chebacco boats—invented in Chebacco Parish (Essex), Ipswich—were favored. Rigged with two sails and less than thirty feet long, the double-enders were especially seaworthy, easy to handle, and within the budget of most Gloucester fishermen. They were sailed relatively close to home, off the Maine coast or within 100 miles of Eastern Point, Gloucester. Here their crews bottom-fished for cod, cusk, haddock, and pollack, barely eking out a living. Typically, their home ports were Loblolly, Pigeon, and Folly coves, and other inlets along Sandy Bay to the Annisquam River. Chebacco Parish, Ipswich, harbored a smaller fleet of about fifty pinkies; a few bankers and bay fishermen docked along the winding Ipswich River. Nearly 250 of Ipswich's population were fishermen, twice the number of Manchester; however, with fivefold more inhabitants, the town was not as fisheries-dependent. Newburyport concentrated on near shore and bay fisheries, but, with only ten major vessels involved, neither was key to its prosperity. Upriver, a few vessels home-based at West Salisbury and Amesbury. Whether counted by vessels employed (over 360), tonnage (over 13,000), or manpower (about 2,100), between 60 and 70 percent of the Massachusetts codfishery centered in Essex County.[14]

By 1790, Essex County's fishing fleet was substantially rebuilt, but exports continued below prewar levels. On July 4, 1789, Congress granted a five-cent bounty on every quintal of dried fish or barrel of pickled fish that was exported. Congressman Benjamin Goodhue and Sen. Elbridge Gerry had helped spearhead the drive. Larger export allowances brought further relief during ensuing years. With federal help and the general revival of commerce, codfishery soon flourished.

Shipbuilding

Rising levels of commerce and fishing sparked new life into county shipbuilding. Elias Hasket Derby engaged the shipwright Enos Briggs from Pembroke, Massachusetts, to construct a new, mammoth—564 tons—*Grand Turk*. On March 27, 1790, the keel was laid, the likes of which was not seen again until Briggs built the frigate *Essex* in 1799. In 1790, Ebenezer Mann, emerging from a three-year hiatus, launched three vessels, including Simon Forrester's 171-ton barque *Good Intent*. After seven languishing years, Retire Becket, the fourth generation of expert Salem shipwrights, resumed work early in 1792.[15] Elsewhere, in New Mills and, especially, along the Merrimack, signs were equally encouraging. The prewar British market had gone, but, with support from the new government, better times were anticipated.

The center of shipbuilding in New England was along the Merrimack, from Joppa in Newbury upriver to Mitchell's Falls in Haverhill. Proximate to the ocean, the protected river towns benefited from vast supplies of northern wood and timber that were cut and floated or rafted downstream. In the shipyard located at the foot of Muzzey's Lane, Newbury (now Marlboro Street, Newburyport), Woodwell & Hale constructed ten vessels between 1783 and 1790.[16] With peacetime, business had increased, though to nowhere near the volume of pre-Revolutionary days. Eleazer Johnson's Newburyport shipyard, situated since the 1690s near Federal Street, and other valley shipyards suffered the same lean times.

On July 4, 1789, legislation passed to aid the export trade also boded well for shipbuilding and may have helped stimulate a flurry of activity along the Merrimack. In 1789, William Cross bought a plot at the foot of Merrill Street, Newburyport, and began to build ship stocks. To the north, in the Belleville section of Newbury (now Newburyport), at or near Moggaridge Point, shipbuilding had been well established. Here, in 1790, beside Jacob Coffin's yard, Orlando B. Merrill purchased land and began his shipyard operation. (During the War of 1812, Merrill and Cross would jointly construct the famous sloop-of-war *Wasp*.) Further north (near the present Chain Bridge), Elias Jackman founded a shipyard. Within a few years, these men became prominent, respected names in New England shipbuilding.[17]

Salisbury Point in West Salisbury was bustling. Adjacent to the Point, near the mouth of the Powow River, was the Ferry district of Amesbury; shipbuilding had made it the most populous, prosperous section of town. In September 1790, Rev. William Bentley observed as he passed through Amesbury and was ferried toward Newburyport: "on the banks of the river [Powow] at the entrance there is a convenient draw Bridge, which has a good effect as seen from the River [Merrimack]. Several vessels of considerable burden were upon the Stocks, & many under repairs in view as we passed." Indeed, after years of decline, the shoreline was revitalized.[18]

Shipbuilding could be found upriver as far as South Amesbury (Merrimacport), Bradford, and Haverhill. Since the 1720s, first John Atwood, and then others, had shaped vessels on the Bradford shoreline. Three shipyards were situated in Haverhill, including one at "the Rocks," near South Amesbury. Though when Reverend Bentley visited in 1790, only one vessel, being superintended by Capt. Henry Elkins of Salem, was on the stocks. Operations concentrated on smaller, light-burden craft, which could navigate the shoals and shallow waters.[19]

The labor-intensive industry required a large force of shipwrights and laborers. It also spawned an array of about thirty related trades: block-and-tackle makers, rope makers, braziers, blacksmiths, mast makers, caulkers, sail makers. Consequently, the stir in shipbuilding stimulated a host of opportunities in shipyard towns.

Census of 1790

The federal census of 1790 counted nearly 58,000 people living in Essex County—nearly 7,000 (14 percent) more residents than fourteen years earlier, before the war. The towns most heavily engaged in commerce, fisheries, and shipbuilding (Beverly, Gloucester, Marblehead, Newbury, Newburyport, and Salem) accounted for nearly the entire growth. Indeed, since 1776, several agrarian, inland towns (Andover, Boxford, Haverhill, Methuen, and Wenham) had lost numbers. With dismal prospects in agriculture, many residents had emigrated to seaports, or out of state.[20]

Manufacturing

During postwar years, New Englanders had become vulnerable to English imports. Excessive spending on these products had exacerbated specie drain, hard times, and popular unrest. Most informed people believed that the region's economic revitalization hinged partly on the growth of domestic manufacturing.

For generations, home industries had been producing goods for market. Ipswich was renowned for silk and thread manufacture, a skill handed down from mother to daughter. By 1790, women were producing about 40,000 yards of lace, annually. Flax was grown in Lynn, along the Merrimack Valley, and elsewhere, to make tow cloth for garments. The war had left in Manchester nearly 100 destitute widows and 135 fatherless children, a large proportion of whom earned a livelihood by weaving cloth for Salem. Hatters operated in Amesbury, Haverhill, and Salisbury, with their goods going to Newburyport, Salem, and Boston for export. Lynn was noted for manufacture of women's shoes. Though most cordwainers were farmers by summer, shoemakers by winter, the year-round employment of resident apprentices and journeymen was increasing. A factory system, however, was still over a generation away.[21]

Since early colonial days, in each hamlet, water-powered mills had been grinding grain, fulling (finishing) wool cloth, and sawing lumber for villagers and, more recently, also for export. On July 1, 1788, Alice Tucker of Newbury reflected on the "pretty rural Village" of Salisbury Mills along the Powow River, of "the hand of ingenuity and industry, the rapid motion of many Wheels going at once and the constant dashing of the water fills."[22] Several brick, potash, and pearl ash works, tanneries, and rum distilleries also operated in Essex County. More recently, a brewery had opened in Newburyport; Robert Laird's beer, porter and ale enjoyed wide popularity. And the existing furnace and mill operations would flourish for generations.

The spinning jenny, an English invention, was employed in Essex County's first manufactories. Compared to methods used in home industry, these machines were complex and the work more specialized; versus mill operations, manufactories required greater skills.

The "very ingenious mechanic" Samuel Blodgett set up a multiple spinning machine in Haverhill to spin flax for duck. Reverend Bentley wrote in his diary: "He has eight looms going, & room for eight more. He has many good specimens of his duck, which by a small anchor he lays in the river for necessary soaking, &c." He also noted three distilleries in Haverhill, one recently converted to a brewery, and, later, a second duck manufactory in Salem that employed twelve spinners and four weavers. In Essex County, and elsewhere along the northeast coast, entrepreneurs were sowing the first seeds of industrial independence.[23]

Beverly's Cotton Factory

A series of English inventions introduced the factory system to the textile industry. England had been shipping inexpensive textiles to America, thus undercutting native home spinning and weaving industries. Though British laws prohibited export of the newly invented machines, or designs, disassembled models and knowledgeable workmen found their way to America.

In the late 1780s, two British artisans, James Leonard and Thomas Somers, left home for America to capitalize on their knowledge. The *Salem Mercury* reported on May 6, 1788, that they were experienced in "the making and finishing of velvets, corduroys, jeans, fustians, denims, Marseilles, quiltings, dimity, muslins, etc." Beverly's foremost merchant-investor, George Cabot, eyeing Leonard's and Somers's talents, subsidized their move into town, with their families.

Cabot convinced a group of local businessmen to associate and invest in the establishment of a cotton factory. Through Leonard and Somers, they acquired a set of cotton carding and spinning machines. Shortly, a successful working experiment was under way.

In August 1788, John Cabot, a local merchant and brother of George, with Dr. Joshua Fisher, a Beverly physician, bought five acres in North Beverly—along present Dodge Street near the firehouse—by Baker's tavern. On this site, Cabot, Fisher, and associated investors constructed a three-story brick building, sixty by twenty-five feet. By October 1788, the first cotton factory in America was operating.[24]

The entrepreneur investors saw themselves achieving a twofold purpose: firstly, to make a profit; secondly, and equally important, to help the state grow less dependent on English textiles. Believing their efforts would be beneficial to the entire commonwealth, the investors petitioned for assistance since costs of perfecting the manufacturing process and training employees had far exceeded their estimates. On February 3, 1789, the General Court incorporated the proprietors as the "Beverly Cotton Manufactory." Two weeks later, shareholders—Andrew, Deborah, George, and John Cabot, Moses Brown, Isaac Chapman, Joshua Fisher, Henry Higginson of Boston, Israel Thorndike—were awarded commonwealth-owned "Eastern lands" valued at five hundred pounds, specie. During the difficult times, legislators wanted to encourage "the most extensive & profitable employment to its citizens."[25]

The factory owners, however, sought further remuneration. They argued that they had helped curb specie drain, since their raw Caribbean cotton was paid for with cod, thus infusing new life into local fisheries. Consumers now could buy Beverly-produced domestic cottons. In addition, the factory provided jobs, especially for infirm women and for children, who otherwise would be on public welfare. In March 1791, the General Court granted shareholders seven hundred tickets in the lotteries, a state revenue scheme begun in December 1790. The tickets helped recoup losses, but Reverend Bentley noted "however wise [it] is not a popular measure."[26]

George Cabot then wrote to Cong. Benjamin Goodhue seeking federal help. The proprietors, Cabot explained, had trusted that their risks would be underwritten if the experiment appeared "a practicable and useful manufacture in this country." Besides, other cotton mills, including the "Rhode Island undertakers" of the Slater mill in Pawtucket, gained by luring its trained work force. While this was "prejudicial" to the Beverly operation, Cabot judged it "beneficial to the public," justifying "the propriety of Government assistance." A congressional delegation—Congressmen Goodhue and Mason and Senator Ellsworth of Connecticut—visited, but no help resulted.[27]

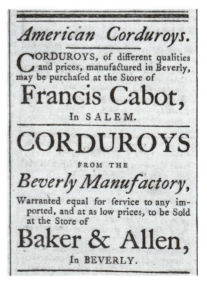

By December 1, 1789, when Francis Cabot and Baker & Allen were advertising in the *Salem Mercury*, Beverly-made corduroys had become common wearing apparel. Courtesy, Essex Institute, Salem, Mass.

American Corduroys.

CORDUROYS, of different qualities and prices, manufactured in Beverly, may be purchased at the Store of

Francis Cabot,
In SALEM.

CORDUROYS
FROM THE
Beverly Manufactory,
Warranted equal for service to any imported, and at as low prices, to be Sold at the Store of

Baker & Allen,
In BEVERLY.

The factory was a multi-level operation. Housed on the first floor were four or five jennies and about a dozen looms, "weaving cotton denim, thicksett, corduroys, velveret, &c." On the second, "a roping jenny of 42 spindles; & a machine on which a person usually doubles & twists, in a day, a cotton warp of 50 yards." The top story was dedicated to carding, warping, and cutting. In the basement, a pair of sturdy horses, driven in a circle by a boy, delivered two "horse power" to a wheel; also underneath were large vats for dyeing cloth.[28]

An estimated 10,000 yards of mostly coarse fabric were produced each year. By December 1, 1789, Baker & Allen in Beverly and Francis Cabot in Salem were selling Beverly corduroys, advertised as "equal for service to any imported, and at as low price." About forty people were employed; by now, Beverly corduroys had become common apparel.[29]

On September 24, 1790, chronicler Bentley visited the textile factory, noting: "Two Jennies were at work below, which carried about 70 spindles each. Several looms were at work, & the remarkable circumstance to us was the moving the shuttle by Springs, which gives great velocity, & allows the greatest number of strokes." The Congregational pastor judged that "the cloth was various & good." Nearly a year later, Bentley returned to write: "Found more hands employed than ever, & the machines all in motion." The Beverly Cotton Manufactory, the first in the nation, continued operation until shortly before the Embargo Act of 1807.[30]

Meanwhile, other far-sighted risk takers were busily planning their entries into uncharted territory. In the summer of 1789, thirty-year-old Nathan Reed was cruising Waters River in Danvers. Reed was propelling a small boat by hand-operated paddle wheels, a precursor to Fulton's steam-driven design. A few years later, Dr. John Manning introduced the factory system to Ipswich. In 1792, a two-story building was erected, and the Massachusetts Woolen Company was organized for the carding, spinning, and weaving of blankets, broad cloths, flannels. Two years later, the Newburyport Woolen Manufactory was incorporated; the proprietors built a factory in Byfield, Newbury, along the Parker River. The national government recognized the importance of manufacturing when Congress passed the first tariff law on July 4, 1789, both to raise revenue and to encourage domestic industry. Creative inventors and skilled mechanics, fueled by adventurous entrepreneurs, already were laying the foundation of America's industrial revolution.

Essex Bridge

Since the late 1630s, nearly every day, a ferry had shuttled over bay waters between Green's Point, Salem, and Ellinwood's wharf,

Beverly. Once again, George Cabot figured prominently when local investors, mostly from Beverly, sought to construct a bridge near the ferry crossing. Shareholders—the largest George and John Cabot, Joseph Lee, Moses Brown, Israel Thorndike, Zachariah Gage, and Hugh Hill—with business ties dating from Revolutionary days signed an agreement on June 13, 1787.

Boston-Portsmouth traffic normally traveled via the Bay road through Danvers. If the destination was Marblehead or Salem, travelers usually turned onto Boston road at the Bell tavern in Danvers, now Peabody. From Danversport, a secondary way wound through North Fields across the North River into Salem.

To build a bridge required an act of the General Court. George Cabot spearheaded an effective lobbying campaign within Essex County. At town meeting on June 25, Newburyporters stated that the existing route,

> from the whole Eastern part of the Commonwealth, to the large commercial Towns of Salem and Marblehead, is circuitous, and, at many Seasons of the year, founderous and bad, that the road through the Town of Beverly and thence across the ferry to Salem is much shorter and better, but from the Inconvenience of said ferry and particularly from the want of proper attention in the helpers thereof, your petitioners and others are extremely incommoded by passing in that rout.[31]

Other Essex County towns, including Beverly, Gloucester, Ipswich, Marblehead, Middleton, Topsfield, and Wenham, sent petitions.

There was, however, widespread vocal opposition. Not only would Danvers no longer be situated along a major thoroughfare, townspeople feared that their ocean access would be obstructed, ruining the town's fisheries and the Down East firewood and lumber trade. They voted unanimously opposed on July 2, 1787; two influential citizens, Israel Hutchinson and William Shillaber, were appointed to lobby against the proposed bridge. West and North Salem residents, particularly North River fishermen, also were adamant, demanding that, if any bridge were to be built, it should cross from Orne's Point, above North River. While South and East Salem residents favored Cabot's proposal, opponents prevailed at a June 25 meeting: 164 yeas and 187 nays were counted. On July 3, a committee (Major Joseph Sprague, Nathaniel Ropes, and Samuel Ward) was appointed to oppose Cabot's petition. With more than thirty vessels—which included two-thirds of Salem's fishing fleet—harbored in the North River, they feared the "fatal Consequences." Not to be outdone, proponents sent a minority petition and a delegation (Capt. John Fisk, Francis Cabot, and Capt. Joseph White). Over the summer, into the fall, the issue engendered heated, acrimonious debate.[32]

Opponents convinced the General Court to delay approval of the bridge. Before proroguing for the summer, the court sent a five-member delegation to Beverly, Danvers, and Salem for an on-site evaluation. Back in session on October 31, the House heard a favorable committee report read, and then adjourned. The following day, however, they voted opposed.

While both sides maneuvered, Cabot's rallying of northern and eastern Essex County paid dividends. Once again, petitions inundated the General Court: from Amesbury, Andover, Ipswich, Manchester, Methuen, and Wenham; from Newburyport, signed by John Mycall, agent; from House members representing Amesbury, Beverly, Boxford, Gloucester, Ipswich, Methuen, Newburyport, and Rowley. A Manchester petition dated November 6 apprised them that the town's mostly poor and indigent widows and their children manufactured clothes from materials they purchased across the river in Salem. Their fishermen and traders also would benefit from the more convenient bridge route when buying supplies during the winter months. On the same day, Wenham drafted a petition explaining that using a bridge would be superior to sending produce to Salem over the longer, rougher, Danvers route. Three days later, Ipswich

A view across the Essex Bridge from near the toll booth. On opening day, September 24, 1788, throngs passed over. Etching by H. R. Blaney. Courtesy, Essex Institute, Salem, Mass.

voters passed a petition noting that Salem accounted for most of its trade—hay, fish, and bait—in exchange for country produce. During the winter, should they navigate through the ice-clogged Ipswich River, a sail around Cape Ann was treacherous. Their already renowned Ipswich clams—150 tons annually—were needed for bait in Marblehead, Salem, and Beverly, particularly in February and early March for first fares. John Mycall, speaking for Newburyport, observed that goods taken in exchange, as well as rigging, sails, and ships' stores, must be transported by roadway during the cold months. After the Senate accepted the petition on October 25, Cabot's concerted pressure finagled the House's concurrence, on November 10, by an overwhelming majority.[33]

On November 17, 1787, the General Court incorporated the investors, authorizing them to construct the Essex Bridge and to set tolls for persons, horses, coaches, chariots, and other conveyances for seventy years. To facilitate upriver travel, toll-free, owners were required to build "a convenient and sufficient draw, or passage way, at least thirty feet wide." For "the ferry ways," Salem was to receive forty pounds annually, while Danvers would receive a ten-pound nuisance fee. The town sought revenge by constructing a bridge at New Mills, known for years as "spite" (now Liberty) bridge, to draw traffic from Beverly.[34]

A proprietors' meeting was held December 13 at the Sun tavern in Salem. Seven Beverly and Salem subscribers were chosen directors: Andrew and George Cabot, Capt. George Dodge, Capt. John Fisk, Capt. Joseph Lee, Edward Pulling, Capt. Joseph White. George Cabot was made president. The project was under way. On May 3, 1788, the first pier was sunk in a mudsill; four and one-half months later, the bridge was completed.[35] It was 1,484 feet from abutment to abutment and 32 feet wide, sporting a draw 30 feet wide "which plays with such ease," wrote the Salem and Newburyport papers, "that two boys of ten years old may raise it."[36]

No toll was charged on the opening day, September 24, 1788. With the bridge decked out in flags of all nations, a throng of sightseers—on foot, on horseback and in carriages—streamed across, marveling at the achievement. "Vast numbers Past. We all Rode over," noted Mrs. Mary Holyoke of Salem. The proprietors celebrated at Leach's tavern near the bridge in Beverly, dining with Lt. Governor Lincoln and Jonathan Jackson, while workers feasted nearby at the Cabot ropewalk. It was a day many would dearly remember.[37]

The *Salem Mercury* proudly noted: "Within the space of twenty miles, stand, as honorary monuments of the ingenuity and industry of the citizens of Massachusetts, three Bridges (Charles River, Malden and Essex) . . . which, for magnitude, [are] not equalled by any thing of the kind in America."[38]

The Essex Bridge opened a new thoroughfare between Boston and Portsmouth. To interior towns north of Beverly, the more direct route to Marblehead and Salem was a blessing. For short-haul coastal traffic, the bridge offered an option to the occasional vagaries of the sea lanes.

During the next decade, beginning with the Essex Merrimack Bridge between Newbury (now Newburyport) and Salisbury (now Amesbury), several timber bridges were to span the Merrimack, connecting northern Essex County with points south. In the 1790s, ferry travel was fast becoming obsolete, as a network of bridges simplified travel and facilitated trade.

A New Dawning: Epilogue

Essex County in 1790 was at the dawning of a commercial resurgence, a boom of epochal proportions. Led by their merchant-shippers, maritime towns would prosper enormously. And the good times

In the 1790s—at the dawning of an epochal commercial boom—schooners and other sailing vessels streamed out of Essex County ports. Watercolor by unknown artist. Courtesy, Beverly Historical Society.

would spread to all groups, even penetrating to farmers in the interior. As the county stood on the threshold of expansion, however, few people would have believed what was lying over the horizon.

With his political and mercantile connections, Congressman Benjamin Goodhue had an excellent vantage point. In spite of this, he was given to dire forebodings. Writing to his brother, Stephen, on May 16, 1790, Goodhue related his grave concerns:

> I am sensible of the decline of trade and business in our quarter and consequently the increase of poverty. I have a long time seen this coming, and I think the Town of Salem and our other Towns have seen their best days, and am grieved at the reflection, but I do not know how to help it, as to the fisheries I do not know what can be effectively done for them. I hope the Government will do what little they can, but I fear people expect more than is in their power.[39]

Hard times had driven hundreds of people from the county in search of better economic opportunities. Thousands of those remaining were impoverished. The recent uphill trend in fisheries had suffered a setback. American-flagged vessels and home products, notably the sacred cod, were closed out of many foreign ports. The new Baltic and East Asian trade routes would take years to develop. In fact, at the time of Goodhue's letter, the first returning Indiaman had not entered Salem harbor.

Despite negative forecasts, the 1790s began well for Essex County. The commercial protections of the new national government had set the stage. Shortly, the region would begin to reap tremendous dividends from world trade. Then, in 1793, Europe became embroiled in war, which lasted almost continuously for twenty-two years. The warring nations became dependent on the United States, the largest neutral trading nation, especially for foodstuffs. Ports heretofore closed were opened, with buyers willing to pay exorbitant prices. The neutral trade, compounded by the expanding worldwide market, would produce an unparalleled prosperity, with the glory days lasting for twenty years.

As the Revolutionary era closed, the sun dawned on a new republic destined for greatness. During the Revolutionary upheaval, the uncertain war years, and the subsequent economic-political dislocation, Essex County's resolve was unrelenting. The sacrifices and heroism of its people were immeasurable. Their passion for liberty demanded their independence; once they achieved it, their undaunted courage won the peace. Their yearning for a stable, sturdy sovereignty created the Constitution of the United States of America. For their contributions to our "more perfect union," they have earned our eternal gratitude.

1. Journal of Alice Tucker, 1784–1791, MS, Private Collection.

2. James Duncan Phillips, "Salem Ocean-Borne Commerce," *EIHC*, 75 (1939):135–44.

3. Edwin M. Stone, *History of Beverly* (Boston: James Munroe, 1843), 200; Port of Beverly—Entries—Imports and Imposts—1787–1789, MS, BHS.

4. Benjamin W. Labaree, *Patriots and Partisans* (Cambridge: Harvard University Press, 1962), 94–98; Caleb Cushing, *The History and Present State of Newburyport* (Newburyport: F. W. Allen, 1826), 84–85.

5. James Duncan Phillips, *Salem and the Indies* (Boston: Houghton Mifflin, 1947), 71–91; Joseph B. Felt, *Annals of Salem*, 2nd ed. (Salem: W. & S. B. Ives, 1849), 2:298.

6. James R. Pringle, *History of Gloucester* (Gloucester: James R. Pringle, 1892), 84; John J. Babson, *History of the Town of Gloucester* (Gloucester: Procter Bros., 1860), 267–71, 477–78.

7. Raymond McFarland, *A History of New England Fisheries* (New York: D. Appleton, 1911), 131; Samuel Eliot Morison, *The Maritime History of Massachusetts* (Boston: Houghton Mifflin, 1921), 82–84; Phillips, *Salem and the Indies*, 169–70; Records—Naval Office—Beverly 1784–1800: Manifests, vol. 6, 1788–89, BHS, MSS, 6698, 6705, 6706, 6710, 6711, 6712, 6714, 6716.

8. Felt, 2:292; *Diary of William Bentley* (Salem: Essex Institute, 1905), 1:104, 105–06, 123; "A Strange Epistle of a Century Ago," *EIHC*, 25 (1888):311–12.

9. Octavius Thorndike Howe, *Beverly Privateers in the American Revolution* (Cambridge: John Wilson, 1922), 423; Phillips, *Salem and the Indies*, 39–43.

10. 44–60; Freeman Hunt, *Lives of American Merchants* (New York: Derby & Jackson, 1858), 2:58–60.

11. Samuel Roads, Jr., *The History of Traditions of Marblehead* (Marblehead: N. Allen Lindsey, 1897), 211–13.

12. *Salem Mercury*, December 18, 1787; Morison, 139; D. Hamilton Hurd, *History of Essex County* (Philadelphia: J. W. Lewis, 1888), 2:1098; Roads, 207.

13. McFarland, 131; Morison, 139–40.

14. Book of Clearance and Reports of Fishing Vessels 1788–1789, MS, BHS; McFarland, 131, 147–49; Morison, 141–44; Chap. 27, Acts, 1787, MA Archives.

15. Phillips, *Salem and the Indies*, 148–52; Bentley, 1:156, 202; William Leavitt, "Materials for the History of Ship Building in Salem," *EIHC*, 6 (1864): 138–39; William Leavitt, "Retire Becket," *EIHC*, 7 (1865): 207–09.

16. E. Vale Smith, *History of Newburyport* (Newburyport: E. Vale Smith, 1854), 263.

17. Sarah Anna Emery, *Reminiscences of a Nonagenarian* (Newburyport, William H. Huse, 1879), 225; Smith, 263.

18. *Diary of William Bentley*, 1:200.

19. Gardner B. Perry, *History of Bradford, Mass.* (Haverhill: C.C. Morse & Son, 1872), 9; George Wingate Chase, *History of Haverhill* (Haverhill: George Wingate Chase, 1860), 450; *Diary of William Bentley*, 1:197–98.

20. *Heads of Families 1790 Massachusetts* (Washington: Bureau of the Census, 1908), 9.

21. Hurd, 1:283; 2:1528, 1543; Thomas Franklin Waters, *Ipswich in the Massachusetts Bay Colony* (Ipswich: Ipswich Historical Society, 1917), 2:368–69; Chap. 27, Acts, 1787, MA Archives.

22. Journal of Alice Tucker.

23. *Diary of William Bentley*, 1:198–99, 202.

24. Robert S. Rantoul, "The First Cotton Mill in America," *EIHC*, 33 (1897):15–16.

25. *Acts and Laws*, 1788–89, 71–73, 362–63.

26. *Diary of William Bentley*, 1:236; Rantoul, "The First Cotton Mill," 23–28.

27. Rantoul, "The First Cotton Mill," 37–39.

28. *Salem Mercury*, November 3, 1789.

29. *Salem Mercury*, December 1, 1789; Felt, 2:162.

30. *Diary of William Bentley*, 1:200–01, 289.

31. Newburyport Town Records, June 25, 1787, 1:494–95.

32. Danvers Town Records, 3:356; Salem Town Records, EI, 5:756–62; *The Diary of William Bentley*, 1:79–80; *Salem Mercury*, November 6, 1787.

33. Chap. 27, Acts, 1787, MA Archives; see volumes 8 of House and Senate journals.

34. *Acts and Laws*, 1786–87, 582–86.

35. *Salem Mercury*, December 18, 1787; May 6, 1788.

36. *Salem Mercury*, September 23, 1788; *The Essex Journal & New-Hampshire Packet*, October 8, 1788.

37. *Salem Mercury*, September 23, 1788; *Diary of William Bentley*, 1:100, 104–05; "Diary of Mrs. Mary (Vial) Holyoke," *The Holyoke Diaries, 1709–1856* (Salem: Essex Institute, 1911), 119.

38. *Salem Mercury*, September 23, 1788.

39. Benjamin Goodhue to Stephen Goodhue, ALS, Goodhue Family Papers, EI.

APPENDIX A

Militia Companies that Answered the Lexington Alarm
Central and Northern Essex County

TOWN COMMANDER	NUMBER IN COMPANY	DAYS	MILES (ROUND TRIP)
Amesbury			
Capt. Timothy Barnard 1	65	5–10	100
Capt. John Currier 2	39	7	86
Capt. Mathais Hoyt 2	62	4	43
Capt. Caleb Pillsbury	15	4	80
Andover			
Capt. Henry Abbot	59	1 1/2	50
Lt. John Adams 3,4	50	3 1/2	55
Capt. Benjamin Ames 2,6	50	7	
Lt. Peter Poor	45	2 1/2–3 1/2	55
Capt. Thomas Poor 2,6	55	7	35
Capt. Joshua Holt 5	70	1 1/2	30
Beverly			
Capt. Caleb Dodge	32	1–2	24–48
Lt. Peter Shaw	42	2	46
Capt. Larkin Thorndike	49	2 1/2	48
Boxford			
Capt. John Cushing 3	33	1–6	24–60+
Capt. Jacob Gould 3	57	3–6	57–65
Capt. William Perley 2,6	52	7	40
Bradford			
Sgt. Abel Kimball	15	5	62
Capt. Nathaniel Gage 2	49	7	36
Capt. John Savory 3,11	50	3–5+	70
Haverhill			
Capt. Richard Ayer 3,11	34	3–5	70
Lt. Israel Bartlet	13	5–7	70
Capt. Ebenezer Colby 3	29	2–6	70
Capt. Joseph Eaton 3	23	2–9	70
Lt. Samuel Clements 3,10	24	4–7	70
Capt. James Sawyer 2,6	50		40
Capt. Timothy Eaton 3	30	4–6	70
Ipswich			
Capt. Jonthn Cogswell, Jr.	63	3	60
Capt. Abram How	43	1–2	12–80
Capt. Moses Jewett 7,8	33	3	60
Capt. James Patch 9	38	4	48
Capt. Daniel Rogers	51	4	60
Capt. Nathaniel Wade 2	51	3	88

Capt. Elisha Whitney **2**	39	4–20	48–108
Capt. Thomas Burnham	60	3	50

Methuen

Major Samuel Bodwell	45	2–5	70
Capt. John Davis **2,6**	49	7	
Capt. James Jones	32	4	60
Capt. James Mallone	24	3–6	60

Newbury

Capt. John Brickett **8**	19	4	80
Capt. Jacob Gerrish	41	6	80
Capt. Moses Little **2**	31	5	60
Capt. John Moody	22	3–6	42–84
Capt. Thomas Noyes	32	4	80
Capt. William Rogers **2,12**	42	3–9	40
Capt. Gideon Woodwell	14	6	86
Capt. Jonathan Poor **12**	19	3–6	86

Newburyport

Capt. Moses Nowell	132	4	75

Rowley

Capt. Thomas Mighill **2**	60	5	35
Capt. Edward Payson	45	2–4	
Capt. Eliphalet Spafford **12**	46	6	66

Salisbury

Capt. Jonathan Evans **2,6**	44	7	50–100
Capt. Joseph Page	16	4–7	100
Capt. Stephen Merrill **12**	35	3 1/2	60
Capt. Henry Morrill	46	4–8	90

Topsfield

Capt. Joseph Gould **7**	63	2–5	60
Capt. Stephen Perkins	47	21/1	60

Wenham

Capt. Thomas Kimball **7**	37	2–4	50
Capt. Billy Porter **2,7**	20	4–5	50

1 East Parish
2 Minuteman Company
3 Samuel Johnson's Regiment
4 Nathaniel Lovejoy's Company
5 Fourth Foot, 9 aged men followed in a provision wagon
6 James Frye's Regiment
7 John Baker's Regiment
8 Horse Troop
9 Hamlet and Ipswich
10 Daniel Hills's Company
11 Samuel Gerrish's Regiment
12 Caleb Cushing's Regiment
Source: Revolutionary Rolls, MA Archives, Vols: 11, 12, 13, 15, 20.

APPENDIX B

Essex County Dead, Battle of Bunker Hill, June 17, 1775

REGIMENT	TOWN	COMPANY COMMANDER
Col. James Frye		
Philip Abbot	Andover	Benjamin Ames
James Boynton 1	Boxford	William Perley
Joseph Chandler	Andover	Benjamin Ames
John Eaton	Haverhill	James Sawyer
William Haggett	Andover	Benjamin Ames
Ebenezer Herrick	Methuen	John Davis
Joseph Hibbard 2	Dracut (Methuen)	John Davis
Jesse Holt 3	Andover	Benjamin Ames
David Huntington	Amesbury	John Currier
James Ingalls 4	Methuen	John Davis
Ichabod March	Amesbury	William H. Ballard
Simeon Pike	Haverhill	James Sawyer
Joseph Simmons	Boxford	William Perley
Col. Moses Little		
Daniel Callahan	Gloucester	Nathaniel Warner
Samuel Nelson	Newburyport	Benjamin Perkins
Moses Pigeon	Newburyport	Benjamin Perkins
Benjamin Smith	Gloucester	Nathaniel Warner
Jesse Story	Ipswich	Abraham Dodge
Col. Ebenezer Bridge		
Josiah Brooks	Gloucester	John Rowe
Samuel Bailey, Jr.	Andover	Charles Furbush
William Parsons	Gloucester	John Rowe
Francis Pool	Gloucester	John Rowe
Daniel Carmichael	Marblehead	Samuel R. Trevett
William Jackson	Marblehead	Samuel R. Trevett
Col. Samuel Gerrish		
Thomas Doyl	Deserted from King's Troops	William Rogers
Col. John Glover		
Thomas Allen	Marblehead	Joel Smith
Unassigned		
Lt. Benjamin West	Salem	

1 Died June 28.
2 Died June 20.
3 Died June 21.
4 Died July 8.

APPENDIX C

Officers, Marblehead Regiment[1]
May 1775

Colonel John Glover
Lieutenant Col. John Gerry
Major Gabriel Johonnot
Adjutant Caleb Gibbs

Captains:

William Bacon
William Blackler
Nicholson Broughton
William Courtis
Thomas Grant
William R. Lee
John Merritt
John Selman
Joel Smith
Francis Symonds

Lieutenants:

John Bray
William Bubier
Nathaniel Clark
Isaac Collyer
John Glover, Jr.
Robert Harris
William Mills
Joshua Prentice
William Russell
John Stacey

Ensigns:

Edward Archbald
Thomas Courtis
John Devereaux, Jr.
Ebenezer Graves
Edward Holman
Seward Lee
George Sinecross
Robert Nimblett
Joshua Orne, Jr.
Nathaniel Pearce

1. Except for Capt. William R. Lee, his lieutenant, John Glover, and his ensign, E. Archbald, all were commissioned by the Provincial Congress on June 23, 1775. See Peter Force, ed., *American Archives*, 4th Series, 2:828.

INDEX